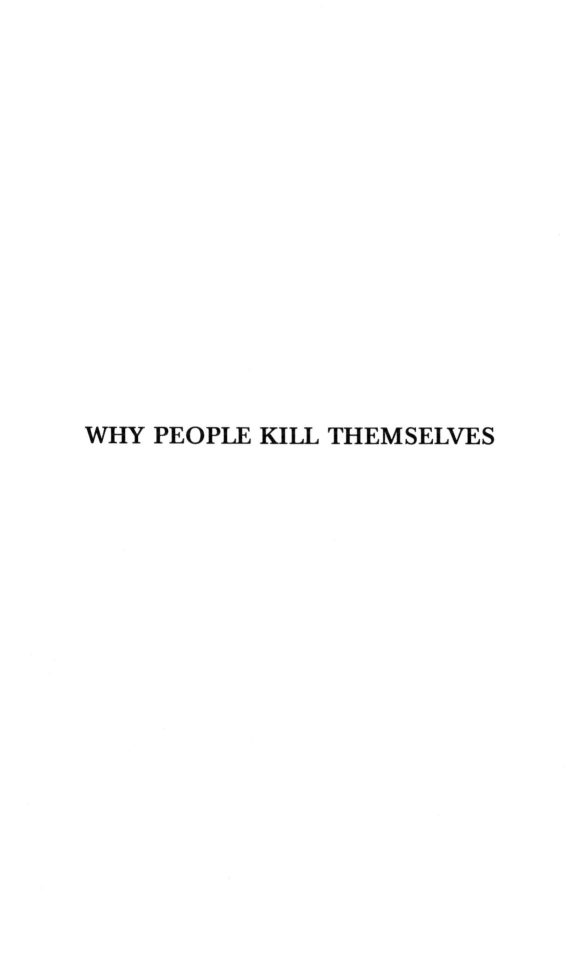

WHY PEOPLE KILL THEMSELVES

Fourth Edition

WHY PEOPLE KILL THEMSELVES

A 2000 Summary of Research on Suicide

By

DAVID LESTER, Ph.D

Professor of Psychology
The Richard Stockton College of New Jersey

Charles C Thomas
PUBLISHER • LTD.
SPRINGFIELD • ILLINOIS • U.S.A.

Published and Distributed Throughout the World by

CHARLES C THOMAS • PUBLISHER, LTD.
2600 South First Street
Springfield, Illinois 62704

© 2000 by CHARLES C THOMAS • PUBLISHER, LTD.

ISBN 0-398-07114-4 (cloth)
ISBN 0-398-07115-2 (paper)

Library of Congress Catalog Card Number: 00-056370

Printed in the United States of America
MR-R-3

Library of Congress Cataloging-in-Publication Data

Lester, David, 1942-
    Why people kill themselves : a 2000 summary of research on suicide / by David
Lester. -- 4th ed.
        p.cm.
    Third ed. has subtitle: a 1990s summary of research findings on suicidal behavior.
    ISBN 0-398-07114-4 (cloth) -- ISBN 0-398-07115-2 (pbk.)
    1. Suicide. 2. Suicidal behavior. I. Title.

HV6545 .L43 2000

00-056370

PREFACE

O ver the last 40 years, I have made an effort to read or peruse everything written in the English language since 1897 on suicidal behavior, the year of publication of Durkheim's classic book on suicide. The results of these reviews have been published in three volumes (Lester, 1972, 1983, 1992), which review the research up to 1969, in the 1970s, and in the 1980s, respectively. This is the fourth and final volume by me in this series, reviewing the research published during the period 1990 to 1997. The four volumes together will, therefore, review one hundred years of research and theory into suicidal behavior.

As before, the present book reviews only current research and theory. It does not review clinical papers dealing with the treatment of suicidal clients. The book assumes knowledge of the previous three books and mentions earlier works only if these works were not cited in the earlier volumes. The books differ in how critical they are of the research and theory. The first edition was highly critical of the research, whereas the second and third editions summarized the research without major criticisms of the goals of the research or the methodology. The change in focus was intentional, since the goal of the books is to review what we know about suicidal behavior, rather than show how "ignorant" previous researchers have been – a switch from a negative to a positive focus. The present book adopts the same uncritical approach throughout, except for the final chapter in which I present my personal evaluation of the research, particularly of the 1990s.

The major sources for locating the scholarly literature on suicidal behavior have been *Biological Abstracts*, *Index Medicus*, *Psychological Abstracts*, and *Sociological Abstracts*, but I have also used other abstracts, primarily in anthropology, criminal justice and women's studies.

The number of papers on suicidal behavior has risen dramatically over the last few decades, from one "shoe box" of 4 x 6 index cards for the 1960s to two for the 1970s, three for the 1980s and five for the 1990s up to 1997. It is partly this increasing quantity of papers and books on suicide that makes the task of reviewing the literature daunting at the present time and led me to make this my last review. My advancing age and my interests in other issues in thanatology also contributed to my decision. I also find that the modern techniques for searching abstracts make the task more difficult, since the on-line and CD-ROM abstract services identify many more irrelevant articles than the paper-bound abstracts of times past. Rather than having an informed person decide whether the article deals with suicidal behavior, modern techniques search for the word "suicide," regardless of whether the articles explore suicidal behavior or merely mention it in passing.

This, then, completes my review of the scholarly literature on suicidal behavior, and I pass the burden on to scholars of the future to continue this task.

REFERENCES

Durkheim, E. *Le suicide.* Paris: Felix Alcan, 1897.

Lester, D. *Why people kill themselves,* 1st Edition. Springfield, IL: Charles Thomas, 1972.

Lester, D. *Why people kill themselves,* 2nd Edition. Springfield, IL Charles Thomas, 1983.

Lester, D. *Why people kill themselves,* 3rd Edition. Springfield, IL Charles Thomas, 1992.

CONTENTS

WHY PEOPLE KILL THEMSELVES

Chapter 1

THE INHERITANCE OF SUICIDAL INCLINATIONS

Studies of the inheritance of suicide have focused on the study of twins (and other closely related individuals) and gene frequencies.

Twin Studies

Roy et al. (1991, 1994) identified twin pairs with one completed suicide and found that the monozygotic (MZ) twins had a significantly higher concordance rate than the dizygotic (DZ) twins. The same result was found for concordance rates when attempted suicide was included as a criterion, and the same result was found in an analysis of the world literature on completed suicide in twins. However, twins in these samples were not separated at birth and raised apart.

Roy et al. (1995) located MZ and DZ twin pairs, one of whom had completed suicide. The MZ surviving twins had a higher incidence of attempted suicide than the surviving DZ twins. In contrast, Segal and Roy (1995) found no differences in attempted suicide in MZ and DZ twin survivors after the cotwin died of nonsuicidal causes, although the MZ twin survivors tended to have more suicidal ideation.

Sibling Studies

Tejerina-Allen et al. (1994) followed up sibling pairs for 12 years. There was zero concordance for attempted suicide and 17 percent concordance for suicidal ideation. Across families, suicidal ideation was more common if there was also suicidal behavior in first-degree relatives (and less if there was close bond with the mother). Within families, suicidal ideation was associated only with more severe punishment.

Gene Studies

Nielsen et al. (1994, 1996) studied alcoholic offenders and found that the frequency of attempted suicide was associated with a lower frequency of the U and UU alleles in the DNA and a higher frequency of UL and LL alleles (where the tryptophan hydroxylase gene has two alleles, U and L). The genotype was not associated with impulsivity and diagnosis. Consistent with this finding, Rylander et al. (1997) studied MZ twin pairs, one of whom had completed suicide. The surviving twins more often had UL and LL genotypes than control groups.

In contrast, Abbar et al. (1995) found no differences in genotypic and allelic frequencies at the tryptophan hydroxylase gene site between attempted suicides and normal controls. Mann et al. (1997) found that attempted suicides more often than non-suicide inpatients had the tryptophan hydroxylase U allele in their serum DNA.

Attempting suicide was predicted in a multiple regression by UU, but not by depression or borderline personality disorder.

Belliver et al. (1997) found no differences between suicidal and nonsuicidal manic-depressive patients in their serotonin transporter gene. Persson et al. (1997) found no differences in blood DNA frequencies of tyrosine hydroxylase alleles between attempted suicides and normals, although the attempters with adjustment disorders had more TH-K3 (but not K1, K2, K4 or K5) alleles.

Other Studies

Mitteraurer (1990) studied suicides in a hospital from 1897–1977. For the manic-depressive and schizoaffective patients, if a relative had completed suicide, 48 percent had an endogenous psychosis; if no relative had completed suicide, 52 percent had an endogenous psychosis, a nonsignificant

difference. As a result of this, Mitteraurer claimed that suicide must have a genetic component independent of endogenous psychoses.

Swift et al. (1991) studied patients with the Wolfram syndrome. Their blood relatives had a history of more suicidal behavior (and psychiatric hospitalizations) than did their spouses. For patients with Ataxia-Telangiectasia, there were no differences.

Discussion

The studies of suicidal behavior in twins have not yet located MZ twins separated early in life and raised apart, a necessary group for demonstrating a genetic effect for any behavior. The allele studies on the tryptophan hydroxylase gene have been conducted by Nielsen and his colleagues, and they await replication by other research groups before we can be sure of their validity.

REFERENCES

Abbar, M., Courtet, P., Amadeo, S., Caer, Y., Mallet, J., Baldy-Moulinier, M., Castelnau, D., & Malafosse, A. Suicidal behaviors and the tryptophan hydroxylase gene. *Archives of General Psychiatry*, 1995, 52, 846-849.

Belliver, F., Laplanche, J. L., Leboyer, M., Feingold, J., Bottos, C., Allilaire, J. F., & Launay, J. M. Serotonin transporter gene and manic-depressive illness. *Biological Psychiatry*, 1997, 41, 750-752.

Mann, J. J., Malone, K., Nielsen, D. A., Goldman, D., Erdos, J., & Gelernter, J. Possible association of a polymorphism of the tryptophan hydroxylase gene with suicidal behavior in depressed patients. *American Journal of Psychiatry*, 1997, 154, 1451-1453.

Mitteraurer, B. A contribution to the discussion of the role of the genetic factor in suicide. *Comprehensive Psychiatry*, 1990, 31, 557-565.

Nielsen, D. A., Goldman, D., Virkkunen,
M., Tokola, R., Rawlings, R., & Linnoila, M. Suicidality and 5-HIAA concentration associated with a tryptophan hydroxylase polymorphism. *Archives of General Psychiatry*, 1994, 51, 34-38.

Nielsen, D. A., Goldman, D., Virkkunen, M., Tokola, R., Rawlings, R., & Linnoila, M. TPH replication study. *Archives of General Psychiatry*, 1996, 53, 964-965.

Persson, M. L., Wasserman, D., Geijer, T., Jonsson, E. G., & Terenius, L. Tyrosine hydroxylase allelic distribution in suicide attempters. *Psychiatry Research*, 1997, 72, 73-80.

Roy, A., Segal, N., Centerwall, B. S., & Robinette, C. D. Suicide in twins. *Archives of General Psychiatry*, 1991, 48, 29-32.

Roy, A., Segal, N., & Sarchiapone, M. Attempted suicide among living co-twins of twin suicide victims. *American Journal of Psychiatry*, 1995, 152, 1075-1076.

Roy, A., Segal, N., Sarchiapone, M., & Lavin, M. Suicidal behavior in twins. In D. Lester (Ed.) *Suicide '94*. Denver: AAS, 1994, 129.

Rylander, G., Asberg, M., Roy, A., & Nielsen, D. A. Genetic studies of suicidal behavior. In J. McIntosh (Ed.) *Suicide '97*. Washington, DC: AAS, 1997, 143–145.

Segal, N. L., & Roy, A. Suicide attempts in twins whose co-twins' deaths were non-suicides. *Personality & Individual Differences*, 1995, 19, 937–940.

Swift, R. G., Perkins, D. O., Chase, C. L., Sadler, D. B., & Swift, M. Psychiatric disorder in 36 families with Wolfram syndrome. *American Journal of Psychiatry*, 1991, 148, 775–779.

Tejerina-Allen, M., Wagner, B. M., & Cohen, P. A comparison of across-family and within-family parenting predictors of adolescent psychopathology and suicidal ideation. In E. M. Hetherington, D. Reiss & R. Plomin (Eds.) *Separate social worlds of siblings*. Hillsdale, NJ: Lawrence Erlbaum, 1994, 143–158.

Chapter 2

PHYSIOLOGICAL FACTORS

A great deal of research continues to appear on the cerebrospinal fluid, brain tissue, blood, and to a lesser extent, urine of suicidal individuals.

Cerebrospinal Fluid

Attempted Suicide

Gardner et al. (1990) compared female suicide attempters with borderline personality disorder to normal controls and found that the attempters had lower levels of 5-HIAA, but similar levels of MHPG and HVA. The level of 5-HIAA was not associated with violence toward others or self-mutilation.

Jones et al. (1990) compared elderly depressed patients who had attempted suicide with those who had not. The attempters had lower levels of 5-HIAA and HVA. The two groups did not differ in psychopathology, aggression scores on the Buss and Durkee Hostility Inventory, depression scores, or recent stressors.

Cremniter et al. (1994) found lower levels of 5-HIAA in attempted suicides using violent methods (versus medical controls), but only if schizophrenic patients were excluded.

Cooper et al. (1992) followed up schizophrenics. Those who attempted suicide had lower 5-HIAA levels, but no differences in levels of HVA or MHPG. Those using violent methods had lower levels of HVA (but not 5-HIAA or MHPG) than those using nonviolent methods. The groups did not differ in age or depression.

Mann et al. (1992b) found that high-intent attempters had lower CSF levels of 5-HIAA as compared to low-intent attempters and nonattempters in a sample of psychiatric inpatients. Levels of 5-HIAA were not associated with the severity of medical damage in the attempters.

Traskman-Bendz et al. (1992a) found that suicide attempters using violent methods had lower levels of 5-HIAA and higher levels of MHPG than those using nonviolent methods. Suicidal intent scores and prior attempts were not associated with these levels. Subsequent attempters had higher levels of MHPG; subsequent completed suicides had lower levels of 5-HIAA and higher levels of MHPG.

On the other hand, Lemus et al. (1990) compared schizophrenics with a history of attempted suicide to those with none and found no differences in 5-HIAA. In alcoholics, Roy et al. (1990) found no differences between suicide attempters and nonattempters (or normal controls) in levels of 5-HIAA, HVA, MHPG, or norepinephrine. Roy and Pollack (1994) found that depressive patients who had attempted suicide did not differ in CSF 5-HIAA or HVA from those who had not.

Mann et al. (1996c) found no differences between depressed patients who had attempted suicide and those who had not in 5-HIAA, HVA, or MHPG. Planned attempts were associated with lower levels of 5-HIAA, and more damaging attempts were associated with lower levels of 5-HIAA and HVA. CSF levels were not associated with violent versus nonviolent method

Kruesi et al. (1992) found that subsequent attempted suicide in children was not predicted by cerebrospinal fluid levels of 5-HIAA or HVA, after controls for age (nor by autonomic nervous system variables such as heart rate).

Bayard-Burfield et al. (1996) found that attempted suicides had higher CSF/blood albumin ratios than healthy controls. Attempters with high (versus low) ratios did not differ in diagnosis, substance use, or CSF levels of HVA, 5-HIAA, and MHPG; they were, however, more likely to use paracetamol for their attempt.

In a sample of attempted suicides, Mann and Malone (1997) found that CSF levels of 5-HIAA (but not HVA or MHPG) were lower if the attempt involved more planning and more serious damage. Levels of 5-HIAA were not associated with use of a violent method.

Among a sample of attempted suicides, Wasserman et al. (1997) found that the depressed attempters had higher levels of 5-HIAA (but not HVA or MHPG). Those who later completed suicide did not differ in these levels, nor was the method used associated with the levels. Those who abused alcohol had lower levels of cortisol.

Roy (1992) compared depressed patients who had attempted suicide with those who had not and found no differences in the CSF CRH. A follow-up of repeaters found no differences in CSF CRH.

In a sample of depressed patients, Roy (1993) found no differences in the CSF concentrations of neuropeptide Y, somatostatin, diazepam-binding inhibitor, GABA, or corticotropin-releasing hormone of repeaters, first-time attempters, and nonattempters.

Completed Suicide

Nordstrom et al. (1994) followed up attempted suicides and found no differences in the CSF concentrations of 5-HIAA, HVA, or MHPG in those completing suicide and those not doing so, although the suicides tended to have lower levels of 5-HIAA and HVA at the time of their attempt. However, Nordstrom et al. (1996) reported that attempted suicides who subsequently completed suicide had lower CSF levels of 5-HIAA than those who did not.

Lester (1991b) found that suicides had lower levels of DOPAC and MHPG, but not HVA or 5-HIAA as compared to those dying of heart attacks. Axelsson and Lagerkvist-Briggs (1992) found no differences in the CSF of psychotics who completed suicide and those who did not in 5-HIAA, HVA, MHPG, albumin, or IgG (nor between violent and nonviolent methods); the CSF/serum ratio of albumin did not differ either.

Roy (1990) followed up depressed patients for five years. Those who repeated their attempt or completed suicide had lower 5-HIAA and HVA levels at intake.

Violent Methods

Traskman-Bendz et al. (1993) found that attempted suicides using violent and nonviolent methods did not differ in CSF levels of 5-HIAA, MHPG, or HVA.

Repeaters

In a sample of attempters, Traskman-Bendz et al. (1992b) found that repeaters had lower levels of cortico-releasing hormone, but not somatostatin, delta-sleep-inducing peptide, neuropeptide Y, beta-endorphins, or vasopressin. Those using violent and nonviolent methods for suicide did not differ in these measures.

Meta-Analyses

Lester (1995) conducted a meta-analysis of research and found that lower levels of 5-HIAA were associated with prior attempts; lower levels of MHPG may also have had association. Subsequent suicidal actions were associated only with lower levels of 5-HIAA. Prior violent suicide attempts were associated with lower levels of 5-HIAA and HVA. On the whole, the studies reviewed in this section support Lester's conclusions.

The Brain

Beta-Endorphins

Scarone et al. (1990) compared completed suicides with controls and found that the left hemisphere caudate nucleus, temporal cortex and frontal cortex had lower beta-endorphin levels in the suicides than in the controls; this was not evident in the right hemisphere. (There were no differences in the hypothalamus or thalamus.)

Serotonin Receptors

Arango et al. (1990), comparing the brains of suicides and controls, found increased 5-HT2 receptor binding in the brains of the suicides in the prefrontal cortex, but not in the temporal cortex. Arango et al. (1995) sampled 103 areas in the prefrontal cortex and found higher 5-HT1a receptor binding and lower serotonin transport binding, especially in centrolateral regions.

Arato et al. (1991a, 1991b) found no differences between suicides and controls in the asymmetry of 3H-imipramine binding in the mediofrontal cortex; they did, however, find differences in Brodmann's area nine of the frontal cortex. The suicides had a higher Bmax on the left side than on the right, while the controls had the reverse pattern. The difference appeared to hold only for suicides using violent methods. However, Arora and Meltzer (1991) failed to replicate this latter finding.

Arango et al. (1992) found higher levels of 5-HT binding in the prefrontal (but not the temporal) cortex of suicides.

Hrdina et al. (1993) found that depressed suicides had higher levels of 5-HT2 receptors than controls in the prefrontal cortex and amygdala (but no differences in Kd), only when the receptors were labeled with 3H-ketanserin, not with 3H-paroxetine.

On the other hand, Cheetham et al. (1990) compared the brains of depressed, drug-free suicides with control brains for 5-HT1 binding sites. No differences were found in the frontal or temporal cortex. In the hippocampus and amygdala, the affinity (Kd) was lower in the suicides, but there were no differences in Bmax.

Dillon et al. (1991) found no differences in 5-HT receptors (Bmax or Kd) in the cortex, hippocampus, or basal ganglia of suicides and controls. Laurence et al. (1990a, 1990b) found no differences between suicides and controls in 5-HT uptake sites in 22 regions of the brain. For suicides using nonviolent methods only, the Bmax was lower in the putamen. There were also no differences between the two hemispheres.

Andersson et al. (1992) found no differences between suicides and controls in 5-HT uptake sites (Bmax or Kd) in the frontal cortex, cingulate cortex, or hypothalamus. Depressed and nondepressed suicides did not differ; nor did those using violent and nonviolent methods.

Ohmori et al. (1992) found higher levels of HVA, but not 5-HIAA or tryptophan, in the frontal cortex of suicides versus those dying of physical disease. Those using violent versus nonviolent methods did not differ in any of these measures.

Arranz et al. (1994) found that suicides from drug overdose (but not other methods) had lower 5-HT1A Kd values than controls. They did not differ in Bmax values, nor in 5-HT1D, 5-HT2 Bmax or Kd values. Depressed suicides had low Kd values of 5-HT1D, while the nondepressed suicides had lower Bmax values of 5-HT1D.

Lowther et al. (1994) found no differences in 5-HT2 binding sites in several brain regions (frontal, parietal and temporal cortex, hippocampus, caudate, and thalamus), but the suicides had higher Kd values than controls in the frontal and parietal cortex. This difference was found only for suicides using nonviolent methods and disappeared after controls for antidepressant use. Lowther et al. (1997a) found no differences between suicides and controls in 5-HT1a binding sites in the frontal or occipital cortex, hippocampus, or amygdala, and no differences between those using violent and nonviolent methods.

Mann et al. (1996a) found no differences between suicides and controls in the levels of 5-HT3 receptors, serotonin, 5-HIAA, or tryptophan in the frontal cortex. Mann et al. (1996b) found no differences in the prefrontal or temporal cortex for 5-HIAA, 5-HT, or tryptophan, but the suicides had fewer 3H-paroxetine binding sites (transporter and nontransporter). Naylor et al. (1996) found no differences in 3H-paroxetine binding in the hippocampus of schizophrenic suicides and deceased nonsuicides.

Arranz et al. (1997) found no differences in the frontal cortex, gyrus cinguli, or hypothalamus of suicides and controls in 5-HT, 5-HIAA, or the serotonin precursor 5-hydroxy-L-tryptophan (or in NA, DA, DOPAC, and HVA).

Little et al. (1997a) found no differences between suicides and controls in serotonin transporter sites in the midbrain, hippocampus, or frontal cortex or 5-HTT mRNA levels in the dorsal and median raphe nuclei.

Stockmeier et al. (1997) found no differences between suicides and controls in 5-HT1A and 5-HT2A receptors in either the right prefrontal cortex or hippocampus.

In contrast, Gross-Isseroff et al. (1990c) found fewer 5-HT2 receptors in the prefrontal cortex and hippocampus of suicides versus controls (Bmax only, not Kd), but only in subjects under the age 50.

Matsubara et al. (1991) found that violent suicides had lower Bmax levels for 5-HT1A binding in the frontal cortex, while nonviolent suicides had higher levels compared to controls. Kd differences were nonsignificant.

Lawrence et al. (1997) found lower levels of 5-HT uptake sites (and Kd values) in the putamens of suicides versus controls, but no differences in nine other regions.

In Brodmann areas eight and nine, Pandey et al. (1997b) found reduced levels of protein kinase C (and hence serotonin-2a receptors) in suicides as compared to controls.

Rosel et al. (1997) found fewer 3H-imipramine binding sites in the hippocampus of suicides versus controls, but not in the cortex, amygdala, or hypothalamus.

Holden (1995) proposed a theory that the association between suicide and serotonin levels in the brain was a result of uncontrolled fluctuations in brain glycemic levels due to glucose metabolism and insulin activity.

Adrenergic Binding

Arango et al. (1990) compared the brains

of suicides with controls and found that there was increased beta-adrenergic receptor binding in both the prefrontal and temporal cortex of the suicides. Arango et al. (1993) found an increase in alpa-1-adrenergic receptors, but not alpha-2 receptors, in some layers of the frontal cortex (but not the temporal cortex) of suicides as compared to controls. Norepinephrine levels were also higher in the temporal cortex of the suicides.

Garcia-Sevilla et al. (1992) found increased binding (Bmax) of alpha-2-adrenoceptors in the frontal cortex of suicides versus those dying of other violent causes for at least one measure. Increased levels were not found in the hippocampus, hypothalamus, amygdala, caudate nucleus, or brain stem, and no differences were found in Kd. The difference was clearer for the depressed suicides.

Meana et al. (1992) compared depressed and nondepressed suicide victims and found that the depressed suicides had increased levels of alpha-2-adrenoceptors (Bmax) in the frontal cortex and hypothalamus. Meana et al. (1993) found increased non-alph-2-adrenergic binding (but not alpha-2-adrenoceptor binding) in the frontal cortex of violent suicides versus nonsuicidal control brains. Gonzalez et al. (1994) found an increase in alpha-2-adrenoceptors in the hippocampus and frontal cortex of suicides (especially depressed suicides) as compared to controls.

Ordway et al. (1994b) found that agonist binding to alpha-2-adrenoceptors in the locus coeruleus of suicides was greater than in controls. (Antagonist binding did not differ significantly, nor did epinephrine.)

In contrast, De Paermentier et al. (1990) compared nine regions of the brain of depressed antidepressant-free suicides and controls. The suicides had fewer beta-adrenoceptors in the temporal cortex; the suicides using violent methods had fewer in the frontal cortex; and those using non-violent methods had fewer in the occipital cortex. No significant differences were found in the caudate nucleus, thalamus, amygdala, hippocampus, or putamen. De Paermentier et al. (1991) found fewer beta-adrenoceptor binding sites in the temporal cortex and thalamus of suicides as compared to controls, but only the difference in the temporal cortex was unrelated to the medication status of the subjects.

De Paermentier et al. (1992, 1997a) found fewer beta and beta-1-adrenoceptors in the temporal cortex of depressed (medication-free) suicides than in normal controls. Suicides using violent methods had fewer beta and beta-1-adrenoceptors in the frontal cortex and fewer beta-1-adrenoceptors in the temporal cortex. Those using nonviolent methods had fewer beta-adrenoceptors in the occipital cortex and few beta and beta-1-adrenoceptors in the temporal cortex. Suicides on antidepressants had fewer beta-adrenoceptors in the temporal cortex and thalamus. Suicides and nonsuicides did not differ in adrenoceptors in the pineal.

Andorn (1991) found an absence of an alpha-2-adrenergic binding site type (3H-clonidine binding) in the prefrontal cortex of suicides as compared to controls.

On the other hand, Stockmeier and Meltzer (1991) found no differences between suicides and controls in beta-adrenergic receptors (Bmax or Kd) in the frontal cortex, nor between suicides using violent versus nonviolent methods.

Little et al. (1993) found lower levels of beta-adrenergic binding in the frontal cortex of suicide brains than in controls. The suicides also had experienced more recent stress and had less good functioning.

However, Sastre and Garcia-Sevilla (1997) found no differences in the frontal cortex in alpha-2-adrenoceptors (or MAO-B sites), but the suicides had fewer I2-receptors and decreased 29/30 kDa imidazoline receptor protein. Little et al. (1997b) found no differences between suicides and controls in pineal beta-adrenergic receptor sites.

De Paermentier et al. (1997b) found no differences between suicides and controls in alpha-1 or alpha-2a-adrenoceptors in nine regions of the brain. The medication-free suicides did have more alpha-2-adrenoceptors in the temporal cortex, while those on antidepressants had fewer alpha-2-adrenoceptors in the occipital cortex and hippocampus and fewer alpha-2a-adrenoceptors in the caudate and amygdala.

Joyce et al. (1992) found that suicides and controls (but not schizophrenics) had greater beta-2-adrenergic receptor density in the right hippocampus than in the left.

Biegon and Fieldust (1992) found that suicides had less tyrosine hydroxylase (the rate-limiting enzyme in norepinephrine synthesis) in their locus coeruleus than controls, but no differences in dopamine beta-hydroxylase (the last enzyme in the synthesis).

Arango et al. (1996a, 1996b) found that suicides had more and denser pigmented locus coeruleus neurons than normals, restricted to the rostral two-thirds of the locus coeruleus. This suggested altered adrenergic function in the suicides. The suicides seemed to experience greater loss of neurons in this region with age than controls.

Mu-Opioid Receptors

Gross-Isseroff et al. (1990b) found an increase in mu-opioid receptor density (Bmax only, not Kd) in some regions of the brains of suicides versus controls (frontoparietal region, but not the thalamus or prefrontal region), but only in subjects under the age of 40. Gabilondo et al. (1995) found a higher Bmax in the frontal cortex and caudate, but not in the thalamus, of suicides versus control; no differences were found in the Kd.

Dopamine Receptors

Ruiz et al. (1992) compared the brains of schizophrenic suicides and nonschizophrenic controls. The Bmax for dopamine binding sites was higher in the caudate nucleus of suicides than in controls (with no differences in the Kd), but was not higher in the frontal cortex. However, nonschizophrenic suicides did not differ from controls, and so the authors concluded that the schizophrenia was responsible for the former difference. Galva et al. (1995) found that suicides had higher levels of HVA and DOPAC in the frontal cortex, but not MHPG, 5-HIAA, 3H-lazabemide binding, MAO-A or MAO-B activity.

In contrast, Murray et al. (1995) found no differences in dopamine receptors between suicides and normals in the striatum or nucleus accumbens, but both of these groups had lower levels than schizophrenics. Sumiyoshi et al. (1995) found no differences in D4-dopamine receptors in the caudate nucleus of suicides and controls. Wyatt et al. (1995) found no differences between suicides and schizophrenics or normals in the concentrations of HVA, DOPAC, MHPG, dopamine, norepinephrine, or normetanephrine in the anterior cingulate cortex. Knable et al. (1996) found no differences in D1-dopamine receptors in the prefrontal or cingulate cortex of suicides and controls. Allard and Norlen (1997) found no differences in dopamine uptake sites in the caudate nucleus of depressed suicides and controls. Bowden et al. (1997b) found no differences in dopamine receptor binding in these regions in antidepressant-free suicides.

Bowden et al. (1997a) found no differences in the basal ganglia of suicides and controls in dopamine and HVA, but nonviolent suicides had lower DOPAC (a dopamine metabolite along with HVA) in the caudate and putamen. All suicides had lower levels of DOPAC in the nucleus accumbens. Differences in the amygdala and hippocampus were not significant. Bowden et al. (1997c) found no differences in dopamine uptake sites in the caudate, putamen, and nucleus accumbens of suicides and controls.

Noradrenergic Binding

Gross-Isseroff et al. (1990a) found lower binding to alpha-1-receptors of tritiated prazosin as a ligand in some regions of the brains of suicides versus controls (only the prefrontal cortex, the caudate nucleus, and the temporal cortex). Klimek et al. (1997) found a reduced level of norepinephrine transporters in the locus coeruleus (the mid-caudal portion only) in suicides versus controls, but no differences in noradrenergic cells.

In contrast, Freed et al. (1993) found more glutamate-mediated binding in the caudate nucleus (but not the frontal cortex) of suicides versus both normal and psychotic controls. Arango et al. (1993) found higher concentrations of norepinephrine in the temporal cortex (but not the prefrontal cortex) of suicide brains versus controls. Ordway et al. (1994a) found that the concentration of tyrosine hydroxylase (relevant to noradrenergic neurotransmission) in the locus coeruleus of suicides was greater than in controls.

Other

Harro et al. (1992) found no differences in the Bmax or Kd for benzodiazepine receptors (relevant to the GABA system) in the frontal cortex of suicides and controls. Stocks et al. (1990) found no differences in benzodiazepine binding sites in the amygdala and hippocampus between depressed suicides and control brains, again suggesting no differences in GABA receptors. Arranz et al. (1992) found no differences in GABA-B binding in the frontal cortex of suicides and controls (nor in depressed/nondepressed or violent/nonviolent methods). Rochet et al. (1992) found no significant differences in Bmax for benzodiazepine binding sites in the hippocampi of suicides using violent methods and nonsuicidal controls, although the suicides had higher Kd values. Pandey et al. (1997a) found that suicides had higher levels of benzodiazepine receptors in the cortex than controls, primarily because of the higher levels in violent suicides. Sundman et al. (1997) found no differences in GABA uptake sites in the frontal cortex of suicides and controls, as well as no differences between suicides using violent and non-violent methods.

Harro et al. (1992) found higher Bmax and Kd values for cholecystokinin receptors in the frontal cortex of suicides versus controls, (for those using both violent and nonviolent methods and for depressed suicides but only for those under the age of 60). In the cingulate cortex, the suicides under 60 had higher Bmax scores, while those over the age of 60 had lower Bmax scores. Bachus et al. (1997) found no differences in cholecystokinin mRNA in the entorhinal cortex of suicides and controls, but the suicides did have elevated levels in the dorsolateral prefrontal cortex. Hurd et al. (1997) found that suicides had increased levels of prodynorphin mRNA in the patch compartment of the caudate nucleus (but not in the putamen or nucleus accumbens. They did not differ in D1- and D2-dopamine receptors, suggesting the involvement of endogenous opioid neuropeptides.

Holeman et al. (1993) found no significant differences in glutamate receptors in nine regions of the brain, either between suicides and controls or between those using violent and nonviolent methods. Nowak et al. (1995) found that suicides had less glutamate receptor binding in the frontal cortex than controls. Noga et al. (1997) found an increase in AMPA receptor sites (glutamate receptors) in the caudate nucleus of suicides and schizophrenics as compared to controls (but not in the putamen or nucleus accumbens), but no increase in NMDA or KA receptor binding.

Sandyk and Kay (1991) found that psychiatric patients who were suicidal had higher levels of choroid plexus calcification.

Sherif et al. (1991) found higher levels of MAO-A in the hypothalamus of suicides as compared to controls, but only in the depressed suicides and not in the frontal cortex or cingulate cortex. The groups did not differ in GABA-T or MAO-B concentrations.

Widdowson et al. (1992) found that completed suicides had lower neuropeptide Y immunoreactivity in the frontal cortex and caudate nucleus, but not in the temporal cortex or cerebellum. The difference was stronger in the depressed suicides. However, Ordway et al. (1995) found no such differences in the frontal cortex of depressed or alcoholic suicides versus controls. Arranz et al. (1996) found no differences between suicides and controls in neuropeptide Y, somatostatin, or cortico-releasing factor in the frontal cortex, gyrus cinguli, or hypothalamus.

Cowburn et al. (1994) found reduced adenylyl cyclase activity in the frontal cortex of suicides versus controls, especially if they used violent methods and if there was history of depression. G-protein levels differed only for some subunits (such as G-1-alpha). But Lowther et al. (1996) found no differences in adenylyl cyclase activity in the frontal and parietal cortex of depressed suicides and controls.

Palmer et al. (1994) found no differences in the frontal and parietal cortexes of suicides and controls in glycine, redox, zinc modulator sites and thus no differences in the N-methyl-D-aspartate receptor-channel complex.

Gilad et al. (1995) found no differences in the frontal cortex and hippocampus between suicides and normal controls in polyamines or their metabolizing enzymes.

Hui et al. (1995) found that schizophrenic suicides had less PSA-100 (puromycin-sensitive aminopeptidase-100) but more PSA-170 in their brains than controls.

Sastre et al. (1995) found decreased binding of I2-imidazoline receptors (Bmax but not Kd) in the frontal cortex of suicides. The total immunoreactivity of the receptors was reduced in the 20-30Kd band of protein but increased in the 45Kd band.

Garcia-Sevilla, et al. (1996) found increased 45Kd band imidazoline receptor proteins in the frontal cortex of suicides and decreased 29/30Kd proteins as compared to controls.

Pacheco et al. (1996) found decreased phosphoinositide signaling in the prefrontal cortex of depressed suicides versus controls (deficits in G-protein mediated 3H-phosphoinositide hydrolysis), suggesting enhanced cyclic AMP production.

Hucks et al. (1997) found that suicides and normals did not differ from controls in corticotropin-releasing factor binding sites in the frontal and motor cortex (and neither did the suicides using violent versus nonviolent methods).

Kato et al. (1997) found no differences between the brains of bipolar disorder suicides and controls in mitochondrial DNA deletion.

Lowther et al. (1997b) found no differences in cAMP binding sites in five different brain regions of antidepressant-free suicides and controls.

Shimon et al. (1997) found that suicides and bipolar patients had lower inositol levels (but not inositol monophosphate activity) than normals in the frontal cortex, but not in the cerebellum or occipital cortex.

Hippocampal Size

Altshuler et al. (1990) compared the size of the hippocampus and parahippocampus in schizophrenics, suicides, and those dying suddenly. The groups did not differ in the size of the hippocampus. The parahippocampus of the schizophrenics was smaller overall – smaller on the right side for both the schizophrenics and suicides and smaller on the left side for only the schizophrenics.

Comment

This body of research urgently needs meta-analyses in order to determine which results are reliable and which are not, especially with regard to the regions of the brain involved.

Blood And Platelet Studies

Cortisol

Dahl et al. (1991) found that adolescents with major depressive disorders had more elevated plasma cortisol levels around sleep onset than normals, and this difference was pronounced in the suicidal adolescents.

In contrast, Pitchot et al. (1995a) found that depressed attempters have a lower delta cortisol response to flesinoxam than controls and a lower delta temperature response, suggesting the involvement of 5-HT1a receptors. Cleare et al. (1996) administered d-fenfluramine (a 5-HT releasing agent) orally and found that serum levels of cortisol were reduced in those who had attempted suicide as compared to healthy controls, while the prolactin response did not differ.

However, Traskman-Bendz et al. (1992a) found no differences in the blood levels of

cortisol (or MAO) between attempters using violent and nonviolent methods for suicide. Inder et al. (1997) found that unipolar affective disorder patients who had attempted suicide had higher levels of arginine vasopressin (but not corticotropin-releasing hormone, cortisol, or adrenocorticotrophic hormone) than those who had not attempted suicide.

New et al. (1997) found a blunted prolactin and cortisol response to dl-fenfluramine (suggesting serotonin involvement) in attempted suicides and self-mutilators versus controls in a sample of patients with personality disorders.

Serotonin

Biegon et al. (1990) compared young men who were suicidal (attempters or ideators) with normal controls and found that the suicidal men had higher levels of 5-HT2 receptor binding. The more depressed suicidal men had higher levels of receptor binding.

Pandey et al. (1990, 1992) found higher levels of platelet serotonin-2 receptor binding (Bmax) in suicidal depressed patients as compared to nonsuicidal depressed patients. Pandey et al. (1995) found that suicidal psychiatric inpatients (attempters and ideators) had higher levels (Bmax) of serotonin-2A receptors, but no differences in Kd. Attempters and ideators did not differ.

Simonsson et al. (1991) found increased transduction of serotonin-2-receptors in the blood of attempted suicides as compared to normal controls and lower MAO activity, but no differences in serotonin. The results of these analyses were not associated with diagnosis or violent/nonviolent method for suicide.

Van Kempen et al. (1992) repeatedly tested nine chronically suicidal women. As their depression scores decreased, their 5-HT levels increased, while the levels of MAO did not change. Arora and Meltzer (1993) found that schizophrenics with a history of suicide attempts had higher Bmax levels (but not Kd levels) for 5-HT2 binding sites than schizophrenics who had not attempted suicide.

In contrast, Marazziti et al. (1990) compared the blood from attempted suicides, depressed patients, and normal controls and found lower levels (Bmax) of 3H-imipramine binding in the attempters (but no differences in Kd). For 5-HT uptake, the Bmax was lower in the attempters, but not the Kd. Those using violent methods for suicide did not differ from those using non-violent methods. Marazziti concluded that serotonin was involved in suicidal behavior. Marazziti and Conti (1991) and Marazzati et al. (1993) confirmed this and noted that the suicide attempters had higher scores on all the Buss and Durkee scales of hostility.

De Leo et al. (1991) found lower Bmax values for 3H-imipramine binding in the blood of attempted suicides as compared to normal controls (but no differences in Kd values).

Mann et al. (1992a) found that attempted suicides had lower levels of serotonin in their platelets (but not in their blood) as compared to nonsuicidal patients with major depressive disorders. Serotonin levels were not associated with suicidal intent or lethality in the attempted suicides.

Mann et al. (1992b) found no differences in platelet 5-HT2 Bmax among high-intent attempters, low-intent attempters, and non-attempters in a sample of psychiatric inpatients. The severity of medical damage in the attempters was associated with the platelet 5-HT2 Bmax levels.

Ashton et al. (1994) compared attempted suicides with normal controls and found lower levels of 5-HT but not 5-HIAA, HVA,

tryptophan, paroxetine-binding or monoamine oxidase. Repeaters had lower levels of 5-HT and HVA than the controls.

McBride et al. (1994) found no differences between major depressive disorder patients who had attempted suicide and those who had not in Bmax and Kd for 5-HT2 receptor binding sites. The Bmax values and suicidal intent were not associated for the attempters, but the Bmax values and the lethality of the attempt were positively associated. The attempters did have lower indices when adenosine diphosphate was added in combination with 5-HT over adenosine diphosphate alone.

Rao et al. (1994) found that suicidal female schizoaffective patients had lower blood levels of serotonin than nonsuicidal patients.

Marazziti et al. (1995) found that attempted suicides had lower Bmax for 3H-imipramine binding (but similar values of Kd) and lower 5-HT uptake levels (Vmax but not Kd) than normals. They did not differ in the enzyme sulphotransferase.

Mock-Seler et al. (1996) found that suicidal ideators among a group of psychotic depressed patients had lower platelet levels of 5-HT. This was found only for the men.

However, Pine et al. (1995) found that adolescent suicide attempters and normals did not differ in platelet 5-HT functioning (3H-imipramine binding). They found that the attempters showed a seasonal fluctuation in Bmax values, with a peak in the summer, while the normals did not.

In a sample of affective disorder patients who had attempted suicide, Rossi et al. (1996) found no differences in platelet 5-HT uptake or 3H-imipramine platelet binding between those who abused alcohol and those who did not.

Verkes et al. (1996) did not find differences in platelet 5-HT (or MAO activity) between recurrent suicide attempters and bulimics. Verkes et al. (1997) found that attempted suicides with higher Kd values for platelet serotonin and 3H-paroxetine binding were more likely to repeat their attempt in the next year. Bmax values and MAO levels did not predict future attempts. Suicidal ideation and Kd values were associated even after controls for sex, age, and alcohol abuse.

In a sample of suicide attempters, Castrogiovanni et al. (1990) found that the Bmax for platelet 3H-imipramine binding (a serotonergic marker) was negatively associated with irritability and indirect hostility scores on the Buss and Durkee Hostility Inventory. The correlations in samples of normals and depressives were not statistically significant.

Lester (1991a) found that Bmax and Kd values for platelet imipramine binding sites in samples of normal people in eight nations was positively associated with the national suicide rates.

Adrenergic System

Pitchot et al. (1994) found that attempted suicides had a weaker response to an alpha-2-adrenergic agonist than depressed controls. Depression scores were not associated with this response, and attempters using violent and nonviolent methods did not differ in their response.

Pitchot et al. (1995c) found no differences in growth hormone responses to a clonidine test between depressed male psychiatric inpatients who had attempted suicide and those who had not.

NK-Cells

Wasserman et al. (1992, 1993, 1997) found that attempters using violent methods had a lower percentage of NK cells and diminished NK-cell activity in their blood as compared to attempters using nonviolent methods and to normal controls. Alcoholic attempters also had lower mean NK-cell activity.

Other

Axelsson and Lagerkvist-Briggs (1992) found no differences in the blood levels of IgG or albumin between psychotics who completed suicide and those who did not.

Pitchot et al. (1992) gave apomorphine to psychiatric depressed inpatients and found that those with a history of attempted suicide had higher levels of growth hormone in their blood 20 to 120 minutes later. The use of violent versus nonviolent methods of suicide was not associated with this measure.

Nassberger and Traskman-Bendz (1993) found that suicide attempters had higher levels of soluble interleukin-2 receptor concentrations, suggesting activation of T-lymphocytes and a disturbance in the immune system.

Sandyk and Awerbuch (1993) found lower levels of melatonin in the blood of suicidal patients with multiple sclerosis (ideators and attempters) than in nonsuicidal patients with MS. Rao and Devi (1993) also reported that low levels of melatonin in the blood (and urine) were associated with subsequent suicidality.

Zonda and Lester (1993) found no differences from expectations in the blood type of completed suicides, although the suicides were more often rh-negative than expected.

Bergman and Brismar (1994) found no differences between male alcoholics who had attempted suicide and those who had not in cortisol, testosterone, sex hormone binding globulin, dehydroepiandrosterone sulfate, estrone, or estrone sulfate.

Rommelspacher et al. (1994) found that MAO-B activity was lower in abstinent alcoholics if they had attempted suicide in the prior few months. Tripodianakis et al. (1995) found that female attempted suicides (but not males) had lower platelet MAO activity than normals. Those using violent versus nonviolent methods did not differ. Reichborn-Kjennervd et al. (1996) studied patients with seasonal affective disorder. Those who attempted suicide during the depression had lower levels of platelet MAO activity.

Mann et al. (1995) studied the prolactin blood response to oral dl-fenfluramine (which assesses serotonergic responsivity) and found that it was not related to a history of attempted suicide or to suicidal intent. Malone et al. (1996) found that attempted suicides of high lethality had a lower prolactin response to fenfluramine than those of low lethality, suggesting lower serotonergic function.

Rommelspacher et al. (1995) found that alcoholics had higher levels of plasma salsolinol (a derivative of dopamine) than normals; if the alcoholics had attempted suicide, however, their levels were lower.

Serres et al. (1995) found that schizophrenics who had attempted suicide had lower Vmax values for erithrocyte L-tryptophan uptake than those who had not. The method of suicide was not related to the Vmax level.

Wolfersdorf et al. (1995) found that depressed patients who later completed a violent suicide did not differ in red cell or serum foliate levels.

Repo et al. (1997) found no differences in blood glucose nadir during an oral glucose tolerance test between firesetters who had attempted suicide and those who had not.

Aggregate Studies

Maes et al. (1996) took weekly blood samples from normals and compared the levels of ingredients with weekly totals of Belgium violent suicides. Weeks with more violent suicides had normals with lower blood levels of L-tryptophan, cholesterol, and lymphocytes (CD4+/CD8+ ratio, cd20+B cells). There were no differences in paroxetine binding, melatonin, calcium, or magnesium.

Dexamethasone Suppression Test

Completed Suicide

Norman et al. (1990) found that depressed inpatients who later completed suicide had higher cortisol levels at 1600 hours but not at 2300 hours post-DST than nonsuicidal depressed inpatients. Depressed inpatients who later attempted suicide did not differ from nonsuicidal depressed inpatients, although those making serious attempts were more likely to be nonsuppressors.

Axelsson and Lagerkvist-Briggs (1992) found no differences in the DST response of psychotics who completed suicide and those who did not.

Lester (1991c) found that the percentage of depressed patients who were nonsuppressors and the mean serum cortisol levels were not associated with national suicide rates over 10 nations.

Attempted Suicide

Coryell (1990) followed up patients with a major depressive disorder. Nonsuppressors made more serious attempts at suicide. Nonsuppressing was not predictive of subsequent mild attempts or of prior attempts.

Roy (1992) compared depressed patients who had attempted suicide with those who had not and found no differences in the DST response. A follow-up of repeaters found no differences in DST response. More attempters using violent methods were nonsuppressors than those using nonviolent methods. Jones et al. (1994) found no differences in DST suppression among schizophrenics who differed in past history of attempted suicide.

Pitchot et al. (1995b) found no differences in the DST between unipolars who had attempted suicide and those who had not, nor between attempters using violent versus nonviolent methods. Traskman-Bendz et al. (1992a) found no differences in DST response between attempters using violent and nonviolent methods.

Suicide Attempts and Ideation

Pfeffer et al. (1991) compared suicidal child psychiatric patients with depressed controls and found no differences in pre-DST cortisol levels at admission, although the controls had lower levels at 4 p.m. after seven weeks. The two groups did not differ in nonsuppression.

Lewis et al. (1996) found no differences in the DST between nonsuicidal schizophrenics and schizophrenics who had attempted suicide or had suicidal ideation.

Suicidal Ideation

Oei et al. (1990) found that suicidal depressed patients did not differ from nonsuicidal patients on the DST, but suicidal and anhedonic patients were more likely to be nonsuppressors.

Meta-analysis

Lester (1992a) carried out a meta-analysis of the research on the DST and suicide. DST results predicted subsequently completed suicide (all eight studies found this, with an average correlation of .19). However, DST results were not associated with a history of attempted suicide.

Urinary Studies

Mancini and Brown (1992) found that attempted suicides had higher levels of urinary norepinephrine than patients with only suicidal ideation. This was especially so for those using violent methods. They did not differ in the levels of dopamine, epinephrine, free cortisol, or serum cortisol or in depression, hopelessness, or suicidal intent scores.

Roy (1992) compared depressed patients who had attempted suicide with those who had not and found no differences in the urinary free cortisol. A follow-up of repeaters found no differences in urinary free cortisol. Roy and Lavin (1994; Roy and Pollack, 1994) found that depressive inpatients who had previously attempted suicide had less HVA, DOPAC, and dopamine in their urine. In a follow-up study, those who subsequently attempted or completed suicide had lower levels of these three substances than those who did not.

Roy et al. (1992) found that depressed patients who had attempted suicide had lower urine levels than nonattempters of HVA and DOPAC, but not dopamine. In a follow-up, the repeaters had lower levels of HVA and DOPAC than nonrepeaters, but not dopamine.

Traskman-Bendz et al. (1992a) found no association in suicide attempters between suicide intent scores and urinary levels of 5-HIAA or MHPG. Attempters using violent and nonviolent methods did not differ in levels of cortisol or the norepinephrine/epinephrine ratio.

Garvey and Noel (1993) found that the level of n-acetyl-beta-glucosaminidase was negatively associated in bipolar patients with depression and with suicidal ideation. Garvey and Underwood (1997) found that serious attempters had lower levels of N-acetyl-beta-glucosaminidase levels than nonserious attempters, depressed patients, and normals.

Garvey et al. (1994) found that current suicidality (but not past suicide attempts) in depressed female outpatients was associated with lower levels of MHPG.

Lithium

Schrauzer and Shrestha (1990) compared Texas counties with high, moderate, and low levels of lithium in their drinking water. Counties with higher levels had lower completed suicide rates.

The Pineal Gland

Milin et al. (1990) compared completed suicides with accident victims. The pinealocyte nuclei of the suicides had the same volume as the controls. The suicides seemed to have a more frequent occurrence of acervuli and the destruction of the endocrine parenchyma secondary to an infiltration and dispersion of glia cells.

Sparks and Little (1990) found that the pineals of suicides had lower serotonin binding than those of control brains, suggesting either fewer 5-HT receptors or reduced affinity.   .

Sleep

Dahl et al. (1990) compared suicide attempters and ideators with nonsuicidal adolescents with major depressive disorders. The suicidal adolescents had longer sleep latencies but did not differ in REM variables, total sleep, or the proportion of the different stages of sleep.

Goetz et al. (1991) found that suicidal young depressive patients had higher REM density than nonsuicidal depressives, but did

not differ on 20 other sleep measures.

Sabo et al. (1991) found that major depressive disorder patients who had previously attempted suicide had longer sleep latencies, slept less, and had fewer late-night delta wave counts. The nonsuicidal patients had less REM sleep in period two and more delta wave counts in period four. The groups did not differ on 29 other sleep variables.

Keshavan et al. (1994) compared psychotic inpatients who had shown prior suicidal behavior with those who had not. The suicidal patients showed increased REM activity and REM time.

Lewis et al. (1996) found that schizophrenics who had been suicidal (ideators and attempters) had increased REM time and REM activity (but not REM latency or slow-wave sleep) over nonsuicidal schizophrenics. No differences were found between recent attempters and less-recent attempts or between those using violent versus nonviolent methods.

Agargun et al. (1997a, 1997b) found that patients with major depression who had insomnia or hypersomnia had more suicidality than those with normal sleep. The suicidal patients had worse sleep quality, latency, and duration, but did not differ in sleep disturbance or medication.

Vignau et al. (1997) found that school students who were poor sleepers had more often attempted suicide or thought about suicide than good sleepers.

Other Variables

Adrenal Gland

Stein et al. (1993) found no differences in the weight of the adrenal gland between suicides (violent and nonviolent) and other sudden deaths. However, Szigethy et al. (1994) found that the adrenal gland (especially the left one) was heavier in completed suicides than controls, perhaps as a result of cortical hypertrophy.

Biorhythms

Caine (1976) found no association between suicides and critical days according to biorhythms. Demuth (1979) found no biorhythm effects in samples of attempted and completed suicides.

EEG

Ashton et al. (1994) found that attempted suicides had less contingent negative variation and more post-imperative negative variation in their EEGs as compared to normal controls, but no differences in the auditory evoked potential. Repeaters had less contingent negative variation than first-timers.

Hansenne et al. (1994) studied depressed psychiatric inpatients. Those who had attempted suicide had lower responses to auditory stimuli (cerebral P300 amplitude and contingent negative variation amplitude). Juckel and Hegerl (1994) found that attempted suicides had a weaker intensity dependence of auditory-evoked potentials. Hansenne et al. (1996) reported that depressed patients who had attempted suicide had reduced amplitudes on electro-oculograms and electroencephalograms compared with those who had not attempted suicide.

Graae et al. (1996) found that female adolescent suicide attempters had no asymmetry in their alpha waves, whereas normals had greater alpha activity in the right hemisphere.

Electrodermal Responses

Keller et al. (1991) found that suicide attempters in a group of depressed patients using violent methods were fast habituators more often than other attempters and controls, but did not differ on other variables. In a follow-up, those completing suicide were more often slow habituaters.

Wolfersdorf et al. (1993) found that depressed psychiatric inpatients (females only) who had attempted suicide by violent methods had higher tonic skin conductance than those using nonviolent methods and nonsuicidal patients. Males only also showed more rapid habituation of the phasic reaction. Those using violent methods were also less depressed and anxious and more satisfied with life. Wolfersdorf et al. (1996) found that the lowered electro-dermal response and faster habituation in suicide attempters is more likely to be true for those using violent methods and for males.

Wolfersdorf and Straub (1994) found that depressive inpatients who later completed suicide did not differ in electro-dermal responsiveness from those who did not do so. Those using violent methods, however, were faster habituators (as were attempters using violent methods), but their data indicate only a tendency in this direction.

Heart

Rechlin et al. (1994) found no differences in heart rate variability between attempted suicides and normal controls.

General Brain Damage

Lester (1992b) discussed the possibility that suicidal behavior could result from a "rage dyscontrol" syndrome.

Pituitary

Lopez et al. (1992) found an increase in

pro-opiomelano-cortin (POMC) in the pituitaries of completed suicides as compared to controls. The POMC-mRNA density per cell was also greater (but not the GR-mRNA density), and the corticotrophic size larger.

Thyrotropin Stimulating Hormone (TSH)

Corrigan et al. (1992) found that the TSH response to the thyroid-releasing hormone was reduced in unipolar patients with high suicidal intent and high suicidal lethality.

Jordan et al. (1992) found that while normal people had asymmetry in TRH content in their left and right intrahypothalamic structures, completed suicides did not.

Discussion

As mentioned earlier, this large body of research urgently needs a series of meta-analyses in order to identify the reliable results. The two that have been published (on the DST and on cerebrospinal fluid monoamines) revealed several consistent findings, but these phenomena were perhaps more amenable to meta-analyses than the brain studies. In addition, sample sizes need to be increased, and since the research is often carried out to explore the biochemical bases for depression, in order to further our understanding of suicide the suicides and the controls must be matched for depression and depressive disorders.

REFERENCES

Agargun, M. Y., Kara, H., & Solmaz, M. Sleep disturbance and suicidal behavior in patients with major depression. *Journal of Clinical Psychiatry*, 1997a, 58, 249–251.

Agargun, M. Y., Kara, H., & Solmaz, M. Subjective sleep quality and suicidality in patients with major depression. *Journal of Psychiatric Research*, 1997b, 31, 377–381.

Allard, P., & Norlen, M. Unchanged density of caudate nucleus dopamine uptake sites in depressed suicide victims. *Journal of Neural Transmission*, 1997, 104, 1353–1360.

Altshuler, L. L., Casanova, M. F., Goldberg, T. E., & Kleinman, J. The hippocampus and parahippocampus in schizophrenics, suicides, and control brains. *Archives of General Psychiatry*, 1990, 47, 1029–1034.

Andersson, A., Eriksson, A., & Marcusson, J. Unaltered number of brain serotonin uptake sites in suicide victims. *Journal of Psychopharmacology*, 1992, 6, 509–513.

Andorn, A. C. The low affinity component of [3H] clonidine binding is absent in the prefrontal cortex of presumptive suicide victims. *Brain Research*, 1991, 568, 276–278.

Arango, V., Ernsberger, P., Marzuk, P., Chen, J. S., Tierney, H., Stanley, M., Reis, D. J., & Mann, J. J. Autoradiographic demonstration of increased serotonin 5-HT2 and beta-adrenergic receptor binding sites in the brains of suicide victims. *Archives of General Psychiatry*, 1990, 47, 1038–1047.

Arango, V., Ernsberger, P., Sued, A. F., & Mann, J. J. Quantitative autoradiography of alpha-1 and alpha-2 adrenergic receptors in the cerebral cortex of controls and suicide victims. *Brain Research*, 1993, 630, 271–282.

Arango, V., Underwood, M. D., Gubbi, A. V., & Mann, J. J. Localized alterations in pre- and post-synaptic serotonin binding sites in the ventrolateral prefrontal cortex of suicide victims. *Brain Research*, 1995, 688, 121–133.

Arango, V., Underwood, M. D., & Mann, J. J. Alterations in monoamine receptors in the brain of suicide victims. *Journal of Clinical Psychopharmacology*, 1992, 12, suppl. 2, 8–12.

Arango, V., Underwood, M. D., & Mann, J. J. Fewer pigmented locus coeruleus neurons in suicide victims. *Biological Psychiatry*, 1996a, 39, 112–120.

Arango, V., Underwood, M. D., Pauler, D. K., Kass, R. E., & Mann, J. J. Differential age-related loss of pigmented locus coeruleus neurons in suicides, alcoholics, and alcoholic suicides. *Alcoholism Clinical & Experimental Research*, 1996b, 20, 1141–1147.

Arato, M., Frecska, E., MacCrimmon, D. J., Guscott, R., Saxena, B., Tekes, K., & Tothfalusi, L. Serotonergic interhemispheric asymmetry. *Progress in Neurology & Psychopharmacology*, 1991a, 15, 759–764.

Arato, M., Tekes, K., Tothfalusi, L., Magyar, K., Palkovits, M., Frecska, E., Falus, A., & MacCrimmon, D. J. Reversed hemispheric asymmetry of imipramine binding in suicide victims. *Biological Psychiatry*, 1991b, 29, 699–702.

Arora, R. C., & Meltzer, H. Y. Laterality and 3H-imipramine binding. *Biological Psychiatry*, 1991, 29, 1016–1022.

Arora, R. C., & Meltzer, H. Y. Serotonin 2 receptor binding in blood platelets of schizophrenic patients. *Psychiatry Research*, 1993, 47, 111–119.

Arranz, B., Blennow, K., Ekman, R., Eriksson, A., & Marcusson, J. Brain neuropeptidergic function in suicide victims. *Human Psychopharmacology*, 1996, 11, 451–461.

Arranz, B., Blennow, K., Eriksson, A., Mansson, J. E., & Marcusson, J. Serotonergic, noradrenergic, and dopaminergic measures in suicide brains. *Biological Psychiatry*, 1997, 41, 1000–1009.

Arranz, B., Cowburn, R., Eriksson, A., Vestling, M., & Marcusson, J. Gamma-aminobutyric acid-B (GABAB) binding sites in postmortem suicide brains. *Neuropsychobiology*, 1992, 26, 33–36.

Arranz, B., Eriksson, A., Mellerup, E., Plenge, P., & Marcusson, J. Brain 5-HT1A, 5-HT1D, and 5-HT2 receptors in suicide victims. *Biological Psychiatry*, 1994, 35, 457–463.

Ashton, C. H., Marshall, E. F., Hassanyeh, F., Marsh, V. R., & Wright-Honari, S. Biological correlates of deliberate self-harm. *Acta Psychiatrica Scandinavica*, 1994, 90, 316–323.

Axelsson, R., & Lagerkvist-Briggs, M. Factors predicting suicide in psychotic patients. *European Archives of Psychiatry*, 1992, 241, 259–266.

Bachus, S. E., Hyde, T. M., Herman, M. M., Egan, M. F., & Kleinman, J. E. Abnormal cholecystokinin mRNA levels in entorhinal cortex of schizophrenics. *Journal of Psychiatric Research*, 1997, 31, 233–256.

Bayard-Burfield, L., Allin, C., Blennow, K., Jonsson, S., & Traskman-Bendz, L. Impairment of the blood-CSF barrier in suicide attempters. *European Neuropsychopharmacology*, 1996, 3, 195–199.

Bergman, B., & Brismar, B. Hormone levels and personality traits in abusive and suicidal male alcoholics. *Alcoholism: Clinical & Experimental Research*, 1994, 18, 311–316.

Biegon, A., & Fieldust, S. Reduced tyrosine hydroxylase immunoreactivity in locus coeruleus of suicide victims. *Synapse*, 1992, 10, 79–82.

Biegon, A., Grinspoon, A., Blumenfeld, B., Bleich, A., Apter, A., & Mester, R. Increased serotonin 5-HT2 receptor binding on blood platelets of suicidal men. *Psychopharmacology*, 1990, 100, 165–167.

Bowden, C., Cheetham, S. C., Lowther, S., Katona, C. L. E., Crompton, M. R., & Horton, R. W. Reduced dopamine turnover in the basal ganglia of depressed suicides. *Brain Research*, 1997a, 769, 135–140.

Bowden, C., Cheetham, S. C., Lowther, S., Katona, C. L. E., Crompton, M. R., & Horton, R. W. Dopamine uptake sites, labelled with [3H]GBR12935, in brain samples from depressed suicides and controls. *European Neuropsychopharmacology*, 1997c, 7, 247–252.

Bowden, C., Theodorou, A. E., Cheetham, S. C., Lowther, S., Katona, C. L. E., Crompton, M. R., & Horton, R. W. Dopamine D1 and D2 receptor binding sites in brain samples from depressed suicides and controls. *Brain Research*, 1997b, 752, 227–233.

Caine, R. L. Biorhythms and suicide. In B. S. Comstock & R. Maris (Eds.), *Proceedings of the 8th Annual Meeting*. Denver: AAS, 1976, 163–165.

Castrogiovanni, P., Fabiani, R., Toschi, D., Marazziti, D., & Conti, L. Aggressive behavior and suicidal attempts. In G. Ferrari, M. Bellini & P. Crepct (Eds.), *Suicidal behavior and risk factors*. Bologna: Monduzzi-Editore, 1990, 749–755.

Cheetham, S. C., Crompton, M. R., Katona, C. L. E., & Horton, R. W. Brain 5-HT1 binding sites in depressed suicides.

Psychopharmacology, 1990, 102, 544–548.

Cleare, A. J., Murray, R. M., & O'Keane, V. Reduced prolactin and cortisol responses to d-fenfluramine in depressed compared to healthy matched controls. *Neuropsychopharmacology*, 1996, 14, 349–354.

Cooper, S. J., Kelly, C. B., & King, D. J. 5-hydroxyindoleacetic acid in cerebrospinal fluid and prediction of suicidal behavior in schizophrenics. *Lancet*, 1992, 340, 940–941.

Corrigan, M. H. N., Gillette, G. M., Quade, D., & Garbutt, J. C. Panic, suicide, and agitation. *Biological Psychiatry*, 1992, 31, 984–992.

Coryell, W. DST abnormality as a predictor of course in major depression. *Journal of Affective Disorders*, 1990, 19, 163–169.

Cowburn, R. F., Marcusson, J. O., Eriksson, A., Wiehager, B., & O'Neill, C. Adenylyl cyclase activity and G-protein subunit levels in postmortem frontal cortex of suicide victims. *Brain Research*, 1994, 633, 297–304.

Cremniter, D., Thenault, M., Jamain, S., Meidinger, A., Delmas, C., & Gaillard, M. Serotonin and suicide. *Progress in Neuropsychopharmacology & Biological Psychiatry*, 1994, 18, 871–878.

Dahl, R. E., Puig-Antich, J., Ryan, N. D., Nelson, B., Dachille, S., Cunningham, S. L., Trubnick, L., & Klepper, T. P. EEG sleep in adolescents with major depression. *Journal of Affective Disorders*, 1990, 19, 63–75.

Dahl, R. E., Ryan, N. D., Puig-Antich, J., Nguyen, N. A., Al-Shabbout, M., Meyer, V. A., & Perel, J. 24-hour cortisol measures in adolescents with major depression. *Biological Psychiatry*, 1991, 30, 25–36.

De Leo, D., Caneva, A., Marazziti, D., & Conti, L. Platelet imipramine binding in intensive case unit suicidal patients. *European Archives of Psychiatry*, 1991, 241, 85–87.

Demuth, P. Wobbly biorhythms. *Human Behavior*, 1979, 8(4), 52–55.

De Paermentier, F. Cheetham, S. C., Crompton, M. R., Katona, C. L. E., & Horton, R. W. Brain beta-adrenoceptor binding sites in antidepressant-free depressed suicide victims. *Brain Research*, 1990, 525, 71–77.

De Paermentier, F. Cheetham, S. C., Crompton, M. R., Katona, C. L. E., & Horton, R. W. Brain beta-adrenceptor binding sites in

depressed suicide victims. *Psychopharmacology*, 1991, 105, 283–288.

De Paermentier, F., Crompton, M. R., Katona, C. L. E., & Horton, R. W. Beta-adrenoceptors in brain and pineal from depressed suicide victims. *Pharmacology & Toxicology*, 1992, 71, S1, 86–95.

De Paermentier, F., Lowther, S., Crompton, M. R., Katona, C. L. E., & Horton, R. W. Beta-adrenoceptors in human pineal glands are unaltered in depressed suicides. *Journal of Psychopharmacology*, 1997a, 11, 295–299.

De Paermentier, F., Mauger, J. M., Lowther, S., Crompton, M. R., Katona, C., & Horton, R. W. Brain alpha-adrenoceptors in depressed suicides. *Brain Research*, 1997b, 757, 60–68.

Dillon, K. A., Gross-Isseroff, R., Israeli, M., & Biegon, A. Autoradiographic analysis of serotonin 5-HT1A receptor binding in the human brain postmortem. *Brain Research*, 1991, 554, 56–64.

Freed, W. J., Dillon-Carter, O., & Kleinman, J. E. Properties of [3H]AMPA binding in postmortem human brain from psychotic subjects and controls. *Experimental Neurology*, 1993, 121, 48–56.

Gabilondo, A. M., Meana, J. J., & Garcia Sevilla, J. A. Increased density of mu-opioid receptors in the postmortem brain of suicide victims. *Brain Research*, 1995, 682, 245–250.

Galva, M. D., Bondiolotti, G. P., Olasmaa, M., & Picotti, G. B. Effect of aging on lazabemide binding, monoamine oxidase activity, and monoamine metabolites in human frontal cortex. *Journal of Neural Transmission*, 1995, 101, 83–94.

Garcia-Sevilla, J. A., Escriba, P. V., Sastre, M., Walzer, C., Busquets, X., Jacquet, G., Reis, D., & Guimon, J. Immunodetection and quantitation of imidazoline receptor proteins in platelets of patients with major depression and in brains of suicide victims. *Archives of General Psychiatry*, 1996, 53, 803–810.

Garcia-Sevilla, J. A., Meana, J. J., Barturen, F., & Pazos, A. Alpha-2-adrenoceptors in the brain of depressed suicide victims. *Clinical Neuropharmacology*, 1992, 15, suppl., 321A–322A.

Gardner, D. L., Lucas, P. B., & Cowdry, R. W. CSF metabolites in borderline personality disorder compared with normal controls. *Biological Psychiatry*, 1990, 28, 247–254.

Garvey, M. J., Holon, S. D., & Tuason, V. B. Relationship between 3-methoxy-4-hydroxyphenylglycol and suicide. *Neuropsychobiology*, 1994, 29, 112–116.

Garvey, M. J., & Noel, M. Association of levels of n-acetyl-beta-glucosaminidase with specific psychiatric symptoms. *Psychiatry Research*, 1993, 47, 129–139.

Garvey, M. J., & Underwood, K. Association of N-acetyl-beta-glucosaminidase levels with seriousness of suicide attempts. *Biological Psychiatry*, 1997, 42, 286–289.

Gilad, G. M., Gilad, V. H., Casanova, M. F., Casero, R. A. Polyamines and their metabolizing enzymes in human frontal cortex and hippocampus. *Biological Psychiatry*, 1995, 38, 227–234.

Goetz, R. R., Puig-Antich, J., Dahl, R. E., Ryan, N. D., Asnis, G. M., Rabinovich, H., & Nelson, B. EEG sleep of young adults with major depression. *Journal of Affective Disorders*, 1991, 22, 91–100.

Gonzalez, A. M., Pascual, J., Meana, J. J., Barturen, F., del Arco, C., Pazos, A., & Garcia-Sevilla, J. A. Autoradiographic demonstration of increased alpha2-adrenoceptor agonist binding sites in the hippocampus and frontal cortex of depressed suicide victims. *Journal of Neurochemistry*, 1994, 63, 256–265.

Graae, F., Tenke, C., Bruder, G., Rotheram, M. J., Piacentini, J., Castro-Blanco, D., Leite, P., & Towey, J. Abnormality of EEG alpha asymmetry in female adolescent suicide attempters. *Biological Psychiatry*, 1996, 40, 706–713.

Gross-Isseroff, R., Dillon, K. A., Fieldust, S. J., & Biegon, A. Autoradiographic analysis of alpha1-noradrenergic receptors in the human brain post-mortem. *Archives of General Psychiatry*, 1990a, 47, 1049–1053.

Gross-Isseroff, R., Dillon, K. A., Israeli, M., & Biegon, A. Regionally selective increases in mu-opoid receptor density in the brains of suicide victims. *Brain Research*, 1990b, 530, 312–316.

Gross-Isseroff, R., Salama, D., Israeli, M., & Biegon, A. Autoradiographic analysis of [3H]ketanserin binding in the human brain postmortem. *Brain Research*, 1990c, 507, 208–215.

Hansenne, M., Pitchot, W., Moreno, A. G., Torrecilas, J. G., Mirel, J., & Ansseau, M. Psychophysiological correlates of suicidal behavior in depression. *Neuropsychobiology*, 1994, 30, 1–3.

Hansenne, M., Pitchot, W., Moreno, A. G., Zaldua, I. U., & Ansseau, M. Suicidal behavior in depressive disorder. *Biological Psychiatry*, 1996, 40, 116–122.

Harro, J., Marusson, J., & Oreland, L. Alterations in brain cholecystokinin receptors in suicide victims. *European Neuropsychopharmacology*, 1992, 2(1), 57–63.

Holden, R. J. Schizophrenia, suicide, and the serotonin story. *Medical Hypotheses*, 1995, 44, 379–391.

Holeman, S. De Paermentier, F., Horton, R. W., Crompton, M. R., Katona, C. L. E., & Maloteaux, J. M. NMDA glutamatergic receptors, labelled with [3H] MK-801, in brain samples from drug-free depressed suicides. *Brain Research*, 1993, 616, 138–143.

Hrdina, P. D., Demeter, E., Vu, T. B., Solonyi, P., & Palkovitz, M. 5-HT uptake sites and 5-HT2 receptors in brain of antidepressant-free suicide victims/depressives, *Brain Research*, 1993, 614, 37–44.

Hucks, D., Lowther, S., Crompton, M. R., Katona, C. L. E., & Horton, R. W. Corticotropin-releasing factor binding sites in cortex of depressed suicides. *Psychopharmacology*, 1997, 134, 174–178.

Hui, M., Budai, E. D., Lajtha, A., Palkovits, M., & Hui, K. S. Changes in puromycin-sensitive aminopeptidases in postmortem schizophrenic brain regions. *Neurochemistry International*, 1995, 27, 433–441.

Hurd, Y. L., Herman, M. M., Hyde, T. M., Bigelow, L. B., Weinberger, D. R., & Kleinman, J. E. Prodynorphin mRNA expression is increased in the patch versus matrix compartment of the caudate nucleus in suicide subjects. *Molecular Psychiatry*, 1997, 2, 495–500.

Inder, W. J., Donald, R. A., Prickett, C. R., Frampton, C. M., Sullivan, P. F., Mulder, R. T., & Joyce, P. R. Arginine vasopressin is associated with hypercortisolemia and suicide attempts in depression. *Biological Psychiatry*,

1997, 42, 744–747.

Jones, J. S., Stanley, B., Mann, J. J., Frances, A. J., Guido, J. R., Traskman-Bendz, L., Winchel, R., Brown, R. D., & Stanley, M. CSF 5-HIAA and HVA concentrations in elderly depressed patients who attempt suicide. *American Journal of Psychiatry*, 1990, 147, 1225–1227.

Jones, J. S., Stein, D. J., Stanley, B., Guido, J. R., Winchel, R., & Stanley, M. Negative and depressive symptoms in suicidal schizophrenics. *Acta Psychiatrica Scandinavica*, 1994, 89, 81–87.

Jordan, D., Borson-Chazot, F., Veisseire, M., Deluermoz, S., Malicier, D., Dalery, J., & Kopp, N. Disappearance of hypothalamic TRH asymmetry in suicide patients. *Journal of Neural Transmission*, 1992, 89(1–2), 103–110.

Joyce, J. N., Lexow, N., Kim, S. J., Artymyshyn, R., Senzon, S., Lawrence, D., Cassanova, M. F., Kleinman, J. E., Bird, E. D., & Winokur, A. Distribution of beta-adrenergic receptor subtypes in human post-mortem brain. *Synapse*, 1992, 10, 228–246.

Juckel, G., & Hegerl, U. Evoked potentials, serotonin, and suicidality. *Pharmacopsychiatry*, 1994, 27, suppl. 1, 27–29.

Kato, T., Stine, O. C., McMahon, F. J., & Crowe, R. R. Increased levels of a mitochondrial DNA deletion in the brain of patients with bipolar disorder. *Biological Psychiatry*, 1997, 42, 871–875.

Keller, F., Wolfersdorf, M., Straub, R., & Hole, G. Suicidal behavior and electrodermal activity in depressive patients. *Acta Psychiatrica Scandinavica*, 1991, 83, 324–328.

Keshavan, M. S., Reynolds, C. F., Montrose, D., Miewald, J., Downs, C., & Sabo, E. M. Sleep and suicidality in psychotic patients. *Acta Psychiatrica Scandinavica*, 1994, 89, 122–125.

Klimek, V., Stockmeier, C., Overholser, J., Meltzer, H. Y., Kalka, S., Dilley, G., & Ordway, G. A. Reduced levels of norepinephrine transporters in the locus coeruleus in major depression. *Journal of Neuroscience*, 1997, 17, 8451–8458.

Knable, M. B., Hyde, T. M., Murray, A. M., Herman, M. M., & Kleinman, J. E. A post-mortem study of frontal cortical dopamine D1 receptors in schizophrenics, psychiatric con-

trols, and normal controls. *Biological Psychiatry*, 1996, 40, 1191–1199.

Kruesi, M. J. P., Hibbs, E. D., Zahn, T. P., Keysor, C. S., Hamburger, S. D., Bartko, J. J., & Rapoport, J. L. A 2-year follow-up study of children and adolescents with disruptive behavior disorders. *Archives of General Psychiatry*, 1992, 49, 429–439.

Laurence, K. M., De Paermentier, F., Cheetham, S. C., Crompton, M. R., Katona, C. L. E., & Horton, R. W. Brain 5-HT uptake sites, labelled with 3H-paroxetine, in antide-pressant-free depressed suicides. *Brain Research*, 1990a, 526, 17–22.

Laurence, K. M., De Paermentier, F., Cheetham, S. C., Crompton, M. R., Katona, C. L. E., & Horton, R. W. Symmetrical hemi-spheric distribution of 3H-paroxetine binding sites in postmortem human brain from con-trols and suicides. *Biological Psychiatry*, 1990b, 28, 544–546.

Laurence, K. M., De Paermentier, F., Lowther, S., Crompton, M. R., Katona, C., & Horton, R. W. Brain 5-hydroxytryptamine uptake sites labeled with 3H-paroxetine in antidepressant drug-treated depressed suicide victims and controls. *Journal of Psychiatry & Neuroscience*, 1997, 22, 185–191.

Lemus, C. Z., Lieberman, J. A., Johns, C. A., Pollack, S., Bookstein, P., & Cooper, T. B. CSF 5-hydroxyindoleacetic acid levels and suicide attempts in schizophrenia. *Biological Psychiatry*, 1990, 27, 926–929.

Lester, D. The association between platelet imipramine binding sites and suicide. *Pharmacopsychiatry*, 1991a, 24, 232.

Lester, D. Concentration of cerebrospinal fluid monoamine metabolites in suicide. *Psychological Reports*, 1991b, 68, 146.

Lester, D. National differences in dexam-ethasone suppression test results and suicide rates. *Psychological Reports*, 1991c, 69, 878.

Lester, D. The dexamethasone suppression test as an indicator of suicide. *Pharmacopsychiatry*, 1992a, 25, 265–270.

Lester, D. Rage dyscontrol and suicide. *South African Journal of Psychology*, 1992b, 22, 27–28.

Lester, D. The concentration of neurotrans-mitter metabolites in the cerebral spinal fluid of suicidal individuals. *Pharmacopsychiatry*, 1995, 28, 45–50.

Lewis, C. F., Tandon, R., Shipley, J. E., DeQuardo, J. R., Jibson, M., Taylor, S. F., & Goldman, M. Biological predictors of suicidality in schizophrenia. *Acta Psychiatrica Scandinavica*, 1996, 94, 416–420.

Little, K. Y., Clark, T. B., Rana, J., & Duncan, G. E. Beta-adrenergic receptor binding in frontal cortex from suicide victims. *Biological Psychiatry*, 1993, 34, 596–605.

Little, K. Y., McLaughlin, D. P., Ranc, J., Gilmore, J., Lopez, J. F., Watson, S. J., Carroll, F. I., & Butts, J. D. Serotonin transporter binding sites and mRNA levels in depressed persons committing suicide. *Biological Psychiatry*, 1997a, 41, 1156–1164.

Little, K. Y., Ranc, J., Gilmore, J., Patel, A., & Clark, T. B. Lack of pineal beta-adrenergic receptor alterations in suicide victims with major depression. *Psychoneuroendocrinology*, 1997b, 22(1), 53–62.

Lopez, J. F., Palkovits, M., Arato, M., Mansour, A., Akil, H., & Watson, S. J. Localization and quantification of pro-opiomelano-cortin mRNA and glucocorticoid receptor mRNA in pituitaries of suicide victims. *Neuroendocrinology*, 1992, 56, 491–501.

Lowther, S., Crompton, M. F., Katona, C. L. E., & Horton, R. W. GTP gamma S and forskolin-stimulated adenylyl cyclase activity in post-mortem brains from depressed suicides and controls. *Molecular Psychiatry*, 1996, 1, 470–477.

Lowther, S., De Paermentier, F., Cheetham, S. C., Crompton, M. R., Katona, C., & Horton, R. W. 5-HT1A receptor binding sites in post-mortem brain samples from depressed suicides and controls. *Journal of Affective Disorders*, 1997a, 42, 199–207.

Lowther, S., De Paermentier, F., Crompton, M. F., Katona, C. L. E., & Horton, R. W. Brain 5-HT2 receptors in suicide victims. *Brain Research*, 1994, 642, 281–289.

Lowther, S., Katona, C., Crompton, M. R., & Horton, R. W. Brain [3H]cAMP binding sites are unaltered in depressed suicides, but decreased by antidepressants. *Brain Research*, 1997b, 758, 223–228.

Maes, M., Scharpe, S., D'hondt, P., Peeters, D., Wauters, A., Neels, H., & Verkerk, R. Biochemical, metabolic, and immune correlates of seasonal variation in violent suicide. *European Psychiatry*, 1996, 11, 21–23.

Malone, K. M., Corbitt, E. M., Li, S., & Mann, J. J. Prolactin response to fenfluramine and suicide attempt lethality. *British Journal of Psychiatry*, 1996, 168, 324–329.

Mancini, C., & Brown, G. M. Urinary catecholamines and cortisol in parasuicide. *Psychiatry Research*, 1992, 43, 31–42.

Mann, J. J., Arango, V., Henteleff, R. A., Lagattuta, T. F., & Wong, D. T. Serotonin 5-HT3 receptor binding kinetics in the cortex of suicide victims are normal. *Journal of Neural Transmission*, 1996a, 103, 165–171.

Mann, J. J., Henteleff, R. A., Lagattuta, T. F., Perper, J. A., Li, S., & Arango, V. Lower 3H-paroxetine binding in cerebral cortex of suicide victims is partly due to fewer high affinity, non-transporter sites. *Journal of Neural Transmission*, 1996b, 10-3, 1337–1350.

Mann, J. J., & Malone, K. M. Cerebrospinal fluid amines and high-lethality suicide attempts in depressed inpatients. *Biological Psychiatry*, 1997, 41, 162–171.

Mann, J. J, Malone, K. M., Sweeney, J. A., Brown, R. P., Linnoila, M., Stanley, B., & Stanley, M. Attempted suicide characteristics and cerebral spinal fluid amine metabolites in depressed inpatients. *Neuropsychopharmacology*, 1996c, 15, 576–586.

Mann, J. J., McBride, A. P., Anderson, G. M., & Mieczkowski, T. A. Platelet and whole blood serotonin content in depressed inpatients. *Biological Psychiatry*, 1992a, 32, 243–257.

Mann, J. J., McBride, A., Brown, R. P., Linnoila, M., Leon, A. C., DeMeo, M., Mieczkowski, T., Myers, J. E., & Stanley, M. Relationship between central and peripheral serotonin indexes in depressed and suicidal psychiatric inpatients. *Archives of General Psychiatry*, 1992b, 49, 442–446.

Mann, J. J., McBride, A., Malone, K. M., DeMeo, M., & Keilp, J. Blunted serotonergic responsivity in depressed inpatients. *Neuropsychopharmacology*, 1995, 13, 53–64.

Marazziti, D., & Conti, L. Aggression and suicide attempts. *European Neuropsychopharmacology*, 1991, 1(2), 169–172.

Marazziti, D., Di Muro, A., Castrogiovani, P., & Conti, L. Suicide attempt and peripheral serotonergic markers. In G. Ferrari, M. Bellini & P. Crepet (Eds.), *Suicidal behavior and risk factors*. Bologna: Monduzzi-Editore, 1990, 663–667.

Marazziti, D., Presti, S., Silvertri, S., Battistini, A., Mosti, L., Balestri, C., Palego, L., & Conti, L. Platelet markers in suicide attempters. *Progress in Neuropsychopharmacology & Biological Psychiatry*, 1995, 19(3), 375–383.

Marazziti, D., Rotondo, A., Presta, S., Pancioli-Guadagnucci, M. L., Palego, L., & Conti, L. Role of serotonin in human aggressive behavior. *Aggressive Behavior*, 1993, 19, 347–353.

Matsubara, S., Arora, R. C., & Meltzer, H. Y. Serotonergic measures in suicide brain. *Journal of Neural Transmission*, 1991, 85, 181–194.

McBride, P. A., Brown, R. P., DeMeo, M., Kelp, J., Mieczkowski, T., & Mann, J. J. The relationship of platelet 5-HT2 receptor indices to major depressive disorder, personality traits, and suicidal behavior. *Biological Psychiatry*, 1994, 35, 295–308.

Meana, J. J., Barturen, F., & Garcia-Sevilla, J. A. Alph2-adrenoceptors in the brain of suicide victims. *Biological Psychiatry*, 1992, 31, 471–490.

Meana, J. J., Barturen, F., Martin, I., & Garcia-Sevilla, J. A. Evidence of increased non-adrenoceptor [3H] idazoxan binding sites in the frontal cortex of depressed suicide victims. *Biological Psychiatry*, 1993, 34, 498–501.

Milin, J., Previtera, L., Sovljanski, M., Previtera, M., & Milin, R. The pineal gland morphofunctional disorder. In G. Ferrari, M. Bellini & P. Crepet (Eds.), *Suicidal behavior and risk factors*. Bologna: Monduzzi-Editore, 1990, 693–698.

Mock-Seler, D., Jakovljevic, M., & Pivac, N. Platelet 5-HT concentrations and suicidal behavior in recurrent major depression. *Journal of Affective Disorders*, 1996, 39, 73–80.

Murray, A. M., Hyde, T. M., Knable, M. B., Herman, M. H., Bigelow, L. B., Carter, J. M., Weinberger, D. R., & Kleinman, J. E. Distribution of putative D4-dopamine receptors in postmortem striatum from patients with schizophrenia. *Journal of Neuroscience*, 1995, 15, 2186–2191.

Nassberger, L., & Traskman-Bendz, L. Increased soluble interleukin-2 receptor concentrations in suicide attempters. *Acta Psychiatrica Scandinavica*, 1993, 88, 48–52.

Naylor, L., Dean, B., Opeskin, K., Pavey, G., Hill, C., Keks, N., & Copolov, D. Changes in the serotonin transporter in the hippocampus of subjects with schizophrenia using 3H-paroxetine. *Journal of Neural Transmission*, 1996, 103, 749–757.

New, A. S., Treatman, R. L., Mitropouplou, V., Benishay, D. S., Coccaro, E., Silverman, J., & Siever, L. J. Serotonergic function and self-injurious behavior in personality disorder patients. *Psychiatry Research*, 1997, 69, 17–26.

Noga, J. T., Hyde, T. M., Herman, M. M., Spurney, C. F., Bigelow, L. B., Weinberger, D. R., & Kleinman, J. E. Glutamate receptors in the postmortem striatum of schizophrenics, suicides, and control brains. *Synapse*, 1997, 27, 168–176.

Nordstrom, P., Gustavsson, P., Edman, G., & Asberg, M. Temperamental vulnerability and suicide risk after attempted suicide. *Suicide & Life-Threatening Behavior*, 1996, 26, 380–394.

Nordstrom, P., Samuelsson, M., Asberg, M., Traskman-Bendz, L., Aberg-Wistedt, A., Nordin, C., & Bertilsson, L. CSF 5-HIAA predicts suicide risk after attempted suicide. *Suicide & Life-Threatening Behavior*, 1994, 24, 1–9.

Norman, W. H., Brown, W. A., Miller, I. W., Keitner, G. I., & Overholser, J. C. The dexamethasone suppression test and completed suicide. *Acta Psychiatrica Scandinavica*, 1990, 81, 120–125.

Nowak, G., Ordway, G. A., & Paul, I. A. Alterations in the N-methyl-D-aspartate (NMDA) receptor complex in the frontal cortex of suicide victims. *Brain Research*, 1995, 675, 157–164.

Oei, T. I., Verheoven, W. M. A., Westenberg, H. G. M., Zwart, F. M., & van Pee, J. M. Anhedonia, suicide ideation, and dexamethasone nonsuppression in depressed patients. *Journal of Psychiatric Research*, 1990, 24, 25–35.

Ohmori, T., Arora, R. C., & Meltzer, H. Y. Serotonergic measures in the suicide brain. *Biological Psychiatry*, 1992, 32, 57–71.

Ordway, G. A., Smith, K. S., & Haycock, J.

W. Elevated tyrosine hydroxylase in the locus coeruleus of suicide victims. *Journal of Neurochemistry*, 1994a, 62, 680–685.

Ordway, G. A., Stockmeier, C. A., Meltzer, H. Y., Overholser, J. C., Jaconetta, S., & Widdowson, P. S. Neuropeptide Y in frontal cortex is not altered in major depression. *Journal of Neurochemistry*, 1995, 65, 1646–1650.

Ordway, G. A., Widdowson, P. S., Smith, K. S., & Halaris, A. Agonist binding to alpha 2-adrenoceptors is elevated in the locus coeruleus from victims of suicide. *Journal of Neurochemistry*, 1994b, 63, 617–624.

Pacheco, M. A., Stockmeier, G., Meltzer, H. Y., Overholser, J. C., Dilley, G. E., & Jope, R. S. Alterations in phospoinositide and G-protein levels in depressed suicide brain. *Brain Research*, 1996, 723, 37–45.

Palmer, A. M., Burns, M. A., Arango, V., & Mann, J. J. Similar effects of glycine, zinc, and an oxidizing agent on [3H]dizocilpine binding to the N-methyl-D-aspartate receptor in neocortical tissue from suicide victims and controls. *Journal of Neural Transmission*, 1994, 96(1), 1–8.

Pandey, G. N., Conley, R. R., Pandey, S. C., Goel, S., Roberts, R. C., Tamminga, C. A., Chute, D., & Smialek, J. Benzodiazepine receptors in the post-mortem brain of suicide victims and schizophrenic subjects. *Psychiatry Research*, 1997a, 71, 137–149.

Pandey, G. N., Dwivedi, Y., Pandey, S. C., Conley, R. R., Roberts, R. C., & Tamminga, L. A. Protein kinase C in the postmortem brain of teenage suicide victims. *Neuroscience Letters*, 1997b, 228(2), 111–114.

Pandey, G. N., & Pandey, S. C., Dwivedi, Y., Sharma, R. P., Janicak, P. G., & Davis, J. M. Platelet serotonin-2A receptors. *American Journal of Psychiatry*, 1995,152, 850–855.

Pandey, G. N., Pandey, S. C., Janicak, P. G., & Davis, J. M. Serotonin receptors in depression and suicidal behavior. In D. Lester (Ed.), *Suicide '92*. Denver: AAS, 1992, 239–240.

Pandey, G. N., Pandey, S. C., Janicak, P. G., Marks, R. C., & Davis, J. M. Platelet serotonin-2 receptor binding sites in depression and suicide. *Biological Psychiatry*, 1990, 28, 215–222.

Pfeffer, C. R., Stokes, P., & Shindledecker, R. Suicidal behavior and hypothalamic-pituitary-adrenocortical axis indices in child psychiatric inpatients. *Biological Psychiatry*, 1991, 29, 909–917.

Pine, D. S., Trautman, P. D., Shaffer, D., Cohen, L., Davies, M., Stanley, M., & Parsons, B. Seasonal rhythm of platelet [3H]-imipramine binding in adolescents who attempted suicide. *American Journal of Psychiatry*, 1995, 152, 923–925.

Pitchot, W., Ansseau, M., Moreno, A. G., Lembreghts, M., Hansenne, M., Wauthy, J., Reel, C., Jammaer, R., Papart, P., Sulon, J., & Legros, J. The flesinoxam 5-HT1A receptor challenge in major depression and suicidal behavior. *Pharmacopsychiatry*, 1995a, 28, suppl. 2, 91–92.

Pitchot, W., Ansseau, M., Moreno, A. G., Wauthy, J., Hansenne, M., & Van Frenckell, R. Relationship between alpha2-adrenergic function and suicidal behavior in depressed patients. *Psychiatry Research*, 1994, 52, 115–123.

Pitchot, W., Hansenne, M., Moreno, A. G., & Ansseau, M. Suicidal behavior and growth hormone response to apomorphine test. *Biological Psychiatry*, 1992, 31, 1213–1219.

Pitchot, W., Hensenne, M., Moreno, A. G., & Ansseau, M. The dexamethasone suppression test in violent suicide attempters with major depression. *Biological Psychiatry*, 1995b, 37, 272–274.

Pitchot, W., Hensenne, M., Moreno, A. G., & Ansseau, M. Growth hormone response to clonidine in nondepressed patients with a history of suicide attempts. *Biological Psychiatry*, 1995c, 38, 201–203.

Rao, A. V., & Devi, S. Hopelessness, melatonin, and suicidal behavior. In K. Bohme, R. Freytag, C. Wachtler, & H. Wedler (Eds.), *Suicidal behavior*. Regensburg: S. Roderer, 1993, 805–806.

Rao, M. L., Braunig, P., & Papassotiropoulos, A. Autoaggressive behavior is closely related to serotonin availability in schizoaffective disorder. *Pharmacopsychiatry*, 1994, 27, 202–206.

Rechlin, T., Weis, M., Spitzer, A., & Kaschka, W. P. Are affective disorders associated with alterations of heart rate variability? *Journal of Affective Disorders*, 1994, 32, 271–275.

Reichborn-Kjennervd, T., Lingjaerde, O., &

Oreland, L. Platelet monoamine oxidase activity in patients with winter seasonal affective disorder. *Psychiatry Research*, 1996, 62, 273–280.

Repo, E., Virkkunen, M., Rawlings, R., & Linnoila, M. Suicidal behavior among Finnish fire setters. *European Archives of Psychiatry*, 1997, 247, 303–307.

Rochet, T., Kopp, N., Vedrinne, J., Delvermoz, S., Debilly, G., & Miachon, S. Benzodiazepine binding sites and their modulators in hippocampus of violent suicide victims. *Biological Psychiatry*, 1992, 32, 922–931.

Rommelspacher, H., Baum, S. S., Dufeu, P., & Schmidt, L. G. Determination of (R)- and (S)-salsolinol sulfate and dopamine sulfate levels in plasma of nonalcoholics and alcoholics. *Alcohol*, 1995, 12, 309–315.

Rommelspacher, H., May, T., Dufeu, P., & Schmidt, L. G. Longitudinal observations of monoamine oxidase B in alcoholics. *Alcoholism: Clinical & Experimental Research*, 1994, 18, 1322–1329.

Rosel, P., Arranz, B., Vallejo, J., Oros, M., Menchon, J. M., Alvarez, P., & Navarro, M. A. High affinity [3H] imipramine and [3H] paroxetine binding sites in suicide brains. *Journal of Neural Transmission*, 1997, 104, 921–929.

Rossi, A., Toschi, D., Carratori, F., & Conti, L. Alcohol abuse and suicidal attempt. *Alcoholism (Zagreb)*, 1996, 31(1), 61–68.

Roy, A. CSF monoamine metabolites and suicidal behavior in depressed patients. In G. Ferrari, M. Bellini, & P. Crepet (Eds.), *Suicidal behavior and risk factors*. Bologna: Monduzzi-Editore, 1990, 21–25.

Roy, A. Neuropeptides in relation to suicidal behavior in depression. *Neuropsychobiology*, 1993, 28, 184–186.

Roy, A. Hypothalamic-pituitary-adrenal axis function and suicidal behavior in depression. *Biological Psychiatry*, 1992, 32, 812–816.

Roy, A., Karoum, F., & Pollack, S. Marked reduction in indices of dopamine metabolism among patients with depression who attempt suicide. *Archives of General Psychiatry*, 1992, 49, 447–450.

Roy, A., Lamparski, D. DeJong, J., Adinoff, B., Ravitz, B., George, D. T., Nutt, D., & Linnoila, M. CSF monoamine metabolites in alcoholic patients who attempt suicide. *Acta Psychiatrica Scandinavica*, 1990, 81, 58–61.

Roy, A., & Lavin, M. Marked reduction in indexes of dopamine metabolism among patients with depression who attempt suicide. In D. Lester (Ed.), *Suicide '94*. Denver: AAS, 1994, 125–126.

Roy, A., & Pollack, S. Are cerebrospinal fluid or urinary monoamine metabolite measures stronger correlates of suicidal behavior in depression. *Neuropsychobiology*, 1994, 29, 164–167.

Ruiz, J., Gabilondo, A. M., Meana, J. J., & Garcia-Sevilla, J. A. Increased [3H] raclopride binding sites in postmortem brains from schizophrenic violent suicide victims. *Psychopharmacology*, 1992, 109, 410–414.

Sabo, E., Reynolds, C. F., Kupfer, D. J., & Berman, S. R. Sleep, depression, and suicide. *Psychiatry Research*, 1991, 36, 265–288.

Sandyk, R., & Awerbuch, G. I. Nocturnal melatonin secretion in suicidal patients with multiple sclerosis. *International Journal of Neuroscience*, 1993, 71, 173–182.

Sandyk, R., & Kay, S. R. Choroid plexus calcification. *International Journal of Neuroscience*, 1991, 57, 95–97.

Sastre, M., Escriba, P. V., Reis, D. J., & Garcia-Sevilla, J. A. Decreased number and immunoreactivity of I2-imidazoline receptors in the frontal cortex of suicide victims. *Annals of the New York Academy of Sciences*, 1995, 763, 520–522.

Sastre, M., & Garcia-Sevilla, J. A. Densities of I2-imidazoline receptors, alpha2-adrenoceptors and monoamine oxidase B in brains of suicide victims. *Neurochemistry International*, 1997, 30(1), 63–72.

Scarone, S., Gambini, O., Calabrese, G., Sacerdote, P., Bruni, M., Carucci, M., & Panerai, A. E. Asymmetrical distribution of beta-endorphin in cerebral hemispheres of suicides. *Psychiatry Research*, 1990, 32, 159–166.

Schrauzer, G. N., & Shrestha, K. P. Lithium in drinking water and the incidence of crimes, suicides and arrests related to drug addictions. *Biological Trace Element Research*, 1990, 25, 105–113.

Serres, F., Dassa, D., Azorin, J. M., & Jeanningros, R. Decrease in red blood cell L-tryptophan uptake in schizophrenic patients.

Progress in Neuropsychopharmacology, 1995, 19, 903–913.

Sherif, F., Marcusson, J., & Oreland, L. Brain gamma-aminobutyrate transaminase and monoamine oxidase activities in suicide victims. *European Archives of Psychiatry*, 1991, 241, 139–144.

Shimon, H., Agam, G., Belmaker, R. H., Hyde, T. M., & Kleinman, J. E. Reduced frontal cortex inositol levels in postmortem brain of suicide victims and patients with bipolar disorder. *American Journal of Psychiatry*, 1997, 154, 1148–1150.

Simonsson, P., Traskman-Bendz, L. Allinder, C., Oreland, L., Regnell, G., & Ohman, R. Peripheral serotonergic markers in patients with suicidal behavior. *European Neuropsychopharmacology*, 1991, 1, 503–510.

Sparks, D. L., & Little, K. Y. Altered pineal serotonin binding in some suicides. *Psychiatry Research*, 1990, 32, 19–28.

Stein, E., McCrank, E., Schaefer, B., & Goyer, R. Adrenal gland weight and suicide. *Canadian Journal of Psychiatry*, 1993, 38, 563–566.

Stockmeier, C. A., Dilley, G. E., Shapiro, L. A., Overholser, J. C., Thompson, P. A., & Meltzer, H. Y. Serotonin receptors in suicide victims with major depression. *Neuropsychopharmacology*, 1997, 16, 162–173.

Stockmeier, C. A., & Meltzer, H. Y. Beta adrenergic receptor binding in frontal cortex of suicide victims. *Biological Psychiatry*, 1991, 29, 183–191.

Stocks, G. M., Cheetham, S. C., Crompton, M. F., Katona, C. L. E., & Horton, R. W. Benzodiazepine binding sites in amygdala and hippocampus of depressed suicide victims. *Journal of Affective Disorders*, 1990, 18, 11–15.

Sumiyoshi, T., Stockmeier, C. A., Overholser, J. C., Thompson, P. A., & Meltzer, H. Y. Dopamine D4 receptors and effects of guanine nucleotides on [3H]raclopride binding in postmortem caudate nucleus of subjects with schizophrenia or major depression. *Brain Research*, 1995, 681, 109–116.

Sundman, I., Allard, P., Eriksson, A., & Marcusson, J. GABA uptake sites in frontal cortex from suicide victims and in aging. *Neuropsychobiology*, 1997, 35, 11–15.

Szigethy, E., Conwell, Y., Forbes, N. T., Cox, C., Caine, E. D. Adrenal weight and morphology in victims of completed suicide. *Biological Psychiatry*, 1994, 36, 374–380.

Traskman-Bendz, L., Alling, C., Alsen, M., Regnell, G., Simonsson, P., & Ohman, R. The role of monoamines in suicidal behavior. *Acta Psychiatrica Scandinavica*, 1993, Suppl. 371, 45–47.

Traskman-Bendz, L., Alling, C., Oreland, L., Regnell, G., Vinge, E., & Ohman, R. Prediction of suicidal behavior from biological tests. *Journal of Clinical Psychopharmacology*, 1992a, 12, Suppl. 2, 21–26.

Traskman-Bendz, L., Ekman, R., Regnell, G., & Ohman, R. HPA-related CSF neuropeptides in suicide attempters. *European Neuropsychopharmacology*, 1992b, 2, 99–106.

Tripodianakis, J., Markianos, M., Sarantidis, D., Istikoglou, C., Andara, A., & Bistolaki, E. Platelet monoamine oxidase in attempted suicide. *European Psychiatry*, 1995, 10, 44–48.

Van Kempen, G. M., Notten, P., & Hengeveld, M. W. Repeated measures of platelet MAO activity and 5-HT in a group of suicidal women. *Biological Psychiatry*, 1992, 31, 529–530.

Verkes, R. J., Fekkes, D., Zwinderman, A. H., Hengeveld, M. W., van der Mast, R. C., Tuyl, J. P., Kerkhof, A., & van Kempen, G. Platelet serotonin and 3H-paroxetine binding correlated with recurrence of suicidal behavior. *Psychopharmacology*, 1997, 132, 89–94.

Verkes, R. J., Pijl, H., Meinders, A. E., & Van Kempen, G. Borderline personality, impulsiveness, and platelet monoamine measures in bulimia nervosa and recurrent suicidal behavior. *Biological Psychiatry*, 1996, 40, 173–180.

Vignau, J., Bally, D., Duhamel, A., Vervaecke, P., Beuscart, R., & Collinet, C. Epidemiologic study of sleep quality and troubles in French secondary school adolescents. *Journal of Adolescent Health*, 1997, 21, 343–350.

Wasserman, D. E., Hellstrom, C., Wasserman, J., Beck, O., Andersson, E., & Asberg, M. Natural killer cell activity and CSF monoamine metabolites in suicide attempters. *Archives of Suicide Research*, 1997, 3, 153–169.

Wasserman, D. E., Wasserman, J., Asberg, M., Hellstrom, C., & Beck, O. NK-cells and suicidality. In D. Lester (Ed.), *Suicide '92.* Denver: AAS, 1992, 188–189.

Wasserman, D. E., Wasserman, J., Asberg, M., Hellstrom, C., & Beck, O. NK-cells a peripheral marker for suicidality? In K. Bohme, R. Freytag, C. Wachtler & H. Wedler (Eds.), *Suicidal behavior.* Regensburg: S. Roderer, 1993, 779–782.

Widdowson, P. S., Ordway, G. A., & Halaris, A. E. Reduced neuropeptide Y concentrations in suicide brain. *Journal of Neurochemistry,* 1992, 59, 73–80.

Wolfersdorf, M., Keller, F., Maier, V., Froscher, W., & Kaschka, W. P. Red-cell and serum foliate levels in depressed inpatients who commit violent suicide. *Pharmacopsychiatry,* 1995, 28, 77–79.

Wolfersdorf, M., & Straub, R. Electrodermal reactivity in male and female depressive patients who later died by suicide. *Acta Psychiatrica Scandinavica,* 1994, 89, 279–284.

Wolfersdorf, M., Straub, R., & Barg, T. Electrodermal activity (EDA) and suicidal behavior. *Crisis,* 1996, 17(2), 69–77.

Wolfersdorf, M., Straub, R., & Hole, G. Electrodermal activity in depressed men and women with violent or nonviolent suicide attempts. *Schweizer Archiv fur Neurologie & Psychiatrie,* 1993, 144, 173–184.

Wyatt, R. J., Karoum, F., & Casanova, M. F. Decreased DOPAC in the anterior cingluate cortex of individuals with schizophrenia. *Biological Psychiatry,* 1995, 38, 4–12.

Zonda, T., & Lester, D. Blood type and suicide. *Biological Psychiatry,* 1993, 33, 850–851.

Chapter 3

SEX, SEXUAL ORIENTATION, AND SUICIDE

THE BASIC SEX DIFFERENCE

The well-documented sex difference in suicidal behavior is that men complete suicide more than women, although women attempt suicide more than men. Koczan and Ozsvath (1990) calculated rates of suicidal behavior in one Hungarian county for 1984–1986. The completed suicide rate for men was 87 and for women 28; the attempted suicide rate for men was 261 and for women 348. In Israel, 1977–1986, Sharlin and Lowenstein (1997) found more completed suicides among Israeli males than females 65 and older (373 versus 259) and more attempted suicides among elderly females (648 versus 404). The completed and attempted suicides did not differ in age, origin, or marital status. The completed suicides more often were depressed and had physical illnesses, while the attempted suicides more often had psychiatric disorders and relationship problems. The presence of mental illness rose for both groups over the period.

Data has been published for 10 percent of the population of China indicating a higher completed suicide rate for women than for men in both urban and rural areas (Lester, 1990c), a finding that was reported many times during the 1990s by various authors. The most common motive for suicide in women was family conflict (He and Lester,

1997). The sex difference in completed suicide in China is found only for those under the age of 60 (Zhao et al., 1994). He and Lester (1997) found that the association was negative between the gender ratio in the population and the gender ratio for suicide rates over age groups.

Other reversals have been noted. In Jhansi City (India) from 1986–1987, the female completed suicide rate exceeded the male rate (Shukla et al., 1990). The most popular method for men was the train and for women burning. In Honiara in the Solomon Islands, both completed suicide and attempted suicide seem to be more common in females than in males (Pridmore, 1997). In Helsinki in 1989, Ostamo and Lonnqvist (1990) found, based on general hospital data, an attempted suicide rate of 321 for men and 233 for women. In Gent (Belgium), Van Heeringen (1994) found that the highest odds ratio for attempted suicides was for males aged 30–45 who were unemployed. In Belgium, Anonymous (1992) found that female attempted suicide rates were higher than male rates for those under the age of 60, but lower for the elderly. The women had made more prior attempts. In the Netherlands, Kingma (1994) found that male/female ratio for suicide attempters in trauma units declined after the age of 40.

In Northern Ireland, Donnelly (1995)

found that male students aged 11–15 more often agreed with the statement "I want to kill myself" than did female students. On the other hand, Kirby et al. (1997) found no sex differences in suicidal ideation in the elderly in Dublin (Ireland). Those with depressive disorders and those aged 65–74 had more suicidal ideation. Lester and Abdel-Khalek (1997) found that female American and Kuwaiti college students had higher scores regarding current suicidal ideation than males in both samples combined, but not significantly higher in either sample separately.

In Norwegian psychiatric patients, Gotestam et al. (1995) found that women with eating disorders had higher rates of attempted suicide, suicidal ideation, and depressive disorders than men with eating disorders.

Maxim and Keane (1992) found that male and female completed suicide rates did not converge in Canada from 1950–1986. Lester (1994c) found little evidence of convergence for 1970–1984 in 23 nations.

Sex Differences in Suicidal Behavior

Attempted Suicide

Spirito et al. (1993) compared adolescent male and female attempters. The males more often had a conduct disorder and the females an adjustment reaction. They did not differ in age, race, social class, living with parents, prior attempts, prior psychiatric contacts, risk-rescue scores, suicidal intent, depression, hopelessness or the characteristics of the attempt. Suominen et al. (1996) found that male attempted suicides were more clinically depressed and more often had an antisocial personality disorder, whereas female attempted suicides more often had depressive syndromes and borderline personality disorder.

Welcher et al. (1993) found that female suicide attempters were less often single, living alone, and alcoholics than male attempters. Repeaters were also more often female (as well as 25–54, schizophrenics, substance abusers, unmarried, living alone, and pensioners). Among self-poisoners in Dublin (Ireland), Coakley et al. (1994) found that the men had more often drunk some alcohol before the suicide attempt. Vrabichev (1992) found that men with sexual problems were more often suicidal than those without such problems, but no such differences were found for women.

Among high school students making one suicide attempt, Mazza and Reynolds (1994) found that the girls were more depressed than the boys, but did not differ in suicidal ideation. For those making two or more attempts, there were no sex differences. The multiple attempters were more depressed than the single attempters, and for the girls, had more suicidal ideation.

Waeld et al. (1994) found that current suicidal ideation in college students was predicted by masculinity scores (but not femininity scores) for both women and men. Suicidal ideation in men was associated with achievement-related stressors and in women with interpersonal stressors.

Vannatta (1997) found that suicidality in the prior 30 days was associated with forcible sex, school misconduct, unfair/strict rules and home environment factors for boys and with over-the-counter drug use, cigarette use, and forcible sex factors in girls.

Bjerke et al. (1990) found that male attempters more often abused alcohol, were more often unemployed or self-employed, were more often single, and more often had jail experience or police contact; they were less often victims of violence, living with parents or children, or on disability pensions. The same differences were found for first-timers and for repeaters.

Among schizophrenic outpatients who attempted suicide in Athens (Greece), Kontaxakis et al. (1990) found that the men were more often single and living with parents, while the women were more often married and living with their spouse. The men and women did not differ in age, education, unemployment, method for suicide, prior attempts, or prior psychiatric hospitalizations.

In Sweden, Mutzell (1997) found that male attempters were older than female attempters, more often had a criminal record, and more often died during the 20-year follow-up period (although the causes of death were similar in male and female attempters).

Hawton and Fagg (1992) found that adolescent male attempters in England were more likely to have had prior psychiatric treatment and recent financial and legal problems (though not more overall stressors). They also more often had ingested alcohol in the six hours prior to the attempt, more often had criminal convictions and drug dependency, and were more likely to be unemployed, not living with relatives/friends, and violent toward others.

Completed Suicide

In Ireland, Daeid (1997) confirmed that marriage had a greater protective effect on suicide rates for men than for women.

Henriksson et al. (1993) found that female suicides in Finland were less often diagnosed as alcohol abusers and more often as having depressive disorders and borderline personality disorders than were male suicides. Comorbidity was common in both groups, but more so among the males.

Marttunen et al. (1995) studied teenage suicides in Finland and found that the females more often had major depressive disorders, borderline personality disorders,

psychosocial impairment, and comorbidity than the males and more often had made previous suicide attempts. Ferrence (1989) found that women attempters and completers were less often alcohol abusers and less often intoxicated during the suicidal action than men.

Nordstrom et al. (1995) followed up attempted suicides and found that more of the men subsequently completed suicide than the women and that more of the older women completed suicide than younger women under the age of 35.

Gill et al. (1996) found no differences in suicidal intent (or the components of suicidal intent) between male and female suicides, except that the acts by males were more open to possible intervention. More younger men than older men had made prior attempts, whereas more older women than younger women had made prior attempts. Older females used less-violent methods than younger females. Older suicides also had more suicidal intent than younger suicides.

Among suicides of young adults, Runeson et al. (1996a) found that the women had made more prior attempts than the men, with longer intervals between the first suicidal communication and the completed suicide. Differences were not found in the presence of alcohol or drugs in their bodies. The women had fewer deceased parents and less suicide in their families (attempted and completed).

In Northern Ireland, O'Connor and Sheehy (1997) found that female completed suicides were older than males, more often married and living with a partner, were more likely to have health problems and major depressive disorders, and had made more prior attempts. Females used poisons more and hanging less. They did not differ in employment or contacts with general practitioners.

Seiden and Gleiser (1990) compared

suicides by male and female chemists. The women's suicides were more often related to work problems (slow promotion, isolation at work, and discrimination). Fewer women were married or had tenure, and they more often had a psychiatric disturbance. Cyanide was the most popular method for suicide among both sexes.

In Lothian (Scotland), Squires and Busuttil (1991) found that male elderly suicides were more often drunk at the time of the suicide and more often left a suicide note than did female elderly suicides.

In India, Mahanta and Trivedi (1993) found that family problems were more common in female suicides than in male suicides, although they were present in a good proportion of both men and women.

Wolfersdorf et al. (1993) found that whereas female completed suicides were more often diagnosed with a depressive disorder, male suicides were more often diagnosed with a personality disorder and alcoholism.

Maris (1981) found that more female suicides had made prior suicide attempts, were drug abusers, and were hopeless; they were less often beer drinkers and had less intergenerational mobility than male completers. The men and women did not differ in early trauma, sexual deviance, depression, or physical health.

Hormones

In a sample of high school students, Martin et al. (1997) found that males who had attempted suicide had higher levels of progesterone (especially if they also used alcohol or marihuana) than nonattempters. Females with suicidal ideation had lower levels.

Method

Frierson and Lippman (1990) found that black male attempted suicides in Kentucky used guns for their attempt more than women and were more often schizophrenic; the females used overdoses more, and they more often had a major depressive disorder. The men and women did not differ in age. Rogers (1990) noted that use of guns by women for suicide in the United States increased during the 1980s.

Lester (1990b) analyzed suicidal injury data from men and women who jumped from heights of 6 to 12 meters. The sexes did not differ in injury severity when jumping from similar heights. Thus, there is no evidence that women die from suicidal acts less often than men simply because they injure less easily or are physiologically hardier.

Stone (1990) in Dallas for 1985–1988 found that male and female completed suicides who used long guns shot themselves in the body (versus the head) equally often. Among those using handguns, however, women were more likely than men to shoot themselves in the body (31 percent versus 16 percent).

Hulten and Wasserman (1992) noted that young females (10–29 years old) in Sweden turned to violent methods for suicide more often during the period 1974–1986. Male and female youth suicides were less often married and more often divorced or single than young people in general.

Lester (1992b) found that the similarity in methods men and women used for suicide was associated with the percentage using guns for suicide over the states of the United States. Thus, the more frequently that guns were used for suicide in a state, the greater the similarity in methods used by men and women for suicide.

In 25 nations, Lester (1994a) found that in 1980 male suicide rates were higher than female rates for all methods, except the use of solids/liquids. Lester (1993c) argued that the sex difference in suicide rates was accounted for by the use of violent methods. Lester showed that in 25 nations men and women have similar rates of suicide by non-violent methods and suggested that testosterone was responsible for the high rate of violent suicide by men.

Sex Roles

Street and Kromrey (1995) found that prior suicidality was less common in androgynous men and women and masculine men and more common in feminine men and masculine women.

Friends

Wallace and Kral (1994) found that female undergraduates had more friends who had been suicidal than had male undergraduates. Kalafat and Elias (1992) found that ninth grade girls were more likely than boys to know an attempted suicide, to know a completed suicide, and to have talked to a suicidal person.

Research on Women

Bettridge and Favreau (1995) found no differences in trait dependency between female adolescent attempters and normal controls. The attempters had social networks and intimate relationships that were less available and less adequate. They did not differ in recent loss or conflicts or completed suicide in their families. The attempters had experienced more severe conflicts, more attempted suicide in their families, and more physical and sexual abuse. They were less certain that their relationships would continue for life.

Runeson et al. (1996b) compared hospitalized female suicide attempters with normal controls. The attempters more often

had a mental disorder, had been unemployed, and used anxiolytics more.

Merrill et al. (1990) noted that Asian women (mainly from the Indian subcontinent) in England who attempted suicide often hold non-traditional values and so came into conflict with their parents. This conflict, combined with hopelessness, led to a high suicidal intent.

Arcel et al. (1992) found that women who attempted suicide in Denmark and Greece frequently had poor relationships with their husbands or lovers.

Battering and Abuse

Stark and Flitcraft (1995) found that female attempted suicides seen in the emergency room who had been battered were more often pregnant at the time of the battering, had more miscarriages, had attempted suicide more often, used more violent means, and were more often African Americans.

In a sample of women in bad relationships, Vitanza et al. (1995) found that attempting suicide was associated with private self-consciousness scores. In the women severely abused, attempting suicide was associated with cognitive failure (difficulties with perception, memory, and motor functions).

In a domestic-violence program in Florida, Stawar (1996) found a higher rate of suicide among the participants than expected. Roberts et al. (1997) found that domestic violence victims had more current and prior suicidality than other emergency room patients. Bergman and Brismar (1991a, 1991b) found that battered wives had made many more suicide attempts than controls.

Anderson et al. (1993) found that 57 percent of a group of women who had been sexually abused as children had attempted suicide.

Suicide and the Menstrual Cycle

Lester (1990a) carried out a meta-analysis of studies on attempted and completed suicide over the menstrual cycle. The only significant variation was for attempted suicide to decline in the third week of the cycle. Targum et al. (1991) found no differences in menstrual phase between suicide attempters and other emergency psychiatric admissions. Rupani and Lema (1993) found that suicidal tendencies were rare in Kenyan nurses premenstrually (only in about one percent).

In India, Chaturvedi et al. (1995) found that women who became suicidal during the premenstrual phase were less likely to be housewives and more likely to be college women in arts and working women in industry. The suicidal women were more irritable and depressed and had more mood swings and water retention.

Vanezis (1990) found an excess of completed suicides (and natural and accidental deaths, but not homicides) during days 6–15 of the menstrual cycle (the proliferative phase) and a deficit in the menstrual phase (days 1–5) and early secretory phase (days 16–19). Chia (1981) found more completed suicides during the premenstrual phase than in the menstrual or other phases of the cycle.

Menstrual Problems

Merikangas et al. (1993) found that young female adults with menstrual problems were more likely than females with no menstrual problems to have a major depressive disorder (and phobias) and tended to attempt suicide more often.

Pregnancy

Appleby (1991) calculated SMRs for women in England for 1973–1984. The ratio was below normal during pregnancy, for the first postnatal year, for teenage mothers, and for unmarried mothers; it was average for women who had stillbirths. In New York City, Marzuk et al. (1997) found an under-representation of pregnant women among the suicides (only one third as many as expected).

Dannenberg et al. (1995) found that women currently or recently pregnant in New York City had a rate of suicide similar to nonpregnant women, although there was an increase in suicides postpartum. Hogberg et al. (1994) appeared to report a high rate of suicide in the first year of motherhood (31 suicides in 134 maternal deaths).

Gissler et al. (1996) found that 73 suicides in Finland out of 1347 among women aged 15–49 were associated with pregnancy: 30 with birth, 29 with abortion, and 14 with miscarriage. The suicide rate was significantly lower after the birth (except for teenagers aged 15–19 for whom it was higher); it was higher after a miscarriage and abortion. Those women who completed suicide after pregnancy were more often unmarried and lower class. Bagedahl-Strindlund (1997) found that mothers with postpartum mental illness were more likely to complete suicide than mothers without.

Appleby and Turnbull (1995) found that the attempted suicide rate was lower in the first postnatal year than in women at other times. Czeizel and Mosonyi (1997) found that attempting suicide with poisons was most common in the first month of pregnancy. Klompenhouwer et al. (1995) found that postpartum suicidality was more common in women with depressive disorders.

Abortion

Clare and Tyrrell (1994) reviewed available data and concluded that suicide was rare during pregnancy if the woman was refused an abortion.

Misic-Pavkov et al. (1993) found that suicidal ideation, prior suicide attempts, and depression were more common in women who had nonapproved late abortions (after ten weeks) than in those with approved abortions or earlier abortions. Morgan et al. (1997) found a rate of attempted suicide prior to the event higher in women who had a miscarriage than in those who had an abortion; the latter had a higher rate than women delivering their babies. After the pregnancy, the attempted suicide rate was highest in those with an induced abortion, less for women who had a miscarriage, and least in those delivering.

Sexual and Physical Abuse

Amaro et al. (1990) compared poor, urban, pregnant minority women who had been physically or sexually abused during their pregnancy with those who had not. The abused women more often were depressed, substance abusers, and with a history of attempted suicide.

The Sex Ratio

Javanainen (1990) looked at the male/female suicide rate ratio for completed suicide in Finland and found that it was lower in the more educated, the upper social class, and in urban regions. By income, the ratio was lower in the richer, primarily due to a relatively lower suicide rate in richer men.

Lester (1990d) noted that the ordering of the sex ratios for estimates of depressed females/males in Hong Kong, the Netherlands, and the United States matched the ratios for the numbers of female/male completed-plus-attempted suicides, but not the ratios for female/male completed suicides.

Lester (1990e) looked at the male/female completed suicide rate ratio for 31 nations.

The ratio was lower in wealthier nations for older adults, and higher in wealthier nations for younger adults suggesting that the sex ratio may be differently determined in youths and older adults.

Looking at 23 nations in 1974 and 1986, Pritchard (1990) concluded that the trend was for the male/female suicide rate ratio to widen. Lester (1993a) found the male/female suicide rate ratio increased in the majority of nations from 1970–1984. The ratio in the nations in 1970 was associated only with the proportion of elderly and not with gender equality. Lester (1994b) found that the sex ratio for suicide rates was not associated with measures of occupational sex segregation or sex egalitarianism in 24 industrialized nations.

Lester (1992a) found that subscriptions to *MS Magazine* per capita were associated neither with female or male suicide rates, nor with the ratio of, or the difference between, the male and female suicide rates.

Lester (1993b) found that the sex ratio of completed suicides in the United States was not associated with the sex ratio found in samples of attempted suicides during the period 1940–1980.

Homosexuality

Nonfatal Suicidality

Bigagli and Grillini (1990) found in a survey in Italy that 6 percent of attempted suicides and 22 percent of those with suicidal ideation were motivated in part by their homosexuality. This was especially true among teenagers in small villages in the south of Italy.

In a community survey of young adult males in Alberta, Bagley and Tremblay (1997) found a history of suicidal ideation and attempts to be most common in celibate homosexuals, less common in active homosexuals and bisexuals, and least common in heterosexuals.

Remafedi et al. (1991, 1993) studied gay and bisexual males aged 14–21. Thirty percent had attempted suicide, with about one-third of the attempts precipitated by homosexual turmoil. These attempters had earlier homosexual and heterosexual experience, used illicit drugs more, had more arrests, and had experienced more sexual abuse. They had higher depression scores, lower masculinity scores, and were classified as more feminine and less masculine or androgynous. They did not differ in hopelessness, attitudes toward homosexuality, family psychiatric history, running away, prostitution, peers completing suicide, or parental support for homosexuality.

Schneider et al. (1991a, 1991b) found that 27 percent of gay and bisexual men had suicidal ideation in the prior six months. Suicidal ideation was associated with depression, loneliness, hopelessness, having a partner die from AIDS, having a close friend with ARC, and having an ARC diagnosis. The HIV-positive men with suicidal ideation had more mood disorders, loneliness, and AIDS-related stressors. The HIV-negative men with suicidal ideation had more current depression, hopelessness, and perceived AIDS risk. The HIV-positive and negative ideators did not differ in suicidal intent, loneliness, depression, hopelessness, or support from confidantes.

Hammelman (1993) found that 29 percent of gay college students had attempted suicide in the past, and 48 percent had suicidal ideation. The mean ages for their suicidality were 17 and 16, respectively, and about two-thirds said that their homosexuality played a role in precipitating their suicidality. Brann and Stroup (1994) found that homosexual and bisexual men had attempted suicide more than heterosexuals after controls for race, education, alcohol abuse, drug abuse, depression, and anxiety.

Proctor and Groze (1994) found that gay and lesbian youths had a high rate of suicidal behavior: 40 percent had attempted suicide and 26 percent had thought about it. The attempters scored lowest on family scales, school environment scales, and self-perception measures.

In a national survey of lesbians, Bradford et al. (1994) found that 18 percent had attempted suicide, more so in the younger women and in African Americans and Latinas. Bridget and Lucille (1996) report a high incidence of attempted suicide in a non-random sample of lesbians (70 percent). Gibson (1994) found that for lesbian women attempting suicide in the past was predicted by sexual abuse (especially outside of the family), being a victim of violence, criticism/humiliation at home, and becoming a lesbian at an earlier age. Predictors also included anger/fighting in the family, violence from the parents, losing jobs due to discrimination, antilesbian harassment, many family moves, and family members with psychiatric problems. Attempting suicide was also associated with drug/alcohol abuse, running away, prostitution, anxiety, violence toward others, and depression. Seventy percent related their attempts to their lesbianism. Mathy (1996) found a high incidence of prior suicidality in a group of lesbians and bisexuals. The attempters were younger when first attracted to women and experienced more maternal verbal abuse, but did not differ in physical, sexual, or emotional abuse; age; or age at first homosexual act.

In a sample of adolescent psychiatric patients, Olsen et al. (1994) found no differences in the depression and suicidality of heterosexual, bisexual/homosexual, and unsure students.

Rotheram-Borus et al. (1994) found that 39 percent of gay and bisexual male adolescents had attempted suicide. The attempters more often were school dropouts, lived outside their homes, had suicidal friends and relatives, and had experienced gay-related stressors (especially coming out to parents and siblings). They did not differ in age, race, gay versus bisexual, grade point average, education, or nongay-life stressors. Rotheram-Borus et al. (1995) found that homosexual and bisexual male adolescents had a steady rate of attempting suicide over the two-year period of study.

Hershberger and D'Augelli (1995) found that attempting suicide in homosexual and bisexual adolescents was predicted by family protection and relationships, self-esteem, and having been attacked (verbally, materially or physically). Hershberger et al. (1997) found that the attempters were aware of their sexual orientation earlier, had more same-sex partners, were more open about their sexual orientation, had more close homosexual friends, had lost more friends, had experienced more insults and assaults, and had lower self-esteem but better relationships with their families. They used drugs/alcohol more, were more depressed, were less satisfied with their sex life, had more problems in close relationships, and had more current suicidal ideation.

Completed Suicide

Shaffer et al. (1995) found similar proportions of homosexuals in youths completing suicide and in community controls. The three homosexual suicides were all psychiatrically disturbed, and their suicides were not a result of stigmatization.

Transsexuals

Cole et al. (1997) found that female-to-male transsexuals were more likely to have attempted suicide than male-to-female transsexuals, but did not differ in the incidence of psychiatric illness. Most of the attempts were precipitated in part by gender dysphoria.

Discussion

Two trends in this research are noteworthy. First, there remains almost no research on theories of the sex difference in rates of attempted and completed suicide. Even with the publicity given the reversal in Chinese completed suicide rates, no tests of the explanations of this reversal have appeared. Second, there has been a growth of interest in suicidal behavior in homosexuals. Again, however, the research is not theory-based, and the correlates of suicidal behavior in homosexuals appear to be similar to those in heterosexuals.

REFERENCES

Amaro, H., Fried, L. E., Cabral, H., & Zuckerman, B. Violence during pregnancy and substance use. *American Journal of Public Health,* 1990, 80, 575–579.

Anderson, G., Yasenik, L., & Ross, C. A. Dissociative experiences and disorders among women who identify themselves as sexual abuse survivors. *Child Abuse & Neglect,* 1993, 17, 677–686.

Anonymous. Suicide attempts. *Weekly Epidemiological Record,* 1992, 67(25), 187–190.

Appleby, L. Suicide during pregnancy and in the first postnatal year. *British Medical Journal,* 1991, 302, 137–140.

Appleby, L., & Turnbull, G. Parasuicide in the first postnatal year. *Psychological Medicine,* 1995, 25, 1087–1090.

Arcel, L. T., Mantonakis, J., Petersson, B.,

Jemos, J., & Kaliteraki, E. Suicide attempts among Greek and Danish women and the quality of their relationships with husbands or boyfriends. *Acta Psychiatrica Scandinavica*, 1992, 85, 189–195.

Bagedahl-Strindlund, M. Postpartum mental illness. *Acta Psychiatrica Scandinavica*, 1997, 95, 389–395.

Bagley, C., & Tremblay, P. Suicidal behaviors in homosexual and bisexual males. *Crisis*, 1997, 18, 24–34.

Bergman, B., & Brismar, B. A five-year follow-up study of 117 battered women. *American Journal of Public Health*, 1991a, 81, 1486–1489.

Bergman, B., & Brismar, B. Suicide attempts by battered women. *Acta Psychiatrica Scandinavica*, 1991b, 83, 380–384.

Bettridge, B. J., & Favreau, O. E. The dependency needs and perceived availability and adequacy of relationships in female adolescent suicide attempters. *Psychology of Women Quarterly*, 1995, 19, 517–531.

Bigagli, A., & Grillini, F. Suicide and risk of suicide among the Italian homosexuals. In G. Ferrari, M. Bellini & P. Crepet (Eds.), *Suicidal behavior and risk factors*. Bologna: Monduzzi-Editore, 1990, 773–777.

Bjerke, T., Jorgensen, P. T., Rygnestad, T., Riaunet, A., & Stiles, T. Repetition of parasuicide. In G. Ferrari, M. Bellini & P. Crepet (Eds.), *Suicidal behavior and risk factors*. Bologna: Monduzzi-Editore, 1990, 453–457.

Bradford, J., Ryan, C., & Rothblum, E. D. National lesbian health care survey. *Journal of Consulting & Clinical Psychology*, 1994, 62, 228–242.

Brann, E. A., & Stroup, N. E. Suicide attempts in men who report sex with men. In D. Lester (Ed.), *Suicide '94*. Denver: AAS, 1994, 168.

Bridget, J., & Lucille, S. Lesbian Youth Support Information Service. *Journal of Community & Applied Social Psychology*, 1996, 6, 355–364.

Chaturvedi, S. K., Chandra, P. S., Gururaj, G., Pandian, R. D., & Beena, M. B. Suicidal ideas during premenstrual phase. *Journal of Affective Disorders*, 1995, 34, 193–199.

Chia, B. H. *Suicidal behavior in Singapore.*

Tokyo: Southeast Asian Medical Information Center, 1981.

Clare, A. W., & Tyrrell, J. Psychiatric aspects of abortion. *Irish Journal of Psychological Medicine*, 1994, 11, 92–98.

Coakley, F., Hayes, C., Fennell, J., & Johnson, Z. A study of deliberate self-poisoning in a Dublin hospital. *Irish Journal of Psychological Medicine*, 1994, 11, 70–72.

Cole, C. M., O'Boyle, M., Emory, L. E., & Meyer, W. J. Comorbidity of gender dysphoria and other major psychiatric diagnoses. *Archives of Sexual Behavior*, 1997, 26, 13–26.

Czeizel, A. E., & Mosonyi, A. Monitoring of early human fetal development in women exposed to large doses of chemicals. *Environmental & Molecular Mutagenesis*, 1997, 30, 240–244.

Daeid, N. N. Suicide in Ireland, 1982 to 1992. *Archives of Suicide Research*, 1997, 3, 31–42.

Dannenberg, A. L., Carter, D. M., Lawson, H. W., Ashton, D. M., Dorfman, S. F., & Graham, E. H. Homicide and other injuries as causes of maternal deaths in New York City, 1987 through 1991. *American Journal of Obstetrics & Gynecology*, 1995, 172, 1557–1564.

Donnelly, M. Depression among adolescents in Northern Ireland. *Adolescence*, 1995, 30, 339–350.

Ferrence, R. G. Sex differences in alcohol related casualties. In N. Giesbrecht, R. Gonzales, M. Grant, E. Osterberg, R. Room, I. Rootman & L. Towle (Eds.) *Drinking and casualties*. London: Tavistock/Routledge, 1989, 343–355.

Frierson, R. L., & Lippman, S. B. Attempted suicide by black men and women. *Journal of the Kentucky Medical Association*, 1990, 88, 287–292.

Gibson, S. A. Suicide attempts among young lesbian women. In D. Lester (Ed.), *Suicide '94*. Denver: AAS, 1994, 200–201.

Gill, D., Conwell, Y., Duberstein, P., & Cox, C. Gender differences in lethal suicide behavior. In J. McIntosh (Ed.), *Suicide '96*. Washington, DC: AAS, 1996, 149–150.

Gissler, M., Hemminki, E., & Lonnqvist, J. Suicides after pregnancy in Finland, 1987–94. *British Medical Journal*, 1996, 313, 1431–1434.

Gotestam, K. G., Eriksen, L., & Hagen, H.

An epidemiological study of eating disorders in Norwegian psychiatric institutions. *International Journal of Eating Disorders*, 1995, 18, 263–268.

Hammelman, T. L. Gay and lesbian youth. *Journal of Gay & Lesbian Psychotherapy*, 1993, 2(1), 77–89.

Hawton, K., & Fagg, J. Deliberate self-poisoning and self-injury in adolescents. *British Journal of Psychiatry*, 1992, 161, 816–823.

He, Z. X., & Lester, D. The gender difference in Chinese suicide rates. *Archives of Suicide Research*, 1997, 3, 81–89.

Henriksson, M. M., Aro, H. M., Marttunen, M. J., Heikkinen, M. E., Isometsa, E. T., Kuoppasalmi, K. I., & Lonnqvist, J. K. Mental disorders and comorbidity in suicide. *American Journal of Psychiatry*, 1993, 150, 935–940.

Hershberger, S. L., & D'Augelli, A. R. The impact of victimization on the mental health and suicidality of lesbian, gay, and bisexual youths. *Developmental Psychology*, 1995, 31, 65–74.

Hershberger, S. L., Pilkington, N. W., & D'Augelli, A. R. Predictors of suicide attempts among gay, lesbian, and bisexual youths. *Journal of Adolescent Research*, 1997, 12, 477–497.

Hogberg, U., Innala, E., & Sandstrom, A. Maternal mortality in Sweden, 1980–1988. *Obstetrics & Gynecology*, 1994, 84, 240–244.

Hulten, A., & Wasserman, D. Suicide among young people aged 10-29 in Sweden. *Scandinavian Journal of Social Medicine*, 1992, 20, 65–72.

Javanainen, M. Sex ratio in suicide mortality in Finland. In G. Ferrari, M. Bellini & P. Crepet (Eds.), *Suicidal behavior and risk factors*. Bologna: Monduzzi-Editore, 1990, 95–99.

Kalafat, J., & Elias, M. Adolescents' experience with and response to suicidal peers. *Suicide & Life-Threatening Behavior*, 1992, 22, 315–332.

Kingma, J. The young male peak in different categories of trauma victims. *Perceptual & Motor Skills*, 1994, 79, 920–922.

Kirby, M., Bruce, I., Radic, A., Coakley, D., & Lawlor, B. A. Hopelessness and suicidal feelings among the community dwelling elderly in Dublin. *Irish Journal of Psychological Medicine*, 1997, 14, 124–127.

Klompenhouwer, J. L., Van Hulst, A. M., Tulen, J. H., Jacobs, M. L., Jacobs, B. C., & Segers, F. The clinical features of postpartum psychosis. *European Psychiatry*, 1995, 10, 355–367.

Koczan, G., & Ozsvath, K. Suicide events in county Baranja 1984–1987. In G. Ferrari, M. Bellini & P. Crepet (Eds.), *Suicidal behavior and risk factors*. Bologna: Monduzzi-Editore, 1990, 113–118.

Kontaxakis, V. P., Christodoulou, G. N., Havaki-Kontaxakis, B. J., & Skoumbourdis, T. Attempted suicide among schizophrenic outpatients in Athens. In G. Ferrari, M. Bellini & P. Crepet (Eds.), *Suicidal behavior and risk factors*. Bologna: Monduzzi-Editore, 1990, 627–631.

Lester, D. Suicide and the menstrual cycle. *Medical Hypotheses*, 1990a, 31, 197–199.

Lester, D. Sex differences in severity of injury of attempted suicides who jump. *Perceptual & Motor Skills*, 1990b, 71, 176.

Lester, D. Suicide in mainland China by sex, urban/rural location, and age. *Perceptual & Motor Skills*, 1990c, 71, 1090.

Lester, D. If women are more often depressed, why don't more of them kill themselves? *Psychological Reports*, 1990d, 66, 258.

Lester, D. The sex distribution of suicides by age in nations of the world. *Social Psychiatry & Psychiatric Epidemiology*, 1990e, 25, 87–88.

Lester, D. Women's liberation and rates of personal violence (suicide and homicide). *Psychological Reports*, 1992a, 71, 304.

Lester, D. Sex differences in the methods used for suicide. *Psychological Reports*, 1992b, 71, 1234.

Lester, D. The changing sex ratio in suicidal and homicidal deaths. *Italian Journal of Suicidology*, 1993a, 3, 33–35.

Lester, D. The sex ratio in samples of attempted and completed suicides over time. *Perceptual & Motor Skills*, 1993b, 77, 402.

Lester, D. Testosterone and suicide. *Personality & Individual Differences*, 1993c, 15, 347–348.

Lester, D. Sex differences in methods for suicide. *Perceptual & Motor Skills*, 1994a, 79, 418.

Lester, D. Gender equality and the sex

differential in suicide rates. *Psychological Reports*, 1994b, 75, 1162.

Lester, D. Gender and the risk of violent death in Canada. *Psychological Reports*, 1994c, 75, 858.

Lester, D., & Abdel-Khalek, A. Gender and depression in undergraduate populations. *Psychological Reports*, 1997, 81, 1210.

Mahanta, J., & Trivedi, B. V. Family distress, suicide, and its prevention. *Indian Journal of Criminology*, 1993, 21(1), 21–22.

Maris, R. W. *Pathways to suicide*. Baltimore: Johns Hopkins University, 1981.

Martin, C. A., Mainous, A. G., Mainous, R. O., Oler, M. J., Curry, T., & Vore, M. Progesterone and adolescent suicidality. *Biological Psychiatry*, 1997, 42, 956–958.

Marttunen, M. J., Henriksson, M. M., Aro, H. M., Heikkinen, M., Isometsa, E. T., & Lonnqvist, J. K. Suicide among female adolescents. *Journal of the American Academy of Child & Adolescent Psychiatry*, 1995, 34, 1297–1307.

Marzuk, P. M., Tardiff, K., Leon, A. C., Hirsch, C. S., Portera, L., Hartwell, N., & Iqbal, M. I. Lower risk of suicide during pregnancy. *American Journal of Psychiatry*, 1997, 154, 122–123.

Mathy, R. M. Parasuicide among lesbians. In J. McIntosh (Ed.), *Suicide '96*. Washington, DC: AAS, 1996, 95–96.

Maxim, P. S., & Keane, C. Gender, age, and the risk of violent death in Canada, 1950–1986. *Canadian Review of Sociology & Anthropology*, 1992, 29, 329–345.

Mazza, J. J., & Reynolds, W. M. Gender differences in multiple suicide attempters. In D Lester (Ed.), *Suicide '94*. Denver: AAS, 1994, 179–180.

Merikangas, K. R., Foeldenyi, M., & Angst, J. The Zurich study. *European Archives of Psychiatry*, 1993, 243, 23–32.

Merrill, J., Owens, J., Wynne, S., & Whittington, R. Asian suicides. *British Journal of Psychiatry*, 1990, 156, 748–749.

Misic-Pavkov, G., Selakovic-Bursic, S., & Vuckovic, N. The role of unwanted pregnancy in suicidal behavior. In K. Bohme, R. Freytag, C. Wachtler & H. Wedler (Eds.), *Suicidal behavior*. Regensburg: S. Roderer, 1993, 729–735.

Morgan, C. L., Evans, M., Peters, J. R., &

Currie, C. Suicides after pregnancy. *British Medical Journal*, 1997, 314, 902.

Mutzell, S. Survival after attempted suicide in Sweden. *International Journal of Adolescence & Youth*, 1997, 6, 315–328.

Nordstrom, P., Samuelsson, M., & Asberg, M. Survival analysis of suicide risk after attempted suicide. *Acta Psychiatrica Scandinavica*, 1995, 91, 336–340.

O'Connor, R. C., & Sheehy, N. P. Suicide and gender. *Mortality*, 1997, 2, 237–254.

Olsen, E. D., King, C. A., Brand, E., Ghaziuddin, N., & Naylor, M. W. Adolescent suicide. In D. Lester (Ed.), *Suicide '94*. Denver: AAS, 1994, 202–204.

Ostamo, A., & Lonnqvist, J. Parasuicide in Helsinki. In G. Ferrari, M. Bellini & P. Crepet (Eds.), *Suicidal behavior and risk factors*. Bologna: Monduzzi-Editore, 1990, 185–188.

Pridmore, S. Suicidal behavior in the Honiara area of the Solomon Islands. *International Journal of Mental Health*, 1997, 25(4), 33–38.

Pritchard, C. Suicide, unemployment, and gender variations in the Western World 1964–1986. *Social Psychiatry & Psychiatric Epidemiology*, 1990, 25, 73–80.

Proctor, C. D., & Groze, V. K. Risk factors for suicide among gay, lesbian, and bisexual youths. *Social Work*, 1994, 39, 504–513.

Remafedi, G., Farrow, J. A., & Deisher, R. W. Risk factors for attempted suicide in gay and bisexual youth. *Pediatrics*, 1991, 87, 869–875.

Remafedi, G., Farrow, J. A., & Deisher, R. W. Risk factors for attempted suicide in gay and bisexual youth. In L. D. Garnets & D. C. Kimmel (Eds.), *Psychological perspectives on lesbian and gay male experiences*. New York: Columbia University, 1993, 486–499.

Roberts, G. L., Lawrence, J. M., O'Toole, B. I., & Raphael, B. Domestic violence in the emergency department. *General Hospital Psychiatry*, 1997, 19, 5–11.

Rogers, J. R. Female suicide. *Journal of Counseling & Development*, 1990, 69, 37–38.

Rotheram-Borus, M. J., Hunter, J., & Rosario, M. Suicidal behavior and gay-related stress among gay and bisexual male adolescents. *Journal of Adolescent Research*, 1994, 9,

498–508.

Rotheram-Borus, M. J., Rosario, M., Van Rossem, R., Reid, H., & Gillis, R. Prevalence, course, and predictors of multiple problem behaviors among gay and bisexual male adolescents. *Developmental Psychology*, 1995, 31, 75–85.

Runeson, B., Beskow, J., & Waern, M. The suicidal process in suicides among young people. *Acta Psychiatrica Scandinavica*, 1996a, 93, 35–42.

Runeson, B., Eklund, G., & Wasserman, D. Living conditions of female suicide attempters. *Acta Psychiatrica Scandinavica*, 1996b, 94, 125–132.

Rupani, N. P., & Lema, V. M. Premenstrual tension among nurses in Nairobi, Kenya. *East African Medical Journal*, 1993, 70, 310–313.

Schneider, S. G., Taylor, S. E., Hammen, C., Kemeny, M. E., & Dudley, J. Factors influencing suicide intent in gay and bisexual ideators. *Journal of Personality & Social Psychology*, 1991a, 61, 776–788.

Schneider, S. G., Taylor, S. E., Kemeny, M. E., & Hammen, C. AIDS-related factors predictive of suicidal ideation of low and high intent among gay and bisexual men. *Suicide & Life-Threatening Behavior*, 1991b, 21, 313–328.

Seiden, R. H., & Gleiser, M. Sex differences in suicide among chemists. *Omega*, 1990, 21, 177–189,

Shaffer, D., Fisher, P., Hicks, R. H., Parides, M., & Gould, M. Sexual orientation in adolescents who commit suicide. *Suicide & Life-Threatening Behavior*, 1995, 25, suppl., 64–71.

Sharlin, S. A., & Lowenstein, A. Suicide among the elderly in Israel. *Death Studies*, 1997, 21, 361–375.

Shukla, G. D., Verman, B. L., & Mishra, D. N. Suicide in Jhansi City. *Indian Journal of Psychiatry*, 1990, 32(1), 44–51.

Spirito, A., Bond, A., Kurkjian, J., Devost, L., Bosworth, T., & Brown, L. K. Gender differences among adolescent suicide attempters. *Crisis*, 1993, 14, 178–184.

Squires, T. J., & Busuttil, A. Elderly suicides in the Lothian and Borders region of Scotland, 1983–1988. *Medicine, Science & the Law*, 1991, 31, 137–146.

Stark, E., & Flitcraft, A. Killing the beast within. *International Journal of Health Services*, 1995, 25, 43–64.

Stawar, T. L. Suicide and homicidal risk for respondents, petitioners, and family members in an injunction program for domestic violence. *Psychological Reports*, 1996, 79, 553–554.

Stone, I. C. Observations and statistics relating to suicide weapons. *Journal of Forensic Sciences*, 1990, 35, 10–12.

Street, S., & Kromrey, J. D. Gender roles and suicidal behavior. *Journal of College Student Psychotherapy*, 1995, 9(3), 41–56.

Suominen, K., Henriksson, M., Suokas, J., Isometsa, E., Ostamo, A., & Lonnqvist, J. Mental disorders and comorbidity in attempted suicide. *Acta Psychiatrica Scandinavica*, 1996, 94, 234–240.

Targum, S. D., Caputo, K. P., & Ball, S. K. Menstrual cycle phase and psychiatric admissions. *Journal of Affective Disorders*, 1991, 22, 49–53.

Vanezis, P. Deaths in women of reproductive age and relationship with menstrual cycle phase. *Forensic Science International*, 1990, 47, 39–57.

Van Heeringen, K. Epidemiological aspects of attempted suicide. *Crisis*, 1994, 15, 116–122.

Vannatta, R. A. Adolescent gender differences in suicide-related behaviors. *Journal of Youth & Adolescence*, 1997, 26, 559–568.

Vitanza, S., Vogel, L., & Marshall, L. Distress and symptoms of post-traumatic stress disorder in abused women. *Violence & Victims*, 1995, 10, 23–34.

Vrabichev, I. Sexual problems and suicide. *4th European Symposium on Suicide*, University of Odense, 1992.

Waeld, L. C., Silvern, L., & Hodges, W. F. Stressful life events. *Sex Roles*, 1994, 30, 1–22.

Wallace, M. D., & Kral, M. J. Sex differences in suicide. In D. Lester (Ed.), *Suicide '94*. Denver: AAS, 1994, 119–120.

Welcher, B., Rubin, P., & Nordentoft, M. Admission of self-poisoned patients during one year at the Poison Treatment Centre, Copenhagen, Denmark. *Acta Psychiatrica Scandinavica*, 1993, Suppl. 371, 38–44.

Wolfersdorf, M., Faust, V., Brehm, M., Moser, K., Holzer, R., & Hole, G. Suicide in the Ravensburg area. In K. Bohme, R.

Freytag, C. Wachtler & H. Wedler (Eds.), *Suicidal behavior.* Regensburg: S. Roderer, 1993, 890–895.

Zhao, S., Qu, G., Peng, Z. L., & Peng, T. S. The sex ratio of suicide rates in China. *Crisis*, 1994, 15, 44–48.

Chapter 4

CHILDHOOD, ADOLESCENCE, AND CHILDHOOD EXPERIENCES

Siblings and Birth Order

In a sample of psychiatric patients, Schierbeak and Newlon (1990) found that substance abuse and/or attempted suicide was more common in first borns, but in a sample of high school students, more common in last borns. Maris (1981) found more first borns in samples of attempted and completed suicides than those dying of natural deaths.

Akande and Lester (1994) found among Yoruban college students in Nigeria that prior (but not current) suicidal ideation was positively associated with sibship size, but suicidality was not associated with birth order.

Bergman et al. (1997) found no differences in past suicidality in students with full versus step/half siblings or in the age, sex, and number of siblings.

Childhood Depression

Harrington et al. (1994) followed up child psychiatric patients for 18 years. More of those who had been depressed subsequently attempted suicide. Those who had a conduct disorder (but not depression) also attempted suicide more subsequently. Childhood anxiety, sex, race, and social class did not predict later suicidality. Childhood suicid-

ality and adult depression also were associated with attempting suicide.

Lewinsohn et al. (1994a, 1994b, 1994c) found in a sample of adolescents who had suffered from a major depressive disorder that suicidal ideation was associated with a longer episode and shorter time to reoccurrence, while attempted suicide was associated with earlier onset and a shorter time to recurrence. Attempting suicide (along with prior depressions, lifetime physical symptoms, and internalizing problem behaviors) predicted future depressions in the following year. The correlates of prior attempts (current depression, suicidal ideation, self-esteem, etc.) were different from the predictors of future attempts (younger mothers, less educated parents, externalizing problem behaviors, social support from family, etc.).

Developmental Stage

Borst and Noam (1993) studied female adolescents who had attempted suicide or who were nonsuicidal and who were in a conformist, versus preconformist, stage of development. In both developmental stages, the suicidal girls had more internal symptoms, but did not differ in external symptoms. The groups did not differ in defense mechanisms used, although the suicidal girls had more affective disorders and fewer conduct disorders. The suicidal conformist girls reported more hopelessness than the suicidal preconformist girls.

In school children in grades two and four, Sack et al. (1994) found that Native American children reported more suicidal ideation but less depression than non-native American children. Teachers and parents differed from the self-reports in their evaluation of the children's depression, however.

Loss and Trauma

Bron et al. (1991) studied a sample of patients over the age of 45 with major depressive disorder, dysthymic disorder or adjustment disorder with depressed mood. Those who had experienced loss before the age of 15 through the separation of parents had the highest lifetime incidence of attempted suicide. They were followed by those who lost a parent through death, with the fewest in those with no loss. The age at loss was not significant, and the difference was found only for the loss of fathers.

Green et al. (1994) followed up for 17 years children who survived a dam collapse. They claimed that the survivors had shown more suicidal behavior, but less depression, than controls and no differences in psychiatric diagnosis. Warheit et al. (1996) examined adolescents after Hurricane Andrew. Having suicidal ideation afterwards was associated with being female, experiencing hurricane-related stress, having a low level of family support and pre-hurricane suicidal ideation, and pre- and post-hurricane depression level.

Lester (1994) found that 6 of 24 famous suicides had experienced loss of a parent (at a median age of ten), and eight had experienced disrupted relationships with parents.

Schutt et al. (1994) found that childhood trauma and social supports predicted suicidal ideation in sheltered homeless adults. Sex, race, monetary benefits, shelter satisfaction, physical health, substance abuse, and psychological treatment did not play a role in the prediction.

In a sample of psychiatric emergency patients, Viinamak et al. (1995) found that childhood trauma, such as being illegitimate or losing parents because of divorce, was not associated with attempted suicide as a precipitating event for the emergency.

Adam et al. (1996) found that adolescent psychiatric patients who had attempted or thought about suicide had experienced slightly more trauma (loss by death, abuse, and separation from parents) than non-suicidal patients, but they had more often failed to resolve the trauma. The males' response was more often a disorganized or dismissing response, the females' response a disorganized or autonomous response.

Music Preferences

Ballard and Coates (1995) played rap and heavy metal music with nonviolent, suicidal and homicidal themes for college students. The type of lyric did not differentially affect the students' depression scores.

Parents

In a sample of adolescent psychiatric patients, Armsden et al. (1990) found that a history of attempted suicide or a history of major depression was associated with less-secure attachment to the parents. Thus, the association of attempted suicide with parental attachment was confounded by the presence of depressive disorders in this study. The adolescents' parental attachments were not associated with suicidality in the parent.

Benjaminsen et al. (1990) found that

attempted suicides did not differ from psychiatric controls in their memories of 28 child-rearing practices. Their parents were more often divorced, but not more often deceased.

Hyer et al. (1990) compared the childhoods of Vietnam veterans with posttraumatic stress disorder who had attempted suicide with the childhoods of veterans who had not attempted suicide. The fathers of the attempters were more inconsistent in their love, less egalitarian, and exerted more punitive, strict, and hostile control. Their mothers did not differ.

Weissman et al. (1992) found that parents with a major depressive disorder had offspring who made more suicide attempts and more often had major depressive disorders and anxiety disorders than the offspring of normal parents.

Kaplan and Maldaver (1993) found that parents whose child completed suicide were older and had higher self-reported pathology in individuation/attachment and congruency. The fathers saw their families as less structured and more flexible than the control families, while the mothers saw their families as less active-recreational. The fathers of the suicides saw their sons as more feminine, but the mothers did not differ in their perceptions of the children.

Maris (1981) found that attempted suicides had experienced more physical punishment by mothers than completed suicides and those dying of natural deaths, while both completers and attempters had experienced more physical punishment by fathers. In addition, the attempters had higher early trauma scores, more negative relationships with others, more multiproblem families of origin, more dissatisfaction with their accomplishments, more problems in life (including rape, arrests, abortion, drug use, sexual deviance, and unemployment), and felt less close to their parents. They appeared to be the most socially deviant. The completers had fewer close friends, more social isolation, higher unemployment, more suicidal relatives, and more rigid thinking, but also greater upward mobility. Those dying of natural deaths were more often disabled and retired. Kaplan et al. (1997) found that physically abused adolescents did not differ from community controls in attempting suicide. Among the physically abused adolescents, the attempters did not differ in family stressors or hopelessness, but had less family cohesion, less caring mothers, and more hostility.

Adam et al. (1994) studied adolescent psychiatric patients and found that attempters had lower maternal-care scores and higher maternal-overprotection scores. The attempters plus ideators had lower paternal-care scores and higher overprotection scores (but only for the female subjects).

Adams et al. (1994a) found that suicidal psychiatric patients and high school students had more family dysfunction and mother-adolescent problems (but not father-adolescent problems) than did controls. They were also more depressed and hopeless and had lower self-esteem. The suicidal and nonsuicidal adolescents did not differ in having intact families.

In a sample of high school students, Martin and Waite (1994) found that attempters had lower maternal and paternal care-and-protection scores on a survey of parental bonding, but they were also more depressed, a variable that was not controlled.

Pfeffer et al. (1994) found that the parents and siblings of child psychiatric patients who had attempted suicide were more likely to have an antisocial personality and to abuse drugs and attempt suicide than the first-degree relatives of nonsuicidal psychiatric controls. They did not differ in completed suicide, assaultive behavior, alcohol abuse, or mood disorders. No differences were found for second-degree relatives.

Allison et al. (1995) found that suicidal high school students reported more parental criticism. Suicidality was associated with low parental care, high parental overprotection, high parental criticism, and hopelessness.

Blanton-Lacy et al. (1995) found that suicidal African American college students perceived less family support and were more depressed and hopeless. Lewis et al. (1995) found that suicidal ideation was associated with family cohesion and perception of family support (but not communal orientation) in a sample of black college students.

King et al. (1995) found that families with adolescent psychiatric inpatients had more depression and suicidal ideation than families with normal children. Suicidal ideation in the adolescent inpatients was not associated with marital adjustment, satisfaction, or conflict over child rearing.

Levy et al. (1995) found that family dysfunction (and social class) were not associated with suicidal ideation or suicidal intent in attempters (but hopelessness was).

Shagle and Barber (1995) found that suicidal ideation in school kids was associated with family conflict, parent-child conflict, parental acceptance, and self-derogation, as well as school performance, and religiosity (but not peer involvement, sex, or grade).

Silverman and Overholser (1995) found that adolescent psychiatric inpatients and their parents who had attempted suicide did not differ in their perceptions of family functioning from the nonsuicidal patients and their parents. The few differences that emerged were in the direction of the nonsuicidal adolescents and their parents perceiving *more* discrepancy. For the suicidal adolescents, hopelessness correlated with the perception of family functioning.

Hollis (1996) found that suicidal adoles-cent psychiatric patients more often had family discord, disturbed mother-child relationships, and a lack of warmth, as well as conduct symptoms and differences in sex and age as compared to nonsuicidal patients.

Hustead et al. (1996) followed up adolescent suicide attempters and psychiatric controls. The attempters did not differ during the next four weeks in terms of daily activities, spending time with friends and parents, or recent stressors. Six months later, however, suicidal ideation was associated with time spent with the parents and family sickness/injuries.

Kerfoot et al. (1996) found that adolescent attempters more often than psychiatric out-patients had broken homes, families on benefits, and families with worse functioning. They were less often bullied; more often knew an attempter; and did not differ in psychiatric diagnosis, current suicidal ideation, hopelessness, criminal record, or having no friends.

Garnefski and Diekstra (1997b) found that adolescents with stepparents had made more attempts at suicide than those from one-parent families, who in turn had made more attempts than those from intact families.

In Victoria (Australia), Krupinski et al. (1997) found that youth completed suicides had close and warm families more often than attempted suicides. They also were more often male, 20-24 (versus 15–19), with psychiatric problems; they used more violent methods, less often sought help from doctors/family/friends, and more often left a suicide note.

In a sample of Indian adolescents in South Africa, Pillay and Wassenaar (1997a, 1997b) found that attempted suicides had more recent stress; more problems with intimacy, romance, and school; less family adaptability, cohesion, and satisfaction; and more hopelessness and psychiatric distur-bance compared with normal adolescents.

Seventy-seven percent had experienced conflict with parents in the 12 hours prior to the attempt.

Rainieri and Lester (1997) found that students who lived with both biological parents for their first 18 years did not differ in current or past suicidality from those who did not.

In the Netherlands, Spruijt and de Goede (1997) found that adolescents from single-parent families and families with conflict more often had thought of suicide in the prior year than those from stable families or families with stepparents.

Perinatal Events

De Leo et al. (1993) followed-up over four thousand premature or difficult births. The attempted and completed suicide rates for these individuals were the same as for the general population. A study of completed suicides found no excess of difficult births.

Barker et al. (1995) followed up large samples of babies and found that later suicide was not associated with low birth weight, being breast-fed exclusively or being weaned by one year. Suicides weighed less at one year.

Physical and Sexual Abuse

Runaway Youth

Rotheram-Borus (1993) found that 37 percent of runaway youth had attempted suicide, almost half in the prior month. Attempted suicide was more common in females, but did not differ by race. Greene (1996) found that attempted suicide in runaway and street youths was associated with drug use (especially sedatives, hallucinogens, and inhalants) and use of drugs by family members. Those attempting suicide were more often white, female, and

older (18–21).

Powers et al. (1990) found that a sample of maltreated adolescents who were runaways and homeless were more often suicidal and female than national samples of runaways and homeless adolescents; they were not more often substance abusers, learning disabled, or depressed. Kurtz et al. (1991) studied runaways in shelters and found that depression, suicidality, and alcohol/drug abuse was greater in those abused physically or sexually and most common in those abused both physically and sexually.

Adolescents and Children

Lanktree et al. (1991) interviewed child psychiatric outpatients and found that those who were abused sexually reported more suicide attempts and were more depressed than those not abused. Bayatpour et al. (1992) found that, in a sample of pregnant adolescents, prior suicidal ideation and attempts were associated with physical and sexual abuse.

Riggs et al. (1990) found that high school students who had attempted suicide were more often girls and more likely to have been physically abused and sexually abused. They did not differ in age or whether living with two parents, but the attempters were less often Southeast Asians.

Wozencraft et al. (1991) found that 42 percent of a sample of sexually abused children had suicidal thoughts. Suicidal ideation was also associated with age, mother's resistance to treatment and investigation, remaining in the home, and being abused by a family member. In a sample of abused children, Livingston et al. (1993) found that only experience of loss predicted suicidal ideation, not depressive disorder, conduct disorder, type of abuse, age, or other stressors.

Cunningham et al. (1992) found that a

history of being beaten, raped, or sexually abused was associated with suicidal ideation and attempts (and violence toward others) in a sample of inner-city youths (mainly black females) seen at public health clinics, even after controls for race and sex.

De Wilde et al. (1992) found that adolescent attempters and depressed adolescents had experienced more physical abuse and more sexual abuse than nondepressed adolescents. The attempters had experienced somewhat more sexual abuse than the depressed adolescents, as well as more parental losses, school failures, and total stressors. This excess of stress was found in early years, teenage years, and in the prior year.

Among male ninth and twelfth graders, Hernandez et al. (1993) found that attempted suicide was more common in those who were sexually and physically abused. The ethnic difference (with blacks attempting suicide more than whites) was eliminated after controls for abuse.

Schiff and Cavaiola (1993) found that abused drug-dependent youths had more often attempted suicide than those who had not been abused, and both of these groups had been more suicidal than normal youths.

Shaunesey et al. (1993) found that adolescent psychiatric inpatients who were physically and sexually abused were more likely to have attempted suicide and to have suicidal ideation. The frequency of physical abuse (but not sexual abuse) was associated with greater suicidality. The duration of abuse was not associated with suicidality.

Stone (1993) found that child-guidance patients who had been abused or neglected had more often made suicide attempts and threats than those not abused. They also more often had a major depression or dysthymia.

De Bellis et al. (1994a, 1994b) found that sexually abused girls had more prior suicidal ideation and attempts than controls, as well as dysthymia, hypothalamic-pituitary-adrenal axis dysregulation, and urinary HVA.

Among adolescents in residential treatment for drug abuse, Deykin and Buka (1994) found that attempting suicide was associated with physical and sexual abuse only in the boys. In this sample, suicidal ideation was a better predictor of attempting suicide than was a depressive disorder. Suicidal ideation and attempting suicide were associated in this sample.

Wagner et al. (1995) found that high school students who had attempted suicide had more often than nonsuicidal students experienced physical abuse, run away from home, were not living with biological parents, had stress from parents, and knew someone who had completed suicide. They also had fewer social supports, and more stress from the police, and more sexual concerns.

In a survey of school children in Minnesota from grades six, nine and twelve, attempted suicide was more common in ninth and twelfth grade girls (Anonymous, 1995). Attempting suicide was associated with sexual abuse, physical abuse, substance abuse, antisocial behavior, alienation, low self-esteem, and emotional distress.

Beautrais et al. (1996) found that youths making serious suicide attempts more often had a disadvantaged childhood, including sexual abuse and poor relationships with parents, as well as more psychiatric disturbance and socioeconomic disadvantages (such as unemployment and poverty) than community controls.

Chandy et al. (1996) found that the experience of sexual abuse and parental alcoholism increased the incidence of suicide attempts and ideation (as well as other nonsuicidal problems such as drug abuse) in seventh through twelfth graders; a combination of both factors increased the incidence still further. Protective factors were being African American, under the age of 15, religious, recently depressed, discipline problems, and less worry about family finances.

Evans et al. (1996) found that, for incarcerated juvenile delinquents who were gang members, experience of sexual (but not physical) abuse was associated with suicidal ideation. For females only, sexual abuse was also associated with prior suicide attempts.

Fergusson et al. (1996) found that sexually abused children more often had a major depressive disorder, anxiety disorder, conduct disorder, and substance abuse disorder and had more often attempted suicide, especially if the abuse involved sexual intercourse.

Martin (1996) found that prior experience of sexual abuse or rape in school students was associated with more drug use, higher depression scores, and more attempted suicide. Experience of sexual abuse was a more powerful determinant of suicidal behavior than having a dysfunctional family.

In a follow-up study of kindergarten children, Silverman et al. (1996) found that physical abuse or sexual abuse resulted in more suicidal ideation and attempts later (in females only), although the researchers failed to control for depression.

Chandy et al. (1997) found that sexually abused male high school students were more likely to have attempted and thought about suicide; they also showed other problems such as binge eating and vandalism.

Fergusson and Lynskey (1997) found that 18 year olds who had been physically punished had more often attempted suicide (and shown other problem behaviors such as substance abuse and criminal behavior) than those who had not. Lynskey and Fergusson (1997) found similar results for sexual abuse.

Garnefski and Diekstra (1997a) found that both male and female high school students with a history of sexual abuse or physical abuse had shown more suicidality (and other problems such as criminality) than those without.

Hustead and Wagner (1997) found that adolescent attempters and psychiatric controls did not differ in experience of sexual abuse, but the attempters had experienced more physical punishment (especially from mothers). They also were more hopeless and had more symptoms of depression.

Among sixth, ninth, and twelfth graders, Neumark-Sztainer et al. (1997) found that past suicidality was associated with physical and sexual abuse, as well as risk-taking, religiosity, self-esteem, emotional well-being, family connectedness and school achievement and connectedness.

In a survey of Native-American youth, Pharris et al. (1997) found that those who had been sexually abused had more often attempted and thought about suicide. Protection factors against suicidality for boys were family attention and caring family, parents, and school, and for girls age, caring family, school and tribal leaders, positive feelings about school, and doing well in school.

Swantson et al. (1997) found that sexually abused children made more suicide attempts and were more depressed in the following five years.

On the other hand, among adolescent suicide attempters seen at a clinic, psychotherapist-rated suicidality was not associated with a history of physical or sexual abuse, running away, or having an intact family (Woznica and Shapiro, 1990). Adolescents who felt unwanted or a burden to their families were more suicidal. Brand et al. (1994, 1996) compared depressed adolescent inpatients with and without experience of sexual abuse. Those with sexual abuse had more PTSD but were similar in depression and suicidality. Cohen et al. (1996) found no association between experiences of sexual or physical abuse and suicidality in a sample of adolescent psychiatric inpatients.

Adults

In a sample of women, Schei (1990) found that the experience of childhood sexual abuse was associated with a history of suicidality, while sexual abuse by the spouse was not.

Lester (1991c) found that a prior history of attempted suicide was associated in prisoners with parental physical abuse and physical punishment from their fathers, and in addition, violent behavior in prison, the violence of the crime, and feeling less close to their fathers.

Brown and Anderson (1991) found that psychiatric patients with childhood experience of physical or sexual abuse or both were more suicidal later in life, and had other problems such as drug/alcohol abuse and personality disorders.

Van der Kolk et al. (1991) studied a sample of patients with personality disorder or bipolar affective disorder type II. Those who had attempted suicide in the past had experienced more sexual abuse and more physical abuse (and witnessed violence) but had not experienced neglect or separations. Prior suicidal ideation was not associated with abuse. Subsequent attempted suicide was associated with a history of sexual abuse and neglect.

Collings (1992) found that male college students who reported sexual molestation as children more often had a history of suicidality and had experienced more recent life stress.

Mullen et al. (1993) studied adults and found that those who had been sexually abused (especially involving intercourse) were more suicidal as adults (and had more drug abuse and psychopathology).

Van Egmond et al. (1993) compared female suicide attempters with a history of sexual abuse to those without such a history. The sexually abused attempters were younger, had more prior attempts, more serious suicidal ideation, and more relatives and friends who had attempted or completed suicide. They had more interpersonal problems, more experience of physical abuse, and more substance abuse. They did not differ in age at the time of abuse, the amount of abuse, or the identity of the abuser (relative or nonrelative).

In a community sample of men, Bagley et al. (1994) found that those who had been sexually abused on several occasions (but not those abused just once) were more depressed currently and had shown more suicidal ideation and attempts than those not abused.

Gould et al. (1994) found a greater history of attempted suicide in adults who reported childhood abuse, especially if the abuse was sexual or emotional.

Wagner and Linehan (1994) studied female outpatients with borderline personality disorder who had attempted suicide in the past. Those with a history of sexual abuse made attempts with higher suicidal intent and medical risk and less manipulative intent. They did not differ in the impulsivity of the attempt, depression, or hopelessness. The severity of the sexual abuse did not correlate with the type of attempt.

Yellowlees and Kaushik (1994a, 1994b) found that adult female psychiatric patients with a history of childhood sexual abuse had more often attempted suicide, abused alcohol and tranquilizers, and been victims of domestic violence. They did not differ in diagnosis. The percentage attempting suicide was greater in those with personality disorders, schizophrenia, and depressive neuroses. Those with personality disorders had more often attempted suicide and abused alcohol and drugs, but had fewer medical problems.

Boudewyn and Liem (1995) found that both male and female college students reported more suicidal ideation and attempts if they had been sexually abused as children.

Among female college students, Bryant and Range (1995a, 1995b) found that the experience of both sexual and physical/psychological abuse combined in childhood resulted in more suicidal ideation as students. Sexual, physical, or psychological abuse alone or physical punishment resulted in only moderate levels of suicidal ideation. Bryant and Range (1997) found that sexual and physical abuse were both associated with greater suicidality in undergraduates and had an additive effect. The more severe the abuse, the more severe the suicidality.

Fullerton et al. (1995) found that adult eating disorder patients who had been sexually or physically abused had more often attempted suicide; they also had more alcohol problems, were more depressed, and shoplifted more often.

Kaplan et al. (1995) found that prior suicide attempts in psychiatric outpatients were associated with sexual abuse, especially at a younger age and by a parent; with physical abuse, especially by a parent; and with physical assault. They were not associated with sexual assault as an adult. The interaction of childhood and adult experiences was complex, but experience of both was associated with more attempts and attempts at an earlier age.

In a sample of college students, Peters and Range (1995) found that those who had been sexually abused either by peers or by adults were more suicidal currently. They did not differ in reasons for living scores. Those actually abused (genital touching) were more suicidal than those merely exploited.

Romans et al. (1995) found that women living in community homes who had been sexually abused as children had attempted suicide more often; they also had more depression, eating disorders, and substance abuse disorders. Among those sexually abused, those attempting suicide had more force used, more intercourse, greater frequency, and more often a father/stepfather perpetrator. They also had more sexual assaults after the age of 15, more often moved away from home, and were more psychiatrically disturbed.

Silk et al. (1995) found that women with borderline personality disorder who had been more severely sexually abused as children made more suicide attempts. Attempting suicide was associated with penetration and ongoing abuse.

In a study of female college students, Valliant et al. (1995) found that those who were sexually abused as children had more suicidal ideation and more psychopathology on some MMPI scales.

Windle et al. (1995) found that both male and female alcoholic inpatients who had been physically or sexually abused or both had more often attempted suicide than those not abused, and the men also more often had depressive disorders.

In female college students, Yama et al. (1995) found that suicidality was associated with childhood sexual abuse, parental alcoholism, and family functioning (conflict, cohesion, and attitudes such as intellectual-cultural and moral-religious orientations).

Elliott et al. (1996) compared serious and gesture attempters and found that the serious attempters had experienced sexual and physical abuse less often. In addition, they had higher suicidal intent, fewer prior attempts, fewer life stressors, more often a major depression, and less often borderline personality disorder and bipolar affective disorder. The groups did not differ in method, alcohol intoxication, or psychiatric history.

Farber et al. (1996) found that pregnant women referred for psychiatric evaluations had more current suicidal ideation if they had been physically or sexually abused (or both) and more prior attempts if they had been sexually abused (or both).

Kroll et al. (1996) found that female outpatients who had experienced sexual abuse as children were more depressed and made more serious suicide attempts. Experience of physical abuse was not associated with these sequelae.

Tobin and Griffing (1996) found that eating-disorder patients who had been sexually abused had attempted suicide more than those patients who had not been abused. They also had higher levels of anxiety, depression, and hostility.

Cloitre, et al, (1997) found that women who were sexually assaulted both in childhood and as adults had the highest incidence of prior attempted suicide, compared to women assaulted only as adults and those not assaulted at all. Sixty percent of the suicide attempts occurred during the childhood abuse or between the childhood and adult abuse.

Among patients in outpatient drug abuse treatment, Gil-Rivas et al. (1997) found that women (but not men) who had been sexually abused showed more prior suicidality (ideation and attempts) than those not abused. Men (but not women) who had been physically abused showed more prior suicidal ideation.

Among women in substance abuse treatment, Jarvis and Copeland (1997) found that those who had been sexually abused had attempted suicide in the past more often than those not abused. Attempting suicide in the sample was associated with low self-esteem, a high dissociation score, adult physical abuse, parental substance abuse,

emotional neglect, and a younger age at intoxication.

McCauley et al. (1997) found that women in primary care who had been sexually or physically abused as children were more depressed and currently suicidal and had attempted suicide more often in the past. The same associations were found for current abuse.

In psychiatric patients, Modestin et al. (1997) found that attempted suicide was associated with sexual abuse and broken homes, but only for the females and those with a borderline personality disorder.

Among female college students, Stepakoff (1997) found that adult and childhood sexual victimization increased the likelihood of prior attempted suicide (even after controls for hopelessness), while only adult sexual victimization increased the likelihood of prior suicidal ideation.

Incest

Stone (1992) followed up psychiatric patients. Those with a borderline personality disorder who completed suicide had a greater incidence of incest experiences than those with other diagnoses.

Consensual Sex

Resnick and Blum (1994) found that high school students who had consensual sex before the age of ten had attempted suicide more in the prior year; they had worse school performance, more gang involvement, more mental health treatment, and parents who abused drugs and alcohol.

Orr et al. (1991) compared virgin and nonvirgin junior high school students. Only nonvirgin girls in the sample had more often attempted suicide and thought about suicide.

Valois et al. (1997) found that past suicidal

ideation in psychiatrically disturbed adolescents was associated positively with having sex between the ages of 13 and 18, but not with having sex before the age of 13.

Corporal Punishment

Straus and Kantor (1994; Straus, 1995) found that experience of corporal punishment in adolescence was associated with adult depression, suicidal ideation, and alcohol abuse. Suicidal ideation as an adult was predicted by corporal punishment in adolescence, social class, gender, age, parents' marital violence, assaulting one's wife, and alcohol use. Suicidal ideation was predicted by experience of corporal punishment, sex, husband-wife violence, and violence between parents.

Comment

In a review of five studies, Beitchman et al. (1992) concluded that there was an association between suicidality and physical and sexual abuse.

The results of these studies have good consistency, but most of them have failed to control for psychiatric disturbance. It seems that sexual and physical abuse in childhood increases the likelihood of many psychiatric symptoms later, of which suicidal behavior is merely one. Future research must explore whether suicidal behavior per se is the result of such experiences rather than a result of the increased level of general psychiatric disturbance.

Psychiatric Disorder

Completed Suicide

Rao et al. (1993) followed up adolescent psychiatric patients for several years and found that only those with major depressions

later committed suicide (3 percent); none of those with anxiety disorders or no disorder did so.

Marttunen et al. (1994a, 1994b, 1994c) compared male adolescent completed suicides who had no diagnosis or simply an adjustment disorder with those who were more disturbed. The less-disturbed suicides experienced less parental violence and alcohol abuse, showed less antisocial behavior, had fewer psychiatric contacts, and experienced less major stress in the prior year. The process leading to their suicides seemed to be of shorter duration, and they were withdrawn/narcissistic. The stress was primarily interpersonal conflict, and they made more communications of intent. Those with antisocial personality disorder experienced more parental violence and alcohol abuse and were more often separated from their parents. They also abused alcohol more themselves and had comorbid diagnoses. Those who abused alcohol were often unemployed, had problems with finances or the law, and had more recent stressors, especially interpersonal separations.

Gould et al. (1996) compared adolescent suicides with community controls and found that the suicides had fewer intact families, worse parent-child relationships, more stressful life events, more mood disorders in mothers, police trouble with fathers, and a family history of suicidal behavior.

Pelkonen et al. (1996) followed up adolescent psychiatric outpatients and found that the subsequent suicides were more often living alone, had more psychiatric referrals, and had been more suicidal in the past.

Shaffer et al. (1996) compared suicides under the age of 20 with normal controls. The suicides were judged more often to have been psychiatrically disturbed, expecially the older suicides. The male suicides were more often diagnosed with substance abuse and the females with major depressive disorders. For the suicides, prior suicide attempts were associated with having a mood disorder but not with the probability of having any psychiatric disorder. Compared to the controls, completing suicide was associated with prior attempts, mood disorder, and substance abuse for males and with prior attempt and mood disorder for females.

Nonfatal Suicidal Behavior

Among child psychiatric inpatients aged 5–13, Milling et al. (1994) found that suicidality peaked at age seven. The seriousness of the suicidality was not associated with age, sex, social class, or custody status.

Apter et al. (1995) found that suicidal behavior was more common in adolescent psychiatric inpatients who were depressed, had endogenous features to their depression, and showed violent behavior. Anorexics and conduct-disorder patients were also more suicidal.

Halfon et al. (1995) found that suicidal adolescent psychiatric inpatients less often than nonsuicidal patients had parents still married, more often had a borderline personality disorder or mood disorder, and less often had a psychosis. They did not differ in the suicidality of psychiatric disorder in their parents.

Lewinsohn et al. (1995) found that high school students with major depressive disorders had made more prior suicide attempts than those with substance abuse disorder or no disorder.

McCarthy et al. (1995) found that attempting suicide was more common in adolescent psychiatric patients with major depressive disorders than in those with conduct disorder, attention deficit disorder, or schizophrenia and other psychoses. The attempters were older, had made more prior

attempts, and had experienced less abuse by parents. Suicidal and assaultive behavior were not associated in these patients.

In a sample of adolescent female psychiatric inpatients, Walsh (1995) found that those who had been self-destructive on many occasions more often were learning disabled and had academic problems, had experienced recent loss, had been physically and sexually abused, had run away from home, were isolated from peers, were involved with satanism, had suicidal fantasies, and had parents who were substance abusers, violent, suicidal, and mentally ill.

Williamson et al. (1995) compared adolescents with major depressive disorders to normal adolescents. The groups did not differ in completed or attempted suicide in their relatives. However, adolescents with major depressive disorder plus suicidal ideation had more suicidal first-degree relatives (as well as more first-degree relatives with major depressive disorder) than those with a major depressive disorder but no suicidal ideation.

Booth and Zhang (1996) studied runaway and homeless youths and found a high percentage of attempted suicide (almost 70 percent) in those with conduct disorder and those with aggressive behavior.

Borchardt and Meller (1996) compared adolescents and pre-adolescents with affective disorder and found more attempted suicide in the adolescent group.

Braun-Scharm (1996) found that suicidality was higher in adolescent psychiatric inpatients with acute stress reactions, emotional disorders, and personality disorders and lower in those with conduct disorders, eating disorders, and schizophrenia.

Buddeberg et al. (1996) studied Swiss adolescents and found that those who had attempted suicide had more eating disorders, mental impairment, and physical impairment than suicidal ideators and normal youths. The attempters used cigarettes and hashish more than the normals, and the ideators used cigarettes and alcohol more. The suicidal youths were more often female, and the attempters were younger than the ideators.

Goldston et al. (1996) found that adolescent psychiatric inpatients who had attempted suicide more than once or who had recently attempted suicide had higher depression and trait anxiety scores and less trait anger than recent attempters with no prior attempts (but did not differ in state anxiety or state anger). Curiously, attempters at any time in the past had the most trait anger.

King et al. (1996) found no differences in current suicidal ideation or past suicidality between depressed adolescent inpatients with major depressions who abused substances and those who did not.

Klein et al. (1996) found that hypomanic traits were associated with attempted suicide in adolescents in school.

Peterson et al. (1996) studied child psychiatric emergencies aged 2–15 years. The suicidal ideators were more often females, older, white, and seen on weekdays during the school year. The attempters were more often female, older, minorities, and seen on weekends. In a follow-up study, the future attempters were older, had more often been hospitalized, and had been seen in vacation months. Future ideators were more often minorities and had suicidal ideation initially.

In a sample of high school students, Wagner et al. (1996) found that attempted suicide was associated with drug use, alcohol use, depression, and conduct problems; it was especially common in those with depression plus one of the other problems.

In a follow-up study, Wolk and Weissman (1996) found that children with major depressive disorders were more likely to attempt suicide (and more often had a tendency to complete suicide) than children with anxiety disorders or normal children.

Patton et al. (1997) found that attempted suicide in 15–16-year-old Australian students was predicted by psychological disturbance, alcohol use, sexual activity and for girls only, parental divorce, antisocial behavior, and marihuana use.

Pelkonen et al. (1997) found that suicidality in adolescent psychiatric outpatients was associated with prior psychiatric care, depressive disorders, and poorer psychosocial functioning (but not with age, parental divorce or death, living at home, legal problems, substance abuse or personality disorder).

Suicide In Adolescents

Suicidal Ideation

Choquet and Menk (1990) found that 14 percent of boys aged 13–16 in a community sample near Paris (France) and 23 percent of girls reported prior suicidal ideation. The ideators had more health problems (tiredness, nightmares, nervousness, and insomnia), drug use (alcohol, tobacco, and illegal drugs), delinquent behavior, school absences, violence, and interpersonal problems.

Meneese and Yutrzenka (1990) found that suicidal ideation in ninth graders was predicted by family environment variables (family organization and conflict) but not by sex, life events, or depression scores. In high school students, Meneese et al. (1992) found that suicidal ideation was more common in females and associated with depression, hopelessness, trait anxiety, negative life stress, utilization of coping behaviors, and family cohesiveness (but not grade level).

Kandel et al. (1991) found that illicit drug use was associated with prior suicidal ideation (and attempts) only in ninth and eleventh grade girls, not boys. Alcohol and cigarette use was not associated with suicidality. Suicidal ideation was associated with depression, not being close to mother and father, delinquency, risk-taking, psychiatric illness (girls only), medical illness (boys only), eating problems, life events, not attending church, and not finding school meaningful (girls only). Suicidality was not associated with party attendance, dating, or associating with peers after school.

Kelly et al. (1991) found that 15.6 percent of Swedish 13–18 year olds had considered suicide in the past year. Suicidal ideation was associated with being female, not feeling healthy, more alcohol and tobacco use, living with one or no parents, being a dropout, and illicit drug use.

Kirkpatrick-Smith et al. (1991-1992) found that suicidal ideation in high school students was predicted by depression, hopelessness, loneliness, life stress, substance abuse, alcohol use, parents' use of alcohol, and negatively, with reasons for living.

In Australia, Rey and Bird (1991) found that adolescents in a psychiatric unit were more likely to have suicidal ideation if they were girls, older, with more stressors, and with an affective disorder.

Beer and Beer (1992) found that suicidal ideation in high school students was associated with frequent absences, but not with low grade-point averages, low self-esteem, being in special education classes, and being eligible for free lunches.

De Man et al. (1992) found that suicidal ideation in adolescents was associated with depression, negative stressors, self-esteem, worse health, fewer interpersonal and family resources, and less satisfaction with these resources, but not with age, similar to the associations found in adults. De Man et al. (1993a) found that suicidal intent in high school students was associated with higher levels of parental control, not seeing parents as sources of support, and being female (but not associated with age or parents' marital status). De Man et al. (1993b, 1993c; De Man and Leduc, 1994, 1995) found that suicidal ideation was associated with being female, low self-esteem, less internal locus of control, depression, alcohol use, drug use, stress, experience of physical violence, school achievement, social support, and anomie (but not with absenteeism, age, or external locus-of-control scores).

In a sample of hospitalized children who were psychiatric patients, Livingston and Bracha (1992) found that the suicidal children had more psychotic symptoms, and in particular, visual hallucinations (but not auditory hallucinations, persecutory ideas, and ideas of reference); they more often had a major depressive disorder.

Ward (1992) found that suicidal ideation in high school students and college freshmen was associated with family conflict, depression, suicidal models inside and outside the family, conduct problems, substance abuse and worries about pregnancy, but not recent stress.

Workman and Beer (1992) found that suicidal ideation in high school students was not associated with sex, grade level, parents' alcohol use, or parents' marital status.

Choquet et al. (1993) found that suicidal ideation in teenagers in Quebec and France was associated with tobacco use, illicit drug use, the use of psychotropic medications, depression, and bad relationships with parents, but not with involvement in sports.

King et al. (1993a) found that suicidal ideation in inpatient girls was associated with depression, family functioning and alcohol use. King et al. (1993b) also found in a mixed-sex sample that the suicidal adolescents had more depressed fathers, less good relationships with their fathers, and fathers who perceived more family problems.

Mothers of the two groups did not differ.

In a sample of adults, Newcomb et al. (1993) found that prior suicidal ideation was positively predicted by increased polydrug use during middle school, especially cigarettes and cannabis (but not by the presence versus absence of polydrug use), emotional distress, depression, psychoticism, hostility, anxiety, and disorganized thinking; it was negatively predicted by social conformity, social supports, purpose in life, and self-derogation.

Steer et al. (1993) found in a multiple regression analysis that suicidal ideation in adolescent psychiatric inpatients was associated with age and hopelessness, but not with gender, ethnicity, mood disorder, past attempts, depression, or anxiety.

Butler et al. (1994) found that suicidal ideation in elementary and high school students was associated with poorer motivation for schooling, academic self-concept, sense of control over performance, and instructional mastery.

Chartier and Lassen (1994) found that past suicidal ideation was more common in female high school students than in males, but was not associated with grade level.

Cohen (1990) compared adolescents with suicidal ideation to clinical and normal control groups. The ideators were more depressed and hopeless, had more desire to hurt themselves, and saw suicide as a better solution. They did not have more stressors, but used denial less often as a defense mechanism. They had more need of psychological support from their mothers and fathers and were more angry at their mothers and fathers, but were not angry at peers.

Siemen et al. (1994) found, in a small sample of adolescent psychiatric inpatients, that suicidal ideation was associated with school-related problems, poor self-concept, poor family support, and being overly sensitive.

Thompson et al. (1994) found that suicidal ideation in high-risk adolescents was associated with depression, self-esteem, family strain, stressors, anger, and drug use. The predictors differed a little for boys and girls.

Goldney et al. (1995a, 1995b) tested high school students and followed them up for eight years. Suicidal ideation at follow-up was predicted by high school measures of self-esteem, depression, and locus of control, as well as four-year follow-up measures of anomie and hopelessness. Those dissatisfied with employment had the highest rate of suicide, along with the unemployed.

Kumar and Steer (1995) found that suicidal ideation in adolescent psychiatric inpatients was predicted by depression, hopelessness, anxiety, and internalization and externalization scale scores; it was not predicted by physical abuse, sexual abuse, mood disorders, substance use, or prior suicide attempts. Current attempted suicide was associated only with prior attempts.

LaFromboise and Howard-Pitney (1995) found that Zuni high school females had been more suicidal in the prior year than Cherokee females. Suicidality was associated with liking school, self-efficacy, social support, and psychological distress, but the correlates of suicidality differed for the two ethnic groups. For example, depression and social support were associated with attempting suicide in the Zuni girls but not in Cherokee girls.

Reinherz et al. (1995) found that current suicidal ideation in male youths was associated with family arguments/violence, failed hearing test at age five, health problems at age nine, parents separated/divorced, phobias at age 14, alcohol/drug abuse, and dependency on mother at age five.

In sixth through eighth graders in New Mexico, suicidal ideation was more common in Mexican Americans girls over the age of 14 (Roberts and Chen, 1995). Depression was associated with suicidal ideation in both Mexican American and Anglo American kids. In a multiple regression, race, sex, speaking English, having two parents, depression, and loneliness were associated with ideation.

Adams and Adams (1996) found that suicidal ideation was associated with scores on a problem-solving alternatives scale and stressful life events in adolescent psychiatric patients.

In fourth through sixth graders, Crocker and Hakim-Larson (1997) found that suicidal ideation was associated with parental support and depression, but not with scholastic competence or behavior and conduct.

Attempted Suicide

Beratis (1990) compared adolescent suicide attempters with normal controls. The attempters were more often psychiatrically disturbed, had more disrupted families, had more parental restrictiveness on personal freedom and forced isolation, had more quarrels and friction with parents, had worse academic performance, and had made more prior suicide attempts. They did not differ in physical health, physical abuse, or suicidality in the family. Beratis found that adolescents who were repeating suicide attempts differed from first-timers in having less restrictive parents and more often being psychiatrically disturbed.

Berman and Schwartz (1990) studied drug-abusing adolescent outpatients. Those who had attempted suicide were more often female, depressed, and accident prone and had more temper tantrums, chronic diseases (such as asthma), and parents in conflict. They found that drug-abusing first-time adolescent suicide attempters more often

had family members abusing drugs than did repeaters. First-timers and repeaters did not differ in Beck Depression Inventory depression scores.

Borst and Noam (1990) found that suicidal adolescent psychiatric inpatients more often than nonsuicidal patients had an affective disorder, were more often girls, and were more often at the conformist developmental stage (as defined by Jane Loevinger) than at the preconformist stage.

Gilliland (1990) compared adolescents who had attempted suicide with nonsuicidal psychiatric patients. The attempters had more friends attempt suicide, were more integrated socially, had fewer concerns with school, and had fewer alcoholic fathers. They did not differ in broken homes or parents who had received psychiatric treatment. Thus, the attempters were better functioning than the controls.

Kienhorst et al. (1990) compared adolescent school pupils who had attempted suicide in the past with those who had not. The attempters were more often girls and abused drugs and alcohol more; they had more parent divorces, deaths outside of the family, unemployed fathers, and worse living situations (single parents or living in an institution). They had higher hopelessness and depression scores, lower self-esteem, and worse relationships with their parents. They did not differ in rational thinking. Kienhorst et al. (1992) found that adolescents who had attempted suicide, as compared to depressed nonsuicidal adolescents, had experienced more stressors; were more likely to have run away from home; were more pessimistic, withdrawn, and permissive toward suicide; had more psychiatric symptoms and more suicidality in significant others; and were less often bipolar. De Wilde and Kienhorst (1993) compared adolescent suicide attempters with nonsuicidal depressed adolescents. The attempters had experienced more physical abuse, separation from parents, and total stressors in the first 12 years of life, and more parental separations, changes in living conditions, and total stressors as teenagers. De Wilde et al. (1993) found that these two groups did not differ in anxiety, locus of control, self-esteem, hopelessness, or family environment, but the two groups did score differently from nondepressed adolescents on these variables. De Wilde and Kienhorst (1994) found that recent attempters had more fights with parents, got more girls pregnant, and attempted suicide at an earlier age. They ran away from home more and had more stressful life events. De Wilde et al. (1994) found that students at high risk for suicide had made more prior attempts, had more stressful life events, and were more hopeless, but did not differ in family support or substance use/abuse. Kienhorst et al. (1991) compared attempted suicides with depressed 12–21 year olds and found the attempters to be more often from broken homes, runaways, with absent fathers, and with less support from parents. Of 171 variables, 36 were statistically significant.

King et al. (1990a) compared adolescent female suicide attempters from a low-income urban area with normal controls and found the attempters to be less often living with their mother, with worse family relations, more depressed, more often delinquent, with fewer support persons and confidantes, and having experienced more stressful life events.

Looking at a group of adolescent psychiatric inpatients, King et al. (1990b) found that the suicidal and nonsuicidal adolescents did not differ in scores on a social adjustment inventory or in the self-perception of their competency.

Ritter (1990) compared adolescent attempters who made serious and gesture attempts. The male serious attempters were more depressed and had more internalizing symptoms, but did not differ in competence, externalizing symptoms, or delinquent and aggressive syndromes. The female serious attempters were more competent and had more internalizing symptoms.

Adcock et al. (1991) found that 16 percent of eighth and tenth grade children in Alabama had attempted suicide, more girls than boys, but no differences by race or rural/urban location. Adolescents who used alcohol and who were no longer virgins had a higher incidence of prior suicide attempts. Females, whites, urban kids, those who had sexual experience, and those who had used alcohol had more knowledge about suicide.

On a Navajo reservation, attempted suicide in sixth to twelfth graders was more likely if they were female and alienated from family and the community; if they had a history of physical abuse, sexual abuse, poor physical health, psychiatric disturbance, family/friends who had attempted suicide; and if they used hard liquor (Grossman et al., 1991). They did not differ in parental use of alcohol, having friends complete suicide, or having parents absent or divorced.

Larsson et al. (1991) surveyed Swedish adolescents aged 13–18. Three percent had pronounced current suicidal ideation (levels two or three on the Beck Depression Inventory), 4 percent had attempted suicide in the past, and 16 percent had a family member or friend who had attempted suicide. Girls had attempted suicide more than boys. Attempting suicide was associated with having a family member or friend attempt suicide.

Paluszny et al. (1991) found that adolescents who had attempted suicide were more often female; came from more chaotic families; were more disturbed, depressed, and constricted; had less insight; and more problems with school, family, girl/boy friends, acting out, and drug abuse as compared to controls. They did not differ in race or whether their families were enmeshed or intact.

Pfeffer et al. (1991) followed up adolescent suicidal children for six to eight years. The predictors of later suicide attempts were having made prior attempts, more severe suicidal behavior at intake for the first admission, and having a mood disorder.

Razin et al. (1991) compared Hispanic adolescent females who attempted suicide with normal controls. The attempters did not differ in psychiatric/medical problems, alcohol/drug abuse, criminal behavior in family, sexual/physical abuse, father absent, close friends, sexually active, or loss of close friends. The attempters more often had a boyfriend, were more often behind in grade level, and were more often a parentified child. They also had mothers with fewer friends.

Swedo et al. (1991) found that adolescent suicide attempters were more hopeless than psychiatric controls and had more psychiatric symptoms. Compared to normals, both groups had a poorer self-image, more drug/alcohol use, a worse relationship with fathers, more hopelessness, and more psychiatric symptoms.

Andrews and Lewinsohn (1992) found that prior attempts in high school students were associated with being female, coming from a single-parent home, having father absent, and the father having no college education, but not associated with race or repeating a grade. Eighty percent of the attempters had a psychiatric disorder, most commonly major depression, alcohol/drug abuse, or disruptive conduct disorder. Attempted suicide in the next year was predicted by prior attempts, prior suicidal ideation, and having a psychiatric disorder.

Among students at a school administered by the Bureau of Indian Affairs, native American youths who had attempted suicide had poorer school performance. They also drank alcohol more, abused drugs more, were more likely to become pregnant, had experienced more physical and sexual abuse, and were more likely to have friends and family attempt or complete suicide (Blum et al., 1992).

Garnefski et al. (1992) found that a history of attempted suicide in adolescents was associated with sexual abuse, loneliness, depressed mood, low self-esteem, drug use, (for girls) physical abuse, and (for boys) low academic achievement.

Grossi and Violato (1992) found that adolescents at a residential treatment center who had attempted suicide had more often failed a grade, lacked an emotional significant other and moved residences and differed in their age at separation from their parents. They did not differ in intelligence test scores, MMPI scores, self-esteem, hopelessness, or scores on the Stroop Color and Word Tests and the Porteus Maze Test.

Among Zuni adolescents, Howard-Pitney et al. (1992; LaFromboise and Howard-Pitney, 1994) found that the attempters were more often female and users of drugs/alcohol, were more depressed and hopeless, and had experienced more stressors. Both attempters and ideators liked school less, had worse interpersonal communication, and had parents who abused drugs/alcohol. They did not differ in measure of traditionality.

Slap et al. (1992) found that attempted suicides among a sample of adolescent patients at a medical clinic were more often female; came without a guardian; used marihuana; had received prior mental health care; more often had sexually-transmitted diseases, pregnancy, and contraception as the complaint; had worse family relationships; and were more depressed, delinquent and aggressive. They did not differ in age, race, parents' occupation or use of alcohol/drugs.

In a sample of African American female adolescent suicide attempters, the more depressed girls were more schizoid, hyperactive, delinquent, unpopular, and internalizing and externalizing, according to their parents. They were more delinquent, internalizing and externalizing and had more thought disorder, according to their own self-report (Summerville et al., 1992).

Gasquet and Choquet (1993) found that adolescent suicide attempters more often than normal adolescents smoked, got drunk, abused tranquilizers, and (for boys only) used illicit drugs. They also had more psychiatric symptoms.

Lewinsohn et al. (1993) compared high school students who had attempted suicide with those who had not. The attempters (after controls for depression scores) more often had a prior psychiatric disorder (especially depressive disorder and substance abuse), school problems, health problems, and internalizing and externalizing symptoms.

Madianos et al. (1993) found that adolescent suicide attempters in Greece, compared to normal controls, more often had prior psychiatric contacts, mental illness in family, divorced parents, licit and illicit drug use, poor scholastic performance, and physical illness in family; they did not differ in depression, absent fathers, immigrant parents, familial alcohol use, or current physical illness.

Morano et al. (1993) compared suicide attempters with nonattempters, matching all psychiatric inpatients for depression. The attempters had more hopelessness and recent loss and less family support (but no differences in other supports).

Sadowski and Kelley (1993) found that adolescent suicide attempters were more hopeless and depressed than psychiatric controls and had worse social problem-solving skills. Suicidal lethality and intent were, however, not related to problem-solving skills.

Tousignant et al. (1993) found that high school students who had attempted suicide more often had broken homes and poor quality of care from parents.

Adams et al. (1994b) found that adolescent psychiatric patients who had attempted suicide had not experienced more overall stressors than normal adolescents, but had experienced more major events and more exits.

Bjarnason and Thorlindsson (1994) found that attempted suicide by ninth and tenth graders associated positively with poor grades and truancy; attending rock concerts and writing poetry; parties and break-ups with friends; using cigarettes, alcohol, caffeine, and drugs; and having peers who attempted or completed suicide. It was associated negatively with sports participation, socializing in school, and having both parents in the home.

De Maso et al. (1994) found that adolescent suicide attempters seen at an emergency room who had depressive disorders had higher suicidal intent than attempters with other diagnoses, but did not differ in method or medical seriousness of the attempt.

Eggert et al. (1994) found that prior suicide attempts in high-risk high school students were associated with anger, drug use, satisfaction with family support, and being a victim of violence, but were not associated with depression, hopelessness, stressful events, or the presence of family support. The lethality of the attempt and the frequency and intensity of suicidal ideation had somewhat different correlates.

Felix-Ortiz et al. (1994) found that prior attempted suicide in Mexican-American adolescents was associated with the use of cigarettes, alcohol, marihuana, inhalants, and hard drugs (frequency and quantity).

Reynolds and Mazza (1994) found that school students who had attempted suicide used more drugs (especially sedatives and stimulants) and alcohol (beer, wine, and liquor) than nonattempters.

Summerville et al. (1994) studied black adolescent suicide attempters. Those who were more depressed came from more-dysfunctional families (especially regarding cohesiveness) and made more internal-global-stable attributions for events.

Tulloch et al. (1994) found that attempted suicides differed from medical controls in more often living on their own or with non-parents, experiencing more physical and more sexual abuse, more unemployment, more substance use (especially tobacco, alcohol, and marihuana), and more often having no close confidante.

Bryant et al. (1995) found that attempted suicide in severely emotionally disturbed teenagers was associated with being female, alcohol use, and illicit drug use, but not with race. Suicidal ideation was associated only with alcohol use.

Eskin (1995) found that attempting suicide had similar correlates in Swedish and Turkish high school students: previous psychiatric contacts, being female, family members attempting suicide, and poor family support. Other correlates differed – for example, parents being immigrants in Sweden and parents being divorced in Turkey. Current suicidal risk had similar correlates.

Garnefski and Diekstra (1995) found that prior attempted suicide in high school students was associated with more smoking, alcohol and marihuana use; felony assaults, vandalism and theft; anxiety, depression, loneliness, and low self-esteem; and learning difficulties and concentration problems.

Pfeffer et al. (1995) found that adolescent suicide attempters showed more projection, regression, compensation, and reaction formation than nonsuicidal adolescents. Only repression was associated with attempting suicide during follow-up (the attempters showed less repression), but controls for mood disorder and social adjustment eliminated this association. The use of compensation and impulse control predicted a good outcome at follow-up for the attempters.

Pillay and Wassenaar (1995) found that South African adolescent attempters were more depressed and hopeless than community and medical controls.

Reinherz et al. (1995) found that attempted suicide in female adolescents was predicted by later birth order (third or higher), family arguments/violence, major depressive disorders, alcohol abuse, and behavior problems (especially aggression) at age five.

Walter et al. (1995) found that Latino junior high school students who had attempted suicide were more often female, but did not differ in acculturation or substance use. They had more adverse social circumstances, academic problems, depressive disorders, and suicidal acquaintances; and they were more violent and sexually active.

Ward (1995) found that Latino students had less suicidality if Spanish was used in the home and if the families used esperatistas (native healers). The correlates of suicidality differed a little for Latinos, African Americans and whites and more so for boys and girls. For example, white and Latino male suicidality was associated with depression and avoidant behavior; for white and Latino females associated with low self-esteem, high family conflict, and suicidal models.

Kirmayer et al. (1996) found that Inuit youths in Canada who had attempted suicide more often were male and first-borns, used inhalants, had friends who had attempted/completed suicide, had higher alienation scores, had more personal and mental health problems, attended church less, and lived in more crowded homes with parents who abused drugs/alcohol.

. Ng (1996) found that suicidal intent in adolescents who attempted suicide was associated with living longer with both biological parents, fewer years in the town, one biological parent at home at the time of the attempt, and more prior attempts.

Rotheram-Borus et al. (1996) found that adolescents seen at a youth service agency who had attempted suicide had more prior suicidal ideation and attempts; were more often angry and depressed; more often had trouble at home, conduct problems, and substance abuse; and less often had multiple arrests. They had more attempted suicide within the families but not more among their peers.

In native Hawaiian high school students, Yuen et al. (1996) found that previous attempted suicide was associated with sex, depression, substance abuse, and family support.

In a national sample of high school students, Woods et al. (1997) found that prior attempted suicide was associated with physical fights in the prior year, cigarette use, gun carrying, lifetime drug use, being native American, and being female. The predictors varied by gender.

Attempters and Ideators

Pronovost (1990; Pronovost et al., 1990) compared suicidal and nonsuicidal adolescents and found that the suicidal adolescents were more often in the later grades, girls, depressed, and had serious ailments (in themselves and their families). They were less likely to be in special education classes, to be from two-parent homes; or to confide in parents, siblings, and relatives.

In Budapest, Czorba and Huszar (1993) found that suicidal adolescent girls differed from nonsuicidal girls in having one-parent families, parents who disagreed over child rearing, emotional distress, and low expectations for the future. The suicidal girls also had worse relationships with parents, warm-permissive mothers and cold fathers, and lack of peer acceptance; they drank wine and spirits more (and beer less).

Fremouw et al. (1993) found that suicidal adolescents differed from psychiatric controls in being more depressed and hopeless and having experienced more negative stressors, but did not differ on an interpersonal problem-solving test. The psychiatric controls were more rigid on an alterative uses test. The suicidal adolescents and psychiatric controls had fewer reasons for living and less family cohesion than normal controls.

Garrison et al. (1993) studied suicidal ideation and attempts in the prior year in high school students and found the incidence to be higher in girls and associated with aggressive behavior, alcohol use, drug use, and cigarette use, but not with race.

Gartrell et al. (1993) studied native Canadian junior high school students. Those who had thought about or attempted suicide in the past had more suicidal behavior in their family members and more often used alcohol, tobacco, and marihuana. Employment of mothers or fathers and having a mother present in the home were not significant correlates of suicidality. In addition, past suicidal ideation was associated with father's absence and with being a girl.

Tousignant and Hanigan (1993) found that suicidal high school students (ideators and attempters) more often had experienced a serious and unexpected loss in a love relationship that was positive up until the breakup, were upset longer, saw kin less often, had more conflict with kin, and were less likely to tell their social network of their loss. They did not differ in having a confidante or in satisfaction with their support.

Vega et al. (1993a, 1993b) found that recent suicidal ideation was most common in African American sixth and seventh graders in Miami, then in whites, Nicaraguans, and finally, Cubans. The order for suicide attempts was Nicaraguans, African Americans, Cubans and whites. The ethnic groups had different levels of the risk factors – for example, the African American children were the most depressed – and the predictive strength of the risk factors differed for each ethnic group. In the Hispanics, acculturation was positively associated with attempting suicide. Overall, drug use, alcohol use, and cigarette smoking predicted attempting suicide in the following year.

Bjarnason (1994) found that suicidality in ninth and tenth graders was associated with depression, suicidal behavior in significant others, and lack of both mental and material support by their families.

DeSimone et al. (1994) found that alcohol use was not associated with past suicidality in high school or college students, after controls for age, sex, and depression.

Ferdinand and Verhulst (1994) found that internalizing scores predicted subsequent suicide attempts and ideation in school children ages 12–16, as did social dysfunction on the GHQ-28 and anxiety on the SCL-90.

Juon et al. (1994) found that suicidal ideation and attempts in Korean high school students were associated with gender, academic stress, hostility, depression, and alcohol use; they were associated less consistently with the use of tranquilizers, stimulants, and inhalants.

Miller (1994) found that adolescents with behavior and emotional disorders had more prior suicidal ideation (males only) and attempts (males and females) than those with no disorders. The two groups did not differ in their rationales for suicide.

Oler et al. (1994) found that high school students on sports teams were less depressed and showed less suicidality than the rest of the students. They also used cigarettes, alcohol, and drugs less.

Reinecke and DuBois (1994) found that suicidality in adolescent psychiatric inpatients was associated with depression, anxiety, hopelessness, self-esteem, dysfunctional attitudes, and social support, but not with stressors or daily hassles.

Wagner and Cohen (1994) found that the siblings of adolescents who had attempted suicide or who had suicidal ideation also showed elevated suicidal ideation. For younger siblings only, suicidal ideation was associated with less maternal warmth and more maternal discipline.

In a national sample, Achenbach et al. (1995) found that later suicidality in boys was predicted by aggression and stress scores, while later suicidality in girls was predicted by delinquency and earlier suicidality. Anxiety and depression scores did not predict later suicidality. It appeared, then, that externalizing symptoms were more predictive of later suicidality than internalizing symptoms.

Ardila and Bateman (1995) found that university students in Colombia who used drugs attempted and thought about suicide more.

Burge et al. (1995) surveyed ninth through twelfth graders and found that sexual activity and alcohol and marihuana use were associated with suicidal ideation and attempts, while cocaine use also was associated with suicide attempts. Multiple attempters used cocaine and alcohol more and engaged in more sexual activity, but did not differ in marihuana use.

Donahue and Benson (1995) surveyed high school students and found that suicidality was negatively associated with religious involvement and educational ability and aspiration and associated positively with having a single-parent home and being female.

Fergusson and Lynskey (1995a, 1995b, 1995c) compared adolescent suicide attempters in the general population with the nonattempters. The attempters had more anxiety, mood, conduct, and substance-abuse disorders. They had more been involved in more juvenile offenses, had more police contacts, more often dropped out of school and had lower self-esteem. They came more often from the lower social classes, had a family history of offending and alcohol/drug abuse, and had received less maternal emotional responsiveness. Similar results were found for suicidal ideation.

In South Africa, Fisher and Charlton (1995) found that coloured teenagers who were high school dropouts were more often substances abusers but less often suicidal (ideation and attempts) than the others.

Guiao and Esparza (1995; Guiao, 1994) found that suicidality in Mexican American teenagers was associated with depression, coping efficiency, and family cohesion, but not with life stress, coping frequency, or family adaptability.

Martin et al. (1995) found that recent suicidal ideation in high school students was associated with family dysfunction, although controls for depression and the marital status of the parents eliminated this association. Suicide attempts were associated with depression, a history of sexual abuse, and having friends who had attempted suicide.

Among youths in correctional facilities, Morris et al. (1995) found that suicidal ideation and attempts were associated with being female and white, drug use, sexual abuse, and being under age 13. Attempts

were also associated with gang membership and having a sexually transmitted disease.

Among a sample of Australian juvenile offenders, Putnins (1995) found that suicidality was associated with greater use of alcohol, hallucinogens, narcotics, stimulants, inhalants, and sedative/hypnotics, but not marihuana.

Reifman and Windle (1995) found that depression, alcohol use, and suicidality predicted suicidality six month later in high school students. Social support and hopelessness did not contribute to the prediction.

Trammel et al. (1995) found that recent (but not long-term) drug use differentiated college students who attempted suicide (but not who had thought about suicide) from those who had not; only marihuana use gave significant differences, not alcohol or hard drugs.

Flisher et al. (1996) found that attempted suicide in school children was associated with alcohol and cannabis use, having sexual intercourse, carrying a knife, smoking cigarettes, not using seat belts, being physically injured by a family member, injuring another, and going out alone at night.

Neumark-Sztainer et al. (1996) found that native American and Hispanic school students had attempted suicide more than whites (as well as girls more than boys and older students more than younger students). Suicidal ideation in the students was associated with delinquent behavior, sexual activity, substance abuse, and unhealthy weight loss.

Vannatta (1996) found that prior suicidality was associated in male senior high school students with violence, home environment, forcible sex, strict rules, alcohol use, and school misconduct. For females, the correlates were violence, home environment, forcible sex (as the offender), strict rules, use of over-the-counter drugs, sexual activity, hard-drug use, school misconduct, and miscommunication with parents.

Zhang (1996) found that depression, family cohesion, and a pro-suicide attitude predicted suicidality in college students in the United States and in China, while religiosity had opposite associations in the two samples.

In sixth through eighth graders, Roberts et al. (1997) found that suicidality in the prior two weeks was more common in Mexican, Pakistani, and Vietnamese Americans; those of mixed ancestry; females; the lower-socioeconomic-status students; and 14–15 year olds.

Attempters Versus Ideators

Kosky et al. (1990) compared adolescent suicide attempters with ideators and found that the attempters more often abused drugs and alcohol, had more family discord, and for the boys, more loss. They did not differ in clinical symptoms, depression, anxiety, or irritability.

Dinges and Quang (1992–1993, 1994) studied adolescent suicide attempters and ideators among American Indians and native Alaskans. Suicide ideation was associated with family/parent conflicts and pregnancy fears. Attempted suicide was associated with family/parent conflicts, school environment, and interpersonal conflicts/tension. Suicidality was also associated with depression, alcohol use, and drug use.

Shaunesey et al. (1993) found that adolescent psychiatric inpatients who were attempters were of lower social class than ideators and nonsuicidal youths.

Culp et al. (1995) found that high school students who had attempted suicide in the past were more currently depressed than those who had thought about suicide in the past.

Wetzler et al. (1996) found that adolescent inpatients who had attempted suicide were the most aggressive and depressed (especially if no medical treatment was necessary), while ideators were the most impulsive. The groups did not differ in overall psychopathology.

Completed Suicides

Graham and Burvill (1992) compared adolescent suicides (15–19) with young adults (20–24) and older adults (45–59) in western Australia. The adolescent suicides were more often single and aborigines. Their method for suicide was more active, and they used carbon monoxide more and poisons less. The adolescents and young adults were more often intoxicated, but the groups did not differ in total stress or the duration of the stress. The stressors were different, with the adolescents experiencing more unemployment and legal/disciplinary problems. The adolescents more often had a personality or conduct disorder; the young adults schizophrenia; and the older adults physical illness, alcohol abuse, and major depression.

Hawton et al. (1993) followed up a sample of adolescents who had attempted suicide and found that subsequent completed suicide was predicted by unemployment, substance abuse, personality disorder, prior suicide attempts, prior psychiatric inpatient treatment, and social class (V).

Queralt (1993) found that completed Latino adolescent suicides in Miami had more school problems (such as truancy), learning disabilities, special education needs, antisocial behavior, emotional symptoms, and family problems than normal controls. They did not differ in migration, acculturations, or psychiatric disorder.

Ward (1993) compared adolescent completers with normal adolescents. The suicides scored higher on scales to measure conduct problems, avoidant behavior, drug abuse, depression and negative affect; they scored lower on scales to measure self-esteem, social support, and family conflict.

Brent et al. (1994a, 1994b, 1994c) compared adolescent completed suicides with community controls. The suicides more often had a personality disorder (especially histrionic, narcissistic, borderline, antisocial, avoidant, passive-aggressive, dependent, and compulsive, but not paranoid, schizoid, or schizotypal). They also had more psychiatric disorders (especially anxiety and depressive disorders and substance abuse). After control for Axis I disorders, they did not differ in personality disorders. The suicides also had more family stressors, relatives with problems, nonintact homes, a family history of depression and substance abuse, and parent-child discord. For those suicides with affective disorders, they were more likely to have a substance abuse disorder, an anxiety disorder, and a family with a history of affective disorder and attempted suicide.

Krausz et al. (1995) followed up schizophrenic adolescent suicide attempters. Those completing suicide had been hospitalized for longer periods, had more prior suicidality, and had more recent hospitalizations. They did not differ in age, diagnosis, sex, or sibling position.

Childhood Predictors of Later Suicide

De Chateau (1990) followed up several thousand child guidance clinic patients after 30 years and compared those completing suicide with those dying from other causes. The suicides had acted out more as children and had parents who more often had psychiatric disorders.

Lester (1991a) compared the suicides in Terman's sample of gifted children with a nonsuicide group matched for mental distur-

bance in adulthood. The suicides had more neurotic symptoms as children. They did not differ in parent or teacher ratings, pregnancy length, birth weight, intelligence test scores, experience of loss, length of breast feeding, health as children, or parents' ages. Lester (1991b) found that the suicides in Terman's sample did not differ from the rest of the sample in intelligence test scores. However, their age at the time of their suicides was associated with the length of pregnancy (negatively); and experience of loss, especially fathers through death, and length of period of breast feeding (positively).

Caspi et al. (1996) found that behavior at age three predicted attempted suicide by age 21. The attempters had been rated more often as inhibited or undercontrolled, and less often as well adjusted, but did not differ in being reserved or confidant. The inhibited children became more depressed, whereas the undercontrolled children became more antisocial.

Discussion

The research on these issues is extensive and typically unsound methodologically. As mentioned earlier, much of the research does not control for psychiatric disturbance in general. Comparing completed suicides with normal controls, for example, is of less value than comparing them with equally disturbed but nonsuicidal controls.

Second, there needs to be some meta-analyses of the results of this research. Each variable has been studied many times, and yet we have no idea of the consistency with which each variable correlates with suicidality (and with which type of suicidality).

Third, there are more than a hundred variables involved here – variables concerned with psychiatric disorder, drug use, delinquent behavior, school behavior, parental variables, stressors, and personality traits. Kienhorst et al. (1991) studied 171 variables, of which 36 correlated significantly with suicidality! A selection of these variables is typically placed in a multiple-regression analysis, and the few significant correlates identified. The variables need to be clustered, and they may not simply increase the risk of suicidal behavior in a simple linear additive model. Other possibilities need to be explored.

REFERENCES

Achenbach, T. M., Howell, C. T., McConaughy, S. H., & Stanger, C. Six year predictors of problems in a national sample of children and youth. *Journal of the American Academy of Child & Adolescent Psychiatry*, 1995, 34, 488–498.

Adam, K. S., Keller, A., West, M., Larose, S., & Goszer, L. B. Parental representation in suicidal adolescents. *Australian & New Zealand Journal of Psychiatry*, 1994, 28, 418–425.

Adam, K. S., Sheldon-Keller, A. E., & West, M. Attachment organization and history of suicidal behavior in clinical adolescents. *Journal of Consulting & Clinical Psychology*, 1996, 64, 264–272.

Adams, D. M., Overholser, J. C., & Lehnert, K. L. Perceived family functioning and adolescent suicide. *Journal of the American Academy of Child & Adolescent Psychiatry*, 1994a, 33, 498–507.

Adams, D. M., Overholser, J. C., & Spirito, A. Stressful life events associated with adolescent suicide attempts. *Canadian Journal of Psychiatry*, 1994b, 39, 43–48.

Adams, J., & Adams, M. The association among negative life events, perceived problem-solving alternatives, depression, and suicidal ideation in adolescent psychiatric patients. *Journal of Child Psychology & Psychiatry*, 1996, 37, 715–720.

Adcock, A. G., Nagy, S., & Simpson, J. A. Selected risk factors in adolescent suicide attempts. *Adolescence*, 1991, 26, 817–825.

Akande, A., & Lester, D. Psychological health, suicidal ideation, and family size among Nigerian Yoruba students. *Individual Psychology*, 1994, 50, 203–206.

Allison, S., Pearce, C., Martin, G., Miller, K., & Long, R. Parental influence, pessimism and adolescent suicidality. *Archives of Suicide Research*, 1995, 1, 229–242.

Andrews, S. A., & Lewinsohn, P. M. Suicide attempts among older adolescents. *Journal of the American Academy of Child & Adolescent Psychiatry*, 1992, 31, 655–662.

Anonymous. *Perspective on youth.* St Paul, MN: Minnesota Department of Children, Families and Learning, 1995.

Apter, A., Gothelf, D., Orbach, I., Weizman, R., Ratzoni, G., Har-Even, D., & Tyano, S. Correlation of suicidal and violent behavior in different diagnosis categories in hospitalized adolescent patients. *Journal of the American Academy of Child & Adolescent Psychiatry*, 1995, 34, 912–918.

Ardila, A., & Bateman, J. R. Psychoactive substance use. *Addictive Behaviors*, 1995, 20, 549–554.

Armsden, G. C., McCauley, E., Greenberg, M. T., Burke, P. M., & Mitchell, J. R. Parent and peer attachment in early adolescent depression. *Journal of Abnormal Child Psychology*, 1990, 18, 683–698.

Bagley, C., Wood, M., & Young, L. Victim to abuser. *Child Abuse & Neglect*, 1994, 18, 683–697.

Ballard, M. E., & Coates, S. The immediate effects of homicidal, suicidal, and nonviolent heavy metal and rap songs on the moods of college students. *Youth & Society*, 1995, 27, 148–168.

Barker, D. J., Osmond, C., Rodin, I., Fall, C. H., & Winter, P. D. Low weight gain in infancy and suicide in later life. *British Medical Journal*, 1995, 311, 1203.

Bayatpour, M., Wells, R. D., & Holford, S. Physical and sexual abuse as predictors of substance use and suicide among pregnant teenagers. *Journal of Adolescent Health*, 1992, 13, 128–132.

Beautrais, A. L., Joyce, P. R., & Mulder, R. T. Risk factors for serious suicide attempts among youths aged 13 through 24 years. *Journal of the American Academy of Child & Adolescent Psychiatry*, 1996, 35, 1174–1182.

Beer, J., & Beer, J. Depression, self-esteem, suicide ideation, and GPAs of high school students at risk. *Psychological Reports*, 1992, 71, 899–902.

Bergman, K. J., & Carmel, L. H., & Lester, D. Birth order, suicidal preoccupation, and scores suggesting manic-depressive tendencies. *Psychological Reports*, 1997, 80, 442.

Beitchman, J. H., Zucker, K. J., Hood, J. E., DaCosta, G. A., Akman, D., & Cassavia, E. A review of the long-term effects of child sexual abuse. *Child Abuse & Neglect*, 1992, 16, 101–118.

Benjaminsen, S., Krarup, G., & Lauritsen, R. Personality, parental rearing behavior, and parental loss in attempted suicide. *Acta Psychiatrica Scandinavica*, 1990, 82, 389–397.

Beratis, S. Factors associated with adolescent suicidal attempts in Greece. *Psychopathology*, 1990, 23, 161–168.

Berman, A. L., & Schwartz, R. H. Suicide attempts among adolescent drug users. *American Journal of Diseases of Childhood*, 1990, 144, 310–314.

Bjarnason, T. The influence of social support, suggestion, and depression on suicidal behavior among Icelandic youth. *Acta Sociologica*, 1994, 37, 195–206.

Bjarnason, T., & Thorlindsson, T. Manifest predictors of past suicide attempts in a population of Icelandic youth. *Suicide & Life-Threatening Behavior*, 1994, 24, 350–358.

Blanton-Lacy, M., Molock, S. D., Kimbrough, R., Williams, S., Nicholson, M., & Hamilton, D. Validity of the use of suicide scales with African Americans. In D. Lester (Ed.), *Suicide '95*. Washington, DC: AAS, 1995, 117.

Blum, R. W., Harman, B., Harris, L., Bergeisen, L., & Resnick, M. D. American Indian-Alaska native youth health. *Journal of the American Medical Association*, 1992, 267, 1637–1644.

Booth, R. E., & Zhang, Y. Severe aggression and related conduct problems among runaway and homeless adolescents. *Psychiatric Services*, 1996, 47, 75–80.

Borchardt, C. M., & Meller, W. H. Symptoms of affective disorder in pre-adolescent versus adolescent inpatients. *Journal of Adolescence*, 1996, 19, 155–161.

Borst, S. R., & Noam, G. G. A developmental approach to adolescent suicidality. In D. Lester (Ed.), *Suicide '90*. Denver: AAS, 1990, 260–261.

Borst, S. R., & Noam, G. G. Developmental psychopathology in suicidal and nonsuicidal adolescent girls. *Journal of the American Academy of Child & Adolescent Psychiatry*, 1993, 32, 501–508.

Boudewyn, A. C., & Liem, J. H. Childhood sexual abuse as a precursor to depression and self-destructive behavior in adulthood. *Journal of Traumatic Stress*, 1995, 8, 445–459.

Brand, E. F., King, C. A., Olson, E., Ghaziuddin, N., & Naylor, M. Depressed adolescents with histories of sexual abuse. In D. Lester (Ed.), *Suicide '94*. Denver: AAS, 1994, 52–53.

Brand, E. F., King, C. A., Olson, E., Ghaziuddin, N., & Naylor, M. Depressed adolescents with histories of sexual abuse. *Journal of the American Academy of Child & Adolescent Psychiatry*, 1996, 35, 34–41.

Braun-Scharm, H. Suicidality and personality disorders in adolescence. *Crisis*, 1996, 17, 64–68.

Brent, D. A., Johnson, B. A., Perper, J., Connolly, J., Bridge, J., Bartle, S., & Rather, C. Personality disorder, personality traits, impulsive violence, and completed suicide in adolescents. *Journal of the American Academy of Child & Adolescent Psychiatry*, 1994a, 33, 1080–1086.

Brent, D. A., Perper, J. A., Moritz, G., Baugher, M., Schweers, J., & Roth, C. Suicide in affectively ill adolescents. *Journal of Affective Disorders*, 1994b, 31, 193–202.

Brent, D. A., Perper, J. A., Moritz, G., Liotus, L., Schweers, J., Balach, L., & Roth, C. Familial risk factors for adolescent suicide. *Acta Psychiatrica Scandinavica*, 1994c, 89, 52–58.

Bron, B., Strack, M., & Rudolph, G. Childhood experiences of loss and suicide attempts. *Journal of Affective Disorders*, 1991, 23, 165–172.

Brown, G. R., & Anderson, B. Psychiatric morbidity in adult inpatients with childhood histories of sexual and physical abuse. *American Journal of Psychiatry*, 1991, 148, 55–61.

Bryant, E. S., Garrison, C. Z., Valois, R. F., Rivard, J. C., & Hinkle, K. T. Suicidal behavior among youth with severe emotional disturbance. *Journal of Child & Family Studies*, 1995, 4, 425–443.

Bryant, S. L., & Range, L. M. Suicidality in college women who report multiple versus single types of maltreatment by parents. *Journal of Child Sexual Abuse*, 1995a, 4(3), 87–94.

Bryant, S. L., & Range, L. M. Suicidality in college women who were sexually and physically abused and physically punished by parents. *Violence & Victims*, 1995b, 10, 195–201.

Bryant, S. L., & Range, L. M. Type and severity of child abuse. *Child Abuse & Neglect*, 1997, 21, 1169–1176.

Buddeberg, C., Buddeberg-Fischer, B., Gnam, G., Schmid, J., & Christen, S. Suicidal behavior in Swiss students. *Crisis*, 1996, 17, 78–86.

Burge, V., Felts, M., Chenier, T., & Parrillo, A. V. Drug use, sexual activity, and suicidal behavior in U.S. high school students. *Journal of School Health*, 1995, 65, 222–227.

Butler, J. W., Novy, D., Kagan, N., & Gates, G. An investigation of differences in attitudes between suicidal and nonsuicidal student ideators. *Adolescence*, 1994, 29, 623–638.

Caspi, A., Moffitt, T. E., Newman, D. L., & Silva, P. A. Behavioral observations at age 3 years predict adult psychiatric disorders. *Archives of General Psychiatry*, 1996, 53, 1033–1039.

Chandy, J. M., Blum, R. W., & Resnick, M. D. History of sexual abuse and parental alcohol misuse. *Child & Adolescent Social Work Journal*, 1996, 13, 411–432.

Chandy, J. M., Blum, R. W., & Resnick, M. D. Sexually abused male adolescents. *Journal of Child Sexual Abuse*, 1997, 6(2), 1–16.

Chartier, G. M., & Lassen, M. K. Adolescent depression. *Adolescence*, 1994, 29, 859–864.

Choquet, M., Kovess, V., & Poutignat, N. Suicidal thoughts among adolescents. *Adolescence*, 1993, 28, 649–659.

Choquet, M., & Menk, H. Suicidal thoughts during early adolescence. *Acta Psychiatrica Scandinavica*, 1990, 81, 170–177.

Cloitre, M., Scarvalone, P., & Difeda, J. Posttraumatic stress disorder, self- and interpersonal dysfunction among sexually retraumatized women. *Journal of Traumatic Stress*, 1997, 10, 437–452.

Cohen, D. R. *A multidimensional study of adolescent suicidal ideation.* Doctoral dissertation, University of Windsor, 1990.

Cohen, Y., Spirito, A., Sterling, C., Donaldson, D., Seifer, R., Plummer, B., Avila, R., & Ferrer, K. Physical and sexual abuse and their relationship to psychiatric disorder and suicidal behavior among adolescents who are psychiatrically hospitalized. *Journal of Child Psychology & Psychiatry*, 1996, 37, 989–993.

Collings, S. J. Suicidal thoughts and behaviours in men who were sexually molested as children. In L. Schlebusch (Ed.), *Suicidal behaviour*. Durban: University of Natal, 1992, 182–186.

Crocker, A. D., & Hakim-Larson, J. Predictors of preadolescent depression and suicidal ideation. *Canadian Journal of Behavioural Science*, 1997, 29, 76–82.

Culp, A. M., Clyman, M. M., & Culp, R. E. Adolescent depressed mood, reports of suicide attempts, and asking for help. *Adolescence*, 1995, 30, 827–837.

Cunningham, R. M., Stiffman, A. R., & Dore, P. Abuse as a precursor to suicidality and violence. In D. Lester (Ed.), *Suicide '92*. Denver: AAS, 1992, 233–234.

Czorba, J., & Huszar, I. Some family and health background characteristics of Hungarian adolescent girls at risk of suicide. *Psychiatria Danubina*, 1993, 5(1–2), 91–101.

De Bellis, M. D., Chrousos, G. P., Dorn, L. D., Burke, L., Helmers, K., Kling, M. A., Trickett, P. K., & Putnam, F. W. Hypothalamic-pituitary-adrenal axis dysregulation in sexually abused girls. *Journal of Clinical Endocrinology & Metabolism*, 1994a, 78, 249–255.

De Bellis, M., Lefter, L., Trickett, P. K., & Putnam, F. W. Urinary catecholamine excretion in sexually abused girls. *Journal of the American Academy of Child & Adolescent Psychiatry*, 1994b, 33, 320–327.

De Chateau, P. Mortality and aggressiveness

in a 30-year follow-up study in child guidance clinics in Stockholm. *Acta Psychiatrica Scandinavica*, 1990, 81, 472–476.

De Leo, D., Longhin, N., Ormskerk, S. C. R., & Saia, S. O. Perinatal disorders as antecedents of suicidal behavior. In K. Bohme, R. Freytag, C. Wachtler & H. Wedler (Eds.), *Suicidal behavior*. Regensburg: S. Roderer, 1993, 702–705.

De Man, A. F., Labreche-Gauthier, L., & Leduc, C. P. Parent-child relationships and suicidal ideation in French-Canadian adolescents. *Journal of Genetic Psychology*, 1993a, 154, 17–23.

De Man, A. F., & Leduc, C. P. Validity and reliability of a self-report suicide ideation scale for use with adolescents. *Social Behavior & Personality*, 1994, 22, 261–266.

De Man, A. F., & Leduc, C. P. Suicidal ideation in high school students. *Journal of Clinical Psychology*, 1995, 51, 173–181.

De Man, A. F., Leduc, C. P., & Labreche-Gauthier, L. Correlates of suicide ideation in French-Canadian adults and adolescents. *Journal of Clinical Psychology*, 1992, 48, 811–816.

De Man, A. F., Leduc, C. P., & Labreche-Gauthier, L. Correlates of suicidal ideation in French-Canadian adolescents. *Adolescence*, 1993b, 28, 819–830.

De Man, A. F., Leduc, C. P., & Labreche-Gauthier, L. A French-Canadian scale for suicidal ideation for use with adolescents. *Canadian Journal of Behavioral Science*, 1993c, 25, 126–134.

De Maso, D. R., Ross, L., & Beardslee, W. R. Depressive disorders and suicidal intent in adolescent suicide attempters. *Journal of Developmental & Behavioral Pediatrics*, 1994, 15(2), 74–77.

DeSimone, A., Murray, P., & Lester, D. Alcohol use, self-esteem, depression, and suicidality in high school students. *Adolescence*, 1994, 29, 939–942.

De Wilde, E. J., & Kienhorst, I. Jacobs revisited. In K. Bohme, R. Freytag, C. Wachtler & H. Wedler (Eds.), *Suicidal behavior*. Regensburg: S. Roderer, 1993, 698–701.

De Wilde, E. J., & Kienhorst, I. Life events and suicide attempts in depressed adolescents. In D. Lester (Ed.), *Suicide '94*. Denver: AAS, 1994, 33–34.

De Wilde, E. J., Kienhorst, I., Diekstra, R., & Wolters, W. The relationship between adolescent suicidal behavior and life events in childhood and adolescence. *American Journal of Psychiatry*, 1992, 149, 45–51.

De Wilde, E. J., Kienhorst, I., Diekstra, R., & Wolters, W. The specificity of psychological characteristics of adolescent suicide attempters. *Journal of the American Academy of Child & Adolescent Psychiatry*, 1993, 32, 51–59.

De Wilde, E. J., Kienhorst, I., Diekstra, R., & Wolters, W. Social support, life events, and behavioral characteristics of psychologically distressed adolescents at high risk for attempting suicide. *Adolescence*, 1994, 29, 49–60.

Deykin, E. Y., & Buka, S. L. Suicidal ideation and attempts among chemically dependent adolescents. *American Journal of Public Health*, 1994, 84, 634–639.

Dinges, N. G., & Quang, D. T. Stressful life-events and co-occurring depression, substance abuse, and suicidality among American Indian and Alaska Native adolescents. *Culture, Medicine & Psychiatry*, 1992–1993, 16, 487–502.

Dinges, N. G., & Quang, D. T. Suicide ideation and suicide attempts among American Indian and Alaska Native boarding school adolescents. *Alaska Native & American Indian Mental Health Research*, 1994, 4, [Monograph] 167–188.

Donahue, M. J., & Benson, P. L. Religion and the well-being of adolescents. *Journal of Social Issues*, 1995, 51(2), 145–160.

Eggert, L. L., Thompson, E. A., & Herting, J. R. A measure of adult potential for suicide (MAPS). *Suicide & Life-Threatening Behavior*, 1994, 24, 359–381.

Elliott, A. J., Pages, K. P., Russo, J., Wilson, L. G., & Roy-Byrne, P. A profile of medically serious suicide attempts. *Journal of Clinical Psychiatry*, 1996, 57, 567–571.

Eskin, M. Suicidal behavior as related to social support and assertiveness among Swedish and Turkish high school students. *Journal of Clinical Psychology*, 1995, 51, 158–172.

Evans, W., Albers, E., Macari, D., & Mason, A. Suicide ideation, attempts and abuse among incarcerated gang and nongang delinquents. *Child & Adolescent Social Work Journal,*

1996, 13, 115–126.

Farber, E. W., Herbert, S. E., & Reviere, S. L. Childhood abuse and suicidality in obstetrics patients in a hospital-based urban prenatal clinic. *General Hospital Psychiatry*, 1996, 18, 56–60.

Felix-Ortiz, M., Munoz, R., & Newcomb, M. D. The role of emotional distress in drug use among Latino adolescents. *Journal of Child & Adolescent Substance Abuse*, 1994, 3(4), 1–22.

Ferdinand, R. F., & Verhulst, F. C. The prediction of poor outcome in young adults. *Acta Psychiatrica Scandinavica*, 1994, 89, 405–410.

Fergusson, D. M., Horwood, L. J., & Lynskey, M. T. Childhood sexual abuse and psychiatric disorder in young adulthood. *Journal of the American Academy of Child & Adolescent Psychiatry*, 1996, 35, 1365–1374.

Fergusson, D. M., & Lynskey, M. T. Childhood circumstances, adolescent adjustment, and suicide attempts in a New Zealand birth cohort. Journal of the *American Academy of Child & Adolescent Psychiatry*, 1995a, 34, 612–622.

Fergusson, D. M., & Lynskey, M. T. Antisocial behavior, unintentional and intentional injuries during adolescence. *Criminal Behavior & Mental Health*, 1995b, 5, 321–329.

Fergusson, D. M., & Lynskey, M. T. Suicide attempts and suicidal ideation in a birth cohort of 16-year-old New Zealanders. *Journal of the American Academy of Child & Adolescent Psychiatry*, 1995c, 34, 1308–1317.

Fergusson, D. M., & Lynskey, M. T. Physical punishment/maltreatment during childhood and adjustment in young adulthood. *Child Abuse & Neglect*, 1997, 21, 617–630.

Fisher, A. J., & Charlton, D. O. High-school dropouts in a working-class South African community. *Journal of Adolescence*, 1995, 18, 105–121.

Flisher, A. J., Ziervogel, C. F., Chalton, D. O., Leger, P. H., & Robertson, B. A. Risk behavior of Cape Peninsular high-school students. *South African Medical Journal*, 1996, 86, 1090–1098.

Fremouw, W., Callahan, T., & Kashden, J. Adolescent suicidal risk. *Suicide & Life-Threatening Behavior*, 1993, 23, 46–54.

Fullerton, D. T., Wonderlich, S. A., & Gosnell, B. A. Clinical characteristics of eating disorder patients who report sexual or physical abuse. *International Journal of Eating Disorders*, 1995, 17, 243–249.

Garnefski, N., & Diekstra, R. F. W. Suicidal behavior and the co-occurrence of behavioral, emotional, and cognitive problems among adolescents. *Archives of Suicide Research*, 1995, 1, 243–260.

Garnefski, N., & Diekstra, R. F. W. Child sexual abuse and emotional and behavioral problems in adolescence. *Journal of the American Academy of Child & Adolescent Psychiatry*, 1997a, 36, 323–329.

Garnefski, N., & Diekstra, R. F. W. Adolescents from one parent, step-parent and intact families. *Journal of Adolescence*, 1997b, 20, 201–208.

Garnefski, N., Diekstra, R. F. W., & de Heus, P. A population-based survey of characteristics of high school students with and without a history of suicidal behavior. *Acta Psychiatrica Scandinavica*, 1992, 86, 189–196.

Garrison, C. Z., McKeown, R. E., Valois, R. F., & Vincent, M. L. Aggression, substance use, and suicidal behavior in high school students. *American Journal of Public Health*, 1993, 83, 179–184.

Gartrell, J. W., Jarvis, G. K., & Derksen, L. Suicidality among adolescent Alberta Indians. *Suicide & Life-Threatening Behavior*, 1993, 23, 366–373.

Gasquet, I., & Choquet, M. Gender role in adolescent suicidal behavior. *Acta Psychiatrica Scandinavica*, 1993, 87, 59–65.

Gilliland, D. Attempted suicide among adolescents. *British Journal of Social Work*, 1990, 20, 365–371.

Gil-Rivas, V., Fiorentine, R., Anglin, M. D., & Taylor, E. Sexual and physical abuse. *Journal of Substance Abuse Treatment*, 1997, 14, 351–358.

Goldney, R. D., Winefield, A. H., Tiggeman, M., & Winefield, H. R. Suicidal ideation and unemployment. *Archives of Suicide Research*, 1995a, 1, 175–184.

Goldney, R. D., Winefield, A. H., Tiggeman, M., & Winefield, H. R. Persistent suicidal ideation and its enduring morbidity. In B. L. Mishara (Ed.), *The impact of suicide*. New York:

Springer, 1995b, 123–129.

Goldston, D. B., Daniel, S., Reboussin, D. M., Kelley, A., Ievers, C., & Brunstetter, R. First-time suicide attempters, repeat attempters, and previous attempters on an adolescent inpatient psychiatric unit. *Journal of the American Academy of Child & Adolescent Psychiatry,* 1996, 35, 631–639.

Gould, D. A., Stevens, N. G., Ward, N. G., Carlin, A. S., Sowell, H. E., & Gustafson, B. Self-reported childhood abuse in an adult population in a primary care setting. *Archives of Family Medicine,* 1994, 3, 252–256.

Gould, M. S., Fisher, P., Parides, M., Flory, M., & Shaffer, D. Psychosocial risk factors of child and adolescent suicide. *Archives of General Psychiatry,* 1996, 53, 1155–1162.

Graham, C., & Burvill, P. W. A study of coroners' records of suicide in young people, 1986–1988, in Western Australia. *Australian & New Zealand Journal of Psychiatry,* 1992, 26, 30–39.

Green, B. L., Grace, M. C., Vary, M. G., Kramer, T. L., Gleser, G. C., & Leonard, A. C. Children of disaster in the second decade. *Journal of American Academy of Child & Adolescent Psychiatry,* 1994, 33, 71–79.

Greene, J. M. Youth and familial substance use's association with suicide attempts among runaway and homeless youth. *Substance Use & Misuse,* 1996, 31, 1041–1058.

Grossi, V., & Violato, C. Attempted suicide among adolescents. Canadian *Journal of Behavioural Science,* 1992, 24, 410–413.

Grossman, D. C., Milligan, C., & Deyo, R. A. Risk factors for suicide attempts among Navajo adolescents. *American Journal of Public Health,* 1991, 81, 870–874.

Guiao, I. Z. Suicidality correlates in Mexican-American teens. In D. Lester (Ed.), *Suicide '94.* Denver: AAS, 1994, 43–44.

Guiao, I., & Esparza, D. Suicidality correlates in Mexican American teens. *Issues in Mental Health Nursing,* 1995, 16, 461–479.

Halfon, O., Laget, J., & Barrie, M. An epidemiological approach to adolescent suicide. *European Child & Adolescent Psychiatry,* 1995, 4, 32–38.

Harrington, R., Bredenkamp, D., Groothues, C., Rutter, M., Fudge, H., & Pickles, A. Adult outcomes of childhood and adolescent depression. *Journal of Child Psychology & Psychiatry,* 1994, 35, 1309–1319.

Hawton, K., Fagg, J., Platt, S., & Hawkins, M. Factors associated with suicide after parasuicide in young people. *British Medical Journal,* 1993, 306, 1641–1644.

Hernandez, J. T., Lodicu, M., & DiClemente, R. J. The effects of child abuse and race on risk-taking in male adolescents. *Journal of the National Medical Association,* 1993, 85, 593–597.

Hollis, C. Deprivation, family environment, and adolescent suicidal behavior. *Journal of the American Academy of Child & Adolescent Psychiatry,* 1996, 35, 622–630.

Howard-Pitney, B., LaFromboise, T. D., Basil, M., September, B., & Johnson, M. Psychological and social indicators of suicidal ideation and suicide attempts in Zuni adolescents. *Journal of Consulting & Clinical Psychology,* 1992, 60, 473–476.

Hustead, L., & Wagner, B. History of abuse and adolescent suicide attempts. In J. McIntosh (Ed.), *Suicide '97.* Washington, DC: AAS, 1997, 125–128.

Hustead, L., Wagner, B., Tobin, J., Aiken, C., & Derousa, J. Daily activities of adolescent suicide attempters. In J. McIntosh (Ed.), *Suicide '96.* Washington, DC: AAS, 1996, 79–82.

Hyer, C. L., McCranie, E. W., Woods, M. G., & Boudewyns, P. A. Suicidal behavior among chronic Vietnam theater veterans with PTSD. *Journal of Clinical Psychology,* 1990, 46, 713–721.

Jarvis, T. J., & Copeland, J. Child sexual abuse as a predictor of psychiatric comorbidity and its implications for drug and alcohol treatment. *Drug & Alcohol Dependence,* 1997, 49, 61–69.

Juon, H. S., Nam, J. J., & Ensminger, M. E. Epidemiology of suicidal behavior among Korean adolescents. *Journal of Child Psychology & Psychiatry,* 1994, 35, 663–676.

Kandel, D. B., Raveis, V. H., & Davies, M. Suicidal ideation in adolescence. *Journal of Youth & Adolescence,* 1991, 20, 289–309.

Kaplan, J., & Maldaver, M. Parental marital style and completed adolescent suicide. *Omega,* 1993, 27, 131–154.

Kaplan, M. L., Asnis, G. M., Lipschitz, D. S., & Chorney, P. Suicidal behavior and abuse in psychiatric outpatients. *Comprehensive Psychiatry*, 1995, 36, 229–235.

Kaplan, S. J., Pelcovitz, D., Salzinger, S., Mandel, F., & Weiner, M. Adolescent physical abuse and suicide attempts. *Journal of the American Academy of Child & Adolescent Psychiatry*, 1997, 36, 799–808.

Kelly, K. B., Ehrver, M., Erneholm, T., Gundevall, C., Wennerberg, I., & Wettergren, L. Self-reported health status and use of medical care by 3500 adolescents in western Sweden. *Acta Paediatrica Scandinavica*, 1991, 80, 837–843.

Kerfoot, M., Dyer, E., Harrington, V., Woodham, A., & Harrington, R. Correlates and short-term course of self-poisoning in adolescents. *British Journal of Psychiatry*, 1996, 168, 38–42.

Kienhorst, C. W. M., De Wilde, E. J., Diekstra, R. F. W., & Wolters, W. H. G. Construction of an index for predicting suicide attempts in depressed adolescents. *British Journal of Psychiatry*, 1991, 159, 676–682.

Kienhorst, C. W. M., De Wilde, E. J., Diekstra, R. F. W., & Wolters, W. H. G. Differences between adolescent suicide attempters and depressed adolescents. *Acta Psychiatrica Scandinavica*, 1992, 85, 222–228.

Kienhorst, C. W. M., De Wilde, E. J., van den Bout, J., Diekstra, R. F. W., & Wolters, W. H. G. Characteristics of suicide attempters in a population-based sample of Dutch adolescents. *British Journal of Psychiatry*, 1990, 156, 243–248.

King, C. A., Ghaziuddin, N., McGovern, L., Brand, E., Hill, E., & Naylor, M. Predictors of comorbid alcohol and substance abuse in depressed adolescents. *Journal of the American Academy of Child & Adolescent Psychiatry*, 1996, 35, 743–751.

King, C. A., Hill, E. M., Naylor, M., Evans, T., & Shain, B. Alcohol consumption in relation to other predictors of suicidality among adolescent inpatient girls. *Journal of the American Academy of Child & Adolescent Psychiatry*, 1993a, 32, 82–88.

King, C. A., Radpour, L., Naylor, M. W., Segal, H. G., & Jouriles, E. N. Parents' marital functioning and adolescent psychopathology, *Journal of Consulting & Clinical Psychology*, 1995, 63, 749–753.

King, C. A., Raskin, A., Gdowski, C. L., Butkus, M., & Opipari, L. Psychosocial factors associated with adolescent female suicide attempts. *Journal of the American Academy of Child & Adolescent Psychiatry*, 1990a, 29, 289–294.

King, C. A., Segal, H. G., Naylor, M., & Evans, T. Family functioning and suicidal behavior in adolescent inpatients with mood disorders. *Journal of the American Academy of Child & Adolescent Psychiatry*, 1993b, 32, 1198–1206.

King, C. A., Shain, B. N., Naylor, M., & Evans, T. L. Social adjustment and adolescent suicidal behavior. In D. Lester (Ed.), *Suicide '90*. Denver: AAS, 1990b, 230–232.

Kirkpatrick-Smith, J., Rich, A. R., Bonner, R., & Jans, F. Psychological vulnerability and substance abuse as predictors of suicide ideation among adolescents. *Omega*, 1991–1992, 24, 21–33.

Kirmayer, L. J., Malus, M., & Boothroyd, L. J. Suicide attempts among Inuit youth. *Acta Psychiatrica Scandinavica*, 1996, 94, 8–17.

Klein, D. N., Lewinsohn, P. M., & Seeley, J. R. Hypomanic personality traits in a community sample of adolescents. *Journal of Affective Disorders*, 1996, 38, 135–143.

Kosky, R., Silburn, S., & Zubrick, S. R. Are children and adolescents who have suicidal thoughts different from those who attempt suicide? *Journal of Nervous & Mental Disease*, 1990, 178, 38–43.

Krausz, M., Muller-Thomsen, T., & Haasen, C. Suicide among schizophrenic adolescents in the long-term course of illness. *Psychopathology*, 1995, 28, 95–103.

Kroll, J., Fiszdon, J., & Crosby, R. Childhood abuse and three measures of altered states of consciousness (dissociation, absorption and mysticism) in a female outpatient sample. *Journal of Personality Disorders*, 1996, 10, 345–354.

Krupinski, J., Tiller, J., Burrows, G. D., & Mackenzie, A. Predicting suicide risk among young suicide attempters. In T. Munakata, F. N. Onuoha & S. Suwa (Eds.), *Crisis behavior toward solidarity and growth*. Chiba, Japan: International Conference of Health Behavioral

Science, 1997, 72–76.

Kumar, G., & Steer, R. A. Psychosocial correlates of suicidal ideation in adolescent psychiatric inpatients. *Suicide & Life-Threatening Behavior*, 1995, 25, 339–346.

Kurtz, P. D., Kurtz, G. L., & Jarvis, S. V. Problems of maltreated runaway youth. *Adolescence*, 1991, 26, 543–555.

LaFromboise, T. D., & Howard-Pitney, B. The Zuni life skills development curriculum. *American Indian & Alaska Native Mental Health Research*, 1994, 4, 98–121.

LaFromboise, T. D., & Howard-Pitney, B. Suicidal behavior in American Indian female adolescents. In S. S. Canetto & D. Lester (Eds.), *Women and suicidal behavior*. New York: Springer, 1995, 157–173.

Lanktree, C., Briere, J., & Zaidi, L. Incidence and impact of sexual abuse in a child outpatient sample. *Child Abuse & Neglect*, 1991, 15, 447–453.

Larsson, B., Melin, L., Brectholtz, E., & Andersson, G. Short-term stability of depressive symptoms and suicide attempts in Swedish adolescents. *Acta Psychiatrica Scandinavica*, 1991, 83, 385–390.

Lester, D. Completed suicide among the gifted. *Journal of Abnormal Psychology*, 1991a, 100, 604–606.

Lester, D. Childhood predictors of later suicide. *Stress Medicine*, 1991b, 7, 129–131.

Lester, D. Physical abuse and physical punishment as precursors of suicidal behavior. *Stress Medicine*, 1991c, 7, 255–256.

Lester, D. Experience of loss and subsequent suicide. *Perceptual & Motor Skills*, 1994, 79, 730.

Levy, S. R., Jurkovic, G. L., & Spirito, A. A multisystems analysis of adolescent suicide attempters. *Journal of Abnormal Child Psychology*, 1995, 23, 221–234.

Lewinsohn, P. M., Clarke, G. N., Seeley, & Rohde, P. Major depression in community adolescents. *Journal of the American Academy of Child & Adolescent Psychiatry*, 1994a, 33, 809–818.

Lewinsohn, P. M., Gotlib, I. H., & Sedey, J. R. Adolescent psychopathology. *Journal of the American Academy of Child & Adolescent Psychiatry*, 1995, 34, 1221–1229.

Lewinsohn, P. M., Roberts, R. E., Seeley, J. R., Rohde, P., Gotlib, I. H., & Hops, H. Adolescent psychopathology. *Journal of Abnormal Psychology*, 1994b, 103, 302–315.

Lewinsohn, P. M., Rohde, P., & Seeley, J. R. Psychosocial characteristics of adolescents with a history of suicide attempts. *Journal of the American Academy of Child & Adolescent Psychiatry*, 1993, 32, 60–68.

Lewinsohn, P. M., Rohde, P., & Seeley, J. R. Psychosocial risk factors for future adolescent suicide attempts. *Journal of Consulting & Clinical Psychology*, 1994c. 62. 297–305.

Lewis, T. T., Molock, S. D., Williams, S., Kimbrough, R., Blanton-Lacy, M., Hamilton, D., & Nicholson, M. Suicide ideation among African-American college students. In D. Lester (Ed.), *Suicide '95*. Washington, DC: AAS, 1995, 112.

Livingston, R., & Bracha, H. S. Psychotic symptoms and suicidal behavior in hospitalized children. *American Journal of Psychiatry*, 1992, 149, 1585–1586.

Livingston, R., Lawson, L., & Jones, J. G. Predictors of self-reported psychopathology by children abused repeatedly by a parent. *Journal of the American Academy of Child & Adolescent Psychiatry*, 1993, 32, 948–953.

Lynskey, M. T., & Fergusson, D. M. Factors protecting against the development of adjustment difficulties in young adults exposed to childhood sexual abuse. *Child Abuse & Neglect*, 1997, 21, 1177–1190.

Madianos, M. G., Madianou-Gefou, D., & Stenfanis, C. N. Depressive symptoms and suicidal behavior among general population adolescent and young adults across Greece. *European Psychiatry*, 1993, 8, 139–146.

Maris, R. W. *Pathways to suicide*. Baltimore: Johns Hopkins University, 1981.

Martin, G. Reported family dynamics, sexual abuse, and suicidal behaviors in community adolescents. *Archives of Suicide Research*, 1996, 2, 183–195.

Martin, G., Rozanes, P., Pearce, C., & Allison, S. Adolescent suicide, depression, and family dysfunction. *Adolescence*, 1995, 92, 336–344.

Martin, G., & Waite, S. Parental bonding and vulnerability to adolescent suicide. *Acta Psychiatrica Scandinavica*, 1994, 89, 246–254.

Marttunen, M. J., Aro, H. M., Henriksson, M. M., & Lonnqvist, J. K. Adolescent suicides with adjustment disorders or no psychiatric diagnosis. *European Child & Adolescent Psychiatry*, 1994a, 3(2), 101–110.

Marttunen, M. J., Aro, H. M., Henriksson, M. M., & Lonnqvist, J. K. Antisocial behavior in adolescent suicide. *Acta Psychiatrica Scandinavica*, 1994b, 89, 167–173.

Marttunen, M. J., Aro, H. M., Henriksson, M. M., & Lonnqvist, J. K. Psychosocial stressors more common in adolescent suicides with alcohol abuse compared with depressive adolescent suicides. *Journal of the American Academy of Child & Adolescent Psychiatry*, 1994c, 33, 490–497.

McCarthy, J. B., Nahas, A. D., & Welson, R. J., Suicidal and assaultive behavior in hospitalized adolescents. *Research Communications in Biology, Psychology & Psychiatry*, 1995, 20(1–2), 69–80.

McCauley, J., Kern, D. E., Kolodner, K., Dill, L., Schroeder, A. F., DeChant, H. K., Ryden, T., Derogatis, L. R., & Bass, E. B. Clinical characteristics of women with a history of childhood abuse. *Journal of the American Medical Association*, 1997, 277, 1362–1368.

Meneese, W. B., & Yutrzenka, B. A. Correlates of suicidal ideation among rural adolescents. *Suicide & Life-Threatening Behavior*, 1990, 20, 206–212.

Meneese, W. B., Yutrzenka, B. A., & Vitale, P. An analysis of adolescent suicidal behavior. *Current Psychology*, 1992, 11, 51–58.

Miller, D. Suicidal behavior of adolescents with behavior disorders and their peers without disabilities. *Behavioral Disorders*, 1994, 20, 61–68.

Milling, L., Campbell, N., Laughlin, A., & Bush, E. The prevention of suicidal behavior among preadolescent children who are psychiatric inpatients. *Acta Psychiatrica Scandinavica*, 1994, 89, 225–229.

Modestin, J., Oberson, B., & Erni, T. Possible correlates of DSM-III-R personality disorders. *Acta Psychiatrica Scandinavica*, 1997, 96, 424–430.

Morano, C. D., Cisler, R. A., & Lemerond, J. Risk factors for adolescent suicidal behavior. *Adolescence*, 1993, 28, 851–865.

Morris, R. E., Harrison, E. A., Knox, G. W., Tromanhauser, E., Marquis, D. K., & Watts, L. L. Health risk behavioral survey from 39 juvenile correctional facilities in the United States. *Journal of Adolescent Health*, 1995, 17, 334–344.

Mullen, O. E., Martin, J. L., Anderson, J. C., Romans, S. E., & Herbison, G. P. Childhood sexual abuse and mental health in adult life. *British Journal of Psychiatry*, 1993, 163, 721–732.

Neumark-Sztainer, D., Story, M., French, S., Cassuto, N., Jacobs, D. R., & Resnick, M. D. Patterns of health-compromising behaviors among Minnesota adolescents. *American Journal of Public Health*, 1996, 86, 1599–1606.

Neumark-Sztainer, D., Story, M., French, S., & Resnick, M. D. Psychosocial correlates of health compromising behaviors among adolescents. *Health Education Research*, 1997, 12, 37–52.

Ng, B. Characteristics of 61 Mexican American adolescents who attempted suicide. *Hispanic Journal of Behavioral Science*, 1996, 18, 3–12.

Newcomb, M. D., Scheier, L. M., & Bentler, P. M. Effects of adolescent drug use on adult mental health. *Experimental & Clinical Psychopharmacology*, 1993, 1, 215–241.

Oler, M. J., Mainous, A. G., Martin, C. A., Richardson, E., Haney, A., Wilson, D., & Adams, T. Depression, suicidal ideation, and substance use among adolescents. *Archives of Family Medicine*, 1994, 3, 781–785.

Orr, D. P., Beiter, M., & Ingersoll, G. Premature sexual activity as an indicator of psychosocial risk. *Pediatrics*, 1991, 87, 141–147.

Paluszny, M., Davenport, C., & Kim, W. J. Suicide attempts and ideation. *Adolescence*, 1991, 26, 209–215.

Patton, G. C., Harris, R., Carlin, J. B., Hibbest, M. E., Coffey, C., Schwartz, M., & Bowes, G. Adolescent suicidal behaviors. *Psychological Medicine*, 1997, 27, 715–724.

Pelkonen, M., Marttunen, M., Pulkkinen, E., Koivisto, A. M., Laippala, P., & Aro. H. Excess mortality among former adolescent male outpatients. *Acta Psychiatrica Scandinavica*, 1996, 94, 60–66.

Pelkonen, M., Marttunen, M., Pulkkinen, E., Laippala, P., & Aro. H. Characteristics of outpatient adolescents with suicidal tendencies.

Acta Psychiatrica Scandinavica, 1997, 95, 100–107.

Peters, D. K., & Range, L. M. Childhood sexual abuse and current suicidality in college men and women. *Child Abuse & Neglect*, 1995, 19, 335–341.

Peterson, B. S., Zhang, H., Lucia, R. S., King, C. A., & Lewis, M. Risk factors for presenting problems in child psychiatric emergencies. *Journal of the American Academy of Child & Adolescent Psychiatry*, 1996, 35, 1162–1173.

Pfeffer, C. R., Hurt, S. W., Peskin, J. R., & Siefker, C. A. Suicidal children grown up. *Journal of the American Academy of Child & Adolescent Psychiatry*, 1995, 34, 1318–1325.

Pfeffer, C. R., Klerman, G. L., Hurt, S. W., Lesser, M., Peskin, J. R., & Siefker, C. A. Suicidal children grown up. *Journal of the American Academy of Child & Adolescent Psychiatry*, 1991, 30, 609–616.

Pfeffer, C. R., Normandin, L., & Kakuma, T. Suicidal children grown up. *Journal of the American Academy of Child & Adolescent Psychiatry*, 1994, 33, 1087–1097.

Pharris, M. D., Resnick, M. D., & Blum, R. W. Protecting against hopelessness and suicidality in sexually abused American Indian adolescents. *Journal of Adolescent Health*, 1997, 21, 400–406.

Pillay, A. L., & Wassenaar, D. R. Psychosocial intervention, spontaneous remission, hopelessness, and psychiatric disturbance in adolescent parasuicides. *Suicide & Life-Threatening Behavior*, 1995, 25, 386–392.

Pillay, A. L., & Wassenaar, D. R. Family dynamics, hopelessness, and psychiatric disturbance. *Australian & New Zealand Journal of Psychiatry*, 1997a, 31, 227–231.

Pillay, A. L., & Wassenaar, D. R. Recent stressors and family satisfaction in suicidal adolescents in South Africa. *Journal of Adolescence*, 1997b, 20, 155–162.

Powers, J. L., Eckenrode, J., & Jaklitsch, B. Maltreatment among runaway and homeless youth. *Child Abuse & Neglect*, 1990, 14, 87–98.

Pronovost, J. Prevalence of suicidal ideations and behaviors among adolescents. In G. Ferrari, M. Bellini & P. Crepet (Eds.), *Suicidal behavior and risk factors*. Bologna: Monduzzi-Editore, 1990, 427–431.

Pronovost, J., Coté, L., & Ross, C. Epidemiological study of suicidal behaviour among secondary-school students. *Canada's Mental Health*, 1990, 38(1), 9–15.

Putnins, A. L. Recent drug use and suicidal behavior among young offenders. *Drug & Alcohol Review*, 1995, 14, 151–158.

Queralt, M. Risk factors associated with completed suicide in Latino adolescents. *Adolescence*, 1993, 28, 831–850.

Rainieri, N., & Lester, D. Parental loss, depression, and suicidality. *Psychological Reports*, 1997, 80, 378.

Rao, U., Weissman, M. M., Martin, J. A., & Hammond, R. W. Childhood deprivation and risk of suicide. *Journal of the American Academy of Child & Adolescent Psychiatry*, 1993, 32, 21–27.

Razin, A. M., O'Dowd, M. A., Nathan, A., Rodriguez, I., Goldfield, A., Martin, C., Goulet, L., Scheftel, S., Mezan, P., & Mosca, J. Suicidal behavior among inner-city Hispanic adolescent females. *General Hospital Psychiatry*, 1991, 13, 45–48.

Reifman, A., & Windle, M. Adolescent suicidal behaviors as a function of depression, hopelessness, alcohol use, and social support. *American Journal of Community Psychology*, 1995, 23, 329–354.

Reinecke, M. A., & DuBois, D. L. Schemata, life events, and suicidality among adolescents. In D. Lester (Ed.), *Suicide '94*. Denver: AAS, 1994, 62–63.

Reinherz, H. Z., Giaconia, R. M., Silverman, A. B., Friedman, A., Pakiz, B., Frost, A. K., & Cohen, E. Early psychosocial risks for adolescent suicidal ideation and attempts. *Journal of the American Academy of Child & Adolescent Psychiatry*, 1995, 34, 599–611.

Resnick, M. D., & Blum, R. W. The association of consensual sexual intercourse during childhood with adolescent health risk and behaviors. *Pediatrics*, 1994, 94, 907–911.

Rey, J. M., & Bird, K. D. Sex differences in suicidal behavior of referred adolescents. *British Journal of Psychiatry*, 1991, 158, 776–781.

Reynolds, W. M., & Mazza, J. J. Suicidality and substance abuse in adolescents. In D. Lester (Ed.), *Suicide '94*. Denver: AAS, 1994, 130–131.

Riggs, S., Alario, A. J., & McHorney, C.

Health risk behaviors and attempted suicide in adolescents who report prior maltreatment. *Journal of Pediatrics*, 1990, 116, 815–821.

Ritter, D. R. Adolescent suicide. *School Psychology Review*, 1990, 19, 83–95.

Roberts, R. E., & Chen, Y. R. Depressive symptoms and suicidal ideation among Mexican American and Anglo adolescents. *Journal of the American Academy of Child & Adolescent Psychiatry*, 1995, 34, 81–90.

Roberts, R. E., Chen, Y. R., & Roberts, C. R. Ethnocultural differences in prevalence of adolescent suicidal behaviors. *Suicide & Life-Threatening Behavior*, 1997, 27, 208–217.

Romans, S. E., Martin, J. L., Anderson, J. C., Herbison, G. P., & Mullen, P. E. Sexual abuse in childhood and deliberate self-harm. *American Journal of Psychiatry*, 1995, 152, 1336–1342.

Rotheram-Borus, M. J. Suicidal behavior and risk factors among runaway youths. *American Journal of Psychiatry*, 1993, 150, 103–107.

Rotheram-Borus, M. J., Walker, J. U., & Ferns, W. Suicidal behavior among middle-class adolescents who seek crisis services. *Journal of Clinical Psychology*, 1996, 52, 137–143.

Sack, W. H., Beiser, M., Baker-Brown, G., & Redshirt, R. Depressive and suicidal symptoms in Indian school children. *American Indian & Alaska Native Mental Health Research*, 1994, 4, 81–96.

Sadowski, C., & Kelley, M. L. Social problem solving in suicidal adolescents. *Journal of Consulting & Clinical Psychology*, 1993, 61, 121–127.

Schei, B. Prevalence of sexual abuse history in a random sample of Norwegian women. *Scandinavian Journal of Social Medicine*, 1990, 18, 63–68.

Schierbeak, M. L., & Newlon, B. J. Substance abuse and attempted suicide. *Individual Psychology*, 1990, 46, 358–364.

Schiff, M., & Cavaiola, A. A. Child abuse, adolescent substance abuse, and "deadly violence." *Journal of Adolescent Chemical Dependency*, 1993, 2, 131–141.

Schutt, R. K., Meschede, T., & Rierdan, J. Distress, suicidal thoughts, and social support among homeless adults. *Journal of Health &*

Social Behavior, 1994, 35, 134–142.

Shaffer, D., Gould, M. S., Fisher, P., Trautman, P., Moreave, D., Kleinman, M., & Flory, M. Psychiatric diagnosis in child and adolescent suicide. *Archives of General Psychiatry*, 1996, 53, 339–348.

Shagle, S. C., & Barber, B. K. A social-ecological analysis of adolescent suicidal ideation. *American Journal of Orthopsychiatry*, 1995, 65, 114–124.

Shaunesey, K., Cohen, J. L., Plummer, B., & Berman, A. L. Suicidality in hospitalized adolescents. *American Journal of Orthopsychiatry*, 1993, 63, 113–119.

Siemen, J. R., Warrington, C. A., & Mangano, E. L. Comparison of the Millon Adolescent Personality Inventory and the Suicide Ideation Questionnaire-Junior with an adolescent inpatient sample. *Psychological Reports*, 1994, 75, 947–950.

Silk, K. R., Lee, S., Hill, E. M., & Lohr, N. E. Borderline personality disorder symptoms and severity of sexual abuse. *American Journal of Psychiatry*, 1995, 152, 1059–1064.

Silverman, A. B., Reinherz, H. Z., & Giaconia, R. M. The long-term sequelae of child and adolescent abuse. *Child Abuse & Neglect*, 1996, 20, 709–723.

Silverman, E. J., & Overholser, J. C. Family functioning and suicidal tendencies. In D. Lester (Ed.), *Suicide '95*. Washington, DC: AAS, 1995, 106–108.

Slap, G. B., Vorters, D. F., Khalid, N., Margulies, S. R., & Forke, C. M. Adolescent suicide attempters. *Journal of Adolescent Health*, 1992, 13, 286–292.

Spruijt, E., & de Goede, M. Transitions in family structure and adolescent well-being. *Adolescence*, 1997, 32, 897–911.

Steer, R. A., Kumar, C., & Beck, A. T. Self-reported suicidal ideation in adolescent psychiatric inpatients. *Journal of Consulting & Clinical Psychology*, 1993, 61, 1096–1099.

Stepakoff, S. Effects of sexual victimization on suicidal ideation and behavior in U.S. college women. *Suicide & Life-Threatening Behavior*, 1997, 27, 107–126.

Stone, M. H. Suicide in borderline and other adolescents. *Adolescent Psychiatry*, 1992, 18, 289–305.

Stone, N. Parental abuse as a precursor to childhood onset depression and suicidality. *Child Psychiatry & Human Development*, 1993, 24(1), 13–24.

Straus, M. A. Corporal punishment of children and adult depression and suicidal ideation. In J. A. McCord (Ed.), *Coercion and punishment in long-term perspective.* New York: Columbia University, 1995, 59–77.

Straus, M. A., & Kantor, G. K. Corporal punishment for adolescents by parents. *Adolescence*, 1994, 29, 543–561.

Summerville, M. B., Abbate, M. F., Siegel, A. M., Serravezza, J., & Karlow, N. J. Psychopathology in urban female minority adolescents with suicide attempts. *Journal of the American Academy of Child & Adolescent Psychiatry*, 1992, 31, 663–668.

Summerville, M. B., Kaslow, N. J., Abbate, M. F., & Cronan, S. Psychopathology, family functioning, and cognitive style in urban adolescents with suicide attempts. *Journal of Abnormal Child Psychology*, 1994, 22, 221–235.

Swantson, H. Y., Tebbutt, J. S., O'Toole, B. I., & Oates, R. K. Sexually abused children 5 years after presentation. *Pediatrics*, 1997, 100, 600–608.

Swedo, S. E., Rettew, D. C., Kuppenheimer, M., Lum, D., Dolan, S., & Goldberger, E. Can adolescent suicide attempters be distinguished from at-risk adolescents? *Pediatrics*, 1991, 88, 620–629.

Thompson, E. A., Moody, K. A., & Eggert, L. L. Discriminating suicide ideation among high-risk youth. *Journal of School Health*, 1994, 64, 361–367.

Tobin, D. L., & Griffing, A. S. Coping, sexual abuse, and compensatory behavior. *International Journal of Eating Disorders*, 1996, 20, 143–148.

Tousignant, M., Bastien, M. F., & Hamel, S. Suicidal attempts and ideations among adolescents and young adults. *Social Psychiatry & Psychiatric Epidemiology*, 1993, 28, 256–261.

Tousignant, M., & Hanigan, D. Crisis support among suicidal students following a loss event. *Journal of Community Psychology*, 1993, 21, 83–96.

Trammel, R. L., Metha, A., Robinson, S., & Chen, E. Suicide and substance abuse in college students. In D. Lester (Ed.), *Suicide '95.* Washington, DC: AAS, 1995, 121–123.

Tulloch, A. L., Blizzard, L., Hornsby, H., & Pinkus, Z. Suicide and self-harm in Tasmanian children and adolescents. *Medical Journal of Australia*, 1994, 160, 775–780.

Valliant, P. M., Maksymchuk, L. L., & Antonowicz, D. Attitudes and personality traits of female adult victims of childhood abuse. *Social Behavior & Personality*, 1995, 23, 205–215.

Valois, R. F., Bryant, E. S., Rivard, J. C., & Hinkle, K. T. Sexual risk-taking behaviors among adolescents with severe emotional disturbance. *Journal of Child & Family Studies*, 1997, 6, 409–419.

Vannatta, R. A. Risk factors related to suicidal behavior among male and female adolescents. *Journal of Youth & Adolescence*, 1996, 25, 149–160.

Van der Kolk, B. A., Perry, J. C., & Herman, J. L. Childhood origins of self-defeating behavior. *American Journal of Psychiatry*, 1991, 148, 1665–1671.

Van Egmond, M., Garnefski, M., Jonkers, D., & Kerkhof, A. The relationship between sexual abuse and female suicidal behavior. *Crisis*, 1993, 14, 129–139.

Vega, W. A., Gil, A., Warheit, G., Apospori, E., & Zimmerman, R. The relationship of drug use to suicidal ideation and attempts among African American, Hispanic, and white non-Hispanic male adolescents. *Suicide & Life-Threatening Behavior*, 1993a, 23, 110–119.

Vega, W. A., Gil, A., Zimmerman, R., & Warheit, G. Risk factors for suicidal behavior among Hispanic, African American, and non-Hispanic white boys in early adolescence. *Ethnicity & Disease*, 1993b, 3, 229–241.

Viinamak, H., Niskanen, L., Haatainen, J., Purhonen, M., Vaananen, K., & Lehtonen, J. Do mental traumas in childhood predict worse psychosocial functioning in adulthood? *Nordic Journal of Psychiatry*, 1995, 49, 11–15.

Wagner, A. W., & Linehan, M. M. Relationship between childhood sexual abuse and topography of parasuicide among women with borderline personality disorder. *Journal of Personality Disorders*, 1994, 8, 1–9.

Wagner, B. M., & Cohen, P. Adolescent

sibling differences in suicidal symptoms. *Journal of Abnormal Child Psychology*, 1994, 22, 321–337.

Wagner, B. M., Cole, R. E., & Schwartzman, P. Psychsocial correlates of suicide attempts among junior and senior high school students. *Suicide & Life-Threatening Behavior*, 1995, 25, 358–372.

Wagner, B. M., Cole, R. E., & Schwartzman, P. Comorbidity of symptoms among junior and senior high school suicide attempters. *Suicide & Life-Threatening Behavior*, 1996, 26, 300–307.

Walsh, B. Poly-self-destructiveness in adolescents. In D. Lester (Ed.), *Suicide '95*. Washington, DC: AAS, 1995, 20–21.

Walter, H. J., Vaughan, R. D., Armstrong, B., Krakoff, R. Y., Maldonado, L. M., Tuzzi, L. & McCarthy, J. F. Sexual, assaultive and suicidal behaviors among urban minority junior high school students. *Journal of the American Academy of Child & Adolescent Psychiatry*, 1995, 34, 73–80.

Ward, A. J. Adolescent suicide and other self-destructive behaviors. *Residential Treatment for Children & Youth*, 1992, 9(3), 49–64.

Ward, A. J. AAS scores in 36 completed adolescent suicides. In D. Lester (Ed.), *Suicide '93*. Denver: AAS, 1993, 163–165.

Ward, A. J. Multicultural aspects of adolescent suicide. In D. Lester (Ed.), *Suicide '95*. Washington, DC: AAS, 1995, 25–27.

Warheit, G. J., Zimmerman, R. S., Khoury, E. L., Vega, W. A., & Gil, A. G. Disaster related stress, depressive signs and symptoms, and suicidal ideation among a multi-racial/ethnic sample of adolescents. *Journal of Child Psychology & Psychiatry*, 1996, 37, 435–444.

Weissman, M. M., Fendrich, M., Warner, V., & Wickramaratne, P. Incidence of psychiatric disorder in offspring at high and low risk for depression. *Journal of the American Academy of Child & Adolescent Psychiatry*, 1992, 31, 640–648.

Wetzler, S., Asnis, G. M., Hyman, R. B., Virtue, C., Zimmerman, J., & Rathus, J. H. Characteristics of suicidality among adolescents. *Suicide & Life-Threatening Behavior*, 1996, 26, 37–45.

Williamson, D. E., Ryan, N. D., Birmaher, B., Dahl, R. E., Kaufman, J., Rao, U., & Puig-Antich, J. A case-control family history study of depression in adolescents. *Journal of the American Academy of Child & Adolescent Psychiatry*, 1995, 34, 1596–1607.

Windle, M., Windle, R. C., & Scheidt, D. M. Physical and sexual abuse and associated mental disorders among alcoholic inpatients. *American Journal of Psychiatry*, 1995, 152, 1322–1328.

Wolk, S. I., & Weissman, M. M. Suicidal behavior in depressed children grown up. *Psychiatric Annals*, 1996, 26, 331–335.

Woods, E. R., Lin, Y. G., Middleman, A., Beckford, P., Chase, L., & DuRant, R. H. The association of suicide attempts in adolescents. *Pediatrics*, 1997, 99, 791–796.

Workman, M., & Beer, J. Depression, suicidal ideation, and aggression among high school students whose parents are divorced and use alcohol at home. *Psychological Reports*, 1992, 70, 503–511.

Wozencraft, T., Wagner, W., & Pellegrini, A. Depression and suicide ideation in sexually abused children. *Child Abuse & Neglect*, 1991, 15, 505–511.

Woznica, J. G., & Shapiro, J. R. An analysis of adolescent suicide attempts. *Journal of Pediatric Psychology*, 1990, 15, 789–796.

Yama, M. F., Tovey, S. L., Fogas, B. S., & Morris, J. The relationship among childhood sexual abuse, parental alcoholism, family environment, and suicidal behavior in female college students. *Journal of Child Sexual Abuse*, 1995, 4(4), 79–93.

Yellowlees, P. M., & Kaushik, A. V. An examination of the associations between life events and psychiatric disorders in a rural psychiatric population. *Australian & New Zealand Journal of Psychiatry*, 1994a, 28, 50–57.

Yellowlees, P. M., & Kaushik, A. V. A case control study of the sequelae of childhood sexual assault in adult psychiatric patients. *Medical Journal of Australia*, 1994b, 160, 408–411.

Yuen, N., Andrade, N., Nehulu, L., Makini, G., McDermott, J. F., Danko, G., Johnson, R., & Waldron, J. The rate and characteristics of suicide attempters in the Native Hawaiian adolescent population. *Suicide & Life-Threatening Behavior*, 1996, 26, 27–36.

Zhang, J. Determinants of suicide ideation. *Adolescence*, 1996, 31, 451–467.

Chapter 5

SOCIOLOGICAL THEORIES OF SUICIDE

Sociological theories of suicide have been reviewed by Lester (1989). This chapter will review recent research on the theories.

Durkheim

Lester (1990b) factor-analyzed suicide rates by method over the states of the USA in 1980 and identified three clusters: (1) hanging, cutting, and jumping; (2) gas and drowning; and (3) solids/liquids and firearms. Of the clusters of social variables identified by factor-analysis, social disintegration correlated with suicide rates only by solids/liquids and by firearms; and so Durkheim's theory of suicide was confirmed only for suicide by some methods.

Lester (1991a) also found that the correlates of social variables with suicides over a sample of nations varied for each method. For example, divorce rates were associated with the suicide rate by solids/liquids but not with the suicide rate by hanging. Thus, Durkheim's theory did not apply to each component of the total suicide rate. On the other hand, Lester (1996c) found that the suicide rates by solids/liquids, firearms, and by all methods were similarly associated over the USA in the same way with longitude and the percent born in state.

Lester (1996a) found that correlates of the time-series suicide rates by different methods also differed over time in England for 1950–1985.

Travis (1990) argued that Durkheim saw suicide as a result of social disorganization, whereas Halbwachs saw suicide as a result of social isolation. To test these two assumptions, Travis examined suicides in Alaska natives. The suicide rate was higher in males and those under the age of 30, but was not related to unemployment or marital status. For those suicides committed only on holidays or in new communities, Travis found that suicide rates were higher in men and in those who were single. The relevance of these results to the two theories is obscure.

Nations

Lester (1991c) found that the suicide rates of 16 Caribbean islands were associated with their population, suggesting that the smaller, perhaps more socially integrated, islands had lower suicide rates.

Primitive Societies

Lester (1992e) measured social integration and social regulation independently in a sample of primitive societies. He found that arranging societies into a three-by-three array based on their scores on both dimensions did not reveal significant differences in suicide rates by cell. However, social integration by itself was positively associated with the suicide rate of the societies.

Earlier Times

Lester (1993a) found that predictions from Durkheim's theory were better supported in 1980 than in 1880 for a sample of European nations.

Abstract Versus Concrete Qualities

Both Taylor (1990) and Moksony (1990) argued that social indicators such as divorce rates did not directly affect the suicide rate. Rather, such social indicators were measures of broader social qualities that affect the suicide rate. Lester (1993d) noted that the consistency of suicide rates of immigrants with suicide rates in their home nations and the association of broad factors of social variables with suicide rates supported the views of Taylor and Moksony.

Lester (1995f) looked at the social correlates of the suicide rates in the states of those born out of state, in non-contiguous states, and abroad. The social correlations were nonsignificant for the suicide rates of those born in state, suggesting that selective migration accounted for the ecological correlations.

Durkheim and Naroll

Lester (1995a) examined similarities and differences between Durkheim's theory and the thwarting disorientation theory of Raoul Naroll.

Alternative Measures

Lester (1995e) found that, in time-series studies of 27 nations, the divorce and marriage rates were better predictors of the suicide rate for the majority of nations than the divorce/marriage-rate ratio.

Gibbs And Martin

Stafford et al. (1990) examined the association between suicide rates of whites and measures of occupational status integration in the United States in 1960 and 1980. On the whole, the associations were negative, as predicted by status-integration theory. The associations were, however, more consistent for male suicide rates than for female suicide rates.

Lester (1992d) compared the success of status-integration measures to predict suicide rates versus other social variables. Over the USA, the percentage born out of state was a stronger correlate of suicide rates. Over nations, however, status integration was a stronger correlate than single social variables.

Lester (1995b) found that state measures of status integration were negatively associated with longitude, urbanism, divorce, and median family income. Thus, the measure may be derivative of more-fundamental social indicators.

Henry And Short

Lester has predicted from Henry and Short's theory of suicide that suicide rates should be higher in nations with a higher quality of life. Lester (1990a) found that the suicide rates in a sample of 43 nations were associated with the quality of life. The association was significant for components concerned with education, health, women's status, demography, and welfare; they were not significant for components concerned with defense, the economy, geography, political stability, political participation, and cultural diversity. Changes in the quality of life from 1970 to 1980 were not associated with changes in the suicide rates. Limiting the sample to 18 industrialized nations produced different results. Lester (1993b) found that the quality of life in urban counties was positively associated with their suicide rates in the USA. However, Lester (1996b) found no association between the quality of life and suicide rates over 12 regions of Great Britain.

Lester (1990c) applied Henry and Short's theory to the rising adolescent suicide rate in some nations, arguing that this could be a result of the increase in the quality of life of adolescents.

Holinger's Cohort Theory

Holinger and Lester (1991) found that the association over the USA between suicide rates and the percentage in the population was positive for those aged 15–24, 25–34 and 35–44 as predicted; and negative for those aged 55–64, 65–74 and 75 and over. Lester (1996d) found that the positive association between youth cohort size and youth suicide rates over the USA was positive in 1970 and but not significantly different from zero in 1989. Absolute changes in both variables over this period were negatively associated, while percentage changes in both were not associated.

Lester (1991b) explored the cohort-size theory in Japan for 1961–1979, and the results did not completely replicate Holinger's study. The negative association was found for youth (aged 15–24) suicide rates, but also for those aged 55 and over.

Lester (1992a) found that, over nations, the suicide rate of each age group and its proportion in the population was negative for those aged 5–14 and positive for those aged 25–34, 35–44, and 65–74. The negative association for youth was not consistent with the above results.

Leenaars and Lester (1996) found support for the cohort-size hypothesis for youth suicide rates (20–34 years old) in Canada for 1969–1987 using a variety of cohort-size measures.

Louks et al. (1996) looked at the suicide rates of young males born in several years during the 1940s and 1950s and found that the suicide rate was higher in the larger cohorts, as well as in those born in the 1950s.

Pampel (1996) looked at 18 nations for 1953–1986 and confirmed the cohort-size hypothesis for youths and young adults using a multiple-regression design controlling for other social indicators. The effect was stronger for men than for women, for the 1950s and 1960s, and for nations with less-collectivist institutions. Stack (1996) also looked at a sample of nations over a 30-year period and found that relative cohort size predicted youth suicide rates in a multiple regression with other variables, overall and separately for nations with market, mixed, and command economies.

Other Theories

Lester (1997a) tested two hypotheses from Thomas Masaryk's theory of suicide. First, he showed that suicide rates had increased with modernization (from 1901 to 1988 in 12 nations and from 1875 to 1975 in 14 nations.) Secondly, he showed that suicide rates were associated with religiosity (church attendance) over the USA.

Lester (1997b) tested a Mohave theory of suicide that individualism leads to suicide by finding a positive association between employee individualism scores and national suicide rates in 34 nations.

Moksony (undated) outlined three theories of regional suicide rates: (1) selective migration, in which suicidal people are more likely to move to some regions; (2) composition, in which the regions differ in the percentage of high-risk individuals (such as the divorced); and (3) the local social environment directly affects the suicide rate. In case three, the region causes suicide, in case one the region attracts suicidal people, and in case two there is no areal input.

Lester's Social-Deviancy Theory

Lester (1992b) compared suicide rates for Asian immigrants in Hawaii and California and in the rest of the USA. The Chinese suicide rate was higher in the rest of the USA, consistent with social-deviancy theory (Lester, 1992c), but Japanese and Filipino suicide rates were lower in the rest of USA.

Lester (1993c) found no association over the USA between the percentage of white foreign-born residents and the suicide rate of the foreign born.

In Canada, Lester (1994b) found no association between the suicide rates of 22 immigrants groups and their proportion in the population. Lester (1995c) found no association between the proportion of native Canadians and their suicide rates over nine Canadian regions.

Lester's Critical-Mass Theory

Lester (1993e) found no association between the suicide rates of nations in 1975 and the absolute increase in the suicide rate by 1985, thereby failing to confirm Lester's critical-mass theory of suicide. Lester (1995d) found that nations with higher suicide rates in 1970 had larger increases by 1980, whereas nations with higher suicide rates in 1980 had smaller increases by 1990.

Lester (1994a) found no support for his critical-mass theory of suicide for changes in young-adult suicide rates in the states the USA for 1970 to 1989. The higher the suicide rate in 1970, the smaller the increase in the next 20 years.

A Natural Suicide Rate

Arguing from Durkheim's ideas, Yang and Lester (1991) suggested that the societal suicide could never be zero. They explored several regression equations predicting suicide rates, set the predictor variables to zero, and found that the resulting suicide rate was always positive.

General Issues

Lester and Yang (1995) explored ways in which suicide impacts the society, in addition to ways in which the society impacts suicide. In addition, they pointed out that cross-sectional and time-series studies typically give very different results, and they suggested that different sociological theories may be required for these two situations.

Discussion

Few new sociological theories of suicide have appeared in recent years, and few researchers have made efforts to test the classic or newer theories explicitly. Theory has been neglected in favor of purely empirical research, presented with only a minimal theoretical justification.

REFERENCES

Holinger, P. C., & Lester, D. Suicide, homicide, and demographic shifts. *Journal of Nervous & Mental Disease*, 1991, 179, 574–575.

Leenaars, A. A., & Lester, D. Testing the cohort-size hypothesis of suicide and homicide rates in Canada and the United States. *Archives of Suicide Research*, 1996, 2, 43–54.

Lester, D. *Suicide from a sociological perspective.* Springfield, IL: Charles Thomas, 1989.

Lester, D. Suicide, homicide, and the quality of life in various countries. *Acta Psychiatrica Scandinavica*, 1990a, 81, 332–334.

Lester, D. The regional variation of suicide by different methods. *Crisis*, 1990b, 11, 32–37.

Lester, D. Suicide prevention in schools. *High School Journal*, 1990c, 73, 161–163.

Lester, D. Are the societal correlates of suicide and homicide rates the same for each lethal weapon? *European Journal of Psychiatry*, 1991a, 5, 5–8.

Lester, D. Size of youth cohort and suicide rate in Japan. *Perceptual & Motor Skills*, 1991b, 73, 508.

Lester, D. Social integration and suicide in the Caribbean islands. *Perceptual & Motor Skills*, 1991c, 73, 742.

Lester, D. Demographic determinants of youth suicide rates. *Journal of Nervous & Mental Disease*, 1992a, 180, 272.

Lester, D. Suicide among Asian Americans and social deviancy. *Perceptual & Motor Skills*, 1992b, 75, 1134.

Lester, D. *Why people kill themselves.* Springfield, IL: Charles Thomas, 1992c.

Lester, D. Testing Gibbs and Martin's theory of suicide. *Psychological Reports*, 1992d, 70, 1010.

Lester, D. A test of Durkheim's theory of suicide in primitive societies. *Suicide & Life-Threatening Behavior*, 1992e, 22, 388–395.

Lester, D. Testing Durkheim's theory of suicide in 19th and 20th Century Europe. *European Archives of Psychiatry*, 1993a, 243, 54–55.

Lester, D. The quality of life in urban areas and suicide. *Perceptual & Motor Skills*, 1993b, 77, 482.

Lester, D. A test of a social deviancy theory of suicide using the foreign-born. *Psychological Reports*, 1993c, 73, 58.

Lester, D. The influences of society on suicide. *Quality & Quantity*, 1993d, 27, 195–200.

Lester, D. The critical-mass theory of suicide. *Psychological Reports*, 1993e, 73, 78

Lester, D. The critical-mass hypothesis of suicide in adolescents. *Perceptual & Motor Skills*, 1994a, 79, 306.

Lester, D. Suicide in immigrant groups as a function of their proportion in the country. *Perceptual & Motor Skills*, 1994b, 79, 994.

Lester, D. Thwarting disorientation and suicide. *Cross-Cultural Research*, 1995a, 29, 14–26.

Lester, D. Measures of status integration in theory of suicide. *Perceptual & Motor Skills*, 1995b, 81, 1042.

Lester, D. Suicide rates in Canadian aboriginals and size of population. *Perceptual & Motor Skills*, 1995c, 81, 1282.

Lester, D. Changes in national suicide rates, 1980–1990. *Psychological Reports*, 1995d, 77, 906.

Lester, D. Suicide and alternative measures of domestic integration. *Psychological Reports*, 1995e, 77, 1322.

Lester, D. Explaining regional differences in suicide rates. *Social Science & Medicine*, 1995f, 40, 719–721.

Lester, D. Are murders and suicides committed by different methods intrinsically different? *Medicine, Science & the Law*, 1996a, 36, 28–30.

Lester, D. The quality of life and suicide in Great Britain. *Perceptual & Motor Skills*, 1996b, 82, 1386.

Lester, D. The geographic variation of suicide rates by solids and liquid substances. *Perceptual & Motor Skills*, 1996c, 83, 98.

Lester, D. Youth cohort size and suicide rates. *Perceptual & Motor Skills*, 1996d, 83, 306.

Lester, D. An empirical examination of Thomas Masaryk's theory of suicide. *Archives of Suicide Research*, 1997a, 3, 125–131.

Lester, D. Notes on a Mohave theory of suicide. *Cross-Cultural Research*, 1997b, 31,

268–272.

Lester, D., & Yang, B. Suicide and society. In B. L. Mishara (Ed.), *The impact of suicide.* New York: Springer, 1995, 215–226.

Louks, J. L., Otis, G. D., Smith, J. R., Hayne, C. H., & Trent, H. E. Male violent death during the Vietnam War. In J. McIntosh (Ed.), *Suicide '96.* Washington, DC: AAS, 1996, 147–148.

Moksony, F. *Explaining areal differences in suicide.* Budapest, Hungary, undated.

Moksony, F. Ecological analysis of suicide. In D. Lester (Ed.), *Current concepts of suicide.* Philadelphia: Charles Press, 1990, 121–138.

Pampel, F. C. Cohort size and age-specific suicide rates. *Demography,* 1996, 33, 341–355.

Stack, S. The impact of relative cohort size on national suicide trends, 1950–1980. *Archives of Suicide Research,* 1996, 2, 213–222.

Stafford, M. C., Martin, W. T., & Gibbs, J. P. Marital status and suicide. *Family Perspectives,* 1990, 24(1), 15–31.

Taylor, S. Suicide, Durkheim, and sociology. In D. Lester (Ed.), *Current concepts of suicide.* Philadelphia: Charles Press, 1990, 225–236.

Travis, R. Halbwachs and Durkheim. *British Journal of Sociology,* 1990, 41, 225–243.

Yang, B., & Lester, D. Is there a natural suicide rate for a society? *Psychological Reports,* 1991, 68, 322.

Chapter 6

THE RELIABILITY AND VALIDITY OF SUICIDE RATES

Accuracy of Certification

Ajiki et al. (1991) studied one prefecture in Japan and found that the calculated standard mortality rate for suicide depended on whether data from medical practitioners or medical examiners were used. On the other hand, in Finland, Lindeman et al. (1995) found that data from Forensic Pathology Units identified 97 percent of the suicides recorded in the Central Statistical Office.

Cantor et al. (1997) argued that the rise in suicide rates in Ireland in the 1970s was due in part to more-accurate recording. In a rural section of County Limerick, Ireland, Kirwan (1991) calculated a suicide rate of 18.0 from an examination of coroner records, compared to the official suicide rate of 7.1. Connolly and Cullen (1995; Connolly et al., 1995) found 220 suicides in County Mayo, of which only 143 were officially recorded as suicides – of the rest 41 were undetermined, 15 accidents, 16 unregistered and 5 were missing. There was more misrecording for drowning deaths. Sex, marital status, employment, and age were not associated with misrecording. Of 134 single road deaths of people over the age of 15, only six were possibly suicides. Naughton et al. (1996) found in Kerry (Ireland) that official records listed 19 suicides in 1988, postmortem listed records 16, and each missed some. There

was a total of 23 suicides. Clarke-Finnegan and Lucey (1997) found a suicide rate of 16.0 for one Irish county in 1986–1990, compared to an official rate of 12.5. The official rate misclassified suicides due to drowning more than those using other methods. Walsh et al. (1990) studied deaths in County Kildare (Ireland) in 1978–1987. They found 58 suicides. The Central Statistical Office recorded 55, adding six that Walsh did not label, but missing nine of Walsh's suicides.

In a follow-up of a sample of conscripts in Sweden, Allebeck et al. (1991) found 195 suicides recorded out of 683 deaths. A close examination of the death certificates found that one labeled suicide was not so, and 12 suicides had been missed.

In the Canary Islands, Rodriguez-Pulido et al. (1991) found an official suicide rate of 4.8 in 1980, but they found a rate of 8.6 by searching through medical examiner files. Dukes et al. (1992) in Wellington (New Zealand) noted that of 239 deaths due to alcohol/drugs/poisons, 164 were ruled suicide, 55 accidental, 10 "uncertain," and 10 "misadventure."

In the Netherlands from 1905–1910, Van Poppel and Day (1996) found that the Protestants had higher mortality rates from suicide and accidents, while Catholics had higher mortality rates from sudden deaths and ill-defined/unspecific causes, suggesting the Catholic suicides were hidden in these categories.

Van de Voorde et al. (1993) compared the suicides in Leuven, Belgium, as recorded by the death certificates and by the Public Prosecutor's Office. The Prosecutor's Office had fewer of those dying by hanging, drowning, and jumping, and fewer who died during transport or at the hospital. The death certificates had fewer of those using cutting and fewer who died at home.

Jarvis et al. (1991) gave Canadian medical examiners vignettes to certify. Their classification of a case as suicide was affected by the religion of the medical examiners, the size of their town, and their experience.

Phillips and Ruth (1993) noted that more suicides in California occurred at symbolic ages (30, 40, 50, etc.). The same phenomenon was found for deaths from barbiturates, single-car crashes, and undetermined causes (but not natural causes or multiple-car crashes). They argued that this suggested that suicides, who do show the "symbolic age" effect, are also misclassified into these other three categories. They therefore concluded that suicidal deaths are sometimes misclassified, more so for blacks than for whites and more for females than for males.

Wetzel et al. (1976) introduced a standard report form for medical examiners and found that use of the form improved the quality of information in the files. Furthermore, several cases initially judged as "open" verdicts were found to have signs indicating suicide. Also, in the United States, Neimetz et al. (1997) found that an autopsy was more likely in the case of suicidal deaths (and in addition, for male, nonwhites, in urban areas, and for other associated characteristics of the death). Sorenson et al. (1997) found that suicides in California, as compared to undetermined deaths, were more often males, whites, used firearms and hanging more often (and poison/gas less often), occurred in the home, without autopsy, and with death instantaneous.

England

Neeleman (1996) claimed (without data) that suicide rates did not rise in England after suicide was decriminalized in 1961. Kelleher et al. (1996) noted that the undetermined death rate had declined from 1976–1992 in Ireland, whereas this rate had increased in England over the same period.

There is good evidence that English suicide rates are grossly underestimated and that official statistics are quite meaningless. Many suicides are classified as open verdicts. In a study in Avon, Vassilas and Morgan (1993) noted 83 recorded suicides, and they judged 61 open and accidental verdicts to be suicides also. If this result is generalized for the whole country, the official English suicide rate is underestimated by 42 percent.

In South Yorkshire, Cooper and Milroy (1994, 1995) found 536 suicides in 1985–1991 whereas only 323 were certified as suicides. (The rest were open verdicts.) Thus, 40 percent of the suicides were misclassified. A suicide verdict was more likely for males, the young, and deaths by gas and hanging.

O'Donnell and Farmer (1995) examined 242 suicides on the London Underground. Only 59 percent were certified as suicides – 22 percent were open verdicts, and 19 percent were accidental. More of the male suicides were misclassified than the female suicides. The accuracy also varied by which coroner's court certified the death.

In Wolverhampton, Scott (1994) calculated a suicide rate of 10.5, compared to the official rate of 6.2. Nowers and Gunnell (1996) found that only 76 percent of the suicides from the Clifton Suspension Bridge were ruled by coroners to be suicide.

In London, Neeleman et al. (1997) found that a coroner's verdict of nonsuicide was more likely if the suicide was female, used passive methods, and was a minority member or a white not born in England and Wales; it was not associated with age.

Salib (1996) also explored the factors leading to a coroner's verdict of suicide versus an open verdict. Suicide was the verdict more often if there was evidence of intent, no problems with alcohol, a prior psychiatric history, and use of a method other than an overdose (but not sex, age, marital status, or prior suicide attempts). Salib et al. (1997) looked at the verdict for former psychiatric patients. A suicide versus an open verdict was predicted by more suicidal intent, absence of an alcohol-related diagnosis, presence of schizophrenia and depressive disorder, and the use of hanging. (Inpatient versus outpatient, sex, marital status, prior attempts, and social isolation did not predict the verdict.) In a study of one coroner, Salib (1997) found that classification of an elderly death as an open verdict (rather than suicide) was more likely if the method was drowning (rather than hanging), if there was no psychiatric history, and if the suicidal intent was less evident. No effect was found from sex, marital status, prior attempts, social isolation, or alcohol problems.

Neeleman and Wessely (1997) found that the ratio of open/suicide verdicts by coroners increased between 1974 and 1991 in England. Open verdicts were more common for drownings, jumping, and drug overdoses. Medically trained coroners gave a greater proportion of open verdicts, and there was an association with geographic area and age, but not sex. In 1989–1991, the ratio of open verdicts to suicide verdicts was 1:1.96.

Suicide and Accidental Death Rates

Lester (1990) studied United States rates from 1950–1984. The suicide and accidental death rates were positively associated for solid/liquid poisoning, gas poisoning, drowning, car exhaust, and barbiturates. The association for firearms was negative. On the whole, therefore, suicidal deaths do not appear to be disguised as accidental deaths, which would necessitate a negative association. Furthermore, if accidental death rates can be viewed as a legitimate index of the availability of methods for suicide, the positive associations for five of the six methods supports an availability hypothesis for the choice of method for suicide. Over 17 nations, Lester (1994a) found suicide and accidental death rates from similar causes positively associated. These results argue against some accidental deaths being disguised suicides.

On the other hand, for the nine regions of the USA, Young (1991) found that prisoner suicide rates were not associated with prisoner accidental death rates or unspecified death rates.

Rockett and Smith (1993) noted that, among eight nations, the unintentional death rates from drowning were deviant for the elderly in Japan, suggesting that these may contain hidden suicides.

Suicide and Undetermined Death Rates

In Australia from 1968 to 1985, as the suicide rate decreased, the undetermined death rate decreased also (a positive association), indicating that the declining suicide rate was not due to covering up suicides by labeling them as undetermined (Cantor and Dunne, 1990). In Italy for 1951–1988, Carollo and De Leo (1996) found that association between suicide rates and deaths from unknown or unspecified causes for the elderly were positive for most sex-by-age groups, suggesting no disguising of suicides, except for the use of poisons and gasses.

Over 17 nations, Lester (1994a) found suicide and undetermined death rates from similar causes not significantly associated. These results argue against some undetermined deaths being disguised suicides.

On the other hand, in Ireland for 1946–1992, Swanwick and Clare (1997) found that the number of suicides and the number of undetermined deaths were negatively associated. Lester (1997) found that suicide and undetermined death rates were negatively associated for 1968-1990 in the United States, but not significantly associated over the states in 1980.

In Germany from 1968–1988, elderly suicide rates by age and sex were inconsistently associated with death rates from senility, sudden/unknown causes, unclear causes, and undetermined deaths (Schmidtke and Weinacker, 1991). However, death rates from unclear causes and nonviolent suicide methods were consistently correlated in a negative manner, suggesting that the unclear cases could be hidden suicides.

Lester (1992a) added the undetermined and one tenth of the accidental death rates to the suicide rates of 15 nations and found that it hardly changed their relative rankings based simply on their suicide rates.

In Sweden, Ferrada-Noli et al. (1996) found that undetermined deaths and suicides did not differ in blood alcohol levels. Among the undetermined deaths, those who were foreign born more often had blood alcohol than Swedish born, but these two groups did not differ in blood alcohol among the suicides.

Attempted and Completed Suicide

Hawton et al. (1997) found that attempted suicide rates in Oxford and completed suicide rates in England were positively associated over time for 1985–1995 for all age-by-sex groups.

The Impact of Changes in Codes

In Canada in 1950–1982, Speechley and Stavraky (1991) found no increase in accidental deaths due to drowning, firearms, poisons, and other causes after 1969 when the undetermined category was made available and equivocal suicides were no longer assigned to accidental causes.

The Stability of Suicide Rates

Lester (1992b) found that the suicide rates in the USA in 1920 and in 1980 were only weakly associated ($r = .27$). The mean suicide rate was the same in both periods, but the standard deviation was lower in 1980. Lester (1993) found that the suicide rates of 20 nations in the 1910s and 1920s were strongly associated with the suicide rates in 1960, indicating great stability.

Immigrants

In Canada, Lester (1994c) found a positive association between the suicide rates of 22 immigrant groups and the suicide rates in their home nations. Ferrada-Noli (1997) replicated this association for immigrants to Sweden. Burvill (1995) found that the suicide rates of elderly immigrants in Australia were higher than those of native-born Australians, but were in the same rank order as the suicide rates in their home nations. However, Johansson et al. (1997) in Sweden found a positive association only for males. Females had a negative association (as did the male/female suicide rate ratio).

Lester (1994b) found that the ratios of violent/nonviolent suicide methods for seven immigrant groups in Australia were positively associated with these ratios in their home nations.

Accuracy of Information

Fishman and Weimann (1997) compared the motives for suicides recorded officially in Israel and for suicides reported in the press. The two groups differed significantly in their motives for suicide and in the correlates (by sex, marital status, and nationality) of the motives. Thus, research based on press-reported suicides may be biased.

Safer (1997) reviewed surveys of suicidality in adolescents and found that anonymous surveys reported lower incidences than identifiable surveys.

Tests and Measurements

Spirito et al. (1991) found that the risk-rescue rating scale in a sample of adolescent suicide attempters had poor inter-judge reliability and a low variation in scores. Jobes et al. (1997) found that patients and clinicians gave different answers when completing a suicide status form for the subjects.

Discussion

On the whole, national suicide rates appear to be relatively comparable, and the existence of open verdicts and undetermined deaths does not appreciably change the relative rankings of national suicide rates. However, greater accuracy in suicide rates, especially in Ireland and England, would be welcomed for sound epidemiological research.

REFERENCES

Ajiki, W., Fukunaga, T., Saijoh, K., & Sumino, K. Recent status of the medical examiner system in Japan. *Forensic Science International,* 1991, 51, 35–50.

Allebeck, P., Allgulander, C., Henningsohn, L., & Jakobsson, S. W. Causes of death in a cohort of 50,465 young men. *Scandinavian Journal of Social Medicine,* 1991, 19, 242–247.

Burvill, P. W. Suicide in the multiethnic elderly population of Australia, 1979–1990. *International Psychogeriatrics,* 1995, 7, 319–333.

Cantor, C. H., & Dunne, M. P. Australian suicide data. *Australian & New Zealand Journal of Psychiatry,* 1990, 24, 381–384.

Cantor, C. H., Leenaars, A. A., & Lester, D. Underreporting of suicide in Ireland 1960–1989. *Archives of Suicide Research,* 1997, 3, 5–12.

Carollo, G., & De Leo, D. Relationship between suicide and undetermined causes of death among the elderly. *Omega,* 1996, 33, 215–231.

Clarke-Finnegan, M., & Lucey, M. Suicide rates in an Irish county. *Irish Medical Journal,* 1997, 90, 76.

Connolly, J. F., & Cullen, A. Underreporting of suicide in an Irish county. *Crisis,* 1995, 16, 34–38.

Connolly, J. F., & Cullen, A., & McTigue, O. Single road traffic deaths. *Crisis,* 1995, 16, 85–89.

Cooper, P. N., & Milroy, C. M. Violent suicide in South Yorkshire, England. *Journal of Forensic Sciences,* 1994, 39, 657–667.

Cooper, P. N., & Milroy, C. M. The coroner's system and underreporting of suicide. *Medicine, Science & the Law,* 1995, 35, 319–326.

Dukes, P. D., Robinson, G. M., Thomson, K. J. & Robinson, B. J. Wellington coroner autopsy cases 1970–89. *New Zealand Medical Journal,* 1992, 105, 25–27.

Ferrada-Noli, M. A cross-cultural breakdown of Swedish suicide. *Acta Psychiatrica Scandinavica,* 1997, 96, 108–116.

Ferrada-Noli, M., Ormstad, K., & Asberg, M. Pathoanatomic findings and blood alcohol analysis at autopsy (BAC) in forensic diagnoses of undetermined suicide. *Forensic Science International,* 1996, 78, 157–163.

Fishman, G., & Weimann, G. Motives to commit suicide. *Archives of Suicide Research,*

1997, 3, 199–212.

Hawton, K., Fagg, J., Simkin, S., Bale, E., & Bond, A. Trends in deliberate self-harm in Oxford, 1985–1995. *British Journal of Psychiatry*, 1997, 171, 556–560.

Jarvis, G. K., Boldt, M., & Butt, J. Medical examiners and manner of death. *Suicide & Life-Threatening Behavior*, 1991, 21, 115–133.

Jobes, D. A., Jacoby, A. M., Cimbolic, P., & Hustead, L. Assessment and treatment of suicidal clients in a university counseling center. *Journal of Counseling Psychology*, 1997, 44, 368–377.

Johansson, L. M., Sundquist, J., Johansson, S. E., Bergman, B., Qvist, J., & Traskman-Bendz, L. Suicide among foreign-born minorities and native Swedes. *Social Science & Medicine*, 1997, 44, 181–187.

Kelleher, M. J., Corcoran, P., Keeley, H. S., Dennehy, J., & O'Donnell, I. Improving procedures for recording suicide statistics. *Irish Medical Journal*, 1996, 89(1), 14–15.

Kirwan, P. Suicide in a rural Irish population. *Irish Medical Journal*, 1991, 84(1), 14–15.

Lester, D. Accidental death rates and suicide. *Activitas Nervosa Superior*, 1990, 32, 130–131.

Lester, D. Miscounting suicides. *Acta Psychiatrica Scandinavica*, 1992a, 85, 15–16.

Lester, D. The stability and variability of suicide rates in the states of the USA. *Perceptual & Motor Skills*, 1992b, 75, 494.

Lester, D. The stability of national suicide rates over time. *Perceptual & Motor Skills*, 1993, 77, 42.

Lester, D. Are suicides disguised as accidental and undetermined deaths? *European Journal of Psychiatry*, 1994a, 8(2), 89–92.

Lester, D. Choice of violent versus nonviolent methods for suicide by immigrants. *Perceptual & Motor Skills*, 1994b, 79, 718.

Lester, D. Suicide in immigrant groups as a function of their proportion in the country. *Perceptual & Motor Skills*, 1994c, 79, 994.

Lester, D. Time-series analysis of suicidal and undetermined deaths. *Perceptual & Motor Skills*, 1997, 85, 1242.

Lindeman, S. M., Hirvonen, I. I., Hakko, H. H., & Lonnqvist, J. K. Use of the National Register of Medico-Legal autopsies in epidemiology suicide research. *International Journal of Legal Medicine*, 1995, 107, 306–309.

Naughton, M., Doyle, A., Melia, P., & Barry, D. Suicide in Kerry. *Irish Journal of Psychological Medicine*, 1996, 13, 147–148.

Neeleman, J. Suicide as a crime in the United Kingdom. *Acta Psychiatrica Scandinavica*, 1996, 94, 252–257.

Neeleman, J., Mak, V., & Wessely, S. Suicide by age, ethnic group, coroners' verdicts, and country of birth. *British Journal of Psychiatry*, 1997, 171, 463–367.

Neeleman, J., & Wessely, S. Changing classification in suicide in England and Wales. *Psychological Medicine*, 1997, 27, 467–472.

Neimetz, P. N., Leibson, C., Naessens, J. M., Beard, M., Tangalos, E., & Kurland, L. T. Determinants of the autopsy decision. *American Journal of Clinical Pathology*, 1997, 108, 175–183.

Nowers, M., & Gunnell, D. Suicide from the Clifton Suspension Bridge. *Journal of Epidemiology & Community Health*, 1996, 50, 30–32.

O'Donnell, I., & Farmer, R. The limitations of official suicide statistics. *British Journal of Psychiatry*, 1995, 166, 458–461.

Phillips , D. P., & Ruth, T. E. Adequacy of official suicide statistics for scientific research and public policy. *Suicide & Life-Threatening Behavior*, 1993, 23, 307–319.

Rockett, I. R., & Smith, G. S. Covert suicide among elderly Japanese females. *Social Science & Medicine*, 1993, 36, 1467–1472.

Rodriguez-Pulido, F., Sierra, A., Gracia, R., Doreste, J., Delgado, S., & Gonzalez-Rivera, J. L. Suicide in the Canary Islands. *Acta Psychiatrica Scandinavica*, 1991, 84, 520–523.

Safer, D. J. Self-reported suicide attempts by adolescents. *Annals of Clinical Psychiatry*, 1997, 9, 263–269.

Salib, E. Predictors of coroner's verdict. *Medicine, Science & the Law*, 1996, 36, 237–241.

Salib, E. Coroner's verdicts in the elderly. *International Journal of Geriatric Psychiatry*, 1997, 12, 481–483.

Salib, E., Joseph, A., & Cawley, S. Unexpected death of psychiatric patients. *Medicine, Science & the Law*, 1997, 37, 210–214.

Schmidtke, A., & Weinacker, B. Covariation

of suicides and undetermined deaths among elderly persons. *Crisis*, 1991, 12(2), 44–58.

Scott, K. W. Suicide in Wolverhampton. *Medicine, Science & the Law*, 1994, 34, 99–105.

Sorenson, S. B., Shen, H., & Kraus, J. F. Undetermined manner of death. *Evaluation Review*, 1997, 21, 43–50.

Speechley, M., & Stavraky, K. M. The adequacy of suicide statistics for use in epidemiology and public health. *Canadian Journal of Public Health*, 1991, 82, 38–42.

Spirito, A., Brown, L., Overholser, J., Fritz, G., & Bond, A. Use of the risk-rescue rating scale with adolescent suicide attempters. *Death Studies*, 1991, 15, 269–280.

Swanwick, G. R., & Clare, A. W. Suicide in Ireland 1945–1992. *Irish Medical Journal*, 1997, 90, 106–108.

Van de Voorde, H., Hooft, P., & Mulkers, U. On the influence of data source in aggregated data studies. *Journal of Epidemiology & Community Health*, 1993, 47, 73–75.

Van Poppel, F., & Day, L. H. A test of Durkheim's theory of suicide. *American Sociological Review*, 1996, 61, 500–507.

Vassilas, C. A., & Morgan, H. G. G.P.'s contact with victims of suicide. *British Medical Journal*, 1993, 307, 300–301.

Walsh, D., Cullen, A., Cullivan, R., & O'Donnell, B. Do statistics lie? *Psychological Medicine*, 1990, 20, 867–871.

Wetzel, R. D., Murphy, G. E., Gantner, G. E., & Risch, J. Improvement in death investigation through standardized report forms. In B. S. Comstock & R. Maris (Eds.), *Proceedings of the 8th Annual Meeting*. Denver: AAS, 1976, 69–74.

Young, T. J. Accidental and unspecified deaths among prisoners as disguised suicides. *Psychological Reports*, 1991, 69, 577–578.

Chapter 7

SOCIOLOGICAL CORRELATES

Abortion Laws

Lester (1995h) found that *Roe v. Wade*, liberalizing abortion laws in the United States, was followed by a decrease in the suicide rate of women aged 35–54.

Age

Completed Suicide

Lester (1994p) reviewed the features of suicidal behavior as they vary with age, and Lester and Yang (1992b) reviewed research on the social correlates of elderly suicide rates.

Girard (1993) examined the variation in suicide rate by age in different countries and found that, as the GNP per capita increased, the suicide rate rose among the elderly.

Lester (1993g) calculated correlation coefficients between suicide rates and age groups for each nation. These values were associated with a number of social variables such as the gross domestic product per capita and birth rates. The correlations were stronger in the more-developed nations, urban nations with older populations.

In a psychological autopsy study of suicides over the age of 50, Conwell et al. (1990) found that those over the age of 75 were more often male, widowed, and used a violent method, and less often had alcohol in their blood and previous psychiatric treat-

ment. Those over 75 had experienced more recent physical illness and loss, while those aged 50–74 had experienced more job, financial, and family stress. Genz (1993) found that in one region of East Germany, elderly suicides (over the age of 65) had less often received psychiatric treatment in the past.

Ajiki et al. (1991) found that the suicide rate in the regions of one prefecture in Japan varied positively with the percentage of elderly (and negatively with population density).

Attempted Suicide

In England, Hawton and Fagg (1990) found a higher attempted suicide rate in those aged 55–64 than in those aged 65 and older. The older attempters also showed a more balanced sex ratio. The attempted suicide rate was higher in the divorced men and women and lowest in the married men and single women. The rate was highest in social classes IV and V. The men were more often alcoholics and intoxicated prior to attempting.

Merrill and Owens (1990) found that elderly (older than 65, versus those younger than 35) attempted suicides in England were more often widowed, living alone, with a psychiatric illness, using tranquilizers and antidepressants, and with higher suicidal intent. They were less often single and using analgesics.

Alcohol Consumption and Alcohol-Control Laws

Jones et al. (1992) found that a lower drinking age in American states from 1979–1984 was associated with a lower suicide rate for those below the legal age. However, changing the legal age did not appear to have an impact during this period.

Cherpited (1996) compared a dry county in Mississippi with a wet county in California. The dry county had a higher suicide rate and a higher percentage of suicides who were intoxicated.

Wasserman et al. (1994) found that as alcohol consumption rates dropped in the former Soviet republics so did the suicide rates. Furthermore, the association between alcohol consumption and suicide rates was positive over the ten regions.

Assisted Suicide

Lester (1997e) found that prohibiting assisted suicide in the states of the USA was associated with an older population in the states but not with other social variables.

Attempted and Completed Suicide

Lester (1991g) found that rates of attempted suicide and completed suicide were moderately associated in seven European nations. Lester (1993i) found that estimates of rates of attempted suicide and completed suicides in 12 European nations were positively associated.

Climate

Lester (1991a) found that suicide rates

were negatively associated with coldness and precipitation, but not elevation, for a sample of SMSAs in America.

Cohort

Wasserman (1989) tried to disentangle the effects of age, period, and cohort in Canada and the United States, a task that is statistically impossible. However, Wasserman concluded that men in Canada showed only an age effect, while white men in the United States showed age and cohort effects. Bille-Brahe and Jessen (1994) reported an age-period cohort analysis for Denmark. In Austria for 1951–1990, Etzerdorfer et al. (1996) found that male suicide rates increased both with age and cohort, while female suicide rates increased only with age.

Cohort Size

Lester (1994g) found that the cohort size of youths aged 15–24 was associated with their suicide rate in the United States for 1933–1985, even after controls for social variables.

Leenaars and Lester (1994) failed to find an association between youth suicide rates and youth cohort size in time-series studies for 1969–1988 in Canada and the United States.

Lester (1994e) found that the suicide rates of native Americans over the states of America were positively associated with the percentage of native Americans in the states.

The Uematsu-Lester Cohort Hypothesis

Lester (1994f) found no support for this hypothesis in Denmark from 1922–1991. Cohorts with a high suicide rate in one period did not have lower suicide rates in other periods. Lester (1995a) found no support for the cohort theory in England from 1941–1965.

Collectivism

Lester (1992f) found no association over nations between suicide rates and a measure of collectivism based on a psychological test given to samples of the population in the nations.

Community Size

In a northern region of Italy with 51 communes, Sangiorgi et al. (1990) found that smaller communities had a higher completed suicide rate, but did not differ in the attempted suicide rate. In the regions of British Columbia (Canada), Agbayewa (1993) found that the elderly suicide rate was negatively associated with population size.

Conception

Lester (1997a) found that the monthly suicide rate in 1980 in the United States was negatively associated with the monthly conception rate, but not significantly associated with the monthly birth rate.

Country Music

Stack and Gundlach (1992) found that the hours of country music on the radio in metropolitan areas was positively associated with white suicide rates, as was the divorce rate and being in the South – poverty and gun availability were not. The associations with black suicide rates were all non-significant. Stack and Gundlach (1995) failed to replicate this result, but in their new analysis the association held for cities with high divorce rates. In national samples, those preferring country music were more likely to be divorced/separated and to own guns.

Criminal-Justice Variables

Lester (1990c) found that the presence of a death penalty in the American states in 1965 was not associated with the states suicide rates, but gun control law strictness was negatively associated with the suicide rate.

Decriminalizing Suicide

Lester (1992g) found that the suicide rate in Canada was higher after decriminalization in 1972, but the slope of the increase was less after decriminalization than before. Lester (1993h) found that decriminalization of suicide in New Zealand in 1961 did not change the suicide rate.

Domestic Terror

Lester (1995e) found that the suicide rate was negatively associated with the number of domestic terrorism incidents in Canada for 1960–1985.

The Economy

Lester and Yang (1997) reviewed theory and research on the economy and suicide. Yang and Lester (1992) found that the time-series suicide rate in the United States was associated with the "misery index," the sum of the inflation and unemployment rates. Lester (1993n) found no association between the misery index and suicide rate by presidential term (from Truman to Reagan).

Lester (1997b) found that the percentage change in the gross domestic product in 72 nations from 1965–1980 was not associated with 1980 suicide rates. Lester (1997c) found that the suicide rate in these nations was associated with industrialization but not urbanization.

Ferrada-Noli (1996) found that the richest

county in Sweden had a lower suicide rate than the poorest one. Lester (1997d) found no association between welfare spending and suicide rates over 18 affluent nations, nor in changes in these variables.

Education

Saucier (1993) found that the percentages finishing high school or college in the states of United States were not associated with the states suicide rates.

Kachur et al. (1995) calculated suicides for the United States in 1980 by education. Those with some college education had lower suicide rates, with the difference no longer significant for those over the age of 70.

Ethnic Groups and Nations

United States

McCord and Freeman (1990) found a low suicide rate in Harlem (New York) in 1979–1981. Kposowa et al. (1995) found that the nativity of white males was not associated with their suicide rate. Suicide rates were predicted by being divorced, living alone and in the center of cities, age, and low family income.

United States: Asian Americans

Lester (1992n) reviewed research on suicide in Chinese Americans. Lester (1994c) found that Japanese American, Chinese American, and Filipino American suicide rates in the United States were lower than white suicide rates, but in the same rank order as rates in the home nations. The Asian American male and female suicide rates were more similar than for whites or blacks, and Asian Americans used firearms less often for suicide.

Shiang et al. (1997) found that Asians in San Francisco had a lower female suicide rate than whites and a peak in older females. Asian male suicide rates were lower than those of whites. The peak in old age was similar, and the Asian suicides used alcohol/drugs less often immediately prior to the suicidal act, used hanging more and guns less, and were using medication less often at the time of the act.

United States: Hispanics

In New Mexico in 1958–1962 and in 1983–1987, Beck et al. (1990) found that age-adjusted male suicide rates were highest in native Americans, then non-Hispanic whites, and lowest in Hispanics. In contrast, female suicide rates were highest in non-Hispanic whites, then Hispanics, and lowest in native Americans.

In 15 states, Maurer et al. (1990) found higher suicide rates in non-Hispanic whites, then Hispanics, and lowest in non-Hispanic blacks. Cuban immigrants had the highest suicide rate. They also presented suicide rates by sex and age.

Among young adults in California, Sorenson and Shen (1996) found that the suicide rates of foreign born were lower. Foreign-born suicides were less educated than American-born suicides and used poisoning less and hanging more. Among the foreign born, suicide rates were highest in the non-Hispanic whites and lowest in the Hispanics. For males, suicide rates were highest in American-born Mexican Americans, then Mexican-born Mexican Americans, and lowest in Mexicans. For women, all Mexican Americans had higher suicide rates than Mexicans.

Lester and Anderson (1992) found that Hispanic-American high school students had higher depression and current suicidal ideation scores than African Americans and were more often living with parents, but did not differ in hopelessness. Reynolds (1992) found that suicidal ideation in high school students was most common in Hispanics, then African Americans and least common in whites. (Females had more suicidal ideation than males.)

United States: Native Americans

Lester (1997j) reviewed research and theory on suicide in native Americans.

Sievers et al. (1990) reported 51 completed suicides for the Pima tribe (native Americans) in 1975–1984. Young and French (1992, 1993) found a suicide rate in the 12 Indian Health Service regions of 18.6 and a suicide rate peak for those aged 15–24. The male and female native American suicide rates were higher than the suicide rate for white men but lower that for white women. Gessner (1997) found higher teen suicide rates in native Alaskans than in Alaskan whites.

Young (1990) found that native American suicide rates were associated with the percentage in poverty over the 12 health areas of the Indian Health Service. Native American suicide rates were not associated with death rates from cirrhosis or motor vehicle accidents (Young, 1991c) or relative income (Young and French, 1996), but they were associated with poverty and household size (Young, 1991d, 1992a). Young (1992b) found that the sum and difference of the suicide and homicide rates were not associated with other causes of death over these regions. Young and French (1995) found that the percent of females in the labor force was associated with the male and female suicide rates. In trying to replicate these findings, Lester (1995d) found that the only significant correlate of these suicide rates was the number of households. In a multiple regression, the number of households and poverty

both contributed significantly. Lester (1997f) found that the percentage of suicides committed by men was not associated with any of the social variables of the 12 Indian Health Service regions.

Kettl and Bixler (1991) reported a high rate of suicide among Alaskan natives. Suicide was most common in those aged 15–24 and between midnight and 3 a.m. Kettl and Bixler (1993) found that Alaska native suicides who had been patients at the health service agencies were more likely to abuse alcohol and have prior suicidal behavior than control patients. They did not differ in diagnosis, tuberculosis, seizures, or congenital problems.

Hisnanick (1994) found that native American and Alaskan native suicide rates decreased from 1973–1988, although the male/female rate ratio increased. The age-adjusted suicide rate for these groups was higher than that for the total United States population.

Van Winkle and May (1993; May and Van Winkle, 1994) found that the suicide rates of Apache in New Mexico were higher than those of Pueblo, who in turn had higher suicide rates than Navajo. The modal native American suicide was male, single, employed, intoxicated with alcohol, and completing suicide at home. For males, native American suicide rates were higher than those of Hispanic whites, with Anglo whites having the lowest rates. For females, the order was Anglo whites, Hispanic whites, and native Americans.

Zitzow and Desjarlait (1994) found that the modal Ojibway attempted suicide was 15–19, female, unemployed or a student, using pills, at home, from 6 p.m. to midnight, and on Saturdays.

Lester (1994h) found that native American suicide rates and white suicide rates were not associated over the states of America.

United States: African Americans

Lester (1993e) found that the relative economic status of African Americans in the period 1967–1986 did not predict their absolute or relative suicide rates. Suicidal behavior in African Americans has been reviewed by Lester (1998).

Australia

Hunter (1991) found that aborigines who completed suicide differed from other aborigines in living more often in towns, being heavy drinkers, and having more suicidality in the past. They did not differ in history of psychosis, work history, or whether of full descent. Fasher et al. (1997) found no differences in prior suicidality between aboriginal and nonaboriginal juvenile detentioners.

Canada

Bagley et al. (1990) found that rates of suicide and suicide plus self-destructive deaths (such as open verdicts, some accidental deaths, single motor-vehicle accidents, and cirrhosis deaths) were higher in young men aged 15–34 living on native Canadian reserves, and among the reserves, in the northern reserves. Bagley (1991) reported that, in Alberta, the suicide rate of young native males was higher in the northern reserves and in reserves farther from towns. He noted that the northern reserves were characterized by greater poverty. Norton et al. (1995) found that Anglo Canadian and native Canadian alcoholics seeking treatment did not differ in suicidality. In both groups, suicidality was predicted by panic attacks in the prior four weeks, higher depression scores, and higher alcohol-abuse scores.

Elliott et al. (1990) found that, among adolescents in Manitoba, 27 percent of native Canadians had attempted suicide versus only 12 percent of whites. The attempters among the native Canadians were older than the nonsuicidal youth, had more prior suicidal ideation, and more often knew someone who had attempted suicide. For the whites, the attempters were more depressed, had experienced more stressors, and had more prior suicidal ideation and attempts.

Also in Manitoba, Malchy et al. (1997) found that aborigines had a higher suicide rate and the aboriginal suicides were younger than the white suicides, had higher blood levels of alcohol, and had less often received psychiatric care. Aborigines on reserves had higher suicide rates than those off reserves, but did not differ in age, blood alcohol levels, or psychiatric care. Sigurdson et al. (1994) found that native Canadian youths had a higher suicide rate in Manitoba than nonnative youths.

Aldridge and St. John (1991) found that native-Canadian youth (10–19) had a high suicide rate on the northern coast of Labrador, but a very low rate elsewhere in the province. (The peak was on Saturdays, but the numbers were very small in the data set.)

Cooper (1995) found that reserves in British Columbia with high suicide rates had less-educated residents, larger households, more children, more single parents, fewer elders, and lower incomes. Compared to white suicides in British Columbia, the aboriginal suicides came from families with more alcohol abuse, child abuse and suicide, were more often alcohol/drug abusers, experienced more violence (as victim and perpetrator), were younger, were more often intoxicated at the time of the suicide, and less often had a history of mental illness. They did not differ in the number of stressors.

Mao et al. (1992) found higher suicide rates for men and women living on Indian reserves in Canada and in registered Indians than in Canadians as a whole. Lester (1995c) found that the regional native Canadian suicide rate was not associated with the proportion of native Canadians in the nine regions (thereby not supporting Lester's social deviancy theory) or with the native Canadian motor-vehicle death rate.

Feather et al. (1993) found that suicide rates for those aged 15–44 were higher in northern Saskatchewan than in the southern part. They noted that the population in the north was younger, with a lower life expectancy, a higher homicide rate, lower income, higher unemployment, and more native Canadians.

Trovato (1986) correlated suicide with social variables over nine ethnic groups in Canada. Suicide rates were higher in the English-speaking groups, those with a religion other than Roman Catholicism, the more educated, the wealthier, those with smaller household sizes, and those less urban. Trovato (1992) found that the violent and accidental mortality of four immigrant groups in Canada (Americans, English, Scots, and Italians) was roughly in the same rank order as in their home countries.

Strachan et al. (1990) found that the Canadian-born had higher suicide rates in 1986 than first-generation Canadians for those aged 15–64, but lower rates for those older than 65. This was found only for men; Canadian-born women had lower suicide rates than first-generation Canadian women. The rates were especially high in first-generation Asian women.

Chinese Populations

Lester (1994m) examined the epidemiology of suicide in Chinese populations in

six nations.

England and Wales

Raleigh et al. (1990) found that completed suicide rates were relatively low in men and elderly immigrants from the Indian subcontinent, but relatively high in young women, especially those who were married, and Hindus. By social class, suicide rates were higher in the highest and lowest social classes, whereas rates in the general population were higher in the middle classes. Raleigh and Balarajan (1992) looked at immigrant groups entering England in 1979–1983. Caribbean males and females and Indian males had low suicide rates; Indian females and East African (mainly Indian) males and females had high suicide rates. Suicide by burning was especially common in both men and women. Raleigh (1996) noted that men from the Indian subcontinent had low suicide rates, while women from the Indian subcontinent and East Africa had high suicide rates.

Handy et al. (1991) found that Asian adolescent suicide attempters more often came from intact families than white adolescent attempters. They did not differ in birth order. The Asian attempters more often had their attempt precipitated by cultural conflict, including fights with their family, whereas the white attempters more often had discipline problems with their families.

Kingsbury (1994) found that adolescent attempted suicides from the Indian subcontinent socialized less with friends than white attempters, experienced more parental control, and tended to be more depressed and hopeless, but have lower suicidal intent.

Neeleman et al. (1996) found that females had higher rates of attempted suicide than males in one region of London. For males, however, Asians and Indians had the highest rate, while for females, Indians had the highest rate. The white attempters were more often unemployed and drug/alcohol abusers. The groups did not differ in prior attempts or psychiatric disorder.

Finno-Ugrians

Kondrichin (1995) hypothesized that Finno-Ugrians (including Finns and Hungarians) had high suicide rates, and Kondrichin and Lester (1997) found that the proportion of Finno-Ugrians in 30 European nations was positively associated with the national suicide rates.

Hong Kong

Simpson and Ng (1992) found that Filipino attempted suicides and self-mutilators in Hong Kong did not differ from Chinese attempters in age or suicidal intent. They were, however, more often married, had less of a psychiatric history, were more often domestic workers, less often semi-skilled, and used less serious means than the Chinese attempters.

Hungary

Zonda and Lester (1990) reported higher attempted suicide rates, but lower completed suicide rates in Hungarian Gypsies.

Israel

Kohn et al. (1997) found that, among Israeli teenagers, the completed suicide rate was highest in the Druze, then Jews, Moslem Arabs, and lowest in Christian Arabs. These differences were clear in males and less clear in females.

Micronesia

Rubenstein (1992) attributed the rise in youth suicide rates in Micronesia to (1) loss of community and family cohesiveness, (2) gain of new functions for the family (due to shift from lineage structure to nuclear-family structure), (3) blocked opportunities, and (4) dependency conflicts for adolescents and loss of socialization supports.

The Netherlands

Grootenhuis et al. (1994) found differences in the personal characteristics of attempted suicides in Oxford (England) and Utrecht (the Netherlands). For example, the Dutch attempters were older, less often intoxicated, and had more socioeconomic problems.

New Zealand

Langley and Johnston (1990) found completed suicide rates higher in whites, but attempted suicide rates higher in the Maori. Skegg et al. (1995) also reported lower suicide rates in Maori men and women.

Singapore

Peng and Choo (1990) reported a completed suicide rate in 1986 of 13.1 in Singapore and an attempted suicide rate of 92.8. For men, completed suicide was most common in Indians, then in Chinese, and lowest in Malays. For women, completed suicide was most common in Chinese, then Indians, and lowest in Malays. Among the elderly, Ko and Kua (1995) found that the Chinese had the highest suicide rates and the Malays the lowest. Elderly Chinese and Indians used similar methods, both preferring to jump.

Kua and Ko (1992) found that Indians had the highest suicide rate, followed by Chinese, and then Malay. Among the elderly, however, the Chinese had a higher suicide rate than the Indians. The Indians and Chinese used similar methods for suicide, but differed from the Malay. Peng and Choo (1992) confirmed the ethnic differences in completed suicide rates. Kok and Tsoi (1993) reported the highest suicide rates in Chinese, followed by Indians and Malays. Lim and Ang (1992) found that attempted suicide was most common in Indian conscripts in the military and least common in the Malays.

South Africa

Flisher and Parry (1994) reported that the completed suicide rate in South Africa was highest in whites, then Asians, and then coloureds and blacks. Whites used firearms more, Asians and blacks used hanging, male coloureds used hanging, and female coloureds used solids and liquids.

Lerer (1992) found that white female suicides in South Africa averaged 59 years old, while coloured and black South Africans averaged 29 years old. The groups did not differ in having alcohol in their blood (nor did they differ in this from female homicide victims). Van Zyl (1988) found that black and white suicide rates were similar in Pretoria in 1968–1973.

Gangat (1990) reported that, among the Indians in Durban, suicide rates were higher in the Tamils and Hindus and lower in the Gujerati, Urdu, Telegu, and Muslim. Forster and Keen (1988) found that 86 percent of male and female Zulus in all regions found suicide unacceptable.

Flisher et al. (1993) found that attempted suicide among high school students in the past year was more common in Afrikaans than in English students and more common in these groups than in the Xhosa students. Lester and Akande (1997) found that South African Xhosa, Nigerian Yoruba, and American college students did not differ in

current suicidal ideation.

Sweden

In Sweden, Wasserman and Eklund (1991) found that attempted suicide rates were higher in Finns than in Swedes (and also higher in women, the single more than the married, and the divorced more than the widowed). Rates peaked at ages 25–34 in women and 45–54 in men.

Taiwan

Wolf (1975) found that the suicide rate in Taiwan in 1905–1930 (when ruled by the Japanese) was higher in the Hokkien than in the Hakka (a minority group).

Among the aboriginal groups, Cheng and Hsu (1992; Cheng, 1995) found that the Atayal and Bunun had relatively high suicide rates. The Ami and Paiwan had relatively low suicide rates, similar to those of the Taiwanese. The groups did not differ in attempted suicide rates. The aboriginal suicides more often had a family history of depression, suicide, and alcoholism than the Taiwanese; and more dysthymia, alcohol abuse, and comorbidity.

Zimbabwe

Lester and Wilson (1990) documented adolescent suicide rates in Zimbabwe in the 1980s and noted a rising trend in self-immolation among adolescent females in Harare.

Fertility

Lester and Yang (1992a) found that birth rates and suicide rates were associated over time in the United States for the total suicide rate, for the suicide rates of men and women, for those aged 15–44, and for white females, and nonwhite males and females.

Gangs

Evans et al. (1996) found that male delinquents who were gang members had shown less prior suicidal ideation and made fewer attempts than nongang members.

Gender Equality

Lester (1992e) found no association over the American states between suicide rates and an index of gender equality. Suicide rates were, however, associated with indices of legitimate violence and social disorganization.

Height

Lester (1995i) found that the average height of people in English counties was associated with the county suicide rates, but not after controls for other social variables. Lester (1996b) found that the average height of nations was associated with the gross domestic product per capita and that both of these variables were associated with the suicide rates.

Homelessness

Kales et al. (1995) reported a high incidence of past attempted suicide and affective disorder (30 percent and 27 percent) in homeless adults in emergency shelters. Geissler et al. (1995) found that attempted suicide was more common in seasoned female homeless substance abusers than in the newly homeless, but they did not differ in psychiatric diagnosis. Sibthorpe et al. (1995) found that homeless and potentially homeless teenagers had a high incidence of attempting suicide (45 percent), and attempting was associated with sex, binge drinking, and sexual abuse.

Households

Amran (1993) found in Japan that the suicide rate for both men and women in households with employees was lower than in households with self-employed persons, which in turn was lower than in agricultural households. Amran suggested that this was a "healthy worker" effect, direct for men and indirect for women (mainly their wives).

Dodge and Austin (1990) found that the suicide rate among elderly females in Japan from 1967–1985 was negatively associated over time with the gross national product per capita and positively with the percentage of households with three generations living together. However, once gross national product per capita was controlled for, the sign for three-generation households was negative, indicating a beneficial effect for living with children and grandchildren. Lester (1993f) found that the proportion of three-generation households in Japan from 1967–1986 was positively associated with elderly suicide rates in correlational analyses, but negatively in multiple regressions.

Olsson and Wasserman (1991) found that the attempted suicide rate was similar for married people with and without children. For those living alone, the rate was higher for those with children.

Lester (1993q) found that marriage and divorce rates were more strongly associated with the suicide rates of American states than ratio measures (divorces/marriages, etc). Lester (1991h) found that the percentage of women aged 45–49 who were childless was not associated with suicide rates over 21 nations.

Human Rights

Lester (1993k) found no association between national suicide rates and human-rights violations.

Immigrants

Stellman (1996) found that Korean immigrants to New York City had higher suicide rates than American whites.

Chandrasena et al. (1991) compared Canadian-born and immigrant suicides in Canada. The immigrants were older, had experienced more life stress, were more educated, had less mental illness in their families, and used firearms less often; they used hanging, drowning, and overdoses more often. They did not differ in unemployment, prior suicide attempts, or prior psychiatric hospitalizations.

Ferrada-Noli et al. (1995) found that Finnish immigrants, an impoverished group in Sweden, had higher suicide rates than the Swedish people. Ferrada-Noli (1997) found that immigrants to Sweden had higher suicide rates and were younger when completing suicide than Swedish suicides. The rates were especially high for Russians, Finns, Germans, Danes, and Norwegians; they were low for those from Iran, Iraq, England, Chile, Italy, and Yugoslavia. The suicide rates of the immigrants were higher than in their home nations, but in roughly the same rank order. Both immigrants and Swedes had higher suicide rates in low-income areas than in high-income areas (Ferrada-Noli and Asberg, 1997). Johansson et al. (1997a, 1997b, 1997c, 1997d) found that the foreign born in Sweden had higher suicide rates than native-born Swedes, especially immigrants from eastern Europe or outside Europe and those immigrating prior to 1967. In a multiple regression versus community controls, the suicide rate was associated with being single, not employed and foreign born, and with somatic disease. In a follow-up of community residents, suicide was predicted by living alone, somatic illness, being foreign born, male, urban, and having a psychiatric illness.

In Australia, Hassan (1995) found that suicide in recent immigrants (less than 10 years) was highest in the English, Germans, and Indians; for longer-term immigrants, suicide rates were highest in Russians, Poles, and New Zealanders.

Among Russian immigrants to Israel, Ponizovsky et al. (1997) found that recent suicidal ideation was associated with being nonmarried, less social support, depression, distress and loneliness (but not time in Israel, sex, age, education, or occupation).

In a review of data from several nations, Patel and Gaw (1996) found that young female immigrants from the Indian subcontinent had higher suicide rates than young immigrant men and women in the home nations. Violent methods of suicide were more common, and the suicide rate was especially high in Hindus.

Lester (1991i) found that the emigration rate from 13 European nations was negatively associated with the suicide rates. Nations with higher suicide rates had lower rates of emigration.

Institutional Characteristics

Osgood and Brant (1990) found that long-term care facilities for the elderly reported suicidal behavior in their patients more often if they had a high staff turnover, and were larger, more expensive, and religious. The suicidal and indirect life-threatening behavior rate was 95, with men and whites more commonly engaging in these behaviors.

Intelligence

Lester (1993m) found no association between suicide rates and mean intelligence test scores over the regions of France. Lester

(1995f) found a positive association over the 12 regions of Ireland and Great Britain, but not when intelligence scores were placed in a multiple regression with other variables.

Marital Status

Studies continue to report suicide rates by marital status. For example, Bucca et al. (1994) found that suicides were more often unmarried, than the general population in Genoa, Italy (but did not differ in education or whether living in a working-class neighborhood). Burnely (1994, 1995) found lower suicide rates in the married in New South Wales (Australia), as well as associations with such variables as living alone, poverty, and education.

In the United States in 1980, Kachur et al. (1995) calculated suicide rates by marital status by age. The divorced had higher suicide rates for all ages. In a study in Maryland, Li (1995) found that the higher suicide rate of widowed over married was found for elderly males, but not elderly females. In a study of 10,906 deaths in 1986, Stack and Wasserman (1993) found that suicide was more common in the non-married, males, nonblacks, and those with high alcohol consumption.

Kowalski (1990) found that both divorce rates and interstate migration rates correlated with suicide rates over the states of the USA in 1970 and 1980. However, the size of the association between divorce and suicide rates was less in 1980 than in 1970, even after controls for other variables.

Stack (1990) found that from 1959–1980, the suicide rate of divorced men under the age of 30 increased, while the suicide rate of divorced men over the age of 30 declined. The ratio of the suicide rates for divorced/married declined over the period for most age-by-sex groups. Looking at the change in the suicide rate from 1950 to 1979

in the sex-by-age-by-marital-status cells (120 cells in all), sex, marital status, and the proportion in each cell had no significant effect, but age had a negative effect. In a time-series study from 1933 to 1971, Lester (1997g) found that the suicide rate was negatively associated with the first-marriage rate, the remarriage rate, and the divorce rate.

Trovato (1991) found that married people in Canada had a lower suicide rate, with no change from 1951 to 1981, a similar effect for all age groups, and the effect greater for men than for women.

Mastekaasa (1993) found that the divorced in Norway had a high suicide rate, but that the high suicide of widows/widowers disappeared after controls for age. The never married had a higher suicide rate than the married, increasingly so for men over the period 1961–1990.

Mastekaasa (1995) looked at several nations and found a general trend for suicide rates to show a disadvantage for the never married over the married that peaks for those 30–40 years of age.

Medical Resources

Lester (1990d) found that the more hospital beds per capita in the state (but not the more physicians per capita), the lower the suicide rate. The availability of beds, physicians and nurses per capita in western European nations, however, was not associated with suicide rates. Young (1991a) found that hospital beds/capita was not associated with suicide rates over the Indian Health Services regions.

Lester (1992b) used infant mortality as an index of medical resources, but infant mortality was negatively associated with suicide rates over nations and over the states of the USA, a direction opposite to the prediction.

Migrants

Lester (1994n) found that state suicide rates were associated with the percentage of returnees to the home state (1975–1980), as well as the percentage born in state and the percentage living in the same house (negatively) and the percentage from other states (positively).

Military

Foreign Nations

In Australia, O'Toole and Cantor (1995) compared Vietnam-era veterans who completed suicide with those who did not. The suicides had lower intelligence test scores and less education, were more unskilled and more often had a prior criminal record. They went AWOL more, committed more offenses while in the service, more often received a psychiatric discharge, and had more psychiatric problems.

In Belgium, Cosyns et al. (1993) found that army personnel had lower completed suicide rates than males aged 20–29 but similar attempted suicide rates. The soldiers used guns and poisons more than the general population and hanging less. Among the soldiers, completed suicide rates were higher in the French speakers (versus Flemish speakers) and professionals (versus conscripts), but did not differ between those stationed in Germany and those stationed at home. Attempted suicide rates were higher in those stationed in Germany and the French speakers, but lower in the professionals.

In Finland, Schroderus et al. (1992) found that the yearly variation in the suicide rate of military conscripts for 1972–1987 was less for young men not in the military. Partonen et al. (1994) found that suicide in military conscripts in Finland peaked during the first 40 days and in days 100–160 (during early

specialization training). Suicides did not differ from nonsuicides in fitness or psychiatric diagnosis, but the suicides were more often married. Also in Finland, Marttunen et al. (1997) found that conscripts who completed suicide, as compared to nonmilitary male suicides of similar age, more often had intact families; were less often substance abusers, under the influence of alcohol and with physical/psychiatric illnesses; had less psychosocial impairment; but had more recent stress (especially interpersonal) and more stress in the prior 24 hours.

Fishman et al. (1990) studied induction data for Israeli military personnel. Those completing suicide did not differ in scholastic ability, combat suitability, or education. The suicides were more psychiatrically disturbed, but this was found only for the noncombat population. The suicides were overrepresented in the combat troops and underrepresented in the noncombat troops. Combat personnel completing suicide in the first three months of service differed in having lower scholastic ability and combat suitability than those not completing suicide. They did not differ in their medical profiles. Noncombat personnel completing suicide in the first three months of service had worse medical profiles (fitness and limitations), but did not differ in scholastic ability and combat suitability from those not completing suicide. Also in Israel, Dycian et al. (1994) found that completed suicides among the military were judged to be more combat suitable than those making nonlethal self-injuries. The two groups did not differ in time in the service. Apter et al. (1993) found that males aged 18–21 who completed suicide in the Israeli military more often had divorced or widowed parents and were more often Ashkenazic than the general population, but did not differ in religion, education, or kibbutz rearing.

Gigantino (1990) found that military suicide rate in Italy for 1976–1987 was lower than the civilian suicide rate: 4.1 versus 4.8 for 18–25 year olds and 4.9 versus 8.3 for 26–60 year olds.

Mehleim (1990) compared Norwegian conscripts who attempted suicide while in training with those who did not. The attempters had lower intelligence test scores, more disturbed parents, were more disturbed themselves and had more disciplinary problems. They typically attempted between 7:30 p.m. and 1:30 a.m. in the barracks. The lethality of the attempt and suicidal intent were strongly associated. The attempters with a personality disorder had more prior attempts and made attempts of lower lethality and intent than the other attempters. Mehlum (1995) found a higher-than-expected suicide rate among Norwegian troops serving under the United Nations in Lebanon 1978-1991.

United States

Rothberg et al. (1990) reported a suicide rate of 14 in the United States Army in 1985–1986. The rate was higher in males, whites, those over the age of 40, enlisted personnel, and the divorced/separated. Suicides peaked in July and on Thursdays. Rothberg (1991) found that the monthly suicide rate in the army was associated with the relocation rate for those aged 17–21 but not for older soldiers.

Sentell et al. (1997) found that civilians had higher suicide rates than military personnel and males higher than females, but that the four major armed services did not differ in suicide rates.

Fagan (1991) reviewed research on suicidal behavior in the army. Attempted suicides as compared to completed suicides were more often female, younger, black, from the junior ranks, and used overdoses. They did not differ in marital status. The rates of both attempted and completed suicide were higher in soldiers in the United States than in those overseas.

Kawahara and Palinkas (1991) found that the navy suicide rate in 1974–1985 was lower than rates in the army or the general population. The rate was higher in those aged 25–29, men, whites, and apprentices/recruits and blue-collar employees.

Helmkamp (1995) found that the marines had a slightly higher suicide rate than the army, followed by the air force, and, last, the navy. The modal military suicide was a white male, aged 17–24, using a firearm. Enlisted personnel had higher rates, as did men, whites, and those aged 17–24.

Helmkamp (1996) reported that the modal military suicide was male, enlisted, 20–34 years old, white, and using firearms. He also found that the occupation was associated with the suicide rate. For example, in the navy, masters-at-arms had a higher suicide rate than radiomen.

Bohnker et al. (1992) found a high incidence of suicide in personnel on an aircraft carrier.

Koshes (1992) found that army soldiers who attempted suicide differed from other psychiatric referrals in more often having an adjustment disorder, being female, being married, and having the rank of E2.

Veterans

Terry et al. (1991) found no differences in suicide rates between women veterans who served in Vietnam and those who did not. Their suicide rates also did not differ from non-veteran women. Bullman and Kang (1996) found a higher suicide rate in wounded Vietnam veterans than men in the general population, especially if they were hospitalized and wounded more than once.

Post-Traumatic Stress Disorder

Hendin and Haas (1991) found that 19 percent of Vietnam veterans with PTSD attempted suicide after service in Vietnam and 15 percent had suicidal ideation. Attempted suicide was associated with guilt about combat actions, survivor guilt, depression, anxiety, severe PTSD, and feelings of being out of control during their service. Actual combat behavior did not distinguish the attempters.

Modernization

Moksony (1995) found that the suicide rate of Hungarian villagers in the 1980s was associated with the percent in agriculture in 1960 but not in 1930. Also, the larger the population loss from 1949–1969, the higher the suicide rate. Thus, Moksony felt that modernization rather than backwardness led to higher suicide rates.

National Character

Lester (1993j) found that suicide rates of nations were associated with national levels of neuroticism (negatively), but not extraversion, psychoticism, or stress. Controls for the gross national product per capita eliminated the association with neuroticism, but resulted in a negative association with extraversion.

Lester and Lynn (1993) found that national suicide rates were associated (negatively) with national measures of achievement, competitiveness, and an occupational preference for business.

Lester (1996c) extended Lynn's notion of national character to the USA and found similar factors for measures of extraversion and neuroticism. Suicide rates loaded positively on the neuroticism factor and negatively on the extraversion factor.

Nutrition

Lester (1991c) found that suicide rates were not associated with the per capita consumption of chocolate or confectionery over a sample of European nations, but the suicide rate divided by the suicide plus homicide rate was positively associated with chocolate consumption. Lester (1997i) found no association between tryptophan intake from diet and suicide rates over 30 nations.

Occupation

Goodman et al. (1994) found that 88 people died from suicide while working in 1980–1990 in the United States, as compared to 106 murdered and 122 dying in car crashes.

Rosenberg et al. (1993) presented mortality data by occupation and industry by sex for 12 states of the USA in 1984. For men, health diagnosis and treatment occupations, technicians, and service occupations had the highest suicide rates; for women, professional specialties had the highest suicide rates. Burnett et al. (1992) examined data for white males from 26 states for 1979–1988 and found greatly increased suicide mortality rates for psychologists, pharmacists, physicians, financial sales people, and lawyers. Stack (1996a, 1996b, 1997a) reported elevated suicide rates for dentists and for artists in the United States after controls for other characteristics, while Stack and Tsoudis (1997) found a high rate for correctional officers, but not after controls for other variables.

In 12 states of the United States, Anonymous (1993) found that male transportation and communication workers, railroad workers, and those in personal services and health services had high suicide rates, while manufacturing and social service workers had low suicide rates. For women, transportation and communication workers, and entertainment and recreation workers had high suicide rates, while manufacturing workers had low suicide rates.

In Alabama, Liu and Waterbor (1994) found suicide rates highest among construction and mining workers and lowest among public administrators and the wholesale trade. Suicide rates were not associated with the income level of occupations. Miller and Beaumont (1995) found an elevated suicide rate in Californian veterinarians (male and female, self-employed, employee, and educators), but only if they had been in the profession for less than 30 years.

Baris and Armstrong (1990) found no increased mortality from suicide in electrical workers in England and Wales. (Only two of the ten occupations had high suicide rates – radio and radar mechanics and telegraph operators.) Also in England, Dunnell (1994) found higher suicide rates in veterinarians, pharmacists, dentists, farmers, and medical practitioners, with lower rates in physiotherapists, education officers, and machine tool operators. The variation by social class was nonlinear. Kelly et al. (1995) found increased suicide mortality in male veterinarians, dentists, farmers, and pharmacists and female veterinarians, government inspectors, medical practitioners, and ambulance workers. Wives of doctors, dentists, and farmers also had high suicide rates. Those in social classes I and II, especially medicine-related, had high suicide rates.

In Ireland, Daeid (1997) found higher suicide rates in veterinarians, dentists, farmers, unskilled workers, the unemployed, and the retired, with lower rates in professionals and employers, nurses, and electricians.

Guidotti (1992) found an average suicide

rate in bus drivers. Gunnarsdottir and Rafnsson (1992) found an average suicide rate in women manual workers in Iceland. In West Berlin (Germany), Heim (1990) found high suicide rates in police officers/security personnel, scientists/artists, and physicians, with low suicide rates in car mechanics and textile/leather workers. In New Zealand, Langley and Johnston (1990) found high completed suicide rates in painters and low rates in drivers. For attempted suicide, rates were high in hotel staff and low in service workers.

In Finland, Valkonen and Martelin (1988) found that the suicide rate in men was highest in unskilled workers and the lower occupational classes, even after controls for other variables. In Australia, Hassan (1995) noted high suicide rates in sailors and nurses and low rates in engineers and pastors. The lower the prestige of the occupation, the higher the suicide rate for men. In New South Wales (Australia), Burnley (1995) found higher suicide rates in farmers, transport workers, and tradesmen, with lower rates in miners and service/sports/ recreational workers. These rates varied by age and sex.

Reviewing recent literature, Boxer et al. (1995) concluded that suicide rates were elevated in chemists, farmers, law enforcement, and physicians (especially women physicians).

Chemical Exposure

Green (1991) found a high suicide rate in forestry workers exposed to phenoxy acid herbicides.

College Students

Schwartz (1990) reviewed research on the topic and concluded that male college and university students had a lower suicide rate than nonstudents, as did females, although less so. Completed suicide was more common in students if they were psychotic, depressed, or had contact with campus mental health services. College student suicide tended to peak in September, January, and March, on Mondays through Thursdays and from midnight to 6 a.m.

Silverman (1993) reviewed research on student suicide and found higher suicide rates for four campuses out of 13 (Oxford, Cambridge, Berkeley, and Harvard). Eight multisite studies found low suicide rates for students. In the USA, Silverman et al. (1997) found a low suicide rate at the Big Ten universities as compared to the general population. The suicide rate was higher in students over the age of 25 than in younger students.

Niemi and Lonnqvist (1993) found that male Finnish college students had a low suicide rate, while female college students had the expected suicide rate. Bjerke et al. (1993) found that students aged 16–19 in Norway had a lower completed suicide rate than nonstudents.

Zhai et al. (1993) found a slightly higher suicide rate for university students in China than for the general population, but they did not control for age and sex.

Hawton et al. (1995a, 1995b) found that Oxford University college students had a lower attempted suicide rate than non-university youths in town. The college attempters were of higher social class, but had less prior psychiatric treatment and had made fewer prior attempts than the "town" youths. They did not differ in alcohol intoxication or method used. Among the university attempters, more were in arts and fewer in science than expected. There was no excess during the final year. The completed suicide rate of the students was, however, higher than expected. Most of the suicides had academic worries. There were no differences in risk by under-graduate/graduate, year, or major.

In Australia, Schweitzer et al. (1995) found that suicidal ideation was higher in Asians, those living alone, and those with no religion.

Electrical Workers

Baris et al. (1996) found an increased suicide rate for electrical workers, but only for those with medium exposure.

Farmers

In 15 states from 1980–1985, Ragland and Berman (1990–1991) found that farmers had a higher completed suicide than truck drivers (although farmers and forestry workers did not differ). By state, the suicide rate for farmers was positively, but not significantly, associated with farm debt/asset ratio.

Stallones (1990) found that Kentucky farmers had a higher suicide rate than other males. The suicide rate was higher only for farmers aged 25–34 and over the age of 45, and it was lower for those under the age of 25 and 35–44. Farmers tended to use firearms more for suicide than other males. In Iowa, Zwerling et al. (1995) found higher suicide rates only in white male farmers over the age of 65.

Gunderson et al. (1993) found that suicide rates were higher in full-time ranchers and farmers than in farm laborers and home-makers. Burnley (1994) found a high suicide rate in farmers (and also manual workers) in New South Wales (Australia).

Notkola et al. (1993) found that farmers had the expected suicide rate in Finland (as did skilled construction workers), whereas forestry workers and semiskilled construction workers had higher rates than expected. Green (1993) found increased suicide rates in forestry workers at a public utility company in Canada.

In Ontario, Pickett et al. (1993) found a low rate of suicide for farmers and no association between this rate and economic indices (such as farm bankruptcies, farm income, unemployment rate, etc.)

Inskip et al. (1996) reported high suicide rates in male and female farmers in England and in farmers' wives. Malmberg et al. (1997) found that English farmers preferred hanging for suicide.

Laborers

In the United States, Stack (1995a, 1995b) found high suicide rates for laborers (109 for men and 39 for women). However, controls for other social variables eliminated the high risk for laborers.

Medical Staff

Lindeman et al. (1997a, 1997b) found that Finnish male physicians had a higher completed suicide rate than other professionals, but not higher than the general male population. Female physicians had a higher suicide rate than both comparison groups. The suicide rate was highest in psychiatrists and obstetricians/gynecologists and lowest in ophthalmologists/internists. Physicians used medications for suicide more than engineers and teachers.

Schlicht et al. (1990) found that male physicians in Victoria (Australia) followed up from the 1950s to 1986 had a normal completed suicide rate, while female physicians had a higher suicide rate than the general female population (SMR = 501).

Hall et al. (1991) found high suicide rates among British pathologists. Peipins et al. (1997) found a high rate of suicide in female American nurses.

Stefansson and Wicks (1991) found a high suicide rate in male dentists, physicians and nurses in Sweden during the 1970s, not during the 1960s or 1980s. Females in these occupations had high rates in all decades. In Iceland, Gunnarsdottir and Rafnsson (1995) found that nurses had an average suicide rate overall, but that nurses with less than 20 years of experience had an elevated suicide rate.

Seagrott and Rooney (1993) found a higher rate than expected for male and for female doctors in England, with the rates similar for male and female doctors.

In a review of the literature, Lindeman (1996; Lindeman et al. 1996) found that male and female doctors and, particularly psychiatrists, had higher suicide rates than the general population and than other professionals.

Olkinuora et al. (1990, 1992) found that 0.6 percent of Finnish physicians had attempted suicide. There were no differences by sex or between specialists and non-specialists. The highest incidences of suicidality (attempts and ideation) were in male psychiatrists, neurologists, general practitioners, occupational health, and anesthesiologists and in women psychiatrists and radiologists. Hendrie et al. (1990) found that male medical students less often had suicidal ideation than male house staff, while the reverse was true for females.

Police Officers

Josephson and Reiser (1990) reported a suicide rate for the Los Angeles Police Department in 1970–1976 of 8.1 and in 1977–1988 of 12.0. The modal suicide was white, 35 years old, a patrolman, an alcohol abuser, separated or seeking a divorce, and with experience of significant loss. Hill and Clawson (1988) found an average suicide rate for police officers in Washington State in 1950-1971. In Buffalo, Violanti et al. (1996) found higher suicide rates in police officers than in municipal workers, although the police suicide rate seemed to be average for adult men. Stack and Kelly (1994) found that police officers did not have a higher rate of suicide in a national mortality study of deaths in 16 states in 1985, once marital status, age, race, and sex were controlled for. In Buffalo, Violanti (1995) found no long-term trend in the police suicide rate from 1950-1990, although it was thought that rates increased after 1970.

Lester (1993p) found that police officers who abused alcohol and completed suicide in New York City in the 1930s were younger, had more current job stress, and had stronger interpersonal motives for their suicide.

In Queensland (Australia), Cantor et al. (1995, 1996) found that the modal police suicide was male, married, a constable, 25–29 years old, used a firearm, 6 a.m. to noon. Compared to the nonsuicides, they did not differ in sex and rank. The rate seems to have declined since 1871. Service, and psychiatric and alcohol problems were each common in about half of the suicides, with health and domestic problems each common in about a third.

Lester (1992c) reported suicide rates for police officers in 26 nations. Their suicide rates were not associated with the national suicide rates in these nations.

Janik and Kravitz (1994) studied police officers who were required to have fitness-for-work evaluations. Those who had previously attempted suicide had more marital problems and suspensions and fewer complaints of administrative harassment. They did not differ in age, years of service, sex, race, alcohol abuse, citizen complaints, drug problems, or stress. In Australia, Lennings (1995) found that depression was associated with suicidal ideation in both police officers and criminal justice students, while negative life events were associated

with suicidal ideation for police but not for students. Age and coping style were not associated with suicidal ideation.

Radiochemical Plants

Komleva et al. (1994) found a high rate of suicide in workers at a Russian radiochemical plant as compared to the general population, but lower death rates from murder and traffic accidents. The more exposure to radiation, the lower the suicide rate!

Writers

Lester (1994d) documented frequent suicide among writers in the USSR, Great Britain, and Japan.

Prisoners

A review of the literature on suicide in prisons was provided by Lester and Danto (1993).

Attempted Suicide

Bland et al. (1990) found that male prisoners had a higher lifetime incidence of suicide attempts (and psychiatric disorders) than the general population.

In England, Griffiths (1991) found that prisoners who had previously attempted suicide did not differ from other prisoners except that they more often had a history of psychiatric treatment, drug abuse, prior convictions, and prior suicide attempts.

Ivanoff (1992) found that male inmates who had attempted suicide (before or during prison time) more often had been homeless, been in psychiatric treatment, were drug abusers, had suicidal behavior and arrests in their social network, and got lower social-desirability scores on a psychological test. They did not differ in age, race, education, criminal history, stressors, or alcohol abuse. Ivanoff et al. (1996) found that attempting suicide in prison by male felons was associated with psychiatric history, suicidal ideation, and if an alcohol abuser, low hopelessness. Current suicidal ideation was associated with coping ability, psychiatric history, hopelessness, depression, and reasons for living scores.

Among juvenile delinquents, Harris and Lennings (1993) found that suicidal ideation or attempts in the prior six months was associated only with depression and not with family background (sexuality, losses, transitions, strains, substance use, or legal conflicts) or hopelessness.

Liebling (1993) compared young offenders who had attempted suicide in prison with those who had not. The attempters had more prior offenses, and had been in prison longer, higher levels of family violence, poorer school performance and more prior psychiatric treatment, substance abuse, isolation/alone in prison, time in seclusion, complaints and disciplinary problems; they had fewer visits and wrote fewer letters. They spent more time in their cells, more often did nothing their cells, were more bored, had more insomnia, had less hope for the future, and felt worse off than other prisoners.

In a second report, Liebling (1995) found that those attempting suicide in prison had more often been bullied at school, sexually abused as children, and self-injured previously. In prison, the attempters got less involved in physical education or jobs, were less active in their cells, had more difficulties with other inmates, more often had no release plans, received fewer letters, had more sleeping problems, and were more hopeless. Liebling observed three types of attempters: poor copers, psychiatrically ill, and long sentences.

In Scotland, Power and Moodie (1997) found a higher suicide risk among prisoners on admission than during custody. Power et al. (1997) found that prisoners who had attempted suicide in the past (or who had prior psychiatric treatment) had a more-difficult time adjusting to prison.

Smyth and Ivanoff (1994) compared inmates who had attempted suicide who were healthier and those less healthy according to depression, anxiety, and prison-behavior scores. They differed in their needs, with the healthier prisoners wanting more activity and social stimulation and the less-healthy prisoners wanting freedom and privacy.

In Canada, Holley et al. (1995) found a higher incidence of prior suicide attempts in prisoners. The attempters were more likely to have a psychiatric disorder, especially a mood or personality disorder, less education, and more violent-criminal behavior. The age at the first attempt was not associated with sex, aboriginal status, psychiatric disorder, attempting suicide in custody, or use of a violent method for suicide. Those who were college educated were older at their first attempt.

Smith et al. (1996) found a tendency for prisons where the warden's office was outside the facility to have more attempted suicides (but not completed suicides).

Among adolescents in a juvenile detention center, Mace et al. (1997) found that females showed more suicidality than males, but there were no racial differences. Current suicidal ideation was predicted for males by depression, stressors, loneliness, and fewer close relatives and predicted for females by depression, age, and impulsivity. Prior attempted suicide was predicted for males by current suicidal ideation, ineffective coping behavior, and not living with a biological parent and predicted for females by stressors, impulsivity, and not living with a biological parent.

Completed Suicide

Dooley (1990b) compared the completed suicides in English prisons with all other prisoners. For 1972–1975, the suicide rate was 31 per 100,000 per year and for 1984–1987 56. The suicides had more often committed violent crimes and less often property crimes, were more often on remand and had received longer sentences. They did not differ in sex or race. The suicides occurred more often in July to September and from midnight to 8 a.m. The suicides were evenly distributed over the days of the week. Liebling (1994) found a suicide rate for women in English prisons of 37 for 1972–1987 and 62 for 1988–1989, comparable to the male prisoner suicide rate of 73 for 1988–1989.

Dooley (1990a) compared prisoners in England who completed suicide with those who died from accidental self-injuries. The self-injurers were more often female, never married, psychotic, and taking major tranquilizers; they used fire to injure themselves during the daytime. They were less often on remand, but did not differ in the violence of their offense or history of attempted suicide.

Crighton and Towl (1997) found high rates of suicide in English prisons, increasing from the 1980s to the 1990s. The rate was lower after sentencing, for sentences less than life, for blacks, and if there was a psychiatric history. Rates were higher on the first day. McHugh (1995) reported a suicide rates of 82 in English prisons for 1983–1993. In England, Pritchard et al. (1997) reported a higher-than-expected suicide rate for male probationers.

In Scotland, Bogue and Power (1995) found a high suicide rate for prisoners. It was even higher in those over the age of 30, in for more than 18-month sentences, who had committed violent or sexual crimes, and

who had fewer prior convictions. The modal suicide used hanging, in the cell, in the first three months of the sentence, from 9 p.m. to 6 a.m., and was a substance abuser.

Laishes (1997) found that the modal suicide in Canadian prisons was male, white, single, 30–39 years old, in a medium-security prison, a recent transfer, with a history of extreme violence and alcohol/drug abuse, a prison management problem, coming from a dysfunctional family background, with no prior suicide attempts or intent, using hanging at night.

Green et al. (1993) found that the modal Canadian federal prisoner suicide was male, white, single, by hanging in the cell, and imprisoned for a nonsexual violent offense. Lester (1995b) found that the time-series suicide rate in Canadian prisoners in 1960–1985 had similar correlates as the general male suicide rate, indicating that the prison suicide rate responded to the same social pressures.

Skegg and Cox (1993) found that Maori and non-Maoris had similar completed suicide rates in New Zealand prisons, even though Maoris were over-represented in prisons compared to their proportion of the general population. Skegg and Cox (1991) found that restrictions on the transfer of psychiatrically disturbed prisoners was followed by an increase in the prison suicide rate.

In the Netherlands from 1973–1984, Kerkhoff and Bernasco (1990) reported that the suicide rate of prisoners varied from 62 to 208 over the years. The completed suicides were older, incarcerated for more violent crimes, with longer sentences compared to nonsuicidal inmates, typically used hanging, occurred in the first three months, and showed no clustering over time. The attempted suicides were younger, committed more violent crimes, had longer sentences than nonsuicidal inmates, and used wrist cutting and swallowing objects. Blaauw et al. (1997) reported high suicide rates in Dutch prisons/jails and in police lockups. The modal police station suicide was male, 32 years old, with a history of arrests, mental health care and substance abuse, intoxicated, in solitude, by hanging, within 18 hours of arrest, and between 6 p.m. and midnight.

Morrison (1996) found that suicides in Australian prisons were younger than those dying from other causes. They did not differ in the day, month, or year of death. The modal suicide was on remand, in the first three months, and from 8 p.m. to 4 a.m., but did not differ in offense. Aborigines did not have a higher proportion of deaths from suicide, but their suicides occurred more often in police lockups. Suicides in police lockups in general were younger and used hanging more. In Queensland, Australia, Reser (1989) found that aboriginal suicides seemed to cluster. Six of the eight in 1986–1987 knew one another, most came from small communities, and most were aged 17-23.

Boiko and Lester (1995) presented cases of suicide by Russian prisoners. Spinellis and Themeli (1997) found a very high suicide rate in Greek prisons, with the modal suicide occurring by hanging, in the cell, at night.

Joukamaa (1997) found a higher rate in Finnish prisoners than for Finnish males in general. The suicide rate was higher in central and provincial prisons, for those in remand, for property offenders, and younger prisoners; it was lower in those arrested for drunken driving. The suicides did not differ in the number of prior convictions. The modal suicide was alone in his cell, used hanging, had spent 3–12 months in prison, died between 6 a.m. and 9 a.m., was single/divorced, and had sought a mental health contact in the prior week. The suicides did not vary by day of week or season.

Salive et al. (1990) calculated a completed suicide rate of 40 for Maryland prisoners in 1979–1987, higher than expected based on the demographic characteristics of the inmate population. Maruschak (1997) reported a state prison suicide rate of only 17 in 1993–1995.

Wooldredge and Winfree (1992) found that suicide rates in American jails were higher in the large prisons, with smaller staff/inmate ratios, and where urine tests were not taken. Suicide rates dropped when jail standards were implemented, capacities decreased, staff ratios increased, doctors made more available, and urine samples taken. Mays and Thompson (1988) found that the suicide rate in small jails (less than 10 inmates) was higher than in large jails.

Haycock (1992) found that sex offenders in mental-penal institutions in two states had lower suicide rates than other inmates, whereas a later study (Haycock, 1993b) reported higher rates. Haycock (1993a) found that suicide rates were highest among involuntary inmates of state hospitals, then in institutions for the sexually dangerous, then addiction centers/prisons, and lowest in institutions for defective delinquents.

In the Detroit jail, DuRand et al. (1995) found that the modal suicide used hanging, from 7 p.m. to 7 a.m., and during days 1–31. Suicide was more likely if the charge was murder/manslaughter.

Lester (1990a) found that the suicide rate of prisoners by state in the USA was negatively associated with the percentage of inmates in multiple-occupancy cells, but not with the average square footage per inmate. Over the nine regions of America, Young (1991b) found that the state prisoner suicide rate and the suicide rate of the general population were associated.

Lester (1992h) found that jail suicide rates

and the existence of state standards for suicide prevention were not associated over the states of the USA. Jail suicide rates were higher in states with lower jail populations.

Religion

Kunz (1987) found no higher rate of suicide among Mormons in Utah as compared to residents with other religions.

Lester (1992i) found that the suicide rate in nations was associated negatively with the degree to which people in the nations believed in God and in life after death.

Stack and Wasserman (1992) analyzed responses to the General Social Survey and found that church attendance, being non-ecumenical, and being more religiously conservative were associated with more negative attitudes toward suicide.

Residence

Pearson (1993) found that residents of a region who completed suicide were more often female and less often had previously attempted suicide than nonresidents who completed suicide, but did not differ in alcohol or medical history.

Rural/Urban

Rural suicide rates were reported to be higher than urban suicide rates in Ireland (Kelleher and Daly, 1990), mainland China (Lester, 1990b), the Peloponnese in southern Greece (Gabriel et al., 1993), Japan (Yamamoto, 1992), the USSR (Varnik and Wasserman, 1992), the Ukraine (Mokhovikov, 1995), in one rural county in Wales (Pollock et al., 1996), and in a Hungarian county (Jegesy et al., 1995). Beratis (1991) reported that teenage suicide rates in Greece were higher in rural areas than in urban areas.

On the other hand, completed suicide rates were higher in urban areas in Italy (Micciolo et al., 1991) and Lithuania (Gailiene et al., 1995). Urban attempted suicide rates were higher in Finland (Ostamo and Lonnqvist, 1991); in addition, male rates were higher than female rates, and the male attempters were more often intoxicated with alcohol. For men, rates peaked for those aged 30–39 while rates for women peaked for those aged 15–19 and 30–34. Ahmadi et al. (1991) found higher youth (15–24) suicide rates in SMSAs in Connecticut than in non-metropolitan areas.

Hassan (1995), however, noted that urban/rural differences in Australia were inconsistent, with no clear trends apparent, while Cantor and Slater (1997) reported high rural suicide rates for men in Queensland and higher metropolitan rates for women.

Watanabe et al. (1995) found a higher suicide rate in a rural district of Japan as compared to an urban district. They noted that, over time in the rural district, there were more nuclear families and fewer three-generation families. Yet most of the elderly suicides lived in the three-generation families and none lived alone.

Lester and Frank (1990) found no differences in suicide rates in farming, urban, and other regions in Arkansas in 1980. Schneider and Greenberg (1994) found no differences between urban and rural areas of New Jersey. Cantor and Coory (1993) found no urban/rural differences in suicide rates of those aged 15–29 in Queensland (Australia). Dudley et al. (1992) found that teenage suicide rates in New South Wales (Australia) were higher in urban areas in 1964–1973 but higher in rural areas in 1984–1988.

Lester (1991f) found that the suicide rates of 50 SMSAs in the United States did not differ from the suicide rates of the states in which they were located, and the correlation between the two sets of rates was 0.86. Stack

(1997b) found a higher suicide rate in Memphis than in the rest of Tennessee. (Suicide rates in Memphis were associated with being male, nonblack, divorced, and youth.)

Gallagher and Sheehy (1994) reviewed European suicide rates and found them rising, especially in rural areas.

Isometsa et al. (1997) compared rural and urban completed suicides in Finland. The urban suicides more often were substance abusers, had cluster B personality disorders and comorbid disorders, were white-collar workers, were younger, had recent separations, and had fewer physical disorders.

Attempted Suicide

Lyster and Youssef (1995) found few differences between urban and rural attempters in Ireland (none in age, marital status, occupation, social class, diagnosis, method, or prior attempts), except that the proportion of males was higher in urban areas. The modal attempter was single, unemployed, and lower class.

Social Class

Kreitman (1990) noted that both completed and attempted suicide rates in Edinburgh (Scotland) were higher in the lower social classes. Kreitman et al. (1991) found that in England and Wales, male completed suicide rates increased with age and were higher in the lower social classes. The increase in suicide rates by age was found only in social classes I to IV. In social class V (the lowest), the rates peaked at age 35–44. The same phenomenon was found in Scotland.

In New Zealand, Langley and Johnston

(1990) found that the attempted suicide rate was higher in the middle class while the completed suicide rate was higher in the lower class.

Social and Political Threat

McCann and Stewin (1990) had history professors rate each year from 1920–1986 for social and political threat. This index was positively associated with the suicide rate. Lester (1993d) confirmed this, but found that the association was no longer significant in a multiple regression with other social indicators.

State Initiatives

Lester (1992j) found that state initiatives for preventing youth suicide were associated with less of an increase in youth suicide rates over time. Youth participation in suicide-prevention programs, however, was associated with more of an increase in youth suicide rates.

Suicide Prevention Centers

Lester (1991b) found that the number of suicide prevention centers in each state (and the number per capita) predicted a lesser increase in the suicide rate in the next ten years from 1970–1980. Lester (1997k) conducted a meta-analysis of all studies on this issue, concluding that suicide prevention centers demonstrated a preventive effect.

Television

Centerwall (1990) found that over the nine major regions of the United States the percentage of households with televisions in 1955 did not predict the rise in the youth suicide rate in the next 10 or 20 years.

Totalitarianism

Lester (1991d) found that suicide rates were not associated with government sanctions over a sample of industrialized nations.

Unemployment

In Japan, from 1961–1979, Snyder (1990) found that, while unemployment and the overall male completed suicide rate were positively associated, the association was positive only for those aged 25–54 – it was negative for those aged 55–74.

In Australia for 1967–1992, Eckersley (1992) found that the amount and duration of unemployment predicted suicide rates for those aged 15–19 and 20–24. Morrell et al. (1993) found that for 1966-1990 in Australia the association between unemployment and suicide was stronger for men than for women, particularly for men aged 20–24.

Ancarani et al. (1990) found no differences in the unemployment rate in a sample of suicides in one region of Italy and the general population. Crepet et al. (1991) found that the unemployed in Italy in 1979–1989 had a higher completed suicide rate. In addition, the correlation over time between suicide and unemployment rates was positive.

Platt et al. (1992a, 1992b) found that suicide rates in Italy both for men and women were higher in the unemployed. Over time, from 1977–1987, the association between suicide and unemployment rates was positive for men but not significant for women. Over the provinces of Italy, the suicide and unemployment rates were negatively associated for men and for women, and well as for the employed and for the unemployed. Changes in the suicide and unemployment rates were not associated over the regions.

In Northern Ireland for 1961–1979, Snyder (1992) found that only the suicide rate of young men aged 15–24 was positively associated with suicide rates; the association was negative for men aged 45–54 and nonsignificant for all other groups of men and women.

In Sweden, Johansson and Sundquist (1997) found that the unemployed had higher suicide rates (as did men and people who were single, renting, with bad health status, and in their 40s). The high rate for the unemployed was found even after controls for the other variables.

Lester (1992d) found no association between unemployment rates and suicide rates over 23 metropolitan areas of the United States. Lester (1994i) found that suicide rates and unemployment rates were positively associated consistently from 1957–1986 when he examined each month separately. That is, they were associated over the 30 Januaries and over the 30 Februaries, etc. For marriage rates, the association was consistently negative. Lester (1997h) found that the unemployment rate in New Mexico was associated positively with the suicide rate of young native Americans in Mexico for 1960–1986. Lester (1996a) found that native American suicide rates were not associated with unemployment rates in the United States for 1955–1987.

In Nuremberg (Germany), Moesler et al. (1990, 1991) found that the completed suicide rate was higher in men aged 16–30 and 36–55 but lower in men aged 31–35 and 56–60. The attempted suicide rate was higher in men of all ages. From 1979-1985, the annual rates of attempted and completed suicide were positively associated with the annual unemployment rate. Monthly changes in the rates were not, however, associated with monthly changes in the unemployment rate. Employed and unemployed suicidal persons did not differ in the methods used, but the unemployed were more often drug abusers and had more often made prior suicide attempts. Langley and Johnston (1990) found that the unemployed in New Zealand had higher completed and attempted suicide rates.

Crombie (1990) examined changes in the unemployment and suicide rates from 1973 to 1983 in 16 modern nations. For men, the unemployment rate rose in all 16 nations and the suicide rate in 14; for women, the unemployment rate rose in all 16 nations, the suicide rate in only seven. Thus, unemployment seemed more closely related to the male suicide rate.

Pritchard (1992) found that unemployment rates were positively associated with overall and with youth male suicide rates in the majority of industrialized nations from 1973–1987

Viinamak et al. (1995) found in a sample of adult Finns that unemployment (as well as mental health impairment) was associated with having suicidal ideation in the prior year.

Pritchard (1990) looked at 23 nations in 1964–1973 and found that the unemployment rate at the end of the period and the change in the suicide over the period were not associated over the nations. However, from 1974–1986, the associations were positive for both male and female suicide rates.

Lester and Yang (1993) found a positive association between unemployment rates and suicide rates over time in four European nations. In ten nations for 1950–1985, Yang and Lester (1996) found that unemployment had a stronger impact on male suicide rates than on female suicide rates.

Platt and Kreitman (1990) found that the attempted suicide and unemployment rates both increased in Edinburgh (Scotland) from 1968 to 1980. Then the attempted suicide rate fell, while the unemployment rate continued to rise. The attempted suicide rate fell in the employed after 1977 and in the unemployed after 1973.

In New Zealand, Fergusson et al. (1997) found that unemployed youths aged 16–18 attempted suicide more, but not after controls for family functioning, intelligence test scores, sex, etc.

Velamoor and Cernovsky (1990) found no differences between unemployed and employed suicide attempters in England in sex, age, presence of children, prior attempts, prior psychiatric treatment, suicide or psychiatric treatment in the families, suicidal intent, or precipitants.

Jones et al. (1991) found that members of a group of attempted suicides were more often unemployed than community controls. Attempters who were unemployed did not differ from employed attempters in recent stressors, and the stressors facing the unemployed attempters did not change from before to after the loss of employment. Jones felt that the data did not support a vulnerability model (stress followed by unemployment leads to attempted suicide) or an indirect causation model (unemployment leads to stress, which leads to attempted suicide). He felt that unemployment separately adds to stress and increases the risk of suicide.

Veterans

Bullman et al. (1990) found no differences between the suicide rates of veterans who had served in Vietnam and those who did not.

Farberow et al. (1990) compared Vietnam veterans dying from suicide with those dying in motor vehicle accidents. The suicides won fewer medals and more often had post-traumatic stress disorder, but did not differ on nine other combat variables (such as being fired upon and witnessing atrocities). Among non-Vietnam veterans, the suicides had more disciplinary actions.

Pollack et al. (1990) calculated a suicide rate of 25.1 for Vietnam veterans, a normal rate. A review of other studies found nine with normal rates, one with a lower rate, and three with higher rates.

War

Lester (1992k) reviewed research on the effect of war on suicide rates. Lester (1994a) confirmed that suicide rates dropped in most nations during World War I and World War II.

Hall (1996; Hall and Cipriano, 1996) found that the suicide rate for American soldiers in Haiti was higher than for those in Somalia or the Persian Gulf War. Vrankovic et al. (1996) found that rates of attempted and completed suicide by gunshot wounds to the head in northeastern Croatia were higher during the war (1991–1994) than prior to the war (1987–1990). Skorupan et al. (1997) found that suicide increased in Zagreb (Croatia) during the 1991–1995 war. The use of firearms for suicide increased and hanging decreased. Gojanvoic et al. (1997) found no changes in the South Croatian suicide rate during the war in 1988–1993, although the suicide rate did increase in the town of Split. Kozaric-Kovacic et al. (1992) found that alcoholic inpatients in Croatia were somewhat more suicidal in 1991 (wartime) than in 1988 (peacetime). In northern Sri Lanka, Somasundaram and Rajadurai (1995) found that the suicide rates dropped once the civil war started in 1984.

Lester and Ausenda (1992) found that changes in suicide rates were not consistent predictors of impending war prior to World War I or World War II. Lester (1994b) found the bellicosity of nations over 150 years was not significantly associated with their modern suicide rates.

Time-Series Studies

Lester (1991e) found that the number of war movies and the military participation rate were both associated with suicide rates in the United States over the period 1940–1986. Lester (1992m) found that the percentage of scholarly articles on war in *Psychological Abstracts* from 1933–1986 predicted suicide rates (along with divorce and unemployment rates) as well as indices of military involvement.

Lester and Yang (1991a, 1991b) found that the suicide rate was associated with the military participation rate in the United States for 1933–1986, but not with yearly changes in the size of the military and not after controls for unemployment. Yang and Lester (1997) for the same period, found that various measures (percentage of the budget spent on defense, absolute expenditures, and the military participation rate) were all negatively associated with suicide rates in multiple-regression analyses, along with divorce and unemployment rates. Lester (1993a, 1993c) found that the lower suicide rates during times of a high military-participation rate were found both for the overall male suicide rate and for the Army suicide rate.

Lester (1992a) found that the threat of nuclear war was not associated with American suicide rates over time since the Second World War.

In France 1826–1913, Lester (1993b) found that suicide rates were lower for both sexes during times of war, for major and for all wars. In Austria for 1873–1913, Lester (1994j) found a negative association between the military-participation rate and the suicide rate. Lester (1994k) found a negative association between involvement in wars and suicide rates for England 1901–1965. In

France 1850–1913, Lester (1995g) found no association between the suicide rate and the military-participation rate or the occurrence of war.

Well-Being

Veenhoven (1993) found that the happiness of residents in 27 nations as rated from national surveys was not associated with the nations suicide rates.

Discussion

It is difficult to summarize the results of the research studies reviewed in this section. Several variables appear to be important correlates (and perhaps determinants) of the suicide rate, including age, marital status, ethnicity, occupation, unemployment, and war. In Chapter 9, the results of multivariate studies are reviewed, studies that attempt to place several of these variables in the statistical analysis at the same time in order to see which are more important. These studies are perhaps more useful for advancing our knowledge of suicidology.

REFERENCES

Agbayewa, M. O. Elderly suicide in British Columbia. *Canadian Journal of Public Health*, 1993, 84, 231–236.

Ahmadi, K. S., Goethe, J. W., & Adams, M. L. Suicidal behaviors among Connecticut youth. *Connecticut Medicine*, 1991, 55(2), 76–80.

Ajiki, W., Fukunaga, T., Saijoh, K., & Sumino, K. Recent status of the medical examiner system in Japan. *Forensic Science International*, 1991, 51, 35–50.

Aldridge, D., & St. John, K. Adolescents and pre-adolescent suicide in Newfoundland and Labrador. *Canadian Journal of Psychiatry*, 1991, 36, 432–436.

Amran, A. The effect of occupational type of household on mortality in Japan. Hiroshima *Journal of Medical Science*, 1993, 42(1), 9–20.

Ancarani, A., Rondinini, C., & Bellini, M. Fifteen-year survey of suicides in the 37th Health Service District of Emilia Romagna region. In G. Ferrari, M. Bellini & P. Crepet (Eds.), *Suicidal behavior and risk factors.* Bologna: Monduzzi-Editore, 1990, 249–253.

Anonymous. Mortality by occupation, industry, and cause of death. *Monthly Vital Statistics Report*, 1993, 42(4), supplement.

Apter, A., Bleich, A., King, R. A., Kron, S., Fluch, A., Kotler, M., & Cohen, D. J. Death without warning. *Archives of General Psychiatry*, 1993, 50, 138–142.

Bagley, C. Poverty and suicide among Native Canadians. *Psychological Reports*, 1991, 69, 149–150.

Bagley, C., Wood, M., & Khumar, H. Suicide and careless death in young males. *Canadian Journal of Community Mental Health*, 1990, 9, 127–142.

Baris, D., & Armstrong, B. Suicide among electric utility workers in England and Wales. British *Journal of Industrial Medicine*, 1990, 47, 788–789.

Baris, D., Armstrong, B., Deadman, J., & Theriault, G. A case cohort study of suicide in relation to exposure to electric and magnetic fields among electrical utility workers. *Occupational & Environmental Medicine*, 1996, 53, 17–24.

Beck, T. M., Samet, J. M., Wiggins, C. L., & Key, C. R. Violent death in the West. *Suicide & Life-Threatening Behavior*, 1990, 20, 324–334.

Beratis, S. Suicide among adolescents in Greece. *British Journal of Psychiatry*, 1991, 159, 515–519.

Bille-Brahe, U., & Jessen, G. The frequency of suicide in individual Danish birth cohorts, 1922–1991. *Suicide & Life-Threatening Behavior*, 1994, 24, 275–281.

Bjerke, T., Stiles, T., Rygnestad, T., & Jorgensen, P. Youthful parasuicide in a Norwegian county. In K. Bohme, R. Freytag, C. Wachtler & H. Wedler (Eds.), *Suicidal behavior.* Regensburg: S. Roderer, 1993, 826–829.

Blaauw, E., Kerkhof, A., & Vermunt, R. Suicides and other deaths in police custody. *Suicide & Life-Threatening Behavior*, 1997, 27, 153–163.

Bland, R. C., Newman, S. C., Dyck, R. J., & Orn, H. Prevalence of psychiatric disorders and suicide attempts in a prison population. *Canadian Journal of Psychiatry*, 1990, 35, 407–413.

Bogue, J., & Power, K. Suicide in Scottish prisons, 1976–93. *Journal of Forensic Psychiatry*, 1995, 6, 527–540.

Bohnker, B., McEwen, G., Blanco, J., & Feeks, E. Psychiatric diagnoses aboard an aircraft carrier. *Aviation, Space & Environmental Medicine*, 1992, 63, 1015–1018.

Boiko, I. G., & Lester, D. Suicide in Russian prisoners. *Corrective & Social Psychiatry*, 1995, 41(2), 23–24.

Boxer, P. A., Bernett, C., & Swanson, N. Suicide and occupation. *Journal of Occupational & Environmental Medicine*, 1995, 37, 442–452.

Bucca, M., Ceppi, M., Peloso, P., Arcellaschi, M., Mussi, D., & Fele, P. Social variables and suicide in the population of Genoa, Italy. *Comprehensive Psychiatry*, 1994, 35, 64–69.

Bullman, T. A., & Kang, H. K. The risk of suicide among wounded Vietnam veterans. *American Journal of Public Health*, 1996, 86, 662–667.

Bullman, T. A., Kang, H. K., & Watanabe, K. K. Proportionate mortality among U.S. Army Vietnam veterans who served in Military Region I. *American Journal of Epidemiology*, 1990, 132, 670–674.

Burnett, C. A., Boxer, P. A., & Swanson, N. G. *Suicide and occupation.* Cincinnati, OH: NIOSH, 1992.

Burnley, I. H. Differential and spatial aspects of suicide mortality in NSW and Sydney, 1980 to 1991. *Australian Journal of Public Health*, 1994, 18, 293–304.

Burnley, I. H. Socioeconomic and spatial differentials in mortality and means of committing suicide in New South Wales, Australia, 1985–1991. *Social Science & Medicine*, 1995, 41, 687–698.

Cantor, C. H., & Coory, M. Is there a rural suicide problem? *Australian Journal of Public Health*, 1993, 17, 382–384.

Cantor, C. H., & Slater, P. J. A regional profile of suicide in Queensland. *Australian & New Zealand Journal of Public Health*, 1997, 21, 181–186.

Cantor, C. H., Tyman, R., & Slater, P. J. A historical survey of police suicide in Queensland, Australia, 1843–1992. *Suicide & Life-Threatening Behavior*, 1995, 25, 499–507.

Cantor, C. H., Tyman, R., & O'Brien, D. Police suicide. *Australian Police Journal*, 1996, 50, 189–192.

Centerwall, B. S. Young adult suicide and exposure to television. *Social Psychiatry*, 1990, 25, 149–153.

Chandrasena, R., Beddage, V., & Fernando, M. L. D. Suicide among immigrant psychiatric patients in Canada. *British Journal of Psychiatry*, 1991, 159, 707–709.

Cheng, T. A. Mental illness and suicide. *Archives of General Psychiatry*, 1995, 52, 594–603.

Cheng, T. A., & Hsu, M. A community study of mental disorders among four aboriginal groups in Taiwan. *Psychological Medicine*, 1992, 22, 255–263.

Cherpited, C. J. Regional differences in alcohol and fatal injury. *Journal of Studies on Alcohol*, 1996, 57, 244–248.

Conwell, Y., Rotenberg, M., & Cine, E. D. Completed suicide at age 50 and over. *Journal of the American Geriatric Society*, 1990, 38, 640–644.

Cooper, M. Aboriginal suicide rates. In P. H. Stephenson, S. J. Elliott, L. T. Foster & J. Harris (Eds.), *A persistent spirit.* Victoria: University of Victoria, 1995, 207–222.

Cosyns, P., De Groot, P., & Reniers, J. Suicidal behavior in the Belgian army. In K. Bohme, R. Freytag, C. Wachtler & H. Wedler (Eds.), *Suicidal behavior.* Regensburg: S. Roderer, 1993, 719–722.

Crepet, P., Caracciolo, S., Casoli, R., Fabbri, D., Florenzo, F., Grassi, G. M., Jonus, A., & Tomelli, A. Suicidal behavior in Italy. *Suicide & Life-Threatening Behavior*, 1991, 21, 263–278.

Crighton, D., & Towl, G. Self-inflicted death in prison in England & Wales. *Issues in Criminological & Legal Psychology*, 1997, #28, 12–20.

Crombie, I. K. Can changes in the unemployment rates explain the recent changes in suicide rates in developed countries? *International Journal of Epidemiology*, 1990, 19, 412–416.

Daeid, N. N. Suicide in Ireland, 1982 to 1992. *Archives of Suicide Research*, 1997, 3, 31–42.

Dodge, H. H., & Austin, R. L. Household structure and elderly Japanese female suicide rate. *Family Perspectives*, 1990, 24(1), 83–97.

Dooley, E. Unnatural deaths in prison. *British Journal of Criminology*, 1990a, 30, 229–234.

Dooley, E. Prison suicide in England and Wales, 1972–1987. *British Journal of Psychiatry*, 1990b, 156, 40–45.

Dudley, M., Waters, B., Kelk, N., & Howard, J. Youth suicide in NSW. *Medical Journal of Australia*, 1992, 156, 83–88.

Dunnell, K. Epidemiology and trends in suicide in the UK. In R. Jenkins, S. Griffiths, I. Wylie, K. Hawton, G. Morgan & A. Tylee (Eds.), *The prevention of suicide*. London: HMSO, 1994, 5–21.

DuRand, C. J., Burtka, G. J., Federman, E. J., Haycox, J. A., & Smith, J. W. A quarter century of suicide in a major urban jail. *American Journal of Psychiatry*, 1995, 152, 1077–1080.

Dycian, A., Fishman, G., & Bleich, A. Suicide and self-inflicted injuries. *Aggressive Behavior*, 1994, 20, 9–16.

Eckersley, R. *Failing a generation*. 5th International Conference, Australian Rotary Health Research Fund, Canberra, 1992.

Elliott, C. A., Kral, M. J., & Wilson, K. G. Suicidal concerns among native youth. In D. Lester (Ed.), *Suicide '90*. Denver: AAS, 1990, 283–285.

Etzerdorfer, E., Piribauer, F., & Sonneck, G. Sex differential for suicide among Austrian age cohorts. *Acta Psychiatrica Scandinavica*, 1996, 93, 240–245.

Evans, W., Albers, E., Macari, D., & Mason, A. Suicide ideation, attempters, and abuse among incarcerated gang and nongang delinquents. *Child & Adolescent Social Work Journal*, 1996, 13, 115–126.

Fagan, J. G. Self-destructive behavior among recruits and career army personnel. *Revue Internationale des Services de Santé des Armees de Terre, de Mer et de l'Air*, 1991, 64(1–3), 5–9.

Farberow, N. L., Kang, H. K., & Bullman, T. A. Combat experience and postservice psychosocial status as predictors of suicide in Vietnam veterans. *Journal of Nervous & Mental Disease*, 1990, 178, 32–37.

Fasher, A. M., Dunbar, N., Rothenburg, B. A., Bebb, D. K., & Young, S. The health of a group of young Australians in a New South Wales juvenile justice detention centre. *Journal of Paediatrics & Child Health*, 1997, 33, 426–429.

Feather, J., Irvine, J., Belanger, B., Dumais, W., Gladue, R., Isbister, W., & Leach, P. Promoting social health in Northern Saskatchewan. *Canadian Journal of Public Health*, 1993, 84, 250–253.

Fergusson, D. M., Horwood, L. J., & Lynskey, M. T. The effects of unemployment on psychiatric illness during young adulthood. *Psychological Medicine*, 1997, 27, 371–381.

Ferrada-Noli, M. Social psychological versus socioeconomic hypotheses on the epidemiology of suicide. *Psychological Reports*, 1996, 79, 707–710.

Ferrada-Noli, M. A cross-cultural breakdown of Swedish suicide. *Acta Psychiatrica Scandinavica*, 1997, 96, 108–116.

Ferrada-Noli, M., & Asberg, Psychiatric health, ethnicity, and socioeconomic factors among suicides in Stockholm. *Psychological Reports*, 1997, 81, 323–332.

Ferrada-Noli, M., Asberg, M., Ormstad, K., & Nordstrom, P. Definite and undetermined forensic diagnoses of suicide among immigrants in Sweden. *Acta Psychiatrica Scandinavica*, 1995, 91, 130–135.

Fishman, G., Morris-Duncan, A., & Kotler, M. Suicide in the Israeli army. *Suicide & Life-Threatening Behavior*, 1990, 20, 225–239.

Flisher, A. J., & Parry, C. D. H. Suicide in South Africa. *Acta Psychiatrica Scandinavica*, 1994, 90, 348–353.

Flisher, A. J., Ziervogel, C. F., Chalton, D. O., Leger, P. H., & Robertson, B. A. Risk-taking behaviour of Cape Peninsular high-school students. *South African Medical Journal*, 1993, 83, 474–476.

Forster, H. W., & Keen, A. W. Black attitudes in suicide. In L. Schlebusch (Ed.), *Suicidal behaviour.* Durban: University of Natal, 1988, 98–109.

Gabriel, J., Paschalis, C., & Beratis, S. Suicide in urban and rural southern Greece. *European Journal of Psychiatry*, 1993, 7, 103–111.

Gailiene, D., Domanskiene, V., & Keturakis, V. Suicide in Lithuania. *Archives of Suicide Research*, 1995, 1, 149–158.

Gallagher, A. G., & Sheehy, N. P. Suicide in rural communities. *Journal of Community & Applied Social Psychology*, 1994, 4(3), 145–155.

Gangat, A. E. Suicide in South Africa. In G. Ferrari, M. Bellini & P. Crepet (Eds.), *Suicidal behavior and risk factors.* Bologna: Monduzzi-Editore, 1990, 135–141.

Geissler, L. J., Bormann, C. A., Kwiatkowski, C. F., Braucht, G. N., & Reichardt, C. S. Women, homelessness, and substance abuse. *Psychology of Women Quarterly*, 1995, 19, 65–83.

Genz, A. Suicide and psychiatric disorders of elderly people in East Germany. In K. Bohme, R. Freytag, C. Wachtler & H. Wedler (Eds.), *Suicidal behavior.* Regensburg: S. Roderer, 1993, 222–225.

Gessner, B. D. Temporal trends and geographic patterns of teen suicide in Alaska, 1979–1993. *Suicide & Life-Threatening Behavior*, 1997, 27, 264–273.

Girard, C. Age, gender, and suicide. *American Sociological Review*, 1993, 58, 553–574.

Gigantino, M. The suicidal behavior within the military. In G. Ferrari, M. Bellini & P. Crepet (Eds.), *Suicidal behavior and risk factors.* Bologna: Monduzzi-Editore, 1990, 163–167.

Goodman, R. A., Jenkins, L., & Mercy, J. A. Workplace-related homicide among health care workers in the United States, 1980 through 1990. *Journal of the American Medical Association*, 1994, 272, 1686.

Gojanvoic, M. D., Capkun, V., & Smoljanovic, A. Influence of war on frequency and patterns of homicides and suicides in South Croatia. *Croatian Medical Journal*, 1997, 38(1), 54–58.

Green, C., Kendall, K., Andre, C., Looman, T., & Polvi, N. A study of 133 suicides among Canadian federal prisoners. *Medicine, Science & the Law*, 1993, 33, 121–127.

Green, L. M. A cohort mortality study of forestry workers exposed to phenoxy acid herbicides. *British Journal of Industrial Medicine*, 1991, 48, 234–238.

Green, L. M. Mortality in forestry and construction workers in Finland. *Journal of Epidemiology & Community Health*, 1993, 47, 508–509.

Griffiths, A. W. Correlates of suicidal history in male prisoners. *Medicine, Science & the Law*, 1991, 30, 217–218.

Grootenhuis, M., Hawton, K., van Rooijen, L., & Fagg, J. Attempted suicide in Oxford and Utrecht. *British Journal of Psychiatry*, 1994, 165, 73–78.

Guidotti, T. L. Mortality of urban transit workers. *Occupational Medicine*, 1992, 42, 125–128.

Gunderson, P., Donner, D., Nashold, R., Salkowicz, L., Sperry, S., & Wittman, B. The epidemiology of suicide among farm residents or workers in five north-central states, 1980–1988. *American Journal of Preventive Medicine*, 1993, 9, supplement 3, 26–32.

Gunnarsdottir, H., & Rafnsson, V. Mortality among female manual workers. *Journal of Epidemiology & Community Health*, 1992, 46, 601–604.

Gunnarsdottir, H., & Rafnsson, V. Mortality among Icelandic nurses. *Scandinavian Journal of Work & Environmental Health*, 1995, 21, 24–29.

Hall, A., Harrington, J. M., & Aw, T. C. Mortality study of British pathologists. *American Journal of Industrial Medicine*, 1991, 20, 83–89.

Hall, D. P. Stress, suicide, and military service during Operation Uphold Democracy. *Military Medicine*, 1996, 161, 159–162.

Hall, D. P., & Cipriano, E. D. Frustrated aggression in psychiatric casualties of Operation Uphold Democracy. *Journal of Nervous & Mental Disease*, 1996, 184, 377–378.

Handy, S., Chithiramohan, R. N., Ballard, C. G., & Silveira, W. R. Ethnic differences in adolescent self-poisoning. *Journal of Adolescence*, 1991, 14, 157–162.

Harris, T. E., & Lennings, C. J. Suicide and adolescence. *International Journal of Offender Therapy*, 1993, 37, 263–270.

Hassan, R. *Suicide explained.* Melbourne: Melbourne University, 1995.

Hawton, K., & Fagg, J. Deliberate self-poisoning and self-injury in older people. *International Journal of Geriatric Psychiatry*, 1990, 5, 367–373.

Hawton, K., Haigh, R., Simkin, S., & Fagg, J. Attempted suicide in Oxford University students, 1976–1990. *Psychological Medicine*, 1995a, 25, 179–188.

Hawton, K., Simkin, S., Fagg, J., & Hawkins, M. Suicide in Oxford University Students. *British Journal of Psychiatry*, 1995b, 166, 44–50.

Haycock, J. Sex, sociopathy, and suicide. *Forensic Reports*, 1992, 5, 351–357.

Haycock, J. Comparative suicide rates in different types of involuntary confinement. *Medicine, Science & the Law*, 1993a, 33, 128–136.

Haycock, J. Double jeopardy. *Suicide & Life-Threatening Behavior*, 1993b, 23, 130–138.

Heim, N. Occupation-related suicides in West Berlin. In G. Ferrari, M. Bellini & P. Crepet (Eds.), *Suicidal behavior and risk factors*. Bologna: Monduzzi-Editore, 1990, 101–106.

Helmkamp, J. C. Suicides in the military. *Military Medicine*, 1995, 160, 45–50.

Helmkamp, J. C. Occupation and suicide among males in the US Armed Forces. *Annals of Epidemiology*, 1996, 6(1), 83–88.

Hendin, H., & Haas, A. P. Suicide and guilt as manifestations of PTSD in Vietnam combat veterans. *American Journal of Psychiatry*, 1991, 148, 586–591.

Hendrie, H. C., Clair, D. K., Brittain, H. M., & Fadul, P. E. A study of anxiety/depressive symptoms of medical students, house staff, and their spouses/partners. *Journal of Nervous & Mental Disease*, 1990, 178, 204–207.

Hill, K. Q., & Clawson, M. The health hazards of "street level" bureaucracy. *Journal of Police Science & Administration*, 1988, 16, 243–248.

Hisnanick, J. J. Comparative analysis of violent deaths in American Indians and Alaskan Natives. *Social Biology*, 1994, 41, 96–109.

Holley, H. L., Arboleda-Florez, J., & Love, E. J. Lifetime prevalence of prior suicide attempts in a remanded population and relationship to current mental illness. *International Journal of Offender Therapy*, 1995, 39, 191–209.

Hunter, E. M. An examination of recent suicides in remote Australia. *Australian & New Zealand Journal of Psychiatry*, 1991, 25, 197–202.

Inskip, H., Coggon, D., Winter, P., & Pannett, B. Mortality of farmers and farmers' wives in England and Wales, 1979–80, 1982–90. *Occupational & Environmental Medicine*, 1996, 53, 730–735.

Isometsa, E., Heikkinen, M., Henriksson, M., Marttunen, M., Aro, H., & Lonnqvist, J. Differences between urban and rural suicides. *Acta Psychiatrica Scandinavica*, 1997, 95, 297–305.

Ivanoff, A. Background risk factors associated with parasuicide among male prison inmates. *Criminal Justice & Behavior*, 1992, 19, 426–436.

Ivanoff, A., Jang, S. J., & Smyth, N. Clinical risk factors associated with parasuicide in prison. *International Journal of Offender Therapy*, 1996, 40, 135–146.

Janik, J., & Kravitz, H. M. Linking work and domestic problems with suicide. *Suicide & Life-Threatening Behavior*, 1994, 24, 267–274.

Jegesy, A., Harsanyi, L., & Angyal, M. A detailed study on suicides in Baranya County (Hungary). *International Journal of Legal Medicine*, 1995, 108, 150–153.

Johansson, L. M., Johansson, S. E., Bergman, B., & Sundquist, J. Suicide, ethnicity and psychiatric in-patient care. *Archives of Suicide Research*, 1997c, 3, 253–269.

Johansson, S. E., & Sundquist, J. Unemployment is an important risk factor for suicide in contemporary Sweden. *Public Health*, 1997, 111(1), 41–45.

Johansson, L. M., Sundquist, J., Johansson, S. E., Bergman, B., Qvist, J., & Traskman-Bendz, L. Suicide among foreign-born minorities and native Swedes. *Social Science & Medicine*, 1997a, 44, 1810187.

Johansson, L. M., Sundquist, J., Johansson, S. E., Qvist, J., & Bergman, B. The influence of ethnicity and social and demographic factors on Swedish suicide rates. *Social Psychiatry & Psychiatric Epidemiology*, 1997b, 32, 165–170.

Johansson, L. M., Sundquist, J., Johansson, S. E., & Bergman, B. Ethnicity, social factors, illness and suicide. *Acta Psychiatrica Scandinavica*, 1997d, 95, 125–131.

Jones, N. E., Pieper, C. F., & Robertson, L. S. The effect of legal drinking age on fatal injuries of adolescents and young adults. *American Journal of Public Health,* 1992, 82, 112–115.

Jones, S. C., Forster, D. P., & Hassanyeh, F. The role of unemployment in parasuicide. *Psychological Medicine,* 1991, 21, 169–176.

Josephson, R. L., & Reiser, M. Officer suicide in the Los Angeles Police Department. *Journal of Police Science & Administration,* 1990, 17, 227–229.

Joukamaa, M. Prison suicide in Finland, 1969–1992. *Forensic Science International,* 1997, 89, 167–174.

Kachur, S. P., Potter, L. B., James, S. P., & Powell, K. E. *Suicide in the United States 1980–1992.* Atlanta: CDC, 1995.

Kales, J. P., Barone, M. A., & Bixler, E. Mental illness and substance abuse among sheltered homeless persons in lower-density population areas. *Psychiatric Services,* 1995, 46, 592–595.

Kawahara, Y., & Palinkas, L. A. Suicide in active-duty enlisted Navy personnel. *Suicide & Life-Threatening Behavior,* 1991, 21, 279–290.

Kelleher, M. J., & Daly, M. Suicide in Cork and Ireland. *British Journal of Psychiatry,* 1990, 157, 533–538.

Kelly, S., Charlton, J., & Jenkins, R. Suicide deaths in England and Wales, 1982–92. *Population Trends,* 1995, Summer(80), 16–25.

Kerkhoff, A. J. F. M., & Bernasco, W. Suicidal behavior in jails and prisons in the Netherlands. *Suicide & Life-Threatening Behavior,* 1990, 20, 123–137.

Kettl, P. A., & Bixler, E. O. Suicide in Alaska Natives, 1979–1984. *Psychiatry,* 1991, 54, 55–63.

Kettl, P., & Bixler, E. O. Alcohol and suicide in Alaska Natives. *American Indian & Alaska Native Mental Health Research,* 1993, 5(2), 34–45.

Kingsbury, S. The psychological and social characteristics of Asian adolescent overdose. *Journal of Adolescence,* 1994, 17, 131–135.

Ko, S. M., & Kua, E. H. Ethnicity and elderly suicide in Singapore. *International Psychogeriatrics,* 1995, 7, 309–317.

Kohn, R., Levav, I., Chang, B., Halperin, B.,

& Zadka, P. Epidemiology of youth suicide in Israel. *Journal of the American Academy of Child & Adolescent Psychiatry,* 1997, 36, 1537–1542.

Kok, L. P., & Tsoi, W. F. Season, climate, and suicide in Singapore. *Medicine, Science & the Law,* 1993, 33, 247–252.

Komleva, N. S., Koshurnikova, N. A., Nifatov, A. P., Bolotnikova, M. G., & Okatenko, P. V. Mortality from external causes among the personnel of Mayok's radiochemical plant. *Science of the Total Environment,* 1994, 142(1,2), 33–35.

Kondrichin, S. V. Suicide among Finno-Ugrians. *Lancet,* 1995, 346, 1632–1633.

Kondrichin, S. V., & Lester, D. Finno Ugrians and suicide. *Perceptual & Motor Skills,* 1997, 85, 514.

Koshes, R. J. Parasuicidal behavior on an active duty army training post. *Military Medicine,* 1992, 157, 350–353.

Kowalski, G. S. Marital dissolution and suicide in the US for the 1980s. *Family Perspectives,* 1990, 24(1), 33–39.

Kozaric-Kovacic, D., Folnegovic-Smalc, V., Jakovljevic, M., & Lang, B. Social trauma and stress in alcoholic patients. *Alcoholism (Zagreb),* 1992, 28(1–2), 85–90.

Kposowa, A. J., Breault, K. D., & Singh, G. K. White male suicide in the United States. *Social Forces,* 1995, 74, 315–323.

Kreitman, N. B. Social class and age in relation to suicide and parasuicide in Scotland. In G. Ferrari, M. Bellini & P. Crepet (Eds.), *Suicidal behavior and risk factors.* Bologna: Monduzzi-Editore, 1990, 13–19.

Kreitman, N., Carstairs, V., & Duffy, J. Association of age and social class with suicide among men in Great Britain. *Journal of Epidemiology & Community Health,* 1991, 45, 195–202.

Kua, E. H., & Ko, S. M. A cross-cultural study of suicide among the elderly in Singapore. *British Journal of Psychiatry,* 1992, 160, 558–559.

Kunz, P. R. Religion and suicide. *Dialogue,* 1987, 20, 115–117.

Laishes, J. Inmate suicides in the correctional service of Canada. *Crisis,* 1997, 18, 157–162.

Langley, J. D., & Johnston, S. E. Purposely

self-inflicted injury resulting in death and hospitalization in New Zealand. *Community Health Studies*, 1990, 14, 190–199.

Leenaars, A. A., & Lester, D. Suicide and homicide rates in Canada and the United States. *Suicide & Life-Threatening Behavior*, 1994, 24, 184–191.

Lennings, C. J. Suicide ideation and risk factors in police officers and justice students. *Police Studies*, 1995, 18(3–4), 39–52.

Lerer, L. B. Women, homicide and alcohol in Cape Town, South Africa. *Forensic Science International*, 1992, 55, 93–99.

Lester, D. Overcrowding in prisons. *Perceptual & Motor Skills*, 1990a, 71, 274.

Lester, D. Suicide in mainland China by sex, urban/rural location, and age. *Perceptual & Motor Skills*, 1990b, 71, 1090.

Lester, D. Capital punishment, gun control, and personal violence (suicide and homicide). *Psychological Reports*, 1990c, 66, 122.

Lester, D. Medical resources and suicide prevention. *Psychological Reports*, 1990d, 67, 344.

Lester, D. The climate of urban areas in the United States and their rates of personal violence (suicide and homicide). *Death Studies*, 1991a, 15, 611–616.

Lester, D. Do suicide prevention centers prevent suicide? *Homeostasis*, 1991b, 33, 190–194.

Lester, D. National consumption of chocolate and rates of personal violence (suicide and homicide). *Journal of Orthomolecular Medicine*, 1991c, 6(2), 81–82.

Lester, D. Totalitarianism and fatalistic suicide. *Journal of Social Psychology*, 1991d, 131, 129–130.

Lester, D. The association between involvement in war and rates of suicide and homicide. *Journal of Social Psychology*, 1991e, 131, 893–895.

Lester, D. Suicide rates in major cities and their states. *Psychological Reports*, 1991f, 69, 810.

Lester, D. Rates of attempted suicide and completed suicide in European community nations. *Psychological Reports*, 1991g, 69, 866.

Lester, D. Childlessness, suicide, and homicide. *Psychological Reports*, 1991h, 69, 990.

Lester, D. Emigration from Europe to the

USA. *Psychological Reports*, 1991i, 69, 1082.

Lester, D. The threat of nuclear war and rates of suicide and homicide. *Perceptual & Motor Skills*, 1992a, 75, 1186.

Lester, D. Medical resources and suicide prevention. *Perceptual & Motor Skills*, 1992b, 75, 1254.

Lester, D. Suicide in police officers. *Police Studies*, 1992c, 15, 146–147.

Lester, D. Unemployment, suicide, and homicide in metropolitan areas. *Psychological Reports*, 1992d, 71, 558.

Lester, D. Gender equality, legitimization of violence, social disorganization, and rates of personal violence (suicide and homicide) in America. *Psychological Reports*, 1992e, 71, 626.

Lester, D. Collectivism-individualism and rates of personal violence (suicide and homicide). *Psychological Reports*, 1992f, 71, 714.

Lester, D. Decriminalization of suicide in Canada and suicide rates. *Psychological Reports*, 1992g, 71, 738.

Lester, D. State regulations for suicide prevention in jails and the jail suicide rate. *Psychological Reports*, 1992h, 71, 1170.

Lester, D. Religiosity, suicide and homicide. *Psychological Reports*, 1992i, 71, 1282.

Lester, D. State initiatives in addressing youth suicide. *Social Psychiatry & Psychiatric Epidemiology*, 1992j, 27, 75–77.

Lester, D. War and personal violence. In G. Ausenda (Ed.), *Effects of war on society*. San Marino: AIEP, 1992k, 211–222.

Lester, D. Scholarly research on war as an index of the nation's military involvement. *Psychological Reports*, 1992m, 71, 1246.

Lester, D. Suicide in Chinese Americans. *Advances in Thanatology*, 1992n, 7(2), 77–79.

Lester, D. Suicide in the military as a function of involvement in war. *Acta Psychiatrica Scandinavica*, 1993a, 88,   223.

Lester, D. The effect of war on suicide rates. *European Archives of Psychiatry*, 1993b, 242, 248–249.

Lester, D. Suicide rates in Army personnel in times of peace and war. *Military Medicine*, 1993c, 158(12), A7.

Lester, D. A subjective index of American social, economic, and political threat, war and personal violence. *Perceptual & Motor Skills*,

1993d, 77, 994.

Lester, D. Economic status of African-Americans and suicide rates. *Perceptual & Motor Skills*, 1993e, 77, 1150.

Lester, D. Household structure and suicide in elderly Japanese women. *Perceptual & Motor Skills*, 1993f, 77, 1282.

Lester, D. Age distribution among suicides in nations of the world. *Perceptual & Motor Skills*, 1993g, 77, 1386.

Lester, D. Decriminalization of suicide in New Zealand and suicide rates. *Psychological Reports*, 1993h, 72, 1050.

Lester, D. Rates of attempted suicide and completed suicide in European nations. *Psychological Reports*, 1993i, 72, 1202.

Lester, D. Suicide and homicide rates and national character. *Psychological Reports*, 1993j, 73, 194.

Lester, D. Violations of human rights and personal violence (suicide and homicide). *Psychological Reports*, 1993k, 73, 1146.

Lester, D. Intelligence and suicide in France. *Psychological Reports*, 1993m, 73, 1226.

Lester, D. Suicide and homicide rates during Presidential terms as a function of economic conditions. *Psychological Reports*, 1993n, 73, 50.

Lester, D. A study of police suicide in New York City, 1934–1939. *Psychological Reports*, 1993p, 73, 1395–1398.

Lester, D. Marital integration, suicide, and homicide. *Psychological Reports*, 1993q, 73, 1354.

Lester, D. Suicide rates before, during, and after the world wars. *European Psychiatry*, 1994a, 9, 262–264.

Lester, D. Bellicose nations and rates of personal violence. *International Social Science Review*, 1994b, 69(1–2), 13–16.

Lester, D. Differences in the epidemiology of suicide in Asian Americans by nation of origin. *Omega*, 1994c, 29, 89–93.

Lester, D. Suicide in writers. *Perceptual & Motor Skills*, 1994d, 78, 698.

Lester, D. Suicide rates in Native Americans by state and size of population. *Perceptual & Motor Skills*, 1994e, 78, 954.

Lester, D. Suicide rates in cohorts over time in Denmark. *Perceptual & Motor Skills*, 1994f, 79, 974.

Lester, D. The Holinger/Easterlin cohort hypothesis about youth suicide and homicide rates. *Perceptual & Motor Skills*, 1994g, 79, 1545–1546.

Lester, D. Native American suicide and homicide rates. *Psychological Reports*, 1994h, 74, 702.

Lester, D. Suicide and unemployment. *Psychological Reports*, 1994i, 75, 602.

Lester, D. The military participation rate and suicide rates in Austria, 1873–1913. *Psychological Reports*, 1994j, 75, 894.

Lester, D. Involvement in war and suicide rates in Great Britain, 1901–1965. *Psychological Reports*, 1994k, 75, 1154.

Lester, D. The epidemiology of suicide in Chinese populations in six regions of the world. *Chinese Journal of Mental Health*, 1994m, 7(1), 25–36.

Lester, D. Interstate return migration. *Social Science Journal*, 1994n, 31, 463–465.

Lester, D. Are there unique features of suicide in adults of different ages and different developmental stages? *Omega*, 1994p, 29, 337–348.

Lester, D. Suicide rates in birth cohorts in England and Wales. *Perceptual & Motor Skills*, 1995a, 81, 1146.

Lester, D. Suicide rates in Canadian prisons. *Perceptual & Motor Skills*, 1995b, 81, 1230.

Lester, D. Suicide rates in Canadian aboriginals and size of population. *Perceptual & Motor Skills*, 1995c, 81, 1282.

Lester, D. Suicide and homicide among Native Americans. *Psychological Reports*, 1995d, 77, 10.

Lester, D. Domestic terror and rates of suicide and homicide in Canada, 1960–1985. *Psychological Reports*, 1995e, 77, 42.

Lester, D. Intelligence and suicide in Ireland and the United Kingdom. *Psychological Reports*, 1995f, 77, 122.

Lester, D. War and suicide in France, 1850–1913. *Psychological Reports*, 1995g, 77, 130.

Lester, D. Suicide and abortion. *Irish Journal of Psychological Medicine*, 1995h, 12, 119.

Lester, D. Height and mortality. *Annals of Human Biology*, 1995i, 22, 347.

Lester, D. American Indian suicide and homicide rates and unemployment. *Perceptual*

& Motor Skills, 1996a, 83, 1170.

Lester, D. Height, gross domestic product, and suicide and homicide. *Perceptual & Motor Skills*, 1996b, 83, 1182.

Lester, D. Applying the concept of national character to states within a nation. *Personality & Individual Differences*, 1996c, 21, 1055–1057.

Lester, D. Seasonal depression and suicide. *Perceptual & Motor Skills*, 1997a, 85, 286.

Lester, D. Anxiety, economic growth, and suicide and homicide. *Perceptual & Motor Skills*, 1997b, 85, 382.

Lester, D. Economic development, suicide, and homicide. *Perceptual & Motor Skills*, 1997c, 85, 458.

Lester, D. Welfare and suicide in 18 affluent capitalist democracies. *Perceptual & Motor Skills*, 1997d, 85, 642.

Lester, D. Social characteristics of states which do not prohibit assisted-suicide. *Perceptual & Motor Skills*, 1997e, 85, 654.

Lester, D. The sex ratio in American Indian suicides. *Psychological Reports*, 1997f, 81, 506.

Lester, D. Marriage, remarriage, suicide, and homicide in America. *Psychological Reports*, 1997g, 81, 1082.

Lester, D. Unemployment and suicide in American Indian youth in New Mexico. *Psychological Reports*, 1997h, 81, 58.

Lester, D. Tryptophan and suicide. *Psychological Reports*, 1997i, 81, 234.

Lester, D. *Suicide in American Indians.* Commack, NY: Nova Science, 1997j.

Lester, D. The effectiveness of suicide-prevention centers. *Suicide & Life-Threatening Behavior*, 1997k, 27, 304–310.

Lester, D. *Suicide in African Americans.* Commack, NY: Nova Science, 1998.

Lester, D., & Akande, A. Patterns of depression in Xhosa and Yoruba students. *Journal of Social Psychology*, 1997, 137, 782–783.

Lester, D., & Anderson, D. Depression and suicidal ideation in African-American and Hispanic-American high school students. *Psychological Reports*, 1992, 71, 618.

Lester, D., & Ausenda, G. Suicide and homicide as indicators of social stress leading up to war. *Peace Research*, 1992, 24(1), 57–63.

Lester, D., & Danto, B. L. *Suicide behind bars.* Philadelphia: Charles Press, 1993.

Lester, D., & Frank, M. L. Suicide and homicide in rural areas. *Psychological Reports*, 1990, 66, 426.

Lester, D., & Lynn, R. National character and suicide. *Personality & Individual Differences*, 1993, 14, 853–855.

Lester, D., & Wilson, C. Teenage suicide in Zimbabwe. *Adolescence*, 1990, 25, 807–809.

Lester, D., & Yang, B. The effect of war on personal aggression. *Medicine & War*, 1991a, 7, 215–217.

Lester, D., & Yang, B. Association between war and suicide and homicide. *Psychological Reports*, 1991b, 68, 1030.

Lester, D., & Yang, B. Fertility and suicide rates. *Journal of Biosocial Science*, 1992a, 24, 97–101.

Lester, D., & Yang, B. Social and economic correlates of the elderly suicide rate. *Suicide & Life-Threatening Behavior*, 1992b, 22, 36–47.

Lester, D., & Yang, B. Anticipating the impact of the high rate of unemployment in Eastern Europe. *Current Politics & Economics of Europe*, 1993, 3, 33–35.

Lester, D., & Yang, B. *The economy and suicide.* Commack, NY: Nova Science, 1997.

Li, G. The interaction effect of bereavement and sex on the risk of suicide in the elderly. *Social Science & Medicine*, 1995, 40, 825–828.

Liebling, A. Suicides in young prisoners. *Death Studies*, 1993, 17, 381–409.

Liebling, A. Suicide amongst prisoners. *Howard Journal of Criminal Justice*, 1994, 33(1), 1–9.

Liebling, A. Vulnerability and prison suicide. *British Journal of Criminology*, 1995, 35, 173–187.

Lim, L. C., & Ang, Y. G. Parasuicide in male conscripts. *Military Medicine*, 1992, 157, 401–404.

Lindeman, S. Are psychiatrists more prone to suicide than other specialists? *Psychiatria Fennica*, 1996, 28, 34–41.

Lindeman, S., Laara, E., Hakko, H., & Lonnqvist, J. A systematic review on gender-specific suicide mortality in medical doctors. *British Journal of Psychiatry*, 1996, 168, 274–279.

Lindeman, S., Laara, E., Hirvonen, J., & Lonnqvist, J. Suicide mortality among medical doctors in Finland. *Psychological Medicine*,

1997a, 27, 1219–1222.

Lindeman, S., Laara, E., Vuori, E., & Lonnqvist, J. Suicides among physicians, engineers, and teachers. *Acta Psychiatrica Scandinavica*, 1997b, 96, 68–71.

Liu, T., & Waterbor, J. W. Comparison of suicide rates among industrial groups. *American Journal of Industrial Medicine*, 1994, 25, 197–203.

Lyster, G., & Youssef, H. Attempted suicide in a catchment area of Ireland. *European Journal of Psychiatry*, 1995, 9, 22–27.

Mace, D. E., Rohde, P., & Gnau, V. Psychological patterns of depression and suicidal behavior of adolescents in a juvenile detention facility. *Journal for Juvenile Justice & Detention Services*, 1997, 12(1), 18–23.

Malchy, B., Enns, M. W., Young, T. K., & Cox, B. J. Suicide among Manitoba's aboriginal people, 1988–1994. *Canadian Medical Association Journal*, 1997, 156, 1133–1138.

Malmberg, A., Hawton, K., & Simkin, S. A study of farmers in England and Wales. *Journal of Psychosomatic Research*, 1997, 43, 107–111.

Mao, Y., Moloughney, B. W., Semeniciw, R. M., & Morrison, H. I. Indian reserve and registered Indian mortality in Canada. *Canadian Journal of Public Health*, 1992, 83, 350–353.

Marttunen, M., Henriksson, M., Pelkonen, S., Schroderus, M., & Lonnqvist, J. Suicide among military conscripts in Finland. *Military Medicine*, 1997, 162, 14–18.

Maruschak, L. HIV in prisons and jails, 1995. *Bureau of Justice Statistics Bulletin*, 1997, August, NCJ-164260.

Mastekaasa, A. Marital status and subjective well-being. *Social Indicators Research*, 1993, 29, 249–276.

Mastekaasa, A. Age variations in the suicide rates and self-reported subjective well-being of married and never married persons. *Journal of Community & Applied Social Psychology*, 1995, 5(1), 21–39.

Maurer, J. D., Rosenberg, H. M., & Keemer, J. B. *Deaths of Hispanic origin, 15 reporting states, 1979–1981*. Hyattsville, MD: National Center for Health Statistics, PHS 91-1855, 1990.

May, P. A., & Van Winkle, N. Indian adolescent suicide. *American Indian & Alaska Native Mental Health Research*, 1994, 4, monograph, 5–34.

Mays, G. L., & Thompson, J. A. Mayberry revisited. *Justice Quarterly*, 1988, 5, 421–440.

McCann, S. J. H., & Stewin, L. L. Good and bad years. *Journal of Psychology*, 1990, 124, 601–617.

McCord, C., & Freeman, H. P. Excess mortality in Harlem. *New England Journal of Medicine*, 1990, 322, 173–177.

McHugh, M. J. Managing suicidal behavior among the prison population. *Journal of the Royal Society of Health*, 1995, 115, 117–119.

Mehleim, L. Attempted suicide in the armed forces. *Military Medicine*, 1990, 155, 596–600.

Mehlum, L. Positive and negative consequences of serving in a UN peace-keeping mission. *Revue Internationale des Services de Santé des Forces Armées*, 1995, 68, 289–295.

Merrill, J., & Owens, J. Age and attempted suicide. *Acta Psychiatrica Scandinavica*, 1990, 82, 385–388.

Micciolo, R., Williams, P., Zimmerman-Tansella, C., & Tansella, M. Geographical and urban-rural variation in the seasonality of suicide. *Journal of Affective Disorders*, 1991, 21, 39–43.

Miller, J. M., & Beaumont, J. J. Suicide, cancer, and other causes of death among Californian veterinarians, 1960–1992. *American Journal of Industrial Medicine*, 1995, 27, 37–49.

Moesler, T. A., Pontzen, W., & Rummler, W. The relationship between suicidal acts and unemployment. In G. Ferrari, M. Bellini & P. Crepet (Eds.), *Suicidal behavior and risk factors*. Bologna: Monduzzi-Editore, 1990, 189–193.

Moesler, T. A., Rummler, W., Holl, R., & Lungershausen, E. Correlations between suicidal actions and unemployment in the period between 1976 and 1985 in the municipal area of Nurnberg. *Psychiatria Danubina*, 1991, 3, 322–325.

Mokhovikov, A. N. *Suicide and telecare in the post-totalitarian society*. Kiev: privately published, 1995.

Moksony, F. Victims of change or victims of backwardness. *Szociologiai Szemle (Review of Sociology)*, 1995, special issue, 105–114.

Morrell, S., Taylor, R., Quine, S., & Kerr, C.

Suicide and unemployment in Australia 1907–1990. *Social Science & Medicine*, 1993, 36, 749–756.

Morrison, S. Custodial suicide in Australia. Medicine, *Science & the Law*, 1996, 36, 167–177.

Neeleman, J., Jones, P., Van Os, J., & Murray, R. M. Parasuicide in Camberwell. *Social Psychiatry & Psychiatric Epidemiology*, 1996, 31, 284–287.

Niemi, T., & Lonnqvist, J. Suicides among university students in Finland. *Journal of American College Health*, 1993, 42(2), 64–66.

Norton, G. R., Rockman, G. E., Malan, J., Cox, B. J., & Hewitt, P. L. Panic attacks, chemical abuse, and suicidal ideation. *Alcoholism Treatment Quarterly*, 1995, 13(3), 33–41.

Notkola, V. J., Marlikainen, P., & Leino, P. I. Time trends in mortality in forestry and construction workers in Finland 1970–85 and impact of adjustment for socioeconomic variables. *Journal of Epidemiology & Community Health*, 1993, 47, 186–193.

Olkinuora, M., Asp, S., Juntunen, J., Kauttu, K., Strid, L., & Aarimaa, M. Stress symptoms, burnout, and suicidal thoughts in Finnish physicians. *Social Psychiatry & Psychiatric Epidemiology*, 1990, 25, 81–86.

Olkinuora, M., Asp, S., Juntunen, J., Kauttu, K., Strid, L., & Aarimaa, M. Stress symptoms, burn out, and suicidal thoughts of Finnish physicians. *Scandinavian Journal of Work & Environmental Health*, 1992, 18, S2, 110–112.

Olsson, M., & Wasserman, D. The family. In T. Bjerke & T. C. Stiles (Eds.), *Suicide attempts in Nordic countries*. Trondheim: Tapir Forlag, 1991, 121–129.

Osgood, N. J., & Brant, B. A. Suicidal behavior in long-term care facilities. *Suicide & Life-Threatening Behavior*, 1990, 20, 113–122.

Ostamo, A., & Lonnqvist, J. Parasuicides in four catchment areas in Finland. In T. Bjerke & T. C. Stiles (Eds.), *Suicide attempts in Nordic countries*. Trondheim: Tapir Forlag, 1991, 57–68.

Ostamo, A., Lonnqvist, J., Heinonen, S., Leppavuori, A., Liikkanen, A., Marttila, M., & Monkkonen, J. Epidemiology of parasuicides in Finland. *Psychiatria Fennica*, 1991, 22, 181–189.

O'Toole, B. I., & Cantor, C. Suicide risk factors among Australian Vietnam era draftees. *Suicide & Life-Threatening Behavior*, 1995, 25, 475–488.

Partonen, T., Schroderus, M., Henriksson, M., Aro, H., & Lonnqvist, J. Suicide among draftees. *Military Medicine*, 1994, 159, 299–301.

Patel, S. P., & Gaw, A. C. Suicide among immigrants from the Indian subcontinent. *Psychiatric Services*, 1996, 47, 517–521.

Pearson, V. A. Suicide in North and West Devon. *Journal of Public Health Medicine*, 1993, 15, 320–326.

Peipins, L. A., Burnett, C., Alterman, T., & Lalich, N. Mortality patterns among female nurses. *American Journal of Public Health*, 1997, 87, 1539–1543.

Peng, K. L., & Choo, A. A. Suicide and parasuicide in Singapore. *Medicine, Science & the Law*, 1990, 30, 225–233.

Peng, K. L., & Choo, A. A. Suicide in Singapore. *Australian & New Zealand Journal of Psychiatry*, 1992, 26, 599–608.

Pickett, W., Davidson, J. R., & Brison, R. J. Suicides on Ontario farms. *Canadian Journal of Public Health*, 1993, 84, 226–230.

Platt, S., & Kreitman, N. Long-term trends in parasuicide and unemployment in Edinburgh 1968–1987. *Social Psychiatry & Psychiatric Epidemiology*, 1990, 25, 56–61.

Platt, S., Micciolo, R., & Tansella. M. Suicide and unemployment in Italy. *Social Science & Medicine*, 1992a, 34, 1191–1201.

Platt, S., Micciolo, R., & Tansella. M. Suicide and unemployment in Italy. In P. Crepet, G. Ferrari, S. Platt & M. Bellini (Eds.), *Suicide behaviour in Europe*. Rome: John Libbey, 1992b, 63–77.

Pollack, D. A., Rhodes, P., Boyle, C. A., Decoufle, P., & McGee, D. L. Estimating the number of suicides among Vietnam veterans. *American Journal of Psychiatry*, 1990, 147, 772–776.

Pollock, L. R., Vesey, P., Hollis, J., & Williams, J. M. Suicide in rural Britain. *Lancet*, 1996, 347, 403–404.

Ponizovsky, A., Safro, S., Ginath, Y., & Ritsner, M. Suicide ideation among recent immigrants. *Israel Journal of Psychiatry*, 1997, 34, 139–148.

Power, K., McElroy, J., & Swanson, V.

Coping abilities and prisoners' perceptions of suicidal risk management. *Howard Journal,* 1997, 36, 378–392.

Power, K. G., & Moodie, E. Characteristics and management of prisoners at risk of suicide behavior. *Archives of Suicide Research,* 1997, 3, 109–123.

Pritchard, C. Suicide, unemployment, and gender variations in the Western World 1964–1986. *Social Psychiatry & Psychiatric Epidemiology,* 1990, 25, 73–80.

Pritchard, C. Is there a link between suicide in young men and unemployment? *British Journal of Psychiatry,* 1992, 160, 750–756.

Pritchard, C., Cox, M., & Dawson, A. Suicide and violent death in a six-year-cohort of male probationers compared with pattern of mortality in the general population. *Journal of the Royal Society of Health,* 1997, 117, 180–185.

Ragland, J. D., & Berman, A. L. Farm crisis and suicide. *Omega,* 1990–1991, 22, 173–185.

Raleigh, V. S. Suicide patterns and trends in people of Indian subcontinent and Caribbean origin in England and Wales. *Ethnicity & Health,* 1996, 1, 55–63.

Raleigh, V. S., & Balarajan, R. Suicide and self-burning among Indians and West Indians in England and Wales. *British Journal of Psychiatry,* 1992, 161, 365–368.

Raleigh, V. S, Bulusu, L., & Balarajan, R. Suicides among immigrants from the Indian subcontinent. *British Journal of Psychiatry,* 1990, 156, 46–50.

Reser, J. P. Australian aboriginal suicide deaths in custody. *Australian Psychologist,* 1989, 24, 325–342.

Reynolds, W. M., Measurement of suicidal ideation in adolescents. In D. Lester (Ed.), *Suicide '92.* Denver: AAS, 1992, 230–232.

Rosenberg, H. M., Burnett, C., Maurer, J., & Spiritas, R. Mortality by occupation, industry, and cause of death. *Monthly Vital Statistics Reports,* 1993, 42(4), Supplement 9/30.

Rothberg, J. M. Stress and suicide in the US Army. *Armed Forces & Society,* 1991, 17, 449–458.

Rothberg, J. M., Fagan, J., & Shaw, J. Suicide in US Army personnel, 1985–1986. *Military Medicine,* 1990, 155, 452–456.

Rubenstein, D. H. Suicide in Micronesia and Samoa. *Pacific Studies,* 1992, 15(1), 51–75.

Salive, M. E., Smith, G. S., & Brewer, T. F. Death in prison. *American Journal of Public Health,* 1990, 80, 1479–1480.

Sangiorgi, R., Destro, E., Finotti, L., Pinotti, A., & Stella, S. Suicidary behavior in Rovigo district from 1975 to 1984. In G. Ferrari, M. Bellini & P. Crepet (Eds.), *Suicidal behavior and risk factors.* Bologna: Monduzzi-Editore, 1990, 243–248.

Saucier, P. R. Education and suicide. *Psychological Reports,* 1993, 73, 637–638.

Schlicht, S. M., Gordon, G. J., Ball, J. R. B., & Christie, D. G. S. Suicide and related deaths in Victorian doctors. *Medical Journal of Australia,* 1990, 153, 518–521.

Schneider, D., & Greenberg, M. Violence. *New Jersey Medicine,* 1994, 91, 855–858.

Schroderus, M., Lonnqvist, J. K., & Aro, H. M. Trends in suicide rates among military conscripts. *Acta Psychiatrica Scandinavica,* 1992, 86, 233–235.

Schwartz, A. J. The epidemiology of suicide among students at colleges and universities in the US. *Journal of College Student Psychotherapy,* 1990, 4(3–4), 25–44.

Schweitzer, R., Klayich, M., & McLean, J. Suicidal ideation and behavior among university students in Australia. *Australian & New Zealand Journal of Psychiatry,* 1995, 29, 473–479.

Seagrott, V., & Rooney, C. Suicide in doctors. *British Medical Journal,* 1993, 307, 447.

Sentell, J. W., Lacroix, M., Sentell, J. V., & Finstuen, K. Predictive patterns of suicidal behavior. *Military Medicine,* 1997, 162, 168–171.

Shiang, J., Blinn, R., Bongar, B., Stephens, B., Allison, D., & Schatzberg, A. Suicide in San Francisco, California. *Suicide & Life-Threatening Behavior,* 1997, 27, 80–91.

Sibthorpe, B., Drinkwater, J., Gardner, K., & Bammer, G. Drug use, binge drinking, and attempted suicide among homeless and potentially homeless youth. *Australian & New Zealand Journal of Psychiatry,* 1995, 29, 248–256.

Sievers, M. L., Nelson, R. G., & Bennett, P. H. Adverse mortality experience of a southwestern American Indian community. *Journal of Clinical Epidemiology,* 1990, 43, 1231–1242.

Sigurdson, E., Staley, D., Matas, M.,

Holdahl, K., & Squair, K. A five-year review of youth suicide in Manitoba. *Canadian Journal of Psychiatry*, 1994, 39, 397–403.

Silverman, M. Campus student suicide rates. *Suicide & Life-Threatening Behavior*, 1993, 23, 329–342.

Silverman, M., Meyer, P. M., Sloan, F., Raffel, M., & Pratt, D. M. The Big Ten student suicide study. *Suicide & Life-Threatening Behavior*, 1997, 27, 285–303.

Simpson, A., & Ng, M. L. Deliberate self-harm of Filipino immigrants in Hong Kong. *Psychologia*, 1992, 35(2), 117–120.

Skegg, K., & Cox, B. Impact of psychiatric services on prison suicide. *Lancet*, 1991, 338, 1436–1438.

Skegg, K., & Cox, B. Suicide in custody. *New Zealand Medical Journal*, 1993, 106, 1–3.

Skegg, K., Cox, B., & Broughton, J. Suicide among New Zealand Maori. *Acta Psychiatrica Scandinavica*, 1995, 92, 453–459.

Skorupan, V., Petrovecki, V., & Skavic, J. Suicide epidemiology before and during the war in Croatia. *Croatian Medical Journal*, 1997, 38(1), 59–63.

Smith, R. R., Lombardo, V. S., & Ranson, J. T. Warden's proximity in relation to disciplinary infractions and attempted suicides. *Journal of Offender Rehabilitation*, 1996, 23(1/2), 37–48.

Smyth, N. J., & Ivanoff, A. Maladaptation and prison environmental preferences among inmate parasuicides. *Journal of Offender Rehabilitation*, 1994, 20, 131–146.

Snyder, M. L. Japanese male suicide before and after retirement. *Psychology*, 1990, 27(2), 47–52.

Snyder, M. L. Unemployment and suicide in Northern Ireland. *Psychological Reports*, 1992, 70, 1116–1118.

Somasundaram, D. J., & Rajadurai, S. War and suicide in northern Sri Lanka. *Acta Psychiatrica Scandinavica*, 1995, 91, 1–4.

Sorenson, S. B., & Shen, H. Youth suicide trends in California. *Suicide & Life-Threatening Behavior*, 1996, 26, 143–154.

Spinellis, C. D., & Themeli, O. Suicide in Greek prisons. *Crisis*, 1997, 18, 152–156.

Stack, S. New micro-level data on the impact of divorce on suicide, 1959–1980. *Journal of*

Marriage & the Family, 1990, 52, 119–127.

Stack, S. Gender and suicide among laborers. *Archives of Suicide Research*, 1995a, 1, 19–26.

Stack, S. Suicide risk among laborers. *Sociological Focus*, 1995b, 28, 197–199.

Stack, S. Suicide risk among dentists. *Deviant Behavior*, 1996a, 17, 107–117.

Stack, S. Gender and suicide risk among artists. *Suicide & Life-Threatening Behavior*, 1996b, 26, 374–379.

Stack, S. Suicide among artists. *Journal of Social Psychology*, 1997a, 137, 129–130.

Stack, S. Suicide in Memphis. In J. McIntosh (Ed.), *Suicide '97*. Washington, DC: AAS, 1997b, 150–153.

Stack, S., & Gundlach, J. The effect of country music on suicide. *Social Forces*, 1992, 71, 211–218.

Stack, S., & Gundlach, J. Country music and suicide. *Social Forces*, 1995, 74, 331–335.

Stack, S., & Kelly, T. Police suicide. *American Journal of Police*, 1994, 13(4), 73–90.

Stack, S., & Tsoudis, O. Suicide risk among correctional officers. *Archives of Suicide Research*, 1997, 3, 183–186.

Stack, S., & Wasserman, I. The effect of religion on suicide ideology. *Journal for the Scientific Study of Religion*, 1992, 31, 457–466.

Stack, S., & Wasserman, I. Marital status, alcohol consumption, and suicide. *Journal of Marriage & the Family*, 1993, 55, 1018–1024.

Stallones, L. Suicide mortality among Kentucky farmers, 1979–1985. *Suicide & Life-Threatening Behavior*, 1990, 20, 156–163.

Stefansson, C. G., & Wicks, S. Health care occupations and suicide in Sweden 1961–1985. *Social Psychiatry & Psychiatric Epidemiology*, 1991, 26, 259–264.

Stellman, S. D. Proportional mortality ratios among Korean immigrants to New York City, 1986–1990. *Yonsei Medical Journal*, 1996, 37(1), 31–37.

Strachan, J., Johansen, H., Nair, C., & Nargundkar, M. Canadian suicide mortality rates. *Health Reports*, 1990, 2, 327–341.

Terry, T. L., Kang, H. K., & Dalager, N. A. Mortality among women veterans, 1973–1987. *American Journal of Epidemiology*, 1991, 134, 973–980.

Trovato, F. Suicide and ethnic factors in Canada. *International Journal of Social Psychiatry*, 1986, 32(3), 55–64.

Trovato, F. Sex, marital status, and suicide in Canada. *Sociological Perspectives*, 1991, 34, 427–445.

Trovato, F. Violent and accidental mortality among four immigrant groups in Canada 1970–1972. *Social Biology*, 1992, 39, 82–101.

Valkonen, T., & Martelin, T. Occupational class and suicide. *Helsingin Yliopiston Sociologian Laitoksen*, 1988, #222.

Van Winkle, N. W., & May, P. A. An update on American Indian suicide in New Mexico, 1980–1987. *Human Organization*, 1993, 52, 304–315.

Van Zyl, A. The role of depression and biochemical aspects of suicidal behavior. In L. Schlebusch (Ed.), *Suicidal behaviour*. Durban: University of Natal, 1988, 44–60.

Varnik, A., & Wasserman, D. Suicides in the former Soviet Republics. *Acta Psychiatrica Scandinavica*, 1992, 86, 76–78.

Veenhoven, R. *Happiness in nations*. Rotterdam: Erasmus University, 1993.

Velamoor, V. R., & Cernovsky, Z. Unemployment and the nature of suicide attempts. *Psychiatric Journal of the University of Ottawa*, 1990, 15, 162–164.

Viinamak, H., Kontula, O., Niskanen, L., & Koskela, K. The association between economic and social factors and mental health in Finland. *Acta Psychiatrica Scandinavica*, 1995, 92, 208–213.

Violanti, J. M. Trends in police suicide. *Psychological Reports*, 1995, 77, 688–690.

Violanti, J. M., Vena, J. E., & Marshall, J. R. Suicides, homicides, and accidental death. *American Journal of Industrial Medicine*, 1996, 30, 99–104.

Vrankovic, D., Splavski, B., Hecimovic, I., Mursic, B., Blagus, G., & Kraus, Z. Incidence and outcome of self-inflicted gunshot wounds to the head in peace and war. *Journal of Neurology, Neurosurgery & Psychiatry*, 1996, 61, 654.

Wasserman, D., & Eklund, G. A study of socio-demographic factors in an unselected parasuicide population in Stockholm. In T. Bjerke & T. C. Stiles (Eds.), *Suicide attempts in the Nordic countries*. Trondheim: Tapir Forlag, 1991, 79–89.

Wasserman, D., Varnik, A., & Eklund, G. Male suicides and alcohol consumption in the former USSR. *Acta Psychiatrica Scandinavica*, 1994, 89, 306–313.

Wasserman, I. M. Age, period, and cohort effects in suicide behavior in the United States and Canada in the 20th Century. *Journal of Aging Studies*, 1989, 3, 295–311.

Watanabe, N., Hasegawa, K., & Yoshinaga, Y. Suicide in later life in Japan. *International Psychogeriatrics*, 1995, 7, 253–261.

Wolf, M. Women and suicide in China. In M. Wolff & R. Witke (Eds.), *Women in Chinese society*. Palo Alto: Stanford University, 1975, 111–141.

Wooldredge, J. D., & Winfree, L. T. An aggregate-level study of inmate suicides and deaths due to natural causes in US jails. *Journal of Research on Crime & Delinquency*, 1992, 29, 466–479.

Yamamoto, T. Contemporary social problems in Japan. *International Journal of Japanese Sociology*, 1992, 1(October), 19–33.

Yang, B., & Lester, D. The misery index and an index of misery. *Atlantic Economic Journal*, 1992, 20(3), 98.

Yang, B., & Lester, D. Does unemployment have a greater social impact on men than on women? *Atlantic Economic Journal*, 1996, 24, 380.

Yang, B., & Lester, D. War and rates of personal violence. *Journal of Social Psychology*, 1997, 137, 131–132.

Young, T. J. Poverty, suicide, and homicide among Native Americans. *Psychological Reports*, 1990, 67, 1153–1154.

Young, T. J. Medical resources, suicide, and homicide among Native Americans. *Corrective & Social Psychiatry*, 1991a, 37(3), 47–49.

Young, T. J. Regional suicide rates among prisoners in the United States. *Research Communications in Psychology, Psychiatry & Behavior*, 1991b, 16(1/2), 90–92.

Young, T. J. Native Americans and the constant death instinct hypothesis. *Perceptual & Motor Skills*, 1991c, 72, 814.

Young, T. J. Suicide and homicide among Native Americans. *Psychological Reports*, 1991d,

68, 1137–1138.

Young, T. J. Household size, suicide, and homicide among American Indians. *International Journal of Comparative & Applied Criminal Justice*, 1992a, 16, 125–127.

Young, T. J. Mortality rates and aggression management among Native Americans. *Psychological Reports*, 1992b, 70, 665–666.

Young, T. J., & French, L. A. Suicide and social status among Native Americans. *Psychological Reports*, 1992, 73, 461–462.

Young, T. J., & French, L. Status integration and suicide among Native American women. *Social Behavior & Personality*, 1995, 23, 155–157.

Young, T. J., & French, L. Suicide and homicide rates among US Indian Health Service Areas. *Social Behavior & Personality*, 1996, 24, 365–366.

Zhai, S. T., Zhang, H. B., Yin, S. C., Liu, Z. L., Chi, W. H., Wu, J. H., Tong, H. D., & Fan, Z. L. *Epidemiological investigation on suicide rate for college students*. 17th Congress of the International Association for Suicide Prevention, Montreal, 1993.

Zitzow, D., & Desjarlait, F. A study of suicide attempts comparing adolescents to adults on a Northern Plains American Indian reservation. *American Indian & Alaska Native Mental Health Research*, 1994, 4, Monograph, 35–69.

Zonda, T., & Lester, D. Suicide among Hungarian Gypsies. *Acta Psychiatrica Scandinavica*, 1990, 82, 381–382.

Zwerling, C., Burmeister, L. F., & Jensen, C. M. Injury mortality among Iowa farmers, 1980–1988. *American Journal of Epidemiology*, 1995, 141, 878–882.

Chapter 8

THE VARIATION OF SUICIDE OVER TIME

Hour of Day

Attempted Suicide

Caracciolo et al. (1990) found that self-poisoners seen at an emergency department in a region of Italy who used opiates (with lower suicidal intent) peaked at 8:30 p.m. while those using other substances (with higher suicidal intent) peaked at 6:30 p.m. Manfredini et al. (1994) reported the peak for self-poisoning to be from 8 p.m. to 9 p.m. Caracciolo et al. (1996) found that suicide attempts peaked at noon to 6 p.m. and 6 p.m. to midnight, for both sexes, all methods, first-timers and repeaters, and all diagnoses. Bilora et al. (1995) found that attempted suicides and heroin overdoses peaked at similar times in the evening – 6:30 p.m. and 7:30 p.m. respectively.

Motohashi (1990) studied suicide attempts in Tokyo for 1978–1985 and found a 24 hour rhythm, with a trough at 3–5 a.m. and a peak at 6–7 p.m. In one county in Sweden, Salander-Renberg and Jacobsson (1991) found that attempted suicides peaked at 6 p.m. to midnight. In Dublin, Ireland, Coakley et al. (1994) found that attempted suicide by poison peaked between 6 p.m. and 6 a.m. Buchanan (1991) found that attempted suicides in New Zealand occurred more often in the evening hours.

In South Africa, Schlebusch (1988) found that attempted suicides peaked at 8 p.m. In Sofia (Bulgaria), Milev and Mikhov (1992) found that attempted suicides by poisoning peaked from 8 p.m. to midnight.

Leikin et al. (1994) found that suicidal calls to a poison control center peaked at 8 p.m. to 10 p.m., but the peak varied by age. For those over the age of 50, the peak was at 11 a.m. In Hawaii, Nakamura et al. (1994) found that adolescent attempts peaked at 4 p.m. to 8 p.m.

Completed Suicide

Maldonado and Kraus (1991) found that female suicides peaked during noon to 4 p.m. in 1945–1964 in Sacramento County (CA) and during 8 p.m. to midnight for 1965–1983. The trough for both sexes and all ages was 4 a.m. to 8 a.m. Rocco et al. (1994) found no differences in the hour of day for completed and attempted suicides in Italy. Gallerani et al. (1996) found that in one region of Italy, the time of the act (not the death) peaked in late morning/early afternoon for both men and women.

Day

In West Berlin in 1988, Bohning et al. (1992) found that the daily count of suicides did not fit a simple Poisson distribution, but did fit a mixed Poisson distribution (two

Poisson distributions combined).

Day of Week

Completed Suicide

In the United States as a whole from 1973–1985, McCleary et al. (1991) found that suicides peaked on Mondays, especially the middle-aged suicides. In 22 counties with a high proportion of African Americans, Greenberg and Schneider (1992) reported that suicides in those aged 15–24 peaked on Tuesdays for white males, Thursdays for black males, Mondays for white females and Mondays/Fridays for black females. None of these peaks were statistically significant. In the United States, Chew and McCleary (1994) found peaks in suicide on Monday, but they noted that these trends differed in strength by age and sex. For example, the Monday peak was strongest in men aged 55–60. Rothberg et al. (1990) found that United States Army suicides in 1985–1986 peaked on Thursdays.

Maldonado and Kraus (1991) found a Monday peak and Friday trough for suicides in Sacramento County (CA) for 1925–1983, with variations by sex and age. In New Jersey 1940–1990, Schneider and Greenberg (1994) found a peak on Mondays, with males also showing a secondary peak on Saturdays. On the other hand, Campbell and Lester (1996) found no variation by day of week in Baton Rouge (Louisiana), while Panser et al. (1995) found no daily variation in a small sample of suicides in Minnesota.

In Singapore, Chia (1981) found that completed suicides tended to peak on Mondays and Thursdays. In Australia, Hassan (1994, 1995) found a Monday peak for suicides (weak in women), unless

Monday was a holiday, whereupon Tuesday was the peak; Hassan found a subsidiary peak on Fridays for women. On the other hand, Martin (1990) found no weekday effect in a sample of suicides from Saskatchewan (Canada) for 1984–1989.

In Finland, Pirkola et al. (1997) compared weekend and weekday suicides. The weekend suicides were less often unemployed, but only if they were alcohol abusers. For nonabusers, there were no differences.

Attempted Suicide

In South Africa, Schlebusch (1988) found that attempted suicides peaked on Sundays. In Sofia (Bulgaria), Milev and Mikhov (1992) found that attempted suicides by poisoning peaked on Wednesday and were lowest on Saturday.

For crisis calls, Noble (1996) found that in Portland (Oregon), calls with suicidal ideation peaked on Wednesdays, while calls involving attempted suicide peaked on Sundays. More suicidal ideators called on the 4th–6th of the month but fewer attempted suicides. In Hawaii, Nakamura et al. (1994) found that adolescent attempts peaked on Mondays and Tuesdays.

On the other hand, Anonymous (1992) found that attempted suicides did not vary by day of week in Belgium, while Buchanan (1991) found no variation over days of the week in a sample of attempted suicides in New Zealand.

Daylight Savings

Shapiro et al. (1990) found no differences in Scotland in the completed or attempted suicide rate the week before changes due to daylight savings time versus the week after.

Season

Completed Suicide

Lester and Frank (1990a, 1990b) found that the American suicide rate peaked in April and August in 1980. For large cities (population over one million) the peak was in March, for smaller cities there was no peak, and for rural areas the peaks were in April and July. The seasonal peaks were not greater in northern regions. However, the spring peak was found only for married persons. The seasonal variation by season was not associated with the gross state product per capita over the 48 states. Lester (1997a) found that native American suicides in the United States did not vary by month in 1980. Lester (1997b) found that the proportion of suicides in March–May in the states of the USA was not associated with latitude, longitude or social indicators. Lester (1993) found that the seasonality of suicide in the United States over time from 1957–1986 was not associated with economic growth, though the trend was negative.

In the United States, Chew and McCleary (1994) found peaks in suicide at the beginning of the month and in the spring, but they noted that these trends differed in strength by age and sex. McCleary et al. (1991) also reported that suicides peaked in the first week of each month, especially for elderly males. The peak month was during spring overall and for the elderly suicides, but teenage suicides peaked in winter.

Rothberg et al. (1990) found that United States Army suicides in 1985–1986 peaked in July. In New Jersey 1940–1990, Schneider and Greenberg (1994) found a peak in spring (March). Campbell and Lester (1996) found a winter peak (January to March) in Baton Rouge (Louisiana). On the other hand, Tietjen and Kripke (1994) found no seasonal variation in suicides in Los Angeles and

Sacramento counties, and Maldonado and Kraus (1991) found no variation by month for suicides in Sacramento County (CA) for 1925–1983.

In England in 1485–1715, MacDonald and Murphy (1990) found that suicide peaked in May. The peak varied by region a little, with a May peak in Norwich and a June peak in London in the 1700s. However, Nowers and Gunnell (1996) found no seasonal variation in suicides from the Clifton Suspension Bridge in England in recent times.

In one region of England, Salib (1997) found no monthly variation in elderly suicides, although the peak tended to be in the summer months. For all suicides, Salib and Gray (1997) found no effect from method on the seasonality of suicide.

Micciolo et al. (1991) found in Italy that the monthly variation in suicides was greater in men than in women and in rural than in urban areas. Males had one harmonic in the seasonality, while women had two harmonics. Preti (1997) found a spring peak for completed suicide in Italy, more so for males.

Martin (1990) found no monthly or seasonal effect in a sample of suicides from Saskatchewan (Canada) for 1984–1989.

Daradkeh (1989) found a peak in spring and summer for suicides in Jordan and a trough in February, October, and November. Sex and violent-versus-nonviolent method had nonsignificant effects on this pattern.

In Singapore, Chia (1981) found that completed suicides tended to peak in May, November, and July. Auer (1990) found that suicide by drowning in a region of Finland peaked in the summer. Kunz and Kunz (1997) found that Finnish suicides peaked in May.

In Belgium, Maes et al. (1993) found that violent suicides peaked in the spring, whereas nonviolent suicides showed no seasonal peak. The spring peak was found for men and women. The violent suicides were older and more were male. A spectral analysis showed rhythms for all suicides of 52, 24, 14.5, and 7.5 weeks and for violent suicides of 52 and 23 weeks.

In Bucharest (Romania), Panaitescu et al. (1993) found a peak in July (followed by April) and summer (followed by spring). The peak periods were August 2–12, followed by April 8–19 and July 6–11. These three periods were very hot and very windy.

In Israeli soldiers, Schreiber et al. (1993) found a winter peak in completed suicide, but no variation in attempted suicide. Attempted suicide by firearm peaked in winter, while other methods showed no variation by season.

In Australia, Hassan (1994, 1995) found that male suicides peaked in September/October/November (Australian spring) and female suicides peaked in August/September/December. However, in the Northern Territory in Australia, Cunningham and Condon (1995) found no spring peak overall in men. Those aged 35–49 had a spring peak, while those 15–34 had fewer than expected suicides in the spring.

In Hong Kong, Ho (1996) reported a peak in completed suicides in the months April to August. Ho et al. (1997) reported a single winter trough in both Hong Kong and Taiwan for both men and women, In Beijing, Zhang (1996) found a peak in August and June.

In Zimbabwe, Lester (1991) found that suicides peaked in November (spring) and January (summer), but this latter finding was probably due to registrations accumulating at the end of the year. The number of suicides per month was not associated with sex, age, marital status, or method for suicide. Flisher et al. (1997) found a peak in South Africa in January (and a trough in June). There were no differences in the pattern by age or sex, but the effect was stronger in blacks and coloureds.

Chew and McCleary (1995) looked at the spring peak in suicide in 28 nations. Canada had the smallest peak and Portugal the greatest peak. For 14 nations in 1980, the less-developed nations had lower suicide rates but a greater seasonality.

Attempted Suicide

Buchanan (1991) found no variation over the months in a sample of attempted suicides in New Zealand. In Edinburgh (Scotland), Masterton (1991) found that suicide attempts using poison had nonsignificant peaks in August and November for males and significant peaks in June and August for females. In England, Barker et al. (1994) found that female attempted suicides peaked in spring and summer and May/June, while men showed no variation.

In one county in Sweden, Salander-Renberg and Jacobsson (1991) found that attempted suicides peaked in April and October for men and in July and October for women.

In Dublin, Ireland, Coakley et al. (1994) found that attempted suicide by poison peaked in July and August, but for women only. In Israel, Iancu et al. (1997) found that attempted suicide by adolescents peaked in May. Preti (1997) found a spring peak for attempted suicide in Italy, more so for males. In South Africa, Schlebusch (1988) found that attempted suicides had a trough in summer (December–February). In Sofia (Bulgaria), Milev and Mikhov (1992) found that attempted suicides by poisoning peaked in March and were lowest in August. However, Anonymous (1992) found that attempted suicides did not vary by season in Belgium.

In Hawaii, Nakamura et al. (1994) found that adolescent attempts peaked in January, but not significantly. Leikin et al. (1994) analyzed calls to a poison control center. Suicidal calls peaked December to February for 13–19 year olds. For crisis calls, Noble (1996) found that in Portland (Oregon), calls with suicidal ideation peaked in December/January while calls involving attempted suicide peaked in March and July.

Serious suicide attempts in school children were found by Milman and Bennett (1996) to peak in April, May, and June and to be motivated by school problems.

Explanations

Maes et al. (1995) noted that the level of L-tryptophan (and also tyrosine and phenylalanine) in the blood was lower in the spring in normal people, and this seasonal variation might be the basis for the seasonal variation in suicide rates. They noted that the monthly violent suicide rate in Belgium (but not the nonviolent suicide rate) was inversely associated with this variation in normal L-tryptophan levels.

Births And Birthdays

Kettle et al. (1997) found that native Alaskan suicides were more often born in the summer than in other seasons, a phenomenon not found in other Alaskans or in three other states examined.

No association between death day and suicide day for completed suicides was found by Wasserman and Stack (1994) for elderly suicides in Ohio, by Panser et al. (1995) for a small sample of suicides in Minnesota, by Chuang and Huang (1996) for suicides in Taiwan, by Lester (1997c) for a sample of famous suicides, or by Nakamura et al. (1994) for adolescent attempted suicides in Hawaii.

Astrology

Klein (1992) compared completed suicides with injured people and found that the suicides were more likely to have cuspal birthdates or deathdates. Other astrological variables did not significantly differentiate the suicides. Lester (1994) found that samples of suicides had their death dates (but not their birth dates) more often on cuspal days.

Elections

From 1952–1984 in the United States, there were fewer suicides in Novembers with presidential elections (but not on the day of the election), as compared to other Novembers, regardless of the winning party (Lester, 1990b).

Steels (1993) noted that attempted suicide by poisoning fell after the general election Conservative victory in Nottingham (England), even though Nottingham voted for Labour.

Holidays

Completed Suicide

Panser et al. (1995) found no change in the suicide rate on national holidays in a small sample of suicides in Minnesota. Lester (1990a) did not find an excess of completed suicides on St. Valentine's Day in the United States, compared to the number on February 7th and February 21st.

Attempted Suicide

Buckley et al. (1994) found fewer than expected attempted suicides presenting at an Australian hospital on public holidays and the days immediately before and after and no excess on Fridays falling on the 13th. They did not, however, control for day of the week. Daradkeh (1992) found fewer attempted suicides during Ramadan in Jordan than in the months before and after that month.

Davenport and Birtle (1990) found an excess of attempted suicides presenting at a British emergency room on St. Valentine's Day and on Christmas Day, compared to February 7th and August 15th. Cullum et al. (1993) found a nonsignificant tendency for there to be more attempted suicides on St. Valentine's Day (versus February 7th and August 15th). Attempted suicides were less common on Christmas Day. The ages of the attempters were similar on all four days.

McGibben et al. (1992) looked at deliberate self-poisoning in adolescent school children in Coventry (England) and found more during the school term, but fewer during Christmas and summer holidays (and no significant difference for Easter). Proctor (1992) found lower admission rates for self-poisoning for 12–16 year olds during school holidays, with no differences between the different holidays.

In Hawaii, Nakamura et al. (1994) found that adolescent attempts did not differ on holidays, except that they were higher from January 1st to 7th.

Biorhythms

Lester (1990c) found no association of completed suicides with biorhythms.

Significant Ages

Phillips and Smith (1991) looked at suicides in California and found an excess of suicides aged 20, 25, 30, 35, etc. This was significant only for males and, among males, only for married males. No effect was found for motor vehicle deaths.

Racial Differences

In the United States, Stack (1995) found that the temporal distribution of completed suicide differed for whites and nonwhites. Nonwhite suicide peaked in March, white suicide in May; nonwhite suicide had a trough on Tuesdays and Thursdays; white suicide on Saturdays. Nonwhite suicide increased on national holidays, especially July 4th; white suicide decreased on holidays, except New Year's Day.

Theory

Francis (1990) correlated over the 12 months of the year the American monthly suicide rate and the monthly conception rate and found a negative correlation. Suicide rates were lower in months when conception was more common. Lester (1992) also found that in 1980 the months with most female suicides had the fewest conceptions (but no difference in the numbers of births). Francis thought that result confirmed Gabennesch's "failed promise" theory for the timing of suicide.

Discussion

Many studies appear on the timing of suicide, but there have been no meta-analyses of the studies to determine if there is consistency in the results. Only Chew and McCleary (1995) have studied these phenomena in a sample of nations. Furthermore, the research rarely proposes or tests any theories about the differences found. The study by Maes et al. (1995) on monthly variations in L-tryptophan and Gabennesch's "failed promise" hypothesis are the exceptions in this regard. More theorizing and testing of hypotheses are necessary before the timing of suicidal behavior can be considered to be of interest to suicidologists.

REFERENCES

Anonymous. Suicide attempts. *Weekly Epidemiological Record*, 1992, 67(25), 187–190.

Auer, A. Suicide by drowning in Uusimaa province in southern Finland. *Medicine, Science & the Law*, 1990, 30, 175–179.

Barker, A., Hawton, K., Fagg, J., & Jennison, C. Seasonal and weather factors in parasuicide. *British Journal of Psychiatry*, 1994, 165, 375–380.

Bilora, F., Vigna, G. B., Manfredini, R., Saccaro, G., Chiesci, M., & San Lorenzo, I. Circadian periodicity in suicidal behavior in opiate overdose syndrome. *Research Communications in Biological Psychology & Psychiatry*, 1995, 20(1–2), 63–68.

Bohning, D., Schlattmann, P., & Lindsay, B. G. Re "A statistical method for evaluating suicide clusters and implementing cluster surveillance." *American Journal of Epidemiology*, 1992, 135, 1310–1314.

Buchanan, W. J. A year of intentional self-poisoning in Christchurch. *New Zealand Medical Journal*, 1991, 104, 470–472.

Buckley, N. A., Dawson, A. H., & Whyte, I. M. There are days and moons and public holidays. *Medical Journal of Australia*, 1994, 161, 728.

Campbell, F., & Lester, D. The temporal distribution of suicides in Baton Rouge. *Perceptual & Motor Skills*, 1996, 83, 14.

Caracciolo, S., Manfredini, R., Gallerani, M., & Tugnoli, S. Circadian rhythm of para-suicide in relation to violence of method and concomitant mental disorder. *Acta Psychiatrica Scandinavica*, 1996, 93, 252–256.

Caracciolo, S., Manfredini, R., Tomelli, A., Conti, W., Govoni, M., Tosi, S. P., Pareschi, P. L., Fersini, C., Cicotti, A., & Molinari, S. Parasuicide by deliberate self-poisoning in the emergency department. In G. Ferrari, M. Bellini & P. Crepet (Eds.), *Suicidal behavior and risk factors*. Bologna: Monduzzi-Editore, 1990, 699–704.

Chew, K. S., & McCleary, R. A life course theory of suicide risk. *Suicide & Life-Threatening Behavior*, 1994, 24, 234–244.

Chew, K. S., & McCleary, R. The Spring peak in suicides. *Social Science & Medicine*, 1995, 40, 223–230.

Chia, B. H. *Suicidal behavior in Singapore*. Tokyo: Southeast Asian Medical Information Center, 1981.

Chuang, H. L., & Huang, W. C. Age, birthdays, and suicide in Taiwan. *Journal of Social Psychology*, 1996, 136, 659–660.

Coakley, F., Hayes, C., Fennell, J., & Johnson, Z. A study of deliberate self-poisoning in a Dublin hospital. *Irish Journal of Psychological Medicine*, 1994, 11, 70–72.

Cullum, S. J., Catalan, J., Berelowitz, K., O'Brien, S., Millington, H. T., & Preston, D. Deliberate self-harm and public holidays. *Crisis*, 1993, 14, 39–42.

Cunningham, J., & Condon, J. R. Is there a suicide season in the Northern Territory? *Medical Journal of Australia*, 1995, 163, 654–655.

Daradkeh, T. K. The seasonal variation of suicide in Jordan. *Jordan Medical Journal*, 1989, 23(1), 69–76.

Daradkeh, T. K. Parasuicide during Ramadan in Jordan. *Acta Psychiatrica Scandinavica*, 1992, 86, 253–254.

Davenport, S. M., & Birtle, J. Association between parasuicide and Saint Valentine's Day. *British Medical Journal*, 1990, 300, 783–784.

Flisher, A. J., Parry, C., Bradshaw, D., & Juritz, J. M. Seasonal variation of suicide in South Africa. *Psychiatry Research*, 1997, 66, 13–22.

Francis, R. G. Gabennesch's "failed promise" hypothesis and suicide. *International Social Science Review*, 1990, 65, 68–71.

Gallerani, M., Avato, F. M., Dal Monte, D., Caracciolo, S., Fersini, C., & Manfredini, R.

The time for suicide. *Psychological Medicine*, 1996, 26, 867–870.

Greenberg, M., & Schneider, D. Blue Thursday? *Public Health Reports*, 1992, 107, 264–268.

Hassan, R. Temporal variations in suicide occurrence in Australia. *Australian & New Zealand Journal of Sociology*, 1994, 30, 194–202.

Hassan, R. *Suicide explained.* Melbourne, Australia: Melbourne University Press, 1995.

Ho, T. P. Changing patterns of suicide in Hong Kong. *Social Psychiatry & Psychiatric Epidemiology*, 1996, 31, 235–240.

Ho, T. P., Chao, A., & Yip, P. Seasonal variation in suicides re-examined. *Acta Psychiatrica Scandinavica*, 1997, 95, 26–31.

Iancu, I., Laufer, N., Dannon, P. N., Zohar-Kadouch, R., Apter, A., & Zohar, J. A general hospital study of attempted suicide in adolescence. *Israel Journal of Psychiatry*, 1997, 34, 228–234.

Kettle, P. A., Collins, T., Sredy, M., & Bixler, E. O. Seasonal differences in suicide birth rate. *American Indian & Alaska Native Mental Health Research*, 1997, 8(1), 1–10.

Klein, S. Astrologically predictable patterns in work-related injuries. Doctoral dissertation, University for Humanistic Studies, San Diego, 1992.

Kunz, P. R., & Kunz, J. Depression and suicide in the dark months. *Perceptual & Motor Skills*, 1997, 84, 537–538.

Leikin, J. B., Morris, R. W., & Lipscomb, J. W. Periodicity of suicide attempts reported to a poison control center. *Veterinary & Human Toxicology*, 1994, 36, 415–417.

Lester, D. Suicide and homicide on St. Valentine's Day. *Perceptual & Motor Skills*, 1990a, 71, 994.

Lester, D. Suicide and presidential elections in the USA. *Psychological Reports*, 1990b, 67, 218.

Lester, D. Biorhythms and the timing of death. *Skeptical Inquirer*, 1990c, 14, 410–412.

Lester, D. The seasonal variation of suicide in Zimbabwe. *Perceptual & Motor Skills*, 1991, 73, 18.

Lester, D. Month of suicide and month of conception. *International Social Science Review*, 1992, 67(1), 13–14.

Lester, D. Seasonality in suicide and economic growth. *Perceptual & Motor Skills*, 1993, 77, 10.

Lester, D. Astrological cuspal days and births and deaths of suicides. *Perceptual & Motor Skills*, 1994, 78, 898.

Lester, D. Seasonal variation in American Indian suicide. *Perceptual & Motor Skills*, 1997a, 84, 46.

Lester, D. Spring peak in suicides. *Perceptual & Motor Skills*, 1997b, 85, 1058.

Lester, D. The birthday blues. *Perceptual & Motor Skills*, 1997c, 85, 1090.

Lester, D., & Frank, M. L. The seasonal variation in suicide in urban and rural areas. *Journal of Affective Disorders*, 1990a, 19, 171.

Lester, D., & Frank, M. L. The seasonal variation in suicide rates. *Perceptual & Motor Skills*, 1990b, 70, 57–58.

MacDonald, M., & Murphy, T. R. *Sleepless souls.* Oxford: Clarendon, 1990.

Maes, M., Cosyns, P., Meltzer, H. Y., De Meyer, F., & Peeters. D. Seasonality in violent suicide but not in nonviolent suicide or homicide. *American Journal of Psychiatry*, 1993, 150, 1380–1385.

Maes, M., Scharpe, S., Verkerk, P., D'Hondt, P., Peeters, D., Cosyns, P., Thompson, P., De Meyer, F., Wauters, A., & Neels, H. Seasonal variation in plasma L-tryptophan availability in healthy volunteers. *Archives of General Psychiatry*, 1995, 52, 937–946.

Maldonado, G., & Kraus, J. F. Variation in suicide occurrence by time of day, day of the week, month, and lunar phase. *Suicide & Life-Threatening Behavior*, 1991, 21, 174–187.

Manfredini, R., Gallerani, M., Caracciolo, S., Tomelli, A., Calo, G., & Fersini, C. Circadian variation in attempted suicide by deliberate self-poisoning. *British Medical Journal*, 1994, 309, 774–775.

Martin, S. J. Distal variables in a completed suicide population. Master's thesis, University of Saskatchewan, 1990.

Masterton, G. Monthly and seasonal variation in parasuicide. *British Journal of Psychiatry*, 1991, 158, 155–157.

McCleary, R., Chew, K. S., Hellsten, J. J., & Flynn-Bransford, M. Age- and sex-specific cycles in US suicides, 1973 to 1985. *American*

Journal of Public Health, 1991, 81, 1494–1497.

McGibben, L., Ballard, C. G., Handy, S., & Silveira, W. R. School attendance as a factor in deliberate self-poisoning by 12–15 year old adolescents. *British Medical Journal*, 1992, 304, 28.

Micciolo, R., Williams, P., Zimmerman-Tansella, C., & Tansella, M. Geographical and urban-rural variation in the seasonality of suicide. *Journal of Affective Disorders*, 1991, 21, 39–43.

Milev, V., & Mikhov, D. Attempted suicide by poisoning in the Sofia region. *British Journal of Psychiatry*, 1992, 160, 560–562.

Milman, D. H., & Bennett, A. A. School and seasonal affective disorder. *American Journal of Psychiatry*, 1996, 153, 849–850.

Motohashi, Y. Circadian variation in suicide attempts in Tokyo from 1978 to 1985. *Suicide & Life-Threatening Behavior*, 1990, 20, 352–361.

Nakamura, J. W., McLeod, C. R., & McDermott, J. F. Temporal variation in adolescent suicide attempts. *Suicide & Life-Threatening Behavior*, 1994, 24, 343–349.

Noble, R. Temporal fluctuation in suicide calls to a crisis intervention center. *Suicide & Life-Threatening Behavior*, 1996, 26, 415–423.

Nowers, M., & Gunnell, D. Suicide from the Clifton Suspension Bridge in England. *Journal of Epidemiology & Community Health*, 1996, 50, 30–32.

Panaitescu, V., Teodoreanu, E., & Popescu, I. Correlation between certain meteorological and climatic conditions and the number of suicides. *Buletinul Academiei de Stiinte a Republicii Moldova Stiinte Biologicesi Chimice*, 1993, 0(3), 49–54.

Panser, L. A., McAlpine, D. E., Wallrichs, S. C., Swanson, D. W., O'Fallon, W. M., & Melton, L. J. Timing of completed suicides among residents of Olmstead County, Minnesota, 1951–1985. *Acta Psychiatrica Scandinavica*, 1995, 92, 214–219.

Phillips, D. P., & Smith, D. G. Suicide at symbolic ages. In A. A. Leenaars (Ed.), *Life span perspectives of suicide*. New York: Plenum, 1991, 81–92.

Pirkola, S., Isometsa, E., Heikkinen, M., & Lonnqvist, J. Employment status influences the weekly pattern of suicide among alcohol misusers. *Alcoholism: Clinical & Experimental Research*, 1997, 21, 1704–1706.

Preti, A. The influence of seasonal change on suicidal behavior in Italy. *Journal of Affective Disorders*, 1997, 44, 123–130.

Proctor, E. A. Self-poisoning by adolescents. *British Medical Journal*, 1992, 304, 912.

Rocco, P. L., Madrisotti & Della Gala, C. Comparison between suicidal and parasuicidal victims in a mountain population. In U. Bille-Brahe & H. Schiodt (Eds.), *Intervention and prevention*. Odense: Odense University Press, 1994, 253–254.

Rothberg, J. M., Fagan, J., & Shaw, J. Suicide in US Army personnel, 1985–1986. *Military Medicine*, 1990, 155, 452–456.

Salander-Renberg, E., & Jacobsson, L. Attempted suicide in Vasterbotten County, Sweden. In T. Bjerke & T. C. Stiles (Eds.), *Suicide attempts in the Nordic countries*. Trondheim: Tapir Forlag, 1991, 69–77.

Salib, E. Elderly suicides and weather conditions. *International Journal of Geriatric Psychiatry*, 1997, 12, 937–941.

Salib, E., & Gray, N. Weather conditions and fatal self-harm in North Cheshire 1989–1993. *British Journal of Psychiatry*, 1997, 171, 473–477.

Schlebusch, L. Parasuicide. In L. Schlebusch (Ed.), *Suicidal behaviour*. Durban: University of Natal, 1988, 29–43.

Schneider, D., & Greenberg, M. Violence. *New Jersey Medicine*, 1994, 91, 855–858.

Schreiber, G., Dycian, A., Kaplan, Z., & Bleich, A. A unique monthly distribution of suicide and parasuicide through firearms among Israeli soldiers. *Acta Psychiatrica Scandinavica*, 1993, 87, 110–113.

Shapiro, C. M., Blake, F., Fossey, E., & Adams, B. Daylight saving time in psychiatric illness. *Journal of Affective Disorders*, 1990, 19, 177–181.

Stack, S. Temporal disappointment, homicide, and suicide. *Sociological Focus*, 1995, 28, 313–328.

Steels, M. Self-poisoning and general elections. *British Journal of Psychiatry*, 1993, 162, 127–128.

Tietjen, G. H., & Kripke, D. F. Suicides in California (1968–1977). *Psychiatry Research*, 1994, 53, 161–172.

Wasserman, I., & Stack, S. Age, birthdays, and suicide. *Journal of Social Psychology*, 1994, 134, 493–495.

Zhang, J. Suicides in Beijing, China, 1992–1993. *Suicide & Life-Threatening Behavior*, 1996, 26, 175–180.

Chapter 9

MULTIVARIATE STUDIES

Population Studies

Stack and Lester (1991) used the General Social Survey to show that support for suicide was associated negatively with church attendance, marriage, age, and sex and positively with education (but not with being Roman Catholic). Stack et al. (1994a) found that approval for suicide in America was positively associated with feminist attitudes and education and negatively with church attendance, being black and not married.

In 16 states, Stack (1996–1997) found that not-employed women had a higher suicide rate for those aged 25–44 while employed women had a higher suicide rate for those aged 65 or more. This was found for all marital statuses.

In England and Wales, Charlton (1995) compared suicides with natural deaths and found that young adult male suicides were more often widowed/divorced, not born in the Commonwealth, and aged 20–29. Older male adult suicides were more often single or widowed/divorced and 45–59. Female suicides were more often single or widowed/divorced, and 20–24. Occupation also contributed to the prediction, with veterinarians being more to likely to be suicides in all groups.

Using the World Value Survey for 19 Western nations, Neeleman et al. (1997) found that national suicide rates were associated with national levels of acceptance of suicide and, for women only, religiousness, church attendance, and religious upbringing; they were not associated with religious affiliation or permissive attitudes toward deviant behavior. At the individual level also, suicide tolerance was associated negatively with religiosity.

In the United States, Stack (1996b) found that having attempted suicide for both men and women was predicted by marital status, race, education, having children, and church attendance, but not by full-time/part-time employment or unemployment. Using the Catchment Area Study, Nisbet (1996) found that predictors of attempted suicide in white females and black females differed a little. Income was positively associated with attempting suicide for black females, but negatively associated for white females. However, black and white females differed on many of the predictive factors. For example, black females had lower incomes, were younger, and lived in larger households.

Primitive Societies

Masumura (1979) found that the suicide rate in primitive societies was associated with aggression and murder, but not with wife abuse, theft, crime, feuding, or warfare.

Regional Studies

Lester (1994i) derived a multiple-regression equation to predict suicide rates based on social variables from 17 nations. He used this equation to predict quite accurately a high Hungarian suicide rate, the Italian suicide rate (Lester, 1995x), and the Czechoslovakian suicide rate (Lester, 1996w).

Lester (1995m) examined the association between suicide rates and population density over the regions of different nations. The majority of the associations were not significantly different from zero, while in India the association was positive, and in the United States and Sri Lanka the association was negative.

United States: States

The most comprehensive study of suicide in the American states has been conducted by Lester (1994q, 1995e).

Lester (1996j) found that divorce was a stronger predictor of state suicide rates (by age, sex, and race) than birth or unemployment rates. Lester (1996m) found that social disintegration was a stronger correlate of state suicide rates than an index of social stress.

Lester (1990b) factor-analyzed suicide rates by method over the states of the USA in 1980 and identified three clusters: (1) hanging, cutting, and jumping; (2) gas and drowning; and (3) solids/liquids and firearms. Of the clusters of social variables identified by factor-analysis, social disintegration correlated with suicide rates only by solids/liquids and by firearms. Therefore, Durkheim's theory of suicide was confirmed only for suicide by some methods.

Lester (1990–1991) found that the social disintegration factor and the east-west factor were associated only with white suicide rates over the states, not with African American suicide rates. The north-south variation in suicide rates was negative for whites and positive for African Americans. Thus, African American suicide rates did not appear to conform to Durkheim's theory of suicide. Looking at social indicators in the states by race, the factor pattern for the social variables was different for whites and African Americans and so the correlates of suicide rates were different. Whereas white suicide rates were predicted by white social disintegration, African American suicide rates were predicted by African American education/wealth.

Lester (1991a) found that the factor correlates of suicide rates by age were similar for youth and adult suicide rates. Lester (1991c) found that the correlates were similar in the more-urban states and less-urban states. Lester (1992b) found that the association of suicide rates with social disintegration was found over the 48 states for both urban and rural suicide rates. The degree of urbanization predicted rural suicides rates over the 48 states, which supported Lester's (1992c) social deviancy theory of suicide. Lester (1996u) found that state suicide rates were associated with the murder rates for children ages one to four in 1980 but not in 1990.

Lester (1996-1997) found that the correlates of state suicide rates in 1880 and 1980 were similar in some respects (higher in the west and lower where the percentage of blacks was higher) but differed also. For example, the association with birth rates was negative in 1880 and positive in 1980.

Lester (1990e) criticized prior research indicating an association between suicide rates and female participation in the labor force. He showed female participation in the labor force was strongly associated with other social indicators for the United States (such as the death rate and the percentage of the population over the age of 65) and could not be singled out as the chief causal variable.

Lester (1994e) found that the percentage of suicides in the states using firearms was positively associated with clusters of variables measuring social disintegration, southernness, and Roman Catholicism and negatively with urban/wealth and age.

Lester (1994f) found that the suicide rates of the states were negatively associated with population density and positively with population growth. Lester (1994h) found that SAT scores were associated with the male suicide rates and the urban suicide rates of the states.

Lester (1994g) found that the suicide rates of the foreign born, those born in contiguous states, and those born in noncontiguous states were positively associated, indicating that state of residence affects the suicide rate. However, the suicide rates of those born in state were not associated with the suicide rates of the foreign born or those born in noncontiguous states, indicating that place of birth also affects the suicide rate.

Lester (1995j) found that the divorce rate was positively associated with the suicide rates of the single, married, divorced, and widowed, suggesting that the divorce rate was an indicator of general malaise in a society. Lester (1995k) found that the suicide rate of the states was associated with the remarriage rate but not the new marriage rate. Lester (1995q) found that suicide rates were higher in the western states and the less densely populated states.

Lester (1994p) found that changes in youth suicide rates over the states from 1960–1970 were not associated with television ownership, as had been suggested, but rather with the wealth of the states.

Lester (1995c) looked for correlates of native American suicide rates over the states and found correlates that were different for those of whites, for example with wealth/urban rather than social instability. Lester (1995g) found that the association between suicide rates and social disintegration was stronger in states with weak gun control laws.

Lester (1995d) found that divorce and alcohol consumption (but not alcohol availability or addiction) were associated with state suicide rates. Liu et al. (1995–1996) used a mixed state-by-time design (51 states and 12 years) and found that suicide rates were associated with beer and wine (but not spirits) consumption.

Yang and Lester (1992a) found that the percentage of married women working full time was positively associated with the suicide rates of married men and women, while the percentage of married women working part time was negatively associated with the suicide rates of married men and women. The associations were not significant for the suicide rates of other marital statuses.

In a multivariate study, Zimmerman (1990, 1995) found that suicide rates were negatively associated with state spending for hospitals, but not after controls for other social variables. Public welfare expenditure was a significant predictor of suicide rates only in 1990, whereas divorce was a significant predictor in 1960, 1980, and 1990.

Medoff and Skov (1992) found that state suicide rates were associated with the percent of Fundamentalists and the southern states (positively) and the percent of blacks and employment in manufacturing (negatively). Median income, percent with high school education, median age, and percentage urban population were not associated with the suicide rate.

Joubert (1994b) found that suicide rates of the states were positively associated with the percentage of the population with no religious affiliation, negatively with the percentage of Roman Catholics (Joubert, 1995a), and not significantly with voter turnout (Joubert, 1995b) the percentage of Baptists, or adopting English as the official language (Joubert, 1997a, 1997b). However, Lester (1995u, 1997h) failed to find significant associations between suicide rates and the percentages of Fundamentalists or Roman Catholics.

Maguire and Snipes (1994) found that the state suicide rates were associated with divorce rates, but not with country music air time on the radio. Stack and Gundlach (1994) argued that Maguire and Snipes used incorrect suicide rates. Stack et al. (1994b) found that subscriptions by youth to *Metal Edge*, a heavy-metal magazine, was positively associated with youth suicide rates, along with other variables (such as divorce and percentage blacks).

Bailey and Stein (1995) found that the suicide rates of the states were negatively associated with the percentages of Jews in the states. Lester (1996e, 1997h) found that the percentage of Jews in the states was negatively associated with the suicide rate after controls for other social indicators.

Gruenwald et al. (1995) found that spirit sales combined with income, unemployment, divorce, and age distribution to predict state suicide rates over 21 years (giving 1050 data points). Wine sales were not significant predictors, and beer sales were negatively associated with suicide rates.

Lester (1990d) found that the lethal-aggression rate (suicide plus homicide rates) was strongly associated with the suicide rate and the homicide rate over the states of the USA and correlated with social variables in the same fashion as the homicide rate.

Huff-Corzine et al. (1991) found that the suicide plus homicide rate (the lethal violence rate) was associated with indices of poverty in both whites and blacks; the ratio of the suicide rate to the lethal-violence rate

was associated with poverty in whites and percentage born in the South in both whites and blacks. They also studied other social variables and found differing associations for white and black suicide rates.

Linsky et al. (1995) looked at correlates of estimates of the suicide rate and suicidal thoughts over the states. The suicide rate was associated with a state stress index, suicidal thoughts, and the proportion of blacks. Suicidal thoughts were associated with perceived stress. For men, the suicide rate was associated with overall stress and economic stress, but not family or community stress. For women, only overall stress was significantly associated with the suicide rate.

United States: Counties

Pescosolido (1990) found that the association between the suicide rates of American counties in 1970 with the percentage of different religious groups (27 in all) varied by region. For example, the association with liberal Protestant church membership was positive in the Northeast and negative in the West. The associations also varied with the population density of the county – the negative association with Roman Catholic church membership was found only in high-density counties.

Pescosolido and Wright (1990) looked at age-by-sex suicide rates for American counties and found that the correlates with divorce rates and never-married rates depended upon whether they used divorce and never-married rates for the whole county or for each age-by-sex group. For example, using overall county-level divorce rates, the association with suicide rates was positive and significant for men aged 25–44 and over 65. Using cell-specific divorce rates, none of the associations were statistically significant. Adding the number of children and the interaction term into the multiple regressions also changed the results.

Joubert (1994a) compared alcohol sales in wet and dry counties in Alabama and found that wet counties had lower suicide rates, higher homicide rates, and higher illegitimacy rates. The residents of wet counties were also more often college graduates, but had more poverty. Also in Alabama, Zekeri and Wilkinson (1995) found that the suicide rate was associated positively with rurality, the percentage of elderly, interstate migrants, and divorce rates and associated negatively with poverty and the percentage of males.

United States: SMSAs

Levine et al. (1989) found that the suicide rates of SMSAs were associated positively with divorce rates, crime rates, climate, income, migrants, and an index of alcoholism, and associated negatively with the quality of life in the regions.

Seydlitz et al. (1993) found that suicide rates in Louisiana parishes were associated with higher oil prices and having more oil wells, but the study mixed ecological and time trends. Wasserman and Stack (1993) found that parish suicide rates were not associated with religious composition (nor other social variables, such as the percent nonwhite, urban, or living alone).

Burr et al. (1994) found that SMSA suicide rates were associated with divorce rates, population density, housing construction, and one-person households, but not with religious affiliations once these other variables were controlled. Burr et al. (1997) found that the association between suicide rates and female labor-force participation (by married women with children) varied by year. The association with male suicide rates was positive in 1970 and negative in 1980; the association with female suicide rates was nonsignificant in 1970 and negative in 1980.

Ellison et al. (1997) found that religious homogeneity (but not the percentage of Catholics or church membership) was negatively associated with SMSA suicide rates. The strength of the association varied by region and was greater in the Northeast.

United States: Census Tracts

Wenz (1976) compared four census tracts in Flint (Michigan). One had a high completed suicide rate, one a high attempted suicide rate, and two had low rates of both. A sample of residents in the tract with a high completed suicide rate had the highest anomie scores and lowest self-esteem. A sample of residents in the tract with a high attempted suicide rate had the highest egoism scores. The residents in the census tracts with low rates of completed and attempted suicide had the lowest anomie and egoism scores and the highest self-esteem scores.

In Alaska, Gessner (1997) found that teen suicide rates were associated with a number of census-tract social variables but, in multiple regression, only the percent of married couples was significant (negatively).

United States: City Areas

Wallace (1990) found that the suicide plus homicide rates were associated over areas in the Bronx with the incidence of low-birthweight babies and social class/overcrowding.

United States: Native Americans

Bachman (1992) looked at suicide in 120 counties in America that are partially or totally located on reservation land (so as to ensure a large population of native Americans). The study included: (1) the association of measures of economic deprivation (the percentage of native American families below the poverty line, the percentage of native Americans unemployed, and the percentage of native Americans aged 16 to 19 not enrolled in school and not high school graduates); (2) social disorganization (the percentage of native Americans not living on the reservation in 1979 or 1980); and (3) acculturation (the lower the percentage of native Americans on the reservation). Suicide rates were calculated for 1980–1987 and were found to be most strongly associated with the percentage of native Americans in the population, the percentage unemployed, and the high school dropout rate. In a multiple-regression analysis, unemployment, percentage of native Americans, and percentage in poverty contributed significantly. If homicide rates were included in the analysis, the significant contributors included the homicide rate, poverty, and unemployment. Thus, economic deprivation rather than acculturation seemed to be the strongest correlate of native American suicide rates in this study.

Australia

Burnley (1994, 1995) found that suicide rates over the regions of Sydney were negatively associated with the proportion married, and positively associated with population density, education, unemployment, low income, and one-person households and by indices of social isolation. The results differed by age and sex, with the associations stronger for male suicide rates than for female suicide rates.

Krupinski et al. (1994) found that the male youth suicide rate (but not the female youth suicide rate) was associated with unemployment over the regions of Victoria.

Cantor et al. (1995) found that suicide rates were higher in regions of Queensland that were more disadvantaged (low income, low education, and high unemployment) and that had fewer economic resources (income, home ownership, dwelling size, and number of cars). Results varied a little by age and sex. Hassan (1995) found that the social correlates of suicide rates over the regions of Adelaide differed for metropolitan and for country areas.

Canada

Trovato and Vos (1992) found that, using age-by-sex specific data over the provinces in Canada, male and female suicide rates were associated with the percent having no religion. The divorce rate was a significant predictor only in 1981 (not in 1971). Married female participation in the labor force was positively associated with male and female suicide rates in 1971 and negatively in 1981.

Trovato and Vos (1990) correlated youth suicide rates over the provinces of Canada in 1970 and 1980 and found inconsistent results. For example, unemployment correlated positively with suicide rates for males and females aged 20–29 but correlated negatively for those aged 15–19. One cluster of variables (percent with no religious preference, divorce rate, and married female labor-force participation) was associated positively with all of the suicide rates.

Trovato (1992a) studied youth suicide rates in Canadian provinces over two years. The results of multiple regressions depended upon the year and sex. Only having no religious affiliation was a consistent correlate for both sexes in both years.

Hasselback et al. (1991) studied the 261 census divisions of Canada and found, in a multiple regression, that suicide rates were associated positively with the percentage of native Canadians, the death rate, the percentage of Francophones, the percentage of immigrants, and the percentage with no religious affiliation; they were associated negatively with the population density, unemployment, family income, percentage of the population aged 5–19, social mobility, and longitude.

Over metropolitan areas in Canada, Trovato (1992b) found that male and female suicide rates were not associated. Male suicide rates were predicted by the percent of native Canadians, population growth, and household size.

Bagley et al. (1990) studied the suicide rates of young native Canadian males aged 15–34 on the 26 most-populated Canadian reserves. The suicide (plus careless death) rate was positively associated with per-capita income, the latitude of the reserve, and the distance from a town.

Over census divisions in British Columbia, Lester (1996d) found that aboriginal suicide rates were associated with the percentage of aboriginals on reserves and the non-aboriginal suicide rate.

Caribbean

Yang and Lester (1994b; Lester, 1996s) found that suicide rates in the Caribbean islands were associated with the per-capita gross national product and the population, but the correlations with divorce and female labor-force participation differed for male and female suicide rates. Lester (1995s) found that Caribbean nations with later development of the sugar industry and stronger central bureaucracies had higher suicide rates.

England and Wales

Lester (1993b) examined correlates of suicide rates over English counties and found great differences from the correlates in the United States. For example, the association with birth rates was negative in England and positive in the United States. Over the 12 regions of Great Britain and Ireland, Lester (1996c) found that the suicide rate was associated with per-capita income, infant mortality, and urbanization.

Lewis et al. (1994) found that suicide rates were positively associated with the availability of psychiatric nurses and consultants over the district health authority regions in England, but not with mental health bed availability.

Over 24 regions of Bristol, Gunnell et al. (1995) found that completed and attempted suicide rates were positively associated, and both rates were associated with socio-economic deprivation and psychiatric admissions. Over the electoral wards of northeast London, Congdon (1996) found that both completed and attempted suicides (which were positively, but weakly, associated) had similar social correlates (including social indicators of anomie, deprivation, and psychiatric morbidity). The associations differed, however, by age and sex.

Finland

Lester (1996v) found that the suicide rate of Finnish provinces was associated with unemployment and the incidence of schizophrenia.

France

Over 19 regions of France, Souetre et al. (1990) found that the suicide rate correlated positively with alcoholism, percent in agriculture, the percent with little education, percent working, percent working women, latitude, and longitude. The rate correlated negatively with physicians per capita, mean temperature and sunshine hours, but not with precipitation. In a multiple regression, the weather variables proved to be the best predictors of the suicide rate.

Hungary

In Hungary, Rihmer et al. (1990) found that the suicide rate was negatively associated with the treated depression rate and positively with the divorce and perinatal mortality rate. The suicide rate was not associated with the treated schizophrenia rate or the marriage, birth, migration, and death rates. They concluded that diagnosis and treatment of depression may lead to reduced suicide rates.

Lester and Rihmer (1992) found that regional suicide rates in Hungary were associated with infant mortality and divorce rates. Zonda, et al. (1992) found that the regional suicide rate was associated only with the divorce rate (and not with marriage, birth, death, migration, or infant mortality rates). Lester and Moksony (1994) found that the social correlates of the regional suicide rates in Hungary varied by age. For example, inter-region migration was associated only with the suicide rates of 40–59 year olds.

India

Over the provinces of India, Lester and Agarwal (1990) found that the social correlates of suicide rates and the proportion of suicides that were male were rather different from those over the regions of the United States. Lester (1996i) found no association between the percentage of Muslims in Indian states and the suicide rate.

Ireland

Kelleher et al. (1996) found that the best predictor of the attempted suicide rate over the electoral wards of Cork was unemployment.

Italy

Lester and Ausenda (1993) found that the ecological correlates of suicide in Italy differed greatly from those in the United States. Lester (1997b) found that the suicide rate was higher in the northern regions than in the southern regions, and the two regions differed significantly in social variables.

Lester and Ausenda (1997) found that, in 1870, the suicide rates of Italian regions were associated with illiteracy (negatively) but not with the percentage of Roman Catholics, marriage and death rates, or the percentage of the population in urban areas.

Japan

Kurosu (1991) found that suicide rates were associated with per-capita income and percent urban (negatively) and percent elderly and percent widowed (positively) over the prefectures of Japan. The percentage of variance explained by these variables increased from 1960 to 1970 to 1980. Lester and Abe (1992) found that per-capita income and birth rates were associated negatively and the percentage of elderly associated positively with suicide rates over the prefectures of Japan.

Chandler and Tsai (1993) found that the male suicide rate in Japanese prefectures was associated negatively with the percent of newcomers, per-capita income, urbanization, and the percentage of elderly, and associated positively with female labor-force participation. The female suicide rate was associated positively with the percentage of Buddhists, the percentage married, and female labor-force participation, and associated negatively with the percentage of Christians, divorce rate, percentage of newcomers, unemployment, and urbanization. Chandler and Tsai suggested that the correlates of suicide rates in women suggested that their suicide was altruistic/fatalistic in nature.

Goto et al. (1994) found three factors of social characteristics over the prefectures of Japan: economic activity, social unrest, and marriages/births. All were associated with suicide rates but in different eras. For example, marriages/births were significantly associated with suicide rates only for 1975–1979 and economic activity only after 1978. Suicide rates were higher in rural areas (especially for males). Changes in economic activity were more strongly associated with changes in the suicide rates than were the other two factors.

Yamamoto (1992) found that suicide rates were negatively associated with depopulation (but not with the percentage of elderly) over the communities in one prefecture. This association was stronger for elderly suicide rates.

The Netherlands

Kerkhof and Kunst (1994) found that the suicide rates of regions in the Netherlands was associated with the divorce rate (positively) and the percentage of orthodox Christians, urban population, and Roman Catholics (negatively). The associations varied by sex and age.

Norway

Rossow (1995) found that the suicide rate was associated with alcohol sales and self-reported alcohol use over the regions of Norway (more so for females), and also unemployment and the proportion of single persons and church-affiliated persons.

Portugal

Skog et al. (1995) found that Portuguese suicide rates were associated with smaller households, Roman Catholic marriages, and cirrhosis mortality. Lester (1997e) found that suicide rates were associated with the male/female ratio (positively), as well as birth rates and cirrhosis mortality (negatively).

Russia

Lester (1995f) found that suicide rates were associated positively with beds per capita and negatively with infant mortality over the regions of Russia. In the United States, these associations were not significant. Lester concluded that good medical resources did not appear to prevent suicide.

Spain

Guttierez (1995) found that provincial suicide rates were associated positively with the percentage of elderly, percentage born in province, and the death rate and associated negatively with the population.

Sweden

Over Swedish counties, Norstrom (1995a) found that alcohol consumption, divorce, religiosity, unemployment, and urbanization all contributed to the prediction of suicide rates. Ferrada-Noli (1997a) found that Swedish counties with more of the residents on social assistance had the higher suicide rates, and Ferrada-Noli (1997b) found that the poorest municipalities had the highest suicide rates. In two psychiatric catchment areas, the one with higher suicide rate had more early retirees, higher unemployment, lower income, less home ownership, and denser population (Ferrada-Noli, 1997c).

Lester and Savlid (1997a, 1997b, 1997c) found that the female suicide rate of Swedish counties (but not the male rate) was associated with per-capita income. In a factor-analysis of social indicators, the female suicide rate (but not the male suicide rate) was associated with wealth, but not illegitimacy or birth rates.

Taiwan

Lester and Hu (1993) found very different regional correlates of the suicide rate in Taiwan from those in the United States. Chuang and Huang (1996b, 1997) studied 23 counties in Taiwan for ten years in a mixed-multiple-regression design and identified many correlates of the suicide rate, including poverty, percent of aboriginals, and per-capita income.

Nations

Lester (1996t) carried out a comprehensive multivariate study of predictors of suicide rates around the world.

Lester (1991b) found that the social correlates of suicide rates by each method were different in a sample of nations. For example, divorce was correlated only with suicide rates by solids/liquids, other gas, submersion, and cutting, but not with suicide rates by domestic gas, hanging, firearms, and jumping. Thus, Durkheim's theory did not apply to suicide rates by every method.

Lester (1990f) in a sample of European nations found that the suicide rate was associated with the per-capita consumption of fat, but not protein, stimulants (tea and coffee), alcoholic beverages, or total calories. Lester (1996g) found no association between national suicide rates and participation in

voluntary associations. Lester (1996h) found no association between population size and density and the suicide/suicide plus homicide rates.

Bond (1991) looked at psychological test scores from students in 15 nations and identified two factors: social integration versus cultural inwardness and reputation versus morality. Neither factor score correlated with national suicide rates.

Unnithan and Whitt (1992) found that the suicide rate was negatively associated with income inequality over 31 nations and positively associated with the gross national product per capita.

Sakinofsky and Stolar (1994) explored differences in youth suicide rates in nations where the rates were rising versus those in which they were stable or declining. The latter countries differed in many ways, such as having steeper rates of increase in the consumer price index, unemployment rising more slowly, and lower female labor-force participation.

Fernquist (1995–1996) examined nine nations in 15 consecutive years (giving 135 data points) and found that elderly suicide rates were positively associated with divorce rates and cirrhosis deaths and negatively associated with political integration.

Huang (1996) found that national suicide rates were associated with unemployment, female labor-force participation and Islam-Catholicism. The correlates for male and female rates were somewhat different. Lester (1996f) found that nations with more Roman Catholics and more Muslims had lower suicide rates, but not after controls for gross national product per capita.

Stack (1996a) found that the suicide rate of nations was predicted by cultural approval of suicide and having a communist regime (but not by church attendance or education).

Makinen (1997) found that while social

indicators such as divorce and homicide rates and the proportion of those under the age of 15 predicted suicide rates in a sample of European nations, changes in the social indicators did not predict changes in the suicide rates.

Using data from the World Value Survey, Stack (1997) found that marriage and having children increased acceptance of suicide in the majority of nations studied.

Lester (1990c) explored the correlates of the suicide rate, homicide rate, suicide plus homicide rate (a lethal aggression measure) and suicide/(suicide plus homicide) rate (a direction-of-aggression measure) with social variables over 18 industrialized nations. The correlates of the lethal-aggression measure were the same as those for the suicide rate; the correlates of the direction-of-aggression measure were similar to those for the homicide rate. Lester concluded that these two new measures added little of interest to the study of suicide.

Rahav (1990) studied the suicide/(suicide plus homicide) rate ratio in a sample of nations. This ratio was positively associated with life expectancy, gross national product per capita, and percentage in high school, negatively associated with fertility and infant mortality, and not associated with the percentage divorced.

Changes Over Time Periods

Diekstra (1989) looked at changes in youth suicide rates from 1960–1985 in European nations. The changes were associated with the changes in unemployment, the percentage of the population under the age of 15, women employed, divorce, homicide, alcohol use, and church attendance.

Lester (1995h) found that the increase in youth suicide rates in nations from 1970–1980 was predicted by age structure (positively) and the suicide rate in 1970

(negatively). Lester (1993c) looked at changes in the elderly suicide rate from 1970 to 1980 in a sample of nations and found no social predictors (unlike changes in the overall suicide rate).

Time-Series Studies

Lester (1993a) found different correlates of suicide in the United States for time-series and cross-sectional analyses, indicating that both types of study were important.

Lester (1994b) carried out time-series analyses for 1950–1985 for 29 nations, examining the associations of suicide rates with marriage and birth rates, and Lester (1994t) examined the role of divorce rates as well for 21 nations. Lester (1994c) reported time-series analyses of male and female suicide rates over 17 nations for birth, marriage, and divorce rates. Yang and Lester (1994c) explored the impact of unemployment on suicide rates in 12 nations for 1950–1985 and found that only four of the nations had evidence for a positive association.

Lester (1995a, 1995b) found that suicide rates by sex were positively associated with alcohol consumption and with divorce in the majority of nations studied. Lester (1996a) explored the association of marriage and birth rates with suicide rates for ten nations for 1900–1988 and found that the results differed by nation. Lester (1996b) found that divorce and marriage rates predicted the suicide-plus-homicide rate and the suicide-minus-homicide rate quite well for 19 nations for 1950-1985. Lester (1997c) found that suicide and homicide rates were positively associated over time for 1950–1985 in 13 nations and negatively associated in six.

Lester and Yang (1998) have reported time-series analyses for an even larger sample of nations and for longer time periods.

Australia

Lester and Yang (1991) found different time-series correlates of the suicide rate in the United States and Australia. For example, the effect of the divorces/ marriages ratio was opposite – positive in the United States and negative in Australia.

Using absolute numbers of suicides, Gibb (1956) factor-analyzed 49 socioeconomic variables for 1906–1946. Suicides were associated with two factors: 1) low alcohol consumption, high unemployment, fewer births, and fewer marriages and 2) male/female ratio, less immigration and emigration, more deaths due to alcoholism, and a higher wholesale price index.

Hassan and Tan (1992) found that the male/female suicide rate ratio for 1901–1985 was positively associated with a modernization index and unemployment, negatively with time, and not associated with war.

Lester (1992a) found that for 1966–1985, alcohol consumption was negatively associated with both male and female suicide rates in Australia. Divorces/marriages and unemployment had no effect on male suicide rates, while employment was negatively associated with female suicide rates.

The prediction of the time-series suicide rate in Australia was compared with that for other Pacific Rim nations by Lester (1994r).

Austria

Lester (1995i) found that divorce and employment were good predictors of the suicide rate in Austria for 1970–1990 for all age groups.

Austro-Hungarian Empire

Ausenda et al. (1991) found that the suicide rate in the Austro-Hungarian Empire for 1875–1913 was associated with the marriage rate (negatively) but not the birth, illegitimacy, or infant mortality rates. Over the regions of the Empire, only the birth rate was associated with the suicide rate (negatively).

Bavaria

Wiedenmann and Weyerer (1994) found that suicide rates were negatively associated with birth rates, but not with marriage rates for 1865–1980.

Canada

Leenaars et al. (1993) compared the time-series correlates in Canada and the United States for 1950–1985. In Canada, suicide rates were associated with divorce rates (positively) and birth rates (negatively), as in the United States, but not associated with marriage or unemployment rates. Leenaars and Lester (1994) found that suicide rates in Canada for 1950–1985 were predicted by birth and divorce rates, as in the United States. Leenaars and Lester (1995) explored the predictors of youth suicide rates and found that the results for Canadian youths were similar to those for older adults.

Krull and Trovato (1994), in a study of Quebec for 1931–1986, combined suicide rates every five years for different age groups and a multiple regressions to predict male and female suicide rates. For 1931–1956, no predictors were significant; for 1961–1986, male suicide rates (but not female suicide rates) were predicted by divorce, unemployment and the percent with no religious affiliation.

In Quebec 1951–1986, Lester (1995p) found that unemployment, divorce, birth, and cirrhosis rates predicted male suicide rates, while only divorce and birth rates predicted female suicide rates.

Lester (1997f) studied each province

separately for 1960–1985 and found that divorce rates were a more-consistent predictor of the time-series suicide rates than marriage, birth, or unemployment rates.

Denmark

Stack (1990) found that divorce and unemployment were both correlated positively with the Danish suicide rate for 1951–1980.

England

Lester (1993g) found that divorce and illegitimacy rates correlated negatively with English suicide rates for 1901–1975.

Finland

In a time-series study of Finland for 1950–1985, Lester (1992d) found that divorce rates, but not birth or marriage rates, predicted the Finnish suicide rate. Stack (1992a) found that divorce rates and a religiosity index, but not unemployment, predicted male and female suicide rates for 1952–1978.

For 1950–1991, Makela (1996) found that alcohol consumption predicted male suicide rates for most age groups in a multiple regression, even after controls for divorce, unemployment, and real wages.

For 1878–1994, Viren (1996) found that the suicide rate was predicted by gross domestic product growth, bankruptcies, and unemployment (as well as age). Stack (1993) found suicide rates to be associated with urbanization for the period 1800–1984. For 1752–1988, Lester (1997d) found that marriage and birth rates were better predictors of the suicide rate in recent times (1951–1988) and of little use in earlier times (1751–1800).

France

Gillis (1994) found that suicide rates in France for 1852–1914 were positively associated with literacy rates and negatively associated with homicide rates. For 1853–1908, Lester (1996q) found that suicide rates were associated with lower birth rates and a higher percentage of illegitimate births.

Lester (1994a) found that the French male suicide rate and male prison suicide rate for 1852–1913 both varied with the marriage and birth rates, although the associations were weaker for the prison suicide rate.

Lester (1996k) found that the male (but not female) French suicide rate for 1950–1980 was associated with the mother's average age, but not with divorce or fertility.

Germany

John (1985) found no association between suicide rates and unemployment of age-by-sex groups for 1950–1980. Lester (1996p) found that social protests were not related to the German suicide rate for 1965–1989.

Weyerer and Wiedenmann (1995) found that economic factors (unemployment, real income, and economic growth) were associated positively with the suicide rate in Germany for 1881–1939 but negatively for 1949–1989.

Hong Kong

Lester (1995n) found that marriage and birth rates and gross national product per capita were good predictors of the time-series suicide rate in Hong Kong for 1971–1990. Shiu et al. (1993) found that an index of societal stress was positively associated over time with the Hong Kong suicide rate for 1962–1985.

Hungary

Lester (1993i) found that measures of domestic social integration did not predict the time-series suicide rate in Hungary for 1950–1985. Lester (1995z) found that predictors of the overall Hungarian suicide rate also worked well at the county level and for village, town, and city suicide rates in Hungary.

India

Lester and Natarajan (1995) found that female labor-force participation and fertility predicted the time-series Indian suicide rate, but with opposite signs to the associations for the American suicide rate.

Ireland

Kelleher and Daly (1990) found that the Irish suicide rate rose from 1970 to 1984, along with rising unemployment, illegitimate births, alcohol admissions, indictable crimes and marital separations. Marriages declined. However, they did not carry out a regression analysis on these variables. For 1950–1985, Lester (1993d) found that social correlates of the Irish suicide rate were different from those in Great Britain.

Israel

Lester (1997a) found that marriage rates predicted male and female suicide rates in Israel for 1960–1989, but birth and divorce rates had different associations with male and female suicide rates.

Italy

Lester (1993e) found similar correlates of the time-series suicide rate in Italy and the United States for 1950–1985.

Japan

Motohashi (1991) examined correlates of the suicide rate in Japan for 1953–1986. The correlates differed for 1953–1972, for 1973–1986 and by sex. For example, in 1953–1972 the male suicide rate was associated with unemployment and male labor-force participation; associated in 1973–1986 with the divorce rate and the percentage employed in primary industry.

Lester et al. (1992) found that unemployment and female labor-force participation (but not divorce rates or change in the GNP) predicted Japanese suicide rates for 1953–1982. Stack (1992b) found that unemployment and an index of religiosity (but not divorce rates) predicted male suicide rates for 1950–1980, but not female suicide rates. Lester (1995r) found the male suicide rate in Japan was positively associated with measures of domestic disintegration, whereas the female suicide rate was positively associated with measures of domestic integration.

The Netherlands

Lester (1993h, 1995w) found that measures of domestic integration (primarily divorce rates) predicted the time-series suicide rate in the Netherlands for 1950–1985. Zalman and Stack (1995, 1996) found that decisions concerning euthanasia in 1974 and 1981 did not affect the suicide for 1950–1990; divorce, religiosity, and unemployment did predict the suicide rate.

New Zealand

Lester (1993f) found that the time-series suicide in New Zealand for 1950–1985 conformed to predictions from Durkheim's theory. Lester (1994d) found that Maori and non-Maori male youth suicide rates (but not female rates) were both associated with unemployment for 1970–1989.

Northern Ireland

Lester et al. (1991) found differences in the time-series correlates of suicide in 1960–1984 for the United States and Northern Ireland. In the United States, divorce rates were the primary correlate, whereas in Northern Ireland, marriage and birth rates were the primary correlates.

Norway

Rossow (1993) found that alcohol consumption and divorce rates predicted the male, but not the female, suicide rate in Norway for 1911–1990.

Portugal

Skog et al. (1995) found that Portuguese male suicide rates (but not female rates) were predicted by war (negatively) and per capita alcohol consumption (positively).

Poland

Lester (1994s) compared the time-series prediction of the suicide in Poland, Yugoslavia, and France.

Puerto Rico

Lester (1994k) found that measures of domestic integration did not predict the time-series suicide in Puerto Rico for 1950–1985 as they did for the United States.

Singapore

Lester (1994n) found that measures of domestic integration did not predict the time-series suicide rate in Singapore for 1950–1985.

Spain

Lester and Garcia (1995) found that the success of marriage and birth rates in predicting the time-series Spanish suicide rate depended upon the source of suicide rates (not significant for health authority rates, but significant for the judicial rates). Lester and Garcia (1996) found that marriage and birth rates predicted the time-series Spanish suicide rate.

Sweden

Stack (1991) found that male and female suicide rates in Sweden were not associated with religious book production, divorces, or unemployment. Religious book production and divorces, however, did predict youth suicide rates.

Norstrom (1995a, 1995b) found that alcohol consumption (and unemployment) predicted Swedish suicide rates over time. This was true also in France, but less so. Norstrom suggested that if alcohol consumption was high (as in France, Denmark, and Portugal), it had less impact on the time-series suicide rate than if alcohol consumption was low (as in Sweden, Norway, and Hungary).

Lester (1994m) found that divorce rates were the most consistent predictors of the time-series suicide rate for 1950–1985 in all four Scandinavian nations.

Switzerland

Lester (1996r) found that marriage, birth, and divorce rates predicted the time-series Swiss suicide rate for 1950–1985.

Taiwan

Yang et al. (1992a) found that the time-series suicide rate in Taiwan was predicted by divorce and female labor-force participation, as in the United States. In the United States, however, unemployment, GNP per capita and GNP growth also contributed to prediction of the suicide rate. Lester (1995y) found that unemployment rates were associated with the time-series Taiwanese suicide rate. Chuang and Huang (1996a) found similar predictors of the suicide rate in Taiwan and the United States (unemployment and female labor-force participation), although more social indicators were involved in the predictive equation for the United States (divorce and gross national product). Lester and Yang (1995) found that the time-series suicide rate in Taiwan was positively associated with social integration, suggesting that suicide in Taiwan may be fatalistic/altruistic in nature.

Trinidad and Tobago

Hutchinson and Simeon (1997) found that the male and female suicide rates were both associated with male unemployment, serious crime, and male psychiatric admissions in Trinidad and Tobago for 1978–1992 (but not with emigration, female unemployment, or female psychiatric admissions).

United States

Lester (1995v) factor analyzed a number of variables over time for 1933–1985. Five factors were identified, and suicide rates were associated with military involvement and business failure factor scores.

Reinfurt et al. (1991) found in a multiple-regression analysis that unemployment predicted suicide rates for 1960–1986. Lester (1996n) found that income inequality did not predict black or white suicide rates for 1947–1972. Lester (1997g) found a negative association for 1960–1992 between black suicide rates and riots involving blacks.

In the United States for 1940–1980, Kimenyi and Shughart (1986) found that the suicide rate was associated with the price of health care, unemployment, and divorce. Yang and Lester (1993) found the effect of health care costs to be significant only for those aged 15–34.

In the United States for 1946–1986, McCall (1991; McCall and Land, 1994) found different correlates of the white male suicide rate for those aged 15–24 and those aged 65 and older. A family-dissolution index predicted the youth suicide rate (positively), while a societal-affluence index predicted the elderly suicide rate (negatively). Cohort size had a negative association with youth suicide rates, but no association with elderly suicide rates, while unemployment played no role in either predictive equation.

Yang (1993) found that the economy had a different effect on the suicide rates of young and old for 1940–1984 – negative for 15–44 year olds and positive for ages 45 and older. The effect of social variables (such as divorce and female labor-force participation) was stronger for women. Racial differences in the regression results were small. Yang (1995) found that the impact of the economy varied by age, sex, and race. For youth, the economy had a positive association with the suicide rate, but for elderly a negative association.

Yang and Lester (1994a) found that suicide rates for 1940–1984 were predicted by the per-capita gross national product, unemployment, divorce, and female labor-force participation. Yang and Lester (1995a) found that social and economic stress had a significant effect on the suicide rate for 1933–1985. Lester and Yang (1992) found that the American suicide rate for 1933–1986 was predicted both by unemployment and the military participation rate, but the impact of unemployment was found in more age groups and sex-by-race groups than the impact of the military participation rate.

In the United States for 1940–1984, Yang (1992) found that the suicide rate was associated positively with unemployment, the GNP/capita, divorce, and the percentage of Roman Catholics and negatively with female labor-force participation and war. The associations varied in the different sex-by-race groups. Divorce was significant for all groups, but unemployment was significant only for white males, for example. In the United States for 1957–1986, Yang and Lester (1992b) found that the monthly suicide rate was positively associated with unemployment and negatively associated with marriage rates. By year, only the marriage association was significant.

Yang and Lester (1995b) found that the unemployment rate predicted the time-series American suicide rate, and the percentage change in the unemployment rate predicted the percentage change in the suicide rate. The former association was found in only in a minority of other nations studied, and the latter association was found only in the United States.

Yang and Lester (1990) studied the American suicide rate for 1940–1984 and found that the correlations were different for the suicide rate, the smoothed suicide rate, and deviations from the smoothed suicide rate. For example, growth in the gross national product was positively associated with the unsmoothed and smoothed suicide rate, but negatively associated with deviations. Unemployment was positively associated with all three suicide rate measures.

In the United States for 1940–1984, Yang et al. (1992b) found that, with smoothing, the suicide rate was predicted by divorce, unemployment, female labor-force participation, and GNP growth. Without smoothing the variables only unemployment and female labor-force participation contributed to prediction of the suicide rate.

Sloan et al. (1994) combined a cross-sectional and longitudinal study of the 48 states for 1982–1988. They found that the suicide rate was associated with the price of alcohol (negatively) but not with dram shop laws, mandatory jail for driving under the influence, gun control, police per capita, percentage black residents, or per-capita income.

By month for 1910–1920, Wasserman (1992) found that the suicide rate was positively associated with mortality from the influenza epidemic, alcohol consumption, and suicide stories in peacetime (but not in wartime); negatively associated with war and the business index; and not associated with war casualties.

Males (1994) found that predictors of the suicide rate in California for 1970–1990 differed from those for the United States as a whole. For example, the percentage of nonwhites was negative in the multiple regression for California but positive for the United States. For native Americans in New Mexico, 1958–1986, Lester (1995t) found that the suicide rate was positively associated with the unemployment rate. In Phoenix 1950–1988, Nalla and Alvarez (1995) found that the suicide rate was associated with the homicide rate, motor vehicle accidental death rate, infant mortality, and the percentage of minorities, but not with divorce, unemployment, or population change.

For 1950–1968, Austin et al. (1992) found that the female/male suicide rate ratio was associated positively with the divorce rate, female labor-force participation, and the percentage of degrees earned by women; it was associated negatively with the fertility rate. Apparently, as sex roles converged, so did the suicide rates. The reverse was found for 1969–1984, however.

Wales

Lester (1994j) found that marriage and birth rates predicted the time-series suicide rate in Wales for 1964–1985 the same way they did in England.

Attempted Suicide

Lester (1990a) factor-analyzed social variables over the electoral wards of Edinburgh (Scotland) and identified four factors. The total attempted suicide rate was associated with child abuse/neglect, age structure, and housing pattern; the adolescent attempted suicide rate was associated with child abuse/neglect and misbehavior. Lester concluded that sociological studies of attempted suicide are possible.

Discussion

Multivariate studies have appeared with increasing frequency in the last decade. Several suggestions can be made for future research. First, studies on individual nations are no longer of much value. Studies must be conducted on a large sample of nations simultaneously so that the generality of the findings can be examined. Second, investigators would do well to agree upon a standard set of variables to include in the regression and factor analyses so that the different studies can be compared more easily. Third, once consistent findings are established across nations, reasons for deviations from the general rules can be explored.

REFERENCES

Ausenda, G., Lester, D., & Yang, B. Social correlates of suicide and homicide in the Austro-Hungarian Empire in the 19th Century. *European Archives of Psychiatry*, 1991, 240, 301–302.

Austin, R. L. Bologna, M., & Dodge, H. H. Sex-role change, anomie, and female suicide. *Suicide & Life-Threatening Behavior*, 1992, 22, 197–225.

Bachman, R. *Death and violence on the reservation.* New York: Auburn House, 1992.

Bagley, C., Wood, M., & Khumar, H. Suicide and careless death in young males. *Canadian Journal of Community Mental Health*, 1990, 9, 127–142.

Bailey, W. T., & Stein, L. B. Jewish affiliation in relation to suicide rates. *Psychological Reports*, 1995, 76, 561–562.

Bond, M. H. Chinese values and health. *Psychology & Health*, 1991, 5, 137–152.

Burnley, I. H. Differential and spatial aspects of suicide mortality in NSW and Sydney, 1980 to 1991. *Australian Journal of Public Health*, 1994, 18, 293–304.

Burnley, I. H. Socioeconomic and spatial differentials in mortality and means of committing suicide in New South Wales, Australia, 1985–91. *Social Science & Medicine*, 1995, 41, 687–698.

Burr, J. A., McCall, P. L., & Powell-Griner, E. Catholic religion and suicide. *Social Science Quarterly*, 1994, 75, 300–318.

Burr, J. A., McCall, P. L., & Powell-Griner, E. Female labor-force participation and suicide. *Social Science & Medicine*, 1997, 44, 1847–1859.

Cantor, C. H., Slater, P. J., & Najman, J. M. Socioeconomic indices and suicide rate in Queensland. *Australian Journal of Public Health*, 1995, 19, 417–420.

Chandler, C. R., & Tsai, Y. M. Suicide in Japan and the West. *International Journal of Comparative Sociology*, 1993, 34, 244–259.

Charlton, J. Trends and patterns in suicide in England and Wales. *International Journal of Epidemiology*, 1995, 24, Suppl. 1, 45–52.

Chuang, H. L., & Huang, W. C. A reexamination of "Sociological and economic theories of suicide." *Social Science & Medicine*, 1996a, 43, 421–423.

Chuang, H. L., & Huang, W. C. Suicide rates in Taiwan. *American Journal of Economics & Sociology*, 1996b, 55, 276.

Chuang, H. L., & Huang, W. C. Economic and social correlates of regional suicide rates. *Journal of Socio-Economics*, 1997, 26, 277–289.

Congdon, P. Suicide and parasuicide in London. *Urban Studies*, 1996, 33, 137–158.

Diekstra, R. F. Suicidal behavior and depressive disorders in adolescents and young adults. *Neuropsychobiology*, 1989, 22, 194–207.

Ellison, C. G., Burr, J. A., & McCall, P. L. Religious homogeneity and metropolitan suicide rates. Social Forces, 1997, 76, 273–299.

Fernquist, R. M. Elderly suicide in Western Europe. *Omega*, 1995–1996, 32, 39–48.

Ferrada-Noli, M. Social psychological indicators associated with the suicide rate. *Psychological Reports*, 1997a, 80, 315–322.

Ferrada-Noli, M. Social psychological variables in populations contrasted by income and suicide rate. *Psychological Reports*, 1997b, 81, 307–316.

Ferrada-Noli, M. Health and socioeconomic indicators in psychiatric catchment areas with divergent suicide rates. *Psychological Reports*, 1997c, 81, 611–619.

Gessner, B. D. Temporal trends and geographic patterns of teen suicide in Alaska, 1979–1993. *Suicide & Life-Threatening Behavior*, 1997, 27, 264–273.

Gibb, C. A. Changes in the cultural pattern of Australia, 1906–1946, as determined by the p-technique. *Journal of Social Psychology*, 1956, 43, 225–238.

Gillis, A. R. Literacy and the civilization of violence in 19th-Century France. *Sociological Forum*, 1994, 9, 371–401.

Goto, H., Nakamura, H., & Miyoshi, T. Epidemiological studies on regional differences in suicide mortality and its correlation with socioeconomic factors. *Tokushima Journal of Experimental Medicine*, 1994, 41(3–4), 115–132.

Gruenwald, P. J., Ponicki, W. R., & Mitchell, P. R. Suicide rates and alcohol consumption in the United States, 1970–1989. *Addiction*, 1995, 90, 1063–1075.

Gunnell, D. J., Peters, T. J., Kammerling, R. M., & Brooks, J. Relation between parasuicide, suicide, psychiatric admissions, and socioeconomic deprivation. *British Medical Journal*, 1995, 311, 226–230.

Guttierez, J. M. Social correlates of suicide and homicide in Spain. *European Journal of Psychiatry*, 1995, 9, 172–178.

Hassan, R. *Suicide explained*. Melbourne: Melbourne University, 1995.

Hassan, R., & Tan, G. Women's emancipation and suicide in Australia. *Australian & New Zealand Journal of Sociology*, 1992, 28, 89–104.

Hasselback, P., Lee, K. I., Mao, Y., Nichol, R., & Wigle, D. T. The relationship of suicide rates to sociodemographic factors in Canadian census divisions. *Canadian Journal of Psychiatry*, 1991, 36, 655–659.

Huang, W. C. Religion, culture, economic, and sociological correlates of suicide rates. *Applied Economics Letters*, 1996, 3, 779–782.

Huff-Corzine, L., Corzine, J., & Moore, D. C. Deadly connections. *Social Forces*, 1991, 69, 715–732.

Hutchinson, G. A., & Simeon, D. T. Suicide in Trinidad and Tobago. *International Journal of Social Psychiatry*, 1997, 43, 269–275.

John, J. Economic instability and health. In G. Westcott, P. G. Svensson & H. F. K. Zollner (Eds.), *Health policy implications of unemployment*. Copenhagen: WHO, 1985, 181–204.

Joubert, C. E. Wet or dry county status and its correlates with suicide, homicide, and illegitimacy. *Psychological Reports*, 1994a, 74, 296.

Joubert, C. E. Religious nonaffiliation in relation to suicide, murder, rape, and illegitimacy. *Psychological Reports*, 1994b, 75, 10.

Joubert, C. E. Catholicism and indices of social pathology in the states. *Psychological Reports*, 1995a, 76, 573–574.

Joubert, C. E. Relationship of voters turnout to indices of social distress. *Psychological Reports*, 1995b, 76, 98.

Joubert, C. E. The relation between states adoption of English as their official language to demographic and social pathology variables. *Psychological Reports*, 1997a, 80, 1324–1326.

Joubert, C. E. Correlates of Baptist church membership in the states with social problems.

Psychological Reports, 1997b, 80, 474.

Kelleher, M. J., & Daly, M. Suicide in Cork and Ireland. *British Journal of Psychiatry*, 1990, 157, 533–538.

Kelleher, M. J., Kelleher, M., Corcoran, P., Daly, M., Daly, F., Crowley, M., & Keeley, H. Deliberate self-poisoning, unemployment, and public health. *Suicide & Life-Threatening Behavior*, 1996, 26, 365–373.

Kerkhof, A., & Kunst, A. A European perspective on suicidal behavior. In R. Jenkins, S. Griffiths, I. Wylie, K. Hawton, G. Morgan & A. Tylee (Eds.), *The prevention of suicide*. London: HMSO, 1994, 22–33.

Kimenyi, M. S., & Shughart, W. F. Economics of suicide. *Atlantic Economic Journal*, 1986, 14(1), 121.

Krull, C., & Trovato, F. The quiet revolution and the sex differential in Quebec's suicide rates. *Social Forces*, 1994, 72, 1121–1147.

Krupinski, J., Tiller, J. W. G., Burrows, G. D., & Hallenstein, H. Youth suicide in Victoria. *Medical Journal of Australia*, 1994, 160, 113–116.

Kurosu, S. Suicide in rural areas. *Rural Sociology*, 1991, 56, 603–618.

Leenaars, A. A., & Lester, D. Domestic and economic correlates of personal violence in Canada and the United States. *Italian Journal of Suicidology*, 1994, 4, 7–12.

Leenaars, A. A., & Lester, D. The changing suicide pattern in Canadian adolescents and youth, compared to their American counterparts. *Adolescence*, 1995, 30, 539–547.

Leenaars, A., Yang, B., & Lester, D. The effect of domestic and economic stress on suicide rates in Canada and the United States. *Journal of Clinical Psychology*, 1993, 49, 918–921.

Lester, D. Ecological correlates of adolescent attempted suicide. *Adolescence*, 1990a, 25, 483–485.

Lester, D. The regional variation of suicide by different methods. *Crisis*, 1990b, 11, 32–37.

Lester, D. Lethal aggression, suicide, and homicide. *Deviant Behavior*, 1990c, 11, 293–295.

Lester, D. Social correlates of lethal aggression. *Psychological Reports*, 1990d, 66, 146.

Lester, D. Women in the labor force and suicide. *Psychological Reports*, 1990e, 66, 194.

Lester, D. Fat consumption and suicide. *Journal of Orthomolecular Medicine*, 1990f, 5(1), 20–21.

Lester, D. Mortality from suicide and homicide for African Americans in the USA. *Omega*, 1990–1991, 22, 219–226.

Lester, D. Social correlates of youth suicide rates in the US. *Adolescence*, 1991a, 26, 55–58.

Lester, D. Are the societal correlates of suicide and homicide rates the same for each lethal weapon? *European Journal of Psychiatry*, 1991b, 5, 5–8.

Lester, D. Social correlates of suicide and homicide in urban and rural regions. *Perceptual & Motor Skills*, 1991c, 73, 274.

Lester, D. Alcohol consumption and rates of personal violence in Australia. *Drug & Alcohol Dependence*, 1992a, 31, 15–17.

Lester, D. The etiology of suicide and homicide in urban and rural America. *Journal of Rural Community Psychology*, 1992b, 12(1), 15–27.

Lester, D. *Why people kill themselves*. Springfield, IL: Charles Thomas, 1992c.

Lester, D. The relationship between family integration and suicide and homicide in Finland and the USA. *Psychiatria Fennica*, 1992d, 23, 23–27.

Lester, D. Time-series versus regional correlates of personal violence. *Death Studies*, 1993a, 17, 529–534.

Lester, D. Social correlates of suicide and homicide in England. *European Journal of Psychiatry*, 1993b, 7, 122–126.

Lester, D. An attempt to explain changing elderly suicide rates. *International Journal of Geriatric Psychiatry*, 1993c, 8, 435–437.

Lester, D. Suicide in Ireland from 1950 to 1985. *Irish Medical Journal*, 1993d, 86, 172, 210–211.

Lester, D. Domestic social integration and suicide in Italy and the United States. *Italian Journal of Suicidology*, 1993e, 3, 29–31.

Lester, D. Suicide in New Zealand 1950–1985. *New Zealand Medical Journal*, 1993f, 106, 111.

Lester, D. Domestic integration and suicide in England and Wales, 1901–1975. *Perceptual & Motor Skills*, 1993g, 77, 922.

Lester, D. Social integration and suicide. *Sociale Wetenschappen*, 1993h, 36(3), 52–59.

Lester, D. Durkheim's theory of suicide in Hungary and the United States of America. *Psychiatria Hungarica*, 1993i, 8, 493–496.

Lester, D. Suicide in prison. *European Archives of Psychiatry*, 1994a, 244, 99–100.

Lester, D. Domestic social integration and suicide. *Italian Journal of Suicidology*, 1994b, 4, 13–15.

Lester, D. The preventive effect of marriage for suicide in men and women. *Italian Journal of Suicidology*, 1994c, 4, 83–85.

Lester, D. Maori and non-Maori youth suicide. *New Zealand Medical Journal*, 1994d, 107, 161.

Lester, D. Social correlates of the percentages of suicides and homicides employing firearms. *Perceptual & Motor Skills*, 1994e, 79, 254.

Lester, D. Suicide in wide-open spaces. *Perceptual & Motor Skills*, 1994f, 79, 650.

Lester, D. Suicide by region of birth and region of residence. *Perceptual & Motor Skills*, 1994g, 79, 698.

Lester, D. Scholastic aptitude and rates of personal violence in the USA. *Perceptual & Motor Skills*, 1994h, 79, 738.

Lester, D. Suicide in Hungary. *Psychiatria Hungarica*, 1994i, 9, 225–230.

Lester, D. Predicting the suicide rate in Wales. *Psychological Reports*, 1994j, 75, 1054.

Lester, D. Social integration and suicide in Puerto Rico and the United States. *Puerto Rican Health Sciences Journal*, 1994k, 13(1), 39.

Lester, D. The variation of suicide rates over time in Scandinavia. *Scandinavian Journal of Social Medicine*, 1994m, 22, 159–160.

Lester, D. Comparing the changing suicide rate in Singapore with the rate in England/Wales and the USA, 1950–1985. *Singapore Medical Journal*, 1994n, 35, 490–491.

Lester, D. Young adult suicide and exposure to television. *Social Psychiatry & Psychiatric Epidemiology*, 1994p, 29, 110–111.

Lester, D. *Patterns of suicide and homicide in America*. Commack, NY: Nova Science, 1994q.

Lester, D. Domestic integration and suicide in Pacific Rim nations. *Chinese Journal of Mental Health*, 1994r, 7(1), 21–24.

Lester, D. Domestic social integration, suicide, and homicide in Poland, France, and Yugoslavia. *EuroCriminology*, 1994s, 7, 73–75.

Lester, D. Domestic integration and suicide in 21 nations, 1950–1985. *International Journal of Comparative Sociology*, 1994t, 35(1–2), 131–137.

Lester, D. Suicide, alcohol, and divorce. *Addiction*, 1995a, 90, 985–988.

Lester, D. The association between alcohol consumption and suicide and homicide rates. *Alcohol & Alcoholism*, 1995b, 30, 465–468.

Lester, D. Social correlates of American Indian suicide and homicide rates. *American Indian & Alaska Native Mental Health Research*, 1995c, 6(3), 46–55.

Lester, D. Alcohol availability, alcoholism, and suicide and homicide. *American Journal of Drug & Alcohol Abuse*, 1995d, 21, 147–150.

Lester, D. Explaining the regional variation of suicide and homicide. *Archives of Suicide Research*, 1995e, 1, 159–174.

Lester, D. Medical resources and the prevention of suicide and homicide. *European Journal of Psychiatry*, 1995f, 9, 97–99.

Lester, D. Social integration, the opportunity for suicide, and suicide. *Homeostasis*, 1995g, 36, 35–39.

Lester, D. Why are some nations experiencing an increase in youth suicide rates. *Homeostasis*, 1995h, 36, 232–233.

Lester, D. Suicide in the elderly in Austria. *International Journal of Geriatric Psychiatry*, 1995i, 10, 713–714.

Lester, D. Is divorce an indicator of general or specific malaise? *Journal of Divorce & Remarriage*, 1995j, 23, 203–205.

Lester, D. Remarriage rates and suicide and homicide in the United States. *Journal of Divorce & Remarriage*, 1995k, 23, 207–210.

Lester, D. An extension of the association between population density and mental illness to suicidal behavior. *Journal of Social Psychology*, 1995m, 135, 657–658.

Lester, D. Suicide in Hong Kong, 1971–1990. *Perceptual & Motor Skills*, 1995n, 80, 1230.

Lester, D. Suicide in Quebec, 1951–1986. *Psychological Reports*, 1995p, 76, 122.

Lester, D. To die with your boots on. *Psychological Reports*, 1995q, 76, 529–530.

Lester, D. Are females' suicides in Japan fatalistic? *Psychological Reports*, 1995r, 76, 986.

Lester, D. Suicide, homicide, and a history of oppression in the Caribbean nations. *Psychological Reports*, 1995s, 77, 942.

Lester, D. American Indian suicide rates and the economy. *Psychological Reports*, 1995t, 77, 994.

Lester, D. Fundamentalism, suicide, and homicide. *Psychological Reports*, 1995u, 77, 1338.

Lester, D. Combining opposing methodologies in studies of suicide and homicide. *Quality & Quantity*, 1995v, 29, 67–72.

Lester, D. Does domestic integration predict the Dutch homicide rate? *Sociale Wetenschappen*, 1995w, 38(2), 47–49.

Lester, D. Il suicidio in Italia. *Italian Journal of Suicidology*, 1995x, 5, 33–37.

Lester, D. Domestic integration and the Taiwanese homicide and suicide rate. *Chinese Journal of Mental Health*, 1995y, 8(3), 21–25.

Lester, D. Durkheim ongyilkossag-elmeletenek ellenorzese Magyarorszagon. *Psychiatria Hungarica*, 1995z, 10, 509–511.

Lester, D. Testing Durkheim's theory of suicide. *European Archives of Psychiatry*, 1996a, 246, 112–113.

Lester, D. Lethal violence and marital disintegration. *Italian Journal of Suicidology*, 1996b, 6, 73–75.

Lester, D. Social correlates of suicide in the British Isles. *Perceptual & Motor Skills*, 1996c, 83, 1194.

Lester, D. Aboriginal suicide in British Columbia. *Perceptual & Motor Skills*, 1996d, 83, 1202.

Lester, D. Comment on "Jewish affiliation in relation to suicide rates." *Psychological Reports*, 1996e, 78, 834.

Lester, D. Religion and suicide. *Psychological Reports*, 1996f, 78, 1090.

Lester, D. Membership in associations and suicide rates. *Psychological Reports*, 1996g, 79, 202.

Lester, D. Cultural evolution, suicide, and homicide. *Psychological Reports*, 1996h, 79, 334.

Lester, D. Suicide in Indian states and religion. *Psychological Reports*, 1996i, 79, 342.

Lester, D. A regional study of fertility and suicide rates. *Psychological Reports*, 1996j, 79, 474.

Lester, D. Fertility and suicide. *Psychological Reports*, 1996k, 79, 482.

Lester, D. Social stress, homicide, and suicide. *Psychological Reports*, 1996m, 79, 922.

Lester, D. Inequality of income and rates of violence in Caucasian and black groups. *Psychological Reports*, 1996n, 79, 978.

Lester, D. Domestic protests and rates of personal violence (suicide and homicide) *Psychological Reports*, 1996p, 79, 1006.

Lester, D. The civilization of violence. *Psychological Reports*, 1996q, 79, 1122.

Lester, D. Testing a Durkheimian theory of suicide and homicide in Switzerland. *Swiss Journal of Sociology*, 1996r, 22, 201–204.

Lester, D. Homicide rates in the Caribbean islands. *Psychological Reports*, 1996s, 79, 1070.

Lester, D. *Patterns of suicide and homicide in the world.* Commack, NY: Nova Science, 1996t.

Lester, D. Regional variation in homicide rates of infants and children. *Injury Prevention*, 1996u, 2, 121–123.

Lester, D. On the regional variation of suicide in Finland. *Psychiatria Fennica*, 1996v, 27, 167–169.

Lester, D. Suicide in the former Czechoslovakia. *Homeostasis*, 1996w, 37, 209–213.

Lester, D. The regional variation of suicide in the United States in 1880 and 1980. *Omega*, 1996–1997, 34, 81–84.

Lester, D. Domestic social integration and suicide in Israel. *Israel Journal of Psychiatry*, 1997a, 34, 157–161.

Lester, D. Suicide in Italy. *Italian Journal of Suicidology*, 1997b, 7, 19–21.

Lester, D. The association of suicide and homicide over time in nations. Italian *Journal of Suicidology*, 1997c, 7, 111–112

Lester, D. Suicide in Finland, 1752 to 1988. *Psychiatria Fennica*, 1997d, 28, 26–33.

Lester, D. Social correlates of suicide rates in Portugal. *Psychological Reports*, 1997e, 80, 962.

Lester, D. Domestic integration and suicide rates in the provinces of Canada. *Psychological Reports*, 1997f, 81, 1114.

Lester, D. Black riots and black suicide rates.

Psychological Reports, 1997g, 81, 1134.

Lester, D. Comment on "Catholicism and indices of social pathology in the states." *Psychological Reports*, 1997h, 80, 1005–1006.

Lester, D., & Abe, K. Social integration and suicide/homicide in Japan and the United States. *Japanese Journal of Psychiatry & Neurology*, 1992, 46, 849–851.

Lester, D., & Agarwal, K. Ecological correlates of suicide and homicide in India and the United States. *Psychological Reports*, 1990, 67, 1374.

Lester, D., & Ausenda, G. The regional variation of suicide in Italy and the USA. *Italian Journal of Suicidology*, 1993, 3, 97–99.

Lester, D., & Ausenda, G. Correlates of suicide in Italian regions in 1864–1876. *Perceptual & Motor Skills*, 1997, 84, 106.

Lester, D., Curran, P. S., & Yang, B. Time-series regression results of suicide rates by social correlates for the USA and Northern Ireland. *Irish Journal of Psychological Medicine*, 1991, 8, 26–28.

Lester, D., & Garcia, J. M. G. Suicide and domestic integration in Spain. *Psychological Reports*, 1995, 77, 218.

Lester, D., & Garcia, J. M. G. Domestic integration and suicide in Spain. *Psychological Reports*, 1996, 79, 1162.

Lester, D., & Hu, Y. H. The regional variation of suicide and homicide in the USA and Taiwan. *Crisis*, 1993, 14, 126–128.

Lester, D., & Moksony, F. The social correlates of suicide in Hungary in the elderly. *European Psychiatry*, 1994, 9, 273–274.

Lester, D., Motohashi, Y., & Yang, B. The impact of the economy on suicide and homicide rates in Japan and the United States. *International Journal of Social Psychiatry*, 1992, 38, 314–317.

Lester, D., & Natarajan, M. Predicting the time-series suicide and murder rates in India. *Perceptual & Motor Skills*, 1995, 80, 570.

Lester, D., & Rihmer, Z. Sociodemographic correlates of suicides rates in Hungary and the United States. *Psychiatria Hungarica*, 1992, 7, 453–457.

Lester, D., & Savlid, A. C. Suicide and wealth in Sweden. *Psychological Reports*, 1997a, 80, 34.

Lester, D., & Savlid, A. C. Social psychological indicators associated with the suicide rate. *Psychological Reports*, 1997b, 80, 1065–1066.

Lester, D., & Savlid, A. C. Comment on "Social psychological variables in populations contrasted by income and suicide rate." *Psychological Reports*, 1997c, 81, 1386.

Lester, D., & Yang, B. The relationship between divorce, unemployment, and female participation in the labour force and suicide rates in Australia and America. *Australian & New Zealand Journal of Psychiatry*, 1991, 25, 519–523.

Lester, D., & Yang, B. The influence of war on suicide rates. *Journal of Social Psychology*, 1992, 132, 135–137.

Lester, D., & Yang, B. Do Chinese women commit fatalistic suicide? *Chinese Journal of Mental Health*, 1995, 8, 23–26.

Lester, D., & Yang, B. *Suicide and homicide in the 20th Century*. Commack, NY: Nova Science, 1998.

Levine, R., Miyake, K., & Lee, M. Places rated revisited. *Environment & Behavior*, 1989, 21, 531–553.

Lewis, G., Appleby, L., & Jarman, B. Suicide and psychiatric services. *Lancet*, 1994, 344, 822.

Linsky, A. S., Bachman, R., & Straus, M. A. *Stress, culture, and aggression*. New Haven: Yale University, 1995.

Liu, T., Waterbor, J. W., & Soong, S. J. Relationships between beer, wine, and spirits consumption and suicide rates in United States from 1977 to 1988. *Omega*, 1995–1996, 32, 227–240.

Maguire, E. R., & Snipes, J. B. Reassessing the link between country music and suicide. *Social Forces*, 1994, 72, 1239–1243.

Makela, P. Alcohol consumption and suicide mortality by age among Finnish men. *Addiction*, 1996, 91, 101–112.

Makinen, I. Are there social correlates to suicide? *Social Science & Medicine*, 1997, 44, 1919–1929.

Males, M. California's suicide decline, 1970–1990. *Suicide & Life-Threatening Behavior*, 1994, 24, 24–37.

Masumura, W. T. Wife abuse and other

forms of aggression. *Victimology*, 1979, 4(1), 46–59.

McCall, P. L. Adolescent and elderly white male suicide trends. *Journal of Gerontology*, 1991, 46,(1), S43–S51.

McCall, P. L., & Land, K. C. Trends in white male adolescent, young adult, and elderly suicide. *Social Science Research*, 1994, 23, 57–81.

Medoff, M. H., & Skov, I. L. Religion and behavior. *Journal of Socio-Economics*, 1992, 21, 143–151.

Motohashi, Y. Effects of socioeconomic factors on secular trends in suicide in Japan, 1953–1986. *Journal of Biosocial Science*, 1991, 23, 221–227.

Nalla, M. K., & Alvarez, A. The many faces of violence. *International Journal of Comparative & Applied Criminal Justice*, 1995, 19, 19–31.

Neeleman, J., Halpern, D., Leon, D., & Lewis, G. Tolerance of suicide, religion, and suicide rates. *Psychological Medicine*, 1997, 27, 1165–1171.

Nisbet, P. A. Protective factors for suicidal black females. *Suicide & Life-Threatening Behavior*, 1996, 26, 325–341.

Norstrom, T. The impact of alcohol, divorce, and unemployment on suicide. *Social Forces*, 1995a, 74, 293–314.

Norstrom, T. Alcohol and suicide. *Addiction*, 1995b, 90, 1463–1469.

Pescosolido, B. A. The social context of religious integration and suicide. *Sociological Quarterly*, 1990, 31, 337–357.

Pescosolido, B. A., & Wright, E. R. Suicide and the role of the family over the life course. *Family Perspectives*, 1990, 24(1), 41–58.

Rahav, G. Cross-national variations in violence. *Aggressive Behavior*, 1990, 16, 69–76.

Reinfurt, D. W., Stewart, J. R., & Weaver, N. L. The economy as a factor in motor vehicle fatalities, suicides, and homicides. *Accident Analysis & Prevention*, 1991, 23, 453–462.

Rihmer, Z., Barsi, J., Veg, K., & Katona, C. L. E. Suicide rates in Hungary correlate negatively with reported rates of depression. *Journal of Affective Disorders*, 1990, 20, 87–91.

Rossow, I. Suicide, alcohol, and divorce. *Addiction*, 1993, 88, 1659–1665.

Rossow, I. Regional analyses of alcohol and suicide in Norway. *Suicide & Life-Threatening*

Behavior, 1995, 25, 401–409.

Sakinofsky, I., & Stolar, A. Socio-economic factors in suicide in young people. In D. Lester (Ed.), *Suicide '94.* Denver: AAS, 1994, 29–31.

Seydlitz, R., Laska, S., Spain, D., Triche, E. W., & Bishop, K. L. Development and social problems. *Rural Sociology*, 1993, 58, 93–110.

Shiu, L. P., Hui, W. M., & Lam, S. K. Negative social events, stress, and health in Hong Kong. *Journal of Epidemiology & Community Health*, 1993, 47, 181–185.

Skog, O. J., Teixeira, Z., Barrias, J., & Moreira, R. Alcohol and suicide. *Addiction*, 1995, 90, 1053–1061.

Sloan, F. A., Reilly, B. A., & Schenzler, C. Effects of prices, civil and criminal sanctions, and law enforcement on alcohol-related mortality. *Journal of Studies on Alcohol*, 1994, 55, 454–465.

Souetre, E., Wehr, T. A., Douillet, P., & Darcourt, G. Influence of environmental factors on suicidal behavior. *Psychiatry Research*, 1990, 32, 253–263.

Stack, S. The effect of divorce on suicide in Denmark. *Sociological Quarterly*, 1990, 31, 359–370.

Stack, S. The effect of religiosity on suicide in Sweden. *Journal for the Scientific Study of Religion*, 1991, 30, 462–468.

Stack, S. The effect of divorce on suicide in Finland. *Journal of Marriage & the Family*, 1992a, 54, 636–642.

Stack, S. The effect of divorce on suicide in Japan. *Journal of Marriage & the Family*, 1992b, 54, 327–334.

Stack, S. The effect of modernization on suicide in Finland. *Sociological Perspectives*, 1993, 36, 137–148.

Stack, S. Culture and suicide. In J. McIntosh (Ed.), *Suicide '96.* Washington, DC: AAS, 1996a, 177–179.

Stack, S. Effect of female labor force participation on female suicide attempts. *Death Studies*, 1996b, 20, 285–291.

Stack, S. The effect of labor-force participation on female suicide rates. *Omega*, 1996–1997, 34, 163–169.

Stack, S. A comparative analysis of the effect of domestic institutions on suicide ideology. *Journal of Comparative Family Studies*, 1997, 28,

304–319.

Stack, S., & Gundlach, J. Country music and suicide. *Social Forces*, 1994, 72, 1245–1248.

Stack, S., Gundlach, J., & Reeves, J. L. The heavy metal subculture and suicide. *Suicide & Life-Threatening Behavior*, 1994b, 24, 15–23.

Stack, S., & Lester, D. The effect of religion on suicide ideation. *Social Psychiatry & Psychiatric Epidemiology*, 1991, 26, 168–170.

Stack, S., Wasserman, I., & Kposowa, A. The effects of religion and feminism on suicide ideology. *Journal for the Scientific Study of Religion*, 1994a, 33, 110–121.

Trovato, F. A Durkheimian analysis of youth suicide. *Suicide & Life-Threatening Behavior*, 1992a, 22, 413–427.

Trovato, F. An ecological analysis of suicide. *Internal Review of Modern Sociology*, 1992b, 22(2), 57–72.

Trovato, F., & Vos, R. Domestic/religious individualism and youth suicide in Canada. *Family Perspectives*, 1990, 24(1), 69–81.

Trovato, F., & Vos, R. Married female labor force participation and suicide in Canada, 1971 and 1981. *Sociological Forum*, 1992, 7, 661–677.

Unnithan, N. P., & Whitt, H. P. Inequality, economic development, and lethal violence. International *Journal of Comparative Sociology*, 1992, 33, 182–196.

Viren, M. Suicide and business cycles. *Applied Economics Letters*, 1996, 3, 737–738.

Wallace, R. Urban desertification, public health, and public order. *Social Science & Medicine*, 1990, 31, 801–813.

Wasserman, I. The impact of epidemic, war, prohibition, and media on suicide. *Suicide & Life-Threatening Behavior*, 1992, 22, 240–254.

Wasserman, I., & Stack, S. The effect of religion on suicide. *Omega*, 1993, 27, 295–305.

Wenz, F. V. Completed suicide, attempted suicide, and urban social structure. In B. S. Comstock & R. Maris (Eds.), *Proceedings of the 8th Annual Meeting*. Denver: AAS, 1976.

Weyerer, S., & Wiedenmann, A. Economic factors and the rates of suicide in Germany between 1881 and 1989. *Psychological Reports*, 1995, 76, 1331–1341.

Wiedenmann, A., & Weyerer, S. Testing Durkheim's theory of suicide. *European Archives of Psychiatry*, 1994, 244, 284–286.

Yamamoto, T. Contemporary social problems in Japan. *International Journal of Japanese Sociology*, 1992, 1(October), 19–33.

Yang, B. The economy and suicide. *American Journal of Economics & Sociology*, 1992, 51, 87–99.

Yang, B. The impact of the economy on the elderly suicide rate in the USA. In K. Bohme, R. Freytag, C. Wachtler & H. Wedler (Eds.), *Suicidal behaviour*. Regensburg: S. Roderer, 1993, 196–199.

Yang, B. The differential impact of the economy on suicide in the young and the elderly. *Archives of Suicide Research*, 1995, 1, 111–120.

Yang, B., & Lester, D. Time-series analyses of the American suicide rate. *Social Psychiatry & Psychiatric Epidemiology*, 1990, 25, 274–275.

Yang, B., & Lester, D. The association between working and personal violence (suicide and homicide) in married men and women. *International Journal of Contemporary Sociology*, 1992a, 29, 67–75.

Yang, B., & Lester, D. Suicide, homicide, and unemployment. *Psychological Reports*, 1992b, 71, 844–846.

Yang, B., & Lester, D. Is suicide a rational behavior? *Atlantic Economic Journal*, 1993, 21(3), 95.

Yang, B., & Lester, D. Crime and unemployment. *Journal of Socio-Economics*, 1994a, 23, 215–222.

Yang, B., & Lester, D. Economic and social correlates of suicide in Caribbean nations. *Psychological Reports*, 1994b, 75, 351–352.

Yang, B., & Lester, D. The social impact of unemployment. *Applied Economics Letters*, 1994c, 1, 223–226.

Yang, B., & Lester, D. Social stress and suicide. *Psychological Reports*, 1995a, 76, 553–554.

Yang, B., & Lester, D. Suicide, homicide, and unemployment. *Applied Economics Letters*, 1995b, 2, 278–279.

Yang, B., Lester, D., & Stack, S. Suicide and unemployment. *Journal of Socio-Economics*, 1992b, 21(1), 39–41.

Yang, B., Lester, D., & Yang, C. H. Sociological and economic theories of suicide.

Social Science & Medicine, 1992a, 34, 333–334.

Zalman, M., & Stack, S. The relationship between euthanasia and suicide in the Netherlands. In D. Lester (Ed.), *Suicide '95*. Washington, DC: AAS, 1995, 86–87.

Zalman, M., & Stack, S. The relationship between euthanasia and suicide in the Netherlands. *Social Science Quarterly*, 1996, 77, 577–593.

Zekeri, A. A., & Wilkinson, K. P. Suicide and rurality in Alabama communities. *Social*

Indicators Research, 1995, 36, 177–190.

Zimmerman, S. L. The connection between macro and micro levels. *Suicide & Life-Threatening Behavior*, 1990, 20, 31–55.

Zimmerman, S. L. Psychache in context. *Journal of Nervous & Mental Disease*, 1995, 183, 425–434.

Zonda, T., Rihmer, Z., & Lester, D. Social correlates of deviant behavior in Hungary. *European Journal of Psychiatry*, 1992, 6, 236–238.

Chapter 10

METEOROLOGICAL CORRELATES OF SUICIDE

Weather

Completed Suicide

Martin et al. (1990) studied suicide in Belgium by month for 1969–1984. The number of violent suicides was negatively associated with the temperature and atmospheric pressure (but only when lagged in time by four months) and positively associated with humidity. The number of nonviolent suicides was not associated with weather variables. The results were similar for men and for women.

Linkowski et al. (1992) found no association over months in Belgium between the number of nonviolent suicides and the weather. Male violent suicides, however, were negatively associated with the amount of sunlight, associated positively with humidity, and not associated significantly with temperature and atmospheric pressure. Female violent suicides showed only the association with sunlight.

In Belgium 1979–1987, Maes et al. (1994) found that the weekly incidence of nonviolent suicide was not associated with weather variables. Violent suicide was associated with ambient temperature, sunlight duration, and increased temperature (positively) and relative humidity (negatively), but not associated with air pressure, precipitation, wind speed, or a geomagnetic index.

In Singapore, Kok and Tsoi (1993) correlated suicide rates and weather variables by month over a ten-year period. There was no association for temperature, humidity, rainfall, wind speed, acidity, or smoke, and the association with sunshine was negative. The associations were stronger for the suicide rates of 0–19 year olds: positive with temperature and negative with humidity, rainfall, and wind speed.

Egashira et al. (1989) found that daily sunshine hours and numbers of suicides in ten-day units were positively associated in Kitakyushu (Japan) for November to March, but not for May to September.

Tietjen and Kripke (1994) looked at periods of ten consecutive days with above average sunshine and those with ten consecutive days with below-average sunshine. In Sacramento County (but not in Los Angeles County), suicides increased after a series of below average sunshine days and decreased 21–25 days after a series of above-average sunshine days.

In Italy, Preti (1997) found that the monthly rate of completed suicide was associated with the maximum and minimum temperature, daylight duration, and sunlight (positively) and the humidity and rainfall (negatively).

In one region of England, Salib (1997) found that days on which elderly suicides occurred did not differ in temperature, humidity, or rainfall but did have more hours of sunshine. Salib and Gray (1997) found that suicides took placed on days with more hours of sunshine; the preceding day also had more sunshine and more diurnal variation in temperature. The associations with weather variables were not affected by the method of suicide.

In Alam Ata in Central Asia, Ashkaliyev et al. (1995) found more suicides on days with more perturbation of the geomagnetic field. In Israel, Stoupel et al. (1995a, 1995b) found that suicide was related positively to proton flux, geomagnetic activity, and sudden magnetic disturbances in the ionosphere, but not related to positive or negative ionization of the atmosphere, sunspots, solar radioflux, or radiowave propagation. In Lithuania, however, suicide was related to sunspots and solar flux (negatively) but not geomagnetic activity.

In an ecological study, Agbayewa (1993) found that the elderly suicide rate in the regions of British Columbia (Canada) was not associated with climatic severity (but was negatively associated with population size). Lester (1996) found many correlates of city suicide rates with weather variables in 1970, but only the negative association between wind speed and suicide rates replicated in 1989.

Attempted Suicide

By month in England, Barker et al. (1994) found that attempted suicide was positively associated with cloudiness, rain, and temperature and negatively associated with visibility. Looking at days with extreme weather conditions, male attempts were more common on extremely windy days, while female attempts were more common on very hot and still days. In multiple regressions, only month predicted male attempts, but month

and weather variables predicted female attempts.

In Italy, Preti (1997) found that the monthly rate of attempted suicide was associated with daylight duration and sunlight (positively) and the humidity and rainfall (negatively), similar to the associations for completed suicide.

Lunar Variables

Martin (1990) studied suicides in Saskatchewan (Canada) from 1984–1989 and found no effect for moon phase or lunar distance (overall, by sex, and by method), Maldonado and Kraus (1991) found no variation by lunar phase for suicides in Sacramento County (CA) for 1925–1983, and Gutierrez-Garcia and Tusell (1997) found no lunar association for completed suicides in Madrid, Spain. On the other hand, Hassan (1995) found more completed suicides than expected during the full moon.

Matthew et al. (1991) found a tendency for male attempted suicides to peak during the fourth quarter of the lunar cycle. In contrast, Rogers et al. (1991) found no significant variation in attempted suicides in Edinburgh (Scotland) over the lunar cycle, although there were trends for peaks at the time of full and new moons.

Martin et al. (1992) reviewed 11 studies on completed suicide and the lunar cycle and found no relationship. For 12 studies of attempted suicide and the lunar cycle, there were no consistent trends.

Discussion

On the whole, results from these studies are either inconsistent or nonsignificant. There is a noteworthy absence of any theory behind the studies and, if consistent and significant findings were obtained, their import for the study of suicide would be   questionable.

REFERENCES

Agbayewa, M. O. Elderly suicide in British Columbia. *Canadian Journal of Public Health*, 1993, 84, 231–236.

Ashkaliyev, Y. F., Drobzhev, V. I., Somsikov, V. M., Turkeyeva, B. A., & Yakovety, T. K. Effect of heliogeographical parameters in the ecological situation. *Biophysics*, 1995, 40, 1035–1041.

Barker, A., Hawton, K., Fagg, J., & Jennison, C. Seasonal and weather factors in parasuicide. *British Journal of Psychiatry*, 1994, 165, 375–380.

Egashira, K., Ichii, S., & Abe, K. Correlation between suicides and sunshine hours in Kitakyushu. Annual Congress of the Japanese Society of Biometeorology, 1989.

Gutierrez-Garcia, J. M., & Tusell, F. Suicides and the lunar cycle. *Psychological Reports*, 1997, 80, 243–250.

Hassan, R. *Suicide explained.* Melbourne: Melbourne University, 1995.

Kok, L. P., & Tsoi, W. F. Season, climate, and suicide in Singapore. *Medicine, Science & the Law*, 1993, 33, 247–252.

Lester, D. A hazardous environment and city suicide rates. *Perceptual & Motor Skills*, 1996, 82, 1330.

Linkowski, P., Martin, F., & De Maertelaer, V. Effect of some climatic factors on violent and nonviolent suicides in Belgium. *Journal of Affective Disorders*, 1992, 25, 161–166.

Maes, M., De Meyer, F., Thompson, P., Peeters, D., & Cosyns, P. Synchronized annual rhythms in violent suicide rate, ambient temperature, and the light-dark span. *Acta Psychiatrica Scandinavica*, 1994, 90, 391–396.

Maldonado, G., & Kraus, J. F. Variation in suicide occurrence by time of day, day of the week, month, and lunar phase. *Suicide & Life-Threatening Behavior*, 1991, 21, 174–187.

Martin, F., De Meertelaer, V., & Linkowski,

P. A differential effect of climatic parameters on violent and nonviolent suicide. In G. Ferrari, M. Bellini & P. Crepet (Eds.), *Suicidal behavior and risk factors*. Bologna: Monduzzi-Editore, 1990, 89–93.

Martin, S. J. Distal variables in a completed suicide population. Master's thesis, University of Saskatchewan, 1990.

Martin, S. J., Kelly, I. W., & Saklofske, D. H. Suicide and lunar cycles. *Psychological Reports*, 1992, 71, 787–795.

Matthew, V. M., Lindesay, J., Shanmuganathan, N., & Eapen, V. Attempted suicide and the lunar cycle. *Psychological Reports*, 1991, 68, 927–930.

Preti, A. The influence of seasonal change on suicidal behavior in Italy. *Journal of Affective Disorders*, 1997, 44, 123–130.

Rogers, T. D., Masterton, G., & McGuire, R. Parasuicide and the lunar cycle. *Psychological Medicine*, 1991, 21, 393–397.

Salib, E., Elderly suicides and weather conditions. *International Journal of Geriatric Psychiatry*, 1997, 12, 937–941.

Salib, E., & Gray, N. Weather conditions and fatal self-harm in North Cheshire 1989–1993. *British Journal of Psychiatry*, 1997, 171, 473–477.

Stoupel, E., Abramson, E., Sulkes, J., Martfel, J., Stein, N., Handelman, M., Shimshoni, M., Zadka, P., & Gabbay, U. Relationship between suicide and myocardial infarction with regard to changing physical environmental conditions. *International Journal of Biometeorology*, 1995a, 38, 199–203.

Stoupel, E., Petrauskiene, J., Kalediene, R., Abramson, E., & Sulkes, J. Clinical cosmobiology. *International Journal of Biometeorology*, 1995b, 38, 204–208.

Tietjen, G. H., & Kripke, D. F. Suicides in California (1968–1977). *Psychiatry Research*, 1994, 53, 161–172.

Chapter 11

THE SOCIAL RELATIONSHIPS OF SUICIDAL PEOPLE

Marriage And Children

In the United States, Stack (1996a, 1996b) found that divorced and widowed had higher suicide rates, both for African Americans and for whites. For whites only, the single also had a higher rate of suicide. Age had a negative association with suicide rates for both ethnic groups, but a sex difference was found only for whites.

In Queensland (Australia), Cantor and Slater (1995) found that married people had the lowest suicide rate. The percentage of suicides peaked for men married 15–19 years and 0–4 years, for women 5–9 years and 35–39 years. For married women, those with three or more children had lower suicide rates than those with no children.

Heikkinen et al. (1995) found that Finnish suicides were more often never married, divorced, or widowed than the general population, and more often living alone or living with parents. The male suicides were more often single and less-often widowed than the female suicides, and abused alcohol more. Isometsa et al. (1996) compared suicides with children to those without children in the same sample. Those with children were older at the time of their suicide, more often married at some point in their lives, more often women, and had a

major depression more often and schizophrenia less often.

Calzeroni et al. (1990) found no association between a history of attempted suicide and celibacy or childlessness in a sample of patients with major affective disorders. However, the suicide attempters did have fewer children.

Hoyer and Lund (1993) studied a large sample of women in Norway and found that the risk of completed suicide was higher in those never married and in those with no children. The more children, the lower the risk of suicide both for women aged 25–44 and 45–74

Parental Loss

Du Plessis (1992) found that attempted suicides who had deceased or divorced parents had more past suicidal ideation and a tendency toward more substance abuse, attempted suicide in their family members, and interpersonal problems than attempters with intact families.

Family Functioning

Keitner et al. (1990) studied inpatients with unipolar depressions. They were administered a family assessment device when admitted and then followed up. The patients who subsequently completed, attempted, or thought about suicide differed on only two of the seven scales at intake – their general functioning and problem-solving scores were worse. Their families did not differ on six of the scales, but scored worse on roles. At the initial admission, the patients who were subsequently suicidal reported an earlier onset of the depression.

Shulman (1992) compared famous suicides and those dying of natural deaths in the United States, Japan, and German-speaking countries. The Americans had experienced more conflict with their mothers than controls; the Japanese were more often raised away from their parents than the controls; the German-speaking suicides had more conflict with their fathers than controls.

De Jong (1992) found that college students with prior suicidal ideation and attempts as well as depressed college students had parents who argued more, were more in danger of splitting up, and made more threats to separate than nondepressed students. These groups were also less attached to both parents, and both showed less individuation from the parents. The suicidal group felt that their parents were less available during their childhood. The groups did not differ in parental loss or peer attachments.

Hirsch and Ellis (1995) found that suicidal ideation in college students was predicted by coming from a single-parent family, but not by age, sex, ethnicity, alcohol/drug use, marital status, or past exposure to suicide.

Miller et al. (1992) found that suicidal adolescents saw their families as having less cohesion and less adaptability than did nonsuicidal adolescent psychiatric patients. Compared to normals, both the suicidal and nonsuicidal psychiatric patients saw their families as less cohesive and adaptable, had less communication with mothers and fathers, and had less caring and more over-protective parents.

Mitchell and Rosenthal (1992) found that families with a suicidal adolescent (ideator or attempter) did not differ from those with a nonsuicidal adolescent psychiatric patient in structural family interaction (enmeshed, disengaged, overprotective, neglecting, rigid, flexible, etc). The suicidal families had more sexual dissatisfaction and conventionalism and more marital conflict over child rearing and role orientation.

In a sample of children who were psychiatric patients, Asarnow (1992) found that the attempted suicides described their families as less cohesive, less expressive, and more in conflict. The suicidal children were more depressed, but did not differ in age, social class, sex, or intelligence test scores.

Campbell et al. (1993) looked at children who were psychiatric inpatients and found that the suicidal children reported less family cohesion, more family conflict, less family expressiveness, less family organization, and less family achievement orientation. The parents' ratings of these dimensions and their child's suicidality were less strongly associated.

Couples

Canetto and Feldman (1993) studied couples with a suicidal woman (attempter or ideator). The women scored normally on a measure of covert dependence, while their male mates scored abnormally. The males encouraged dependency more in the women than the women did in the men. The women and men did not differ in overall dependence.

Friends

Welz (1994) found that attempted suicides had fewer regular contacts than normal controls (but more frequent interaction with them) and received less psychological and instrumental support. The attempters living alone belonged to fewer organizations than those living with others, whereas the controls belonged to more.

Kimbrough et al. (1996a) found that suicidal ideation and perceived support from family (but not perceived support from community) were negatively associated both in African American and in white college students. The two groups of students did not differ in friends, acculturation, depression, or suicidal ideation, but the white students perceived more support from teachers.

Kimbrough et al. (1996b) compared black students at predominantly black and predominantly white colleges. The two groups of blacks students did not differ in depression or suicidal ideation. Suicidal ideation was associated with depression, religiosity, and support from family and friends but not with support from school or boy/girl friends.

Latha et al. (1996) found that attempted suicides and depressives had fewer acquaintances and group memberships, less-frequent social contacts, and a poorer quality of social support than normals.

Knott and Range (1997) found that nonsuicidal students perceived suicidal students as having less social support than the suicidal students perceived about themselves.

Interpersonal Functioning

D'Andrea (1990) found that suicidal and depressed college students were both lower in self-centeredness and higher in separation anxiety and dependency denial than normal controls. The suicidal students, however, had the highest engulfment anxiety. (The three groups did not differ in recent stressors.)

Spirito et al. (1990) compared adolescent suicide attempters with psychiatric controls and found no differences in depression or social skills (appropriate social skills, inappropriate assertiveness, impulsive/recalcitrant behavior, overconfidence, or jealousy/withdrawal). Repeaters did not differ in social skills from first-timers but were more depressed.

Resources

Conrad (1991) studied eleventh and twelfth graders and found that those who had attempted suicide more often had no one to talk to, attended church less, had divorced and separated parents more often, and had worse health. D'Attilio et al. (1992) found that suicidal potential in students was associated with having fewer social supports and being less satisfied with those contacts.

Berger (1993) found that the more seriously suicidal medical patients had fewer social supports (and had more past and present suicidality). Eskin (1993) found that suicide risk in Turkish subjects was associated with less perceived social support from friends and family (as well as hopelessness, negative self-evaluation, and hostility). Neeleman and Power (1944) found that depressed patients and attempted suicides were more depressed than medical controls, had less social support, and were more dissatisfied with their social supports.

On the other hand, Whatley and Clopton (1992) found that suicidal ideation in college students was not associated with social supports. It was associated with depression, hopelessness and race – Asians had more suicidal ideation.

Experiencing Suicide in Others

Hazell (1993) followed up the friends of students who had attempted or completed suicide in school and found that they had more depression and suicidal ideation (both current and past) than students who barely knew the suicides. The friends also had more delinquency, drug use and thought disorder.

Ovuga et al. (1995) found that death wishes in Ugandan students were associated with both a personal and a family history of suicidality. Bridge et al. (1997) found that adolescent attempted suicides had more attempted suicide in their relatives than community controls (and also more Axis I psychiatric disorders and conduct disorder in their relatives).

On the other hand, Strang and Orlefsky (1990) found that college students who had experienced attempted or completed suicide in their families or friends were not more likely to have current suicidal ideation than those who had not. The students with current suicidal ideation had less-secure interpersonal attachments than those without.

Johnsen et al. (1995) used a national sample to ask how many people the respondents had known who completed suicide in the last year. The answer was a very small number, suggesting either that suicides are over-counted or the social networks of suicides are very small.

Discussion

In the 1960s, research appeared that examined the social relationships of suicidal individuals close up and in detail, often observing their interaction styles. Recent research has drawn back and used more distal variables and standardized questionnaires, a regrettable change.

REFERENCES

Asarnow, J. R. Suicidal ideation and attempts during middle childhood. *Journal of Clinical Child Psychology*, 1992, 21, 35–40.

Berger, D. Suicide evaluation in medical patients. *General Hospital Psychiatry*, 1993, 15, 75–81.

Bridge, J. A., Brent, D. A., Johnson, B. A., & Connolly, J. Familial aggregation of psychiatric disorders in a community sample of adolescents. *Journal of the American Academy of Child & Adolescent Psychiatry*, 1997, 36, 628–636.

Calzeroni, A., Conte, G., Pennati, A., Vita, A., & Sacchetti, E. Celibacy and fertility rates in patients with major affective disorders. *Acta Psychiatrica Scandinavica*, 1990, 82, 309–310.

Campbell, N. B., Milling, L., Laughin, A., & Bush, E. The psychosocial climate of families with suicidal children. *American Journal of Orthopsychiatry*, 1993, 63, 142–145.

Canetto, S. S., & Feldman, L. B. Covert and overt dependence in suicidal women and their male partners. *Omega*, 1993, 27, 177–194.

Cantor, C. H., & Slater, P. J. Marital breakdown, parenthood, and suicide. *Journal of Family Studies*, 1995, 1, 91–102.

Conrad, H. Where do they turn? *Journal of Psychosocial Nursing*, 1991, 29(3), 14–20.

D'Andrea, I. Interpersonal functioning in suicidal youth. In D. Lester (Ed.), *Suicide '90*. Denver: AAS, 1990, 262–263.

D'Attilio, J. P., Campbell, B. M., Lubold, P., Jacobson, T., & Richard, J. A. Social support and suicide potential. *Psychological Reports*, 1992, 70, 76–78.

De Jong, M. L. Attachment, individuation, and risk of suicide in late adolescence. *Journal of Youth & Adolescence*, 1992, 21, 357–373.

Du Plessis, W. F. Suicidal behaviour and parental dialysis. In L. Schlebusch (Ed.), *Suicidal behaviour*. Durban: University of Natal, 1992, 86–98.

Eskin, M. Reliability of the Turkish version of the Perceived Social Support from Friends and Family Scale, Scale for Interpersonal Behavior, and Suicide Probability Scale. *Journal of Clinical Psychology*, 1993, 49, 515–522.

Hazell, P. Friends of adolescent suicide attempters and completers. *Journal of the American Academy of Child & Adolescent Psychiatry*, 1993, 32, 76–81.

Heikkinen, M. E., Isometsa, E. T., Marttunen, M. J., Aro, H. M., & Lonnqvist, J. K. Social factors in suicide. *British Journal of Psychiatry*, 1995, 167, 747–753.

Hirsch, J., & Ellis, J. B. Family support and other social factors precipitating suicidal ideation. *International Journal of Social Psychiatry*, 1995, 41, 26–30.

Hoyer, G., & Lund, E. Suicide among women related to number of children in marriage. *Archives of General Psychiatry*, 1993, 50, 134–137.

Isometsa, E. T., Heikkinen, M. E., Henriksson, M. M., Aro, H. M., Marttunen, M., & Lonnqvist, J. Parenthood, completed suicide, and mental disorders. *Archives of General Psychiatry*, 1996, 53, 1061–1062.

Johnsen, E. C., Bernard, H. R., Killworth, P. D., Shelley, G. A., & McCarty, C. A social network approach to corroborating the number of AIDS/HIV+ victims in the United States. *Social Networks*, 1995, 17, 167–187.

Keitner, G. I., Ryan, C. E., Miller, I. W., Epstein, N. B., Bishop, D. S., & Norman, W. H. Family functioning, social adjustment, and recurrence of suicidality. *Psychiatry*, 1990, 53, 17–30.

Kimbrough, R., Molock, S. D., & Walton, K. Perception of social support. *Journal of Negro Education*, 1996b, 65, 295–307.

Kimbrough, R., Molock, S. D., Williams, S., & Blanton-Lacy, M. Perception of social support (family and community), acculturation, and their relationship to depression and suicidal ideation. In J. McIntosh (Ed.), *Suicide '96*. Washington, DC: AAS, 1996a, 164–165.

Knott, E. C., & Range, L. M. Accurately imagining suicide. *Journal of Applied Social Psychology*, 1997, 27, 1545–1556.

Latha, K. S., D'Souza, P., & Bhat, S. M. Social support and suicide attempts. *Indian Journal of Social Work*, 1996, 57, 386–395.

Miller, K. E., King, C. A., Shain, B. N., & Naylor, M. W. Suicidal adolescents' perceptions of their family environment. *Suicide & Life-Threatening Behavior*, 1992, 22, 226–239.

Mitchell, M. G., & Rosenthal, D. M. Suicidal adolescents. *Journal of Youth & Adolescence*, 1992, 21, 23–33.

Neeleman, J., & Power, M. J. Social support and depression in three groups of psychiatric patients and a group of medical controls. *Social Psychiatry & Psychiatric Epidemiology*, 1994, 29, 46–51.

Ovuga, E., Buga, J., & Guwatudde, D. Risk factors toward self-destructive behavior among fresh students at Makerere University. *East African Medical Journal*, 1995, 72, 722–727.

Shulman, E. Cultural factors and childhood trauma in suicide. In D. Lester (Ed.), *Suicide '92*. Denver: AAS, 1992, 197–198.

Spirito, A., Hart, H., Overholser, J., & Halverson, J. Social skills and depression in adolescent suicide attempters. *Adolescence*, 1990, 25, 543–552.

Stack, S. The effect of marital integration on African American suicide. *Suicide & Life-Threatening Behavior*, 1996a, 26, 405–414.

Stack, S. The effect of marital integration on African American suicide. In J. McIntosh (Ed.), *Suicide '96*. Washington, DC: AAS, 1996b, 125–126.

Strang, S. P., & Orlefsky, J. L. Factors underlying suicidal ideation among college students. *Journal of Adolescence*, 1990, 13, 39–52.

Welz, R. The social supports of suicide attempters. In D. Lester (Ed.), *Suicide '94*. Denver: AAS, 1994, 135–137.

Whatley, S. L., & Clopton, J. R. Social support and suicidal ideation in college students. *Psychological Reports*, 1992, 71, 1123–1128.

Chapter 12

METHODOLOGICAL ISSUES

Age-Adjusted Suicide Rates

Lester and Motohashi (1992), in a time-series study of suicide in Japan, found that the signs in the multiple regressions using crude and age-adjusted suicide rates were the same for unemployment and female labor-force participation (both negative), divorce rates (negative), and changes in GNP (nonsignificant). However, the absolute values of the regression coefficients did differ.

Lester (1992a) carried out a similar study for the United States and found that the divorce rate was a significant predictor of the crude suicide rate but not the age-adjusted suicide rate. Marriage, birth, and unemployment rates had similar regression coefficients in both analyses. In Canada, Lester (1997) found no differences in the time-series results using crude versus age-adjusted suicide rates.

In a cross-sectional study of the 48 American states, Lester (1993) found that there were significant differences in the size of correlations between suicide rates and social variables when using crude versus age-adjusted suicide rates, although the trends were similar.

Opportunity-Based Suicide Rates

Suicide rates could be calculated based on the number of suicides per available means, such as suicides by car exhaust per 1,000 cars rather than per 100,000 people in the population. Lester (1992b) found identical social correlates of population-based and car-based car exhaust suicide rates over the states of the USA.

Other Measures

Thorson (1993) suggested using the percentage of deaths due to suicide as a measure. Lester (1994) found that this measure was correlated with a measure of social disintegration over the states of the USA, as was the suicide rate, but it was also associated with an age-structure factor.

Spatial Autocorrelation

Few ecological studies have controlled for spatial autocorrelation. However, Wasserman and Stack (1995) found no evidence for spatial autocorrelation in the suicide rates of American states or Louisiana parishes.

Research Issues

Psychological autopsy diagnoses of suicides are always done with knowledge of the occurrence of suicide and so may be biased. However, Kelly and Mann (1996) compared the psychological autopsy diagnoses of deceased psychiatric patients with psychiatric records available and found that the diagnoses matched for 91 percent of the cases.

Molock, et al. (1996) questioned the validity of scales for both black and white Americans. They found different factor structures for the Beck Depression Inventory for the two groups (but similar factor structures for the Suicidal Ideation Scale and the Hopelessness Scale).

Discussion

Very little has been published on methodological issues in suicidology. However, it would make sense for nations to calculated age-adjusted suicide rates or to base the suicide rates on the population 15 years and older rather than on the total population.

REFERENCES

Kelly, T. M., & Mann, J. J. Validity of DSM-III-R diagnoses by psychological autopsy. *Acta Psychiatrica Scandinavica*, 1996, 94, 337–343.

Lester, D. Effect of using age-adjusted suicide rates on time-series studies of the American suicide rate. *Perceptual & Motor Skills*, 1992a, 75, 778.

Lester, D. Social correlates of opportunity-based suicide rates. *Psychological Reports*, 1992b, 71, 154.

Lester, D. Using age-adjusted rates in ecological studies of suicide and homicide. *Perceptual & Motor Skills*, 1993, 77, 270.

Lester, D. An alternative measure of the frequency of suicide and homicide and its social correlates. *Perceptual & Motor Skills*, 1994, 79, 606.

Lester, D. Use of age-adjusted suicide rates in time-series studies in Canada. *Psychological Reports*, 1997, 81, 490.

Lester, D., & Motohashi, Y. Effect of using age-adjusted suicide rates on the results of time-series analysis of the suicide rate. *Perceptual & Motor Skills*, 1992, 75, 310.

Molock, S. D., Williams, S., & Kimbrough, R. Measuring suicidality in African American college students. In J. McIntosh (Ed.), *Suicide '96*. Washington, DC: AAS, 1996, 127–128.

Thorson, J. A. To die with your boots on. *Psychological Reports*, 1993, 72, 843–854.

Wasserman, I. M., & Stack, S. Geographic spatial autocorrelation and United States suicide patterns. *Archives of Suicide Research*, 1995, 1, 121–129.

Chapter 13

THE SUICIDAL ACT

Aborted Attempts

In a sample of psychiatric inpatients, Marzuk et al. (1997) found that 46 percent had attempted suicide and 29 percent had aborted a suicide attempt. Those aborting attempts and those who never actually attempted suicide were more depressed and more often had a family history of suicide. Those both attempting suicide and aborting attempts more often had a borderline or antisocial personality disorder.

Alcohol Intoxication

Goodman et al. (1991) found that suicides were less intoxicated with alcohol than murder victims and accidental deaths. Among the suicides, native Americans were more often intoxicated, as were those completing suicide on the weekend and from 9 p.m. to 6 a.m., Men and women suicides did not differ in intoxication.

In Germany, Kubo et al. (1991) found that alcohol intoxication was more common in suicides than in those dying in general, similar in frequency to accidental deaths, but less common than in those dying from drug intoxication or murder.

In Australia, Hayward et al. (1992) found that suicides who tested positive for blood alcohol (36 percent of the sample) were younger, more often male, and used carbon monoxide. The act was more often precipitated by a break-up, and the suicide more often had a history of drug or alcohol misuse and prior psychiatric illness.

Robicsek et al. (1993) found that 53 percent of suicide attempters were legally intoxicated, compared to 63 percent of assault victims. Nielsen et al. (1993) found that the suicidal intent score of attempters was not associated with alcohol intoxication. The risk of dying and suicidal intent were associated, however, only in the non-alcohol-dependent attempters. Those with high intent did use different methods (more hanging, drowning, jumping, and multiple methods).

Ostamo and Lonnqvist (1993) found that attempted suicides who had ingested alcohol were more often male; aged 20–49 if men, and 30–59 if women; divorced or married; had made prior attempts; and made less-lethal attempts (men only) with less-suicidal intent (men only). They did not differ in method.

Suokas and Lonnqvist (1995) found that attempters who were intoxicated with alcohol were more often male, under the age of 35, divorced, and of lower social class. Men and the younger attempters also had higher levels of alcohol. Those with alcohol present had less wish to die, less suicidal intent, and less certainty of dying; they made less-lethal and more-impulsive attempts. The presence of alcohol did not predict subsequent completed suicide.

Consultation With Physicians

Gorman and Masterton (1990) compared suicide attempters with controls for visits to general practitioners in the previous year. The attempters showed an increase in consultations in the nine months prior to the attempt and in the three months afterwards. There was an increase also in consultations in the previous week. The increase was significant for mental problems and social/family matters, but not for physical problems. Suicidal intent for the attempters was not related to the number of consultations in the previous year or week.

Michel et al. (1997) found that Germans were more likely to discuss their suicidal ideation with the general practitioner than Swedish patients, although they visited their physicians at the same rate in the month prior to the suicide attempt.

In a sample of older suicides (over the age of 50) in Rochester (New York), Caine et al. (1996) found that 53 percent had visited a physician in the prior month, but only 2 percent had received adequate treatment.

Isacsson et al. (1994a, 1994b) found that only 8 percent of completed suicides in San Diego had antidepressants in their system. More than half of the depressed suicides had consulted a physician in the prior 90 days, but less than half of these were prescribed an antidepressant. In Sweden, 16 percent had antidepressants in their system, but most of the suicides were not in treatment.

In Finland, Isometsa et al. (1994a, 1994b) found that only 74 percent of the bipolar completed suicides were receiving psychiatric care, only 32 percent were taking lithium, and none had electroconvulsive therapy in the prior three months. The bipolars had received more prior psychiatric

treatment and hospitalization than the unipolar suicides and used medications more. (The bipolars were also more often divorced, but did not differ in sex, living alone or being retired.) Only half of the suicides with a major depressive disorder were in psychiatric treatment at the time of their death, and few were receiving adequate treatment for their depression – only 3 percent were prescribed antidepressants in adequate doses. In this same sample, Isometsa et al. (1995b) found that females reported their suicidal intent more than males to health care professionals, mostly when in outpatient care. Those communicating intent more often had a major depressive disorder and less often had alcoholism.

In Scotland, Matthews et al. (1994) found that 25 percent of a sample of completed suicides with a psychiatric history and 16 percent of those with no psychiatric history had visited a GP in the prior week. Five percent of the former group mentioned suicide to their GP.

Obafunwa and Busuttil (1994) found that completed suicides in Scotland who had consulted their GP in the prior week were more often female, psychiatric patients, alcohol abusers, used drugs for their suicide, had deteriorating health, and had made prior attempts. They did not differ in urban/rural location, marital status, or unemployment.

Vassilas and Morgan (1993, 1994; Vassilas, 1994) found that recent prior contact with a GP was more common in completed suicides over the age of 35 and if the suicides had prior psychiatric contacts. Compared to controls in the community, elderly suicides had consulted significantly more with their GPs in the prior four weeks, for psychological reasons, but not significantly more often for physical reasons. Also in England, Meats and Solomka (1995) compared completed suicides with other patients of the same GPs. The suicides had seen their GP more often in the prior month, but did not differ in medical contacts over the past year. They had more prior psychiatric contacts lifetime, in the past year, and in the prior month. The suicides who had consulted their GP were more often married, with prior attempts, and impulsive; they did not differ in method or reason for the suicide, age, sex, or warning.

Appleby et al. (1996) found that 49 percent of completed suicides under the age of 35 in England had seen their GP in the prior three months, more so in the last month and the last week than earlier; there were no sex differences in this. Sixty-four percent of them mentioned psychological problems. Forty-four percent of these were prescribed medications, but only 18 percent were prescribed antidepressants in adequate dosage.

Power et al. (1997) found that completed suicides had made more visits to GPs in the prior 10 years than normals, but not in the prior few months. The suicides had more often been diagnosed psychiatrically, given medication, and referred to mental health services.

In a sample of elderly suicides in Ontario (Canada), Duckworth and McBride (1996) found that the women were more often receiving treatment for depression than the men, but that none were being treated with the safer serotonin reuptake inhibitors.

Van Casteren et al. (1993) found that completed and attempted suicides were equally likely to have consulted with a general practitioner in prior week or the prior month (and had a similar incidence of prior suicide attempts, mental disorder, and treatment).

On a native American reservation, Mock et al. (1996) found that the completed suicides were less likely than controls to use

the reservation clinic or hospital in the prior six months, whereas the attempted suicides were more likely to use these services (and to report psychological problems).

Impulsivity

Chess et al. (1997) found that two-thirds of suicidal people went through an orderly sequence of stages – precontemplation, contemplation, preparation, and action – while one-third skipped the early stages.

Brown et al. (1991) compared impulsive and nonimpulsive adolescent suicide attempters. The impulsive attempters were less depressed and hopeless and of lower social class. They did not differ in race, sex, the circumstances of the act, prior attempts, or anger-in/anger-out.

Suominen et al. (1997) found that attempted suicides with alcohol dependence made more impulsive attempts (and had less suicidal intent) than those with major depressive disorder, both, or neither. The attempters with a major depressive disorder were the most hopeless, while those with alcohol dependence had more alcohol in their blood at the time of the attempt. Overall, suicidal intent was associated with hopelessness and impulsivity, but not with age or depression.

Simon and Crosby (1997) surveyed high school students and found that unplanned attempts were carried out more by students who carried guns, used marihuana, dieted in an unhealthy way, initiated sexual intercourse, and made fewer prior attempts in the last year. The unplanned and planned attempters did not differ in physical fights, alcohol use, or cocaine use.

Lethality

Lomonaco et al. (1990) found that the "gravity" of the suicide attempt was higher for women if they were divorced, living alone, with recent bereavement, and psychotic; for men the gravity was higher if they were widowed, living with a non-nuclear relative, with recent bereavement, and psychotic.

In a survey of college freshmen, Meehan et al. (1992) found that 10.4 percent had attempted suicide: 4.6 percent had been injured or ill afterwards, 2.6 percent sought medical care, and 1.0 percent were admitted to a hospital. In the previous year, only 1.9 percent had attempted suicide: 1.0 percent were injured or ill afterwards, 0.4 percent sought medical care, and zero percent had been admitted to a hospital.

Runeson et al. (1996) found that completed suicides who had made prior attempts switched to more-lethal methods for their final act.

Location

Lester and Frank (1990) found that suicides committed out of the home state were more often men, single/divorced, aged 15–34, by hanging, but they did not differ in race.

Motive

Velamoor and Cernovsky (1992) classified a sample of attempted suicides on whether they intend to die. Those who said yes more often left a suicide note and, according to significant others (but not according to self-report), had more often made prior attempts and been in a psychiatric hospital. They did not differ in sex, marital status, psychiatric illness in the family, type of precipitating event, age, or number of children.

Johns and Holden (1997) found that the motive of internal perturbation predicted both prior suicidal ideation and attempts in college students (along with depression and hopelessness), whereas extrapunitive/manipulative motives predicted only prior ideation.

Precipitants

Sorenson and Golding (1990) found that recent (in previous six months) victims of crime in a community survey were more depressed and suicidal than nonvictims. The only crime for which this association was statistically significant was mugging.

Walford et al. (1990) reported cases of suicide in fathers after disclosure of incest with their children. Lester (1991b) reported cases of suicide after loss of reputation, such as after exposure as a pedophile. Lester (1990) reported cases of suicide after restoration of sight.

Loebel et al. (1991) examined the reasons for suicide in the elderly and found that eight suicides gave as a reason anticipation of placement in a nursing home. Four others gave pain as a reason. The fear of a nursing home placement was more common among the married suicides.

Gregory (1994) found a high incidence of loss in Eskimos attempting suicide, but there was no control group. The modal attempter was young, female, and unmarried. Byrne and Rapheal (1997) found an increase in suicidal ideation (but not depression or loneliness) in the year following bereavement in elderly male widows.

Griffith (1994) found that, in addition to suicidal ideation in college students being associated with stressful life events, suicidal ideation was also associated with daily hassles (as well as lack of social supports). Herman and Lester (1994), however, found no association between physical symptoms of stress and suicidal ideation in high school students after controls for depression.

Taylor (1994) found that attempted

suicides more often had worries over debts than fracture patients. The attempters with and without debt worries did not differ in depression scores. Hatcher (1994) compared attempted suicides who had problem debts and those without. Those with debts had more suicidal intent, more depression, more hopelessness after the attempt, more unemployment, less income, and more often were given a psychiatric diagnosis. They did not differ in age, prior attempts, or prior psychiatric contacts.

Smith and Milliner (1994) documented cases of young athletes attempting suicide because of sports-related stressors, such as deterioration in athletic skills or being replaced on the team.

Davidson et al. (1996) found that persons who had been sexually assaulted had higher lifetimes rates of attempting suicide than matched controls. Struckman-Johnson et al. (1996) found that one-third of prisoners raped in prison experienced suicidal ideation afterwards, and one-half were depressed. Bagley et al. (1997) found that school girls sexually assaulted at school (unwanted exposure, unwanted touching, or verbal harassment) were more likely to have attempted suicide than girls not assaulted. Choquet et al. (1997) found that both adolescent boys and girls who had been raped were more likely to have attempted suicide than those not raped.

Steels (1994) found that the incidence of attempted suicides rose in the 12 hours after a major soccer defeat in an English town. Buckley and McDonald (1997) found no increased in attempted suicide as a result of the Hale-Bopp comet, although they found an association between rates of attempted suicide and the share price of Nike! Cohn et al. (1997) found an increase in attempted suicides in the three months around the comet's appearance as compared to previous years.

Sharkey (1997) found that the suicidal overdose rate decreased in the local hospital after a Protestant massacre in Northern Ireland.

Among completed suicides, Heikkinen et al. (1994a, 1994b) found that alcoholics had more financial troubles, unemployment, separations, and family discord and less somatic illness. The alcoholics were also more often male and older. The stressor varied also with age and whether living alone. For the total sample of suicides (alcoholic and nonalcoholic), males had more stressors than females, especially from separations, finances, job, and unemployment. The men more often had no confidantes, were lonely, and lived alone.

The Rationality of Suicide

Mathes (1990) presented students with 20 situations and had them rate the amount of displeasure in each and the likelihood that they might commit suicide in such a situation. The two scores were positively associated over the students, both for men and for women, indicating that the decision was rational.

Repeaters

Bjerke et al. (1990) found that male repeaters differed from first-time attempters in alcohol abuse, intention, and recent contact with health services. For females the discriminators were alcohol abuse, economic position, income, previous imprisonment, and police contact. Gilliland (1995) found that adolescents who repeated overdoses were less likely to live with both parents and more likely to have a parent with a psychiatric history, know someone who overdosed, and have been sexually abused as a child. Gupta et al. (1995) found that repeaters had poorer contacts with their families, were more often divorced/

separated, had more physical violence in their relationships, more unemployment and financial instability, and more often had a psychiatric disorder and higher suicidal-intent scores.

Gilbody et al. (1997) found that attempted suicides who repeated did so with a median interval of 12 weeks. Repeaters were more likely to have made prior attempts, but did not differ in sex from nonrepeaters. Bille-Brahe et al. (1995) found that repeaters are more likely to make subsequent suicide attempts.

Rescue

Pillay and Wassenaar (1991) found that adolescent suicide attempters who did not expect to be rescued tended to have higher hopelessness scores (but not significantly).

Sequelae

Physical Sequelae

Frierson and Lippman (1990) surveyed 260 people who survived suicidal gunshot wounds. Forty had colostomies as a result, 15 organic brain syndrome, 12 seizures, 10 amputations, and 10 infections. Henriksson (1990) has provided graphic descriptions of the reconstructive work needed after attempted suicide by firearms. Biering-Sorensen et al. (1992) found that 13 percent of admissions with spinal cord injuries were due to suicide attempts.

Psychological Sequelae

Kalb (1991) interviewed suicidal people about the perceived consequences of attempting suicide. Attempters saw attempting as much more positive in its effects on themselves than suicidal ideators

did (hypothetically for the latter group) and more positive in social consequences. Attempters also viewed alternatives to attempting as having more negative consequences for themselves than did the ideators.

At a crisis intervention unit, Bronisch (1992) compared patients who had attempted suicide with those who had not. There was no evidence that the suicide attempt had a cathartic effect. Incidentally, the attempters did not differ from the controls on a personality test that measured esoteric tendencies, isolation tendencies, rigidity, extraversion, neuroticism, or frustration tolerance. On the other hand, Davis (1995) found that attempted suicides were less depressed (and less likely to be diagnosed as having a major depressive disorder) after one week than on admission, suggesting a cathartic effect.

Wulsin and Goldman (1993) reported the case of post-traumatic stress disorder in an individual following a suicide attempt.

Social Sequelae

Wagner et al. (1996) found that parents of teens who attempted suicide were most-often worried, then angry, caring, sad, and least-often overwhelmed. The parents of repeaters were more angry and caring, and the parents of high-lethality attempts less angry and caring. Parents who were caring had teenagers who made one-two prior attempts, had a shorter psychiatric history, and made a lower-lethality attempt.

Survivors

Brent et al. (1995) found that 5 percent of the friends of adolescent completed suicides developed post-traumatic stress disorder and that these were more likely to have made prior attempts themselves; they were also more often substance abusers, closer to the victim, and living in discordant families.

Funerals

Lester and Ferguson (1992) found that the funerals of suicides cost less than those of people dying natural deaths.

Stressors

Attempted Suicides

De Vanna et al. (1990) compared suicide attempters with normal controls and found no differences in total stressful life events. The attempters had experienced more major events and more events involving interpersonal relationships and isolation. The attempters had also received more psychiatric treatment in the past and made more prior suicide attempts.

Tatarelli et al. (1990a, 1990b) found that attempted suicides had not experienced more stressors overall in the last five years than depressed patients, but had experienced more chronic stressors. They had experienced more psychiatric illness in themselves and their families, physical illness in themselves, interpersonal conflict, unemployment, and unsatisfactory relationships in childhood. They did not differ in drug and alcohol abuse or early loss.

Vassilas (1990) compared female attempted suicides with appendectomy patients and found that the attempters had more recent stressors (in the past 13 weeks), especially stress with an uncertain outcome and impaired relationships; they were also more depressed and anxious and had received less social support and support from their confidantes.

Clum et al. (1991) found that the recent stressors predicted recent prior suicide attempts in a sample of psychiatric patients and also subsequent suicide attempts in the following year.

Ceyhun et al. (1993) compared attempted suicides who were depressed versus those judged to be in crisis. Six months later, the depressed attempters had experienced less stress than those who had been in crisis.

In India Latha et al. (1994) found that suicide attempters had experienced more life stress in the prior six months than had depressed patients and normals. Beautrais et al. (1997) found that adolescent suicide attempters in New Zealand had experienced more recent stress than normal controls.

Completed Suicides

In Finland, Heikkinen et al. (1990, 1992a, 1992b) looked at recent stress in suicides living with a spouse or partner. The men had more somatic illness and less psychiatric disorder than the women, but did not differ in 17 other stressors. By age, those younger than 45 had more interpersonal discord, separations, childhood adversity, financial trouble, job problems, and unemployment; the older suicides had fewer stressors overall, although they had more somatic illness and retirement problems.

In this Finnish sample of suicides, Heikkinen et al. (1995; Heikkinen and Lonnqvist, 1995) found that men and younger adults had experienced more recent stressors than women and older adults. For example, men had experienced more separations and unemployment than women; older adults had experienced more somatic illness and less unemployment than younger adults. Heikkinen et al. (1997a, 1997b) found that the suicides with personality disorders had more recent stress in the prior week and three months than those with no personality disorder; they more often lived alone, in urban areas, with an opposite sex companion and less often had a psychiatrically disturbed parent. In the same sample, Isometsa et al. (1995a) found that bipolars and unipolars had similar incidence of recent stressors. Marttunen et al. (1993) found that recent stressors were common in Finnish adolescent completed suicides (96 percent in prior month). If parental support was weak, then interpersonal separation was more often a precipitant and there were more stressors.

Rich et al. (1991) found that the stressors in completed suicides differed by age. Conflict-separation stress was most common in younger adults, economic stress rose up to those in their 50s and then declined, and medical illness was most frequent in those over age of 60. Males and females did not differ in total stress, but males did have more economic stress.

In one region of Malaysia, Maniam (1994) found that completed suicides had experienced more loss and failure in the prior year than medical controls. They did not differ in birth order, marital status, age, sex, income, schooling, or religion.

In England, Vassilas and Morgan (1997) found that older suicides did not differ in the total amount of life stress but had less interpersonal stress and more physical and psychiatric problems. The older and younger suicides did not differ in alcohol abuse or unemployment.

Attempted Versus Completed Suicides

Duberstein et al. (1992) found no differences in total stress in the prior year between attempted and completed suicides. There were differences in particular stressors, and these varied with age.

Suicidal Intent

Cazzulo et al. (1990) found that attempted

suicides who had made previous attempts did not differ from first-timers in their suicidal intent.

Hamdi et al. (1991) found that high suicidal intent in suicide attempters in the United Arab Emirates was associated with less often using poisons and making more-lethal attempts. Suicidal intent was associated with age and psychosis positively, but not with being a repeater, sex, marital status, unemployment, or showing problem behavior.

Lester (1991a) found that the correlates of suicidal intent were different in completed suicides and attempted suicides. For example, suicidal intent was higher in completed suicides who were Jewish and who had a recent breakup; suicidal intent was higher in attempted suicides who were white and who attempted suicide at home.

Rygnestad (1997) found that attempted suicides had a high rate of subsequent completed suicide. Suicidal intent for the attempt did not predict subsequent suicide. For women, there were no predictors of subsequent suicide; for men, the suicides were older and more often not imprisoned.

Witnessed Suicides

McDowell et al. (1994) found that 4 percent of suicides in the air force were witnessed by another. They described four types of witnessed suicides: Russian roulette, violent divorces, homicidal rage, and reciprocal abandonment.

Runeson et al. (1996) found that completed suicides who had witnesses to the act more often had a personality disorder.

Discussion

This research addresses many of the circumstances of the suicidal act. Most of the research, however, particularly into precipitants and stressors, has little theoretical relevance beyond establishing that stressors play a role and that precipitants exist. The impulsivity of the suicidal act and whether it was witnessed seem to have more interest, but these areas have not been extensively researched.

REFERENCES

Appleby, L., Amons, T., Tomension, B., & Woodman, M. General practitioners and young suicides. *British Journal of Psychiatry*, 1996, 168, 330–333.

Bagley, C., Bolitho, F., & Bertrand, L. Sexual assault in school, mental health, and suicidal behaviors in adolescent women in Canada. *Adolescence*, 1997, 32, 361–366.

Beautrais, A. L., Joyce, P. R., & Mulder, R. T. Precipitating factors and life events in serious suicide attempts among youths age 13 through 24. *Journal of the American Academy of Child & Adolescent Psychiatry*, 1997, 36, 1543–1551.

Biering-Sorensen, F., Pedersen, W., & Muller, P. G. Spinal-cord injury due to suicide attempts. *Paraplegia*, 1992, 30, 139–144.

Bille-Brahe, U., Jessen, G., & Jensen, B. Monitoring repeated suicidal behavior. In B. Mishara (Ed.), *The impact of suicide*. New York: Springer, 1995, 156–166.

Bjerke, T., Jorgensen, P. T., Rygnestad, T., Riaunet, A., & Stiles, T. Repetition of parasuicide. In G. Ferrari, M. Bellini & P. Crepet (Eds.), *Suicidal behavior and risk factors*. Bologna: Monduzzi-Editore, 1990, 453–457.

Brent, D. A., Perper, J. A., Moritz, G., Liotus, L., Richardson, D., Canobbio, R., Schweers, J., & Roth, C. Post-traumatic stress disorder in peers of adolescent suicide victims. *Journal of the American Academy of Child & Adolescent Psychiatry*, 1995, 34, 209–215.

Bronisch, T. Does an attempted suicide actually have a cathartic effect? *Acta Psychiatrica Scandinavica*, 1992, 86, 228–232.

Brown, L. K., Overholser, J., Spirito, A., & Fritz, G. K. The correlates of planning in adolescent suicide attempts. *Journal of the American Academy of Child & Adolescent Psychiatry*, 1991, 30, 95–99.

Buckley, N. A., & McDonald, J. A. Hale Bopp and knocking on heaven's gate. *Medical Journal of Australia*, 1997, 167, 654–655.

Byrne, G., & Raphael, B. The psychological symptoms of conjugal bereavement in elderly men over the first 13 months. *International Journal of Geriatric Psychiatry*, 1997, 12, 241–251.

Caine, E. D., Lyness, J. M., & Conwell, Y. Diagnosis of late-life depression. *American Journal of Geriatric Psychiatry*, 1996, 4, Suppl. 1, 45–50.

Cazzulo, C. L., Vitali, A., Calchi Novati, N., & Albonetti, S. The suicidal behaviours. In G. Ferrari, M. Bellini & P. Crepet (Eds.), *Suicidal behavior and risk factors*. Bologna: Monduzzi-Editore, 1990, 781–785.

Ceyhun, B., Ergin, G., & Durukan, A. Life stress. In K. Bohme, R. Freytag, C. Wachtler & H. Wedler (Eds.), *Suicidal behavior*. Regensburg: S. Roderer, 1993, 706–709.

Chess, E. M., Coombs, D. W., Ryan, W., Leeper, J., Miller, H. L., Geiger, B. G., Willis, S., & Grimley, D. M. An exploratory study applying the transtheoretical model to the development of suicidal behavior. In J. McIntosh (Ed.), *Suicide '97*. Washington, DC: AAS, 1997, 107–108.

Choquet, M., Darves-Bornoz, J. M., Ledoux, S., Manfredi, R., & Hassler, C. Self-reported health and behavioral problems among adolescent victims of rape in France. *Child Abuse & Neglect*, 1997, 21, 823–832.

Clum, G. A., Luscomb, R. L., & Patsiokas, A. T. On the stress/parasuicide or parasuicide/stress relationship. *Psychological Reports*, 1991, 68, 1317–1318.

Cohn, S. M., Chao, C., Cross, J. H., Bell, M. A., Sawyer, M. D., Burns, G. A., & Angood, P. A. Self-inflicted injuries before the arrival of Hale-Bopp comet. *Journal of Trauma*, 1997, 43, 175–176.

Davidson, J. R., Hughes, D. C., George, L.

K., & Blazer, D. G. The association of sexual assault and attempted suicide within the community. *Archives of General Psychiatry*, 1996, 53, 550–555.

Davis, A. T. Attempted suicide and depression. In B. L. Mishara (Ed.), *The impact of suicide*. New York: Springer, 1995, 130–141.

De Vanna, M., Paterniti, S., Milievich, C., Rigamonti, R., Sulich, A., & Faravelli, C. Recent life events and attempted suicide. *Journal of Affective Disorders*, 1990, 18, 51–58.

Duberstein, P. R., Conwell, Y., & Caine, E. Age differences in the life events prior to attempted and completed suicide. In D. Lester (Ed.), *Suicide '92*. Denver: AAS, 1992, 201–203.

Duckworth, G., & McBride, H. Suicide in old age. *Canadian Journal of Psychiatry*, 1996, 41, 217–222.

Frierson, R. L., & Lippman, S. B. Psychiatric consultation for patients with self-inflicted gunshot wounds. *Psychosomatics*, 1990, 31(1), 67–74.

Gilbody, S., House, A., & Owens, D. The early repetition of deliberate self-harm. *Journal of the Royal College of Surgeons*, 1997, 31, 171–172.

Gilliland, D. An attempt to classify adolescent parasuicide attempters. *British Journal of Social Work*, 1995, 25, 647–657.

Goodman, R. A., Istre, G. R., Jordan, F. B., Herndon, J. L., & Kelaghan, J. Alcohol and fatal injuries in Oklahoma. *Journal of Studies on Alcohol*, 1991, 52, 156–161.

Gorman, D., & Masterton, G. General practice consultation patterns before and after intentional overdose. *British Journal of General Practitioners*, 1990, 40, 102–105.

Gregory, R. J. Grief and loss among Eskimos attempting suicide in Western Alaska. *American Journal of Psychiatry*, 1994, 151, 1815–1816.

Griffith, S. C. The relationship of daily college hassles, negative major life events, and social supports to suicidal ideation among male and female traditional college students. In D. Lester (Ed.), *Suicide '94*. Denver: AAS, 1994, 177–178.

Gupta, K., Sivakumar, K., & Smeeton, N. Deliberate self-harm. *Irish Journal of Psychological Medicine*, 1995, 12, 131–133.

Hamdi, E., Amin, Y., & Mattar, T. Clinical correlates of intent in attempted suicide. *Acta Psychiatrica Scandinavica*, 1991, 83, 406–411.

Hatcher, S. Debt and deliberate self-poisoning. *British Journal of Psychiatry*, 1994, 164, 111–114.

Hayward, L., Zubrick, S. R., & Silburn, S. Blood alcohol levels in suicide cases. *Journal of Epidemiology & Community Health*, 1992, 46, 256–260.

Heikkinen, M., Aro, H., & Lonnqvist, J. Life events and suicide. In G. Ferrari, M. Bellini & P. Crepet (Eds.), *Suicidal behavior and risk factors*. Bologna: Monduzzi-Editore, 1990, 583–588.

Heikkinen, M., Aro, H., & Lonnqvist, J. The partner's views on precipitant stressors in suicide. *Acta Psychiatrica Scandinavica*, 1992a, 85, 380–384.

Heikkinen, M., Aro, H., & Lonnqvist, J. Recent life events and their role in suicide as seen by the spouses. *Acta Psychiatrica Scandinavica*, 1992b, 86, 489–494.

Heikkinen, M., Aro, H., & Lonnqvist, J. Recent life events, social support, and suicide. *Acta Psychiatrica Scandinavica*, 1994a, suppl. 377, 65–72.

Heikkinen, M., Aro, H., Henriksson, M. M., Isometsa, E. T., Sarna, S. J., Kuoppasalmi, K. I. & Lonnqvist, J. Differences in recent life events between alcoholic and depressive non-alcoholic suicides. *Alcoholism: Clinical & Experimental Research*, 1994b, 18, 1143–1149.

Heikkinen, M. E., Henriksson, M. M., Isometsa, E. T., Marttunen, M. J., Aro, H. M., & Lonnqvist, J. K. Recent life events and suicide in personality disorders. *Journal of Nervous & Mental Disease*, 1997a, 185, 373–381.

Heikkinen, M., Isometsa, E. T., Aro, H. M., Sarna, S. J., & Lonnqvist, J. K. Age-related variation in recent life events preceding suicide. *Journal of Nervous & Mental Disease*, 1995, 183, 325–331.

Heikkinen, M. E., Isometsa, E. T., Henriksson, M. M., Marttunen, M. J., Aro, H. M., & Lonnqvist, J. K. Psychosocial factors and completed suicide in personality disorders. *Acta Psychiatrica Scandinavica*, 1997b, 95, 49–57.

Heikkinen, M., & Lonnqvist, J. K. Recent life events in elderly suicide. *International*

Psychogeriatrics, 1995, 7, 287–300.

Henriksson, T. G. Close-range blasts toward the maxillofacial region in attempted suicide. *Scandinavian Journal of Plastic & Reconstructive Surgery & Hand Surgery*, 1990, 24, 81–86.

Herman, S. L., & Lester, D. Physical symptoms of stress, depression, and suicidal ideation in high school students. *Adolescence*, 1994, 29, 639–641.

Isacsson, G., Bergman, U., & Rich, C. L. Antidepressants, depression, and suicide. *Journal of Affective Disorders*, 1994a, 32, 277–286.

Isacsson, G., Holmgren, P., Wasserman, D., & Bergman, U. Use of antidepressants among people committing suicide in Sweden. *British Medical Journal*, 1994b, 308, 506–509.

Isometsa, E., Heikkinen, M., Henriksson, M., Aro. H., & Lonnqvist, J. Recent life events and completed suicide in bipolar affective disorder. *Journal of Affective Disorders*, 1995a, 33, 99–106.

Isometsa, E. T., Henriksson, M. M., Aro, H. M., & Lonnqvist, J. Suicide in bipolar disorder in Finland. *American Journal of Psychiatry*, 1994a, 151, 1020–1024.

Isometsa, E. T., Henriksson, M. M., Aro, H. M., Heikkinen, M. E., Kuoppasalmi, K. I., & Lonnqvist, J. Suicide in major depression. *American Journal of Psychiatry*, 1994b, 151, 530–536.

Isometsa, E., Heikkinen, M., Marttunen, M., Henriksson, M., Aro. H., & Lonnqvist, J. The last appointment before suicide. *American Journal of Psychiatry*, 1995b, 152, 919–922.

Johns, D., & Holden, R. R. Differentiating suicidal motivations and manifestations in a nonclinical population. *Canadian Journal of Behavioural Science*, 1997, 29, 266–274.

Kalb, R. Rational aspects of suicidality. *Psychiatria Danubina*, 1991, 3, 338–340.

Kubo, S. I., Dankworth, G., & Puschel, K. Blood alcohol concentrations of sudden unexpected deaths and nonnatural deaths. *Forensic Science International*, 1991, 52, 77–84.

Latha, K. S., Bhat, S. M., & D'Souza, P. Attempted suicide and recent stressful life events. *Crisis*, 1994, 15, 136.

Lester, D. Suicide after restoration of sight. *Archives of the Foundation of Thanatology*, 1990,

16(2), unpaged.

Lester, D. Does suicidal intent mean the same in completed suicides as it does in attempted suicides? *Psychological Reports*, 1991a, 69, 50.

Lester, D. The trauma of loss of reputation. *Illness, Crises & Loss*, 1991b, 1(3), 61–62.

Lester, D., & Ferguson, M. An exploratory study of funeral costs for suicides. *Psychological Reports*, 1992, 70, 938.

Lester, D. & Frank, M. L. Suicide and homicide away from home. *American Journal of Forensic Medicine & Pathology*, 1990, 11, 298–299.

Loebel, J. P., Loebel, J. S., Dager, S. R., Centerwall, B. S., & Reay, D. T. Acticipation of nursing home placement may be a precipitant of suicide among the elderly. *Journal of the American Geriatric Society*, 1991, 39, 407–408.

Lomonaco, E., Gioeli, A., & Olivetto, L. 10 years of consultation for attempted suicide. In G. Ferrari, M. Bellini & P. Crepet (Eds.), *Suicidal behavior and risk factors*. Bologna: Monduzzi-Editore, 1990, 545–555.

Maniam, T. Family characteristics of suicides in Cameroon Highlands. *Medical Journal of Malaysia*, 1994, 49, 247–251.

Marttunen, M. J., Aro, H. M., & Lonnqvist, J. K. Precipitant stressors in adolescent suicide. *Journal of the American Academy of Child & Adolescent Psychiatry*, 1993, 32, 1178–1183.

Mathes, W. E. Rational suicide. *Psychological Reports*, 1990, 67, 307–310.

Matthews, K., Milne, S., & Ashcroft, G. W. Role of doctors in the prevention of suicide. *British Journal of General Practitioners*, 1994, 44, 345–348.

Marzuk, P. M., Tardiff, K., Leon, A. C., Portera, L., & Weiner, C. The prevalence of aborted suicide attempts among psychiatric inpatients. *Acta Psychiatrica Scandinavica*, 1997, 96, 492–496.

McDowell, C. P., Rothberg, J. M., & Koshes, R. J. Witnessed suicides. *Suicide & Life-Threatening Behavior*, 1994, 24, 213–223.

Meats, P., & Solomka, B. A perspective on suicide in the 90s. *Psychiatry Bulletin*, 1995, 19, 666–669.

Meehan, P. J., Lamb, J. A., Saltzman, L. E., & O'Carroll, P. W. Attempted suicide among young adults. *American Journal of Psychiatry*, 1992, 149, 41–44.

Michel, K., Runeson, B., Valach, L., & Wasserman, D. Contacts of suicide attempters with GPs prior to the event. *Acta Psychiatrica Scandinavica*, 1997, 95, 94–99.

Mock, C. N., Grossman, D. C., Mulder, D., Stewart, C., & Koepsell, T. S. Health care utilization as a marker for suicidal behavior on an American Indian reservation. *Journal of General Internal Medicine*, 1996, 11, 519–524.

Nielsen, A. S., Stenager, E., & Bille-Brahe, U. Attempted suicide, suicidal intent, and alcohol. *Crisis*, 1993, 14(1), 32–38.

Obafunwa, J. O., & Busuttil, A. Clinical contact preceding suicide. *Postgraduate Medical Journal*, 1994, 70, 428–432.

Ostamo, A., & Lonnqvist, J. Alcohol as part of parasuicide. In K. Bohme, R. Freytag, C. Wachtler & H. Wedler (Eds.), *Suicidal behavior.* Regensburg: S. Roderer, 1993, 911–914.

Pillay, A. L., & Wassenaar, D. Rescue expectations and hopelessness in adolescent parasuicides. *Perceptual & Motor Skills*, 1991, 72, 363–366.

Power, K., Davies, C., Swanson, V., Gordon, D., & Carter, H. Case-control study of GP attendance rates by suicide cases with or without a psychiatric history. *British Journal of General Practitioners*, 1997, 47, 211–215.

Rich, C. L., Warsradt, G. M., Nemiroff, R. A., Fowler, R. C., & Young, D. Suicide, stressors, and the life cycle. *American Journal of Psychiatry*, 1991, 148, 524–527.

Robicsek, F., Ribbeck, B., Walker, L. G., Thomason, M. H., Hollenbeck, J. I., & Baker, J. W. The cost of violence. *North Carolina Medical Journal*, 1993, 54, 578–582.

Runeson, B., Beskow, J., & Waern, M. The suicidal process in suicides among young people. *Acta Psychiatrica Scandinavica*, 1996, 93, 35–42.

Rygnestad, T. Mortality after deliberate self-poisoning. *Social Psychiatry & Psychiatric Epidemiology*, 1997, 32, 443–450.

Sharkey, J. The Greysteel massacre. *Irish Journal of Psychological Medicine*, 1997, 14, 55–56.

Simon, T. R., & Crosby, A. E. Planned and unplanned suicide attempts among

adolescents in the United States. In J. McIntosh (Ed.), *Suicide '97.* Washington, DC: AAS, 1997, 170–172.

Smith, A. M., & Milliner, E. K. Injured athletes and the risk of suicide. *Journal of Athletic Training*, 1994, 29, 337–341.

Sorenson, S. B., & Golding, J. M. Depressive sequelae of recent criminal victimization. *Journal of Traumatic Stress*, 1990, 3, 337–350.

Steels, M. D. Deliberate self poisoning. *Irish Journal of Psychological Medicine*, 1994, 11, 76–78.

Struckman-Johnson, C., Struckman-Johnson, D., Rucker, L., Bumby, K., & Donaldson, S. Sexual coercion reported by men and women in prison. *Journal of Sex Research*, 1996, 33(1), 67–76.

Suokas, J., & Lonnqvist, J. Suicide attempts in which alcohol is involved. *Acta Psychiatrica Scandinavica*, 1995, 91, 36–40.

Suominen, K., Isometsa, E., Henriksson, M., Ostamo, A., & Lonnqvist, J. Hopelessness, impulsiveness, and intent among suicide attempters with major depression, alcohol dependence, or both. *Acta Psychiatrica Scandinavica*, 1997, 96, 142–149.

Tatarelli, R., Girardi, P., Terzariol, L., Pepe, I. A., Speranza, E., Ruggiero, F., & Sollazzo, R. Risk factors and stressful events in a sample of attempted suicide patients. In G. Ferrari, M. Bellini & P. Crepet (Eds.), *Suicidal behavior and risk factors.* Bologna: Monduzzi-Editore, 1990a, 717–722.

Tatarelli, R., Girardi, P., Terzariol, L., Pepe, I. A., Speranza, E., Ruggiero, F., & Sollazzo, R. Stressful events in a sample of depressed patients with attempted suicide and a sample of depressed patients without attempted suicide. In G. Ferrari, M. Bellini & P. Crepet (Eds.), *Suicidal behavior and risk factors.* Bologna: Monduzzi-Editore, 1990b, 723–728.

Taylor, S. J. Debt and deliberate self-harm. *British Journal of Psychiatry*, 1994, 164, 848–849.

Van Casteren, V., Van der Veken, J., Tafforeau, J., & Van Oyen, H. Suicide and attempted suicide reported by general practitioners in Belgium, 1990–1991. *Acta Psychiatrica Scandinavica*, 1993, 87, 451–455.

Vassilas, C. A. Differentiating life stresses prior to admission to hospital for appendectomy and parasuicide. *Journal of Psychosomatic Research*, 1990, 34, 699–707.

Vassilas, C. Recent studies of contacts with services prior to suicide. In R. Jenkins, S. Griffiths, I. Wylie, K. Hawton, G. Morgan & A. Tylee (Eds.), *The prevention of suicide.* London: HMSO, 1994, 109–113.

Vassilas, C., & Morgan, H. G. GPs' contact with victims of suicide. *British Medical Journal,* 1993, 307, 300–301.

Vassilas, C., & Morgan, H. G. Elderly suicides' contact with their general practitioner before death. *International Journal of Geriatric Psychiatry*, 1994, 9, 1008–1009.

Vassilas, C., & Morgan, H. G. Suicide in Avon. *British Journal of Psychiatry,* 1997, 170, 453–455.

Velamoor, V. R., & Cernovsky, Z. Z. Suicide with the motive "to die" or "not to die" and its socioanamnestic correlates. *Social Behavior & Personality*, 1992, 20, 193–198.

Wagner, B., Schuman, P. M., Tobin, J., & Aiken, C. Can teen suicide attempts have a family function? In J. McIntosh (Ed.), *Suicide '96.* Washington, DC: AAS, 1996, 90–92.

Walford, G., Kennedy, M. T., Manwell, M. K. C., & McCune, N. Father-perpetrators of child sexual abuse who commit suicide. *Irish Journal of Psychological Medicine*, 1990, 7, 144–145.

Wulsin, L. R., & Goldman, L. Post-traumatic stress disorder following a suicide attempt. *Journal of Traumatic Stress*, 1993, 6, 151–155.

Chapter 14

EPIDEMIOLOGY AND THE INCIDENCE OF SUICIDE

National Trends

Lester (1990a) examined suicide rates from 1970–1984 in 23 nations. The male suicide rate increased significantly over the time period in 18 nations and decreased significantly in one; the female suicide rate increased significantly over the time period in nine nations and decreased significantly in five. Reviews of suicide rates by age in nations of the world were presented by Lester (1991a, 1991b).

Lester (1992) found that, for 14 nations, the mean suicide rate had increased from 1875 to 1986, but the standard deviation/ mean did not change. Lester (1996a) found that most nations of the world experienced rising male and female suicide rates during the 1970s, but this trend did not continue in the 1980s. Lester (1995a) found that, in the 1980s, as many nations experienced an increase in suicide rates as a experienced decrease – overall, for youth, and for the elderly. Nations with the higher rates in 1980 experienced a decrease during the 1980s. Lester (1996b) found that most nations had an increasing suicide rate from 1960–1990. Quadratic trends were less consistent, with 14 nations fitting an inverted-U-shaped curve and 21 a U-shaped curve.

Bahrain

Al-Ansari et al. (1997) calculated attempted suicide rates by overdose for 15–24 year olds and found higher rates in non-Bahraini than in Bahraini (106 versus 39).

Baltic Countries

Wasserman and Varnik (1994) noted that the high suicide rates in Estonia, Latvia, and Lithuania declined from 1984–1987 (during Perestroika), but rose thereafter, especially among the men.

Canada

Leenaars and Lester (1992) compared the epidemiology of suicide in Canada and the United States for 1960–1988.

China

Li and Baker (1991) reported suicide rates for mainland China for 10 percent of the population in 1986. The rate was 17.6 – higher in women than in men; 10.0 for urban areas and 27.7 for rural areas. Rates rose with age for both men and women. Zhang (1996) reported a low suicide rate for Beijing in 1992–1993 (5.1 and 4.6 respectively). Yip (1996) compared the patterns of completed suicide in Taiwan, Hong Kong, and Beijing (China).

Costa Rica

Lester (1995b) reported on the epidemiology of suicide in Costa Rica.

Eastern Europe

Sartorius (1995) found that the total suicide rates in Eastern European nations rose from 1987 to 1992 and the male/female ratio increased, whereas the rates in other European nations declined. The trends for the elderly were less clear, but their rates seemed to decline during this same period in Eastern Europe.

English-Speaking Countries

Cantor et al. (1996; Lester et al., 1997) explored trends in English-speaking countries and found differences between the old-world and new-world nations.

Greenland

Thorslund (1990) documented a rising suicide rate from 1962 to 1986 among those born in Greenland (from 9.4 to 114.1), with suicide rates peaking in the young. He noted a similar increase among the Inuit of Quebec (Canada).

Israel

Arieli et al. (1996) found that Ethiopian Jews in Israel had a higher suicide rate than the general population, with more males aged 20–39 than the general suicides. The most common precipitants for this group were family conflicts, internalized aggression, and depression.

Italy

In the South Tyrol area of Italy, regions with more Italians and fewer Germans had lower suicide rates, especially for males (Deisenhammer et al., 1996). Suicide rates were associated with age, marital status, and community size. The Italians lived in larger communities and were older, but the ethnic association was found even after controls for these variables.

Pacific Islands

Pridmore (1995) reported a suicide rate of 3.9 for the Solomon Islands for 1989–1993. Pridmore et al. (1995) reported a suicide rate of 1.5 for Fiji for 1969–1989 and an attempted suicide rate of 12.0. Suicidal behavior in Fiji (fatal and nonfatal combined) was more common in women than in men and in Indians than in Fijians.

Scotland

Lester (1995d) found that attempted and completed suicide rates were positively associated for men and negatively associated for women in Scotland over the period 1982–1992. The male/female ratio increased for both attempted and completed suicide over the period.

United States

Males (1991) noted a rise in suicide rates for 15–19 year olds from the 1950s to the 1980s for the United States and attributed this to a changing classification in which suicides in this group that used to be ruled accidental are now more accurately coded as suicides.

Lester (1995c) calculated suicide rates by ethnicity in 1890 and 1990. Chinese Americans had the highest suicide rate in 1890, followed by native Americans, whites, and blacks.

Riggs et al. (1996) noted that the peak in male suicides among the oldest had remained constant from 1951–1988, whereas the peak in female suicide rates had declined from the 60 year olds to the 40 year olds.

Nonfatal Suicidal Behavior

In a review of surveys of adolescents, Safer (1997) found that about 9.6 percent of American students had attempted suicide (with a male/female ratio of 1/1.9) as compared to 7.2 percent for students in other nations (with a male/female ratio of 1/1.6).

England

Hawton et al. (1994) calculated attempted suicide rates for the Oxford region. Rates were higher in women; the unemployed;and social classes III, IV, and V. For women, rates peaked at ages 15–19, and were higher for the single and divorced; for men the rates peaked at age 25-29 and were higher in the divorced. Single and married women had higher rates than single and married men; widowed and divorced men had higher rates than widowed and divorced women.

Ethiopia

Kebede and Ketsela (1993) found that pupils 11–18 years old in Ethiopia had a lifetime incidence of attempted suicide of 14.3 percent. The frequency was not associated with sex, age, parental education, or family history of suicide, but was more common in ninth graders, in those with higher hopelessness scores, heavy alcohol use, and suicidal ideation.

Greece

Madianos et al. (1993) found a higher incidence of prior attempted suicide (and suicidal ideation) in females than in males and an increase from 1978–1984. Attempting suicide was associated with depression and problem drinking, being over the age of 35, divorced/widowed, a skilled worker or unemployed, female, a high school graduate,

living in Athens, and having a mentally ill family member.

Hong Kong

Lai-Yeung (1995) found that female university students in Hong Kong reported more suicidal ideation than male students.

Jamaica

Lambert et al. (1994) found no differences in the incidence of suicidal talk in Jamaican and American children aged 6–11, nor differences by sex, age, or social class.

The Netherlands

Arensman et al. (1995) found in one region of the Netherlands that attempted suicide rates were higher in men, the divorced, the less educated, unemployed, and disabled.

Nigeria

Lester and Akande (1995) found no differences between Yoruban and American students in current suicidal ideation.

Norway

Hjelmeland and Bjerke (1996) found attempted suicide rates in one county in Norway to be higher in women, urban areas, the divorced/separated, those aged 35–44, the unemployed, and those with less education. The methods used, the personal characteristics, and the precipitants varied with sex and age.

Reunion

Duval et al. (1997) found a high rate of attempted suicide in Reunion (335), with a higher rate in the southern rural areas of the island, a slight over-representation of women and a frequent use of pesticides and herbicides.

Scandinavia

Wasserman et al. (1994) compared attempted suicide rates by men and women in Scandinavia. They noted that Finns in Sweden had higher rates of attempted suicide than Finns in Finland.

Trinidad

Neehall and Beharry (1994) found a higher rate of attempted suicide for East Indian adolescents, average rate for Africans, and a lower rate for mixed youths.

United States

Birkhead et al. (1993), based on surveillance data from emergency rooms in Cobb County (Georgia), found an attempted suicide rate of 89.0 and a completed suicide rate of 15.0. Attempted suicide peaked (at 317) in those aged 15–19, while completed suicide peaked (at 27) in those aged 55–64. Attempters used primarily drugs/poisons, while completers used primarily guns. Among the attempters, females were more common than males and blacks more than whites.

Lester (1994) found that depression and current suicidal ideation was more common in high school students than in college students (but significantly so only for girls).

Meilman et al. (1994) found a rate of 14.5 for suicide attempts at William and Mary College and 18.4 for suicidal threats. The most common stressors were work/school failure for the attempters, relationship difficulties for the threaters, and social isolation for the general student body.

Swanson et al. (1992) found a higher incidence of suicidal ideation in the past week in American adolescents than in Mexican adolescents (23 percent versus 12 percent). Sex, drug use, and depression were associated with suicidal ideation in the USA; in Mexico it was poverty.

Lester and DeSimone (1995) found no differences between white and black students in current suicidal ideation (or between boys and girls). Among African American college students, Molock et al. (1994) found that females had attempted suicide more than males (16 percent versus 2 percent) and thought about suicide more often (56 percent versus 31 percent). Those with prior and current suicidal ideation were more depressed than those without.

Children

Milling et al. (1991a, 1991b) found suicidal behavior to be quite common among psychiatric inpatients and outpatients aged 4–12. For example, 15 percent of the outpatients and 31 percent of inpatients had thought about, threatened, or attempted suicide during their current illness.

Clarke et al. (1993) found cases of suicide by hanging in three Ohio children aged 8, 10, and 13.

Domenech et al. (1992) found little change in the incidence of suicidal ideation in children from ages 11–14. There were no sex differences, but depression was associated with suicidal ideation.

Adolescents

Completed Suicide

Haring et al. (1991) in Austria found an increase in the incidence of suicide at ages 14–15 and 18–19 (times when the adolescent is changing schools) and also in

February–March (times when school reports come out).

Nonfatal Suicidal Behavior

Lester (1990b) compared the responses of college students and high school students to item nine on Beck's Depression Inventory. More high school students reported some (score 1–3) current suicidal ideation (34 percent versus 23 percent). For lifetime history of suicidal behavior, 5.0 percent of the college students had attempted suicide, 9.1 percent threatened suicide, and 29.2 percent thought about suicide.

Ahmadi et al. (1991) in Connecticut found that 26 percent of high school students had considered suicide as compared to 16 percent of college students; 2.6 percent of the high school students and 0.9 percent of the college students had attempted suicide. Students at a private high school had a lower incidence of prior suicidal ideation, but a higher incidence of prior attempted suicide.

In Oregon in 1988, adolescents under age 18 had a completed suicide rate of 4.6 and an attempted suicide rate of 214.0 (Andrus et al., 1991). Completers tended to be more often male and white and to use firearms and hanging more and overdoses less. There were no urban/rural differences.

In a survey of ninth to twelfth graders in 50 states, 27 percent had thought of suicide in the past year, 16 percent had made serious plans, and 8.3 percent had attempted suicide, with two percent requiring medical attention (Anonymous, 1991). Females, Hispanics, and whites reported more suicidality.

Garrison et al. (1991a, 1991b) surveyed seventh and eighth graders and found that about a quarter had a history of suicidal ideation, more so in girls and in blacks. Tested every year, the correlations between recent suicidal ideation from year to year

was low – 0.35 for a one-year interval and 0.28 for a two-year interval. Suicidal ideation was associated with depression, life events, and family cohesion in one report and with these variables plus not living with parents, depressive disorders, and negatively, with socialized aggressive conduct disorder in the other report.

In seventh to twelfth graders in Minnesota, Harris et al. (1991) found a higher incidence of prior attempted suicide in females and the higher grades.

Kandel et al. (1991) surveyed ninth and eleventh graders and found that 6 percent of the boys and 12 percent of the girls had attempted suicide in the past; 26 percent of the boys and 42 percent of the girls had thought about suicide in the past year.

Farrow and Schwartz (1992) found that suburban white adolescents seen at pediatric clinics had more suicidal ideation than urban blacks (plus fewer school problems and more alcohol use).

In Nevada, Alberg and Evans (1994) found that suicidal ideation was more common in eighth graders than in tenth graders, females, nonwhites, the non-religious, and high achievers. There were no urban/rural differences.

Ward (1994) found that students in a rural white high school and inner-city Hispanics scored highest on a suicide-behavior scale, and African American sixth–eighth graders scored the lowest. The study, however, confounded age, sex, and urban/rural location.

Kienhorst et al. (1990) surveyed students aged 10–20 in the Netherlands and found that 2.2 percent had previously attempted suicide (3.3 percent of girls and 1.3 percent of boys). Boys aged 13 and younger reported a higher incidence than girls, whereas girls aged 14 and older reported a higher incidence than boys. Recent suicidal ideation was reported by 3.5 percent.

Larsson and Melin (1992) found that 20

percent of Swedish 8–13 year olds had suicidal ideation, more so in the girls and in those who were depressed.

Pronovost (1990) surveyed adolescents aged 12–18 in Quebec (Canada) and found that 3.5 percent had attempted suicide in the past and 15.4 percent had seriously thought about suicide. The largest jump in incidence was from age 12 to age 13.

The Elderly

Osgood et al. (1991) studied nursing home patients and found that the suicide rate was 16 (versus 19 in the community), the attempted suicide rate 63, the fatal indirect life-threatening behavior rate 79, and the nonfatal indirect life-threatening behavior rate 228. The rates of all of these were higher in males; the rates of completed suicide and fatal indirect, life-threatening behavior higher in whites; and the rates of attempted suicide and nonfatal life-threatening

behavior higher in nonwhites. Osgood suggested that life-threatening behavior should be taken into account when discussing suicidal behavior in the elderly.

In Calgary (Canada), Bagley and Ramsay (1993) found that 18–24 year olds had more lifetime suicidal ideation than those over the age of 60, as well as poorer mental health, more drug abuse, and more childhood separation from parents. Among the youth, females had more suicidal ideation than the males (but not more "suicidal preoccupation").

Discussion

Lester (1995e) noted that trends in national suicide rates were of little interest unless (a) they generalized to other nations and (b) we could explain differences between nations in the trends. Progress has been made on the first task, but little on the second.

REFERENCES

Ahmadi, K. S., Goethe, J. W., & Adams, M. L. Suicidal behaviors among Connecticut youth. *Connecticut Medicine*, 1991, 55(2), 76–80.

Al-Ansari, A. M. S., Hamadeh, R. R., Matar, A. M., Buzaboon, B., Marhoon, H., & Raees, A. G. Overdose among youth in Bahrain. *Journal of the Royal Society of Health*, 1997, 117, 366–371.

Alberg, E., & Evans, W. Suicidal ideation among a stratified sample of rural and urban adolescents. *Child & Adolescent Social Work Journal*, 1994, 11, 379–389.

Andrus, J. K., Fleming, D. W., Heumann, M. A., Wassell, J. T., Hopkins, D. D., & Gordon, J. Surveillance of attempted suicide among adolescents in Oregon, 1988. *American Journal of Public Health*, 1991, 81, 1067–1069.

Anonymous. Attempted suicide among high school students. *Journal of the American Medical Association*, 1991, 266, 1911–1912.

Arensman, E., Kerkhof, A. J., Hengeveld, M. W., & Mulder, J. D. Medically treated suicide attempts. *Journal of Epidemiology & Community Health*, 1995, 49, 285–289.

Arieli, A., Gilat, I., & Aycheli, S. Suicide among Ethiopian Jews. *Journal of Nervous & Mental Disease*, 1996, 184, 317–319.

Bagley, C., & Ramsay, R. Suicidal ideas and behavior in contrasted populations. *Journal of Community Psychology*, 1993, 21, 26–34.

Birkhead, G. S., Galvin, V. G., Meehan, P. J., O'Carroll, P. W., & Mercy, J. A. The emergency department in surveillance of attempted suicide. *Public Health Reports*, 1993, 108, 323–331.

Cantor, C. H., Leenaars, A. A., Lester, D., Slater, P. J., Wolanowski, A. M., & O'Toole, D. Suicide trends in eight predominantly English-speaking countries 1960–1989. *Social Psychiatry & Psychiatric Epidemiology*, 1996, 31, 364–373.

Clarke, M. A., Feczko, J. D., Hawley, D. A., Pless, J. E., Tate, L. R., & Fardal, P. M. Asphyxial deaths due to hanging in children. *Journal of Forensic Sciences*, 1993, 38, 344–352.

Deisenhammer, E. A., Haring, C., Kemmler, G., Pycha, R., & Hinterhuber, H. Suicide in South Tyrol 1980–1992. *European Archives of Psychiatry*, 1996, 246, 273–278.

Domenech, E., Canals, J., & Fernandez Ballert, J. Suicidal ideation among Spanish school children. *Personality & Individual Differences*, 1992, 13, 1055–1057.

Duval, G., Baillet, A., & Catteau, C. Epidémiologie des tentatives de suicide à l'Ile de la Réunion. *Revue d'Epidémiologie et de Santé Publique*, 1997, 45(1), 23–28.

Farrow, J. A., & Schwartz, R. H. Adolescent drug and alcohol usage. *Journal of the National Medical Association*, 1992, 84, 409–413.

Garrison, C. Z., Addy, C. L., Jackson, K. L., McKeown, R. E., & Waller, J. L. A longitudinal study of suicidal ideation in young adolescents. *Journal of the American Academy of Child & Adolescent Psychiatry*, 1991b, 30, 597–603.

Garrison, C. Z., Jackson, K. L., Addy, C. L., McKeown, R. E., & Waller, J. L. Suicidal behaviors in young adolescents. *American Journal of Epidemiology*, 1991a, 133, 1005–1014.

Haring, C., Biebl, W., Barnas, C., Miller, C. H., & Fleischhacker, W. W. Vulnerable phases in adolescence represented by means of committed suicide. *Crisis*, 1991, 12, 58–63.

Harris, L., Blum, R. W., & Resnick, M. Teen females in Minnesota. *Women & Therapy*, 1991, 11(3/4), 119–135.

Hawton, K., Fagg, J., Simkin, S., & Mills, J. The epidemiology of attempted suicide in the Oxford area, England (1989–1992). *Crisis*, 1994, 15, 123–135.

Hjelmeland, H., & Bjerke, T. Parasuicide in the county of Sor-Trondelag, Norway. *Social Psychiatry & Psychiatric Epidemiology*, 1996, 31, 272–283.

Kandel, D. B., Raveis, V. H., & Davies, M. Suicidal ideation in adolescence. *Journal of Youth & Adolescence*, 1991, 20, 289–309.

Kebede, D., & Ketsela, T. Suicide attempts in Ethiopian adolescents in Addis Ababa high schools. *Ethiopian Medical Journal*, 1993, 31, 83–90.

Kienhorst, C. W. M., de Wilde, E. J., van den Bout, J. Broese van Groenou, M. I., Diekstra, R. F. W., & Wolters, W. H. G. Self-reported suicidal behavior in Dutch secondary education students. *Suicide & Life-Threatening Behavior*, 1990, 20, 101–112.

Lai-Yeung, S. An integrative model of suicide ideation among Hong Kong students. In D. Lester (Ed.), *Suicide '95*. Washington, DC: AAS, 1995, 124–125.

Lambert, M. C., Knight, F., Taylor, R., & Achenbach, T. M. Epidemiology of behavioral and emotional problems among children of Jamaica and the United States. *Journal of Abnormal Child Psychology*, 1994, 22, 113–128.

Larsson, B., & Melin, L. Prevalence and short-term stability of depressive symptoms in school children. *Acta Psychiatrica Scandinavica*, 1992, 85, 17–22.

Leenaars, A. A., & Lester, D. Comparison of rates and patterns of suicide in Canada and the United States, 1960–1988. *Death Studies*, 1992, 16, 417–430.

Lester, D. Changes to suicide rates unique to Canada? *Canadian Journal of Public Health*, 1990a, 81, 240–241.

Lester, D. Depression and suicide in college students. *Personality & Individual Differences*, 1990b, 11, 757–758.

Lester, D. A cross-cultural look at the suicide rates of children and adolescents. In A. A. Leenaars & S. Wenckstern (Eds.), *Suicide prevention in schools*. New York: Hemisphere, 1991a, 17–25.

Lester, D. Suicide across the life-span. In A. A. Leenaars (Ed.), *Life span perspectives of suicide*. New York: Plenum, 1991b, 71–80.

Lester, D. Have national suicide rates increased and converged over the last 100 years? *Perceptual & Motor Skills*, 1992, 75, 1262.

Lester, D. Depression and suicidal preoccupation in high school and college students. *Psychological Reports*, 1994, 75, 984.

Lester, D. Recent trends in national suicide rates. *Italian Journal of Suicidology*, 1995a, 5, 29–32.

Lester, D. Suicide and homicide in Costa Rica. *Medicine, Science & the Law*, 1995b, 35, 316–318.

Lester, D. Suicide rates among Native Americans in 1890. *Perceptual & Motor Skills*,

1995c, 80, 830.

Lester, D. Suicide and parasuicide in Scotland. *Perceptual & Motor Skills*, 1995d, 80, 862.

Lester, D. Secular trends in suicide. *Perceptual & Motor Skills*, 1995e, 80, 1041–1042.

Lester, D. Recent trends in suicide mortality. *Crisis*, 1996a, 17, 94.

Lester, D. Trends in national suicide rates from 1960–1990. *Italian Journal of Suicidology*, 1996b, 6, 71–72.

Lester, D., & Akande, A. Depression in Nigerian and American students. *Psychological Reports*, 1995, 76, 906.

Lester, D., Cantor, C. H., & Leenaars, A. A. Suicide in the United Kingdom and Ireland. *European Psychiatry*, 1997, 12, 300–304.

Lester, D., & DeSimone, A. Depression and suicidal ideation in African American and Caucasian students. *Psychological Reports*, 1995, 77, 18.

Li, G., & Baker, S. P. A comparison of injury death rates in China and the United States, 1986. *American Journal of Public Health*, 1991, 81, 605–609.

Madianos, M. G., Madianou-Gefou, D., & Stefanis, C. N. Changes in suicidal behavior among nation-wide general population samples across Greece. *European Archives of Psychiatry*, 1993, 243, 171–178.

Males, M. Teen suicide and changing cause-of-death certification, 1953–1987. *Suicide & Life-Threatening Behavior*, 1991, 21, 245–259.

Meilman, P. W., Pattis, J. A., & Kraus Zeilmann, D. Suicide attempts and threats on one college campus. *Journal of American College Health*, 1994, 42, 147–154.

Milling, L., Campbell, N. B., Davenport, C. W., & Carpenter, G. Suicidal behavior among psychiatric inpatient children. *Child Psychiatry & Human Development*, 1991a, 22, 71–77.

Milling, L., Gyure, K., Davenport, C. W., & Bair, P. Suicidal behavior among psychiatric outpatient children. *Child Psychiatry & Human Development*, 1991b, 22, 283–289.

Molock, S. D., Kimbrough, R., Lacy, M. B., McClure, K. P., & Williams, S. Suicidal behavior among African American college students. *Journal of Black Psychology*, 1994, 20, 234–251.

Neehall, J., & Beharry, N. Demographic and clinical features of adolescent parasuicides. *West Indian Medical Journal*, 1994, 43, 123–126.

Osgood, N., J., Brant, B. A., & Lipman, A. *Suicide among the elderly in long-term care facilities*. New York: Greenwood, 1991.

Pridmore, S. Suicidal behavior in the Solomon Islands. *Medical Journal of Australia*, 1995, 162, 614–616.

Pridmore, S., Ryan, K., & Blizzard, L. Victims of violence in Fiji. *Australian & New Zealand Journal of Psychiatry*, 1995, 29, 666–670.

Pronovost, J. Prevalence of suicidal ideations and behaviors among adolescents. In G. Ferrari, M. Bellini & P. Crepet (Eds.), *Suicidal behavior and risk factors*. Bologna: Monduzzi-Editore, 1990, 427–431.

Riggs, J. E., McGraw, R. L., & Keefover, R. W. Suicide in the United States, 1951–1988. *Comprehensive Psychiatry*, 1996, 37, 222–225.

Safer, D. J. Self-reported suicide attempts by adolescents. *Annals of Clinical Psychiatry*, 1997, 9, 263–269.

Sartorius, N. Recent changes in suicide rates in selected Eastern European and other European countries. *International Psychogeriatrics*, 1995, 7, 301–308.

Swanson, J. W., Linskey, A. O., Quintero Salinas, R., Pumariega, H. J., & Holzer, C. E. A binational school survey of depressive symptoms, drug use, and suicidal ideation. *Journal of the American Academy of Child & Adolescent Psychiatry*, 1992, 31, 669–678.

Thorslund, J. Inuit suicides in Greenland. *Arctic Medical Research*, 1990, 49(1), 25–33.

Ward, A. J. Mean Suicide Scale (AAS) scores in different groups. In D. Lester (Ed.), *Suicide '94*. Denver: AAS, 1994, 132–133.

Wasserman, D., Fellman, M., Bille-Brahe, U., Bjerke, T., Jacobson, L., Jessen, G., Lonnqvist, J., Njastad, P., Ostamo, O., & Salander-Renberg, E. Parasuicide in the Nordic countries. *Scandinavian Journal of Social Medicine*, 1994, 22, 170–177.

Wasserman, D., & Varnik, A. Increase in suicide among men in the Baltic countries. *Lancet*, 1994, 343, 1504–1505.

Yip, P. S. Suicides in Hong Kong, Taiwan, and Beijing. *British Journal of Psychiatry*, 1996, 169, 495–500.

Zhang, J. Suicides in Beijing, China, 1992–1993. *Suicide & Life-Threatening Behavior*, 1996, 26, 175–180.

Chapter 15

THE METHODS CHOSEN FOR SUICIDE

Marzuk et al. (1992a) classified methods of suicide for their ease of access in the five boroughs of New York City. The suicide rates for methods of similar access in the boroughs were similar, whereas the suicide rates for methods of different access were different. The associations were as predicted for the methods of falling from heights, prescriptions (they used physicians per capita as a proxy measure), carbon monoxide poisoning, and commuter trains; the associations were nonsignificant for subway trains.

Firearms

For reviews of this research see Lester (1993a) and Miller and Hemenway (1999).

The Effect of Strict Handgun Control Laws

Boor and Bair (1990) found that eight elements of state gun control statutes in the United States in 1985 were associated with the state suicide rates. In a multiple regression with control variables, the predictors of the state suicide rates were the divorce rate, the crime rate, restrictions on sellers, and restrictions on buyers. Lester (1990h) found that state gun control law strictness in 1965 was associated with a lower state suicide rate.

Yang and Lester (1991) found gun control strictness was associated with a reduced suicide in the states, after controls for divorce and unemployment rates, for the total suicide rate and for the suicide rate by firearms. Gun control strictness was associated with higher suicide rates by jumping but not with suicide rates by the other methods. Lester (1993e) found that the age-adjusted rate of firearm suicides in the states of America was associated with the strictness of state gun control laws.

Loftin et al. (1991) found that a strict handgun law in Washington, D.C., led to a drop of 23 percent in suicides using firearms but no change in other methods and no change in the neighboring states of Maryland and Virginia.

Cantor and Lewin (1990) noted that Queensland, Australia, had weaker gun control laws than other states. From 1961–1985, Queensland had a higher suicide rate, a higher suicide rate using firearms, and a greater proportion of suicides using firearms. Snowdon and Harris (1992) noted that South Australia restricted firearms in 1980. The male firearm suicide rate declined after this, but there was an increase in the male suicide rate by other methods. In other Australian states, however, both the firearm and nonfirearm suicide rates rose from pre-1980 to post-1980. In 1992, a stricter gun control law took effect in Queensland (Australia). Cantor and Slater (1995) found that the number of firearm suicides dropped afterwards by 21 percent, primarily in men, in urban areas, and for 15–29 year olds. Although the use of drugs and hanging increased in urban areas, the total number of suicides decreased. (In rural areas, the use of methods other than firearms did not change.)

Mundt (1990) found that tightening the gun control law in Canada in 1977 was associated with a lowering of the firearm suicide rate, even though the overall suicide rate increased and firearm ownership increased. Lester and Leenaars (1993, 1994) also found that tightening the gun control law in Canada in 1977 resulted in a decreased use of firearms for suicide in Canada as a whole (both in terms of rate and percentage). There was no definitive evidence that people switched to other methods for suicide, although the effect appears to have been stronger for females than for males (Leenaars and Lester, 1996). Leenaars and Lester (1997) found that the preventive effect was found in those aged 25–64, but the use of guns increased in those over age 75. The use of other methods for suicide increased in those aged 15–34 and over age 75. Rich et al. (1990) documented that the imposition of strict gun control laws in Toronto resulted in a decreased use of guns for suicide and a corresponding increasd use of jumping (primarily in front of subway trains). Thus, apparently, people switched methods for suicide.

Carrington and Moyer (1994a, 1994b) also found that the firearm suicide rate declined after passage of the law, but not the suicide rate by all other methods. Thus, displacement to other methods did not appear to occur. These trends were found in the provinces as well as the whole of Canada.

Sloan et al. (1990) compared suicide in Seattle (USA) and Vancouver (Canada) in 1985–1987. These cities presumably differ in gun ownership and gun control laws. The suicide rates were similar, but the handgun suicide rate was higher in Seattle. In contrast, the suicide rates using poisoning, hanging, and jumping/drowning were higher in Vancouver. Thus, there appeared to be evidence for switching methods when guns were less available in Canada. However, for 15–24 year olds, the suicide rate was higher in Seattle and attributable to guns. Thus, Sloan concluded that gun control might lower the suicide rate in young adults.

The results of the research are not altogether consistent, and different investigators draw different conclusions. For example, while Lester (1993a) has concluded that strict gun control laws do have a preventive effect on suicide, Kleck (1991) concluded that strict gun control laws have no impact on suicide rates.

Attempts to Measure the Extent of Firearm Ownership

There are no measures of firearm ownership for each state of the United States. However, several indirect measures are available.

(1) ACCIDENTAL DEATH RATES. Lester (1993c) found that the accidental death rate using firearms in the states of America was positively associated with the firearm suicide rate, but not with the overall suicide rate. Lester (1992) showed that the accidental death rate from firearms in a sample of nations was positively associated with the suicide rate using firearms and the percentage of suicides using firearms, but not with the suicide rate by all other methods. Lester (1994b) found that the accidental death rate from firearms was positively associated with the suicide rate using firearms over the provinces of Canada (and negatively associated with the suicide rate by all other

methods, suggesting that switching may occur).

(2) PERCENTAGE OF HOMICIDES BY FIREARMS. Lester (1990a) found that the percentage of homicides committed in each of a sample of nations of the world was positively associated with the nations' suicide rates using guns and negatively associated with the suicide rate by all other methods. Lester (1994b) found that the percentage of homicides using firearms was not associated with the suicide rate using firearms over the provinces of Canada.

(3) SUBSCRIPTIONS TO GUN MAGAZINES. Lester (1993e) found that the age-adjusted firearm suicide rates of the states were associated with subscriptions to gun-oriented magazines, but not significantly so.

(4) FIREARMS DEALERS. Lester (1993b) found that the per-capita density of firearms dealers in the states of America was not associated with the age-adjusted firearms death rates in the states.

Gundlach (1990) measured firearm availability in the SMSAs of America by counting retail outlets in telephone book Yellow Pages. For the 77 largest SMSAs, divorce predicted the suicide rate in regions with both high availability and low availability of firearms for both male and female suicide rates. Living alone predicted the suicide rate only when firearm availability was high. For the nine major regions of the United States, the firearm suicide rate was strongly associated with the Yellow Pages measure of firearm availability (measured for only the largest SMSAs in each region) and with the percentages owning guns.

(5) HUNTING LICENSES. Lester (1995c) found that the per-capita purchase of hunting licenses in the states of America was associated with other indirect measures of firearm ownership and appeared to be associated with a lower firearm suicide rate, with no evidence for switching. Simon et al.

(1996) found that the firearm suicide rate in the regions of Quebec (Canada) was associated with the density of hunting licences (and with the total suicide rate).

Actual Firearm Ownership

Killias (1993) and Lester (1996a) both found that estimates of the percentage of households with guns in 12 nations was positively associated with the suicide rate using firearms (the total suicide rate and the percentage of suicides using guns), but not with the suicide rate by all other methods.

Over the provinces of Canada, Carrington and Moyer (1994a) found that the firearm suicide rate (but not the suicide rate by all other methods) was associated with the percentage of households owning guns.

Time-Series Analyses

Boor (1981) found that from 1962–1975 in the United States, as domestic production and importing of firearms increased, so did the suicide rate using firearms. Wintemute (1988) found that the number of domestically produced handguns each year from 1946 to 1985 was positively associated with the firearm suicide rate.

Lester (1990d) found that the accidental death rate from firearms in the United States from 1950 to 1984 was *negatively* correlated with the suicide rate from firearms, results contrary to an availability hypothesis. However, Lester and Abe (1990) found that the accidental death rate and suicide rate from firearms were positively associated over time in Japan. Lester (1991c) found that the suicide rate by firearms was positively associated over time in the United States with the percentage of suicides using firearms, subscriptions to two gun-oriented magazines, and household ownership of handguns; it was negatively associated with the accidental death rate from firearms. Ownership of long guns and the use of firearms for homicide were unrelated to the use of firearms for suicide.

In Northern Ireland, however, the suicide rate using firearms was not related to the accidental death rate from firearms or the percentage of homicides using firearms (Curran and Lester, 1991).

Guns in the Home

Kellermann et al. (1992) found that those committing suicide at home were more likely to have a gun in the home; not graduate from high school; live alone; have been hospitalized for drinking; be on medication; use illicit drugs; and have more quarrels/fights, arrests, and depression/mental illness than living controls from the same communities. The presence of a gun was significant in the multiple regression. The risk of suicide at home was even higher when the gun was a handgun, loaded, and kept in unlocked storage.

Brent et al. (1993b) found that adolescent suicides with no psychiatric diagnosis more often had a loaded gun in the home than adolescent suicides with a psychiatric disorder. Brent et al. (1993a) found that adolescent suicides who used a firearm for their suicide more often had a gun in the home, completed suicide in the home, and were intoxicated with alcohol at the time, white, and of lower social class. They did not differ in psychiatric diagnosis or life stressors. The more handguns in the home, the higher the percentage of suicides using a firearms. This association was found in urban areas only and was stronger in the nondisturbed suicides, but remained significant after controls for psychiatric disturbance and prior suicide attempts. The suicides in general more often than com-munity controls had access to handguns (but not long guns) in the home.

Freeman et al. (1994) found that all of their sample of combat veterans with post-traumatic stress disorder had owned guns and three-quarters still did. Over half had loaded a gun at some point in order to commit suicide, and a third had done this while intoxicated.

Beautrais et al. (1996) found that com-pleted suicides and community controls did not differ in gun ownership. However, using a gun for suicide rather than another method was associated with gun ownership for com-pleters and attempters combined.

Bailey et al. (1997) found that female suicides in three counties in America (in Kentucky, Ohio and Washington) more often had a gun in the home than did neighbors (as well as more often lived alone and had a history of mental illness). Cummings et al. (1997) found that suicides in Washington were more likely to have a handgun in the home than living matched controls and to have made more purchases of handguns; they did not differ in the caliber of the gun in the home.

Firearm Storage

Brent et al. (1991) compared adolescent completed suicide, attempted suicides, and psychiatric controls. Sixty-nine percent of the completers used guns for the suicidal act versus none of the attempters. More of the completers had guns available in the homes, and they had more total guns and more handguns available. They did not differ in the method of storage of guns or whether the gun was stored loaded.

Car Exhaust

Lester (1990d) found that the accidental death rate from car exhaust was positively associated over time in the United States with the suicide rate from car exhaust, and Lester and Abe (1990) replicated this result in Japan. Lester (1995d) found that the accidental death rate from car exhaust from 1950–1984 in the United States did not predict the suicide rate by car exhaust or the percentage of suicides using car exhaust. The percentage of suicides using car exhaust, but not the suicide rate using car exhaust, was associated with the number of cars per capita. Shelef (1994) noted that the decline in suicides from car exhaust in the United States levelled off in 1983, while the accidental deaths continued to decline through 1987.

In Northern Ireland, Curran and Lester (1991) found that, as suicide using car exhaust became more common, suicide by all other methods did not become less common.

Lester (1993c) found that the accidental death rate from car exhaust was positively associated over the states of America with the suicide rate from car exhaust. Lester (1994e) found that the per-capita car ownership in nations of the world was positively associated with the suicide rate from car exhaust.

Domestic Gas

Burvill (1990) noted that, as Australia detoxified its domestic gas by switching to natural gas in 1969–1987, men seemed to switch from domestic gas to car exhaust for suicide, whereas women did not, and the use of gas by men for suicide declined.

Lester (1990b) documented that, as domestic gas was detoxified in the United States in the 1950s, there was a corresponding decrease in the use of domestic gas for suicide. At the same time, car ownership was increasing, and the data for men shows that men may have switched from domestic gas

to car exhaust for suicide. However, switching between these two methods for suicide did not appear to have occurred for women. Lester (1990d) found that the accidental death rates from all gases in the United States from 1950 to 1984 was positively associated with the suicide rate from gases, and Lester and Abe (1990) replicated this result in Japan.

Lester (1990e) found that as domestic gas was detoxified in Switzerland, not only did the suicide rate using domestic gas decline, but so did the overall suicide rate, indicating that people did not switch methods for suicide once domestic gas became less toxic.

Lester (1991a) found that the detoxification of domestic gas in the Netherlands was accompanied by a decrease in its use for suicide, but also by increase in the use of other methods. In Northern Ireland, on the other hand, detoxification of domestic gas was not accompanied by an increase in the rate of suicide using all other methods (Curran and Lester, 1991). In Scotland from 1950 to 1975, Lester and Hodgson (1992) found that, as domestic gas was detoxified, the suicide rate using domestic gas declined, while the suicide rate using all other methods continued to rise at the same pace as before detoxification. The total suicide rate stopped increasing and held steady.

Looking at the effects of detoxification in six nations, Lester (1995b) concluded that the impact was beneficial on the overall suicide rate only when suicide by domestic gas was a common method for suicide (as in Northern Ireland, Scotland, and Switzerland).

Lester (1990c) explored whether the detoxification of domestic gas and the presence of a suicide prevention center both had an effect on the suicide rate of cities in England. He found no significant effects from either variable, but the sample sizes were small and the cities with less-toxic gas at the end of the study period still had high levels of carbon monoxide.

Medications and Poisons

In the United States from 1960 to 1974, Lester (1990f) found that the suicide rate using barbiturates was associated with the annual sales of barbiturates and with the accidental death rate from barbiturates. Lester (1990d) found that in the United States from 1950 to 1984, the accidental death rate from solids and liquids, as well as specifically from barbiturates, was positively associated with the suicide rates from these methods. Lester and Abe (1990) replicated this result in Japan for medicaments in general.

Lester (1993c) found that the accidental death rates from poisoning by solids/liquids and by gases were positively associated over the states of America with the suicide rates by these two methods. Lester (1991b) found that the association between suicidal and accidental deaths rates over time in the United States from 1979 to 1987 was positive and strong for barbiturates and for other sedatives and hypnotics, but not for analgesics/antipyretics/antirheumatics or for tranquilizers/other psychotropic agents.

Lester (1994c) used the per-capita availability of doctors in European nations as a proxy measure of prescription rates and found that the measure was positively associated with the suicide rate using solids and liquids, but not with the suicide rate by all other methods. Lester (1994d, 1995a) replicated this result over the states of America, but failed to replicate it over the regions of Russia.

Bodeker (1991) found in Germany that, when several chlorinated hydrocarbon pesticides were prohibited for agricultural use, their use for suicide dropped – from 111 suicides in 1983 to 5 suicides in 1984. Accidental deaths from the pesticides did not

decline as much.

Jick et al. (1995) tracked patients in England given antidepressants by their GPs. The suicide rate was higher in those who were given more than one type of antidepressant, a higher dose, fluoxetine, and a prescription in the previous 30 days (as well as men and those who were suicidal).

Gunnell et al. (1997) found that British sales of paracetamol and the Oxford rate of attempting suicide with paracetamol were associated for 1976–1993. The same was found also for France as a whole. The attempted and completed suicide rates by paracetamol were positively associated in both Britain and France over time. In France, paracetamol is sold in smaller amounts, and the attempted suicide rate using paracetamol is lower in France than in Britain.

Melander et al. (1991) compared two towns in Sweden, one of which instituted prescription surveillance and an information campaign about medication use. In this town, the use of barbiturates and anxiolytic-hypnotic drugs for suicide decreased, as did the overall suicide rate and the prescription rate for anxiolytic-hypnotic drugs. In the other town, although the use of barbiturates for suicide decreased, the use of anxiolytic-hypnotic drugs did not, the overall suicide rate did not change, while the prescription rate for anxiolytic-hypnotic drugs increased. Thus, the surveillance and campaign worked to reduce the use of these medications for suicide and to reduce the suicide rate.

Isacsson et al. (1995) found that suicide rates were higher for antipsychotics and anxiolytics and lower for analgesics in a region of Sweden. Analysis of their data indicates that the number of suicides by each medication and the number of prescriptions were strongly associated (Spearman rho = 0.93).

Also in Sweden, Carlsten et al. (1996) found that the suicide rate using barbiturates followed the sales of barbiturates from 1969–1992, and the same parallel was found for analgesics and neuroleptics/antidepressants. Sundquist et al. (1996) found that, in southern Sweden, the greater the sales of tranquilizers and hypnotics/sedatives in the municipalities (but not antidepressants or neuroleptics), the higher the suicide rate.

Parron et al. (1996) found that workers in Spain who used pesticides more (such as farmers) used them more often for suicide.

Drowning

Lester (1993f) failed to find an association between suicide rates by drowning and the length of the nations coastline. Lester (1990d) found that the accidental death rate in the United States from drowning from 1950 to 1984 was positively associated with the suicide rate from drowning. Ross and Lester (1991) found the modal suicide using Niagara Falls (in New York State in the United States) lived within ten miles of the Falls, and so convenience appeared to be a factor in the choice of the Falls for suicide.

Jumping

Ellis (1996) reported that England and Australia both had "popular" bridge venues for committing suicide. Lester (1993d) found that fencing-in a bridge that was a popular suicide venue in Washington, D.C., not only reduced the number of suicides from that bridge, but appeared to lower the total number of bridge suicides in the city as a whole. O'Carroll and Silverman (1994) confirmed that suicides from the Ellington Bridge dropped to almost zero, while the number from the Taft Bridge did not increase.

In Singapore, Lester (1994a) found that the suicide rate by leaping from high-rise apartment buildings was positively associ-

ated with their availability, and while the suicide rate by all other methods declined, the total suicide rate rose during the period studied. Chia (1981) found that suicides living in high-rise buildings in Singapore used jumping as their preferred method; suicides living elsewhere used hanging as their preferred method. Furthermore, people living in high-rise buildings had a higher suicide rate than those living elsewhere. Incidentally, suicide rates from high-rise buildings were higher for people living in three-room flats than for those living in one-room flats.

Education

McManus et al. (1997) found that 94 percent of households who brought an attempted suicide to the emergency department had one or more means for committing suicide at home. Those who received education in the emergency-department about restricting access to lethal methods were more likely to do so when they got home than those not educated (86 percent versus 36 percent). In addition, if the attempt was serious, more families restricted access when they returned home.

Characteristics of Those Using Different Methods

Aircraft

Ungs (1994) documented ten suicides by aircraft in the United States over a 12-year period, with 20 more possibilities. The modal suicide was male, white, and married, with a median age of 36.

Burning

Swenson and Dimsdale (1990) found that eight attempted suicides by burning were substance abusers, had organic disorders brought on by this abuse, and were impulsive. In Norway, Rogde and Olving (1996) found that the majority of completed suicides using fire were male.

In England, Sheth et al. (1994) found that attempted suicide by burning was more common in women and in Asians (from the Indian subcontinent). Among the Asians, the women were immigrants, married, housewives, with children, mostly using kerosene. Prosser (1996), also in England, found that the typical suicide by burning was male, aged 43, white/British born, similar to all suicides.

Suk et al. (1991) found that among those attempting suicide in Korea by burning 79 percent died. Their suicidal acts were more often in public or with family present, from noon to 6 p.m. They experienced more political conflict and less family conflict compared to other suicidal persons matched for sex and age.

In India, Rao et al. (1989) found that women using burning as a suicidal action died more often than accidental burning cases. Suicides burned themselves more often on the face and scalp and on the back (rather than the front), compared to accidental cases. Suicides occurred more often in locked rooms and at odd hours of the day. The suicides were more often psychiatrically disturbed, had attempted suicide more in the past, and more often had a family history of burning. Both accidental and suicidal cases occurred most often in the kitchen, but the suicides less often burned themselves in the presence of others and more often locked the door.

Garcia-Sanchez et al. (1994) found that the modal attempted suicide using burning had a prior psychiatric illness, was male, and committed the act at home from noon to 6 p.m. Twenty percent had previously attempted suicide and 30 percent died.

In Verona (Italy), Castellani et al. (1995) found that 39 percent of those with self-inflicted burns died. The average body area burned was 41 percent. The mean age was 38 (with the men younger than the women), and the modal case had a psychiatric disorder and took place at home.

Tuohig et al. (1995) compared patients attempting suicide by burning with those self-mutilating with burning. The attempters burned more of their body; used flammable liquids rather than scalding, chemicals, or contact; had depressions rather than personality or eating disorders; had fewer prior burnings; and more often died. The attempters were more often married, more impulsive, and had less often been sexually abused. The groups did not differ in past psychiatric history, alcohol/drug abuse, or unemployment.

Al-Shlash et al. (1996) found that suicidal burn patients were more likely to die in Saudi Arabia than accidental burn patients, indicating that the suicidal patients had more serious burns.

In Bulgaria, Hadjiiski and Todorov (1996) found that the modal suicide (attempted and completed) using burning was male, 20–40 years old, using a flame (rather than electricity) and that 35 percent died.

Cameron et al. (1997) found that attempted suicides by burning were on average male, 31 years old, with burns over 30 percent of their skin. Fifty-two percent used a flammable liquid, 82 percent needed surgery, and 18 percent died. Compared to accidental burn victims, the suicides were more often male, older, burned a greater area, more often used a flammable liquid; and died; they were more often schizophrenic, depressed, and with a personality disorder.

In Denmark, Leth and Hart-Madsen (1997) found that the modal suicide by self-incineration did so at home, left no suicide note, used gasoline, had a psychiatric disorder, had attempted suicide previously, and was disabled. The sex distribution was even.

In Brazil, Marchesan et al. (1997) found that the modal person using burning for suicide was female, in her 20s, using methyl alcohol, burning more than 60 percent of the body, in the presence of others. Fifty-five percent died.

Car Accidents

In their multi-nation European study of attempted suicide, Schmidtke et al. (1994) identified 29 suicide attempts using car accidents. The modal attempter by car accident was male, in Germany/Switzerland, under the age of 55, on Tuesdays and Saturdays, in May or July, and from 6 p.m. to midnight. Compared to other attempters, there were fewer Catholics and more unemployed people.

Ohberg et al. (1997) compared possible suicides by car with unintentional deaths in cars. The suicides were more often in a passenger car, in a head-on collision, suffering life stress, with a mental disorder and prior suicide attempts with fewer passengers, and fewer other drivers killed. They did not differ in alcohol abuse or physical problems. The suicides classified as such officially were younger and more often alcohol abusers.

Car Exhaust

Busuttil et al. (1994) found that suicide by car exhaust had risen in popularity in Scotland since 1990. The modal suicide using this method was male, 35–44, rural, on Monday/Tuesday and in spring/summer. In Sweden, Ostrom et al. (1996) found that car-exhaust suicides were male and completed suicide outdoors. The suicide rate by this method was higher in rural areas.

In England, McClure (1994) found that an increase in male youth suicide rates from 1960–1990 was due to increased suicide rates only by hanging and car exhaust.

In Vienna, Risser and Schnieder (1995) found that the modal carbon-monoxide suicide was male and used car exhaust. Compared to the accidental deaths from gas, the suicides had higher levels of carboxy hemoglobin in their blood, were younger, showed no monthly variation, and were more often male.

Drowning

Avis (1993) found that 86 percent of those completing suicide by drowning in Newfoundland (Canada) did so in the ocean. They were primarily male (64 percent) and did not differ in age from other suicides.

Firearms

In the United States in 1989–1991, Kaplan et al. (1996) found that the suicide rate by guns for white males over the age of 65 was higher in nonmetropolitan areas, in the divorced/widowed, and in those with less than high school education. For white females over the age of 65, Kaplan et al. (1997) found that completing suicide by gun was less common in those over the age of 85, the nonmarried, the more educated, and in metropolitan areas and the Northeast (and more common in the South). Lester (1996c) noted that the accidental death from firearms in the United States has declined from 1960–1990, while the suicide and homicide rates by firearms have increased.

Miner et al. (1990) found that death in children from gunshot wounds to the brain was associated with suicidal intent, the trajectory of the bullet, and the severity of the coma, but not with age, sex, or the caliber of the bullet.

In the army from 1978-1988, Reed et al. (1990) noted that those using firearms for suicides most commonly used revolvers (38 percent) and pistols (30 percent), followed by rifles (19 percent) and shotguns (12 percent). In Dallas in 1985–1988, Stone (1990) found that 54 percent of the firearm completed suicides used revolvers, 20 percent pistols, 15 percent shotguns, and 11 percent rifles. Also in Dallas, Stone (1992) found that men using handguns for suicide shot themselves in the head more than women did (79 percent versus 62 percent), and the same was true for long guns (61 percent versus 52 percent). Women preferred to use handguns over long guns more than men did (89 percent versus 71 percent).

Riddick et al. (1993) compared suicide and homicide victims by firearm in Mobile, Alabama. The suicides were middle-aged/elderly white males, the homicide victims were young black males. Handguns were used by about two-thirds of both suicides and murderers.

Harruff et al. (1994) noted that the modal person who shot himself during confrontations with police was male, 20–39, white, in a marital/relationship disturbance, using a handgun to shoot himself in the head.

Kaplan et al. (1994) documented the rising use of firearms for suicide among males in the United States from 1979–1988, especially among the elderly. The use of guns was higher in blacks than whites and in the elderly. In Alabama in the 1980s, Liu and Waterbor (1994–1995) found that the use of firearms for suicide was greater in whites, males, older suicides, and in those in rural areas, but declined over the decade.

In the United States in 1988–1990, Sacks et al. (1994) estimated that 66 percent of suicides occurred in the home, and 43 percent of the homes had guns. They calculated that 32 percent of the suicides were attributable to guns being available in the home.

In Massachusetts, Barber et al. (1996) found that completed/attempted suicides using firearms had a high mortality rate – 84 percent died. The attempters, compared to completers, were more often black or Hispanic, urban dwellers, young, and shooting themselves in nonvital regions of the body.

Marzuk et al. (1992b) found that those dying from Russian roulette were more often cocaine abusers than regular handgun suicides. The Russian roulette victims were typically male, young, unemployed, and black/hispanic.

Zwerling et al. (1993) studied firearm suicides in Iowa. Thirty seven percent used handguns, 41 percent shotguns, and 22 percent rifles, as compared to household ownership rates of 32 percent, 66 percent, and 71 percent respectively. Thus, handguns were overrepresented among the suicides. Females preferred handguns, while males preferred shotguns. Zwerling et al. found that the use of handguns for suicide increased from the 1980s to the 1990s to the point that handguns and shotguns were used equally often (with rifles a ranked third).

In Brisbane (Australia), Cantor et al. (1991) found that the most common weapon in firearm suicides was rifles, followed by shotguns and handguns. Firearm suicides were more often male than firearm murders (93 percent versus 80 percent). Ten of the 108 firearm homicides were followed by suicide. Selway (1991) in Victoria (Australia) found that firearm suicides were typically males (97 percent), median age 40, at home (73 percent) and without witnesses (90 percent). They most often shot themselves in the bedroom (32 percent) and in the head (28 percent), with rifles the most common firearm (followed by shotguns and then handguns). About one-third were intoxicated with alcohol.

De Moore et al. (1994) studied Australian attempted suicides by firearm. The modal attempter was male, born in Australia, single, living in an urban area, living with his family, aged 15–19, and with an adjustment disorder and interpersonal conflicts.

Chapman and Milroy (1992) compared suicides and homicides by gun in England. The suicides were more often male, older, and intoxicated with alcohol. The suicides were more often shot in the head and less often in chest or multiple sites, but did not differ in type of gun used. For the suicides, if a shotgun was used, the gun was put in the mouth; if a handgun was used, the shot was more often on the right side of the head.

In England, Nowers (1994) found that firearm suicides occurred more often at home, in anger after a recent relationship dispute, and with fewer prior attempts than did suicides using other methods. The groups did not differ in alcohol use, presence of a suicide note, depression, physical illness, or psychiatric contacts.

In London, Rouse and Dunn (1992) found that 34 percent of firearm fatalities were suicides, 57 percent homicides, and 2 percent accidental. The male suicides were older than the homicide victims, but the female suicides were younger than the homicide victims.

In Stockholm (Sweden), Karlsson et al. (1993) found that firearms for suicide were used primarily by men (99 percent), with shotguns the most common weapon, followed by rifles, service arms, pistols, and revolvers. Shooting in the head (particularly the mouth) was most common. Firearm suicides peaked in August. Firearm suicides more often had ingested alcohol than homicide victims.

In Newfoundland, Avis (1994) found that firearms were the most common method for suicide. Shotguns were the most popular firearm, followed by rifles, with handguns the least common.

In Cape Town (South Africa), MacDonald and Lerer (1994) found no change in the percentage of suicides using guns from 1986–1991.

Armour (1996) compared firearm suicides in Northern Ireland by security forces and civilians. The security forces suicides more often had marital problems (and less often mental ill health), were younger, more often used revolvers and pistols (and less often shotguns), were witnessed, and more often shot themselves in the right temple (and less often in the chest). They did not differ in blood alcohol levels.

In eastern Finland, Hintikka et al. (1997) studied suicides in males aged 15–24 of whom 62 percent used guns (primarily licensed hunting guns). The percentage of suicides using guns was higher in the rural regions. The firearm suicides were more often intoxicated, happened more often after a quarrel, with others close by, witnessed, and at the residence.

Gas

Theilade (1990) found that suicides using domestic gas in Denmark were more often intoxicated with alcohol than those dying accidentally from domestic gas. The proportion of men in the suicides was greater than in the accidental deaths (70 percent versus 51 percent). For those using gas for suicide, those using car exhaust were more often male as compared to those using domestic gas (93 percent versus 70 percent). Suicides using domestic gas were typically middle-age/elderly men and women, single/widowed, and depressed. Suicides using car exhaust were typically younger (especially if the car was situated in the open air), more often married, and more educated than those using domestic gas.

Hanging

In Saudi Arabia, Elfawal and Awad (1994) found that the modal suicide by hanging was male, aged 30–39, an expatriate, Indian, and of lower social class (laborers and domestics). In western Australia, Cooke et al. (1995) found that modal hanging suicide was male, aged 20–24, committing suicide in or around the home.

Injections

Peschel et al. (1995) found that the modal suicide in Munich (Germany) using injection of toxic agents was a physician (or nurse), most commonly injecting an anesthetic or related drug (such as benzodiazepines or barbiturates).

Jumping

Hanzlick et al. (1990) identified 19 suicides in Atlanta in 1967–1986 who jumped from hotels more than 10 stories high. The average jumper was male, 34 years old, alone when jumping, and a local resident. Hotels with high inner atriums had more jumpers. Local residents were less likely to leave a suicide note than out-of-towners.

Isbister and Roberts (1992) studied jumpers in Glasgow (Scotland). Of 58 jumpers, 21 were killed at once and 11 more later. The jumpers were mostly men, single, unemployed and jumping between 7 p.m. and 2 a.m.

Vieta et al. (1992) found that men and women attempting suicide by jumping jumped from similar heights. The injuries were worse in the elderly, widowed, and those with affective disorders (but did not differ by sex). The males more often had a personality disorder or substance abuse, the females an affective disorder. (Those with nonaffective and nonpsychotic diagnoses had experienced more recent stress.)

Fischer et al. (1993) found that those completing suicide by jumping in New York City were more often male, widowed, living alone, elderly, Hispanic, and living in Manhattan. Compared to those using other methods, the jumpers lived higher up, had less access to medication, abused drugs/alcohol less often, and were more often in a nonpenal institution.

Li and Smialek (1994) compared suicides by jumping with accidental deaths from jumping. The suicides used bridges more and ladders less. The suicides were more often female and black.

White et al. (1995) found that patients who jumped from a general hospital were (1) attempted suicides, (2) acutely delirious, or (3) chronically medically ill (with pain, dyspnea, transient confusion, poor prognosis, and recent adverse news). Two-thirds of the jumpers died. Those who jumped were more often males and older, with fewer medical diagnoses and psychiatric disorders than nonfatal jumpers seen in the emergency room.

Richter et al. (1996) compared suicidal and accidental jumpers (almost of all of whom survived). The attempted suicides were more often female, had psychiatric illness more often, used windows more (and ladders/roofs less), and stayed longer in intensive care and in the hospital. They did not differ in the site of the injury, height from which they jumped, age, or alcohol/drug abuse. The attempters showed no seasonal variation, whereas the accidents peaked in Spring and Summer. In Vienna, however, Risser et al. (1996) found that suicides fell from greater heights than accidents.

Jumping From Bridges

Cantor and Hill (1990) examined the characteristics of suicides from two bridges in Brisbane, Australia. Those jumping from the new Gateway Bridge were more often employed, living outside the city core, and married; they less often had a history of psychiatric care than those jumping from the old Story Bridge. Thus, the two populations were quite different. If suicide from one bridge was made impossible, switching probably would not occur.

Lafave et al. (1995) reported that the modal jumper from the Golden Gate Bridge in 1937–1991 (an average of 19.5 per year) was male, white, and 30–39 years old.

Nowers and Gunnell (1996) found that 72 percent of the suicides jumping from the Clifton Suspension Bridge lived in the county. Compared to other suicides, the bridge jumpers did not differ in the distance of their home from the bridge, psychiatric history, diagnosis, age, or sex.

Prevost et al. (1996) found that the typical jumper from the Jacques Cartier Bridge in Montreal (Canada) was male, aged 30, not intoxicated with alcohol, and with a history of psychiatric treatment and attempted suicide.

Medications

Studies continue to look at the mortality rates (suicidal plus accidental) for various antidepressants (e.g., Henry and Antao, 1992; Malmvik et al., 1994). Masica et al. (1992) noted that age-adjusted suicide rates declined after the introduction of Prozac in 1988. Freemantle et al. (1994) found that death rates in the United Kingdom from the older tricyclics were higher than for the newer tricyclics, which were higher than for the serotonin reuptake inhibitors.

Youssef (1990) found that completed and attempted suicides in rural Ireland used different drugs for suicide. The completers used benzodiazepines and neuroleptics more (but not antidepressants). The completers used higher doses and more often used two or more drugs. The groups did not differ in age, sex, marital status, or diagnosis.

In Zagreb, Milcevic and Prpic (1991) found that men used antipsychotic medications more for attempting suicide, while women used anxiolytics (such as diazepam) more. The men were also more often repeaters.

Cugino et al. (1992) found that those attempting suicide with overdoses switched methods on later attempts as often as those using other methods for attempting suicide (about 20 percent switched). Those using overdoses tended less often to use alcohol during the attempt. The method used (and the time between the first and second attempts) was not associated with age, sex, race, education, reason, or season.

Kelleher et al. (1992) found that the increase in the suicide rate in Ireland from 1971–1988 did not appear to be due to the increase in the use of antidepressants for suicide.

O'Donovan et al. (1993) found that self-poisoners using household products (versus medications) were older, had longer hospital stays, and higher mortality.

Valle et al. (1993) found that suicide attempters seen at an emergency room were, more often than other intoxicated patients, females, teenagers, using medications, and died. Attempts also were more common in the winter and spring.

Obafunwa et al. (1994) found that dextropropoxyphene was used in some suicides, and the modal user was male, employed, aged 25–44, urban, depressed, and obtaining the drug via a prescription for self.

Buckley et al. (1996) found that men aged 25–44 used medications for completed and attempted suicide more than expected given the prescription rate.

Ohberg et al. (1996) found that the majority of Finnish completed suicides using poisons used more than one drug.

Myers et al. (1992) surveyed adolescents and found that 23 percent overestimated the amount of acetaminophen needed for death, 41 percent underestimated the amount, and 19 percent were correct. Seventeen percent believed that it was impossible to die with acetaminophen.

Hawton et al. (1995) asked why suicide attempters in England chose paracetamol (acetaminophen in the United States). Sixty-two percent mentioned its availability, yet 42 percent knew of the possible liver damage. Friedman (1996) found that 41 percent of those using paracetamol for attempting suicide knew about the liver damage. Of those taking large overdoses, almost all used bottles and only 7 percent used blister packs, suggesting that marketing the pills in blister packs might reduce the use of paracetamol for large overdoses. Hawton et al. (1996) found that 41 percent of those attempting suicide with paracetamol were impulsive (with less than one hour of premeditation). Those who knew about possible liver damage did not differ in suicidal intent or depression from those who did not.

In England, Neeleman and Wessely (1997) found that attempted suicides used paracetamol more than did completed suicides. The completed suicides more often used paracetamol plus opiates and tricyclics and used a higher mean number of drugs. In America, Schiodt et al. (1997) found that suicide attempters versus accidental overdoses using acetaminophen (paracetamol in England) used twice as much on the average, were less often alcohol abusers, and less often died.

Plastic Bags

Perez-Martinez et al. (1993) found that men and women used plastic bag asphyxiation equally often for suicide. Haddix et al. (1996) found that the modal plastic bag user in Washington state was equally often male or female and had a mean age of 72.

Poisons

Stavemann and Thieme (1993) found that suicide rates rose in Western Samoa during 1976–1983, only for those using paraquat. Bowles (1995) found that sales of paraquat in Western Samoa and its use for completed and attempted suicide were strongly associated in the period 1973–1988. An education program on radio in May 1982 had an impact only for a few months, about the same as the impact from the South Pacific games in August 1983.

In Denmark, Christesen (1994) found that attempting suicide by caustic ingestion was more common in women, in those with a psychiatric history, and took place in the home.

The use of pesticides has been documented in England and Wales by Thompson et al. (1995), with 29 such completed suicides in 1990–1991, mainly men using paraquat.

Klein-Schwartz and Smith (1997) found that 64 percent of fatalities from agricultural/horticultural chemicals in the United States for 1985–1990 were suicides (with a peak in ages 25–44), and 17 percent of nonfatal hospitalizations were attempted suicides.

Stabbing

Start et al. (1992) found that the modal completed suicide by stabbing in Yorkshire (England) was male, made one wound with a kitchen knife on the left side of the chest, in the bedroom from midnight to 6 a.m. There were often tentative marks and an incision rather stabbing (the opposite to homicide).

In Tokyo (Japan), Kuroda et al. (1997) found that suicide by self-stabbing was preferred by men (while women preferred drowning more). The modal self-stabber was aged 40–49 for men and 50–59 for women, stabbed in the neck and chest for men and neck, groin and arms for women, using a kitchen knife, at home, in the living room. The women self-stabbers more often had a psychiatric history.

Switching Methods

Nordentoft et al. (1993) followed up attempters using poisons who subsequently completed suicide. Sixty percent used poisons for their completed suicide, while 40 percent switched methods. Psychotics were more likely to switch.

Trains and Railways

Emmerson and Cantor (1993) found that train suicides in Queensland (Australia) were roughly split between men and women, therefore indicating a higher percentage of women, than for other methods of suicide. More than half of the suicides had been inpatients and more than half were schizophrenic. Schmidtke (1994) reported that the modal railway suicide in West Germany was male, 20–29 years old, in the evening, on Mondays and Tuesdays, and with a peak in the fall.

Cina et al. (1994) found that most train-pedestrian fatalities were accidental and only 4 percent suicides.

Clarke (1994) claimed that, as the length of the railways increased in England from 1860–1910 and the number of passengers increased, the number of railway suicides increased. However, he examined only absolute numbers, not rates.

In England, O'Donnell et al. (1994) followed up attempted suicides by railway for ten years and found that 7 percent had completed suicide.

Underground Trains

O'Donnell et al. (1996) looked at a sample of underground-train jumpers who survived. They had high suicidal intent and were impulsive. The majority were in psychiatric treatment (schizophrenia was the most common diagnosis) and had made prior suicide attempts. Almost half knew someone who used this method.

On the London Underground from 1940–1990, O'Donnell and Farmer (1994; Farmer et al., 1991) identified 3240 suicidal incidents, with a fatality rate of 54 percent. There were fewer on Sundays, more in the spring, and more from 9 a.m. to 5 p.m. The modal suicide was male, aged 25–34. The rate was higher in stations near psychiatric hospitals, and a high proportion of the victims were psychiatric patients. Stations with pits had lower fatality rates. Fatalities were more common in jumps from the first third of the platforms and for the elderly. The percentage of acts that were fatal declined from 1950 (70 percent fatal) to 1990 (55 percent fatal).

Gaylord and Lester (1994) found the modal completed/attempted suicide in Hong Kong was male, committing suicide between 11 a.m. and 3 p.m., with an age in the 30s. The rate peaked in 1986.

In Vienna, Sonneck et al. (1994) found that the number of subway suicides increased from 1984–1987, whereupon the media stopped publicizing them, and the number dropped. The modal suicide was male and 20–24 years old for men and 25–29 years old for women.

Reviewing data from 23 metro systems, O'Donnell and Farmer (1992) found that suicides were primarily males, under the age of 40, with no seasonal variation, occurring most often between 10 a.m. and noon. Lester (1995f) found that subway suicide rates in 17 cities were not associated with the nations overall suicide rates.

Unusual Methods

Durand et al. (1991) reported a suicide attempt by someone injecting herself with HIV–positive blood – she did subsequently test positive for HIV.

Changes Over Time

Lester (1990g) looked at the changes in methods for suicide in 16 developed nations from 1960 to 1980. Overall, the number of suicides rose. The use of car exhaust, hanging, firearms, and "other" methods increased; the use of domestic gas declined; and the use of drowning, cutting, and solids/liquids stayed the same.

In New South Wales (Australia), Dudley et al. (1992) found that the methods used by teenage suicides changed from 1964 to 1988. Firearms and hanging became more common, while poisoning became less common.

In Finland, Ohberg et al. (1995) noted that, as the suicide rate rose from 1947 to 1990, men and women used poisoning and hanging less, while men used car exhaust more. The use of car exhaust paralleled the increased number of cars. Parathion increased in use up until 1958, after which restrictions were introduced; the total suicide rate remained stable, suggesting switching. The use of antidepressants and neuroleptics paralleled their increasing prescription, but the former was true only for the tricyclics and not for the other antidepressants.

In Italy for 1964–1982, De Leo et al. (1995) found that the methods used for suicide by the elderly changed. For men, firearms, jumping, hanging, and the use of car exhaust increased, while the use of drowning, cutting, and domestic gas decreased. For women, the use of domestic gas decreased, while the use of all other methods increased.

McLoone (1996) found that youth suicide rose more in the deprived regions of Scotland during 1981–1992 than in the affluent regions. In the deprived regions, suicide by poisoning and hanging increased more, whereas in the affluent regions suicides by car exhaust increased more. McLoone and Crombie (1996) found that male and female rates of attempting suicide grew closer during this period, and while the use of hypnotics/sedatives for attempting decreased, the use of analgesics (especially paracetamol) increased.

Opportunity-Based Suicide Rates

Over the nine major regions of the United States, Lester (1990i) found that the social correlates of the firearm suicide rate per capita and the firearm suicide rate per household were identical, but differed greatly from the firearm suicide rate per firearm-owning household. Thus, opportunity-based suicide rates may be differently determined than population-based suicide rates.

Correlates of Choice of Method

Heim and Lester (1991) found that the method for suicide in suicides in West Berlin was associated with gender – men used firearms more, while women used solids/liquids more. Medications were used more by older men, while younger men used hanging more. Hanging was also used more by married men. Women used medications more on weekends, jumping at the beginning of the week, and hanging in midweek. Those using medications more often had addiction problems, were psychiatric outpatients and heart patients, and were less often depressed patients. Jumping was used more by psychiatric inpatients and psychotics.

Obafunwa and Busuttil (1994) found that hanging was more popular among completed suicides in Scotland in the young and the elderly, car exhaust in those aged 25–44 and jumping in urban regions. In England and Wales, Kelly et al. (1995) found that occupation was associated with choice of method – pharmacists using poisons more, and farmers and veterinarians used firearms more. In Wolverhampton (England), Scott (1994) found that Asians (from the Indian subcontinent) used hanging more for suicide, the elderly used drowning more, and those with prior psychiatric disorders used drugs and drowning more.

Snyder (1994) documented by sex and year changes in the methods used for suicide in Japan and Ireland. The changes were more similar for men and women in Japan than in Ireland.

In Belgrade, Slavic et al. (1992) found that males used guns and cutting more, while females used poisoning more for completed suicide. Older suicides used hanging more. Urban suicides used jumping more, while rural suicides used hanging more. Suicides whose occupation involved wearing guns (soldiers and police) also used guns more for suicide. Alcoholics used hanging, psychotics used jumping, while those with no psychiatric disorder used guns more.

In New South Wales (Australia), Burnley (1995) found that the methods used for suicide varied by sex, age, occupation, and urban/rural location. For example, firearms were used more by youths, men, farmers, and transport workers and in inland rural areas.

In Finland, Henriksson et al. (1995) found that elderly completed suicides used hanging more and drugs and carbon monoxide less than younger suicides; they also more often had a major depressive disorder and less

often an Axis II or substance abuse disorder. Ohberg et al. (1996) found that alcohol intoxication was most common in male completed suicides in Finland who used poisons, firearms, and jumping under a vehicle and least common in those using cutting or jumping from a height. Alcohol intoxication was more common in female suicides using poisons.

Lester (1997) concluded that choice of method of suicide was more strongly related to situational variables than to psychological variables.

Attempted Suicides

Gupta and Trzepacz (1997) compared serious attempters using overdoses versus other methods. The overdosers more often were female and separated and had a borderline personality disorder. (They did not differ in seasonality.)

Among Israeli adolescent attempted suicide, Iancu et al. (1997) found that those under the age of 13 used violent methods more often.

In Greece, Kontaxakis and Christodoulou (1997) found that attempted suicides using overdoses were more often female, single, employed, and younger, and less often with an affective disorder, schizophrenia, or severe psychiatric disturbance. Those using hanging were older, more often married, unemployed, living with their own family, and suffering from an affective disorder. The jumpers were more often male, and the drowners were more often schizophrenics. The groups did not differ in prior attempts or psychiatric hospitalizations.

Among children who attempted suicide, Li et al. (1997) found that those using firearms were more often boys and were more seriously injured. Those using hanging were more often boys and younger; those using jumping more often were girls, carried out the act away from home, and suffered less injury. The groups did not differ in psychiatric disorder, time of day, or day of the week.

Rating Methods

Rhyne et al. (1995) had lay people and forensic pathologists rate methods of suicide on dimensions. Three clusters emerged: (1) lethal/quick (e.g., hanging), (2) moderate lethality/pain/long (e.g., overdose), and (3) least lethal/pain/moderate time (e.g., car crash). In a sample of suicides, males preferred cluster-one methods while females preferred cluster-two methods.

Classifying Methods

Modern Methods

Lester (1996b) found that both over nations of the world and over time in the United States, men used both technical methods and nontechnical methods for suicide more than did women.

Violent Versus Nonviolent Methods

Van Heeringen et al. (1991) compared attempted suicides using violent and nonviolent methods. Those using violent methods were more often male, older, and had a major depressive disorder (rather than a personality disorder). They did not differ in prior attempts, past or present psychiatric treatment, or substance abuse.

Nordentoft et al. (1993) found that psychotics were more likely to use violent methods for completed suicide.

Cooper and Milroy (1994) studied completed suicides using violent methods. Males used all methods more than females, except jumping from heights. Jumping was more common in those under the age of 40,

and hanging was more common in women if they were aged 40–59. Choice of method was also affected by precipitating stress (for example, hanging was more common after a relationship ended), origin (non-Europeans used hanging more), and alcohol intoxication (intoxicated attempters used drowning less).

Frankenfield et al. (1994) screened unnatural deaths in Maryland and found that suicides who had been taking fluoxetine used more-violent methods than those using tricyclic antidepressants. They suggest that perhaps fluoxetine is less toxic, forcing suicides to switch to other methods; perhaps it is prescribed to different types of patients; or perhaps it induces violence.

Threshold

Wiedenmann and Weyerer (1993) classified methods for suicide according to whether they bypassed phylogenetically existing suppressor mechanisms – painless, innovative, and modern, with no connection to evolutionary historically lethal situations – such as shooting and gas, as opposed to hanging, drowning, and jumping. They claimed that in Germany, the suicide rate peaked in years when the percentage of these "low-threshold" methods was higher.

Lester (1995e) found that the correlation between the suicide rate over time with low-threshold methods was positive in England and in the United States, but not significant in Japan; with high-threshold methods negative in the United States, positive in Japan, and not significant in England.

Discussion

Research on the methods used for suicide has increased in volume during the 1990s. The results suggest that it may be heuristic to consider suicide by different methods as distinctly different acts, perhaps with different motivations and determinants (Lester, 1996c). Lester (1995b) has shown, for example, that the social correlates of suicide rates by different methods over the American states are quite different from one another.

The results also suggest that suicide may be prevented in some cases by restricting access to lethal means for suicide. Research is still required to explore which people would switch methods if some were made less available and why people choose one method over another for suicide.

REFERENCES

Al-Shlash, S., Warnasuriya, N. D., Al Shareef, Z., Filobbos, P., Sarkans, & Al Dusari, S. Eight years experience of a regional burns unit in Saudi Arabia. *Burns*, 1996, 22, 376–380.

Armour, A. A study of gunshot suicides in Northern Ireland from 1989 to 1993. *Science & Justice*, 1996, 36(1), 21–25.

Avis, S. P. Suicidal drowning. *Journal of Forensic Sciences*, 1993, 38, 1422–1426.

Avis, S. P. Suicidal gunshot wounds. *Forensic Science International*, 1994, 67, 41–47.

Bailey, J. E., Kellerman, A. L., Somes, G. W., Banton, J. G., Rivara, F. P., & Rushforth, N. P. Risk factors for violent death of women in the home. *Archives of Internal Medicine*, 1997, 157, 777–782.

Barber, C. W., Ozonoff, V. V., Schuster, M., Hume, B., McLaughlin, H., & Jannelli, L. When bullets don't kill. *Public Health Reports*, 1996, 111, 482–493.

Beautrais, A. L., Joyce, P. R., & Mulder, R. T. Access to firearms and the risk of suicide. *Australian & New Zealand Journal of Psychiatry*, 1996, 30, 741–748.

Bodeker, W. Suicidal pesticide poisoning. *World Health Forum*, 1991, 12(2), 208–209.

Boor, M. Methods of suicide and implications for suicide prevention. *Journal of Clinical Psychology*, 1981, 37, 70–75.

Boor, M., & Bair, J. H. Suicide rates, hand gun control laws and sociodemographic variables. *Psychological Reports*, 1990, 66, 923–930.

Bowles, J. R. Suicide in Western Samoa. In R. F. W. Diekstra, W. Gulbinat, I. Kienhorst & D. De Leo (Eds.), *Preventive strategies on suicide*. Leiden: E. J. Brill, 1995, 173–206.

Brent, D. A., Perper, J. A., Allman, C. J., Moritz, G. M., Wartella, M. E., & Zelenak, J. P. The presence and accessibility of firearms in the homes of adolescent suicides. *Journal of the American Medical Association*, 1991, 266, 2989–2995.

Brent, D. A., Perper, J. A., Moritz, G. M., Baugher, M., & Allman, C. Suicide in adolescents with no apparent psychopathology. *Journal of the American Academy of Child & Adolescent Psychiatry*, 1993b, 32, 494–500.

Brent, D. A., Perper, J. A., Moritz, G. M., Baugher, M., Schweers, J., & Roth, C. Firearms and adolescent suicide. *American Journal of Diseases of Children*, 1993a, 147, 1066–1071.

Buckley, N. A., Dawson, A. H., Whyte, I. M., Hazell, P., Meza, A., & Britt, H. An analysis of age and gender influences on the relative risk for suicide and psychotropic drug self-poisoning. *Acta Psychiatrica Scandinavica*, 1996, 93, 168–171.

Burnley, I. H. Socioeconomic and spatial differentials in mortality and means of committing suicide in New South Wales, Australia, 1985–1991. *Social Science & Medicine*, 1995, 41, 687–698.

Burvill, P. W. The changing pattern of suicide by gassing in Australia, 1910–1987. *Acta Psychiatrica Scandinavica*, 1990, 81, 178–184.

Busuttil, A. A., Obafuna, J. O., & Ahmed, A. Suicide inhalation of vehicular exhaust in the Lothian and Borders region of Scotland. *Human Experimental Toxicology*, 1994, 13, 545–550.

Cameron, D. R., Pegg, S. P., & Muller, M. Self-inflicted burns. *Burns*, 1997, 23, 519–521.

Cantor, C. H., Brodie, J., & McMillen, J. Firearm victims. *Medical Journal of Australia*, 1991, 155, 442–446.

Cantor, C. H., & Hill, M. A. Suicide from river bridges. *Australian & New Zealand Journal of Psychiatry*, 1990, 24, 377–380.

Cantor, C. H., & Lewin, T. Firearms and suicide in Australia. *Australian & New Zealand Journal of Psychiatry*, 1990, 24, 500–509.

Cantor, C. H., & Slater, P. J. The impact of firearm control legislation on suicide in Queensland. *Medical Journal of Australia*, 1995, 162, 583–585.

Carlsten, A., Allebeck, P., & Brandt, L. Are suicide rates in Sweden associated with changes in the prescribing of medications? *Acta Psychiatrica Scandinavica*, 1996, 94, 94–100.

Carrington, P. J., & Moyer, S. Gun availability and suicide in Canada. *Studies on Crime and Crime Prevention*, 1994a, 3, 168–178.

Carrington, P. J., & Moyer, S. Gun control and suicide in Ontario. *American Journal of Psychiatry*, 1994b, 151, 606–608.

Castellani, G., Beghini, D., Barisoni, B., & Marigo, M. Suicide attempt by burning. *Burns*, 1995, 21, 607–609.

Chapman, J., & Milroy, C. M. Firearm deaths in Yorkshire and Humberside. *Forensic Science International*, 1992, 57, 181–191.

Chia, B. H. *Suicidal behavior in Singapore*. Tokyo: Southeast Asian Medical Information Center, 1981.

Christesen, H. B. T. Caustic ingestion in adults. *Journal of Toxicology: Clinical Toxicology*, 1994, 32, 557–568.

Cina, S. J., Koeplin, J. L., Nichols, C. A., & Conradi, S. E. A decade of train-pedestrian fatalities. *Journal of Forensic Science*, 1994, 39, 668–673.

Clarke, M. Railway suicide in England and Wales, 1850–1949. *Social Science & Medicine*, 1994, 38, 401–407.

Cooke, C. T., Cadden, G. A., & Margolius, K. A. Death by hanging in Western Australia. *Pathology*, 1995, 27, 268–272.

Cooper, P. N., & Milroy, C. M. Violent suicide in South Yorkshire. *Journal of Forensic Science*, 1994, 39, 657–667.

Cugino, A., Markovich, E. I., Rosenblatt, S., Jarjoura, D., Blend, D., & Whittier, F. C. Searching for a pattern. *Journal of Psychosocial Nursing*, 1992, 30(3), 23–26.

Cummings, P., Koepsell, T. D., Grossman, D. C., Savarino, J., & Thompson, R. S. The association between the purchase of a handgun and homicide and suicide. *American Journal of Public Health*, 1997, 87, 974–978.

Curran, P. S., & Lester, D. Trends in the methods used for suicide in Northern Ireland. *Ulster Medical Journal*, 1991, 60, 58–62.

De Leo, D., Carollo, G., Dello Buono, M., Conforti, D., & Mastinu, A. Epidemiology of suicide in the elderly population of Italy 1958–1988. *Archives of Suicide Research*, 1995, 1, 3–17.

De Moore, G. M., Plew, J. D., Bray, K. M., & Snars, J. N. Survivors of self-inflicted firearm injury. *Medical Journal of Australia*, 1994, 160, 421–425.

Dudley, M., Waters, B., Kelk, N., & Howard, J. Youth suicide in NSW. *Medical Journal of Australia*, 1992, 156, 83–88.

Durand, E., Le Jeunne, C., & Hugues, F. C. Failure of prophylactic zidovudine after suicidal inoculation of HIV-infected blood. *New England Journal of Medicine*, 1991, 324, 1062.

Elfawal, M. A., & Awad, O. A. Deaths from hanging in the eastern province of Saudi Arabia. *Medicine, Science & the Law*, 1994, 34, 307–312.

Ellis, A. M. Suicide from the Clifton Suspension Bridge in England. *Journal of Epidemiology & Community Health*, 1996, 50, 474.

Emmerson, B., & Cantor, C. Train suicides in Brisbane, Australia, 1980–1986. *Crisis*, 1993, 14, 90–94.

Farmer, R., O'Donnell, I., & Tranah, T. Suicide on the London underground system. *International Journal of Epidemiology*, 1991, 20, 707–711.

Fischer, E. P., Comstock, G. W., Monk, M. A., & Sencer, D. J. Characteristics of completed suicides. *Suicide & Life-Threatening Behavior*, 1993, 23, 91–100.

Frankenfield, D. L., Baker, S. P., Lange, W. R., Caplan, Y., & Smialek, J. E. Fluoxetine and violent death in Maryland. *Forensic Science International*, 1994, 64, 107–117.

Freeman, T., Clothier, J., Thornton, C., & Keesee, N. Firearm collection and use among combat veterans admitted to post-traumatic stress disorder rehabilitation unit. *Journal of Nervous & Mental Disease*, 1994, 182, 592–594.

Freemantle, N., House, A., Song, F., Mason, J. M., & Sheldon, T. A. Prescribing selective serotonin reuptake inhibitors as strategy for prevention of suicide. *British Medical Journal*, 1994, 309, 249–253.

Friedman, T. Paracetamol overdose. *British Journal of Psychiatry*, 1996, 168, 519.

Garcia-Sanchez, V., Palao, R., & Legarre, F. Self-inflicted burns. *Burns*, 1994, 20, 537–538.

Gaylord, M. S., & Lester, D. Suicide in the Hong Kong subway. *Social Science & Medicine*, 1994, 38, 427–430.

Gundlach, J. H. Absence of family support, opportunity, and suicide. *Family Perspectives*, 1990, 24(1), 7–13.

Gunnell, D., Hawton, K., Murray, V., Garner, R., Bismuth, C., Fagg, J., & Simkin, S. Use of paracetamol for suicide and nonfatal poisoning in the UK and France. *Journal of Epidemiology & Community Health*, 1997, 51, 175–179.

Gupta, B., & Trzepacz, P. T. Serious overdosers admitted to a general hospital. *General Hospital Psychiatry*, 1997, 19, 209–215.

Haddix, T. L., Harruff, R. C., Reay, D. T., & Haglund, W. D. Asphyxial suicides using plastic bags. *American Journal of Forensic Medicine & Pathology*, 1996, 17, 308–311.

Hadjiiski, O., & Todorov, P. Suicide by self-inflicted burns. *Burns*, 1996, 22, 381–383.

Hanzlick, R., Masterton, K., & Walker, B. Suicide by jumping from high-rise hotels. *American Journal of Forensic Medicine & Pathology*, 1990, 11, 294–297.

Harruff, R. C., Llewellyn, A. L., Clark, M. A., Hawley, D. A., & Pless, J. E. Firearm suicides during confrontations with police. *Journal of Forensic Science*, 1994, 39, 402–411.

Hawton, K., Ware, C., Mistry, H., Hewitt, J., Kingsbury, S., Roberts, D., & Weitzel, H. Why patients choose paracetamol for self-poisoning and their knowledge of its dangers. *British Medical Journal*, 1995, 310, 164.

Hawton, K., Ware, C., Mistry, H., Hewitt, J., Kingsbury, S., Roberts, D., & Weitzel, H. Paracetamol self-poisoning. *British Journal of Psychiatry*, 1996, 168, 43–48.

Heim, N., & Lester, D. Factors affecting choice of method for suicide. *European Journal of Psychiatry*, 1991, 5, 161–165.

Henriksson, M. M., Marttunen, M. J., Isometsa, E. T., Heikkinen, M. E., Aro, H. M., Kuoppasalmi, K. I., & Lonnqvist, J. K. Mental disorders in elderly suicide. *International Psychogeriatrics*, 1995, 7, 275–286.

Henry, J. A., & Antao, C. A. Suicide and fatal antidepressant poisoning. *European Journal of Medicine*, 1992, 1, 343–348.

Hintikka, J., Lehtonen, J., & Viinamaki, H. Hunting guns in homes and suicides in 15–24 year old males in Eastern Finland. *Australian & New Zealand Journal of Psychiatry*, 1997, 31, 858–861.

Iancu, I., Laufer, N., Dannon, P. N., Zohar Kadouch, R., Apter, A., & Zohar, J. A general hospital study of attempted suicide in adolescence. *Israel Journal of Psychiatry*, 1997, 34, 228–234.

Isacsson, G., Wasserman, D., & Bergman, U. Self-poisonings with antidepressants and other psychotropics in an urban area of Sweden. *Annals of Clinical Psychiatry*, 1995, 7, 113–118.

Isbister, E. S., & Roberts, J. A. Autokabalesis. *Injury*, 1992, 23, 119–122.

Jick, S. S., Dean, A. D., & Jick, H. Antidepressants and suicide. *British Medical Journal*, 1995, 310, 215–218.

Kaplan, M. S., Adamek, M. E., & Geling, O. Sociodemographic predictors of firearm suicide among older white males. *Gerontologist*, 1996, 36, 530–533.

Kaplan, M. S., Adamek, M. E., Geling, O., & Calderon, A. Firearm suicide among older women in the US. *Social Science & Medicine*, 1997, 44, 1427–1430.

Kaplan, M. S., Adamek, M. E., & Johnson, S. Trends in firearm suicide among older American males: 1979–1988. *Gerontologist*, 1994, 34, 59–65.

Karlsson, T., Isaksson, B., & Ormstad, K. Gunshot fatalities in Stockholm, Sweden. *Journal of Forensic Sciences*, 1993, 38, 1409–1421.

Kelleher, M. J., Daly, M., & Kelleher, M. J. A. The influence of antidepressants in overdose on the increased suicide rate in Ireland between 1971 and 1988. *British Journal of Psychiatry*, 1992, 161, 625–628.

Kellermann, A. L., Rivara, F. P., Somes, G.,

Reay, D. T., Francisco, J., Banton, J. G., Prodzinski, J., Fligner, C., & Hackman, B. B. Suicide in the home in relation to gun ownership. *New England Journal of Medicine*, 1992, 327, 467–472.

Kelly, S., Charlton, J., & Jenkins, R. Suicide deaths in England and Wales, 1982–92. *Population Trends*, 1995, Summer(80), 16–25.

Killias, M. International correlations between gun ownership and rates of homicide and suicide. *Canadian Medical Association Journal*, 1993, 148, 1721–1725.

Kleck, G. *Point blank*. New York: Aldine de Gruyter, 1991.

Klein-Schwartz, W., & Smith, G. S. Agricultural and horticultural chemical poisonings. *Annals of Emergency Medicine*, 1997, 29, 232–238.

Kontaxakis, V. P., & Christodoulou, G. N. Attempted suicide by violent methods. In A. J. Botsis, C. R. Soldatos & C. N. Stefanis (Eds.), *Suicide*. Amsterdam: Elsevier, 1997, 187–191.

Kuroda, N., Saito, K., Takada, A., Watanabe, H., Tomita, A., Murai, T., & Yanagida, J. Suicide by self-stabbing in the city of Tokyo. *Japanese Journal of Legal Medicine*, 1997, 51, 301–306.

Lafave, M., Hutton, J., LaPorta, A. J., & Mallory, P. L. History of high-velocity impact water trauma at Letterman Army Medical Center. *Military Medicine*, 1995, 160, 197–199.

Leenaars, A. A., & Lester, D. Gender and the impact of gun control on suicide and homicide. *Archives of Suicide Research*, 1996, 2, 223–234.

Leenaars, A. A., & Lester, D. The impact of gun control on suicide and homicide across the life span. *Canadian Journal of Behavioural Science*, 1997, 29, 1–6.

Lester, D. The availability of firearms and the use of firearms for suicide. *Acta Psychiatrica Scandinavica*, 1990a, 81, 146–147.

Lester, D. The effects of detoxification of domestic gas on suicide in the United States. *American Journal of Public Health*, 1990b, 80, 80–81.

Lester, D. Was gas detoxification or establishment of suicide prevention centers responsible for the decline in the British suicide rate? *Psychological Reports*, 1990c, 66, 286.

Lester, D. Accidental death rates and suicide. *Activitas Nervosa Superior*, 1990d, 32, 130–131.

Lester, D. The effect of the detoxification of domestic gas in Switzerland on the suicide rate. *Acta Psychiatrica Scandinavica*, 1990e, 82, 383–384.

Lester, D. The use of prescribed medications for suicide. *International Journal of Risk & Safety in Medicine*, 1990f, 1, 279–281.

Lester, D. Changes in the methods used for suicide in 16 countries from 1960 to 1980. *Acta Psychiatrica Scandinavica*, 1990g, 81, 260–261.

Lester, D. Capital punishment, gun control, and personal violence (suicide and homicide). *Psychological Reports*, 1990h, 66, 122.

Lester, D. A study of opportunity-based suicide rates. *Psychological Reports*, 1990i, 67, 498.

Lester, D. Effects of detoxification of domestic gas on suicide in the Netherlands. *Psychological Reports*, 1991a, 68, 202.

Lester, D. Iatrogenic concerns in the treatment of suicidal patients. *Pharmacology & Toxicology*, 1991b, 69, 301–302.

Lester, D. Association of different measures of gun ownership over time. *Psychological Reports*, 1991c, 69, 1058.

Lester, D. A secondary prevention tactic for suicide. *Italian Journal of Suicidology*, 1992, 2, 17–18.

Lester, D. Controlling crime facilitators. *Crime Prevention Studies*, 1993a, 1(1), 35–54.

Lester, D. Firearm deaths and the density of firearms dealers in America. *Perceptual & Motor Skills*, 1993b, 76, 978.

Lester, D. Availability of methods for suicide and suicide rates. *Perceptual & Motor Skills*, 1993c, 76, 1358.

Lester, D. Suicide from bridges in Washington, D.C. *Perceptual & Motor Skills*, 1993d, 77, 534.

Lester, D. Firearm deaths in the United States and gun availability. *American Journal of Public Health*, 1993e, 83, 1642.

Lester, D. Suicide by drowning and the extent of the nation's coastline. *Perceptual & Motor Skills*, 1993f, 77, 1118.

Lester, D. Suicide by jumping in Singapore as a function of high-rise apartment availability. *Perceptual & Motor Skills*, 1994a, 79, 74.

Lester, D. Use of firearms for suicide in Canada. *Perceptual & Motor Skills*, 1994b, 79, 962.

Lester, D. Estimates of prescription rates and the use of medications for suicide. *European Journal of Psychiatry*, 1994c, 8, 81–83.

Lester, D. Estimates of prescription rates and the use of medicaments for suicide. *Pharmacology & Toxicology*, 1994d, 75, 231–232.

Lester, D. Car ownership and suicide by car exhaust in nations of the world. *Perceptual & Motor Skills*, 1994e, 79, 898.

Lester, D. Medical resources and the prevention of suicide and homicide. *European Journal of Psychiatry*, 1995a, 9, 97–99.

Lester, D. Effects of the detoxification of domestic gas on suicide rates in six nations. *Psychological Reports*, 1995b, 77, 294.

Lester, D. The availability of guns and the rates of personal violence (homicide and suicide). *Italian Journal of Suicide*, 1995c, 5, 73–76.

Lester, D. The toxicity of car exhaust and its use as a method for suicide. *Psychological Reports*, 1995d, 77, 1090.

Lester, D. The impact of availability, attraction, and lethality of suicide methods on suicide rates in Germany. *Acta Psychiatrica Scandinavica*, 1995e, 92, 318.

Lester, D. Subway suicide rates and national suicide rates. *Perceptual & Motor Skills*, 1995f, 80, 954.

Lester, D. Gun ownership and rates of homicide and suicide. *European Journal of Psychiatry*, 1996a, 10, 83–85.

Lester, D. Gender differences in methods for suicide. *Perceptual & Motor Skills*, 1996b, 82, 1154.

Lester, D. Issues in preventing suicide by firearms. In J. McIntosh (Ed.), *Suicide '96*. Washington, DC: AAS, 1996c, 34.

Lester, D. Determinants of choice of method for suicide and the person/situation debate in psychology. *Perceptual & Motor Skills*, 1997, 85, 497–498.

Lester, D., & Abe, K. The availability of lethal methods for suicide and the suicide rate. *Stress Medicine*, 1990, 6, 275–276.

Lester, D., & Hodgson, J. The effects of the detoxification of domestic gas on the suicide rate in Scotland. *European Journal of Psychiatry*, 1992, 6, 171–174.

Lester, D., & Leenaars, A. A. Suicide rates in Canada before and after tightening firearm control laws. *Psychological Reports*, 1993, 72, 787–790.

Lester, D., & Leenaars, A. A. Gun control and rates of firearms violence in Canada and the United States. *Canadian Journal of Criminology*, 1994, 36, 463–464.

Leth, P., & Hart-Madsen, M. Suicide by self incineration. *American Journal of Forensic Medicine & Pathology*, 1997, 18, 113–118.

Li, G., Ling, J., DiScala, C., Nordenholtz, K., Sterling, S., & Baker, S. Characteristics and outcomes of self-inflicted pediatric injuries. *Injury Prevention*, 1997, 3, 115–119.

Li, L., & Smialek, J. E. The investigation of fatal falls and jumps from heights in Maryland (1987–1992). *American Journal of Forensic Medicine & Pathology*, 1994, 15, 295–299.

Liu, T., & Waterbor, J. W. Declining use of firearms to commit suicide in Alabama in the 1980s. *Omega*, 1994–1995, 30, 145–153.

Loftin, C., McDowall, D., Wiersema, B., & Cottey, T. J. Effects of restrictive licensing of handguns on homicide and suicide in the District of Columbia. *New England Journal of Medicine*, 1991, 325, 1615–1620.

MacDonald, I. L., & Lerer, L. B. A time-series analysis of trends in firearm-related homicide and suicide. *International Journal of Epidemiology*, 1994, 23, 66–72.

Malmvik, J., Lowenhielm, C. G. P., & Melander, A. Antidepressants in suicide. *European Journal of Clinical Pharmacology*, 1994, 46, 291–294.

Marchesan, W. G., da Silva, F. F., Canalli, J. E., & Ferreira, E. Suicide attempted by burning in Brazil. *Burns*, 1997, 23, 270–271.

Marzuk, P. M., Leon, A. C., Tardiff, K., Morgan, E. B., Stajic, M., & Mann, J. J. The effect of access to lethal methods of injury on suicide rates. *Archives of General Psychiatry*, 1992a, 49, 451–458.

Marzuk, P. M., Tardiff, K., Smyth, D., Stajic, M., & Leon, A. C. Cocaine use, risk taking, and fatal Russian roulette. *Journal of the American Medical Association*, 1992b, 267,

2635–2637.

Masica, D. N., Kotsanos, J. G., Beasley, C. M., & Potvin, J. H. Trend in suicide rates since fluoxetine introduction. *American Journal of Public Health*, 1992, 82, 1295.

McClure, G. M. Suicide in children and adolescents in England and Wales 1960–1990. *British Journal of Psychiatry*, 1994, 165, 510–514.

McLoone, P. Suicide and deprivation in Scotland. *British Medical Journal*, 1996, 312, 543–544.

McLoone, P., & Crombie, I. K. Hospitalization for deliberate self-poisoning in Scotland from 1981 to 1993. *British Journal of Psychiatry*, 1996, 169, 81–85.

McManus, B. L., Kruesi, M. J. P., Dontes, A. E., Defazio, C. R., Piotrowski, J. T., & Woodward, P. J. Child and adolescent suicide attempts. *American Journal of Emergency Medicine*, 1997, 15, 357–360.

Melander, A., Henricson, K., Stenberg, P., Lowenhielm, P., Malmvik, J., Sternebring, B., Kaij, L., & Bergdahl, U. Anxiolytic-hypnotic drugs. *European Journal of Clinical Pharmacology*, 1991, 41, 525–529.

Milcevic, G., & Prpic, H. Self-poisoning with psychopharmacological agents in Zagreb. *Human & Experimental Toxicology*, 1991, 10, 305–310.

Miller, M., & Hemenway, D. The relationship between firearms and suicide. *Aggression & Violent Behavior*, 1999, 4, 59–75.

Miner, M. E., Ewing-Cobbs, L., Kopaniky, D. R., Cabrera, J., & Kaufman, P. The results of treatment of gunshot wounds to the brain in children. *Neurosurgery*, 1990, 26, 20–25.

Mundt, R. J. Gun control and rates of firearm violence in Canada and the United States. *Canadian Journal of Criminology*, 1990, 32, 137–154.

Myers, W. C., Otto, T. A., Harris, E., Diaco, D., & Moreno, A. Acetaminophen overdose as a suicidal gesture. *Journal of the American Academy of Child & Adolescent Psychiatry*, 1992, 31, 686–690.

Neeleman, J., & Wessely, S. Drugs taken in fatal and nonfatal self-poisoning. *Acta Psychiatrica Scandinavica*, 1997, 95, 283–287.

Nordentoft, M., Breum, L., Munck, L. K., Nordestgaard, A. G., Hunding, A., & Bjaeldager, P. High mortality by natural and unnatural causes. *British Medical Journal*, 1993, 306, 1637–1641.

Nowers, M. Gunshot suicide in the County of Avon, England. *Medicine, Science & the Law*, 1994, 34(2), 95–98.

Nowers, M., & Gunnell, D. Suicide from the Clifton Suspension Bridge in England. *Journal of Epidemiology & Community Health*, 1996, 50, 30–32.

Obafunwa, J. O., & Busuttil, A. A review of completed suicides in the Lothian and Borders region of Scotland. *Social Psychiatry & Psychiatric Epidemiology*, 1994, 29, 100–106.

Obafunwa, J. O., Busuttil, A., & Al-Oqleh, A. M. Dextropropoxyphene-related deaths. *International Journal of Legal Medicine*, 1994, 106, 315–318.

O'Carroll, P. W., & Silverman, M. M. Community suicide prevention. *Suicide & Life-Threatening Behavior*, 1994, 24, 89–99.

O'Donnell, I., Arthur, A. J., & Farmer, R. D. J. A follow-up study of attempted railway suicides. *Social Science & Medicine*, 1994, 38, 437–442.

O'Donnell, I., & Farmer, R. Suicidal acts on metro systems. *Acta Psychiatrica Scandinavica*, 1992, 86, 60–63.

O'Donnell, I., & Farmer, R. The epidemiology of suicide on the London Underground. *Social Science & Medicine*, 1994, 38, 409–418.

O'Donnell, I., Farmer, R., & Catalan, J. Explaining suicide. *British Journal of Psychiatry*, 1996, 168, 780–786.

O'Donovan, F. C., Owens, J., & Tracey, J. A. Self-poisoning. *Irish Medical Journal*, 1993, 86(2), 64–65.

Ohberg, A., Lonnqvist, J., Sarva, S., Vuori, E., & Penttila, A. Trends and availability of suicide methods in Finland. *British Journal of Psychiatry*, 1995, 166, 35–43.

Ohberg, A., Penttila, A., & Lonnqvist, J. Driver suicides. *British Journal of Psychiatry*, 1997, 171, 468–472.

Ohberg, A., Vuori, E., Ojanpera, I., & Lonnqvist, J. Alcohol and drugs in suicide. *British Journal of Psychiatry*, 1996, 169, 75–80.

Ostrom, M., Thorson, J., & Eriksson, A. Carbon monoxide suicide from car exhausts. *Social Science & Medicine*, 1996, 42, 447–451.

Parron, T., Hernandez, A. F., & Villanueva, E. Increased risk of suicide with exposure to pesticides in an intensive agricultural area. *Forensic Science International*, 1996, 79, 53–63.

Perez-Martinez, A. L., Chui, P., & Cameron, J. M. Plastic bag suffocation. *Medicine, Science & the Law*, 1993, 33, 71–75.

Peschel, O., Betz, P., & Eisenmenger, W. Injection of toxic agents. *Forensic Science International*, 1995, 75, 95–100.

Prevost, C., Julien, M., & Brown, B. P. Suicides associated with the Jacques Cartier Bridge, Montreal, Quebec 1988–1993. *Canadian Journal of Public Health*, 1996, 87, 377–380.

Prosser, D. Suicides by burning in England and Wales. *British Journal of Psychiatry*, 1996, 168, 175–182.

Rao, A. V., Mahendran, N., Gopalakrishnan, C., Reddy, T., Prabhakar, E. R., Swaminathan, R. Belinda, C., Andal, G., Baskaran, S., Prahee, R., Kumar, N., Luthra, U. K., Aynkaran, J. R., & Catherine, I. One hundred female burn cases. *Indian Journal of Psychiatry*, 1989, 31(1), 43–50.

Reed, G. E., McGuire, P. J., & Boehm, A. Analysis of gunshot residue test results in 112 suicides. *Journal of Forensic Sciences*, 1990, 35, 62–68.

Rhyne, C. E., Templer, D. I., Brown, L. G., & Peters, N. B. Dimensions of suicide. *Suicide & Life-Threatening Behavior*, 1995, 25, 373–380.

Rich, C. L., Young, J. G., Fowler, R. C., Wagner, J., & Black, N. A. Guns and suicide. *American Journal of Psychiatry*, 1990, 147, 342–346.

Richter, D., Hahn, M. P., Ostermann, A. W., Ekkernkamp, A., & Muhr, G. Vertical deceleration injuries. *Injury*, 1996, 27, 655–659.

Riddick, L., Wanger, G. P., Fackler, M. L., Carter, R. D., Hoff, C. J., Jinks, J. M., & Becker, J. A. Gunshot injuries in Mobile County, Alabama. *American Journal of Forensic Medicine & Pathology*, 1993, 14, 215–225.

Risser, D., Bonsch, A., Schneider, B., & Baver, G. Risk of dying after a free fall from height. *Forensic Science International*, 1996, 78, 187–191.

Risser, D., & Schneider, B. Carbon monoxide-related deaths from 1984 to 1993 in Vienna, Austria. *Journal of Forensic Sciences*, 1995, 40, 368–371.

Rogde, S., & Olving, J. H. Characteristics of fire victims in different sorts of fires. *Forensic Science International*, 1996, 77, 93–99.

Ross, T. E., & Lester, D. Suicides at Niagara Falls. *American Journal of Public Health*, 1991, 81, 1677–1678.

Rouse, D., & Dunn, L. Firearm fatalities. *Forensic Science International*, 1992, 56, 59–61.

Sacks, J. J., Mercy, J. A., Ryan, G. W., & Parrish, R. G. Guns in the home, homicide, and suicide. *Journal of the American Medical Association*, 1994, 272, 847–848.

Schiodt, F. V., Rochling, F. A., Casey, D. L., & Lee, W. M. Acetaminophen toxically in an urban county hospital. *New England Journal of Medicine*, 1997, 337, 1112–1117.

Schmidtke, A. Suicidal behavior on railways in the FRG. *Social Science & Medicine*, 1994, 38, 419–426.

Schmidtke, A., Kerkhof, A., Bille-Brahe, U., De Leo, D., Bjerke, T., Crepet, P., Garing, C., Hawton, K., Lonnqvist, J., Michel, K., Pommereau, X., Salander-Renberg, E., Querejeta, I., Temesvary, B., Wasserman, D., & Fricke, S. Suicide attempts by "car accident." In D. Lester (Ed.), *Suicide '94*. Denver: AAS, 1994, 124.

Scott, K. W. Suicide in Wolverhampton. *Medicine, Science & the Law*, 1994, 34, 99–105.

Selway, R. Gunshot suicides in Victoria, Australia, 1988. *Medicine, Science & the Law*, 1991, 31, 76–80.

Shelef, M. Unanticipated benefits of automotive emission control. *Science of the Total Environment*, 1994, 146/147, 93–101.

Sheth, H., Dziewulski, P., & Settle, J. Self-inflicted burns. *Burns*, 1994, 20, 334–335.

Simon, R., Chouinard, M., & Gravel, C. Suicide and firearms. In J. McIntosh (Ed.), *Suicide '96*. Washington, DC: AAS, 1996, 35–37.

Slavic, S., Baralic, I., Obradovic, M., Jecmenica, D., Slobodan, K., & Dovic, V. *Modes of suicide of males*. 4th European Symposium on Suicide, University of Odense, 1992.

Sloan, J. H., Rivara, F. P., Reay, D. T., Feris, J. A. J., & Kellerman, A. L. Firearm regulation and rates of suicide. *New England Journal of Medicine*, 1990, 322, 369–373.

Snowdon, J., & Harris, L. Firearm suicides in Australia. *Medical Journal of Australia*, 1992, 156, 79–83.

Snyder, M. L. Methods of suicide used by Irish and Japanese suicides. *Psychological Reports*, 1994, 74, 127–130.

Sonneck, G., Etzerdorfer, E., & Nagel-Kuess, S. Imitative suicide on the Viennese subway. *Social Science & Medicine*, 1994, 38, 453–457.

Start, R. D., Milroy, C. M., & Green, M. A. Suicide by self-stabbing. *Forensic Science International*, 1992, 56, 89–94.

Stavemann, H. H., & Thieme, J. C. Coming to grips with the youth suicide wave in Western Samoa. In L. Bohme, R. Freytag, C. Wachtler & H. Wedler (Eds.), *Suicidal behavior.* Regensburg: S. Roderer, 1993, 859–862.

Stone, I. C. Observations and statistics relating to suicide weapons. *Journal of Forensic Sciences*, 1990, 35, 10–12.

Stone, I. C. Characteristics of firearms and gunshot wounds as markers of suicide. *American Journal of Forensic Medicine & Pathology*, 1992, 13, 275–280.

Suk, J. H., Han, C. H., & Yeon, B. K. Suicide by burning in Korea. *International Journal of Social Psychiatry*, 1991, 37, 141–145.

Sundquist, J., Ekedahl, A., & Johansson, S. E. Sales of tranquillizers, hypnotics/ sedatives, and antidepressants and their relationship with underprivileged area scores and mortality and suicide rates. *European Journal of Clinical Pharmacology*, 1996, 51, 105–109.

Swenson, J. P., & Dimsdale, J. E. Substance abuse and attempts at suicide by burning. *American Journal of Psychiatry*, 1990, 147, 811.

Theilade, P. Carbon monoxide poisoning. *American Journal of Forensic Medicine & Pathology*, 1990, 11, 219–225.

Thompson, J. P., Casey, P. B., & Vale, J. A. Deaths from pesticide poisoning in England and Wales 1990–1991. *Human & Experimental Toxicology*, 1995, 14, 437–445.

Tuohig, G. M., Saffle, J. R., Sullivan, J. J., Morris, S., & Lehto, S. Self-inflicted patient burns. *Journal of Burn Care & Rehabilitation*, 1995, 16, 429–436.

Ungs, T. J. Suicide by use of aircraft in the United States, 1978–1989. *Aviation, Space & Environmental Medicine*, 1994, 65, 953–956.

Valle, M. C., Lloret, J. B. M., Gisbert, S. M., & Ciriquian, J. L. M. Etiology of intoxication. *European Journal of Epidemiology*, 1993, 9, 361–367.

Van Heeringen, C., Jannes, C., & Van Remoortel, L. Characteristics of violent attempted suicides and implications for aftercare. *European Journal of Psychiatry*, 1991, 5, 152–160.

Vieta, E., Nieto, E., Gasto, C., & Cirera, E. Attempted suicide by jumping. *European Psychiatry*, 1992, 7, 221–224.

White, R. T., Gribble, R. J., Corr, M. J., & Large, M. M. Jumping from a general hospital. *General Hospital Psychiatry*, 1995, 17, 208–215.

Wiedenmann , A., & Weyerer, S. The impact of availability, attraction, and lethality of suicide methods on suicide rates in Germany. *Acta Psychiatrica Scandinavica*, 1993, 88, 364–368.

Yang, B., & Lester, D. The effect of gun availability on suicide rates. *Atlantic Economic Journal*, 1991, 19(2), 74.

Youssef, H. A. Psychotropic drugs in suicidal patients. *International Clinical Psychopharmacology*, 1990, 5, 291–294.

Zwerling, C., Lynch, C. F., Burmeister, L. F., & Goertz, U. The choice of weapons in firearm suicide in Iowa. *American Journal of Public Health*, 1993, 83, 1630–1632.

Chapter 16

COMMUNICATION AND THE SUICIDAL ACT

Communication of Suicidal Intent

Asgard (1990), in a study of Swedish women who committed suicide in Stockholm, found that those under the age of 30 more often left a suicide note and made more direct communications of suicidal intent and fewer indirect communications than older female suicides.

Marttunen (1994) found that male adolescent completed suicides in Finland communicated their intent more to peers, while female adolescent suicides communicated more to adults. The girls used hanging more and shooting less often, had more often attempted suicide in the past, and more often had received recent psychiatric care.

Suicide Notes

Who Leaves a Note?

Heim and Lester (1990) found that suicides in West Berlin (Germany) who left a suicide note were more often women, older, and widowed than those not leaving a note. Note writers killed themselves more often on Monday and used poisons.

In subway suicides in London (England), O'Donnell et al. (1993) found that 15 percent of completed suicides and 4 percent of attempted suicides left notes. The note leavers did not differ in sex or age from those not leaving notes.

Attempters Versus Completers

Brevard et al. (1990) compared suicide notes from attempters and completers and found that the notes from attempters less often expressed the wish to be killed (anger-in) but did not differ in the wishes to die (escape) or to kill (anger-out). Lester (1994c) confirmed this after controlling for sex and age, but Leenaars et al. (1992b) found no differences in Menninger's three motives for suicide (to die, to kill, and to be killed) when the notes were matched for age and sex. Brevard and Lester (1991) found that the completers more often addressed their note to someone, said "sorry," and mentioned grandparents. The attempters' notes were more often in the nature of a last will and testament. The completers had a lower total-isolation score.

Leenaars et al. (1992a) found no differences in eight suicidal patterns between notes from attempters and completers. On 20 content dimensions, the attempters more often showed a lack of social integration and suicide as style of life.

Lester (1994b) found the suicidologists could not distinguish suicide notes from completers and attempters, and Black and Lester (1995) found that skilled judges of

237

suicide notes could not distinguish them.

Sex Differences

Lester and Heim (1992) found no differences on 16 content variables between the suicide notes of men and women, but the notes from men had more mention of depression and poor health. Linn and Lester (1996) found no sex differences in a sample of suicide notes. Lester and Linn (1997) found no sex differences in romantic versus work motives for suicide.

Age Differences

Linn and Lester (1996) found that suicide notes from older people had less self-blame, low self-esteem, feelings of unworthiness, and performance failure, but had more grief over loss and mention of incurable illnesses.

Bauer et al. (1997) found that the commonalities in suicide notes from suicides of different ages outweighed the differences. The tendency was for the notes of older suicides to stress more often reunion with loved ones, fears of being a burden, financial devastation, physical deterioration and loss of control over life, a negative attitude to being old, physical illness, instructions to prevent distress to survivors, and sleep problems.

Hoax Notes

Lester et al. (1990) found that the hoax notes had more wish to kill in them, while genuine notes had more wish to be killed and less wish to die as compared to simulated notes.

Differences by Nation

Lester (1997) found that German notes more often had the wish to die than American notes. Leenaars (1992) found that suicide notes from Canada and the United States were similar on 55 of 56 content variables examined. Leenaars et al. (1994) found no differences between suicide notes in Germany and the United States. Leenaars et al. (1996) found no differences in Menninger's motive (to kill, to be killed, and to die) when the notes were matched for age and sex.

Differences by Method

Leenaars (1990) found no differences in eight content dimensions between the suicide notes of those using active and passive methods.

Learning Disabilities

McBride and Siegel (1997) found that suicide notes from adolescents had worse spelling, handwriting, letter errors, and letter quality than those from elderly suicides. Dictating the notes to learning-disabled and normal adolescents indicated that the adolescent suicide notes resembled those written by learning-disabled students and differed from those written by normal students.

Symbolic Ages

Leenaars (1996) found no differences in the content of suicide notes of those killing themselves at symbolic ages (such as 20, 30, etc.).

Type of Note

Heim and Lester (1991) compared those who left instructions with those who left wills/testaments. Those leaving instructions were younger, more often Catholic, male, and married/single, and more often had problems with work, loneliness, and addictions; they less often had problems with the recent death of a partner.

Peck (1989–1990) classified the notes of adolescents into six types: anger, symbolic gestures, requests for forgiveness, reactions to broken friendships, reactions to stress, and failure.

Judgments of Suicide Notes

Lester (1995b) changed the apparent sex of the note writer and found that this had no impact on judgments of the rationality, mental illness, emotional upset, or likelihood of suicide of the writer.

Simulated Notes: Judgments

Lester (1993) obtained two sets of genuine/simulated suicide notes and found that naive judges showed no parallel forms reliability. He found that experts discerned the genuine notes better than chance, while naive judges could not. Lester (1991a) had naive judges guess the genuine note in a sample of genuine/simulated note pairs. The odd-even correlation was moderate, suggesting that the judges were reasonably reliable.

Lester (1991b) found the accuracy of naive judges was associated with extraversion, but not with neuroticism, psychoticism, or Keirsey-Bates temperament scores. Lester (1995a) found that Machiavellian scores did not predict the success of naive judges. Lester (1994a) found that judges more sympathetic to suicide were more accurate in picking out genuine notes.

Leenaars and Lester (1991) found that the genuine note in 19 of 33 pairs of genuine/simulated suicide notes was obvious to the student judges, while in 14 of the pairs it was not. Asking the judges for their reasons for judging a note to be genuine, they focused on traumatic events and idiosyncratic views.

Simulated Notes: Differences

Black (1993) found that the genuine notes were longer and, after controls for length, had more instructions, information, religious ideas, and dates. The simulated notes had more depression, justification, life overwhelming as a reason, and less mention of afterlife.

Discussion

The study of suicide notes remains of great interest to suicidologists, but little advance has been made in the last decade except for the extension of the research to suicide notes form the attempters.

REFERENCES

Asgard, U. A psychiatric study of suicide among urban Swedish women. *Acta Psychiatrica Scandinavica*, 1990, 82, 115-124.

Bauer, M. N., Leenaars, A. A., Berman, A. L., Jobes, D. A., Dixon, J. F., & Bibb, J. L. Late adulthood suicide. *Archives of Suicide Research*, 1997, 3, 91-108.

Black, S. T. Comparing genuine and simulated suicide notes. *Journal of Consulting &*

Clinical Psychology, 1993, 61, 699-702.

Black, S. T., & Lester, D. Distinguishing suicide notes from completed suicides and attempted suicides. *Perceptual & Motor Skills*, 1995, 81, 802.

Brevard, A., & Lester, D. A comparison of suicide notes written by completed and attempted suicides. *Annals of Clinical Psychiatry*, 1991, 3, 43-45.

Brevard, A., Lester, D. & Yang, B. A comparison of suicide notes written by suicide completers and suicide attempters. *Crisis*, 1990, 11, 7-11.

Heim, N., & Lester, D. Do suicides who write notes differ from those who do not? *Acta Psychiatrica Scandinavica*, 1990, 82, 372-273.

Heim, N., & Lester, D. A study of different types of suicide notes. *Homeostasis*, 1991, 33, 109-112.

Leenaars, A. A. Do the psychological characteristics of the suicidal individual make a difference in the method of chosen for suicide? *Canadian Journal of Behavioural Science*, 1990, 22, 385-392.

Leenaars, A. A. Suicide notes from Canada and the United States. *Perceptual & Motor Skills*, 1992, 74, 278.

Leenaars, A. A. Suicide notes at symbolic ages. *Psychological Reports*, 1996, 78, 1034.

Leenaars, A. A., & Lester, D. Myths about suicide notes. *Death Studies*, 1991, 15, 303-308.

Leenaars, A. A., Lester, D., & Heim, N. Menninger's motives for suicide in suicide notes from Germany and the USA. *Crisis*, 1996, 17, 87.

Leenaars, A. A., Lester, D., Wenckstern, S., & Heim, N. Suizid-Abschiedsbriefe. *Suizidprophylaxe*, 1994, 22(3), 99-101.

Leenaars, A. A., Lester, D., Wenckstern, S., McMullin, C., Rudzinski, D., & Brevard, A. Comparison of suicide notes and parasuicide notes. *Death Studies*, 1992a, 16, 331-342.

Leenaars, A. A., Lester, D., & Yang, B. Menninger's motives for suicide in the notes of completed and attempted suicides. *Psychological Reports*, 1992b, 70, 369-370.

Lester, D. Reliability of naive judges of genuine suicide notes. *Perceptual & Motor Skills*, 1991a, 73, 942.

Lester, D. Accuracy of recognition of genuine versus simulated suicide. *Personality & Individual Differences*, 1991b, 12, 765-766.

Lester, D. Reliability of judging genuine and simulated suicide notes. *Perceptual & Motor Skills*, 1993, 77, 882.

Lester, D. Correlates of accuracy in judging genuine versus simulated suicide notes. *Perceptual & Motor Skills*, 1994a, 79, 642.

Lester, D. Can suicidologists distinguish between suicide notes from completers and attempters? *Perceptual & Motor Skills*, 1994b, 79, 1498.

Lester, D. Motives for suicide in suicide notes from completed and attempted suicides. *Psychological Reports*, 1994c, 75, 1130.

Lester, D. Personality correlates of correctly identifying genuine suicide notes. *Perceptual & Motor Skills*, 1995a, 80, 890.

Lester, D. Is the gender of a suicide note writer associated with judgments made about the suicide? *Perceptual & Motor Skills*, 1995b, 81, 50.

Lester, D. Menninger's motives for suicide in suicide notes from America and Germany. *Perceptual & Motor Skills*, 1997, 85, 1194.

Lester, D., & Heim, N. Sex differences in suicide notes. *Perceptual & Motor Skills*, 1992, 75, 582.

Lester, D., & Linn, M. Sex differences in suicide notes. *Psychological Reports*, 1997, 80, 1302.

Lester, D., Seiden, R. H., & Tauber, R. K. Menninger's motives for suicide in genuine, simulated, and hoax suicide notes. *Perceptual & Motor Skills*, 1990, 71, 248.

Linn, M., & Lester, D. Content differences in suicide notes by gender and age. *Psychological Reports*, 1996, 78, 370.

Marttunen, M. Psychosocial maladjustment, mental disorders and stressful life events precede adolescent suicide. *Psychiatria Fennica*, 1994, 25, 39-51.

McBride, H., & Siegel, L. S. Learning disabilities and adolescent suicide. *Journal of Learning Disabilities*, 1997, 30, 652-659.

O'Donnell, I., Farmer, R., & Catalan, J. Suicide notes. *British Journal of Psychiatry*, 1993, 163, 45-48.

Peck, D. L. Teenage suicide expressions. *International Quarterly of Community Health Education*, 1989-1990, 10(1), 53-64.

Chapter 17

PSYCHIATRIC DISORDER AND SUICIDE

Harris and Barraclough (1997) reported a meta-analysis of studies on the risk of suicide in psychiatric disorders. Thirty-six disorders had a significantly increased risk of suicide, five had a nonsignificant increased risk (bulimia nervosa, somatization disorder, transient global amnesia, petit mal epilepsy, and epilepsy seen by general practitioners), and one had an average risk (mental retardation).

Psychiatric Disorder in General

Completed Suicide

In one catchment area in England, King and Barraclough (1990) found that suicides, accidental deaths, and undetermined deaths did not differ in lifetime admissions to psychiatric care, but the undetermined deaths were more often currently in care.

Gabriel and Paschalis (1991) found that completed suicides with a psychiatric history had more prior suicide attempts and more acute stress, whereas those with no psychiatric history had more chronic stress. The groups did not differ in age, marital status, urban/rural living, communication or suicidal intent, leaving a suicide notes, or method for suicide.

In a complete sample of Finnish adolescent suicides in one year, Marttunen et al. (1991) found that 50 of the 53 were diagnosable, with depressive disorder the most common diagnosis (40 percent), followed by personality disorder (21 percent) and adjustment disorder (15 percent).

Among a sample of former psychiatric inpatients, Wolford et al. (1991) found that the suicides were more diagnosed with schizophrenia and affective disorders and were more often white, substance abusers, and not single.

Axelsson and Lagerkvist-Briggs (1992) found higher suicide rates in bipolars, paranoids, schizophrenics, and major depressive disorders. The completed suicides had shown more prior suicidal behavior; had older fathers (but not mothers); had more children; and had been more depressed, paranoid, and elevated in the past. They did not differ in age, alcohol abuse, age at onset, or duration of the illness.

Boyer et al. (1992) compared suicides with those dying in motor vehicle accidents and people in the general population. The suicides were more likely to have Axis I disorders (especially major depression and alcohol/drug dependence) and Axis II disorders (especially borderline and antisocial personality disorders).

Cantor et al. (1992) compared patients in psychiatric community care who completed suicide with those who did not. The groups did not differ on any variable: employment, early loss, diagnosis, depression, substance abuse, prior suicide attempts, family suicidal behavior, mental illness, substance abuse, or history of violence.

In a community rehabilitation service, Pyke and Steers (1992) found that suicides versus controls matched for psychiatric disability, had been hospitalized more during the program, were ill for a shorter period of time, and had more difficulty establishing relationships. They did not differ in diagnosis, substance abuse, living alone, marital status, education, finances, or prior hospitalizations.

Brent et al. (1993c) found that adolescent suicides in the community more often had a psychiatric disorder, prior suicidal behavior, and prior psychiatric treatment than community controls. As compared to community controls, Brent et al. (1993f) found that the adolescent suicides had experienced more recent stressors, especially interpersonal conflict and interpersonal loss. In a regression analysis, suicide was associated with depression, substance abuse, and legal/disciplinary problems.

Brent et al. (1993e) found that adolescent suicides with minimal psychiatric pathology had experienced fewer stressors than the suicides with psychiatric disorders. However, their parents more kept guns, especially loaded guns, in the home.

Brent et al. (1993d, 1993g) found that peers of the suicides had more suicidal ideation (but made no more attempts) in the seven months after the suicides, compared to controls. Their siblings also had more depressive symptoms and suicidal ideation.

Earle et al. (1994) compared psychiatric outpatients who completed suicide with those who did not. The suicides more often had a diagnosis of depression or alcohol abuse and less often schizophrenia. They were also younger, more often male, less often African American, more often single if male, and more often divorced/widowed if female. They had more prior psychiatric hospitalizations, were less often seen in the last two weeks, were more often in counseling/medication programs, and less often in daily programs.

In England, King (1994) found that completed suicide in former psychiatric patients was more common if they were male, unemployed, and widowed/divorced.

Lesage et al. (1994) compared suicides with living controls. The suicides more often had major depressions, schizophrenia, alcohol dependence, drug dependence, antisocial personality disorder, and borderline personality disorder. They had more prior attempts and less education, but did not differ in physical handicaps.

Milne et al. (1994) studied suicides in Scotland who had received primary care. Those who had received a psychiatric diagnosis were more often female and older; those with depression were more often female, older, and less often single; those with physical illnesses were more often female and older; and those abusing alcohol were more often male. Those who had been prescribed antidepressants were more likely to complete suicide by overdose. Those with prior attempts more often had a psychiatric diagnosis and used overdoses.

Runeson and Rich (1994) found that completed suicides with diagnoses of borderline personality disorder and schizophrenia had poor adaptive functioning, while those with adjustment disorders and major depressive disorders had fair adaptive functioning.

Amaddeo et al. (1995) found that the risk of suicide in people with psychiatric illnesses was especially raised in those aged 14–24.

Hewer et al. (1995) found that the percentage of deaths due to suicide was lower in patients with organic mental disorders than in those with functional psychoses and other psychiatric disorders.

Dennehy et al. (1996) compared psychiatric patients completing suicide after discharge with matched controls. The suicides had been more suicidal in the hospital, but did not differ in the duration of their illness, prior attempts, alcohol/drug misuse, unemployment, marital status, or whether living alone.

In Scotland, Ramayya et al. (1996) found that completed suicides differed from undetermined deaths only in having made more prior attempts and not in mental illness, alcohol dependence, current psychiatric treatment, or family history of suicide.

Groholt et al. (1997) found that affective disorder and disruptive disorder differentiated adolescent suicides from normals. Among the suicides, the dropouts differed from the students in more often having a disruptive disorder and living apart from their family.

(1) FOLLOW-UP STUDIES. Alleback and Allgulander (1990b) studied later suicide in Swedish military conscripts. They found that neurotic disorders, personality disorders, and drug dependence at intake increased the risk of later suicide. Too-few conscripts had schizophrenia or affective disorders at intake for these to be studied. The presence of mental retardation and psychosomatic disorders at intake did not predict the risk of later suicide. Once they became inpatients, any diagnosis increased the risk of suicide.

Allgulander et al. (1992) followed up the discharged psychiatric patients and found a suicide rate higher in those with affective disorders, paranoid psychoses, neurotic disorders, and prescription addiction than in other psychiatric patients. Suicide rates were average for patients with schizophrenia, organic psychoses, personality disorders, and drug addiction, and they were lower in alcoholics.

Ferrero et al. (1992) followed up adolescent psychiatric inpatients and found that those abusing drugs were most likely to complete suicide. Subsequent attempted suicide was common in all patients.

In a sample of self-poisoners (accidental and suicidal), Ekeberg et al. (1994) found that subsequent completed suicide was predicted by the poisoning being suicidal, but not by age, sex, substance abuse, or social group.

Among involuntary patients, Engberg (1994) found that predictors of completed suicide varied with cohort. A short length of stay predicted suicide in both cohorts; being a nonpsychotic older male predicted suicide in one cohort, and further commitment for being dangerous predicted suicide in the other cohort.

In a 15-year follow-up of adolescent psychiatric inpatients, Kjelsberg et al. (1994) found a completed suicide rate of 145 for males and 110 for females. The suicides had more depression symptoms, learning difficulties, immature defense mechanisms, verbal abuse from parents, losses in early childhood, and stressors. They were more help-rejecting, and had less self-esteem and parental support.

In a follow-up study of attempted suicides, the completed suicide rate was found to be high (3600) by De Moore and Robertson (1996). Predictors of completed suicide for the attempters included more than one prior attempt, a planned attempt, and use of a narcotics overdose. (Sex, age, suicidal intent, lethality, and use of alcohol were not predictors.)

Lester (1996) found in various studies that estimates of the percentage of attempted suicides subsequently completing suicide were associated only with the length of follow-up and not the year of the study or the sample size.

Hepple and Quinton (1997) followed up a sample of elderly attempted suicides for three and a half years. Those who subsequently completed suicide had made more prior attempts, were more often divorced, and more often had a psychiatric history. They did not differ in age, suicidal intent at the time of the attempt, physical illness, or social class. Those who subsequently attempted or completed suicide more often had a depressive disorder and a subsequent psychiatric illness. The repeaters who attempted suicide were more often female than the repeaters who completed suicide.

(2) POST-DISCHARGE STUDIES. Geddes and Juszczak (1995) found high rates of suicide in the first 28 days after discharge from a psychiatric hospital, but no differences by diagnosis. Geddes et al. (1997) found a high rate of suicide in psychiatric patients after discharge, especially in the first month. Males with nonpsychotic depressions and affective psychoses had the highest suicide rates, while females with personality disorders and nonpsychotic depressions had the highest suicide rates.

Goldacre et al. (1993) found that psychiatric patients, both men and women, had the highest rate of suicide in the first 28 days after discharge. The rates varied by gender, but were higher for depressive disorders and neuroses than for schizophrenia and alcohol dependence. Stark et al. (1995) also found a high rate of suicide in the month after discharge. Isometsa et al. (1993) found that suicide was especially common in psychiatric patients in the first 28 days after discharge (four times higher than expected).

Johansson et al. (1996) found that ex-psychiatric patients had a high suicide rate, with 73 percent completing suicide within one year of discharge. Menezes and Mann (1996) found a high completed suicide rate in the two years after discharge for patients with nonaffective functional psychoses.

Hansen (1997) found a high suicide rate for first-admission patients in the first year after discharge.

(3) INPATIENT SUICIDE. Roy and Draper (1994, 1995) found that inpatient suicides had more prior attempts, were more often involuntary admissions, more often had schizophrenia, and more often lived alone than inpatient controls. They did not differ in alcohol/drug abuse, unemployment, or marital status.

Blain and Donaldson (1995) found that inpatient suicides were more often male, using violent methods (primarily hanging), with 54 percent away from the hospital, and one-third in the first week. The male suicides were younger than the female suicides (40 versus 58).

Read et al. (1993) found that psychiatric patients who completed suicide were more often compulsory admissions, schizophrenics, unmarried, and with prior attempts than those who did not complete suicide; they did not differ in physical health, substance abuse, the number of psychiatric admissions, time since last suicide attempt, or affective disorder.

Taiminen (1993) found that psychiatric inpatients who killed themselves were on lower doses of neuroleptics and more often on benzodiazepines than those not completing suicide; they did not differ in antidepressants, lithium, or antiparkinsonism drugs.

Batten and Kamara (1992) found that the institutional suicide rate in schizophrenics was double that for those with affective disorders among inmates committed for crimes for which they were judged to have diminished responsibility.

Ganesvara and Shah (1997) found that the inpatient completed suicide in Australia in 1973–1993 was 3.7 per 1,000 admissions. By year, the association of the suicide rate with the number of admissions was negative, but not with the population suicide rate.

De Leo (1997) found that modal inpatient suicide used jumping, between 6 a.m. and noon, was male, and had anxiety and insomnia.

Attempted Suicide

Hale et al. (1990) compared psychiatric patients who had attempted suicide with those who had not. The attempters had more mood disorders, schizophrenia, and Axis II diagnoses (especially borderline and passive-aggressive) and fewer adjustment disorders.

In a community survey, Petronis et al. (1990) found that 0.2 percent had attempted suicide in the previous year. These attempters were more often separated/divorced, abused alcohol and cocaine, had a major affective disorder, were less often employed, and less often had advanced education. They did not differ in sex, race, ethnicity, or the abuse of other drugs.

Hagen (1991) compared psychiatric patients who had attempted suicide in the previous year with those who had not. Those with recent suicide attempts were less often schizophrenic and more often diagnosed with anorexia, bulimia, personality disorder, and depressive neurosis. They were younger, more often married or divorced, less often living with a spouse, and more often had marriage and family problems. Attempted suicide rates peaked in men in their 30s and women in their 20s. Rates were highest in the divorced, then in the single, and lowest in the married/widowed.

Hamer et al. (1991) found that 54 percent of a sample of attempted suicides had a DSM-III psychiatric disorder.

In an psychiatric emergency room sample, Palsson et al. (1991) found that attempted suicides were more often female, abusers of alcohol and prescription medications, and suffering from acute stress reactions; other patients were more often diagnosed with affective disorders and had prior psychiatric of alcohol-abuse treatment.

Trautman et al. (1991) looked at a sample of adolescent minority females who had attempted suicide versus psychiatric controls. The attempters did not differ in diagnosis, anorexia, substance abuse, behavioral problems, or anger.

Modestin and Kamm (1990) compared patients attempting suicide in the hospital with those attempting suicide before admission and with nonsuicidal psychiatric controls. The attempts of the patients in the hospital had lower suicidal intent than the attempts made before hospitalization. Compared to nonsuicidal patients, the in-hospital attempters were younger, more frequently depressed, were from rural areas, fell ill at an earlier age, and had made more prior attempts. Compared to pre-hospital attempters, the in-hospital attempters were less well-adjusted vocationally, less often of foreign origin, more often psychotic, more seriously disturbed, and had experienced less stress in recent months.

Van Zyl (1988) found that adolescent attempted suicides more often had an adjustment disorder as compared to depressed nonsuicidal adolescents. They did not differ in family functioning.

Adams and Overholser (1992) studied patients at a psychiatric emergency unit. The attempters were younger, more often female, and had depressive disorders and abused drugs more often than the nonsuicidal patients. They did not differ in alcohol abuse.

Cremniter et al. (1992) found that attempted suicides seen in an emergency room more often had a personality or adjustment disorder, whereas those with suicidal ideation more often had an affective disorder (and more prior psychiatric hospitalizations). The attempters were also more often female and had made more prior attempts.

Lyness et al. (1992) found that elderly

psychiatric inpatients who had attempted suicide during their index episode did not differ in diagnosis or substance abuse from those who did not. They did have more of a suicidal history, but did not differ in sex, age, marital status, or living situation.

Nieto et al. (1992b) found that older suicide attempters (65 years and older) more often had an affective disorder, less often a personality disorder, made more serious attempts, more often had a physical illness, and were more often widowed than younger attempters. They did not differ in sex, prior attempts, or suicide in family members.

In Turkey, Sayil and Gogus (1992) found that psychiatric outpatients who had made suicidal attempts or threats had been diagnosed with depression and were currently depressed more often than those with only suicidal ideation or who were non-suicidal. They were also more often divorced and less often had a university education (but did not differ in sex, age, social class, profession, or religious belief).

In Switzerland, Angst et al. (1993) followed up a community sample of people born in 1959–1960. By age 30, 3.8 percent had attempted suicide. These attempters were more often unskilled, had more often run away and been truant from school, were less popular at school, and had more disciplinary problems at school; they came more often from broken homes, had parents with psychiatric problems and families with conflict and suicidal behavior, had lower self-esteem and more helplessness; and they were more likely to have depressive disorders, anxiety disorders, substance abuse disorders, and antisocial personality disorder.

Asnis et al. (1993) found that a history of suicidal ideation and attempts in psychiatric outpatients was more common in mood-disorder and substance-abuse patients than in anxiety-disorder patients.

Brent et al. (1993b) found that suicidal adolescents (attempters and ideators) were more often substance abusers than non-suicidal adolescent psychiatric patients. Those who attempted suicide in the next six months more often had an affective disorder, a major depressive disorder, prior attempts, deaths of a relative, and family financial problems.

Rifai et al. (1993) studied elderly psychiatric inpatients. Recent attempters more often had a mood disorder, abused alcohol, and had medical problems and less often had an organic mental disorder. They did not differ in EEG abnormalities or age at onset of depressive illness.

Botsis et al. (1994) found that psychiatric inpatients who had attempted suicides had shown more past violence and had lower coping-style scores than nonsuicidal psychiatric inpatients.

Asukai (1995) compared more-lethal and less-lethal suicide attempters. The more-lethal attempters were more often male and older, less often unemployed, and had fewer prior attempts. They more often had a depressive disorder and substance-abuse disorder and less often had a personality disorder. The two groups did not differ in prior psychiatric treatment (or marital status and living alone).

Hornig and McNally (1995) found that prior attempts at suicide were more common in all psychiatric disorders except panic disorder and somatization disorder. Comorbidity with panic disorder significantly significantly increased the risk of prior suicide attempts only in patients with agoraphobia.

Takahashi et al. (1995) found that psychiatric geriatric inpatients who were attempters more often had mood disorders, adjustment disorders, prior psychiatric illnesses and hospitalizations, somatization, and delirium. They had less dementia, were more often living alone, and had more often visited a GP in the prior two weeks.

Beautrais et al. (1996) compared attempted suicides with normals and found more psychiatric disorders in the attempters. These included mood disorders, alcohol abuse, drub abuse, anxiety disorders, eating disorders, antisocial personality disorder, and comorbidity, but not schizophrenia.

In Mexico, Borges and Rosovsky (1996) found that attempted suicides in the emergency room were more often female, over the age of 35, unemployed/housewives, divorced/widowed, habitual drug users, and intoxicated with alcohol than accident patients.

Liu et al. (1996) found that attempted suicide in psychiatric patients was more common in those with an affective disorder and least common in those with an affective disorder and least common in schizophrenics.

Nordstrom et al. (1996) found that attempted suicides admitted to a psychiatric ward scored high on somatic anxiety, psychic anxiety, and muscular tension and scored low on socialization. Those subsequently completing suicide had the highest scores on somatic anxiety and impulsivity and lowest scores on socialization.

Among psychiatric inpatients, Bai et al. (1997) found that schizophrenics more often had attempted suicide prior to admission, but the depressive disorder patients were more suicidal on admission than those with other diagnoses.

Among adolescent African Americans, Jones (1997) found that attempted suicides were more depressed, more often substance abusers, and had more externalizing and internalizing symptoms than other emergency room patients.

Attempted and Completed Suicide

Hanafy (1991) compared 30 completed

suicides from one region in Ireland with 20 attempted suicides from a neighboring region that had experienced no recent completed suicides. The completers had been hospitalized for a longer period during prior attempts, whereas the attempters more often had a family history of mental illness and suicide. The completers used drowning more, while the attempters used overdoses more. The groups did not differ in sex, age, marital status, education, religion, occupation, social class, or diagnosis.

Valente (1993) compared VA psychiatric patients who completed or attempted suicide. The completers were older, had more psychiatric symptoms, gave more suicidal messages, were lower in social class, had more prior psychiatric hospitalizations, and used more-lethal methods. They did not differ in alcohol abuse, loss, years in the armed service, parental deaths, family suicide, or violent behavior.

Hattori et al. (1995) found that psychiatric patients who completed suicide more often had depressive disorders, while those who attempted suicide more often had adjustment disorders. Both of these groups more often had schizophrenia, schizoaffective disorders, and depressive disorders than nonsuicidal patients.

Repeaters

Sakinofsky and Roberts (1990; Sakinofsky et al. 1990) studied attempted suicides and compared repeaters with nonrepeaters. The repeaters had more prior attempts, made attempts of less lethality, had a longer period of disturbance, had more problems, and were younger at their first attempt. The repeaters obtained higher scores for alienation and external hostility. The groups did not differ in age, sex, education, depression and suicidal intent scores, locus of control, or self-esteem. Similar differences were found between those attempters who had resolved their problems and those who had not in a three-month follow-up.

Bjerke et al. (1991) found that women had higher attempted suicide rates in one county of Norway, and the rates peaked in both sexes for those aged 25–29. The attempters were less educated, less often married, more often divorced or separated, and had migrated more than the general population. The repeaters abused alcohol and drugs more, committed more crimes and had more prior psychiatric contacts.

Ojehagen et al. (1991) found that repeaters were less often regularly employed, more often on disability pensions, more often had prior and current psychiatric treatment, and made more impulsive attempts; they did not differ in diagnosis, somatic illnesses or psychiatric problems, and suicidal behavior in their relatives.

Trull and Widiger (1991) found that a history of recurrent suicidal behavior in a sample of psychiatric patients was associated with low energy, low self-esteem, pessimism, and tearfulness.

Morton (1993) studied attempted suicides and found that a history of prior attempts was associated with having prior psychiatric treatment, a personality disorder (as opposed to major depressive disorders), and alcohol abuse, as well as age (the repeaters were older), social class, and unemployment.

Among Israeli attempted suicides, repeaters were more often characterized by mental illness, depression, and social conflicts (Sheiban, 1993).

In a sample of suicidal psychiatric patients, Rudd et al. (1996) found that the multiple attempters were more phobic and had higher scores for suicidal ideation, depression, impaired problem solving, hopelessness, and borderline and schizotypal traits.

Krarup et al. (1991) compared first-ever attempters with repeaters and found the first-evers to have had more parental loss, less unhappy childhoods, and less attempted suicide in families/friends. They did not differ in having a bad relationship with their parents.

Gupta et al. (1992) found that those who repeated suicide attempts more often had a psychiatric diagnosis and more often had a personality disorder than one-time attempters. The repeaters did not differ in the diagnosis of schizophrenia versus depressive disorder, sex, age, religion, marital status, education, or occupation. The rate of attempting was higher in depressive disorder patients than in schizophrenics.

Ojehagen et al. (1992) followed up self-poisoners. Those who repeated in the next year were more hopeless, less often regularly employed, had more prior attempts of less serious intent, and more often had been in psychiatric treatment.

Rygnestad et al. (1992) followed up attempted suicides and found that male repeaters were more often divorced/separated and substance abusers; the female repeaters were more often divorced/single, alcohol abusers, with legal problems, a history of victimization, and prior psychiatric treatment.

Van Aalst et al. (1992) found that attempters who later repeated were more often schizophrenic, younger, with prior attempts and a family history of suicide and not living at home. They did not differ in the severity of the injury.

Jorgensen et al. (1993) found that male repeaters were more often drug abusers, alcohol abusers, never married, living alone, educated, employed, and had been more often convicted of a crime. The female repeaters were more often victims of violence, living with a partner with no children or with children but no partner, and disabled or in a subordinate job.

Van Egmond et al. (1993) found that female suicide attempters who repeated in the following year had more prior attempts and ideation, more psychiatric treatment, higher depression scores, more life stress and sexual abuse, lower self-esteem, more excessive use of medicines and tranquilizers, and more recent losses through death.

Taylor et al. (1994) compared attempted suicides with prior attempts and those without. The repeaters had worse social dysfunction and lower somatic and depression scores on the GHQ, but did not differ in anxiety. The repeaters had more panic symptoms, more PTSD symptoms, a more extensive psychiatric history, and more often had been sexual abused. They did not differ in physical abuse, disrupted childhoods, substance abuse, or unemployment.

Van Heeringen (1994) found that repeated attempted suicides were more often female, living alone, divorced, and with a personality disorder (but did not differ in age, education, or unemployment). For divorced subjects, repetition was predicted by being male, over the age of 54, not living alone, no more than a secondary school education, an Axis I diagnosis, and not being employed.

Fridell et al. (1996) followed up attempters and found the repeaters were more often female and younger, more often had a personality disorder, a parent with psychiatric illness (especially the father), and a less-satisfying social network. They were less often married/cohabitating; they were more often employed/studying and had a worse social adjustment, more recent suicidal ideation, hopelessness, and anxiety; and they had more current problems and psychiatric symptoms.

Hjelmeland (1996) found that repeaters, more often than first-timers, were unmarried, unemployed, abusers of alcohol and drugs, victims of violence, sexually abused, with a criminal record and psychiatric problems, with suicidal friends/relatives, and had moved more often in the last year. Fewer variables predicted subsequent attempts. (Alcohol abuse was one such predictor.)

Suicidal Ideation

Hawley et al. (1991) found that emergency psychiatric patients with suicidal ideation more often had a personality disorder, alcohol dependence, a criminal record, and a record of prior self harm than nonsuicidal patients. They also were more manipulative, in greater distress, and more often male.

In a sample of mental health patients, Mechanic et al. (1991) found that suicidal ideation was associated strongly with depression; associated weakly with legal problems, deviant sexual behavior, drinking problems, and life events; and associated negatively with a general health index.

Zimmerman et al. (1995) found that medical outpatients with suicidal ideation more often had a psychiatric history than those without ideation (and were younger and more often divorced). They did not differ in physician visits in the prior year.

Callahan et al. (1996) found that suicidal ideation in primary care patients was found only in those with depression. Among the depressed patients, those with suicidal ideation did not differ from those without in any characteristic studied (including smoking, cognitive impairment, body weight, alcohol abuse, age, race, sex, and education).

Lambert and Bonner (1996) compared ideators with ideators who also threatened suicide and had been seen at a psychiatric emergency department. Those who also threatened suicide more often were substance abusers, had an antisocial personality disorder, and less often had a major depressive disorder. They were also more often homeless and with legal problems, and were less often married. The two groups did not differ in attempts during the next six months.

Lish et al. (1996) found that general medical outpatients who had suicidal ideation were more often found to have a psychiatric disorder, especially in a major depressive disorder, dysthymia, or panic disorder. In a multiple-regression analysis, suicidal ideation was associated with sex, race, major depressive disorder, panic disorder, drug abuse, PTSD, and generalized anxiety disorder.

Mireault and De Man (1996) found that suicidal ideation in an elderly sample was associated with health status, alcohol use, depression, social isolation, and satisfaction with social supports.

Olfson et al. (1996) found that recent suicidal ideation in primary care patients was associated with poor physical health, poor emotional health, marital distress, health-related work loss, major depressive disorders, general anxiety disorders, and drug abuse.

In a sample of Swedish elderly, Skoog et al. (1996) found that recent suicidal ideation in women was associated with having any diagnosis, particularly depressive, psychotic, and anxiety disorders; and with myocardial infarction, peptic ulcer, use of anxiolytics, and neuroleptics; but not with the use of antidepressants.

Szanto et al. (1996) compared elderly depressed patients with a wish to die versus a wish to attempt suicide. The suicidal patients had more prior suicidal ideation and more current suicidal ideation, but did not differ in hopelessness, depression, or prior attempts. In a multiple-regression analysis, the suicidal ideators differed from the non-ideators in depression and prior suicidal ideation, whereas the active and passive ideators differed only in prior suicidal ideation.

Clum and Weaver (1997) found that, in a sample of chronic, severe suicidal ideators in college, the severity of the ideation was associated with childhood attention deficit hyperactivity disorder and separation anxiety disorder; with major depression, PTSD; and with the number of diagnoses in adulthood.

In German elderly over the age of 70, Linden and Barnow (1997) found that 22 percent wished to die. The more suicidal were more depressed and more often had a psychiatric disorder. However, of those with suicidal intent, at least six patients had no psychiatric disorder and no high scores on scales to measure pathology.

Suicidality

Cohen et al. (1997) found that, among adolescent psychiatric inpatients, Americans were more depressed and had more prior suicidality (attempts and ideation) than Israelis.

Milling et al. (1992) found no association between diagnosis and suicidality in hospitalized preadolescent children.

Bronisch and Whittchen (1994) found in a sample of Germans that attempted suicide and suicidal ideation were more common in those with major depressions, panic attacks and drug abuse, and were most common in those with major depressions plus panic attacks or drug abuse.

Zisook et al. (1994) found that current suicidal ideation was more common in psychiatric outpatients with major depressions or borderline personality disorder, while a lifetime history of attempted suicide was more common in borderline personality disorder patients. Borderline personality as a comorbid condition increased the incidence of suicidality.

King et al. (1995b) followed up adolescent psychiatric inpatients and found that subsequent suicidality was predicted by greater suicidality at hospitalization, a diagnosis of dysthymia, and more family dysfunction (but not by prior attempts or depression scores).

Ahrens and Linden (1996) found that depression, apathy, and low levels of mania predicted suicidality in schizophrenic, schizoaffective, unipolar, and bipolar psychiatric admissions.

In Pakistan, Javed (1996) found that suicidal ideation and attempts in depressed patients were predicted by depression scores, age, sex, and the duration of the mental illness.

Kaplan and Harrow (1996; Kaplan et al., 1996) found that positive symptoms of psychosis (such as hallucinations and delusions) predicted subsequent suicidality for schizophrenics and schizoaffective patients, whereas deficit symptoms (such as psychomotor retardation and concreteness) predicted subsequent suicidality in depressive disorder patients. Post-hospital functioning predicted subsequent suicidality for all patients.

Among patients seen in the emergency room with chest pains, Fleet et al. (1997) found that the presence of current suicidal ideation was associated with a diagnosis of panic disorder, general anxiety disorder, dysthymia, and major depressive disorder (but not with the presence of coronary artery disease).

Florio et al. (1997) found that the presence of suicidal ideation in elderly people referred to a community mental health center was associated with living alone, depressive disorders, anxiety disorders, emotional disturbance, medical problems, family conflict, and relationship loss. Forsell et al. (1997) found that suicidal ideation in the elderly in the community was associated with being female, single, and institutionalized, as well as with physical disability, vision problems, hearing problems, major depression, generalized anxiety syndrome, dementia, and a history of psychiatric disorder.

The Effect of Age

In Ireland, Foster et al. (1997) found that elderly suicides were less often unemployed and more often had an Axis I disorder (unipolar depression, comorbidity, and prior psychiatric contact). Female suicides had more comorbidity than males suicides.

Isometsa et al. (1995) found that young adults in a Finnish sample of suicides were more likely to have psychoses and less likely to have alcoholism than middle-aged suicides, but did not differ in depressive disorders or personality disorders.

Knauer et al. (1993) found that psychiatric patients under the age of 60 who committed suicide were more often schizophrenic and committed suicide while AWOL. Those over the age of 60 more often had affective disorders and committed suicide while on the ward (during the night).

Asgard (1990) looked at female suicides in Stockholm and found that those under the age of 30 more often had adjustment disorders, while those over the age of 30 more often had depressive disorders. Those under the age of 60 were more likely to have attempted suicide previously.

Carney et al. (1994) compared suicides aged 16–30, 31–59, and 60–88. The elderly suicides were more often married or widowed and living alone, and had fewer prior suicide attempts, less talk of suicide, less substance abuse, and more adjustment disorders and depressed mood.

Lonnqvist et al. (1995) found that elderly suicides in Finland more often had depressive disorders, while younger suicides more often had alcohol abuse disorders; adolescents more often had depressive disorders and adjustment disorders than adults. Females had more depressive disorders than males, and elderly males had more comorbidity than elderly females.

Conwell et al. (1996) found that elderly suicides were more likely to have a mood disorder and less likely to have an alcohol abuse disorder. Diagnosis also varied by sex.

In a study of female attempted suicides among psychiatric inpatients in Budapest, Frater et al. (1991) found that those under the age of 60 were mainly addicted or had personality disorders, while those over the age of 60 had organic syndromes. The older women had worse depression, and more physical and psychosocial burdens, but they less often had conflict as a stressor.

Frierson (1991) found that, in elderly suicide attempters over the age of 60, the use of firearms declined with age, while overdoses increased. The use of alcohol in the attempt and having a psychiatric history declined with age, while a history of attempted suicide increased with age.

Trachtenberg et al. (1993) found that elderly suicidal psychiatric patients (attempters and ideators) more often had a depressive disorder and a psychiatric history, whereas younger patients more often had a personality disorder. The two groups did not differ in precipitants or whether living alone.

In elderly psychiatric inpatients, Schmid et al. (1994) found that attempters differed from ideators in being older, more often Protestant and more often living alone (versus in a nursing home). They did not differ in sex, marital status, children, physical illness, diagnosis, prior hospitalization, alcohol abuse, or stressors.

In Singapore, Ko et al. (1997) found that adult and elderly psychiatric inpatients did not differ in prior attempted suicide, but the elderly patients had less suicidal ideation.

Psychotics

Milch (1990) studied hospitalized patients who attempted or completed suicide in the hospital. The psychotics made more serious suicidal acts, with more deaths and fewer gestures. Compared to nonsuicidal patients, the attempters were more hopeless and abused medications more, whereas the completers did not differ from the controls. The completers showed more tension, agitation, and withdrawal than the attempters. During hospitalization, the attempters improved while the completers worsened.

Westermeyer et al. (1991) followed up psychotics (who had a higher incidence of suicide than patients with other diagnoses). The psychotics who later completed suicide were more often white, single, male, with higher intelligence test scores, a gradual onset of the psychosis, and lower prehospital competence and drug abuse than those who did not complete suicide. They did not differ in depression.

Jorgensen and Mortensen (1992) found a higher-than-expected suicide rate among patients with reactive psychoses.

Cohen et al. (1994) found that psychotics who had previously attempted suicide had been more physically violent and depressed than those who had not attempted suicide, hallucinated more, and more often had an affective disorder (but not substance abuse or schizophrenia).

Isometsa et al. (1994a) compared completed suicides with major depressive disorders who were psychotic and nonpsychotic. The psychotics used more violent methods, but they did not differ demographically, in other diagnoses, clinical history, or making suicidal communications.

Affective Disorders

Completed Suicide

Fawcett et al. (1990) followed up major affective disorder patients for ten years. Those completing suicide in the first year of follow-up more often had abused alcohol and had anhedonia, psychic anxiety, insomnia, obsessions and compulsions, indecisiveness, and diminished concentration. Those completing suicide after the first year were more hopeless and indecisive; they had more suicidal ideation, prior suicidal attempts, and diminished concentration. No differences were found for the subtype of major affective disorder. In a later review of his study, Fawcett (1993) found that completed suicide in the first year of patients with a major affective disorder was predicted by anhedonia, anxiety, panic attacks, alcohol abuse, insomnia, and diminished concentration. Completed suicide in years two–ten was predicted by hopelessness, suicidal ideation at intake, and prior suicide attempts.

Young et al. (1992) followed up depressed patients. Those completing suicide were more hopeless, had no child under the age of 18 in the house, more often abused drugs/alcohol, and more often cycled between depression and mania. Hopelessness increased the suicidal risk in substance nonabusers but decreased the risk in abusers.

Andrew et al. (1993) followed up severely depressed female psychiatric inpatients after nine months. Poorer outcome was associated with lower self-esteem and suicidal ideation (but not with endogenicity or depression score).

Bradvik and Berglund (1993) found that male depressive disorder patients who completed suicide differed in marital status, social class, diagnosis, prior suicide attempts,

life stress, experience of parent separation/loss, psychosis in their families, and brittle/sensitive personality. Female suicides differed in being less often married, with more prior attempts, less disharmonious childhoods, and less nonfatal illness. Among the female suicides, those with prior attempts had less psychomotor retardation and more acute onset of the disorder.

Buchholtz-Hansen et al. (1993) found a slightly higher suicide rate than expected in endogenous depressives, especially three–four years after release, and found a much higher suicide rate than expected in nonendogenous depressives, especially in the first year after release.

Roy (1993a) found that anxiety levels did not predict subsequent completed suicide in patients with a major depressive disorder.

Isometsa et al. (1994b) studied suicides with major depressive disorders. Those who had not received medical or psychiatric care were more often substance abusers; those with past psychiatric care were more often female, had anxiety disorders, were taking antidepressants, had attempted suicide in the past, and had made more suicidal communications to professionals.

Young et al. (1994) found that affective disorder patients were more likely to complete suicide in the next five years if, at intake, they were hopeless without substance abuse or, if they were substance abusers, without hopelessness.

In a follow-up study, Nordstrom et al. (1995) found that prior attempts predicted subsequent completed suicide, in all subtypes of depressives, in men and women, and in all ages.

O'Leary (1996) found no differences in completed suicide between endogenous and neurotic depressives.

Blair-West et al. (1997) used data from the Catchment Area Survey to estimate that 70 percent of suicides could be attributed to major depressive disorders.

Nonfatal Suicidality

Brent et al. (1990) compared suicidal and nonsuicidal adolescent inpatients with affective disorders and found that the suicidal patients had an earlier onset, longer duration of the disorder, and higher levels of depression, but not higher levels of hopelessness. The suicidal patients also had more cognitive distortions, less assertiveness, more family suicidality, and more life stressors.

Myers et al. (1991a, 1991b) found that suicidality in adolescent psychiatric patients was associated with depression, hopelessness, self-esteem, conduct problems, life stress, and mother's psychopathology, but not associated with locus of control, separation anxiety, or father's psychopathology. For those with major depressive disorder, depression and conduct problems were the strongest correlates. Over time, the predictors of later suicide in the adolescents with a major depressive disorder were age, anger, and severity of suicidality at intake.

Hori et al. (1993) found that patients with major depressive disorders who were also delusional more often had a history of suicidal ideation and attempts and had made more violent attempts than those without delusions.

In child psychiatric outpatients, Kovacs et al. (1993) found that depression and suicidality were associated. A major depressive disorder increased the risk of suicidality, and a major depressive disorder plus substance abuse/conduct disorder increased the risk even more.

Sarchiapone et al. (1994) found that suicidal ideation and psychomotor activity were positively associated in psychiatric patients with mood disorders.

Cornelius et al. (1995) found that patients with a major depressive disorder plus alcoholism had engaged in more suicidal behavior in the past and had lower self-esteem, more impulsivity, and more functional impairment than patients with only one of these two disorders.

Among depressive adolescent psychiatric inpatients, King et al. (1995a) found that comorbid substance abuse was not related to the severity of the depression or suicidal ideation.

Lepine and Lellouch (1995) found that major depressive disorders plus social phobia were associated with greater suicidality in community men than major depressive disorders alone, but there was no difference for women.

Wallace and Pfohl (1995) found that current suicidal ideation (and depression scores) decreased with age in a sample of psychiatric inpatients.

In a community sample, Hanna and Grant (1997) found that prior suicidality was more common in those with a major depressive disorder plus an alcohol use disorder than in those with only a major depressive disorder.

Attempted Suicide

Papadimitriou et al. (1991) studied suicide attempters with affective disorders. Those using violent methods had more relatives who had completed suicide (especially on the maternal side), whereas those using nonviolent methods had more relatives who completed suicide on the paternal side.

Cole and Casey (1992) found that patients with major depressive disorder who had recently attempted suicide had more acting-out hostility and better social functioning, but did not differ in depression, hopelessness, social supports, suicidal behavior in family and friends, or direction of hostility.

Vieta et al. (1992) compared attempted suicides with affective disorders to those with other diagnoses. The affective disorder attempters were older, more often female, used nonviolent methods, made more serious attempts, and had more physical illness. They did not differ in prior attempts or suicidal behavior in their families.

Cassano et al. (1993) found that 6 percent of psychiatric patients with a single episode of major depressive disorder had attempted suicide. Attempts were more common in those with early onset (younger than 45 years of age). The type of depressive disorder was not associated with the presence of prior attempts (depressive versus hyperthymic versus neither).

Zweig and Hinrichsen (1993) followed up patients with major depressive disorders and found that subsequent attempted suicide was predicted by higher social class, more prior suicidality, and less remission (but not sex, age, marital status, physical health, or depression scores).

Mullick et al. (1994) found that suicide attempters with major depressive disorders had made more prior attempts and had higher suicidal intent than other attempters.

Rifai et al. (1994) found that prior suicide attempts in elderly patients with depressive disorders were associated with hopelessness but not depression scores.

Ahrens et al. (1995) found that affective disorder patients who had previously attempted suicide had an earlier onset of the disorder but did not differ in the duration of the illness or the number of episodes. The rate of attempting suicide was steady during the course of the illness, but was associated with the rate of episodes.

Angst (1995) found that attempting suicide was more common in dysthymics and those with major depression plus dysthymia or brief recurrent depressions.

Malone et al. (1995) compared patients with major depressive disorders who had or had not attempted suicide. The attempters

were younger at the time of their first hospitalization, had more prior hospitalizations, more often had a borderline personality disorder, and were more suicidal when hospitalized. They had more alcohol and drug abuse, more impulsivity and aggression, and more loss of parents; but they did not differ in depression, anxiety, hopelessness, or the number of depressive episodes.

Corbitt et al. (1996) found that a history of repeated attempted suicide was more common in major depressives with comorbid borderline personality disorder than in those without. The former group did not differ in the lethality of their attempts, but made their first attempt at a younger age, had more suicidal ideation, and were more depressed. Borderline and cluster B symptoms predicted prior attempted suicide better than depressive symptoms.

Derecho et al. (1996) found no differences in prior attempted suicide in psychiatric inpatients with atypical versus nonatypical depressions.

Spalletta et al. (1996) found that, among young male psychiatric inpatients, those with major depressive disorders had the highest frequency of prior attempted suicide, followed by dysthymics, and the lowest frequency in those with adjustment disorder with depressed mood. The first two groups had more depression and suicidal ideation than the latter group.

Brodaty et al. (1997) found that all subtypes of depressive patients had a higher-than-expected completed suicide rate subsequently (endogenous, neurotic, and other types).

Attempted/Completed Suicide

Lee et al. (1992) found that subsequent attempted/completed suicide in depressives was predicted by severe dysphoria, psychomotor retardation, previous brain injury, loss through separation, past alcoholism, significant chronic medical illness, and prior attempted suicide (but not by sex, social class, age at onset, previous depression, loss through death, personality disorder, Eysenck Personality Inventory scores, or Leighton Obsessional Inventory scores).

Unipolar Affective Disorder

Winokur and Coryell (1992) found that unipolar depressives who had a family history of alcoholism made more suicide attempts than those with a family history of depression.

Rhode et al. (1991) found more severe suicidal ideation and prior attempts in unipolar adolescent patients who had comorbid disorders.

Brodaty et al. (1993) followed up patients with unipolar depressive disorders and found more completed suicides among the older patients (60 and older) than among the younger patients.

Whisman et al. (1995) found that unipolar patients with high hopelessness had more suicidal ideation than those with low hopelessness. They also had more social and cognitive dysfunction.

Isometsa et al. (1996a) found that completed suicides with unipolar and "other" depressive disorders did not differ in prior attempts at suicide.

Bipolar Affective Disorder

Roy (1993b) found that depressed patients who had attempted suicide were more often bipolar, had their first depression at an earlier age, had more episodes of depression, and were more angry on self-report inventory than nonattempters. They did not differ in depression scores. Those making violent attempts more often had a family history of suicide.

Rihmer et al. (1990) found that half of a sample of suicides had a major affective disorder: 53 percent nonbipolar, 46 bipolar type II, and only a single bipolar type I.

Conti et al. (1980) found that attempted suicides diagnosed with bipolar affective disorder had higher suicidal intent than those who had experienced depressive episodes or than the remaining attempters.

Newman and Bland (1991) found that the standard mortality ratios for completed suicide were highest in patients with major depressive disorders, then bipolar disorders, and lowest in manic disorders.

In a follow-up study of patients treated with lithium, Vestergaard and Aagaard (1991) found that the suicides were all bipolars or of uncertain polarity, younger, and more socially isolated than the survivors.

Wu and Dunner (1993) found no differences in prior attempted suicide between rapid cycling (four–ten episodes per year) and other bipolar patients.

Dilsaver et al. (1994, 1997) found that patients with mania plus depression or depressive mania were more suicidal than patients with pure mania. Among the bipolar patients, psychotics and nonpsychotics did not differ in suicidality.

Sharma and Markar (1994) found that bipolar patients had a higher mortality from suicide than the general population. The bipolars who completed suicide differed from those who did not in being younger at admission, having more admissions, staying longer, being prescribed lithium less often, and more often being unmarried. They did not differ in sex, social class, or living alone.

Angst et al. (1996) found that patients with a major depressive disorder had a higher subsequent completed suicide rate than bipolar patients.

Feinman and Dunner (1996) found that

prior attempts were more common in bipolar patients who were also substance abusers than in those who were not.

Strakowski et al. (1996) found that mixed bipolars had more suicidal ideation than manic bipolars (and were more depressed), but controls for the level of depression eliminated this difference.

Unipolar and Bipolar Disorders

In a meta-analysis of research, Lester (1993c) found an excess of subsequent completed suicide in unipolars and attempted suicide in bipolars. There were no differences in prior attempts.

Chen and Dilsaver (1996) found that bipolars had attempted and thought about suicide more in the past than unipolars. Chen and Dilsaver (1996) found that bipolars had a higher lifetime incidence of attempted suicide than unipolars who had, in turn, a higher incidence than those with other Axis I disorders, even after controls for sex, race, age, social class, marital status, and panic disorder.

Angst and Preisig (1995) followed up unipolars and bipolars and found 17 percent of their deaths in the next 27 years to be from suicide. The suicides were more severely ill since onset, and the unipolars had more episodes per year, but diagnosis did not predict a suicidal outcome.

Stephens and McHugh (1991) followed up affective disorder patients. Unipolars were more likely to complete suicide than bipolars, but did not differ in prior suicide attempts. The depressed patients had more suicidal ideation in the hospital than the manic patients. Those with prior attempts showed less improvement.

Fritze et al. (1992) found that affective disorder patients who had attempted suicide were more often bipolars and schizo-affective, and less often unipolars, than those

completing suicide.

Brief Recurrent Depression

Montgomery et al. (1990) followed 30 suicide attempters for six months and found that they had 87 episodes of brief depression. The median length was three days and the mean severity high. On average, the episodes were 18 days apart.

Maier et al. (1994) found that the presence of a brief recurrent depression did not increase the likelihood of prior suicide attempts unless combined with major depressive episodes. Altamura et al. (1995) found that 9 percent of patients with brief recurrent depression had previously attempted suicide.

Merikangas et al. (1994) found that subsequent attempted suicide was more common in patients with both a brief recurrent depression and a major depressive disorder than in patients with either diagnosis alone.

Weiller et al. (1994a, 1994b) found that a history of attempted suicide was equally common in those with brief recurrent depressions (if at least monthly) and those with major depressive episodes, and more common in these patients than in those with other diagnoses.

Recurrent Major Depression

Bulik et al. (1990) compared patients with recurrent major depression who had attempted suicide with those who had not. The attempters were younger, more often separated or divorced, had higher depression-scale scores, and a more agitated and incapacitating depression (but did not differ in psychotic or endogenous depressions); they more often had a bipolar affective disorder and alcoholism, and were more disturbed on most scales of the SADS and SCL-90. They did not differ in sex, education, or the number of previous episodes of depression.

Seasonal Mood Disorder

Allen et al. (1993) matched seasonal with nonseasonal mood disorder patients for age, sex, and diagnostic subtype. The seasonal patients had less suicidal ideation. Thalen et al. (1995) also found that seasonal depressed patients had less suicidal ideation and depression scores than nonseasonal depressed patients.

Dysthymia

Shain et al. (1990) studied a sample of adolescent inpatients with a major depressive disorder. Those who had previously had dysthymia had a history of more suicidal ideation and suicide attempts.

Paranoia

Wolfersdorf et al. (1990) compared depressed inpatients with and without paranoid delusions. In one sample, the currently suicidal patients were less paranoid, but in another sample there were no differences. In a sample of unipolar patients, the delusional patients were more suicidal during treatment, but not at admission.

Hopelessness

Beck et al. (1990) followed up a sample of psychiatric outpatients and found that those who subsequently completed suicide had scored higher on tests of depression and hopelessness. Beck et al. (1993a) found that mood disorder, depression scores, and hopelessness scores were associated with current suicidal ideation in psychiatric outpatients.

Beck et al. (1993b) found that suicidal ideators more often had mood disorders, personality disorders, and prior suicide attempts; had lower self-concept; and had higher depression and hopelessness scores. For those suicidal ideators with a mood disorder, four scales of dysfunctional attitudes (out of nine) differentiated them (perfectionism, vulnerability, disapproval, and impressing others).

Bonner and Rich (1990) found that suicidal ideation in male prisoners was associated positively with depression, hopelessness, loneliness, and jail stress and associated negatively with reasons for living and irrational beliefs. In a multiple regression, however, the roles of depression and hopelessness were no longer statistically significant.

Chiles et al. (1990) compared suicide attempters and ideators in China and the United States. They did not differ in depression, but the American patients had become suicidal at an earlier age, had made more prior attempts, and had communicated their suicidal intent more. The American attempters more often saw suicide as an effective solution and expressed less social disapproval for suicide. For the Chinese patients, suicidal intent was associated more strongly with depression scores, whereas for the American patients suicidal intent was associated more strongly with hopelessness scores.

Range and Antonelli (1990) found that depression and hopelessness were associated with measures of suicidality in a sample of college students. Rudd (1990) found that suicidal ideation in college students was associated with depression, hopelessness, and social support (from family and friends), but with not recent stressors. Connell and Meyer (1991) found that suicidality in college students was associated with hopelessness and depression scores, as well as with state and trait anxiety and social desirability scores.

Salter and Platt (1990) found that suicidal intent in a sample of attempters was associated with depression and hopelessness scores, but the size of the associations was affected both by the time before the interview and scores on a test of social desirability.

Ivanoff and Jang (1991) found that hopelessness was associated with current suicidal ideation in prisoners who had previously attempted suicide, while hopelessness and depression were associated with current suicidal ideation in prisoners not previously suicidal. In addition to depression and hopelessness, current suicidal ideation was associated in a multiple regression with prior delinquency, commission of violent crimes, and education; it was not associated with life events, length of sentence, income, age, visitors, or social-desirability scores.

Dixon et al. (1992) found that hopelessness (as well as sex, stressors, and hassles) were correlated with suicidal ideation in college students, but hopelessness was the strongest correlate.

In a sample of juvenile delinquents, Kempton and Forehand (1992) found that attempting suicide was associated with depression (for whites only), but not associated with hopelessness, substance abuse, conduct disorder, age, length of incarceration, grade, or reading level.

MacLeod et al. (1993) found that attempted suicides were more generally hopeless than medical patients, especially for expectations of future positive events. They did not differ in expectations of future negative events or general cognitive processing.

Pillay and Wassenaar (1993) found that Indian adolescent suicide attempters in South Africa were more hopeless and depressed than normal controls and had more psychiatric symptoms.

Steiner et al. (1993) found that hopelessness scores did not predict subsequent completed or attempted suicide or suicidal ideation in depressed psychiatric inpatients.

Sociological Studies

Rihmer et al. (1993) found that the suicide rate of the regions of Hungary was positively associated with the rate of diagnosed depression and negatively associated with the prevalence of physicians. They suggested that these results indicated that treatment of depression reduces the suicide rate.

Schizophrenia

Suicidal Ideation

Shuwall and Siris (1994) found that suicidal ideation in schizophrenic inpatients was associated with psychosis, blue mood, somatic anxiety, hallucinations, and phobias.

Meltzer and Okayli (1995) found no differences in the number of prior suicidal episodes in schizophrenics who were neuroleptic resistant and those who were neuroleptic responsive.

Attempted Suicide

Bandelow et al. (1990) found that the current level of depression in schizophrenics was not associated with a history of attempted suicide.

Clerici et al. (1990) interviewed the families of schizophrenics who had attempted suicide and those who had not. The families of the suicide attempters had lower scores for expressed emotion, but not for the other six scales measuring warmth, hostility, criticism, overinvolvement, and positive remarks.

Dassori et al. (1990) compared schizophrenics who had a history of suicidal ideation or attempts with nonsuicidal schizophrenics. The suicidal patients were younger, had been disturbed for less time, showed a worsening trend, had more symptoms (including depression, substance abuse, hypoactivity, and aggression), had less social support, more often had a personality disorder and physical illness, and less often were unemployed or had poor work performance. The groups did not differ in race, sex, religion, marital status, psychiatric disorder in their families, multiple diagnoses, or recent stressors.

Gotze and Orlwoski-Studemann (1990) compared schizophrenic inpatients who had been suicidal (ideation or attempts) with nonsuicidal schizophrenic inpatients. The most important "significant other" for suicidal patients was a parent and for nonsuicidal patients was their partner. The suicidal schizophrenics showed more paranoia, inhibition of aggression, and internal tension. The two groups did not differ in age, sex, coming from a broken home, social class, career decline, length of illness, age at onset, suicide in family and friends, or alcohol and drug abuse.

In a comparison of suicidal and self-injuring psychiatric inpatients, Roy et al. (1990b) found that schizophrenics were overrepresented in both groups. The schizophrenics in the suicidal group made more severe attempts.

Addington and Addington (1992) found that prior suicide attempts and current suicidal ideation in schizophrenics were associated with depression and having a depressive disorder. Prior suicide attempts (but not current suicidal ideation) were associated with being female, less education, and early parental loss. Suicidality was not associated with intelligence test scores.

Bartels et al. (1992) found that alcohol use was associated with suicide attempts and

ideation in both urban and rural schizophrenics, but after controls for depression, the association was nonsignificant.

Nieto et al. (1992a) found that schizophrenic attempters were older, more often single, used more violent methods, attempted more often in the hospital, had less physical illness, and more of a psychiatric history than other attempters; they did not differ in sex, prior attempts, or suicidal behavior in family members. Among the schizophrenic attempters, those with delusions and hallucinations used more violent methods.

Jones et al. (1994) compared schizophrenics who had previously attempted suicide and those who had not. The suicide attempters more often had a major depression, current suicidal ideation, and higher depression and hopelessness scores. They did not differ in positive or negative symptoms.

Gallagher et al. (1995) found that schizophrenics with hallucinations were more likely to have attempted suicide in the past (especially males) and more likely to in the future than schizophrenics without hallucinations, and they were more hopeless.

Amador et al. (1996) found that schizophrenics who had attempted or thought about suicide had more awareness of their negative symptoms (such as delusions, blunter affect, anhedonia, and asociality, but not hallucinations or thought disorder) than nonsuicidal schizophrenics, indicating that greater insight and suicidality are associated in schizophrenics.

Krausz et al. (1996) found that schizophrenics who abused two or more psychotropic substances had attempted suicide more than those who did not abuse these substances.

Lindstrom et al. (1997) found that voluntary and involuntary schizophrenic patients did not differ in prior suicide attempts.

Sullivan et al. (1997) found that schizophrenics who had attempted or threatened suicide were more likely to be readmitted in the following two years than those who had not.

Completed Suicide

Cheng et al. (1990) compared schizophrenics who completed suicide with those who did not and found that the suicides had more prior admissions, suicidality (attempts and ideation), violence, and major depressions. They did not differ in age at onset or duration of the schizophrenia. Lim and Tsoi (1991) reported a suicide rate of 567 in a 15-year follow-up study of schizophrenics in Singapore. The suicides were younger and had fewer delusions than those still alive, but did not differ in sex, race, marital status, prior suicide attempts, hallucinations, or depression.

Cohen et al. (1990) followed up schizophrenics for eight years and compared the suicides with those who survived. The suicides had been younger at their first psychiatric contact and at intake were more hopeless, hostile, depressed, paranoid, and obsessive-compulsive on the self-report SCL. They did not differ in life satisfaction or ratings of symptoms.

Mortensen and Juel (1990) followed up over 6,000 schizophrenics for 29 years and found a higher suicide rate than expected – the SMR was 1.32. Mortensen and Juel (1993) reported significantly higher SMRs for male and female schizophrenics after release, especially in the first year of follow-up.

Test et al. (1990) found that schizophrenics who completed suicide were younger at their first mental health contact and had more distress on five of eight scales of a symptom inventory.

Hu et al. (1991) found that schizophrenics who completed suicide were more often middle/upper class and unemployed; less often married; and had more psychotic symptoms, depression (past and present), and psychiatric admissions. They did not differ in sex, age at onset, ethnicity, religion, education, living alone, or having suicides in the family.

Harrow et al. (1992) followed up schizophrenics and found that completed suicide was more likely in those who were paranoid, in the first year of hospitalization, and in chronic patients, men, whites, and substance abusers.

Modestin et al. (1992) found that schizophrenics who completed suicide were less often foreign born, but more often of lower social class, with early vocational difficulties, chronic disability, early onset, long duration, prior suicide attempts, in-hospital suicidality, and placement under tutelage. Thus, they had early problems, a more severe illness, and more suicidality.

Havak-Kontaxaki et al. (1994) compared schizophrenic suicides in the hospital with living schizophrenic inpatients. The suicides had a longer illness, more prior suicide attempts (especially by violent methods), more prior depressive illness, more prior homicides, were admitted more often for suicidal behavior, and had more alcohol abuse in their families. They did not differ in hallucinations, delusions, subtype of schizophrenia, number of admissions, physical health, sex, age, unemployment, or marital status.

Hoffman (1994) found that suicide risk in schizophrenics was associated with their prior rate of hospitalization, but not their rate of hospitalization in the subsequent two years.

Taiminen and Kujari (1994) found that schizophrenic inpatients who committed suicide had more prior attempts, lower doses of neuroleptics, more depressive symptoms, and fewer positive schizophrenic symptoms.

Stefenson and Cullberg (1995) reported on seven schizophrenics who completed suicide. All were chronically ill, and most were in remission. Their premorbid functioning was good, and they had a sense of losing their former self. They had feelings of being hopelessly handicapped and had experienced negative life events.

Zisook et al. (1995) found that subsequent completed suicide (or prior attempted suicide) was not predicted by the presence of command hallucinations in schizophrenics. Fenton et al. (1997) followed up schizophrenics for 19 years and found that the completed suicides had fewer negative symptoms (especially blunted affect and social withdrawal) and more positive symptoms (especially delusions and suspiciousness). Those who attempted suicide or who had suicidal ideation did not differ from the living controls. The completed suicide risk was highest in the paranoids and lowest in the deficit subtype.

Peuskens et al. (1997) found that schizophrenics who completed suicide were typically male, in the hospital or in the first month after discharge, nonparanoid or schizoaffective, and 28 years old. Compared to living controls, the suicides more often had attempted suicide, a family history of suicide, and experience of family loss; they were more often psychotic and acting-out; they had more admissions, but less duration of illness; they were more depressed; had higher intelligence test scores; and were more often AWOL from the hospital and noncompliant.

Brown (1997) conducted a meta-analysis of research and found an excess of mortality in schizophrenics for suicide (and for all natural causes too). In a meta-analysis of follow-up studies of schizophrenia, Lester (1993d) found that the percentage of suicides was negatively associated with the sample size, but not associated with the length of follow-up.

For a good review of suicide in schizophrenia, see Caldwell and Gottesman (1990).

Sociological Studies

Lester (1993e) found no association between the rates of suicide and schizophrenia over the states of the United States.

Somatization Disorders

Tomasson et al. (1991) found that somatization disorder patients were more likely to have attempted suicide than conversion disorder patients. They also were more likely to have a history of major depression, panic disorder, and substance abuse. Morrison (1989) found more prior attempted suicide in female somatization patients than in primary affective disorder patients.

Anxiety Disorders

Allgulander and Lavori (1991) found an excess of completed suicides over expectations in both men and women patients with pure anxiety neurosis. Allgulander (1994) found excess suicide mortality in patients with anxiety disorders and with depressive disorders.

Post-Traumatic Stress Disorder

Warshaw et al. (1993) found that a history of attempted suicide was more common in anxiety disorder patients with post-traumatic stress disorder than in those with trauma but no PTSD or in other patients.

Bullman and Kang (1994) found that Vietnam veterans had a higher suicide rate than other American men and that those with PTSD had a higher suicide rate than those without. If they also had a comorbid disorder, the suicide rate was even higher.

Kramer et al. (1994) found that Vietnam veterans who had treatment for PTSD were more likely to have had suicidal ideation than those who had not undergone treatment. Suicidal ideation and attempts were more likely only in veterans with both depression and PTSD. Scores on a PTSD scale were positively associated with prior suicidal ideation and attempts in the total sample of Vietnam veterans.

Freeman et al. (1995) found that, among patients with PTSD, those with prior suicide attempts had a higher dissociation experience score, and showed more animal cruelty in the past. They did not differ in gun ownership, alcohol/drug abuse, or combat exposure.

Giaconia et al. (1995) found that attempted suicide and suicidal ideation were more common in those with PTSD than in those with trauma but no PTSD and those with no trauma.

In a sample of methadone maintenance patients, Villagomez et al. (1995) found that lifetime PTSD was associated with past suicidal ideation and attempts and with major depressive disorders.

In a sample of adolescent psychiatric outpatients who had attempted suicide, Rathus et al. (1995) found that those with a current diagnosis of PTSD had more suicidal intent.

Obsessive-Compulsive Disorder

Degonda et al. (1993) found that obsessive-compulsive disorder was not associated with lifetime history of attempted suicide in a Swiss cohort of young adults.

In a community sample, Nestadlt et al. (1994) found that obsessive/compulsives had more suicidal behavior (and alcoholism) in

their relatives.

Chen and Dilsaver (1995) studied unipolar and bipolar patients and those with other Axis I diagnoses. Those with obsessive-compulsive disorder had higher rates of lifetime attempted suicide and rates of suicidal ideation than those without the disorder. The groups did not differ in substance abuse.

Panic Disorder

Arnold et al. (1995) reviewed research and found that estimates of the prevalence of suicide attempts in panic disorder patients range from zero percent to 57 percent.

In a community sample, Johnson et al. (1990) found that the lifetime incidence of attempted suicide was 26 percent in those with panic disorder plus other disorders, 7 percent in those with only panic disorder, and 1 percent in those with no disorder. The lifetime incidence of attempted suicide was higher in those with major depressive disorder plus other disorders (including those with major depressive disorder plus panic disorder) than in those with only major depressive disorder (20 percent versus 8 percent).

Lepine et al. (1990) studied a sample of patients with panic disorder. Sixty percent had considered suicide, and 42 percent attempted suicide. The majority of suicide attempts occurred after the first panic attack. The attempters were more often female, unmarried, with a major depressive disorder, with alcohol or drug abuse, and had their first panic attack in the spring or summer. They did not differ in age.

Lepine et al. (1991, 1993) next compared panic-attack patients who had previously attempted suicide to those who had not. They did not differ in age at referral or age at first attack. There were more suicide attempts after the first attack than before.

The attempters were more depressed and abused drugs/alcohol more. They also had more attacks in the spring and summer. The attempters had a longer duration of panic disorder, more alcohol/substance abuse, and more often had a major depressive disorder (but did not differ in age at first panic attack, age of onset of panic disorder, agoraphobia, and obsessive-compulsive disorder).

Anthony and Petronis (1991) compared attempted suicides with controls and found no differences in the history of panic attacks. The attempted suicides more often had a major depressive disorder. However, in a multiple regression with education, marital status, alcohol abuse, cocaine use, and major depressive disorder, a history of panic attack was significantly associated with attempting suicide.

Beck et al. (1991) found less suicidality in outpatients with panic disorder (with or without agoraphobia) than in patients with a major depressive disorder. Patients with panic disorder resembled "other" patients in their suicidality.

Noyes et al. (1991) found that 18 percent of panic disorder patients completed or attempted suicide in the next seven years. The completers and serious attempters more often had a personality disorder and major depressive disorder, had more social and work impairments, were younger, had an earlier onset, had higher neuroticism scores (but not extraversion scores), had more neurotic traits as children, had more disturbed relatives, and were more disturbed on the SCL-90.

Friedman et al. (1992) found that panic disorder patients who also had a borderline personality had a history of more suicidal ideation and suicide attempts than pure panic disorder patients. The panic disorder patients who attempted suicide more often abused drugs/alcohol and had greater affective instability and a more-chaotic,

empty life.

Leon et al. (1992) found that prior attempted suicide in a community sample was associated with situation-specific panic attacks (not spontaneous ones) not due to drugs, alcohol, or medical complications, and was also associated with the total symptom count.

Mannuzza et al. (1992) examined relatives and friends of panic disorder patients. The rate of attempted suicide in these people was higher in those also diagnosed with panic disorder or "other" disorders, less in those with panic attacks, and least in those with no disorder.

Clayton (1993) followed up patients with major affective disorders for ten years. Completing suicide in the first year of follow-up was associated with high anxiety and panic attacks; completing suicide in years two–nine was associated with hopelessness, prior suicide attempts, and suicidal ideation at intake.

Norton et al. (1993) found that substance abuse patients with panic attacks were more depressed and more likely to have attempted suicide than those without panic disorder. The attempters did not differ from non-attempters in which drug was abused.

Rudd et al. (1993) found that suicidal ideation was more common in patients with mood disorders than in patients with mood disorders plus panic disorder. The groups did not differ in attempted suicide. The risk of future suicide was higher in mood disorder patients with phobias or post-traumatic stress disorder, but not panic disorder.

Andrade et al. (1994) found that prior suicidality was greater in panic disorder patients with comorbid major depressions (and also pure major depressives) than in pure panic disorder patients.

Borden (1994) found that a quarter of suicide attempts and ideation episodes in panic disorder patients was due to the panic attack. The suicidal patients were younger; had more severe panic disorder; an earlier age at onset; and more depression, state and trait anxiety, and psychopathology. They did not differ in duration of the panic disorder, the number of attacks, or secondary diagnoses.

Cox et al. (1994) found prior suicidal ideation equally common in panic disorder patients and social phobia patients, while prior suicide attempts were somewhat more common in the panic disorder patients. Attempting suicide was associated with prior psychiatric hospitalization and treatment for depression (but not substance abuse or anxiety disorders).

King et al. (1995c) found that depressed outpatients with panic attacks more likely to have attempted suicide in the past than those without, especially if the panic attacks were infrequent. The attempts typically occurred in the depression preceding the panic attack. In a multiple regression, however, only a history of psychotic symptoms was associated with attempting suicide.

In panic disorder patients, Warshaw et al. (1995) found that past attempted suicide was more common if patients also had a depressive disorder. Sex, PTSD, substance abuse, eating disorders, and early onset also were associated with past attempts. Future attempts were predicted by early onset, prior attempts, eating disorders, alcohol abuse, PTSD, and borderline personality disorder, as well as a worse global assessment, being younger at intake, not married, and having no children.

Agargun and Kara (1996) found that emergency room patients with chest pain had more recent suicidal ideation and more depression if they had panic disorder than those without panic disorder, even after controls for the presence of a major depressive disorder.

Henriksson et al. (1996) found panic disorder more often in female completed suicides than in male completed suicides. All had a comorbid Axis I diagnosis, most often a major depression.

Lepola et al. (1996) followed up panic disorder patients and found that all those who attempted or completed suicide also had comorbid major depression and alcohol abuse.

Korn et al. (1997) found that panic disorder patients with comorbid disorders had more suicidal ideation during the panic attack and lifetime than pure panic disorder patients (but did not differ in attempted suicide).

On the other hand, in a review of the research, Noyes (1991) found that subsequent attempted suicide in panic disorder patients and completed suicide in anxiety disorder patients were similar in frequency to those outcomes in major depressive disorder patients. Fava et al. (1992) found no differences in suicidal tendencies in affective disorder patients with and without panic disorder. Norton et al. (1996) found no differences in prior attempted suicide between patients with panic disorder and those with social phobia.

Social Phobia

Weissman et al. (1996) found in community surveys over four nations that the percentage of attempted suicides by those with a psychiatric disorder was higher if the people also had a social phobia.

Weiller et al. (1996) found that general-practitioner patients with social phobias more often had suicidal ideation, and if there was also a major depressive disorder present, more often had attempted suicide.

Lecrubier and Weiller (1997) found that primary care patients with social phobias were more likely to have prior suicidal ideation and attempts than those with no social phobia, and even more so if they also had a depressive disorder.

Adjustment Disorder

Greenberg et al. (1995) found that psychiatric emergency admissions with adjustment disorders showed more suicidality as well as more substance abuse disorder, had fewer readmissions, and had shorter stays than those with other diagnoses.

Personality Disorders

In a three-year follow-up of patients diagnosed with personality disorders, Mehlum et al. (1991) found that only 1 percent had completed suicide, a low rate. Cheng et al. (1997) found that, in three ethnic groups in Taiwan, the completed suicides were more likely to have a personality disorder than were living controls. The odds ratio for suicide was highest for those with an impulsive personality disorder plus severe depression.

In a study of adolescent suicide attempters versus psychiatric controls, Brent et al. (1993a) found that the attempters more often had a personality disorder (especially a borderline personality disorder) and an affective disorder. The groups did not differ in aggression, assaultiveness, or impulsive aggression.

Pretorius et al. (1994) found that attempted suicides who went on to repeat their attempts were more likely to have histrionic, narcissistic, borderline, and antisocial personality disorders.

Johnson et al. (1995) found that adolescent attempters were more likely to have a personality disorder than psychiatric controls, but did not differ in having any diagnosis or a major depressive disorder.

In a sample of Finnish suicides, Isometsa et al. (1996a) found that Cluster B types

(borderline, etc.) more often had depressive disorders, substance abuse disorder, prior attempts, and alcohol dependence, and less physical disease than control suicides; Cluster C types (dependent, etc.) did not differ from control suicides.

Borderline Personality Disorder

Links et al. (1990) followed up borderline patients for two years and found that 4.5 percent had completed suicide.

Paris (1990) followed up a sample of borderline personality disorder patients for 15 years. The suicides did not differ in social adaptation, impulse-action, affects, interpersonal relations, affective disorder, age, sex, or marital status from the surviving patients; however, they had lower psychosis scores, fewer losses and separations, fewer problems with their mothers, and more education.

Kjelsberg et al. (1991) compared borderline patients who completed suicide with those still alive. The suicides had more childhood loss, more early and serious suicide attempts, and more often had no contact with a therapist and no anxiety neurosis. They did not differ in loss as adults, prior psychiatric hospitalization, alcohol/drug abuse, impulse control, or risk taking.

Runeson and Beskow (1991) compared completed suicides who had a borderline personality disorder with those who did not. The borderlines more often had an antisocial personality disorder; were substance abusers; and had early parental loss, family substance abuse, financial problems, and more arrests/convictions.

Kullgren et al. (1992) found that borderline patients who completed suicide were more often male, older, nonattached, hostile, depressed; and with antisocial behavior, more prior hospitalizations, and more suicide attempts.

Rich and Runseon (1992) found that borderline personality was a more common diagnosis for youth suicides in Goteborg (Sweden) than in San Diego, but a reassessment of the San Diego suicides revealed a more comparable incidence of borderline personality disorder.

Trull and Widiger (1991) found that high school students who had attempted suicide differed from nonsuicidal students on many scales of the Adolescent Psychopathology scales including borderline personality disorder (and depression).

Lester (1993g) found that having a borderline personality disorder was associated with recent self-mutilation, but with not lifetime suicide attempts, in a sample of suicidal emergency room patients.

Russ et al. (1993) found that self-injuring borderline patients who experienced no pain during the self-injuring were more depressed, impulsive, anxious, dissociated, with more prior trauma and suicide attempts than those reporting pain.

Mehlum et al. (1994) followed up psychiatric patients and found that those with borderline personality disorder had more subsequent (as well as more prior) suicide attempts than patients with other personality disorders or no personality disorder. Those borderline patients who attempted suicide later were more likely to continue to be diagnosed as borderlines.

Soloff et al. (1994) found that borderline patients with prior suicide attempts were older and more depressed, made more impulsive actions, and more often had comorbid antisocial personality disorder than those who did not. The latter had more comorbid paranoid and schizotypal personality disorders. The groups did not differ in major depressions and substance abuse.

Sabo et al. (1995) followed up female borderline patients and found three styles for their suicidality: fluctuating (with higher baseline dysphoria and social isolation), consistently low (with higher baseline drug use), and steadily declining.

Schmidtke and Schaller (1995) found that female borderline patients more often had a history of attempted suicide than females with Munchhausen syndrome.

Oldham et al. (1996) found that suicidal threats were associated with experience of neglect (but not abuse) in a sample of borderline personality disorder patients.

Brodsky et al. (1997) found no association between the number of borderline personality criteria and prior suicide attempts in psychiatric inpatients, although impulsivity and childhood abuse were associated with prior attempts.

Dubo et al. (1997) found that borderline personality disorder patients had shown more suicidality in the past than those with other personality disorders, but did not differ in their ages when suicidal. For the borderline patients, sexual abuse by caregivers was associated with the duration of suicidality, but not age at the time of the attempts or the number of attempts. For those with other personality disorders, suicidality was associated with caregiver emotional withdrawal and denial and lack of a relationship with caregiver.

Compulsive Personality Disorder

Stein et al. (1996) found no differences in prior attempts by compulsive personality disorder patients and all other personality disorder patients.

Conduct Disorder

Schlebusch (1992) compared adolescent suicide attempters diagnosed with conduct disorder versus adjustment disorder. Those with conduct disorders more often had recent disciplinary problems, while those with adjustment disorders more often had emotional problems. This difference was found only if the family was not intact and there were more than five people in the household.

Young et al. (1995) found that a history of attempted suicide in boys with conduct disorder was associated with the number of drugs used and the conduct disorder symptom count, but not depression scores or diagnosis.

Alcohol Abuse

For a review of suicide and alcohol/drug abuse see Lester (1992).

Completed Suicide

Murphy and Wetzel (1990) reviewed previous research and estimated the "lifetime" risk of suicide in alcoholics to be 2 to 3.4 percent. The average age of alcoholic suicides was 49. Gillet et al. (1991) followed up female alcoholics for an average of 46 months and found that 18 of 151 had died including 6 from suicide. Hansen and Simonsen (1991) examined a forensic series of autopsies and found that 6.6 percent of the deaths of alcoholics were from suicide, compared to 14.1 percent of the deaths of nonalcoholics. Lester (1991a) found that the age at death of American writers was associated both with being alcoholics and dying from suicide.

Andreasson et al. (1991) followed up Swedish conscripts for 20 years. Those who were high consumers of alcohol had a higher risk of subsequent completed suicide, whereas moderate consumers and abstainers did not differ in risk. Other predictors of suicide included having a psychiatric diagnosis, number of friends, and having contact with the police.

Lester (1991b) reviewed studies of

alcoholics and found that the rate of suicide was negatively associated with the length of follow-up, living in the United States (versus other nations), and the sample size. The percentage completing suicide was associated only with the first two variables.

Murphy (1992) compared alcoholics who completed suicide with living controls in the community. The suicides had more recent heavy drinking, major depressive disorders, unemployment, living alone, and talk of suicide; less social support; but no differences in medical problems. Compared to alcoholics in treatment, the suicides had more current drinking, major depressive disorders, suicidal ideation, unemployment and living alone; were younger; and had fewer medical problems.

Duberstein et al. (1993) compared suicides with alcohol/substance abuse to those with mood and anxiety disorders. The substance abusers had experienced more stressors involving conflicts/arguments, attachment disruptions, and interpersonal stress over the prior year, especially in the prior six weeks.

In a follow-up study of alcoholics who had been inpatients, Duffy and Kreitman (1993) found no effect from the time of entrance into the cohort, sex, age, social class, or marital status. Suicide was more common in those with a secondary diagnosis of depression for women and personality disorder or drug addiction for men.

Klatsky and Armstrong (1993) found that heavy drinking (more than six drinks a day) was associated with a higher risk of suicide in patients in a medical care program. Mutzell (1994) found that a diagnosis both of alcoholism and drug use increased the proportion of deaths from suicide.

Berglund (1995) followed up alcoholics and found that the suicides were more often married, had peptic ulcers, dysphoria and depression. They were more brittle/sensitive than the others. Both the suicidal and assaultive alcoholics had higher suicide rates than the others.

Rossow and Amundsen (1995) found that alcoholics among former Norwegian military conscripts had a higher suicide rate, especially with advancing age. The risk of suicide decreased with self-confidence but was not associated with birth order.

Attempted Suicide

Roy et al. (1990a) found that alcoholic inpatients who had attempted suicide were more often female, of lower social class, younger, with an earlier onset, and more alcohol intake. For men only, they were more often with a major depression, antisocial personality disorder, panic/phobic disorder, drug abuse, and alcoholic mother and siblings than those who had not attempted suicide.

Selakovic-Bursic (1990) compared alcoholics who had attempted suicide with those who had not. The attempters more often were diagnosed with a depressive disorder and with a personality disorder, had more aggressive personalities, and during their hangovers, were more depressed and less vegetative.

Biro et al. (1991) found that suicidality (ideation and attempts) and major depressive disorder were associated in a sample of alcoholics.

Platt and Robinson (1991) found that alcohol abuse was more common in male attempted suicides than in female attempters (15.3 percent versus 5.6 percent). The alcohol abusers were older, more often separated/divorced/widowed, unemployed, and not psychiatrically ill (but with more prior psychiatric care). They had more prior attempts, drinking at the time of the attempt and violence toward others, and more often were victims of violence and with a criminal record.

Roy et al. (1991) found that early-onset alcoholics (before the age of 20) had more often attempted suicide than those with later onset.

Watson et al. (1991) found that women admitted to the general ward of a hospital for drug overdoses (not necessarily suicidal in nature) were more often problem drinkers than women admitted for other reasons.

Merrill et al. (1992) classified attempted suicides by alcohol consumption (low, moderate, or high) and found no differences in prior attempts or suicidal-intent scores.

Wasserman (1992) found that suicide attempters who abused alcohol were older than those who did not. Attempters in intensive care more often had alcohol-abusing parents, more parental loss from divorce/separation (but not death), and less emotional support from their parents.

Berglund et al. (1993) found that attempted suicide and aggressive behavior were associated in male (but not female) alcoholics. Attempted suicide was associated with the use of alcohol plus benzodiazepines in both male and female alcoholics.

Ojehagen et al. (1993) found that outpatient alcoholics who had attempted suicide were worse abusers and had more treatment for alcoholism and psychiatric problems (but did not differ in sex, marital status, education, employment, family history of alcoholism, or attrition rate).

Robinson and Platt (1993) found that suicide attempters with early onset of alcohol abuse (under the age of 30), were more often single, living with relatives/friends, diagnosed with a personality disorder, drug abusers, and in debt. They had more often experienced separation from father and expressed violence toward others than those with older-age onset of alcohol abuse. They did not differ in social class, separation from mother, or family mental illness and suicide attempts.

In a family practice, Amodei et al. (1994) found that alcohol abusers had a higher incidence of suicide attempts and ideation than nonabusers. Among the abusers, women had more suicidality than men.

Bergman and Brismar (1994a, 1999b) found that male alcoholics with a history of violence had more often attempted suicide than nonviolent alcoholics. They also had more severe alcoholism, more drug abuse, more alcoholic parents, and more violence in their homes as children. Attempting suicide in the sample was associated with physically abusing others.

Burch (1994) found that alcohol-dependent men (with no other psychiatric disorder) who had attempted suicide had more prior drug use and psychiatric treatment (and more in their families) than those who had not attempted suicide. They also had higher Pd and Ma scores on the MMPI and higher depression scores. They did not differ in age, race, familial suicidal behavior or years of alcohol dependency.

Among alcoholics, Windle (1994) found that those who had attempted suicide had more psychiatric disorders and higher MMPI-scale scores on all scales except social introversion. They were also more often single, divorced/widowed, unemployed, and with low income. They did not differ in race, age, education, intelligence, combat exposure, severity of alcoholism, or family history of alcoholism.

Brandell and Ekselius (1995) found that alcoholics with personality disorders had a much higher incidence of prior attempts than those with no personality disorder. The difference was especially pronounced for borderline personality disorder in men and avoidant personality disorder in women.

In a catchment-area survey, Stack and Wasserman (1995) found that attempting suicide was predicted by heavy drinking,

race, sex, age, education, and being non-married.

Cornelius et al. (1996) found that 41 percent of alcoholics with major depressive disorder attempted suicide during the current depressive episode. The attempters had been drinking more heavily in the prior week, but did not differ in suicidal ideation.

Krausz et al. (1996) found that patients with alcoholic psychoses had attempted suicide more than alcoholics.

Rossi et al. (1996) compared attempted suicide with affective disorders who were alcohol abusers and those who were not. The alcohol abusers had made more attempts and, if bipolars, had more negativism and verbal hostility on the Buss and Durkee Hostility Inventory.

Blixen et al. (1997) found that elderly psychiatric patients who also abused drugs/alcohol had higher rates of prior suicide attempts (but not suicidal ideation) than those who did not.

Hawton et al. (1997) found that male attempted suicides were more often alcohol and drug abusers than female attempted suicides. The drug/alcohol abusers more often had attempted suicide, and the drug abusers were also more impulsive, unemployed, and with a criminal record and a personality disorder.

Suicidal Ideation

Workman and Beer (1990) found that high school students who abused alcohol had more suicidal ideation than those who did not. Sex and grade were not associated with suicidal ideation.

In a general medical clinic population, Hunt et al. (1992) found that suicidal ideation/attempts were associated with problem drinking in both men and women (as well as being unmarried in men and smoking, over the age of 65, low income, and unemployment in women). Suicidality was not associated with obesity, inactivity, or hypertension.

Duncan et al. (1997) found that alcohol use in adolescence (especially accelerating use) predicted suicidal ideation (and other problem behaviors) ten years later.

Sociological Studies

In Perth (Australia) from 1968–1984, Smith and Burville (1991) found that wine and spirits consumption (but not beer consumption) were associated with attempted suicide rates for males and females aged 15–39 (but not males and females 40 years of age and older).

Smart and Mann (1990) found that, from 1963–1983 in Ontario, the suicide rates of both men and women were positively associated with alcohol consumption, the alcoholism rate, alcohol-dependent mortality, and liver-cirrhosis mortality. Lester (1993a) found that Canadian suicide rates from 1960–1985 were associated with alcohol consumption and alcohol-cirrhosis death rates, but not with nonalcohol-cirrhosis death rates. The associations were stronger for female suicide rates. Skog and Elekes (1993) found that alcohol sales and suicide rates were associated in Hungary for 1950–1990.

Skog (1993) found that when the price of alcohol increased in 1916–1917 in Denmark (as a result of the war), consumption dropped, and the suicide rate dropped, but only among alcohol abusers.

Across the American states, Lester (1993b) found that restrictions on alcohol through prosecutions (rather than sales) were related to lower suicide rates. Lester (1993f) found no association over nations between suicide rates and per capita consumption of alcohol, rates of alcoholism, or cirrhosis death rates.

Drug Use

General Substance Abuse

Runeson (1990) compared suicides aged 15–29 who had abused psychoactive substances with those who had not. The substance abusers more often had a personality disorder (especially borderline) and were more often intoxicated at the time of the suicide. The nonabusers more often had a major depression or an adjustment disorder. The substance abusers less often left a suicide note, were more often unemployed and had legal problems, and had parents with more substance abuse and attempted suicide. They did not differ in prior attempts, method for suicide, recent separations, or parental loss. The duration of abuse was associated with the duration of suicidality.

Bukstein et al. (1993) compared adolescent completed suicides with community controls, all with substance abuse. The suicides had more active substance abuse, comorbid major depression, alcohol abuse, recent suicidal ideation, a family history of depression and substance abuse, legal problems, and handguns in the home. They did not differ in sex, prior psychiatric treatment, total life events, or long guns in the home.

Frischer et al. (1993) found that 35 percent of the deaths of intravenous drug users in Glasgow (Scotland) were from suicide. Rossow (1994) found that drug addicts in treatment had a higher suicide rate than the general population, especially females aged 15–24.

Felts et al. (1992) found that adolescents in schools who used cocaine/crack, alcohol, and marihuana had less suicidal ideation, but made more suicide attempts in the past year. Those using needle-drugs had more suicidal ideation and made fewer suicide attempts.

Loimer et al. (1992) found that drug addicts in outpatient treatment who had attempted suicide were younger and more often female, polydrug users, alcohol users, and HIV-positive. They began drug use earlier than those who had not attempted suicide.

Dinwiddie et al. (1992) found that prior attempts at suicide were most common in intravenous drug users and then, in order, in users of other drugs, marihuana users, and nonusers. Among the intravenous drug users, the presence of an antisocial personality disorder was not associated with incidence of prior attempts.

Ekeberg et al. (1991) found that substance abusers presenting at an emergency room for self-poisoning were more often there as a result of attempted suicide than were nonabusers. However, the attempters and the nonattempters had similar overall mortality rates in a five-year follow-up.

Madianos et al. (1994) found that illicit drug users in Greece in the general population had more often thought about and attempted suicide than nonusers (especially if involved with polydrug use). The same trend was found for alcohol use/abuse.

Rossow and Wichstrom (1994) found that high school students who had attempted suicide used alcohol, cannabis, solvents/glue, and other drugs more than non-attempters. They were also more depressed and lonely, more often female, not living with parents, and over the age of 18.

Anderson et al. (1995) compared VA patients who had attempted suicide and were substance abusers with those who were not abusers. The abusers were younger and more often from the Vietnam era. They were often married, female, and white. They more often had other psychiatric diagnoses, PTSD, neurosis, and personality disorder.

Chatham et al. (1995) compared methadone maintenance patients who became suicidal during treatment with those who did not. The suicidal clients were more depressed and hostile, more often risk takers, and had more arguments with others in the last six months. They did not differ in self-esteem, anxiety, social conformity or in patterns of drug use. Their parents were supportive of them when younger, but their parents did not differ in drug use or psychiatric problems. They were more often self-referred, in AA, and with previous drug treatment.

Westermeyer et al. (1995) found that suicidal ideation (but not attempted suicide) was more common in substance-abusing patients in treatment if they also had a comorbid anxiety disorder.

Johnsson and Fridell (1997) found that prior attempted suicide in drug abusers in treatment was associated with family members' substance abuse, early loss, psychiatric disorder as a child, being female, and subsequent suicidal ideation. Drug abuse variables were not associated with attempting suicide.

Amphetamines

Baberg et al. (1996) found that psychiatric patients who had used amphetamines also had more often attempted suicide.

Cocaine

Marzuk et al. (1992, 1995b) found that 22 percent of suicides under the age of 60 in New York City in 1985 had cocaine in their systems – 12 percent had cocaine and alcohol. The presence of cocaine was associated with Hispanic ethnicity, firearm suicide, alcohol use, and age 18–30. Cocaine was more often found in accident victims and murder victims than in suicides.

Seibyl et al. (1993) found that schizophrenics who used cocaine prior to admission were more suicidal on admission. Rosseli and

Ardila (1996) found that people who were cocaine or polydrug dependent attempted and thought about suicide more than normal controls and had more completed suicides in their families. Salloum et al. (1996) found a tendency for hospitalized psychiatric patients who abused cocaine and alcohol or only cocaine to have more suicidality than patients abusing only alcohol.

In a follow-up study of African Americans followed from first grade to age 32, Juon and Ensminger (1997) found that attempting suicide was associated with cocaine use, adult depression, and frequent mobility. For males, additional correlates were childhood psychopathology, nonmarried, and living with one parent at age six. For females, assaultiveness in adolescence was associated with attempted suicide.

Heroin

Schifano et al. (1990) found a completed suicide rate in Padua (Italy) of 113 for heroin addicts and 462 for alcoholics.

Marihuana

Andreasson and Allebeck (1990) found that the subsequent suicide rate in Swedish military conscripts was higher if they had used cannabis at a high rate. However, once background variables, such as having had contact with the police, were put into a multiple regression, the effect of cannabis use on the suicide rate was no longer statistically significant.

Medications

Allgulander et al. (1994) found that patients dependent upon medications had a higher-than-expected suicide rate (both those abusing alcohol and street drugs and those not abusing).

Marzuk et al. (1995a) found that 16 percent of suicides in New York City had psychotropic medications present in their bodies, more so in whites and women; 52 percent of these had used the medication for suicide.

Methadone

Magruder-Habib et al. (1992) found that methadone outpatients had attempted and thought about suicide less often in the prior year than residential inpatients and non-methadone outpatients. Females and whites/Hispanics had more suicidality. Being suicidal at entry into the program and a return to weekly or more-frequent drug use predicted suicidal behavior in the following year.

Caplehorn et al. (1996) found that opiate addicts on methadone had a lower suicide rate than those not on methadone.

Solvent Users

Dinwiddie et al. (1990) found that solvent users among a group of alcoholics and felons had attempted and thought about suicide more in the past than nonusers, but they were also more likely to have a unipolar depressive disorder (but not a bipolar affective disorder).

Other Problems

Compulsive Gamblers

Frank et al. (1991) surveyed members of Gamblers Anonymous and found that those who had attempted suicide were more often divorced, had stolen, had borrowed money to pay debts, and had alcoholic relatives; and they bet at an earlier age. They did not differ in other addictions, at which games they bet, whether they had ever written bad checks, their average bet per week, or their annual salary.

Eating Disorders

Theander (1983) conducted a long-term follow-up study of female anorexics and found that about 5 percent of the sample completed suicide. Crisp et al. (1992) found that, of 12 anorexics dead in a 20-year follow-up of 168 patients, five had died from suicide. Sullivan (1995) conducted a meta-analysis of 42 studies of anorexics and found that 27 percent of their deaths were from suicide.

Hatsukami et al. (1986) found that bulimics with affective disorder or substance abuse had attempted suicide more often than pure bulimics. Bulik et al. (1997) found that bulimics who abused alcohol had attempted suicide more than those who did not abuse alcohol.

Smith et al. (1991a, 1991b) found no difference in Exner's Rorschach signs for suicidality between bulimics and normals or between purging and nonpurging bulimics. However, Weisberg et al. (1987) found that bulimics and depressed patients did score higher in suicidality than normals. Gordon et al. (1984) found that anorexics gave more Rorschach signs of suicidality (Appelbaum's signs) than adolescents with conduct disorder.

French et al. (195) found that dieting frequency in adolescents was associated with binge eating, alcohol and tobacco use, and prior suicidality. Both boy and girl purgers were more suicidal.

Favaro and Santonastaso (1996) found that attempted suicide was more common in anorexics if they also vomited, used laxatives, or both. Bulimics were also more likely to have attempted suicide if they purged.

Pryor et al. (1996) found that binging/purging anorexics had more often attempted suicide then restricting anorexics. Favaro and Santonastaso (1997) found that,

among emergency room patients, those with binging/purging anorexia or purging bulimia were likely to have attempted suicide.

Kent et al. (1997) found that women who had attempted suicide were more often to have an eating disorder (and more depression, anxiety, and inward and outward hostility) than other emergency room patients.

Predicting Suicide

The Probability of Suicide

Lester (1990) analyzed follow-up studies of suicide in anxiety neuroses/panic disorder and in alcoholics. The percentage of deaths from suicide was negatively associated with the length of follow-up used in the studies for the anxiety patients but not significantly associated for the studies of alcoholics.

Completed Suicide

Allebeck and Allgulander (1990a) compared Swedish conscripts into the military who later completed suicide with those who did not. The suicides more often had a psychiatric disorder, especially schizophrenia (although not at the time of entry into the military), more inpatient care, high levels of alcohol consumption, poor emotional control, and poor social conditions (such as police contact and few friends).

Allgulander and Fisher (1990) followed up a sample of attempted suicides who used self-poisoning to see who later completed suicide. The predictors for women were age, making prior suicide attempts, having a neurosis or personality disorder, having an affective disorder, the use of drugs and alcohol for the self-poisoning, and having a central nervous system or cardiac disease (although these two last factors were no longer significant in a multiple regression). The predictors for men were age, making prior suicide attempts, using prescription drugs, and cancer (although this last factor was not significant in a multiple regression).

Brown (1990) compared physicians who had completed suicide with a sample of physicians dead from natural causes. The suicides had more often been in psychiatric care and had experienced more recent stressful life events, especially financial stressors.

Nielsen et al. (1990) followed up a sample of attempted suicides for five years, by which time 11.6 percent had completed suicide. The completers had more chronic somatic disease (especially those over the age of 40), and more often a depressive disorder and substance abuse (of their medications). They did not differ in the number of prior attempts.

Psychiatrists were asked by O'Reilly et al. (1990) for their clinical hunches about clues that their patients were about to complete suicide. Three clues were given: withdrawal, considering oneself a burden, and help negation.

Ross et al. (1990) found the following predictors of suicide in a retirement community: widowed/divorced, sleeping more than nine hours per night, drinking more than three alcoholic drinks a day, smoking, and depression scores. Estrogen use did not predict suicide.

Goldstein et al. (1991) followed up patients with affective disorders and found that completed suicide was predicted by sex, suicidal ideation on admission, manic or mixed bipolar type, unipolar with a history of mania, prior suicide attempts, and an unfavorable outcome at discharge.

Graves and Thomas (1991) followed up medical students and found that those who later completed suicide showed more nervous habits as students, including

irritability, urinary frequency, loss of appetite, difficulty sleeping, and the urge to be alone. They did not differ in their parents' ages, number of siblings, loss of parents, alcohol use, or grade point average.

Lonnqvist and Ostamo (1991) followed up attempted suicides for four and a half years and found that 3.4 percent completed suicides, accounting for 47 percent of all deaths. The suicides were more often male, with prior psychiatric outpatient treatment, more lethal first attempts, and greater suicidal intent, but did not differ in age. After five and a half years, Lonnqvist and Suokas (1993) found that the suicides were more often male, over the age of 45, and with prior psychiatric treatment and attempted suicide. Their index attempt was more severe, with more suicidal intent and less impulsiveness.

Rygnestad and Hauge (1991) found that attempted suicide was more common in females, the separated/divorced, those in the city, the unemployed, and those on social security or old-age pensions. Ten years later, completed suicide was predicted by separation from parents in adolescence, a family history of psychiatric disorder, broken marriages, frequent migration, alcohol abuse, and more suicidal intent in the earlier suicide attempt.

Suokas and Lonnqvist (1991) followed up a sample of attempted suicides for five years. Those who completed suicide (3.2 percent with a rate of 589) were more often males, aged 40–59, with previous psychiatric treatment and suicide attempts, who had made a more lethal attempt with higher suicidal intent, and who were less impulsive in their suicidal attempt.

Nordentoft et al. (1993) found that completed suicide was predicted in a sample of attempters by addiction, more than one prior attempt, living alone, age, and making a more serious prior attempt. Nordentoft and Rubin (1993) found that subsequent completed suicide was predicted by unemployment, an affective disorder, and prior attempts (but not by sex, living alone, or substance abuse).

Attempted Suicide

Duggn et al. (1991) followed depressed inpatients for 18 years. Those who subsequently attempted or completed suicide (24 of the former and 5 of the latter) showed at admission more severe dysphoria, retarded psychomotor behavior, brain damage, and losses from separation than those still alive. They did not differ in type of depression, personality disorder, losses by death, prior suicide attempts, extraversion, neuroticism, or obsessions. The predictors of subsequent suicidal behavior, however, differed from the predictors of the frequency of suicide attempts, the suicidal intent, and the medical lethality of the suicidal behavior.

Pfeffer et al. (1993) followed up psychiatric patients and found that a subsequent suicide attempt was predicted by mood disorder, substance abuse disorder, life stressors, and poor social adjustment. The psychiatric patients were more likely to attempt suicide than normal controls, especially if the patients were suicidal initially.

Repeated Suicide Attempts

Allgulander and Fisher (1990) followed up a sample of attempted suicides who used self-poisoning to see who later attempted suicide. For women, age and making prior suicide attempts predicted repeating, whereas for men, age, making prior suicide attempts, and using neuroleptic drugs for the self-poisoning predicted repeating. The presence of medical diseases did not predict repeating.

Leon et al. (1990) followed up a sample of suicide attempters for 28 months. Those who repeated had more prior attempts, but did not differ in sex, age, or suicidal history in their families.

Peterson and Bongar (1990) compared suicide attempters seen once at an emergency room with those seen two or more times. The repeaters were older, more often living alone or in group homes, had more prior attempts and psychiatric hospitalizations, were more often schizophrenic and with a personality disorder, and were more often on antipsychotic, antidepressant, or anti-Parkinsonism medication. They did not differ in sex, race, marital status, affective disorder, or alcohol/substance abuse.

Spirito et al. (1990) followed up a sample of adolescent attempters for three months. Those who repeated during this time made greater preparations, used alcohol and/or drugs, and had greater suicidal intent in their index attempt.

Stenager and Benjaminsen (1991) followed up suicide attempters and found that the repeaters more often had a personality disorder and more often a secondary or a character depression, but did not differ in other diagnoses.

Stocks and Scott (1991) studied in a sample of persons who attempted three times in one week. They were mainly young, unemployed, lower class, lacking a partner, with one or more criminal convictions, with a personality disorder, with prior attempts, and did not leave a suicide note. None had died a year later, although 37 percent had made further attempts.

Treatment

Isacsson et al. (1992) found that completed suicides in Sweden obtained more prescription drugs than living controls, but only 13 percent of the men and 9 percent of the women were given antidepressants.

Discussion

This tremendous body of research is difficult to summarize. However, it is noteworthy that the research is driven by the DSM diagnostic system, which is changed every few years. There have been many criticisms directed toward this diagnostic system, one of which asserts that it is based on a description of symptoms and not on etiological factors. We can expect the system to be revised extensively in the next century, and such revisions would make much of the research reviewed in this chapter irrelevant for an understanding of suicide.

Furthermore, it appears that many of the correlates of suicidal behavior are similar, regardless of the diagnosis of the patient. For example, depression and depressive syndromes are associated with past, present, and future suicidal behavior in almost all diagnostic categories. Thus, it remains open to question as to what extent studies of suicide by diagnosis furthers our understanding of suicide.

REFERENCES

Adams, D. M., & Overholser, J. C. Suicidal behavior and history of substance abuse. *American Journal of Drug & Alcohol Abuse*, 1992, 18, 343–354.

Addington, D. E., & Addington, J. M. Attempted suicide and depression in schizophrenia. *Acta Psychiatrica Scandinavica*, 1992, 85, 288–291.

Agargun, M. Y., & Kara, H. Suicidality in patients with panic disorder. *European Psychiatry*, 1996, 11, 209–211.

Ahrens, B., Berghofer, A., Wolf, T., & Muller-Oerlinghausen, B. Suicide attempts, age, and duration of illness in recurrent affective disorders. *Journal of Affective Disorders*, 1995, 36, 43–49.,

Ahrens, B., & Linden, M. Is there a suicidal syndrome independent of specific major psychiatric disorder? *Acta Psychiatrica Scandinavica*, 1996, 94, 79–86.

Allebeck, P., & Allgulander, C. Suicide among young men. *Acta Psychiatrica Scandinavica*, 1990a, 81, 565–570.

Allebeck, P., & Allgulander, C. Psychiatric diagnoses as predictors of suicide. *British Journal of Psychiatry*, 1990b, 157, 339–344.

Allen, J. M., Lam, R. W., Remick, R. A., & Sadovnnick, A. D. Depressive symptoms and family history in seasonal and nonseasonal mood disorders. *American Journal of Psychiatry*, 1993, 150, 443–448.

Allgulander, C. Suicide and mortality patterns in anxiety neurosis and depressive neurosis. *Archives of General Psychiatry*, 1994, 51, 708–712.

Allgulander, C., Allebeck, P., Przybeck, T. R., & Rice, J. P. Risk of suicide by psychiatric diagnosis in Stockholm county. *European Archives of Psychiatry*, 1992, 241, 323–326.

Allgulander, C., Brandt, L., & Allebeck, P. Suicide and psychology in 1537 patients dependent on prescribed psychoactive medications. *American Journal of Addictions*, 1994, 3, 236–240.

Allgulander, C., & Fisher, L. D. Clinical predictors of completed suicide and repeated self-poisoning in 8895 self-poisoning patients. *European Archives of Psychiatry*, 1990, 239, 270–276.

Allgulander, C., & Lavori, P. W. Excess mortality among 3302 patients with pure anxiety neurosis. *Archives of General Psychiatry*, 1991, 48, 599–602.

Altamura, A. C., Carta, M. G., Carpiniello, B., Piras, A., Maccio, M. V., & Marcia, L. Lifetime prevalence of brief recurrent depression. *European Neuropsychopharmacology*, 1995, 99S–102S.

Amaddeo, F., Bisoffi, G., Bonizzato, P., Micciolo, R., & Tansella, M. Mortality among patients with psychiatric illness. *British Journal of Psychiatry*, 1995, 166, 83–788.

Amador, A. F., Friedman, J. H., Kasapis, C., Yale, S. A., Flaum, M., & Gorman, J. M. Suicidal behavior in schizophrenia and its relationship to awareness of illness. *American Journal of Psychiatry*, 1996, 153, 1185–1188.

Amodei, N., Elkin, B. B., Burge, S. K., Rodriguez-Andrew, S., Lane, P., & Seale, J. P. Psychiatric problems experienced by primary care patients who misuse alcohol. *International Journal of the Addictions*, 1994, 29, 609–626.

Anderson, B. A., Howard, M. O., Walker, R. D., & Suchinsky, R. T. Characteristics of substance-abusing veterans attempting suicide. *Psychological Reports*, 1995, 77, 1231–1242.

Andrade, L., Easton, W. W., & Chilcoat, H. Lifetime comorbidity of panic attacks and major depression in a population-based study. *British Journal of Psychiatry*, 1994, 165, 363–369.

Andreasson, S., & Alleback, P. Cannabis and mortality among young men. *Scandinavian Journal of Social Medicine*, 1990, 18, 9–15.

Andreasson, S., Romelsjo, A., & Allebeck, P. Alcohol, social factors and mortality among young men. *British Journal of Addiction*, 1991, 86, 877–887.

Andrew, B., Hawton, K., Fagg, J., & Westbrook, D. Do psychosocial factors influence outcome in severely depressed female psychiatric inpatients? *British Journal of Psychiatry*, 1993, 163, 747–754.

Angst, J. The epidemiology of depressive disorders. *European Neuropsychopharmacology*, 1995, 5, 95S–98S.

Angst, J., Degonda, M., & Ernst, C. The Zurich study. *European Archives of Psychiatry*, 1993, 242, 135–141.

Angst, J., Kupfer, D. J., & Rosenbaum, J. F. Recovery from depression. *Acta Psychiatrica Scandinavica*, 1996, 93, 413–419.

Angst, J., & Preisig, M. Outcome of a clinical cohort of unipolar, bipolar, and schizoaffective patients. *Schweizer Archiv fur Neurologie & Psychiatrie*, 1995, 146, 17–23.

Anthony, J. C., & Petronis, K. R. Panic attacks and suicide attempts. *Archives of General Psychiatry*, 1991, 48, 1114.

Arnold, D. H., Sanderson, W. C., & Beck, A. T. Panic disorder and suicide. In G. M. Asnis & H. M. van Praag (Eds.), *Panic disorder*. New York: Wiley, 1995, 99–115.

Asgard, U. A psychiatric study of suicide among urban Swedish women. *Acta Psychiatrica Scandinavica*, 1990, 82, 115–124.

Asnis, I., Friedman, T. A., Sanderson, W. L., Kaplan, M. L., Van Praag, H. M., & Harkavy-Friedman, J. M. Suicide behaviors in adult psychiatric outpatients. *American Journal of Psychiatry*, 1993, 150, 108–112.

Asukai, N. Suicide and mental disorders. *Psychiatry & Clinical Neurosciences*, 1995, 49, S1, 91–97.

Axelsson, R., & Lagerkvist-Briggs, M. Factors predicting suicide in psychotic patients. *European Archives of Psychiatry*, 1992, 241, 259–266.

Baberg, H. T., Nelesen, R. A., & Dimsdale, J. E. Amphetamine use. *American Journal of Psychiatry*, 1996, 153, 789–793.

Bai, Y. M., Liu, C. Y., & Lin, C. C. Risk factors for parasuicide among psychiatric inpatients. *Psychiatric Services*, 1997, 48, 1201–1203.

Bandelow, B., Mueller, W., Gaebel, W., Koepcke, W., Linden, M., Mueller-Spahn, F., Pietzcker, A., Resichies, F. M., & Tegeler, J. Depressive syndromes in schizophrenic patients after discharge from hospital. *European Archives of Psychiatry*, 1990, 240, 113–120.

Bartels, S. J., Drake, R. E., & McHugo, G. Alcohol use, depression, and suicidal behavior in schizophrenia. *American Journal of Psychiatry*, 1992, 149, 394–395.

Batten, P. J., & Kamara, S. G. The descriptive epidemiology of unnatural deaths in Oregon's state institutions. *American Journal of Forensic Medicine & Pathology*, 1992, 13, 154–168.

Beautrais, A. L., Joyce, P. R., Mulder, R. T., Fergusson, D. M., Deavoll, B. J., & Nightingale, S. K. Prevalence and comorbidity of mental disorders in person making serious suicide attempts. *American Journal of Psychiatry*, 1996, 153, 1009–1114.

Beck, A. T., Brown, G., Berchick, R. J., Stewart, B. L., & Steer, R. A. Relationship between hopelessness and ultimate suicide. *American Journal of Psychiatry*, 1990, 147, 190–195.

Beck, A. T., Steer, R. A., Beck, J. S., & Newman, C. F. Hopelessness, depression, suicidal ideation, and clinical diagnosis of depression. *Suicide & Life-Threatening Behavior*, 1993a, 23, 139–145.

Beck, A. T., Steer, R. A., & Brown, G. Dysfunctional attitudes and suicidal ideation in psychiatric outpatients. *Suicide & Life-Threatening Behavior*, 1993b, 23, 11–20.

Beck, A. T., Steer, R. A., Sanderson, W. C., & Skeie, T. M. Panic disorder and suicidal ideation and behavior. *American Journal of Psychiatry*, 1991, 148, 1195–1199.

Berglund, M. Mortality data in treatment evaluation. *Alcoholism*, 1995, 31, 47–57.

Berglund, M., Lindberg, S., & Bergman, H. Attempted suicide and other high-risk behaviors in alcoholics related to suicide and violent death. In K. Bohme, R. Freytag, C. Wachtler, & H. Wedler (Eds.), *Suicidal behavior*. Regensburg: S. Roderer, 1993, 409–412.

Bergman, B., & Brismar, B. Characteristics of violent alcoholics. *Alcohol & Alcoholism*, 1994a, 29, 451–457.

Bergman, B., & Brismar, B. Hormone levels and personality traits in abusive and suicidal male alcoholics. *Alcoholism: Clinical & Experimental Research*, 1994b, 18, 311–316.

Biro, M., Selakovic-Bursic, S., & Kapamadzija, B. The role of depressive disorder in the suicidal behavior of alcoholics *Crisis*, 1991, 12, 64–68.

Bjerke, T., Rygnestad, T., & Stiles, T. C. Epidemiological and clinical aspects of parasuicide in the county of Sor-Trondelag, Norway. In T. Bjerke & T. C. Stiles (Eds.), *Suicide attempts in the Nordic countries*. Trondheim: Tapir Forlag, 1991, 91–101.

Blain, P. A., & Donaldson, L. J. The reporting of inpatient suicides. *Public Health*, 1995, 109, 293–301.

Blair-West, G. W., Mellsop, G. W., & Eyeson-Annan, M. L. Down-rating lifetime suicide risk in major depression. *Acta Psychiatrica Scandinavica*, 1997, 95, 259–263.

Blixen, C. E., McDougall, G. J., & Suen, L. J. Dual diagnosis in elders discharged from a psychiatric hospital. *International Journal of Geriatric Psychiatry*, 1997, 12, 307–313.

Bonner, R. L., & Rich, A. R. Psychosocial vulnerability, life stress, and suicide ideation in a jail population. *Suicide & Life-Threatening Behavior*, 1990, 20, 213–224.

Borden, J. W. Panic disorder and suicidality. *Journal of Anxiety Disorders*, 1994, 8, 217–225.

Borges, G., & Rosovsky, H. Suicide attempts and alcohol consumption in an emergency room sample. *Journal of Studies of Alcohol*, 1996, 57, 543–548.

Botsis, A. J., Soldatos, C. R., Liossi, A., Kokkevi, A., & Stefanis, C. N. Suicide and violence risk. *Acta Psychiatrica Scandinavica*, 1994, 89, 92–96.

Boyer, R., Lesage, A. D., Grunberg, F., Morisette, R., Vanier, C., Buteau-Ménard, C., & Loyer, M. Mental illness and suicide. In D. Lester (Ed.), *Suicide '92*. Denver: AAS, 1992, 250–251.

Bradvik, L., & Berglund, M. Risk factors for suicide in melancholia. *Acta Psychiatrica Scandinavica*, 1993, 87, 306–311.

Brandell, A., & Ekselius, L. Personality disorders in alcoholics. *Nordic Journal of Psychiatry*, 1995, 49, 389–392.

Brent, D. A., Johnson, B., Bartle, S., Bridge, J., Rather, C., Matta, J., Connolly, J., & Constantine, D. Personality disorder, tendency to impulsive violence, and suicidal behavior in adolescents. *Journal of the American Academy of Child & Adolescent Psychiatry*, 1993a, 32, 69–75.

Brent, D. A., Kolko, D. J., Allan, M. J., & Brown, R. V. Suicidality in affectively disordered adolescent inpatients. *Journal of the American Academy of Child & Adolescent Psychiatry*, 1990, 29, 586–593.

Brent, D. A., Kolko, D. J., Wartella, M. E., Boyland, M. B., Moritz, G., Baugher, M., & Zelenak, J. P. Adolescent psychiatric inpatients' risk of suicide attempt at six-month follow-up. *Journal of the American Academy of Child & Adolescent Psychiatry*, 1993b, 32, 95–105.

Brent, D. A., Perper, J. A., Moritz, G., Allman, C., Friend, A., Roth, C., Schweers, J., Balach, L., & Baughter, M. Psychiatric risk factors for adolescent suicide. *Journal of the American Academy of Child & Adolescent Psychiatry*, 1993c, 32, 521–529.

Brent, D. A., Perper, J. A., Moritz, G., Allman, C., Schweers, J., Roth, C., Balach, L., Canobbio, R., & Liotus, L. Psychiatric sequelae to the loss of an adolescent peer to suicide. *Journal of the American Academy of Child & Adolescent Psychiatry*, 1993d, 32, 509–517.

Brent, D. A., Perper, J. A., Moritz, G., Baugher, M., & Allman, C. Suicide in adolescents with no apparent psychopathology. *Journal of the American Academy of Child & Adolescent Psychiatry*, 1993e, 32, 494–500.

Brent, D. A., Perper, J. A., Moritz, G., Baughter, M., Roth, C., Balach, L., & Schweers, J. Stressful life events, psychopathology, and adolescent suicide. *Suicide & Life-Threatening Behavior*, 1993f, 23, 179–187.

Brent, D. A., Perper, J. A., Moritz, G., Liotus, L., Schweers, J., Roth, C., Balach, L., & Allman, C. Psychiatric impact of the loss of an adolescent sibling to suicide. *Journal of Affective Disorders*, 1993g, 28, 249–256.

Brodaty, H., Harris, L., Peters, K., Wilhelm, K., Hickie, I., Boyce, P., Mitchell, P., Parker, G., & Eyers, K. Prognosis of depression in the elderly. *British Journal of Psychiatry*, 1993, 163, 589–596.

Brodaty, H., MacCuspie-Moore, C. M., Tickle, L., & Luscombe, G. Depression, diagnostic subtype, and death. *Journal of Affective Disorders*, 1997, 46, 233–242.

Brodsky, B. S., Malone, K. M., Ellis, S. P., Dulit, R. A., & Mann, J. J. Characteristics of borderline personality disorder associated with suicidal behavior. *American Journal of Psychiatry*, 1997, 154, 1715–1719.

Bronisch, T., & Wittchen, H. V. Suicidal ideation and suicide attempts. *European Archives of Psychiatry*, 1994, 244, 93–98.

Brown, R. L. Life events and their effect on suicide. *Advances in Medical Sociology*, 1990, 1, 171–188.

Brown, S. Excess mortality of schizophrenia. *British Journal of Psychiatry*, 1997, 171, 502–508.

Buchholtz-Hansen, P. E., Wang, A. G., & Kragh-Sorensen, P. Mortality in major affective disorder. *Acta Psychiatrica Scandinavica*, 1993, 87, 329–335.

Bukstein, O. G., Brent, D. A., Perper, J. A., Moritz, G., Baughter, M., Schweers, J., Roth, C., & Balach, L. Risk factors for completed suicide among adolescents with a lifetime history of substance abuse. *Acta Psychiatrica Scandinavica*, 1993, 88, 403–408.

Bulik, C. M., Carpenter, L. L., Kupfer, D. J., & Frank, E. Factors associated with suicide attempts in recurrent major depression. *Journal of Affective Disorders*, 1990, 18, 29–37.

Bulik, C. M., Sullivan, P. F., Carter, F. A., & Joyce, P. R. Lifetime comorbidity of alcohol dependence in women with bulimia nervosa. *Addictive Behaviors*, 1997, 22, 437–446.

Bullman, T. A., & Kang, H. K. Posttraumatic stress disorder and the risk of traumatic deaths among Vietnam veterans. *Journal of Nervous & Mental Disease*, 1994, 182, 604–610.

Burch, E. A. Suicide attempt histories in alcohol-dependent men. *International Journal of the Addictions*, 1994, 29, 1477–1486.

Caldwell, C. B., & Gottesman, I. Schizophrenics kill themselves too. *Schizophrenia Bulletin*, 1990, 571–589.

Callahan, C. M., Hendrie, H. C., Nienaber, N. A., & Tierney, W. M. Suicidal ideation among older primary care patients. *Journal of the American Geriatric Society*, 1996, 44, 1205–1209.

Cantor, C. H., Burnett, P. C., Quinn, J., Nizette, D., & Brook, C. Suicide and community psychiatric care. *Acta Psychiatrica Scandinavica*, 1992, 85, 229–233.

Caplehorn, J., Dalton, M., Haldar, F., Pretenas, A., & Nisbet, J. Methadone maintenance addicts' risk of fatal heroin overdose. *Substance Use & Misuse*, 1996, 31, 177–196.

Carney, S. S., Rich, C. L., Burke, P. A., & Fowler, R. C. Suicide over 60. *Journal of the American Geriatric Society*, 1994, 42, 174–180.

Cassano, G. B., Akiskal, H. S., Savino, M., Soriani, A., Musetti, L., & Perugi, G. Single episode of major depressive disorder. *European Archives of Psychiatry*, 1993, 242, 373–380.

Chatham, L. R., Knight, K., Joe, G. W., & Simpson, D. D. Suicidality in a sample of methadone maintenance clients. *American Journal of Drug & Alcohol Abuse*, 1995, 21, 345–361.

Chen, Y. W., & Dilsaver, S. C. Comorbidity for obsessive-compulsive disorder in bipolar and unipolar disorders. *Psychiatry Research*, 1995, 59, 57–64.

Chen, Y. W., & Dilsaver, S. C. Lifetimes rates of suicide attempts among subjects with bipolar and unipolar disorders relative to subjects with other Axis I disorders. *Biological Psychiatry*, 1996, 39, 896–899.

Cheng, A. T., Mann, A. H., & Chan, K. A. Personality disorder and suicide. *British Journal of Psychiatry*, 1997, 170, 441–446; 171, 190.

Cheng, K. K., Leung, C. M., Lo, W. H., & Lam, T. H. Risk factors of suicide among schizophrenics. *Acta Psychiatrica Scandinavica*, 1990, 81, 220–224.

Chiles, J. A., Ping, Z. Y., & Strosahl, D. A Chinese/American cross-cultural study of depression, hopelessness, and suicidal behavior. In G. Ferrari, M. Bellini & P. Crepet (Eds.), *Suicidal behavior and risk factors*. Bologna: Monduzzi-Editore, 1990, 609–614.

Clayton, P. I. Suicide in panic disorder and depression. *Current Therapeutic Research*, 1993, 54, 825–831.

Clerici, M., Bressi, C., Bertrando, P., Albonetti, S., Garavaglia, R., Rapolla, M. R., Invernizzi, G., & Cazzullo, C. R. Family emotions and suicide attempts in schizophrenia. In G. Ferrari, M. Bellini & P. Crepet (Eds.), *Suicidal behavior and risk factors*. Bologna: Monduzzi-Editore, 1990, 633–637.

Clum, G. A., & Weaver, T. L. Diagnostic morbidity and its relationship to severity of ideation for a nonpatient sample of chronic and severe suicide ideators. *Journal of Psychopathology & Behavior Assessment*, 1997, 19, 191–206.

Cohen, L. J., Test, M. A., & Brown, R. L. Suicide and schizophrenia. *American Journal of Psychiatry*, 1990, 147, 602–607.

Cohen, S., Lavelle, J., Rich, C. L., & Bromet, E. Rates and correlates of suicide attempts in first-admission psychotic patients. *Acta Psychiatrica Scandinavica*, 1994, 90, 167–171.

Cohen, Y., Spirito, A., Apter, A., & Sain, S. A cross-cultural comparison. *Child Psychiatry & Human Development*, 1997, 28, 89–102.

Cole, M., & Casey, P. The relationship between depressive illness and parasuicide. In P. Crepet, G. Ferrari, S. Platt & M. Bellini (Eds.), *Suicidal behavior in Europe*. Rome: John Libbey, 1992, 261–270.

Connell, D. K., & Meyer, R. G. Adolescents' suicidal behavior and popular self-report instruments of depression, social desirability, and anxiety. *Adolescence*, 1991, 26, 113–119.

Conti, L., Toschi, D., DiMuro, A., & Marazitti, D. Depression and suicide attempt.

in G. Ferrari, M. Bellini & P. Crepet (Eds.), *Suicidal behavior and risk factors*. Bologna: Monduzzi-Editore, 1990, 669–674.

Conwell, Y., Duberstein, P. C., Cox, C., Harrmann, J. R., Forbes, N. T., & Caine, E. D. Relationships of age and Axis I diagnoses in victims of suicide. *American Journal of Psychiatry*, 1996, 153, 1001–1008.

Corbitt, E. M., Malone, K. M., Haas, G. L., & Mann, J. J. Suicidal behavior in patients with major depression and comorbid personality disorder. *Journal of Affective Disorders*, 1996, 39, 61–72.

Cornelius, J. R., Salloum, I. M., Day, N. L., Thase, M. E., & Mann, J. J. Patterns of suicidality and alcohol use in alcoholics with major depression. *Alcoholism: Clinical & Experimental Research*, 1996, 20, 1451–1455.

Cornelius, J. R., Salloum, I. M. Mazzich, T., Cornelius, M. D., Fabrega, H., Ehler, J. G., Ulrich, R. F., Thase, M. E., & Mann, J. J. Disproportionate suicidality in patients with comorbid major depression and alcoholism. *American Journal of Psychiatry*, 1995, 152, 358–364.

Cox, B. J., Direnfeld, D. M., Swinson, R. P., & Norton, G. R. Suicidal ideation and suicide attempts in panic disorder and social phobia. *American Journal of Psychiatry*, 1994, 151, 882–887.

Cremniter, D., Jamain, S., Meidinger, A., Thenault, M., Payant, C., Delmas, C., Guerin, A., & Fermania, J. Attempts to commit suicide and suicidal thoughts. In P. Crepet, G. Ferrari, S. Platt & M. Bellini (Eds.), *Suicidal behaviour in Europe*. Rome: John Libbey, 1992, 271–276.

Crisp, A. H., Callendar, J. S., Halek, C., & Hsu, L. K. G. Long-term mortality in anorexia nervosa. *British Journal of Psychiatry*, 1992, 161, 104–107.

Dassori, A. M., Mezzich, J. E., & Keshavan, M. Suicidal indicators in schizophrenia. *Acta Psychiatrica Scandinavica*, 1990, 81, 409–413.

Degonda, M., Wyss, M., & Angst, J. The Zurich study. *European Archives of Psychiatry*, 1993, 243, 16–22.

De Leo, D. Suicide in a general hospital. *Crisis*, 1997, 18, 5–6.

De Moore, G. M., & Robertson, A. R. Suicide in the 18 years after deliberate self-harm. *British Journal of Psychiatry*, 1996, 169, 489–494.

Dennehy, J. A., Appleby, L., Thomas, C. S., & Faragher, E. B. Case-control study of suicide by discharged psychiatric patients. *British Medical Journal*, 1996, 312, 1580.

Derecho, C. N., Wetzler, S., & McGinn, L. K. Atypical depression among psychiatric inpatients. *Journal of Affective Disorders*, 1996, 39, 55–59.

Dilsaver, S. C., Chen, Y. W., Swan, A. C., Shoaib, A. M., & Krajewski, K. J. Suicidality in patients with pure and depressive mania. *American Journal of Psychiatry*, 1994, 151, 1312–1315.

Dilsaver, S. C., Chen, Y. W., Swan, A. C., Shoaib, A. M., Tsai-Dilsaver, Y., & Krajesski, K. J. Suicidality, panic disorder and psychosis in bipolar depression, depressive mania, and pure mania. *Psychiatry Research*, 1997, 73, 47–56.

Dinwiddie, S. H., Reich, T., & Cloninger, C. R. Solvent use and psychiatric comorbidity. *British Journal of Addiction*, 1990, 85, 1647–1656.

Dinwiddie, S. H., Reich, T., & Cloninger, C. R. Psychiatric comorbidity and suicidality among intravenous drug users. *Journal of Clinical Psychiatry*, 1992, 53, 364–369.

Dixon, W. A., Rumford, K. G., Heppner, P. P., & Lips, B. J. Use of different sources of stress to predict hopelessness and suicide ideation in a college population. *Journal of Counseling Psychology*, 1992, 39, 342–349.

Duberstein, P. R., Conwell, Y., & Caine, E. D. Interpersonal stressors, substance abuse, and suicide. *Journal of Nervous & Mental Disease*, 1993, 181, 80–85.

Dubo, E. D., Zanarini, M. C., Lewis, R. E., & Williams, A. A. Childhood antecedents of self-destructiveness in borderline personality disorder. *Canadian Journal of Psychiatry*, 1997, 42, 63–69.

Duffy, J., & Kreitman, N. Risk factors for suicide and undetermined death among inpatient alcoholics. *Addiction*, 1993, 88, 757–766.

Duggan, C. F., Sham, P., Lee, A. S., & Murray, R. M. Can future suicidal behavior in depressed patients be predicted? *Journal of Affective Disorders*, 1991, 22, 111–118.

Duncan, S. C., Alpert, A., Duncan, T. E., & Hops, H. Adolescent alcohol use development and young adult outcomes. *Drug & Alcohol Dependence*, 1997, 49, 39–48.

Earle, K. A., Forquer, S. L., Volo, A. M., & McDonnell, P. M. Characteristics of outpatient suicides. *Hospital & Community Psychiatry*, 1994, 45, 123–126.

Ekeberg, O., Ellingsen, O., & Jacobsen, D. Suicide and other causes of death in a five-year follow-up of patients treated for self-poisoning in Oslo. *Acta Psychiatrica Scandinavica*, 1991, 83, 432–437.

Ekeberg, O., Ellingsen, O., & Jacobsen, D. Mortality and causes of death in a 10-year follow-up of patients treated for self-poisoning in Oslo. *Suicide & Life-Threatening Behavior*, 1994, 24, 398–405.

Engberg, M. Mortality and suicide rates of involuntary committed patients. *Acta Psychiatrica Scandinavica*, 1994, 89, 35–40.

Fava, G., Grandi, S., Savron, G., Conti, S., & Rafanelli, C. Panic disorder and suicidal ideation. *American Journal of Psychiatry*, 1992, 149, 1412.

Favaro, A., & Santonastaso, P. Purging behaviors, suicide attempts, and psychiatric symptoms in 398 eating disordered subjects. *International Journal of Eating Disorders*, 1996, 20, 99–103.

Favaro, A., & Santonastaso, P. Suicidality in eating disorders. *Acta Psychiatrica Scandinavica*, 1997, 95, 508–514.

Fawcett, J. The morbidity and mortality of clinical depression. *International Clinical Psychopharmacology*, 1993, 8, 217–220.

Fawcett, J., Scheftner, W. A., Fogg, L., Clark, D. C., Young, M. A., Hedeker, D., & Gibbons, R. Time-related predictors of suicide in major affective disorder. *American Journal of Psychiatry*, 1990, 147, 1189–1194.

Feinman, J. A., & Dunner, D. L. The effect of alcohol and substance abuse on the course of bipolar affective disorder. *Journal of Affective Disorders*, 1996, 37, 43–49.

Felts, W. M., Chenier, T., & Barnes, R. Drug use and suicide ideation and behavior among North Carolina public school students. *American Journal of Public Health*, 1992, 82, 870–872.

Fenton, W. S., McGlashan, T. H., Victor, B. J., & Blyler, C. R. Symptoms, subtype, and suicidality in patients with schizophrenia spectrum disorders. *American Journal of Psychiatry*, 1997, 154, 199–204.

Ferrero, F., Giacomini-Biraud, V., Zabala, I., & Tricot, L. Suicide, suicidal behavior, and mortality in adolescent patients. In P. Crepet, G. Ferrari, S. Platt & M. Bellini (Eds.), *Suicidal behaviour in Europe*. Rome: John Libbey, 1992, 161–167.

Fleet, R. P., Dupuis, G., Kaczorowski, J., Marchand, A., & Beitman, B. D. Suicidal ideation in emergency department chest pain patients. *American Journal of Emergency Medicine*, 1997, 15, 345–349.

Fleet, R. P., Dupuis, G., Marchand, A., Burelle, D., Arsenault, A., & Beitman, B. D. Panic disorder in emergency department chest pain patients. *American Journal of Medicine*, 1996, 101, 371–380.

Florio, E. R., Hendryx, M. S., Jensen, J. E., Rockwood, T. H., Raschko, R., & Dyck, D. G. A comparison of suicidal and nonsuicidal elders referred to a community mental health center program. *Suicide & Life-Threatening Behavior*, 1997, 27, 182–193.

Forsell, Y., Jorm, A. F., & Winblad, B. Suicidal thoughts and associated factors in an elderly population. *Acta Psychiatrica Scandinavica*, 1997, 95, 108–111.

Foster, T., Gillespie, K., & McClelland, R. Mental disorders and suicide in Northern Ireland. *British Journal of Psychiatry*, 1997, 170, 447–452.

Frank, M. L., Lester, D., & Wexler, A. Suicidal behavior among members of Gamblers Anonymous. *Journal of Gambling Studies*, 1991, 7, 249–254.

Frater, R., Hegyi, Z., Nemes, R., & Lajtai, L. Attempted suicide. *Psychiatria Danubina*, 1991, 3, 331–333.

Freeman, T. W., Keesee, N., Thornton, C., Gillette, G., & Young, K. Dissociative symptoms in post-traumatic stress disorder subjects with a history of suicide attempts. *Journal of Nervous & Mental Disease*, 1995, 183, 664–666.

French, S. A., Story, M., Downes, B., Resnick, M. D., & Blum, R. W. Frequent dieting among adolescents. *American Journal of Public Health*, 1995, 85, 695–710.

Fridell, E. J., Ojehagen, A., & Traskman Bendz, L. A five-year follow-up study of suicide attempts. *Acta Psychiatrica Scandinavica*, 1996, 93, 151–157.

Friedman, S., Jones, J. C., Chernen, L., & Barlow, D. H. Suicidal ideation and suicide attempts among patients with panic disorder. *American Journal of Psychiatry*, 1992, 149, 680–685.

Frierson, R. L. Suicide attempts by the old and the very old. *Archives of Internal Medicine*, 1991, 151, 141–144.

Frischer, M., Bloor, M., Goldberg, D., Clark, J., Green, S., & McKeganey, N. Mortality among injecting drug users. *Journal of Epidemiology & Community Health*, 1993, 47, 59–63.

Fritze, J., Schneider, B., & Lanczik, M. Autoaggressive behavior and cholesterol. *Neuropsychobiology*, 1992, 26, 180–181.

Gabriel, J., & Paschalis, C. The psychopathology of suicide in the northwestern Peloponnesus. *Psychopathology*, 1991, 24, 82–87.

Gallagher, A. G., Dinan, T. G., Sheehy, N. P., & Baker, L. J. Chronic auditory hallucinations and suicide risk factors in schizophrenics. *Irish Journal of Psychological Medicine*, 1995, 16, 346–355.

Ganesvara, T., & Shah, A. K. Psychiatric inpatient suicide rates. *Medicine, Science & the Law*, 1997, 37, 202–209.

Geddes, J. R., & Juszczak, E. Period trends in rate of suicide in first 28 days after discharge from psychiatric hospital in Scotland, 1968–1992. *British Medical Journal*, 1995, 311, 357–360.

Geddes, J. R., Juszczak, E., O'Brien, F., & Kendrick, S. Suicide in the 12 months after discharge from psychiatric inpatient care, Scotland, 1968–92. *Journal of Epidemiology & Community Health*, 1997, 51, 430–434.

Giaconia, R. M., Reinherz, H. Z., Silverman, A. B., Pakiz, B., Frost, A. K., & Cohen, E. Traumas and post-traumatic stress disorder in a community population of older adolescents. *Journal of the American Academy of Child & Adolescent Psychiatry*, 1995, 34, 1369–1380.

Gillet, C., Paille, F., Wahl, D., Aubin, H. J., Pirollet, P., & Prime, T. Outcome of treatment in alcoholic women. *Drug & Alcohol Dependence*, 1991, 29, 189–194.

Goldacre, M., Seagroatt, V., & Hawton, K. Suicide after discharge from psychiatric inpatient care. *Lancet*, 1993, 342, 283–286.

Goldstein, R. B., Black, D. W., Nasrallah, A., & Winokur, G. The prediction of suicide. *Archives of General Psychiatry*, 1991, 48, 418–422.

Gordon, D. P., Halmi, K. A., & Ippolito, P. M. A comparison of the psychological evaluation of adolescents with anorexia nervosa and adolescents with conduct disorder. *Journal of Adolescence*, 1984, 7, 245–266.

Gotze, P., & Orlowski-Studemann, E. Suicide in schizophrenic patients. In G. Ferrari, M. Bellini & P. Crepet (Eds.), *Suicidal behavior and risk factors*. Bologna: Monduzzi-Editore, 1990, 621–626.

Graves, P. L., & Thomas, C. B. Habits of nervous tension and suicide. *Suicide & Life-Threatening Behavior*, 1991, 21, 91–105.

Greenberg, W. M., Rosenfeld, D. N., & Ortega, E. A. Adjustment disorder as an admission diagnosis. *American Journal of Psychiatry*, 1995, 152, 459–461.

Groholt, B., Ekeberg, O., Wichstrom, L., & Haldorsen, T. Youth suicide in Norway, 1990–1992. *Suicide & Life-Threatening Behavior*, 1997, 27, 250–263.

Gupta, S. C., Trivedi, J. K., & Singh, H. A study of suicide attempts with special reference to repeaters versus nonrepeaters. *Indian Journal of Clinical Psychology*, 1992, 19(1), 23–27.

Hagen, H. Suicidal attempts among psychiatric patients. In T. Bjerke & T. C. Stiles (Eds.), *Suicide attempts in the Nordic countries*. Trondheim: Tapir Forlag, 1991, 131–145.

Hale, M., Jacobson, J., & Carson, R. A database review in C-L psychiatry. *Psychosomatics*, 1990, 31, 282–286.

Hamer, D., Sanjeev, D., Butterworth, E., & Barczak, P. Using the Hospital Anxiety and Depression Scale to screen for psychiatric disorders in people presenting with deliberate self-harm. *British Journal of Psychiatry*, 1991, 158, 782–784.

Hanafy, A. Y. Sociodemographic aspects and length of stay in hospital in suicide. *European Journal of Psychiatry*, 1991, 5, 147–151.

Hanna, E. Z., & Grant, B. F. Gender differences in DSM-IV alcohol-use disorders and major depression as distributed in the general population. *Comprehensive Psychiatry*, 1997, 38, 202–212.

Hansen, A. U., & Simonsen, J. The manner and cause of death in a forensic series of chronic alcoholics. *Forensic Science International*, 1991, 49, 171–178.

Hansen, V. Long-term mortality after first psychiatric admission. *British Journal of Psychiatry*, 1997, 171, 181.

Harris, E. C., & Barraclough, B. M. Suicide as an outcome for mental disorders. *British Journal of Psychiatry*, 1997, 170, 205–228.

Harrow, M., Westermeyer, J., Kaplan, K., & Butz, C. Schizophrenia and suicide. In D. Lester (Ed.), *Suicide '92*. Denver: AAS, 1992, 206–208.

Hatsukami, D., Mitchell, J. E., Eckert, E. D., & Pyle, R. Characteristics of patients with bulimia only, bulimia with affective disorder, and bulimia with substance abuse problems. *Addictive Behaviors*, 1986, 11, 399–406.

Hattori, T., Taketani, K., & Ogasawara, Y Suicide and suicide attempts in general hospital psychiatry. *Psychiatry & Clinical Neurosciences*, 1995, 49, 43–48.

Havak-Kontaxaki, B. J., Kontaxakis, V. P., Protopappa, V. A., & Christodoulou, G. N. Suicide in a large psychiatric hospital. *Bibliotheca Psychiatrica*, 1994, #165, 63–71.

Hawley, C. J., James, D. V., Birkett, P. L., Baldwin, D. S., de Ruiter, M. J., & Priest, R. G. Suicidal ideation as a presenting complaint. *British Journal of Psychiatry*, 1991, 159, 232–238.

Hawton, K., Simkins, S., & Fagg, J. Deliberate self-harm in alcohol and drug misusers. *Drug & Alcohol Review*, 1997, 16(2), 123–129.

Henriksson, M. M., Isometsa, E. T., Kuoppasalmi, K. I., Heikkinen, M. E., Marttunen, M. J., & Lonnqvist, J. K. Panic disorder in completed suicide. *Journal of Clinical Psychiatry*, 1996, 57, 275–281.

Hepple, J., & Quinton, C. One hundred cases of attempted suicide in the elderly. *British Journal of Psychiatry*, 1997, 171, 42–46.

Hewer, W., Rossler, W., Fatkenheuer, B., & Loffler, W. Mortality among patients in psychiatric hospitals in Germany. *Acta Psychiatrica Scandinavica*, 1995, 91, 174–179.

Hjelmeland, H. Repetition of parasuicide. *Suicide & Life-Threatening Behavior*, 1996, 26, 395–404.

Hoffman, H. Age and other factors relevant to the rehospitalization of schizophrenic outpatients. *Acta Psychiatrica Scandinavica*, 1994, 89, 205–210.

Hori, M., Shiraishi, H., & Koizum, J. Delusional depression and suicide. *Japanese Journal of Psychiatry & Neurology*, 1993, 47, 811–817.

Hornig, C. D., & McNally, R. J. Panic disorder and suicide attempts. *British Journal of Psychiatry*, 1995, 167, 76–79.

Hu, W. H., Sun, C. M., Lee, C. T., Peng, S. L., Lin, S. K., & Shen, W. W. A clinical study of schizophrenic suicides. *Schizophrenia Research*, 1991, 5(1), 43–50.

Hunt, D. K., Lowenstein, S. R., Badgett, R. G., Marine, W. M., Garrett, C. J., & Steiner, J. F. Detection of injury-prone behaviors among internal medicine patients. *Journal of General Internal Medicine*, 1992, 7, 573-582.

Isacsson, G., Boethius, G., & Bergman, U. Low level of antidepressant prescription for people who later commit suicide. *Acta Psychiatrica Scandinavica*, 1992, 85, 444–448.

Isometsa, E. T., Aro, H. M., Henriksson, M. M., Heikkinen, M. E., & Lonnqvist, J. K. Suicide in major depression in different treatment settings. *Journal of Clinical Psychiatry*, 1994b, 55, 523-527.

Isometsa, E., Heikkinen, M., Henriksson, M., Aro, H., Marttunen, M., Kuoppasalmi, K., & Lonnqvist, J. Suicide in nonmajor depression. *Journal of Affective Disorders*, 1996a, 36, 117–127.

Isometsa, E. T., Henriksson, M. M., Aro, H. M., Heikkinen, M. E., Juoppasalmi, K., & Lonnqvist, J. K. Suicide in psychotic major depression. *Journal of Affective Disorders*, 1994a, 31, 187–191.

Isometsa, E., Henriksson, M., Heikkinen, M., Aro, H. M., Marttunen, M. J., Kuoppasalmi, K. I., & Lonnqvist, J. Suicide among subjects with personality disorders. *American Journal of Psychiatry*, 1996b, 153, 667–673.

Isometsa, E., Henriksson, M., Heikkinen, M., & Lonnqvist, J. Suicide after discharge from psychiatric inpatient care. *Lancet*, 1993, 342, 1055-1056.

Isometsa, E. T., Henriksson, M. M., Marttunen, M., Heikkinen, M. E., Aro, H. M., Kuoppasalmi, K., & Lonnqvist, J. K. Mental disorders in young and middle-aged men who commit suicide. *British Medical Journal*, 1995, 310, 1366-1367.

Ivanoff, A., & Jang, S. J. The role of hopelessness and social desirability in predicting suicidal behavior. *Journal of Consulting & Clinical Psychology*, 1991, 59, 394–399.

Javed, M. A. Suicidal symptoms in depressed Pakistani patients. *Journal of the Pakistan Medical Association*, 1996, 46(4), 69–70.

Johansson, L., M., Johansson, S. E., Sundquist, J., & Bergman, Suicide among psychiatric inpatients in Stockholm, Sweden. *Archives of Suicide Research*, 1996, 2, 171–181.

Johnson, B. A., Brent, D. A., Connolly, J., Bridge, J., Matta, J., Constantine, D., Rather, C., & White T. Familial aggregation of adolescent personality disorders. *Journal of the American Academy of Child & Adolescent Psychiatry*, 1995, 34, 798–804.

Johnson, J., Weissman, M. M., & Klerman, G. L. Panic disorder, comorbidity, and suicide attempts. *Archives of General Psychiatry*, 1990, 47, 805–808.

Johnsson, E., & Fridell, M. Suicide attempts in a cohort of drug abusers. *Acta Psychiatrica Scandinavica*, 1997, 96, 362–366.

Jones, G. D. The role of drugs and alcohol in urban minority adolescent suicide attempters. *Death Studies*, 1997, 21, 189–202.

Jones, J. S., Stein, D. J., Stanley, B., Guido, J. R., Winchel, R., & Stanley, M. Negative and depressive symptoms in suicidal schizophrenics. *Acta Psychiatrica Scandinavica*, 1994, 89, 81–87.

Jorgensen, P., & Mortesen, P. B. Cause of death in reactive psychoses. *Acta Psychiatrica Scandinavica*, 1992, 85, 351–353.

Jorgensen, P., Stiles, T. C., Bjerke, T., & Rygnestad, T. Repetition of parasuicide. In K. Bohme, R. Freytag, C. Wachtler & H. Wedler (Eds.), *Suicidal behavior*. Regensburg: S. Roderer, 1993, 755–758.

Juon, H. S., & Ensminger, M. E. Childhood, adolescent, and young-adult predictors of suicidal behaviors. *Journal of Child Psychology & Psychiatry*, 1997, 38, 553–563.

Kaplan, K. J., & Harrow, M. Positive and negative symptoms as risk factors for later suicidal activity in schizophrenics versus depressives. *Suicide & Life-Threatening Behavior*, 1996, 26, 105–121.

Kaplan, K. J., Harrow, M., & Beck, J. Positive and negative symptoms as risk factors for later suicidal activity. In J. McIntosh (Ed.), *Suicide '96*. Washington, DC: AAS, 1996, 93–94.

Kempton, T., & Forehand, R. Suicide attempts among juvenile delinquents. *Behavior Research & Therapy*, 1992, 30, 537–541.

Kent, A., Goddard, K. L., van den Besk, P., Raphael, F. J., McCluskey, S. E., & Lacey, J. H. Eating disorder in women admitted to hospital following deliberate self-poisoning. *Acta Psychiatrica Scandinavica*, 1997, 95, 140–144.

King, C. A., Ghaziuddin, N., McGovern, L., Hill, E., & Naylor, M. Identifying depressed adolescents with comorbid alcohol abuse. In D. Lester (Ed.), *Suicide '95*. Washington, DC: AAS, 1995a, 118–120.

King, C. A., Segal, H., Kaminski, K., Naylor, M., Ghaziuddin, N., & Radpour, L. A prospective study of adolescent suicidal behavior following hospitalization. *Suicide & Life-Threatening Behavior*, 1995b, 25, 327–338.

King, E. Suicide in the mentally ill. *British Journal of Psychiatry*, 1994, 165, 658–663.

King, E., & Barraclough, B. M. Violent death and mental illness. *British Journal of Psychiatry*, 1990, 156, 714–7120.

King, M., Schmaling, K. B., Cowley, D. S., & Dunner, D. L. Suicide attempt history in depressed patients with and without a history of panic attacks. *Comprehensive Psychiatry*, 1995c, 36, 25–30.

Kjelsberg, E., Eikeseth, P. H., & Dahl, A. A. Suicide in borderline patients. *Acta Psychiatrica Scandinavica*, 1991, 84, 283–287.

Kjelsberg, E., Neegaard, E., & Dahl, A. A. Suicide in adolescent psychiatric inpatients. *Acta Psychiatrica Scandinavica*, 1994, 89, 235–241.

Klatsky, A. L., & Armstrong, M. A. Alcohol use, other traits, and risk of unnatural death. *Alcoholism: Clinical & Experimental Research*, 1993, 17, 1156–1162.

Knaurer, E., Bussing, A., & Kerstiens, J. Hospital suicides of elderly people. In K. Bohme, R. Freytag, C. Wachtler & H. Wedler (Eds.), *Suicidal behavior*. Regensburg: S. Roderer, 1993, 251–258.

Ko, S. M., Kua, E. H., & Chow, M. H. Depression of young and elderly patients. *Singapore Medical Journal*, 1997, 38, 439–441.

Korn, M. L., Plutchik, R., & Van Praag, H. M. Panic-associated suicidal and aggressive ideation and behavior. *Journal of Psychiatric Research*, 1997, 31, 481–487.

Kovacs, M., Goldston, D., & Gasonis, C. Suicidal behaviors and childhood-onset depressive disorders. *Journal of the American Academy of Child & Adolescent Psychiatry*, 1993, 32, 8–20.

Kramer, T. L., Linday, J. D., Green, B. L., Grace, M. C., & Leonard, A. C. The comorbidity of post-traumatic stress disorder and suicidality in Vietnam veterans. *Suicide & Life-Threatening Behavior*, 1994, 24, 58–67.

Krarup, G., Nielsen, B., Rask, P., & Petersen, P. Childhood experiences and repeated suicidal behavior. *Acta Psychiatrica Scandinavica*, 1991, 83, 16–19.

Krausz, M., Mass, R., Haasen, C., & Gross, J. Psychopathology in patients with schizophrenia and substance abuse. *Psychopathology*, 1996, 29, 95–103.

Kullgren, G., Armelius, B. A., & Jacobsson, L. Completed suicide among patients with borderline personality disorder. In P. Crepet, G. Ferrari, S. Platt & M. Bellini (Eds.), *Suicidal behaviour in Europe*. Rome: John Libbey, 1992, 143–148.

Lambert, M. T., & Bonner, J. Characteristics and six-month outcome of patients who use suicide threats to seek hospital admission. *Psychiatric Services*, 1996, 47, 871–873.

Lecrubier, Y., & Weiller, E. Comorbidities in social phobia. *International Clinical Psychopharmacology*, 1997, 12, S6, 17–21.

Lee, A. S., Duggan, C., & Murray, R. M. Can one predict the long-term outcome of hospitalized depressives? *Journal of Psychopharmacology*, 1992, 6, (Suppl. 2),

300–303.

Leon, A. C., Friedman, R. A., Sweeney, J. A., Brown, R. P., & Mann, J. J. Statistical issues in the identification of risk factors for suicidal behavior. *Psychiatry Research*, 1990, 31, 99–108.

Leon, A. C., Klerman, G. L., Weissman, M. M., Fyer, A. J., & Johnson, J. Evaluating the diagnostic criteria for panic disorder. *Social Psychiatry & Psychiatric Epidemiology*, 1992, 27, 180–184.

Lepine, J. P., Chignon, J. M., & Teherani, M. Onset of panic disorder and suicide attempts. *Psychiatry & Psychobiology*, 1990, 5, 339–342.

Lepine, J. P., Chignon, J. M., & Teherani, M. Suicidal behavior and onset of panic disorder. *Archives of General Psychiatry*, 1991, 48, 668–669.

Lepine, J. P., Chignon, J. M., & Teherani, M. Suicide attempts in patients with panic disorder. *Archives of General Psychiatry*, 1993, 50, 144–149.

Lepine, J. P., & Lellouch, J. Classification and epidemiology of social phobia. *European Archives of Psychiatry,* 1995, 244, 290–296.

Lepola, U., Koponen, H., & Leinonen, E. A naturalistic six-year follow-up study of patients with panic disorder. *Acta Psychiatrica Scandinavica*, 1996, 93, 181–183.

Lesage, A. D., Boyer, R., Grunberg, F., Vanier, C., Morissette, R., Menard-Buteau, C., & Longer, M. Suicide and mental disorders. *American Journal of Psychiatry*, 1994, 151, 1063–1068.

Lester, D. Mortality from suicide in follow-up studies of psychiatric patients. *Perceptual & Motor Skills*, 1990, 71, 230.

Lester, D. Premature mortality associated with alcoholism and suicide in American writers. *Perceptual & Motor Skills*, 1991a, 73, 162.

Lester, D. Suicide among alcoholics. *Perceptual & Motor Skills*, 199b, 73, 242.

Lester, D. Alcoholism and drug abuse. In R. W. Maris, A. L. Berman, J. T. Maltsberger & R. I. Yufit (Eds.), *Assessment and prediction of suicide*. New York: Guilford, 1992, 321–336.

Lester, D. Alcohol use and abuse in Canada and mortality from suicide. *Canadian Journal of Public Health*, 1993a, 84, 402.

Lester, D. Restricting the availability of alcohol and rates of personal violence (suicide and homicide). *Drug & Alcohol Dependence*, 1993b, 31, 215–217.

Lester, D. Suicidal behavior in bipolar and unipolar affective disorder. *Journal of Affective Disorders*, 1993c, 27, 117–121.

Lester, D. Mortality from suicide in follow-up studies of schizophrenia. *Perceptual & Motor Skills*, 1993d, 77, 114.

Lester, D. Rates of mental illness and suicide by state. *Perceptual & Motor Skills*, 1993e, 77, 330.

Lester, D. Alcohol use and abuse, suicide, and homicide. *Psychological Reports*, 1993f, 73, 346.

Lester, D. Borderline personality disorder and suicidal behavior. *Psychological Reports*, 1993g, 73, 394.

Lester, D. The mortality of attempted suicides in follow-up studies of male suicide attempters. *Perceptual & Motor Skills*, 1996, 83, 530.

Lim, L. C. C., & Tsoi, W. F. Suicide and schizophrenia in Singapore. *Annals of the Academy of Medicine, Singapore*, 1991, 20, 201–203.

Linden, M., & Barnow, S. The wish to die in very old persons near the end of life. *International Psychogeriatrics*, 1997, 9, 291–307.

Lindstrom, E., Wallsten, T., Palmstierna, T., & Van Knorring, L. The need for compulsory care in schizophrenia in relation to symptomatology and side-effects. *European Journal of Psychiatry*, 1997, 11, 72–80.

Links, P. S., Mitton, J. E., & Steiner, M. Predicting outcome for borderline personality disorder. *Comprehensive Psychiatry*, 1990, 31, 490–498.

Lish, J. D., Zimmerman, M., Farber, N., Lush, D., Kuzma, M., & Plescia, G. Suicide screening in a primary care setting at a Veterans Affairs medical center. *Psychosomatics*, 1996, 37, 413–424.

Liu, C. Y., Bai, Y. M., Yang, Y. Y., Lin, C. C., Si, C. B., & Lee, C. H. Suicide and parasuicide in psychiatric inpatients. *Psychological Reports*, 1996, 79, 683–690.

Loimer, N., Werner, E., Hofmann, P., & Presslich, O. Drug addiction, AIDS, and suicidal behavior. In P. Crepet, G. Ferrari, S. Platt & M. Bellini (Eds.), *Suicidal behaviour in Europe.*

Rome: John Libbey, 1992, 307–313.

Lonnqvist, J. K. Henriksson, M. M., Isometsa, E. T., Marttunen, M. J., Heikkinen, M. E., Aro, H. M., & Kuoppasalmi, K. I. Mental disorders and suicide prevention. *Psychiatry & Clinical Neurosciences*, 1995, 49, (Suppl. 1), 111–116.

Lonnqvist, J. K., & Ostamo, A. Suicide following the first suicide attempt. *Psychiatria Fennica*, 1991, 22, 171–179.

Lonnqvist, J. K., & Suokas, J. Risk of lethal outcome in attempted suicide. In K. Bohme, R. Freytag, C. Wachtler & H. Wedler (Eds.), *Suicidal behavior*. Regensburg; S. Roderer, 1993, 498–501.

Lyness, J. M., Conwell, Y., & Nelson, J. C. Suicide attempts in elderly psychiatric inpatients. *Journal of the American Geriatric Society*, 1992, 40, 320–324.

MacLeod, A. K., Rose, G. S., & Williams, J. M. Components of hopelessness about the future of parasuicide. *Cognitive Therapy Research*, 1993, 17, 441–455.

Madianos, M. G., Gefou-Madianou, D., & Stefanis, C. N. Symptoms of depression, suicidal behavior, and use of substances in Greece. *Acta Psychiatrica Scandinavica*, 1994, 89, 159–166.

Magruder-Habib, K., Hubbard, R. L., & Ginzburg, H. M. Effects of drug misuse treatment on symptoms of depression and suicide. *International Journal of the Addictions*, 1992, 27, 1035–1065.

Maier, W., Herr, R., Greensicke, M., Houshangpour, K., & Benkert, O. Recurrent brief depression in general practice. *European Archives of Psychiatry*, 1994, 244, 196–204.

Malone, K. M., Haas, G. L., Sweeney, J. A., & Mann, J. J. Major depression and the risk of attempted suicide. *Journal of Affective Disorders*, 1995, 34, 173–185.

Mannuzza, S., Aronowitz, B., Chapman, T., Klein, D. F., & Fyer, A. J. Panic disorder and suicide attempts. *Journal of Anxiety Disorders*, 1992, 6, 261–274.

Marttunen, M. J., Aro, H. M., Henriksson, M. M., & Lonnqvist, J. K. Mental disorders in adolescent suicide. *Archives of General Psychiatry*, 1991, 48, 834–839.

Marzuk, P. M., Tardiff, K., Leon, A. C.,

Hirsch, C. S., Stajic, M., Hartwell, N., & Portera, L. Use of prescription psychotropic drugs among suicide victims in New York City. *American Journal of Psychiatry*, 1995a, 152, 1520–1522.

Marzuk, P. M., Tardiff, K., Leon, A. C., Stajic, M., Morgan, E. B., & Mann, J. J. Prevalence of cocaine use among residents of New York City who committed suicide during a one-year period. *American Journal of Psychiatry*, 1992, 149, 371–375.

Marzuk, P. M., Tardiff, K., Leon, A. C., Hirsch, C. S., Stajic, M., Portera, L., Hartwell, N., & Iqbal, M. I. Fatal injuries after cocaine use as a leading cause of death among young adults in New York City. *New England Journal of Medicine*, 1995b, 332, 1753–1757.

Mechanic, D., angel, R., & Davies, L. Risk and selection processes between the general and the speciality mental health sectors. *Journal of Health & Social Behavior*, 1991, 32, 49–64.

Mehlum, L., Friis, S., Irion, T., Johns, S., Karterud, S., Vaglum, P., & Vaglum, S. Personality disorders two–five years after treatment. *Acta Psychiatrica Scandinavica*, 1991, 84, 72–77.

Mehlum, L., Friis, S., Vaglum, P., & Kartervd, S. The longitudinal pattern of suicidal behavior in borderline personality disorder. *Acta Psychiatrica Scandinavica*, 1994, 90, 124–130.

Meltzer, H. Y., & Okayli, G. Reduction of suicidality during clozapine treatment of neuroleptic-resistant schizophrenia. *American Journal of Psychiatry*, 1995, 152, 183–190.

Menezes, P. R., & Mann, A. H. Mortality among patients with non-affective functional psychoses in a metropolitan area of Southeastern Brazil. *Revista de Saude Publica*, 1996, 30, 304–309.

Merikangas, K. R., Wicki, W., & Angst, J. Heterogeneity of depression. *British Journal of Psychiatry*, 1994, 164, 342–348.

Merrill, J., Milner, G., Owens, J., & Vale, A. Alcohol and attempted suicide. *British Journal of Addiction*, 1992, 87, 83–89.

Milch, W. E. The change of symptomatology in hospitalized suicidal patients. *Crisis*, 1990, 11, 44–51.

Milling, L., Campbell, N. B., Bush, E., & Laughlin, A. The relationship of suicidality and psychiatric diagnosis in hospitalized preadolescent children. *Child Psychiatry & Human Development*, 1992, 23(1), 41–49.

Milne, S., Matthews, K., & Ashcroft, G. W. Suicide in Scotland 1988–1989. *British Journal of Psychiatry*, 1994, 165, 541–544.

Mireault, M., & De Man, A. F. Suicidal ideation among the elderly. *Social Behavior & Personality*, 1996, 24, 385–392.

Modestin, J., & Kamm, A. Parasuicide in psychiatric inpatients. *Acta Psychiatrica Scandinavica*, 1990, 81, 225–230.

Modestin, J., Zarro, I., & Waldvogel, D. A study of suicide in schizophrenic inpatients. *British Journal of Psychiatry*, 1992, 160, 398–401.

Montgomery, S. A., Montgomery, D., Baldwin, D., & Green, M. The duration, nature, and recurrence rate of brief depressions. *Progress in Neuropsychopharmacology & Biological Psychiatry*, 1990, 14, 729–735.

Morrison, J. Increased suicide attempts in women with somatization disorder. *Annals of Clinical Psychiatry*, 1989, 1, 251–254.

Mortensen, P. B., & Juel, K. Mortality and causes of death in schizophrenic patients in Denmark. *Acta Psychiatrica Scandinavica*, 1990, 81, 372–377.

Mortensen, P. B., & Juel, K. Mortality and cause of death in first-admitted schizophrenic patients. *British Journal of Psychiatry*, 1993, 163, 183–189.

Morton, M. J. Prediction of repetition of parasuicide. *International Journal of Social Psychiatry*, 1993, 39, 87–99.

Mullick, M. S., Karim, M. E., & Khanam, M. Depression in deliberate self-harm patients. *Bangladesh Medical Research Council Bulletin*, 1994, 20(3), 123–128.

Murphy, G. E. *Suicide in alcoholism.* New York: Oxford University Press, 1992.

Murphy, G., & Wetzel, R. D. The lifetime risk of suicide in alcoholism. *Archives of General Psychiatry*, 1990, 47, 383–392.

Mutzell, S. Mortality, suicide, social maladjustment, and criminality among male alcoholic parents and men from the general population and their offspring. *International Journal of Youth & Adolescence*, 1994, 4, 305–328.

Myers, K., McCauley, E., Calderon, R., Mitchell, J., Burke P., & Schloredt, K. Risks for suicidality in major depressive disorder. *Journal of the American Academy of Child & Adolescent Psychiatry*, 1991a, 30, 86–94.

Myers, K., McCauley, E., Calderon, R., & Treder, R. The three-year longitudinal course of suicidality and predictive factors for subsequent suicidality in youths with major depressive disorders. *Journal of the American Academy of Child & Adolescent Psychiatry*, 1991b, 30, 804–810.

Nestadlt, G., Samuels, J. F., Romanoski, A. J., Folstein, M. F., & McHugh, P. Obsessions and compulsions in the community. *Acta Psychiatrica Scandinavica*, 1994, 89, 219–224.

Newman, S. C., & Bland, R. C. Suicide risk varies by subtype of affective disorder. *Acta Psychiatrica Scandinavica*, 1991, 83, 420–426.

Nielsen, B., Wang, A. G., & Bille-Brahe, U. Attempted suicide in Denmark. *Acta Psychiatrica Scandinavica*, 1990, 81, 250–254.

Nieto, E., Vieta, E., Gasto, C., Vallejo, J., & Cirera, E. Suicide attempts of high medical seriousness in schizophrenic patients. *Comprehensive Psychiatry*, 1992a, 33, 384–387.

Nieto, E., Vieta, E., Lazaro, L., Gasto, C., & Cirera, E. Serious suicide attempts in the elderly. *Psychopathology*, 1992b, 25, 183–188.

Nordentoft, M., Breum, L., Munck, L. K., Nordenstgaard, A. G., Hunding, A., & Bjaeldager, P. High mortality by natural and unnatural causes. *British Medical Journal*, 1993, 306, 1637–1641.

Nordentoft, M., & Rubin, P. Mental illness and social integration among suicide attempters in Copenhagen. *Acta Psychiatrica Scandinavica*, 1993, 88, 278–285.

Nordstrom, P., Asberg, M., Aberg-Wistedt, A., & Nordin, C. Attempted suicide predicts suicide risk in mood disorders. *Acta Psychiatrica Scandinavica*, 1995, 92, 345–350.

Nordstrom, P., Gustavsson, P., Edman, G., & Asberg, M. Temperamental vulnerability and suicide risk after attempted suicide. *Suicide & Life-Threatening Behavior*, 1996, 26, 380–394.

Norton, G. R., McLeod, L., Guertin, J., Hewitt, P. L., Walker, J. R., & Stein, M. B. Panic disorder or social phobia. *Behavior Research & Therapy*, 1996, 34, 273–276.

Norton, G. R., Rockman, G. E., Puy, B., & Marion, T. Suicide, chemical abuse, and panic attacks. *Behavior Research & Therapy*, 1993, 31, 37–40.

Noyes, R. Suicide and panic disorder. *Journal of Affective Disorders*, 1991, 22, 1–11.

Noyes, R., Christiansen, J., Clancy, J., Garvey, M. J., Suelzer, M., & Anderson, D. J. Predictors of serious suicide attempts among patients with panic disorders. *Comprehensive Psychiatry*, 1991, 32, 261–267.

Ojehagen, A., Berglund, M., & Apnel, C. P. Long-term outpatient treatment in alcoholics with previous suicidal behavior *Suicide & Life-Threatening Behavior*, 1993, 23, 320–328.

Ojehagen, A., Danielsson, M., & Traskman-Bendz, L. Deliberate self-poisoning. *Acta Psychiatrica Scandinavica*, 1992, 85, 370–375.

Ojehagen, A., Regnell, G., & Traskman-Bendz, L. Deliberate self-poisoning. *Acta Psychiatrica Scandinavica*, 1991, 84, 266–271.

Oldham, J. M., Skodol, A. E., Gallaher, P. E., & Kroll, M. E. Relationship of borderline symptoms to histories of abuse and neglect. *Psychiatric Quarterly*, 1996, 67, 287–295.

O'Leary, D. The endogenous subtype and naturalistic course in depression. *Journal of Affective Disorders*, 1996, 41, 117–123.

Olfson, M., Weissman, M. M., Leon, A. C., Sheehan, D. V., & Farber, L. Suicidal ideation in primary care. *Journal of General Internal Medicine*, 1996, 11, 447–453.

O'Reilly, R. L., Truant, G. S., & Donaldson, L. Psychiatrists' experience of suicide in their patients. *Psychiatric Journal of the University of Ottawa*, 1990, 15, 173–176.

Palsson, S. P., Jonsdottir, G., & Petursson, H. Parasuicidal behavior in an emergency room population. *Nordic Journal of Psychiatry*, 1991, 45, 351–356.

Papadimitriou, G. N., Linkowski, P., Delarbre, C., & Mendelewicz, J. Suicide on the paternal and maternal sides of depressed patients with a lifetime history of attempted suicide. *Acta Psychiatrica Scandinavica*, 1991, 83, 417–419.

Paris, J. Completed suicide in borderline personality disorder. *Psychiatric Annals*, 1990, 20(1), 19–21.

Peterson, L. G., & Bongar, B. Repetitive suicidal crises. *Psychopathology*, 1990, 23, 136–145.

Petronis, K. R., Samuels, J. F., Moscicki, E. K., & Antony, J. C. An epidemiologic investigation of potential risk factors for suicide attempts. *Social Psychiatry & Psychiatric Epidemiology*, 1990, 25, 193–199.

Peuskens, J., De-Hert, M., Cosyns, P., Pieters, G., Theys, P., & Vermote, R. Suicide in young schizophrenic patients during and after inpatient treatment. *International Journal of Mental Health*, 1997, 25(4), 39–44.

Pfeffer, C. R., Klerman, G. L., Hurt, S. W., Kakuma, T., Peskin, J. R., & Siefker, C. A. Suicidal children grown up. *Journal of the American Academy of Child & Adolescent Psychiatry*, 1993, 32, 106–113.

Pillay, A. L., & Wassenaar, D. R. Intervention effects in adolescent suicidal behavior. In D. Lester (Ed.), *Suicide '93*. Denver: AAS, 1993, 57–59.

Platt, S., & Robinson, A. Parasuicide and alcohol. *International Journal of Social Psychiatry*, 1991, 37, 159–172.

Pretorius, H. W., Bodemer, W., Roos, J. L., & Grimbeck, J. Personality traits, brief recurrent depression, and attempted suicide. *South African Medical Journal*, 1994, 84, 690–694.

Pryor, T., Widerman, M. W., & McGilley, B. Clinical correlates of anorexia nervosa subtypes. *International Journal of Eating Disorders*, 1996, 19, 371–379.

Pyke, J., & Steers, M. J. Suicide in a community-based case management service. *Community Mental Health Journal*, 1992, 28, 483–389.

Ramayya, A., Campbell, M., & Callender, J. S. Death by suicide in Grampain 1974–1990. *Health Bulletin*, 1996, 54(1), 37–44.

Range, L. M., & Antonelli, K. B. A factor analysis of six commonly used instruments associated with suicide using college students. *Journal of Personality Assessment*, 1990, 55, 804–811.

Rathus, J., Wetxler, S., & Asnis, G. Post-traumatic stress disorder and the exposure to violence in adolescents. *Journal of the American Medical Association*, 1995, 273, 1734.

Read, D. A., Thomas, C. S., & Mellsop, G. W. Suicide among psychiatric inpatients in the

Wellington region. *Australian & New Zealand Journal of Psychiatry*, 1993, 27, 392–398.

Reynolds, W. M., & Mazza, J. J. Suicide attempts and psychopathology in youth. In D. Lester (Ed.), *Suicide '92*. Denver: AAS, 1992, 109–111.

Rich, C. L., & Runeson, B. S. Similarities in diagnostic comorbidity between suicide among young people in Sweden and the United States. *Acta Psychiatrica Scandinavica*, 1992, 86, 335–339.

Rifai, A. H., George, C. J., Stack, J. A., Mann, J. J., & Reynolds, C. F. Hopelessness in suicide attempters after acute treatment of major depression in late life. *American Journal of Psychiatry*, 1994, 151, 1687–1690.

Rifai, A. H., Mulsant, B. H., Sweet, R. A., & Pasternak, R. E. A study of elderly suicide attempters admitted to an inpatient psychiatric unit. *American Journal of Geriatric Psychiatry*, 1993, 1, 126–135.

Rihmer, Z., Barsi, J., Arato, M., & Demeter, E. Suicide in subtypes of primary major depression. *Journal of Affective Disorders*, 1990, 18, 221–255.

Rihmer, Z., Rutz, W., & Barsi, J. Suicide rate, prevalence of diagnosed depression, and prevalence of working physicians in Hungary. *Acta Psychiatrica Scandinavica*, 1993, 88, 391–394.

Robinson, A., & Platt, S. Age, parasuicide, and problem drinking. *International Journal of Social Psychiatry*, 1993, 39, 81–86.

Rohde, P., Lewinsohn, P. M., & Seeley, J. R. Comorbidity of unipolar depression. *Journal of Abnormal Psychology*, 1991, 100, 214–222.

Ross, R. K., Bernstein, L., Trent, L., Henderson, B. E., & Paganini-Hill, A. A prospective study of risk factors for traumatic deaths in a retirement community. *Preventive Medicine*, 1990, 19, 323–334.

Rosseli, M., & Ardila, A. Cognitive effects of cocaine and polydrug abuse. *Journal of Clinical & Experimental Neuropsychology*, 1996, 18, 122–135.

Rossi, A., Toschi, D., Carratori, F., & Conti, L. Alcohol abuse and suicidal attempt. *Alcoholism (Zagreb)*, 1996, 32(1), 61–68.

Rossow, I. Suicide among drug addicts in Norway. *Addiction*, 1994, 89, 1667–1673.

Rossow, I., & Amundsen, A. Alcohol abuse and suicide. *Addiction*, 1995, 90, 685–691.

Rossow, I., & Wichstrom, L. Parasuicide and use of intoxicants among Norwegian adolescents. *Suicide & Life-Threatening Behavior*, 1994, 24, 174–183.

Roy, A. Anxiety and suicide in depression. *Canadian Journal of Psychiatry*, 1993a, 38, 694–695.

Roy, A. Features associated with suicide attempts in depression. *Journal of Affective Disorders*, 1993b, 27, 35–38.

Roy, A., DeJong, L., Lamparski, D., Adinoff, B., George, T., Moore, V., Garnett, D., Kerich, M., & Linnoila, M. Mental disorders among alcoholics. *Archives of General Psychiatry*, 1991, 48, 423.

Roy, A., & Draper, R. Suicide among psychiatric hospital patients. In D. Lester (Ed.), *Suicide '94*. Denver: AAS, 1994, 127–128.

Roy, A., & Draper, R. Suicide among psychiatric hospital inpatients. *Psychological Medicine*, 1995, 25, 199–202.

Roy, A., Lamparski, D., DeJong, J., Moore, V., & Linnoila, M. Characteristics of alcoholics who attempt suicide. *American Journal of Psychiatry*, 1990a, 147, 761–765.

Roy, S., Hahn, A., Hanson, D., & Herrera, J. Self-injury in psychiatric inpatients. *International Journal of Psychosomatics*, 1990b, 37, 35–36.

Rudd, M. D. an integrative model of suicidal ideation. *Suicide & Life-Threatening Behavior*, 1990, 20, 16–30.

Rudd, M. D., Dahm, P. F., & Rajab, M. H. Diagnostic comorbidity in persons with suicidal ideation and behavior. *American Journal of Psychiatry*, 1993, 150, 928–934.

Rudd, M. D., Joiner, T., & Rajab, M. H. Relationships among suicide ideators, attempters, and multiple attempters in a young-adult sample. *Journal of Abnormal Psychology*, 1996, 105, 541–550.

Runeson, B. Psychoactive substance abuse disorder in youth suicide. *Alcohol & Alcoholism*, 1990, 25, 561–568.

Runeson, B., & Beskow, J. Borderline personality disorder in young Swedish suicides. *Journal of Nervous & Mental Disease*, 1991, 179, 153–156.

Runeson, B., & Rich, C. L. Diagnostic and Statistical Manual of Mental Disorder, 3rd Edition (DSM-III), adaptive functioning in young Swedish suicide. *Annals of Clinical Psychiatry*, 1994, 6, 181–183.

Russ, M. J., Shearin, E. N., Clarkin, J. F., Harrison, K., & Hull, J. W. Subtypes of self-injurious patients with borderline personality disorder. *American Journal of Psychiatry*, 1993, 150, 1869–1871.

Rygnestad, T., & Huage, L. Epidemiological, social, and psychiatric aspects in self-poisoned patients. *Social Psychiatry & Psychiatric Epidemiology*, 1991, 26, 53–62.

Rygnestad, T., Stiles, T. C., Bjerke, T., & Jorgensen, P. Fatal and nonfatal repetition of parasuicide. In P. Crepet, G. Ferrari, S. Platt & M. Bellini (Eds.), *Suicidal behaviour in Europe*. Rome: John Libbey, 1992, 183–190.

Sabo, A. N., Gunderson, J. G., Najavits, L. M., Chauncey, D., & Kisiel, C. Changes in self-destructiveness of borderline patients in psychotherapy. *Journal of Nervous & Mental Disease*, 1995, 183, 370–376.

Sakinofsky, I., & Roberts, R. S. Why parasuicides repeat despite problem resolution. *British Journal of Psychiatry*, 1990, 156, 399–405.

Sakinofsky, I., Roberts, R. S., Brown, Y. B., Cumming, C., & James P. Problem-resolution and repetition of parasuicide. *British Journal of Psychiatry*, 1990, 156, 395–399.

Salloum, I. M., Daley, D. C., Cornelius, J. R., Kirisci, L., & Thase, M. E. Disproportionate lethality in psychiatric patients with concurrent alcohol and cocaine abuse. *American Journal of Psychiatry*, 1996, 153, 953–955.

Salter, D., & Platt, S. Suicidal intent, hopelessness, and depression in a parasuicide population. *British Journal of Psychiatry*, 1990, 29, 361–371.

Sarchiapone, M., Koukopoulos, A., De Risio, S., Bria, P., & Scavo, A. Psychomotor activity and suicide. In D. Lester (Ed.), *Suicide '94*. Denver: AAS, 1994, 134.

Sayil, I., & Gogus, A. K. The distribution of the suicidal thought and attempt among the psychiatric outpatients. In *Crisis*. Ankara: Ankara University, 1992, 6–9.

Schifano, F., Frezza, M., & De Leo, D. Suicide, suicidal desire, or opiate overdose? In G. Ferrari, M. Bellini & P. Crepet (Eds.), *Suicidal behavior and risk factors*. Bologna: Monduzzi-Editore, 1990, 1067–1071.

Schlebusch, L. The relationship between adolescent psychopathology and suicidal behavior. In L. Schlebusch (Ed.), *Suicidal behaviour*. Durban: University of Natal, 1992, 168–175.

Schmid, H., Manjee, K., & Shah, T. On the distribution of suicide ideation versus attempt in elderly psychiatric inpatients. *Gerontologist*, 1994, 34, 332–339.

Schmidtke, A., & Schaller, S. Munchhausen syndrome and suicidal behavior. In D. Lester (Ed.), *Suicide '95*. Washington, DC: AAS, 1995, 109–111.

Seibyl, J. P. Satel, S. L., Anthony, D., Southwick, S. M., Krystal, J. H., & Charney, D. S. Effects of cocaine on hospital course in schizophrenia. *Journal of Nervous & Mental Disease*, 1993, 181, 31–37.

Selakovic-Bursic, S. Aetiopathogenic aspects of suicidal behavior of alcoholics. In G. Ferrari, M. Bellini & P. Crepet (Eds.), *Suicidal behavior and risk factors*. Bologna: Monduzzi-Editore, 1990, 1055–1060.

Shain, B. N., King, C. A., & Naylor M. Dysthymia preceding major depression. In D. Lester (Ed.), *Suicide '90*. Denver: AAS, 1990, 240–241.

Sharma, R., & Markar, H. R. Mortality in affective disorder. *Journal of Affective Disorders*, 1994, 31, 91–96.

Sheiban, B. K. Mental illness and suicide in Israel. *Medicine & Law*, 1993, 12, 445–465.

Shuwall, M., & Siris, S. G. Suicidal ideation in postpsychotic depression. *Comprehensive Psychiatry*, 1994, 35, 132–134.

Skog, O. J. Alcohol and suicide in Denmark 1911–1924. *Addiction*, 1993, 88, 1189–1193.

Skog, O. J., & Elekes, Z. Alcohol and the 1950–1990 Hungarian suicide trend. *Acta Sociologica*. 1993, 36, 33–46.

Skoog, I., Aevarsson, O., Beskow, J., Larsson, L., Palsson, S., Waern, M., Landahl, S., & Ostling, S. Suicidal feelings in a population sample of nondemented 85 year olds. *American Journal of Psychiatry*, 1996, 153, 1015–1020.

Smart, R. G., & Mann, R. E. Changes in

suicide rates after reductions in alcohol consumption and problems in Ontario, 1975–1983. *British Journal of Addiction*, 1990, 85, 463–468.

Smith, D. I., & Burville, P. W. Relationship between alcohol consumption and attempted suicide morbidity rates in Perth, Western Australia, 1968–1984. *Addictive Behaviors*, 1991, 16, 57–61.

Smith, J. E., Hillard, M. C., & Roll, S. Rorschach evaluation of adolescent bulimics. *Adolescence*, 1991a, 26, 687–696.

Smith, J. E., Hillard, M. C., Walsh, R. A., Kubacki, S. R., & Morgan, C. D. Rorschach assessment of purging and nonpurging bulimics. *Journal of Personality Assessment*, 1991b, 56, 277–288.

Soloff, P. H., Lis, J. A., Kelly, T., Cornelius, J., & Ulrich, R. Risk factors for suicidal behavior in borderline personality disorder. *American Journal of Psychiatry*, 1994, 151, 1316–1323.

Spalletta, G., Troisi, A., Saracco, M., Ciani, N., & Pasini, A. Symptom profile, Axis II comorbidity and suicidal behavior in young males with DSM-III-R depressive illness. *Journal of Affective Disorders*, 1996, 39, 141–148.

Spirito, A., Lewander, W., Riggs, S., & Fritz, G. Longitudinal course of adolescent suicide attempters. In G. Ferrari, M. Bellini & P. Crepet (Eds.), *Suicidal behavior and risk factors*. Bologna: Monduzzi-Editore, 1990, 945–950.

Stack, S., & Wasserman, I. Marital status, alcohol abuse, and attempted suicide. *Journal of Addictive Disease*, 1995, 14(2), 43–51.

Stark, C., Hall, D., O'Brien, F., & Smith, H. Suicide after discharge from psychiatric hospitals in Scotland. *British Medical Journal*, 1995, 311, 1368–1369.

Stefenson, A., & Cullberg, J. Committed suicide in a total schizophrenic cohort. *Nordic Journal of Psychiatry*, 1995, 49, 429–437.

Stein, D. J., Trestman, R. L., Mitropoulov, V., Coccaro, E. F., Hollander, E., & Siever, L. J. Impulsivity and serotonergic function in compulsive personality disorder. *Journal of Neuropsychiatry & Clinical Neuroscience*, 1996, 8, 393–398.

Steiner, B., Wolfersdorf, M., Keller, F., & Hole, G. The relationship between hopelessness and the tendency to commit suicide in the course of depressive disorders. In K. Bohme, R. Freytag, C. Wachtler & H. Wedler (Eds.), *Suicidal behavior*. Regensburg: S. Roderer, 1993, 769–774.

Stenager, E. N., & Benjaminsen, S. Repetition of parasuicide, psychiatric diagnosis, and treatment modalities. In T. Bjerke & T. C. Stiles (Eds.), *Suicide attempts in the Nordic countries*. Trondheim: Tapir Forlag, 1991, 171–181.

Stephens, J. H., & McHugh, P. R. Characteristics and long-term follow-up of patients hospitalized for mood disorders in the Phipps Clinic, 1913–1940. *Journal of Nervous & Mental Disease*, 1991, 179, 64–73.

Stocks, R., & Scott, A. I. What happens to patients who frequently harm themselves? *British Journal of Psychiatry*, 1991, 158, 375–378.

Strakowski, S. M., McElroy, S. L., Keck, P. E., & West, S. A. Suicidality among patients with mixed and manic bipolar disorder. *American Journal of Psychiatry*, 1996, 153, 674–676.

Sullivan, G., Young, A. S., & Morgenstern, H. Behaviors as risk factors for rehospitalization. *Social Psychiatry & Psychiatric Epidemiology*, 1997, 32, 185–190.

Sullivan, P. F. Mortality in anorexia nervosa. *American Journal of Psychiatry*, 1995, 152, 1073–1074.

Suokas, J., & Lonnqvist, J. Outcome of attempted suicide and psychiatric consultation. *Acta Psychiatrica Scandinavica*, 1991, 84, 545–549.

Szanto, K., Reynolds, C. F., Frank, E., Steck, J., Fasiczka, A. L., Miller, M., Mulsant, B. H., Mazumdar, S., & Kupfer, D. Suicide in elderly depressed patients. *American Journal of Geriatric Psychiatry*, 1996, 4, 197–207.

Taiminen, T. J. Effects of psychopharmacotherapy on suicide risk in psychiatric inpatients. *Acta Psychiatrica Scandinavica*, 1993, 87, 3, 45–47.

Taiminen, T. J., & Kujari, H. Antipsychotic medication and suicide risk among schizophrenic and paranoid inpatients. *Acta Psychiatrica Scandinavica*, 1994, 90, 247–251.

Takahashi, Y., Hirasawa, H., Koyama, K., Asakawa, O., Kido, M., Onose, H., Udagawa, M., Ishikawa, Y., & Uno, M. Suicide and aging in Japan. *International Psychogeriatrics*, 1995, 7, 239–251.

Taylor, C. J., Kent, G. G., & Huws, R. L. A comparison of the backgrounds of first-time and repeated overdose patients. *Journal of Accident & Emergency Medicine*, 1994, 11, 238–242.

Test, M. A., Burke, S. S., & Wallisch, L. S. Gender differences of young adults with schizophrenic disorders in community care. *Schizophrenic Bulletin*, 1990, 16, 331–344.

Thalen, B. E., Kjellman, B. F., Morkrid, L., & Wetterberg, L. Seasonal and nonseasonal depression. *European Archives of Psychiatry*, 1995, 245, 101–108.

Theander, S. Research on outcomes and prognosis of anorexia nervosa and some results from a Swedish long-term study. *International Journal of Eating Disorders*, 1983, 2, 167–174.

Tomasson, K., Kent, D., & Coryell, W. Somatization and conversion disorders. *Acta Psychiatrica Scandinavica*, 1991, 84, 288–293.

Trachtenberg, D., Kay, G., & Degendorfer, N. Suicidality in psychogeriatric patients. In K. Bohme, R. Freytag, C. Wachtler & H. Wedler (Eds.), *Suicidal behavior*. Regensburg: S. Roderer, 1993, 226–229.

Trautman, P. D., Rotheram-Borus, M. J., Dopkins, S., & Lewin, M. Psychiatric diagnoses in minority female adolescent suicide attempters. *Journal of the American Academy of Child & Adolescent Psychiatry*, 1991, 30, 617–622.

Trull, T. J., & Widiger, T. A. The relationship between borderline personality disorder and dysthymia symptoms. *Journal of Psychopathology & Behavioral Assessment*, 1991, 13, 91–106.

Valente, S. Suicide among psychiatric patients. In K. Bohme, R. Freytag, C. Wachtler & H. Wedler (Eds.), *Suicidal behavior*. Regensburg: S. Roderer, 1993, 217–220.

Van Aalst, J. A., Shotts, S. D., Vitsky, J. L., Bass, S. M., Miller, R. S., Meador, K. G., & Morris, J. A. Long-term follow-up of unsuccessful violent suicide attempts. *Journal of Trauma*, 1992, 33, 457–461.

Van Egmond, M., Garnefski, N., Diekstra, R. F. W., & Hengeveld, M. W. Prediction of repeated suicidal behavior among women. In K. Bohme, R. Freytag, C. Wachtler & H.

Wedler (Eds.), *Suicidal behavior*. Regensburg: S. Roderer, 1993, 759–762.

Van Heeringen, C. Risk factors for the repetition of attempted suicide. In U. Bille-Brahe & H. Schoidt (Eds.), *Intervention and prevention*. Odense: Odense University, 1994, 53–60.

Van Zyl, A. The role of depression and biochemical aspects of suicidal behavior. In L. Schlebusch (Ed.), *Suicidal behavior*. Durban: University of Natal, 1988, 44–60.

Vestergaard, P., & Aagaard, J. Five-year mortality in lithium-treated manic-depressive patients. *Journal of Affective Disorders*, 1991, 21, 33–38.

Vieta, E., Nieto, E., Gasto, C., & Cirera, E. Serious suicide attempts in affective patients. *Journal of Affective Disorders*, 1992, 24, 147–152.

Villagomez, R. E., Meyer, T. J., Lin, M. M., & Brown, L. S. Post-traumatic stress disorder among inner-city methadone maintenance patients. *Journal of Substance Abuse Treatment*, 1995, 12, 253–257.

Wallace, J., & Pfohl, B. Age-related differences in the symptomatic expression of major depression. *Journal of Nervous & Mental Disease*, 1995, 183, 99–102.

Warshaw, M. G., Fierman, E., Pratt, L., Hunt, M., Yonkers, K. A., Massion, A. O., & Keller, M. B. Quality of life and dissociation in anxiety disorder patients with histories of trauma or PTSD. *American Journal of Psychiatry*, 1993, 150, 1512–1516.

Warshaw, M. G., Massion, A. O., Peterson, L. G., Pratt, L. A., & Keller, M. B. Suicidal behavior in patients with panic disorder. *Journal of Affective Disorders*, 1995, 34, 235–247.

Wasserman, D. Attempted suicide and alcoholism. In P. Crepet, G. Ferrari, S. Platt & M. Bellini (Eds.), *Suicidal behaviour in Europe*. Rome: John Libbey, 1992, 287–295.

Watson, H. E., Kershaw, P. W., & Davies, J. B. Alcohol problems among women in a general hospital ward. *British Journal of Addictions*, 1991, 86, 889–894.

Weiller, E., Boyer, P., Lepine, J. P., & Lecrubier, Y. Prevalence of recurrent brief description in primary care. *European Archives of Psychiatry*, 1994a, 244, 174–181.

Weiller, E., Lecrubier, Y., Maier, W., &

Ustus, T. B. The relevance of recurrent brief depression in primary care. *European Archives of Psychiatry*, 1994b, 244, 182–189.

Weiller, E., Bisserbe, J. C., Boyer, B., Lepine, J. P., & Lecrubier, Y. Social phobia in general health care. *British Journal of Psychiatry*, 1996, 168, 169–174.

Weisberg, L. J., Norman, D. K., & Herzog, D. B. Personality functioning in normal weight bulimia. *International Journal of Eating Disorders*, 1987, 6, 615–631.

Weissman, M. M., Bland, R. C., Canino, G. J., Greenwald, S., Lee, C. K., Newman, S. C., Rubio-Stipec, M., & Wickramaratne, P. J. The cross-national epidemiology of social phobia. *International Clinical Psychopharmacology*, 1996, 11, (Suppl. 3), 9–14.

Westermeyer, J., Harrow, M., & Marengo, J. T. Risk for suicide in schizophrenia and other psychotic and nonpsychotic disorders. *Journal of Nervous & Mental Disease*, 1991, 179, 259–266.

Westermeyer, J., Tucker, P., & Nugent, S. Comorbid anxiety disorder among patients with substance abuse disorders. *American Journal of Addictions*, 1995, 4, 97–106.

Whisman, M. A., Miller, I. W., Norman, W. H., & Keitner, G. I. Hopelessness and depression in depressed inpatients. *Cognitive Therapy & Research*, 1995, 19, 377–398.

Windle, M. Characteristics of alcoholics who attempt suicide. *Journal of Studies on Alcohol*, 1994, 55, 571–577.

Winokur, G., & Coryell, W. Familial subtypes of unipolar depression. *Biological Psychiatry*, 1992, 32, 1012–1018.

Wolfersdorf, M., Hole, G., Steiner, B., & Keller, F. Suicide risk in suicidal-versus-non-suicidal depressed inpatients. *Crisis*, 1990, 11, 85–97.

Wolford, K. M., Reihman, J., & Tars, S. E. Psychological autopsy database development. *Forensic Reports*, 1991, 4, 437–450.

Workman, M., & Beer, J. Relationship between alcohol dependency and suicide ideation among high school students. *Psychological Reports*, 1990, 66, 1363–1366.

Wu, L. H., & Dunner, D. L. Suicide attempts in rapid cycling bipolar disorder patients. *Journal of Affective Disorders*, 1993, 29, 57–61.

Young, M. M., Fogg, L., Scheftner, W., & Fawcett, J. Nonadditive models for predicting suicide risk. In D. Lester (Ed.), *Suicide, '92*. Denver: AAS, 1992, 214–215.

Young, M. M., Fogg, L., Scheftner, W., & Fawcett, J. Interactions of risk factors in predicting suicide. *American Journal of Psychiatry*, 1994, 151, 434–435.

Young, S. E., Mikulich, S. K., Goodwin, M. B., Hardy, J., Martin, C. L., Zoccolillo, M. S., & Crowley, T. J. Treated delinquent boys' substance use. *Drug & Alcohol Dependence*, 1995, 37, 149–162.

Zimmerman, M., Lish, J. D., Lush, D. T., Farber, N. J., Plescia, G., & Kuzma, M. A. Suicidal ideation among urban medical outpatients. *Journal of General & Internal Medicine*, 1995, 10, 573–576.

Zisook, S., Byrd, D., Kuck, J., & Jeste, D. V. Command hallucinations in outpatients with schizophrenia. *Journal of Clinical Psychiatry*, 1995, 56, 462–465.

Zisook, S., Goff, A., Sledge, P., & Schuchter, S. R. Reported suicidal behavior and current suicidal ideation in a psychiatric outpatient clinic. *Annals of Clinical Psychiatry*, 1994, 6, 27–31.

Zweig, R. A., & Hinrichsen, G. A. Factors associated with suicide attempts by depressed older adults. *American Journal of Psychiatry*, 1993, 150, 1687–1692.

Chapter 18

MEDICAL ILLNESS

General Physical Illness

Rao (1990) compared suicide attempters in India who were psychiatrically ill or physically ill versus neither. Both ill groups had higher hopelessness scores; the physically ill attempters has less suicidal intent than the psychiatrically ill and fewer recent stressors. Among the physically ill, those with abdominal pain (versus ulcer, dysmenorrhea, and uterine pain) had lower suicidal intent and hopelessness scores.

Conwell et al. (1993) studied the severity of impairment in 13 organ system in a sample of suicides. The impairment was higher in the elderly, but did not vary with sex or education.

In general medical patients, Cooper-Patrick et al. (1994) found that 2.6 percent had thought of suicide in the previous year. The frequency was associated with being white, separated/divorced, and aged 18–30, but not with sex, social class, or education. Suicidal ideation was associated with major depressions, panic disorder, alcoholism, and phobic disorder in the prior year.

Stenager et al. (1994a) found that 52 percent of a sample of attempted suicides had a physical disease. Those with a disease were older, in more pain, more depressed, less Often psychotic, and more often in crisis. They did not differ in sex, prior attempts, psychiatric treatment, suicidal intent, or hopelessness.

Grabbe et al. (1997) found that elderly completed suicides more often had a history of cancer and less often a history of stroke than other decedents; they were more often alcohol abusers, white, male, and with a psychiatric disorder. Compared to injury deaths, the suicides less often had stroke and diabetes, and more often had lung conditions (as well as being more often white, male, non-poor, alcohol abusers, and psychiatrically disturbed).

Meta-Analyses

Harris and Barraclough (1994) found an increased risk of completed suicide in patients with HIV/AIDS, Huntington's disease, malignant neoplasm (all sites), renal disease (hemodialysis and transplants), spinal cord injury (traumatic), systemic lupus erythematosis, multiple sclerosis, peptic ulcer, amputation, heart valve replacement, hormone replacement therapy, intestinal disease, liver disease (and alcoholism), neurofibromatosis, Parkinson's disease, and systemic sclerosis. A lower risk was found for pregnancy and puerperium.

Stenager and Stenager (1992) reviewed research on suicide in neurological disorders and concluded that there was evidence for an increased suicide risk only in multiple sclerosis, spinal cord lesions, and epilepsy.

Specific Diseases

AIDS and HIV

Reviews of the literature confirm the increased incidence of suicidal ideation, attempted suicide and completed suicide in HIV-positive and AIDS patients (Beckett and Shenson, 1993).

Coté et al. (1992) found that the suicide rate for those with AIDS was 165. The rate was higher in whites and those aged 40–49, and the most common method for suicide was by drug overdose. Mancoske et al. (1995) calculated a suicide rate for AIDS patients in Los Angeles of 1750, lower in the metropolitan area than in the nonmetropolitan area. The modal AIDS suicide was male, white, with 12 years of education, and never married. Dannenberg et al. (1996) found that military service applicants who were HIV-positive versus HIV-negative had similar suicide rates in a follow-up study (49 and 36 respectively), but the rates for both groups were higher than that for the general population matched for sex, race, and age. Marzuk et al. (1997) found that 9 percent of suicides in New York City were HIV-positive. Those HIV-positive were more often male, aged 25–54, Hispanic or nonHispanic blacks, and used poisons more and firearms less for their suicide.

Loimer et al. (1990) found that HIV-infected intravenous drug users had attempted suicide more in the past (but had not overdosed more) than noninfected drug users. (The researchers failed to control for sex, however.) Wedler (1991) found that the deaths of HIV-positive intravenous drug users were more often from suicide than HIV-negative intravenous drug users.

Perry et al. (1990) found no increase in current suicidal ideation from before HIV testing to one week after and two months after, regardless of whether the individuals tested positive or negative. Gala et al. (1992) found that about six percent of HIV-positive patients attempted suicide after notification. This was predicted by having a psychiatric history and prior attempted suicide. Ritchie et al. (1992) surveyed HIV-positive patients and found that 55 percent had suicidal ideation after the diagnosis, 8 percent in the prior week to the survey.

In Finland, Vuorio et al. (1990) reported cases of suicide in the patients who had an unfounded fear of AIDS, probably resulting from guilt over their sexual activities. Halttunen et al. (1991; Aro et al., 1994, 1995) found no completed suicides who were HIV-positive in the suicides from one year. Twenty-eight of the 1,397 suicides had a fear of AIDS, and half of these had engaged in HIV-risk behaviors. These suicides were younger, more often had a major depressive disorder, and had made more health contacts. About half had prior psychiatric treatment, and about half had attempted suicide in the past. All were judged to be psychiatrically disturbed with Axis I disorders.

Belkin et al. (1992) found that 16 percent of HIV-positive subjects had thought about suicide in the prior week. Suicidal ideation was associated with sex, symptom intensity, having bad days, and not having medical insurance. It was not associated with race, employment, having AIDS, months since diagnosis, or being an intravenous drug user.

McKegney and O'Dowd (1992) found that suicidal ideation was more common in HIV-positive patients than in HIV-negative patients and AIDS patients. O'Dowd et al. (1993) found that, among psychiatric outpatients, those HIV-positive and with AIDS-related complex had more suicidal ideation than those with AIDS, perhaps a result of denial or central nervous system problems in those with AIDS.

Rajs and Fugelstad (1991) found that HIV-positive persons who completed suicide in Stockholm were more often addicts in 1985–1987 and more often homosexual/bisexual in 1988–1990. Rajs and Fugelstad (1992) found that 0.005 percent of suspicious deaths in Sweden were found to have HIV infections, and 29 percent of the deaths of these HIV-infected persons were due to suicide. Of these 25 suicides, 12 were homosexual/bisexual, 8 were addicts, and 1 was HIV-infected as a result of a blood transfusion.

Rundell et al. (1992) compared HIV-positive patients who attempted suicide with those who did not. The attempters more often abused alcohol, had a personality disorder, an adjustment disorder, and prior major depressive disorders; they had poorer social support and more HIV-related stressors. (They did not differ in race, age, marital status, family history of suicide, alcohol abuse or depression, prior attempts, or other stressors.)

Hendricks (1993) found a higher incidence of suicidal ideation among HIV-positive gay men than HIV-negative gay men. The ideators had smaller social support networks. As the time since diagnosis increased, suicidal ideation became more common and reasons for living less strong, while depression, hopelessness, and satisfaction with support groups did not change.

Lester (1993) found that people with HIV/AIDS who had attempted suicide more often had been in psychiatric treatment, had an antisocial personality disorder, and were currently suicidal (but did not differ in being homosexual/bisexual or in having more than 50 sexual partners).

When suicidal vignettes were given to subjects to read, O'Neal and Range (1993) found that students were less helpful to HIV-positive people than to those with panic attacks.

Rabkin et al. (1993) interviewed gay men with AIDS. Fourteen percent report suicidal ideation before contracting AIDS, 14 percent afterwards, and 29 percent both before and after. Twenty-three percent had attempted suicide prior to contracting AIDS, but only 2 percent afterwards. Twiname (1993) found that HIV-positive patients with no symptoms were more hopeless but less depressed than HIV-positive patients with symptoms or with AIDS. Alfonso et al. (1994) found that psychiatric patients who were HIV-positive or had AIDS were more suicidal than those without. The HIV+/AIDS patients were more often drug abusers and had a mood disorder and were less often schizophrenic.

Cochran and Mays (1994) found that HIV-positive men and women were more suicidal (and depressed) if they had symptoms than if they did not, and they were more suicidal than HIV-negative men. Steer et al. (1994) found that hopelessness predicted current suicidal ideation in IV drug users who were not in treatment but who sought HIV screening and counseling.

Van Haastrecht et al. (1994) studied intravenous drug users tested for HIV. The suicide rate in the next four years did not differ for those testing positive and negative.

Catalan et al. (1995) compared attempted suicides who were HIV-positive with those who were not. The HIV attempters were more often gay/bisexual, unemployed, with a present and past history of psychiatric treatment, with a depressive disorder; they were less often alcohol abusers and more often had health concerns. They did not differ in prior attempts, reason for attempt, or marital status.

Klee (1995) found that amphetamine users who were suicidal before drug use were more often female, with a history of depression, using tranquilizers, and being AIDS tested. Those suicidal during withdrawal were more often homeless, injecting amphetamines, older, taking higher doses with greater frequency, with paranoid delusions, and not in contact with parents. In the polydrug users, attempting suicide was associated with sharing needles, high doses, using injections, being female, with depression and paranoia, and in bad relationships with mothers.

Sherr (1995) found that 10 percent of patients at a clinic attempted suicide prior to their HIV diagnosis, 9 percent afterwards, and 3 percent both before and after.

In Spain, Ayuso Mateos et al. (1996) found that psychiatric patients who engaged in risky behavior with regard to HIV/AIDS had more often attempted suicide than those who had not.

Breitbart et al. (1996) found that support for physician-assisted suicide in AIDS patients was greater in those who were depressed, hopeless, with suicidal ideation, with psychological distress, white, with less social support, with terminal illness in friends/ relatives, and who did not attend church. They did not differ in pain, symptoms, impairment, or extent of the disease.

Judd and Mijch (1996) found that HIV-positive patients who were symptomatic or asymptomatic did not differ in current suicidal ideation.

Domino and Shen (1996–1997) found that HIV-positive gays/bisexuals were more hopeless and depressed than HIV-negative gays/bisexuals and normal heterosexuals. They also saw suicide as less impulsive, more normal, and less morally bad.

Kissinger et al. (1997) found no differences in their CD4 counts between adolescent HIV-positive patients who had attempted suicide, thought about it, or who were nonsuicidal.

Looking at the partners of HIV-positive or negative men, Rosengard and Folkman (1997) found that HIV status did not predict

suicidal ideation, but bereavement did, as did the burden involved in being a caregiver, less social support, less optimism, and use of escape-avoidance coping mechanisms.

Among inner-city black young men who were psychiatric inpatients, Wood et al. (1997) found that those who were HIV-positive were more suicidal, but only if they were schizophrenics, not depressives or substance abusers.

Alzheimer's Disease

Albert et al. (1993) found that Alzheimer's patients in a chronic care facility were more depressed and had more suicidal ideation than the other patients.

Attempted Suicide

Lester (1991) reviewed 45 studies of mortality in attempted suicides. The percentage who went on to complete suicide was associated positively with the length of follow-up and the percentage of missing subjects, and associated negatively with Great Britain (versus other nations). The year of publication of the study, the sample size, and whether the sample was from a general hospital were not significantly associated with the percentage of later suicides. The percentage of attempters repeating attempts was associated only with the percentage of missing subjects.

Pearce and Martin (1994) found that attempted suicides had more prior suicidality. Pfeffer et al. (1994) found that psychiatric patients were more likely than community controls to be suicidal later only if they were suicidal at intake.

Brain Injury

Persinger (1994) found that brain-injured

patients who had episodes of sensed presence had more suicidal ideation than those without this sensed presence. Suicidal ideation was even more common if there was also a fragmentation of self-concept, lowered left-hemisphere linguistic functions, and depression.

Cancer

Shinohara et al. (1990) found that both Korean male and female cancer patients in Japan had significantly higher completed suicide rates as compared to the Japanese. Levi et al. (1991) found a higher SMR for suicide for cancer patients in Switzerland, overall and for men, women, and all age groups. The risk of suicide was highest in the first year after notification and then declined.

In Stockholm, Allebeck and Bolund (1991) found that 0.4 percent of deaths of cancer patients were due to suicide. The standard mortality ratio for suicide was 2.4 for males and 2.7 for females (and the SMRs for attempted suicide were, respectively, 1.7 and 1.3). The SMRs were high for all ages, higher in the first two years after diagnosis, and higher in those with the most tumor sites.

De Leo et al. (1991) found that post-mastectomy patients had a more positive attitude toward suicide than other medical patients and normal controls. The positive attitude was positively associated with irritability, psychoticism, and number of confidants and associated negatively with the number of people in their households, but not associated significantly with time since diagnosis.

Hietanen and Lonnqvist (1991) found that of 1397 suicides in Finland in 1987, 4.3 percent had cancer – 25 patients were in remission, 18 terminal, and 17 in other stages. Those in remission more often had head and neck cancer and lymphoma, other diseases, alcohol abuse, psychiatric treatment, prior suicide attempts, a family history of suicide and mental disorder, and interpersonal conflict; those terminal more often had lung and breast cancer and melanoma, pain, and dependency on others. They did not differ in depression or prior suicidal ideation. Hietanen et al. (1993) found that the cancer suicides, compared with other suicides, were in more pain, were more physically disabled, more often had significant others, and the relatives more readily accepted the suicide decision. They did not differ in family histories of suicide or psychiatric disorder, psychiatric treatment, alcohol abuse, or depression. Henriksson et al. (1995) found no differences in depressive syndromes between cancer and other suicides. Those suicides with cancer in remission versus terminal patients more often had a major depression and substance abuse disorder.

Storm et al. (1992) found that the risk of suicide in cancer patients was higher up to two years after diagnosis for nonlocalized cancers; for tumors of the brain and nervous system; and for lung, stomach, rectal, and kidney cancers. There was no effect of age at diagnosis.

In the Netherlands, Laane (1995) found that those requesting euthanasia/assisted suicide were more likely to have cancer than those dying natural deaths.

Sullivan et al. (1997) found that pain and depression did not affect the interest of cancer patients in hastening death, but the somatic symptom burden did.

On the other hand, Filiberti et al. (1991) found that suicide was rare in cancer patients while in the hospital – in five years with an average capacity of 500 patients, there was only one suicide. Hudson et al. (1997) found that long-term survivors of childhood cancer had an average suicide rate.

Chemical and Radiation Exposure

Michalek et al. (1990) found that the suicide rate of Vietnam veterans exposed to herbicides was normal. However, Rahu et al. (1997) and Vanchieri (1997) found that Estonian clean-up workers at Chernobyl had a higher-than-expected rate of suicide.

Cholesterol

In reviews of previous research, Boston et al. (1996), Conroy (1993), Law et al. (1994) and Muldoon et al. (1990, 1991, 1993) found evidence that the risk of dying from suicide and violence (accidents and homicide) and attempted suicide was higher in those who lowered their cholesterol levels. Law et al. felt that the effect was found only in community cohorts, but not in samples of employed men, and was found for only the first five years. Engelberg (1992) suggested that low cholesterol levels lead to a decrease in brain serotonin, which leads to worse suppression of aggressive behavior. Muldoon et al. (1990) suggested the role of metabolic factors, dietary fat, underlying illness, weight loss, alcohol and tobacco use, social class, and psychiatric disorder. The effect may also be due to changes in depression.

(1) COMPLETED SUICIDE. Lindberg et al. (1992) followed up a large sample of people screened for cholesterol and found that low serum cholesterol was associated with a high suicide rate for the first seven years of follow-up, but not after that. Schuit et al. (1993) found a positive association between a low cholesterol level and mortality due to all external causes, including suicide.

Iribarren et al. (1995) found that serum cholesterol levels predicted completed suicide in a Japanese sample of men. Suicide was not predicted by body mass, systolic blood pressure, blood glucose, percentage of energy from fat, dietary cholesterol, smoking, uric acid, or a physical-activity index.

In a follow-up study of working men, Zureik et al. (1996) found that those who subsequently completed suicide had lower average cholesterol levels and more often showed a decline over time.

On the other hand, Smith et al. (1990) found no evidence for higher cholesterol levels in completed suicides versus those dying from other violent causes, but they did not employ a nondeceased control group. Vartiainen et al. (1994) found no differences in mortality from suicide and other violent causes in a follow-up study of patients with measured serum cholesterol.

In an indirect test of this association, Ginter (1996) found a positive association between suicide rates in 45 nations and the death rate from cardiovascular disease.

(2) ATTEMPTED SUICIDE. Fritze et al. (1992) found that affective disorder patients who had attempted suicide had slightly more hypercholesterolemia than those who had completed suicide, but this difference was confounded by age. The two groups did not differ in serum cholesterol or body mass index, although the completed suicides did have a lower index.

Brunner et al. (1992) found no association between cholesterol level and responses to the question "Have you recently felt that life is not worth living?" Hunt et al. (1992) found no association of high cholesterol with suicidal ideation/attempts in male and female at a a general hospital clinic.

Maes et al. (1994) found that blood levels of free cholesterol and esterified cholesterol were not associated with suicidality in a sample of depressed patients. Maes et al. (1997) found that suicidality in patients with major depression was not associated with serum HDL-C, cholesterol, triglycerides, or vitamin E. Male patients with major depression and a prior attempt at suicide had lower HDL-C levels as compared to healthy controls.

Engstrom et al. (1995) found that use of violent/nonviolent methods, suicidal intent, and hopelessness were not associated with serum cholesterol, triglycerides, or low- and high-density lipoprotein cholesterol in a sample of attempted suicides.

Kunugi et al. (1997) found that attempted suicides had lower cholesterol levels than psychiatric patients and normal people, even after controls for sex, age, psychiatric diagnosis, red blood cell count, and serum total protein.

Wolfersdorf et al. (1996) found no differences in cholesterol or triglycerides between depressed inpatients who had made violent suicide attempts and nonsuicidal depressed inpatients; patients with back pain, however, had higher levels of both than the psychiatric patients.

Saiz et al. (1997) found that attempted suicides had higher levels of triglycerides, cVLDL, cortisol, and prolactin than normals, but not cholesterol, cHDL, clDL, glucose, tirotropin, or somatotropin. Repeaters had higher levels only of somatotropin (and were more depressed) than first-timers.

Seefried and Gumpel (1997) found that attempted suicides did not differ from drug/alcohol intoxicated patients or normals in cholesterol, triglycerides, LDL, or HDL levels.

On the other hand, Glueck et al. (1994) found that child psychiatric inpatients with adjustment disorders or affective disorders were more suicidal and had lower total plasma cholesterol than children with disruptive behavior, attention-deficit disorder, or oppositional defiant disorder.

Modai et al. (1994) found that attempted suicides had lower serum cholesterol than ideators and nonsuicidal psychiatric patients. The difference was found primarily for unipolars and not for bipolars or schizophrenics. Among unipolars, Greenberg (1995) found no differences in serum albumin and protein between attempters, ideators, and nonsuicidal patients, thus ruling out malnutrition as a cause of the differences.

In patients with major depression, Sullivan et al. (1994) found that those who attempted suicide in the prior month had lower cholesterol levels. Suicidality was predicted by cholesterol level, not by triglyceride levels or body-mass index.

Takei et al. (1994) found that attempted suicides had lower cholesterol levels than psychiatric controls and normal controls, even after controls for diagnosis, duration of illness, red blood cell count, total protein, triglyceride level, sex, and age.

Gallerani et al. (1995) found lower levels of cholesterol in attempted suicides versus general hospital patients, in both men and women and in those using violent or nonviolent methods. The levels were related to diagnosis. The attempters also had higher white blood cell counts, but did not differ on 22 other measures (sodium, uric acid, red blood cells, etc.).

Golier et al. (1995) found that male psychiatric patients with low serum cholesterol had fewer prior suicide attempts, after controls for age, weight, race, social class, alcohol use, and depression. For women, there was no association.

However, Ryan and Murray (1995) found that attempted suicides had higher levels of cholesterol than health subjects.

(3) SOCIOLOGICAL STUDIES. Kromhout et al. (1992) found that national levels of cholesterol were not associated with national rates of violent death (suicide plus accidents plus murder) over seven nations.

Cystic Fibrosis

Burke et al. (1994) examined the mothers

of children with inflammatory bowel disease and cystic fibrosis. Their lifetime rates of depression were high, but whereas the mothers of children with cystic fibrosis had more panic attacks, the mothers of the children with bowel disease had made more suicide attempts (primarily when the children were teenagers).

Diabetes

In a 1988 follow-up of children with Type 1 diabetes seen in 1958–1981 (Joner and Patrick, 1991), 20 had died, including two from suicide. Goldston et al. (1994) found that suicide ideation was common in children diagnosed with diabetes (46 percent on follow-up) and was associated only with depression scores and noncompliance (and not with sex, social class, anxiety, severity of illness, age at diagnosis, or prior psychiatric illness).

Kyvik et al. (1994) found a higher-than-expected suicide rate for men with insulin-dependent diabetes diagnosed before the age of 20.

Goldston et al. (1997) found that non-compliance with their medical regime in adolescent diabetics was associated with suicidal ideation, even after controls for psychiatric disorder. Suicidal ideation in the past year was predicted by hopelessness, psychiatric diagnosis, and coming from a two-parent home. Lifetime prevalence of suicidal ideation was predicted by age, duration of the diabetes, hopelessness, and psychiatric diagnosis.

Dementia

Rao et al. (1997) found that suicidal ideation in community residents over the age of 80 was more common in those with mixed dementia (Alzheimer-type) and multi-infarct dementia (but not simple Alzheimer-type dementia, the severity of the dementia, or the awareness of memory problems).

Dyspnea

Horton-Deutsch et al. (1992) found that 19 percent of a sample of elderly suicides suffered from chronic dyspnea.

Ectopic Pregnancy

Farhi et al. (1994) found a higher rate of attempted and completed suicide in the following year in women with ectopic pregnancies than in nonpregnant women.

Epilepsy

Mendez and Doss (1992) found four completed suicides in a sample of 1611 epileptic patients, and all four had partial complex seizures with a temporal lobe focus.

Fear of Illness

Halttunen et al. (1993) found that about two and a half percent of suicides in Finland were motivated in part by a fear of illness. These patients tended to be older, more often with an illness, and if having an actual somatic illness, more in contact with health services.

Fibromyalgia

Stiles (1991) found that fibromyalgia patients attempted suicide less often than depressed patients. Among the fibromyalgia patients, a history of attempting suicide was associated with depressive disorder, anxiety disorder, somatoform disorder, and person-ality disorder (especially avoidant and self-defeating personality disorder). Among the depressed patients, a history of attempting suicide was associated with anxiety disorder, substance abuse disorder, social phobia, and personality disorder (especially avoidant personality disorder).

Gastrectomy

Stael van Holstein et al. (1995) found that patients given partial gastrectomies had a higher-than-expected suicide rate.

Handicapped

Thompson and Newman (1995) found a lower-than-expected suicide rate in handicapped Canadian adolescents and an above-average suicide rate for neglected and abused adolescents.

Headache

Breslau et al. (1991) found that people who suffered from migraine headaches with aura had the highest lifetime incidence of attempted suicide, followed by those with migraines but no aura, and lowest in those with no migraine headaches, even after controls for the presence of major affective disorders. Breslau (1992) reported that those with both migraine headaches with aura and a major depressive disorder had an increased risk of suicidal attempts and ideation.

Lester et al. (1992) found that having tension or migraine headaches was not associated with current and prior suicidality in a sample of college students.

Hormone Replacement Treatment

Hunt et al. (1990) found more suicides than expected in a group of patients undergoing hormone replacement therapy.

Huntington's Disease

After testing 388 people of whom 66 were positive for Huntington's disease, Bloch et al. (1992) found none attempting suicide yet. Lawson et al. (1996) found no differences in suicidal ideation in those tested for Huntington's disease with increased risk or decreased risk and those not tested.

Sorensen and Fenger (1992) found that 5.6 percent of the deaths of Huntington's patients were from suicide, as were 5.3 percent of those at risk (e.g., siblings of patients), compared to 2.7 percent of the deaths of Danes in general.

Di Maio et al. (1993) found that 7.3 percent of Huntington's disease patients and family members died from suicide. Suicide appeared to be more common in those possibly afflicted than in those definitely afflicted or with a lesser chance of being afflicted. The suicides had the disease for a shorter period of time and were younger at the time of death. The suicides seemed also to cluster in some families.

Lipe et al. (1993) compared Huntington's disease patients who completed suicide with controls. The suicides were less likely to have offspring, but did not differ in sex, age, marital status, suicide in the family, depression, alcoholism, dementia, or a history of violence.

Wong et al. (1994) found that 25 percent of family members of patients with Huntington's disease said that they might consider suicide if diagnosed with the disease. This tendency was associated with depression and avoidance coping strategies.

Hyperparathyroidism

Uden and Tibblin (1990) followed up 282

patients with hyperparathyroidism for 7.8 years and found that 3.3 percent of the deaths were from suicide.

Intracranial Hypertension

Mackerle et al. (1990) found two suicides in 38 patients after surgery for intracranial hypertension.

Lupus

Futrell et al. (1992) found that suicidal behavior in lupus patients was not associated with physiological measures or the presence of other diseases.

Motor Neuron Disease

Bak et al. (1994) found no excess of suicide among patients with motor neuron disease.

Multiple Sclerosis

Long and Miller (1991) found that suicidal ideation in multiple sclerosis patients was positively associated with the fear of dying, the fear of death, and fear of premature death; it was negatively associated with the progression of the disease, support from clergy, family and friends, hopelessness, and religiosity; it was not associated with age, race, sex, income, or functional limitations. Hopelessness was the strongest predictor of suicidal ideation.

Sadovnick et al. (1991) found a higher-than-expected rate of suicide in multiple sclerosis patients. The suicides were younger, less disabled, and had the disorder for less time than those dying of other causes. Sadovnick et al. (1992) reported that 10.4 percent of the 115 deaths of multiple sclerosis patients were from suicide in a sample of 2348 patients.

Stenager et al. (1992) found an increased risk of suicide in patients with multiple sclerosis, especially if the age at onset was less than 30, the age at diagnosis less than 40, and in the first five years after diagnosis. Stenager et al. (1996) found no effect on the risk of suicide from age at onset, interval between onset and diagnosis, or symptoms.

Berman and Samuel (1993) found that multiple sclerosis patients who completed suicide were more often male, unemployed, in financial stress, severely disturbed, in the late stages, in psychic pain, unable to express feelings or ask for help, interpersonally withdrawn, and with fewer suicidal friends/family members.

Pain

Fishbain et al. (1991) found that suicide rates were higher than expected in both male and female chronic-pain patients. Varma et al. (1991) found that 40 percent of patients with chronic pain had depression and 8 percent had suicidal plans.

Penttinen (1995) found that suicide in Finnish farmers was associated with back pain, even after controls for smoking, age, and social class.

Parkinson's Disease

Stenager et al. (1994b) found an average rate of suicide in Parkinson's patients. Among Parkinson's patients, Starkstein et al. (1990) found that the depressed patients were more suicidal than the nondepressed patients.

Pesticides

Davies (1995) reviewed evidence to support the hypothesis that exposure to organophosphate pesticides increases the vulnerability to affective disorder and suicide.

Psoriasis

Gupta et al. (1993) found that 5. 5 percent of patients with psoriasis had current suicidal ideation. The more severe the psoriasis and the more severe the depression, the more likely that the patients had suicidal ideation.

Psychogenic Seizures

Peguero et al. (1995) found that patients with psychogenic seizures had a higher incidence of prior suicide attempts than epileptics. Attempting suicide in these patients was associated with incontinence and self-injury during the seizure.

Skin Disorders

Denicoff et al. (1990) compared patients with Darier's disease (a skin disorder) with patients who had other skin disorders. The two groups did not differ in depression scores, but the patients with Darier's disease had a tendency to greater past suicidality.

Smoking

Smith et al. (1992) followed up a large sample of men and found that those who smoked had a higher suicide rate. The suicide rate was higher if the men were white, from low income areas, and had mycardial infarctions (but not diabetes). Hemenway et al. (1993) found that smoking and suicide were associated in a large sample of nurses. Doll et al. (1994) found that smoking was associated with completed suicide in British doctors.

Solvent-Related Disorders

Berlin et al. (1995) found a high suicide rate in these patients.

Spinal Cord Injury

Charlife and Gerhart (1991) found a suicide rate of 59 in spinal cord patients – 54 in paraplegics and 64 in quadriplegics. The suicides had been more active in causing their injury, had more pre-injury family disintegration, alcohol/drug abuse, and depression, and more post-injury depression and alcohol abuse than controls matched for age at injury, sex, and level of injury.

De Vivo et al. (1991) found that persons with spinal cord injury had a higher suicide rate than expected. The rate was higher in the first five years after the injury, in paraplegics (versus quadriplegics), if complete paraplegia (versus incomplete) and for whites, females, and those aged 25–54.

Judd and Brown (1992) found six suicides among 342 patients treated in a five-year period for acute spinal cord injuries. They tended to be male, alcohol/drug abusers, depressed and preferring death, and with a schizoid/depressive/narcissistic personality disorder.

Kishy and Robinson (1996) found that suicidal spinal cord patients more often had a psychiatric history, especially a depressive disorder. Suicidality was not associated with characteristics of the injury.

Steroid Use

Middleman et al. (1995) found that high school students who used steroids were more likely to have attempted suicide, engaged in sexual intercourse and other risky behaviors, and have had a sexually transmitted disease.

Stroke

Kishy et al. (1996a, 1996b) found that suicidal ideation in stroke patients was associated with having a prior stroke, being younger, alcohol abuse, greater social impairment prior to the stroke, and a major depressive disorder. It was not associated with physical impairment (except for sensory deficits), age, education, marital status, handedness, or social class.

Tardive Dyskinesia

Sandyk and Kay (1991) found that psychiatric patients who had previously attempted suicide had more tardive dyskinesia in the neck, trunk, and limbs (but not lips, tongue, or jaw) than patients who had not attempted suicide. They did not differ in sex, diagnosis, age at onset, intelligence, test scores, or duration of illness.

Terminal Illness

Chocinov et al. (1995) found that 14 percent of terminally ill patients had occasional thoughts of suicide, and 8 percent had serious and pervasive thoughts. This latter group was in more pain, had less family support, had higher depression scores, and was more likely to have a depressive disorder.

Thorotrast-Injection Patients

Andersson et al. (1993) found that Thorotrast-injection patients had a higher suicide rate than expected.

Tinnitus

Lewis et al. (1994) identified 20 cases of suicide world-wide with tinnitus. The majority were men, and the mean age was 57. Ten had a prior psychiatric diagnosis, and the duration of the tinnitus average two years.

Transplants

Montandon and Frey (1991) found that 1.4 percent of patients given renal transplants completed suicide in the next 12 years. Those given cyclosporin were less likely to complete suicide.

Weight

Mitchell et al. (1990) found that people more than 30 percent overweight had attempted suicide more often than normal-weight persons and had more depressed families, but did not differ in alcohol abuse or the presence of an affective disorder.

Hospital Characteristics

Bassett and Tsourtos (1993) found that over ten years in a 20-bed inpatient psychiatric unit, the suicide rate increased along with the number of patients, a reduced length of stay, and the proportion of severely disturbed patients.

Discussion

We have witnessed attention given to the 1990s to suicidality in people with HIV infections and AIDS. However, this research has been rather poor. The correlates of suicidality in these patients appear to be quite similar to those in other groups, and this particular illness seems to be nothing more than an additional stressor with which these individuals have to cope. The research has not advanced our understanding of suicidality.

REFERENCES

Albert, M., Jenike, M., Nixon, R., & Nobel, K. Thyrotropin response to thyrotropin-releasing hormone in patients with dementia of the Alzheimer type. *Biological Psychiatry*, 1993, 33, 267–271.

Alfonso, C. A., Cohen, M. A., Aladjem, A. D., Morrison, F., Powell, D. R., Winters, R. A., & Orlowski, B. K. HIV seropositivity as a major risk factor for suicide in the general hospital. *Psychosomatics*, 1994, 35, 368–373.

Allebeck, P., & Bolund, C. Suicides and suicide attempts in cancer patients. *Psychological Medicine*, 191, 21, 979–984.

Andersson, M., Juel, K., & Storm, H. H. Pattern of mortality among Danish Thorotrast patients. *Journal of Clinical Epidemiology*, 1993, 46, 637–644.

Aro, A. R., Henriksson, M., Leinikki, P., & Lonnqvist, J. Fear of AIDS and suicide in Finland. *AIDS Care*, 1995, 7, S2, 187–197.

Aro, A. R., Jallinoja, P. T., Henriksson, M. M., & Lonnqvist, J. K. Fear of acquired immunodeficiency syndrome and fear of other illnesses in suicide. *Acta Psychiatrica Scandinavica*, 1994, 90, 65–69.

Ayuso Mateos, J. L., Lastra, I., & Montanes, F. Research in psychopathology in patients with HIV/AIDS. *AIDS Care*, 1996, 8, 233–239.

Bak, S., Stenager, E. N., Stenager, E., Boldsen, J., & Smith, T. A. Suicide patients with motor neuron disease. *Behavioral Neurology*, 1994, 7, 181–184.

Bassett, D., & Tsourtos, G. Inpatient suicide in general hospital psychiatric unit. *General Hospital Psychiatry*, 1993, 15, 301–306.

Beckett, A., & Shenson, D. Suicide risk in patients with human immunodeficiency virus infection and acquired immunodeficiency syndrome. *Harvard Review of Psychiatry*, 1993, 1(1), 27–35.

Belkin, G. S., Fleishman, J. A., Stein, M. D., Piette, J., & Mor, V. Physical symptoms and depressive symptoms among individuals with HIV infection. *Psychosomatics*, 1992, 33, 416–427.

Berlin, K., Edling, C., Persson, B., Ahlborg, G., Hillert, L., Hogstedt, B., Lundberg, I.,

Svensson, B. G., Thiringer, G., & Orbaeck, P. Cancer incidence and mortality of patients with suspected solvent-related disorders. *Scandinavian Journal of Work, Environment & Health*, 1195, 21, 362–367.

Berman, A. L., & Samuel, L. Suicide among people with multiple sclerosis. *Journal of Neurologic Rehabilitation*, 1993, 7)2), 53–62.

Bloch, M., Adam, S., Wiggins, S., Huggings, M., & Hayden, M. R. Predictive testing for Huntington's disease in Canada. *American Journal of Medical Genetics*, 1992, 42, 499–507.

Boston, P. R., Dursun, S. M., & Reveley, M. A. Cholesterol and mental disorder. *British Journal of Psychiatry*, 1996, 169, 682–689.

Breitbart, W., Rosenfeld, B. D., & Passik, S. D. Interest in physician-assisted suicide among ambulatory HIV-infected patients. *American Journal of Psychiatry*, 1996, 153, 238–242.

Breslau, N. Migraine, suicidal ideation, and suicide attempts. *Neurology*, 1992, 42, 392–395.

Breslau, N., David, G. C., & Adreski, P. Migraine, psychiatric disorders, and suicide attempts. *Psychiatry Research*, 1991, 37, 11–23.

Brunner, E., Smith, G. D., Pilgrim, J., & Marmot, M. Low serum cholesterol and suicide. *Lancet*, 1992, 339, 1001–1002.

Burke, P. M., Kocoshis, S., Neigut, D., Sauer, J., Candra, R., & Orenstein, D. Maternal psychiatric disorders in pediatric inflammatory bowel disease and cystic fibrosis. *Child Psychiatry & Human Development*, 1994, 25, 45–52.

Catalan, J., Seijas, D., Lief, T., Pergami, A., & Burgess, A. Suicidal behavior in HIV infection. *Archives of Suicide Research*, 1995, 1, 85–96.

Charlife, S. W., & Gerhart, K. A. Behavioral and demographic predictors of suicide after traumatic spinal cord injury. *Archives of Physical Medicine & Rehabilitation*, 1991, 72, 488–492.

Chochinov, H. M., Wilson, K. G., Enns, M., Mowchun, N., Lander, S., Levitt, M., & Clinch, J. J. Desire for death in the terminally ill. *American Journal of Psychiatry*, 1995, 152, 1185–1191.

Cochran, S. D., & Mays, V. M., Depressive distress among homosexually active African American men and women. *American Journal of*

Psychiatry, 1994, 151, 524–529.

Conroy, R. M. Low cholesterol and violent death. *Irish Journal of Psychological Medicine*, 1993, 10, 67–70.

Conwell, Y., Forbes, N. T., Cox, C., & Caine, E. D. Validation of a measure of physical illness burden at autopsy. *Journal of the American Geriatric Society*, 1993, 41, 38–41.

Cooper-Patrick, L., Crum, R. M., & Ford, D. E. Identifying suicidal ideation in general medical patients. *Journal of the American Medical Association*, 1994, 272, 1757–1762.

Coté, T. R., Biggar, R. J., & Dannenberg, A. L. Risk of suicide among persons with AIDS. *Journal of the American Medical Association*, 1992, 268, 2066–2068.

Dannenberg, A. L., McNeil, J. G., Brundage, J. F., & Brookmeyer, R. Suicide and HIV infection. *Journal of the American Medical Association*, 1996, 276, 1743–1746.

Davies, D. R. Organophosphates, affective disorders, and suicide. *Journal of Nutritional & Environmental Medicine*, 1995, 5, 367–374.

De Leo, D., Precheri, M., Melodia, C., Vella, J., Forza, G., & de Bertolini, C. Suicide attitude in breast cancer patients. *Psychopathology*, 1991, 24, 115–119.

Denicoff, K. D., Lehman, Z. A., Rubinow, D. R., Schmidt, P. J., & Peck, G. L. Suicidal ideation in Darier's disease. *Journal of the American Academy of Dermatology*, 1990, 22, 196–198.

De Vivo, M. J., Black, K. J., Richards, J. S., & Stover, S. L. Suicide following spinal cord injury. *Paraplegia*, 1991, 29, 620–627.

Di Maio, L., Squitieri, F., Napolitano, G., Campanella, G., Trofatter, J. A., & Conneally, P. M. Suicide risk in Huntington's Disease. *Journal of Medical Genetics*, 1993, 30, 293–295.

Doll, R., Peto, R., Wheatley, K., Gray, R., & Sutherland, I. Mortality in relation to smoking. *British Medical Journal*, 1994, 309, 901–911.

Domino, G., & Shen, D. Attitudes toward suicide in patients with HIV/AIDS. *Omega*, 1996–1997, 34, 15–27.

Engelberg, H. Low serum cholesterol and suicide. *Lancet*, 1992, 339, 727–729.

Engstrom, G., Alsen, M., Regnell, G., & Traskman-Bendz, L. Serum lipids in suicide attempters. *Suicide & Life-Threatening Behavior*,

1995, 25, 393–400.

Farhi, J., Ben-Rafael, Z., & Dicker, D. Suicide after ectopic pregnancy. *New England Journal of Medicine*, 1994, 330, 714.

Filiberti, A., Ripamonti, C., Saita, L., de Conno, F., & Maino, E. Frequency of suicide by cancer patients at the National Cancer Institute of Milan. *Annals of Oncology*, 1991, 2, 610.

Fishbain, D. A., Goldberg, M., Rosomoff, R. S., & Rosomoff, H. Completed suicide in chronic pain. *Journal of Clinical Pain*, 1991, 7(1), 29–36.

Fritze, J., Schneider, B., & Lanczik, M. Autoaggressive behavior and cholesterol. *Neuropsychobiology*, 1992, 26, 180–181.

Futrell, N., Schultz, L. R., & Millikan, C. CNS disease in patients with systemic lupus erythematosus. *Neurology*, 1992, 42, 1649–1657.

Gala, C., Pergami, A., Catalan, J., Riccio, M., Durbano, R., Musicco, M., Baldeweg, T., & Invernizzi, G. Risk of deliberate self-harm and factors associated with suicidal behavior among asymptomatic individuals with HIV infection. *Acta Psychiatrica Scandinavica*, 1992, 86, 70–75.

Gallerani, M., Manfredini, R., Caracciolo, S., Scapoli, C., Molinari, S., & Fersini, C. Serum cholesterol concentrations in parasuicide. *British Medical Journal*, 1995, 310, 1632–1636.

Ginter, E. Re: "Hypothesis: low serum cholesterol, suicide, and interleukin 2." *American Journal of Epidemiology*, 1996, 143, 405.

Glueck, C. J., Kuller, F. E., Hamer, T., Rodriguez, R., Sosa, F., Sieve-Smith, L., & Morrison, J. A. Hypocholesterolemia, hypertriglyceridemia, suicide, and suicide ideation in children hospitalized for psychiatric diseases. *Pediatric Research*, 1994, 35, 602–610.

Goldston, D. B., Kelley, A. E., Reboussin, D. M., Daniel, S. S., Smith, J. A., Schwartz, P. R., Lorentz, W., & Hill, C. Suicidal ideation and behavior and noncompliance with the medical regime among diabetic adolescents. *Journal of the American Academy of Child & Adolescent Psychiatry*, 1997, 36, 1528–1536.

Goldston, D. B., Kovacs, M., Ho, V. Y., Parrone, P. L., & Stiffler, L. Suicidal ideation and suicide attempts among youth with insulin-dependent diabetes mellitus. *Journal of the American Academy of Child & Adolescent Psychiatry*, 1994, 33, 240–246.

Golier, J. A., Marzuk, P. M., Leon, A. C., Weiner, C., & Tardiff, K. Low serum cholesterol level and attempted suicide. *American Journal of Psychiatry*, 1995, 152, 419–423.

Grabbe, L., Demi, A., Camann, M. A., & Potter, L. The health status of elderly persons in the last year of life. *American Journal of Public Health*, 1997, 87, 434–437.

Greenberg, W. M., Serum cholesterol levels and suicidality. *Journal of Clinical Psychiatry*, 1995, 56, 434–435.

Gupta, M. A., Schork, N. J., Gupta, A. K., Kirkby, S., & Ellis, C. I. Suicidal ideation in psoriasis. *International Journal of Dermatology*, 1993, 32, 188–190.

Halttunen, A., Henriksson, M., & Lonnqvist, J. Completed suicide with a fear of having contracted AIDS. In J. Beskow, M. Bellini, J. Faria & A. Kerkhof (Eds.), *HIV and AIDS-related suicidal behavior*. Bologna: Monduzzi-Editore, 1991, 69–76.

Halttunen, A., Henriksson, M., & Lonnqvist, J. Suicides and fear of somatic illness. In K. Bohme, R. Freytag, C. Wachtler & H. Wedler (Eds.), *Suicidal behavior*. Regensburg: A Roderer, 1993, 881–884.

Harris, E. C., & Barraclough, B. M. Suicide as an outcome for medical disorders. *Medicine*, 1994, 73, 281–296.

Hemenway, D., Solnick, S. J., & Colditz, G. A. Smoking and suicide among nurses. *American Journal of Public Health*, 1993, 83, 249–251.

Hendricks, M. L. HIV-associated suicidal ideation in gay men. In D. Lester (Ed.), *Suicide '93*. Denver: AAS, 1993, 154–155.

Henriksson, M. M., Isometsa, E. T., Hietanen, P. S., Aro, H. M., & Lonnqvist, J. K. Mental disorders in cancer suicides. *Journal of Affective Disorders*, 1995, 36, 11–20.

Hietanen, P., & Lonnqvist, J. Cancer and suicide. *Annals of Oncology*, 1991, 2(1), 19–23.

Hietanen, P., Lonnqvist, J., & Jallinoja, P. Cancer suicides compared to suicides among general population. In K. Bohme, R. Freytag,

C. Wachtler & H. Wedler (Eds.), *Suicidal behavior*. Regensburg: A Roderer, 1993, 873–876.

Horton-Deutsch, S. L., Clark, D. C., & Farran, C. J. Chronic dyspnea and suicide in elderly men. *Hospital & Community Psychiatry*, 1992, 43, 1198–1203.

Hudson, M. M., Jones, D., Boyett, J., Sharp, G. B., & Pui, C. H. Late mortality of long-term survivors of childhood cancer. *Journal of Clinical Oncology*, 1997, 15, 2205–2213.

Hunt, D. K., Lowenstein, S. R., Badgett, R. G., Marine, W. M., Garrett, C. J., & Steiner, J. F. Detection of injury-prone behaviors among internal medicine patients. *Journal of General Internal Medicine*, 1992, 7, 573–582.

Hunt, K., Vessey, M., & McPherson, K. Mortality in a cohort of long-term users of hormone replacement therapy. *British Journal of Obstetrics & Gynecology*, 1990, 97, 1080–1086.

Iribarren, C., Reed, D. M., Wergoske, G., Burchfiel, C. M., & Dwyer, J. H. Serum cholesterol level and mortality due to suicide and trauma in the Honolulu Heart Program. *Archives of Internal Medicine*, 1995, 155, 695–700.

Joner, G., & Patrick, S. The mortality of children with Type 1 (insulin-dependent) diabetes mellitus in Norway, 1973–1988. *Diabetologia*, 1991, 34, 29–32.

Judd, F. K., & Brown, D. J. Suicide following acute traumatic spinal cord injury. *Paraplegia*, 1992, 30, 173–177.

Judd, F. K., & Mijch, A. M. Depressive symptoms in patients with HIV infection. *Australian & New Zealand Journal of Psychiatry*, 1996, 30, 104–109.

Kishy, Y., Kosier, J., & Robinson, R. Suicidal plans in patients with acute stroke. *Journal of Nervous & Mental Disease*, 1996a, 184, 274–280.

Kishy, Y., & Robinson, R. Suicidal plans following spinal cord injury. *Journal of Neuropsychiatry & Clinical Neuroscience*, 1996, 8, 442–445.

Kishy, Y., Robinson, R., & Kosier, J. Suicidal plans in patients with stroke. *International Psychogeriatrics*, 1996b, 8, 623–634.

Kissinger, P., Fuller, C., Clark, P. A., & Abdalian, S. E. Psychosocial characteristics of HIV-infected adolescents in New Orleans. *Journal of Adolescent Health*, 1997, 20, 258.

Klee, H. Drug misuse and suicide. *AIDS Care*, 1995, 7, (Suppl. 2), 145–155.

Kromhout, D., Katan, M. B., Menotti, A., Keys, A., & Bloemberg, B. Serum cholesterol and long-term death rates from suicide, accidents, and violence. *Lancet*, 1992, 340, 317.

Kunugi, H., Taki, N., Aoki, H., & Nanko, S. Low serum cholesterol in suicide attempters. *Biological Psychiatry*, 1997, 41, 196–200.

Kyvik, K. O., Stenager, E. N., Green, A., & Svendsen, A. Suicides in men with IDDM. *Diabetes Care*, 1994, 17, 210–212.

Laane, H. M. Euthanasia, assisted suicide, and AIDS. *AIDS Care*, 1995, 7, (Suppl. 2), 163–167.

Law, M. R., Thompson, S. G., & Wald, J. J. Assessing possible hazards of reducing serum cholesterol. *British Medical Journal*, 1994, 308, 373–379.

Lawson, K., Wiggins, S., Green, T., Adam, S., Bloch, M., & Hayden, M. R. Adverse psychological events occurring in the first year after predictive testing for Huntington's Disease. *Journal of Medical Genetics*, 1996, 33, 856–862.

Lester, D. Mortality from suicide in attempted suicides. *Perceptual & Motor Skills*, 1991, 72, 1030.

Lester, D. Sexual versus psychiatric predictors of suicide in men with AIDS-related illnesses. *American Journal of Drug & Alcohol Abuse*, 1993, 19, 139–140.

Lester, D., Ferraro, T. M., & Murphy, J. A. Headache symptoms, depression, and suicidal preoccupation. *Perceptual & Motor Skills*, 1992, 74, 90.

Levi, F., Bulliard, J. L., & La Vecchia, C. Suicide risk among incident cases of cancer in the Swiss canton of Vaud. *Oncology*, 1991, 48, 44–47.

Lewis, J. E., Stephens, S. D. G., & McKenna, L. Tinnitus and suicide. *Clinical Otolaryngology*, 1994, 19(1), 50–54.

Lindberg, G., Rastam, L., Gullberg, B., & Eklund, G. A. Lowe serum cholesterol concentration and short term mortality from injuries in men and women. *British Medical Journal*, 1992, 305, 277–279.

Lipe, H., Schultz, A., & Bird, T. D. Risk factors for suicide in Huntington's disease.

American Journal of Medical Genetics, 1993, 48, 231–233.

Loimer, N., Hollwerer, E., Hofman, P., & Presslich, O. Epidemiology of suicide, parasuicide, and fatalities among drug addicts in Vienna in 1989. In G. Ferrari, M. Bellini & P. Crepet (Eds.), *Suicidal behavior and risk factors*. Bologna: Monduzzi-Editore, 1990, 1049–1054.

Long, D. D., & Miller, B. J. Suicidal tendency and multiple sclerosis. *Health & Social Work*, 1991, 16, 104–109.

Mackerle, S., Neoral, L., Sykora, J., Chrobok, O., & Kosatik, A. Is suicide following surgical management of intracranial hypertension a mere chance phenomenon? *Acta Universitatis Palackianae Olomicensis Facultatis Medicae*, 1990, 125, 243–248.

Maes, M., Delanghe, J., Meltzer, H. Y., Scharpé, S., D'Hondt, P., & Cosyns, P. Lower degree of esterification of serum cholesterol in depression. *Acta Psychiatrica Scandinavica*, 1994, 90, 252–258.

Maes, M., Smith, R., Christophe, A., Vandoolaeghe, E., Van Gastel, A., Neels, H., Demedts, P., Wauters, A., & Maltzer, H. Y. Lower serum high-density lipoprotein cholesterol (DHL-C) in major depression and in depressed men with serious suicidal attempts. *Acta Psychiatrica Scandinavica*, 1997, 95, 212–221.

Mancoske, R. J., Wadsworth, C. M., Dugas, D. S., & Haseny, J. A. Suicide risk among people living with AIDS. *Social Work*, 1995, 40, 783–787.

Marzuk, P. M., Tardiff, K., Leon, A. C., Hirsch, C. S., Hartwell, N., Portera, L., & Iqbal, M. I. HIV seroprevalence among suicide victims in New York City, 1991–1993 *American Journal of Psychiatry*, 1997, 154, 1720–1725.

McKegney, F. P., & O'Dowd, M. A. Suicidality and HIV status. *American Journal of Psychiatry*, 1992, 149, 396–398.

Mendez, M. F., & Doss, R. C. Ictal and psychiatric aspects of suicide in psychiatric patients. *International Journal of Psychiatry in Medicine*, 1992, 22, 231–237.

Michalik, J. E., Wolfe, W. H., & Miner, J. C. Health status of Air Force veterans occupationally exposed to herbicides in

Vietnam. *Journal of the American Medical Association*, 1990, 264, 1832–1836.

Middleman, A. B., Faulkner, A. H., Woods, E. R., Emans, S. J., & DuRant, R. H. High-risk behaviors among high school students in Massachusetts who use anabolic steroids. *Pediatrics*, 1995, 96, 268–272.

Mitchell, J. E., Pyle, R. L., Eckert, E. D., Hatsukami, D., & Soll, E. Bulimia nervosa in overweight individuals. *Journal of Nervous & Mental Disease*, 1990, 178, 324–327.

Modai, I., Valevski, A., Dror, S., & Weizman, A. Serum cholesterol levels and suicidal tendencies in psychiatric inpatients. *Journal of Clinical Psychiatry*, 1994, 55, 252–254.

Montandon, A., & Frey, F. J. Decreased risk of suicide in renal transplant patients on cyclosporin. *Lancet*, 1991, 338, 635.

Muldoon, M. F., Manuck, S. B., & Matthews, K. A. Lowering cholesterol concentrations and mortality. *British Medical Journal*, 1990, 301, 309–314.

Muldoon, M. R., Manuck, S. B., & Matthews, K. A. Mortality experience in cholesterol-reduction trials. *New England Journal of Medicine*, 1991, 324, 322–323.

Muldoon, M. F., Rossouw, J. E., Manuck, S. B., Glueck, C. J., Kaplan, J. R., & Kaufmann, P. G. Low or lowered cholesterol and risk of death from suicide and trauma. *Metabolism*, 1993, 42(9), S1, 45–56.

O'Dowd, M. A., Biderman, D. J., & McKegney, F. P. Incidence of suicidality in AIDS and HIV-positive patients attending a psychiatry outpatient program. *Psychosomatics*, 1993, 34, 33–40.

O'Neal, S. E., & Range, L. M. College students' hypothetical responses to suicidal individuals who are HIV-positive, substance abusing, depressed, or anxious. *Death Studies*, 1993, 17, 143–149.

Pearce, C. M., & Martin, G. Predicting suicide attempts among adolescents. *Acta Psychiatrica Scandinavica*, 1994, 90, 324–328.

Peguero, E., Abou-Khalil, B., Fakhoury, T., & Mathews, G. Self-injury and incontinence in psychogenic seizures. *Epilepsia*, 1995, 36, 586–591.

Penttinen, J. Back pain and risk of suicide among Finnish farmers. *American Journal of Public Health*, 1995, 85, 1452–1453.

Perry, S., & Jacobsberg, L., & Fishman, B. Suicidal ideation and HIV testing. *Journal of the American Medical Association*, 1990, 263, 679–682.

Persinger, M. A. Sense of a presence and suicidal ideation following traumatic brain injury. *Psychological Reports*, 1994, 75, 1059–1070.

Pfeffer, C. R., Hurt, S. W., Kakuma, T., Peskin, J. R., Siefker, C. A., & Nagabhairova, S. Suicidal children grown up. *Journal of the American Academy of Child & Adolescent Psychiatry*, 1994, 33, 225–230.

Rabkin, J. G., Remien, R., Katoff, L., & Williams, J. B. W. Suicidality in AIDS long-term survivors. *AIDS Care*, 1993, 5, 401–411.

Rahu, M., Tekkel, M., Veidebaum, T., Pukkala, E., Hakulinen, T., Auvinen, A., Ryptomaa, T., Inskip, P. D., & Baice, J. D. The Estonian study of Chernobyl cleanup workers. *Radiation Research*, 1997, 147, 653–657.

Rajs, J., & Fugelstad, A. HIV-related suicides in Stockholm. In J. Beskow, M. Bellini, J. Faria & A. Kerkhof (Eds.), *HIV and AIDS-related suicidal behavior*. Bologna: Monduzzi-Editore, 1991, 33–39.

Rajs, J., & Fugelstad, A. Suicide related to human immunodeficiency virus infection. *Acta Psychiatrica Scandinavica*, 1992, 85, 234–239.

Rao, A. V. Physical illness, pain, and suicidal behavior. *Crisis*, 1990, 11(2), 48–55.

Rao, V., Dening, T., Brayne, C., & Huppert, F. A. Suicidal thinking in community residents over eighty. *International Journal of Geriatric Psychiatry*, 1997, 12, 337–343.

Ritchie, E. C., Radke, A. Q., & Ross, B. Depression and support systems in male Army HIV+ patients. *Military Medicine*, 1992, 157, 345–349.

Rosengard, C., & Folkman, S. Suicidal ideation, bereavement, HIV serostatus, and psychosocial variables. *AIDS Care*, 1997, 9, 373–384.

Rundell, J. R., Kyle, K. M., Brown, G. R., & Thomason, J. L. Risk factors for suicide attempts in a human immunodeficiency virus screening program. *Psychosomatics*, 1992, 33(1), 24–27.

Ryan, M., & Murray, F. E. Scottish study

does not replicate findings. *British Medical Journal*, 1995, 311, 807.

Sadovnick, A. D., Ebers, G. C., Wilson, R. W., & Paty, D. W. Life expectancy in patients attending multiple sclerosis clinics. *Neurology*, 1992, 42, 991–994.

Sadovnick, A. D., Eisen, K., Ebers, G. C., & Paty, D. W. Cause of death in patients attending multiple sclerosis clincis. *Neurology*, 1991, 41, 1193–1196.

Saiz, P. A., Bobes, J., Gonzales, M. P., Cocana, I., Gonzalez-Quiros, P., & Bousono, M. Searching for a predictive peripheral biological model in parasuicidal behavior. *European Psychiatry*, 1997, 12, 75–81.

Sandyk, R., & Kay, S. R. Suicidal behavior and tardive dyskinesia. *International Journal of Neuroscience*, 1991, 57, 269–271.

Schuit, A. J., Dekker, J. M., Schouten, E. G., & Kok, F. J. Low serum cholesterol and death due to accidents, violence, or suicide. *Lancet*, 1993, 341, 827.

Seefried, G., & Gumpel, K. Low serum cholesterol and triglycerides and risk of death from suicide. *Archives of Gerontology & Geriatrics*, 1997, 25, 111–117.

Sherr, L. Suicide and AIDS. *AIDS Care*, 1995, 7, (Suppl. 2), 109–116.

Shinohara, S., Kono, A., Ahn, Y. O., & Shigematsu, T. Cancer and other causes of death among Koreans in Fukuoka, Japan, 1976–1986. *Japanese Journal of Cancer Research*, 1990, 81, 866–870.

Smith, G. D., Phillips, A. N., & Neaton, J. D. Smoking as an independent risk factor for suicide. *Lancet*, 1992, 340, 709–712.

Smith, G. D., Shipley, M. J., Marmot, M. G., & Patel, C. Lowering cholesterol concentrations and mortality. *British Medical Journal*, 1990, 301, 552.

Sorensen, S. A., & Fenger, K. Causes of death in patients with Huntington's disease and in unafflicted first-degree relatives. *Journal of Medical Genetics*, 1992, 29, 911–914.

Stael van Holstein, C. C., Anderson, H., Eriksson, S., & Holdt, B. Mortality after remote surgery for gastroduodenal disease. *Gut*, 1995, 37, 617–622.

Starkstein, S. E., Preziosi, T. J., Forrester, A. W., & Robinson, R. G. Specificity of affective and autonomic symptoms of depression in Parkinson's disease. *Journal of Neurology, Neurosurgery & Psychiatry*, 1990, 53, 869–873.

Steer, R. A., Iguchi, M. Y., & Platt, J. J. Hopelessness in IV drug users not in treatment and seeking HIV testing and counseling. *Drug & Alcohol Dependence*, 1994, 34, 99–103.

Stenager, E. N., Kocj-Henriksen, N., & Stenager, E. Risk factors for suicide in multiple sclerosis. *Psychotherapy & Psychosomatics*, 1996, 65, 86–90.

Stenager, E. N., & Stenager, E. Suicide and patients with neurological diseases. *Archives of Neurology*, 1992, 49, 1296–1303.

Stenager, E. N., Stenager, E., & Jensen, K. Attempted suicide, depression, and physical diseases. *Psychotherapy & Psychosomatics*, 1994b, 61, 65–73.

Stenager, E. N., Stenager, E., Koch-Henriksen, N., Bronnum-Hansen, H., Hyllested, K., Jensen, K., & Bille-Brahe, U. Suicide and multiple sclerosis. *Journal of Neurology, Neurosurgery & Psychiatry*, 1992, 55, 542–545.

Stenager, E. N., Wermuth, L., Stenager, E., & Boldsen, J. Suicide in patients with Parkinson's disease. *Acta Psychiatrica Scandinavica*, 1994a, 90, 70–72.

Stiles, T. C. Axis I and Axis II disorders in primary fibromyalgia and major depressed patients with and without a lifetime history of parasuicide. In T. Bjerke & T. C. Stiles (Eds.), *Suicide attempts in the Nordic countries*. Trondheim: Tapie Forlag, 1991, 147–155.

Storm, H. H., Christensen, N., & Jensen, O. M. Suicides among Danish patients with cancer. *Cancer*, 1992, 69, 1507–1512.

Sullivan, M., Rapp, S., Fitzgibbon, D., & Chapman, C. R. Pain and the choice to hasten death in patients with painful metastatic cancer. *Journal of Palliative Care*, 1997, 13(3), 18–38.

Sullivan, P. F., Joyce, P. R., Bulik, C. M., Mulder, R. T., & Oakley-Browne, M. Total cholesterol and suicidality in depression. *Biological Psychiatry*, 1994, 36, 472–477.

Takei, N., Kunugi, H., Nanko, S., Aoki, H., Iyo, R., & Kazamatsuri, H. Low serum cholesterol and suicide attempts. *British Journal of Psychiatry*, 1994, 164, 702–703.

Thompson, A. H., & Newman, S. C. Mortality in a child welfare population. *Child Welfare*, 1995, 74, 843–857.

Twiname, B. G. The relationship between HIV classification and depression and suicidal intent. *Journal of the Association of Nurses for AIDS Care*, 1993, 4(4), 28–35.

Uden, P., & Tibblin, S. Mortality in patients surgically treated for primary hyperparathyroidism due to solitary adenome. *Annales Chirurgicae & Gynaecologiae*, 1990, 79, 123–128.

Vanchieri, C. Chernobyl liquidators show increased risk of suicide, not cancer. *Journal of the National Cancer Institute*, 1997, 89, 1750–1752.

Van Haastrecht, H. J., Mientjes, G. H., van den Hoek, A. J., & Coutintio, R. A. Death for suicide and overdose among drug injectors after disclosure of first HIV test result. *AIDS*, 1994, 8, 1721–1725.

Varma, V. K., Chaturvedi, S. K., Malhotra, A., & Chari, P. Psychiatric symptoms in patients with non-organic chronic pain. *Indian Journal of Medical Research*, Section B, 1991, 94 (February), 60–63.

Vartiainen, E., Puska, P., Pekkanen, J., Tuomilehto, J., Lonnqvist, J., & Ehnholm, C. Serum cholesterol concentration and mortality from accidents, suicide, and other violent causes. *British Medical Journal*, 1994, 309, 445–447.

Vuorio, K. A., Aareka, E., & Lehtinin, V. Eight cases of patients with unfounded fear of AIDS. *International Journal of Psychiatry in Medicine*, 1990, 20, 405–411.

Wedler, H. L. Suicidal behavior in the HIV-infected population. In J. Beskow, M. Bellini, J. Faria & A. Kerkhof (Eds.), *HIV and AIDS-related suicidal behavior*. Bologna: Monduzzi-Editore, 1991, 41–44.

Wolfersdorf, M., Michelsen, A., Keller, F., Maier, V., Froscher, W., & Kaschka, W. P. Serum cholesterol, triglycerides and suicide in depressed patients. *Archives of Suicide Research*, 1996, 2, 161–170.

Wong, M. T., Chang, P. C., Yu, Y. L., Chan, Y. W., & Chan, V. Psychosocial impact of Huntington's disease on Hong Kong Chinese families. *Acta Psychiatrica Scandinavica*, 1994, 90, 16–18.

Wood, K. A., Nairn, R., Kraft, H., & Siegel, A. Suicidality among HIV-positive psychiatric inpatients. *AIDS Care*, 1997, 9, 385–389.

Zureik, M., Courbon, D., & Ducimetiere, P. Serum cholesterol concentration and death from suicide in men. *British Medical Journal*, 1996, 313, 649–652.

Chapter 19

SUGGESTION AND SUICIDE

Suicide Clusters

Completed Suicide

Gibbons et al. (1990) examined suicides by young people aged 1–19 in Cook County by month for 11 years and found that the distribution fit a Poisson distribution. Thus, there was no evidence for clustering. Kirch and Lester (1990) examined data on 11 patients who jumped to their deaths from one psychiatric hospital and found no evidence for clustering. James and Silcocks (1992) found no evidence for clustering in suicides by hanging in Cardiff (Wales) over a 15-year period. Taiminen and Helenius (1994) found no evidence of clustering for 58 suicides in one hospital in Finland from 1967–1992. Nowers and Gunnell (1996) found no clustering in suicides from the Clifton Suspension Bridge in England. Gessner (1997) found no evidence of clustering of teen suicides in Alaska; that is, they found no more in the same census tract within 7 days or 30 days than expected by chance.

On the other hand, using the same statistical technique, Haw (1994) found that 14 suicides in one year in a psychiatric unit did show clustering.

Gould et al. (1990a, 1990b) examined clustering of suicides within counties for 15–19 year olds in the United States for 1978–1984 and found an excess of suicides over the expected number within 7 days of one another, within 14 days, and within 30 days. Data from 11 states by town of residence showed a similar excess of observed clustering over expected. The clustering for counties was observed for 15–19 year olds and 20–24 year olds. Seven day clustering was also found for 55–64 year olds and 30 day clustering for 25-29 year olds, 55-64 year-olds, and 65–74 year olds.

Cox and Skegg (1993) looked at men committing suicide in prisons and police cells in New Zealand by month. They identified four clusters in prisons and three in police cells, defined as more suicides per month than expected by chance. The clusters in police cells were of longer duration than those in prisons; the two sets of clusters were not associated with each other.

Attempted Suicide

King et al. (1993, 1995) failed to find clustering of attempted suicide in adolescent psychiatric inpatients.

Gould et al. (1994) examined the clustering of attempted suicides in New Zealand hospitals for a three-year period. There was clustering, consistently only for 15–19 year olds (for 7, 14, 30, and 90-day intervals). Other groups showed the clustering for only some intervals.

Suicide Pacts

Brown et al. (1995) found that 2.5 percent of suicides in Southampton (England) in 1974–1993 were suicide pacts. The nine pairs were all man/woman, completing suicide the same day and place, and using the same method. The modal pair used car exhaust, were married, and were mentally ill (especially with major depressive disorders). Usually one member of the pair was suicidal and the other devoted or dependent. The major motive was relief of medical illness or mental disorders.

Brown and Barraclough (1997) found that suicide pacts accounted for 0.6 percent of all suicides in England. The majority of pacts involved married couples, male/female pairs, with peak in April to June (like other suicides), with little evidence of coercion of one member by the other. The pact suicides were older than other suicides.

Granboulan et al. (1997) found that double adolescent attempters had more often experienced parental deaths, separation/divorce, and foster homes/residential care than single attempters. They did not differ in sex or psychiatric disturbance in their parents.

Suicide Venues

Ross and Lester (1991) found an average of 12.8 suicides at Niagara Falls each year. The peak was during May–August and 10 a.m. to 8 p.m. The modal suicide lived within ten miles of the Falls.

Social Transmission

Sorenson and Rutter (1991) surveyed community residents and found that 6.6 percent had a family member attempt suicide, more so for women, non-Hispanic whites, and those with a high school education. Those who had a history of suicidal ideation or attempted suicide had a higher incidence of family members attempting suicide. Those with suicidal ideation, as compared to nonsuicidal residents, had more parents attempting suicide; more parental mental disturbance; and more often were disturbed themselves, female, unmarried, and over the age of 65. The attempters more often had parental mental disturbance, more often were disturbed themselves, and were more often female and unmarried.

Chiles et al. (1985) found that attempted suicides, as compared to psychiatric controls, saw suicide as a more efficacious solution to problems, but knew fewer people who had attempted or completed suicide. Those that they did know were more interpersonally distant.

Conrad (1992) found that high school students who had attempted suicide knew more people who had completed suicide and who had attempted suicide than did nonsuicidal students. The groups did not differ in attribution of causes for suicide.

Platt (1993) found no differences in lifetime contact with attempted or completed suicides between attempters and normal controls, but the attempters had more contact in the last three months with suicidal friends and relatives. Repeaters had more nonintensive contact with suicidal people than nonrepeaters (that is with more distant suicidal people). The more contact with suicidal people, the more negative the opinions about suicide.

Brent et al. (1996a) found that adolescent suicides had more psychiatric disorder, personality disorder, attempted suicide, suicidal ideation, and assaultive behavior in their first- and second-degree relatives, compared to community controls. This suggests modeling or genetic transmission of psychiatric disorder.

Brent et al. (1996b) followed up friends of adolescent completed suicides and found that they did not differ in suicidal behavior in the next three years as compared to controls. Brent et al. (1994) found that adolescents who had a friend complete suicide did not show an increased rate of attempted suicide or suicidal ideation as compared to controls. Fekete and Schmidtke (1996a) found that attempted suicides did not have more suicide models in their families than normals.

Gutierrez et al. (1996) found that adolescent psychiatric inpatients who had a friend/relative attempt or commit suicide had different attitudes toward life and death than those who did not. For example, they had a weaker attraction to life. Those with a completed suicide in a friend/relative had a stronger attraction to death, and those with an attempted suicide in a friend/relative had a stronger repulsion by life. In addition, the suicidal and the depressed adolescents (ideators and attempters) also had a stronger attraction to death, a weaker attraction to life, and a stronger repulsion by life.

Martin (1996) found that recent suicidal ideation in high school students was associated with real-life experience of suicide, but not with exposure to television suicides. Recent attempts at suicide were, however, associated with both. A high rate of exposure to real-life suicides or to television suicides was associated with greater depression, substance use, risk taking, and suicidality.

Wallace and Kral (1996) found that the acceptability of suicide in college students was not associated with having been exposed to suicidality in others, but was associated with knowing someone with serious suicidal ideation and having someone close complete suicide. (Suicide acceptability was also associated with having prior suicidal ideation but not prior attempts.) Suicidal ideation and attempts in the past were associated with knowing a completed suicide who was close or an attempted suicide.

Williams et al. (1996) presented students with vignettes of stressed individuals. If the individual had a best friend who had completed suicide (sensationalized or not), students increased their prediction of suicide as an outcome. The sex and race of the individual played no role in predicting a suicidal outcome.

Final Exit

Marzuk et al. (1993) found an increase in suicide by use of a plastic bag in New York City in the year after the publication of *Final Exit* compared to the year before (33 versus 8), but no change in the use of other methods. Nine of the 33 suicides had the book with them. The 33 versus the 8 did not differ in demographics, medical illness, prior suicide attempts, and prior psychiatric hospitalization. Over the United States, Marzuk et al. (1994) found an increase in suicides by asphyxiation and poisoning in the year *Final Exit* was published, but no increase in suicides by other methods.

In Switzerland, Michel et al. (1994a, 1994b) found that 12.2 percent of all completed suicides used drugs, and 16 percent of these suicides used the drug combination recommend by *EXIT*, an organization to help people commit suicide. Attempters tended to use nonopiate analgesics more than the completers, but the modal drug of choice for both groups was the benzodiazepines. Lester (1994) found no effect in Germany, however, of the availability of a do-it-yourself manual there.

Publicity

Fekete and Macsai (1990) explored suicide in Hungary after a beauty queen killed herself with Lidocain in 1985, and a film and books on her appeared. Although prescriptions for the drug declined after 1985, its use for suicide increased from 1986–1989, an increase found only in females aged 15–39. Fekete et al. (1993) confirmed that the suicide of the beauty queen had no impact on suicides in the elderly; neither did newspaper reports in the 1980s of suicides using paraquat and railway trains, suggesting that the elderly are less responsive to modeling influences.

Riaunet et al. (1991) studied reports in newspapers and on television in Norway about suicide and found no increase in attempted suicides on these days.

Sonneck et al. (1992; Etzerdorfer et al., 1992) noted that subway suicides in Vienna (Austria) declined after the media abstained from reporting them, much more than the decline in other suicides. (More of the subway suicides occurred on Mondays and Tuesdays and more in the less busy stations.)

Jobes et al. (1996) found an increase in calls to the Seattle Crisis Center after the suicide of Kurt Cobain, but no increase in the number of completed suicides in King County (Washington). Martin and Koo (1997) found no increase in completed suicide in the 30 days after Kurt Cobain's suicide.

Newspapers

Gundlach and Stack (1990) found that monthly suicide rates in New York City from 1910–1920 were associated with economic conditions (a business activity index), influenza epidemics, and prohibition, but not with newspaper publicity of suicides. The relationship between monthly suicide rates and publicity was nonlinear – the suicide rate peaked for six stories per month. Wasserman (1993) re-analyzed these data adding alcohol consumption and found that the effect of suicide coverage in the New York Times was no longer significant – only business activity and alcohol consumption were associated with suicide.

Stack (1990b) looked at suicide stories in newspapers by month for 1948–1980. In a multiple regression, unemployment and publicity had an impact on the number of suicides. The effect of publicity was significant for publicized cases involving marital problems, celebrities, and spouse murder/ suicides. Stack (1990d) found that the monthly number of suicides from 1950–1980 was affected by newspaper stories on suicide, both for celebrities and noncelebrities (but less so). Unemployment contributed, too, but not war. However, Stack (1992) found that suicide publicity had no association with monthly suicide rates in the United States from 1933–1939 (nor did business activity or a presidential election).

Wasserman (1990) looked at monthly suicide numbers for 1970–1983 and found that the association with publicized celebrity suicides was eliminated after correction for autocorrelation. War and unemployment were not associated with monthly suicide numbers, while divorces/(divorces plus marriages) was significant only after correction for autocorrelation. Wasserman et al. (1994) found that monthly coverage of suicides by the *New York Times* was associated only with war and not circulation, presidential elections, or the suicide rate.

In Japan in 1954–1986, Ishii (1991) found that both males and females showed an increase in suicides after newspaper stories about suicide. Also in Japan, Stack (1996) found that the monthly suicide rate was affected by stories about Japanese suicides but not by non-Japanese suicides.

In Baden-Wurttemberg (Germany) 1968–1980, newspaper stories on suicide were followed by a significant increase in suicide in the following week (Jonas, 1992).

In Australia, Hassan (1995a, 1995b) found that suicide stories in newspapers in Sydney and Melbourne were followed on the two following days by an increase in the number of male suicides; females did not show this effect.

Fekete and Schmidtke (1995) examined newspaper stories on suicide in Hungary and West Germany. The German newspapers carried more stories about attempted suicide, stressed the negative consequences more, and had more murder-suicide stories. The Hungarian newspaper stories stressed the positive consequences more and more often mentioned the geographic site. The researchers did not look at the impact of these stories on suicide, however.

Fekete and Schmidtke (1996b) found that Hungary and United States newspapers differed in their suicide stories. In Hungary there were more reports of prominent persons who completed suicide, but fewer of celebrity suicides and suicide-murders. American newspapers had more science and statistics and more about the negative consequences of suicide.

Television: Completed Suicide

Stack (1990a) studied the effect of televised suicide news stories by month from 1968–1980. He noted an increase in elderly suicides after the stories, and if the news story involved an elderly person, an even larger increase in elderly suicides. The effect was found only for celebrity suicides in the news stories. In a multiple regression, in addition to publicity, unemployment had no impact, but war had a positive impact on the number of suicides. Stack (1993) found that monthly suicide rates were associated with television suicide stories and unemployment, but not war, in the United States from 1968–1980.

Stack (1991) explored monthly suicide rates from 1968–1980 and found that age-specific television suicide stories (both celebrity and noncelebrity) were associated with suicide rates only for 15–34 year olds and those 65 or older. Divorce, unemployment, and war were also significant predictors of suicide rates for some of the age groups.

Stack (1990c) looked at the number of teenage suicides by day and found no impact from four television films involving teenage suicide aired in 1984–1985.

Television: Attempted Suicide

Although Waldron et al. (1993) found an increase in overdoses in their region of England in the week after a televised show featuring an overdose as compared to the week before; they noted that other weeks of the year had equally high rates of overdose. Simkin et al. (1995) found no increase in overdoses using paracetamol after television broadcasts showing attempted suicide with paracetamol.

Discussion

The research on these four topics (clustering, suicide pacts, social transmission, and publicity) all indicate that suicidal behavior can (but not always does) increase the risk of suicidal behavior in others. Little research has appeared, however, on who is susceptible to these "suggestion" effects and who is not.

REFERENCES

Brent, D. A., Bridge, J., Johnson, B. A., & Connolly, J. Suicidal behavior runs in families. *Archives of General Psychiatry*, 1996a, 53, 1145–1152.

Brent, D. A., Moritz, G., Bridge, J., Perper, J., & Canobbio, R. Long-term impact of exposure to suicide. *Journal of the American Academy of Child & Adolescent Psychiatry*, 1996b, 35, 646–653.

Brent, D. A., Perper, J., Moritz, G., Liotus, L., Schweers, J., & Canobbio, R. Major depression or uncomplicated bereavement? *Journal of the American Academy of Child & Adolescent Psychiatry*, 1994, 33, 231–239.

Brown, M., & Barraclough, B. M. Epidemiology of suicide pacts in England and Wales. *British Medical Journal*, 1997, 315, 286–287.

Brown, M., King, E., & Barraclough, B. M. Nine suicide pacts. *British Journal of Psychiatry*, 1995, 167, 448–451.

Chiles, J., Strosahl, K., McMurtray, L., & Linehan, M. Modeling effects on suicidal behavior. *Journal of Nervous & Mental Disease*, 1985, 173, 477–481.

Conrad, N. Stress and knowledge of suicidal others as factors in suicidal behavior of high school students. *Issues in Mental Health Nursing*, 1992, 13, 95–104.

Cox, B., & Skegg, K. Contagious suicide in prisons and police cells. *Journal of Epidemiology & Community Health*, 1993, 47, 69–72.

Etzerdorfer, E., Sonneck, G., & Nagel-Kuess, S. Newspaper reports and suicide. *New England Journal of Medicine*, 1992, 327, 502–503.

Fekete, S., Koczan, G., Varga, J., & Osvath, K. Getting out of life. In K. Bohme, R. Freytag, C. Wachtler & H. Wedler (Eds.), *Suicidal behavior*, Regensburg: S. Roderer, 1993, 188–191.

Fekete, S., & Macsai, E. Hungarian suicide models. In G. Ferrari, M. Bellini & P. Crepet (Eds.), *Suicidal behavior and risk factors*. Bologna: Monduzzi-Editore, 1990, 149–155.

Fekete, S., & Schmidtke, A. The impact of mass media reports on suicide and attitudes toward self-destruction. In B. L. Mishara (Ed.), *The impact of suicide*. New York: Springer, 1995, 142–155.

Fekete, S., & Schmidtke, A. Suicidal models. *Omega*, 1996a, 33, 233–241.

Fekete, S., & Schmidtke, A. Attitudes toward suicide in the media. In J. McIntosh (Ed.), *Suicide '96*. Washington, DC: AAS, 1996b, 131–133.

Gessner, B. D. Temporal trends and geographic patterns of teen suicide in Alaska, 1979–1993. *Suicide & Life-Threatening Behavior*, 1997, 27, 264–273.

Gibbons, R. D., Clark, D. C., & Fawcett, J. A statistical method for evaluating suicide clusters and implementing cluster surveillance. *American Journal of Epidemiology*, 1990, 132, S183–S191.

Gould, M. S., Petrie, K., Kleinman, M. H., & Wallenstein, S. Clustering of attempted suicide. *International Journal of Epidemiology*, 1994, 23, 1185–1189.

Gould, M. S., Wallenstein, S., & Kleinman, M. Time-space clustering of teenage suicide. *American Journal of Epidemiology*, 1990a, 131, 71–78.

Gould, M. S., Wallenstein, S. Kleinman, M., O'Carroll, P., & Mercy, J. Suicide clusters. *American Journal of Public Health*, 1990b, 80, 211–212.

Granboulan, V., Zivi, A., & Basquin, M. Double suicide attempt among adolescents. *Journal of Adolescent Health*, 1997, 21, 128–130.

Gundlach, J. H., & Stack, S. The impact of hyper media coverage on suicide. *Social Science Quarterly*, 1990, 71, 619–627.

Gutierrez, P., King, C. A., & Ghaziuddin, N. Adolescent attitudes about death in relation to suicidality. *Suicide & Life-Threatening Behavior*, 1996, 26, 8–18.

Hassan, R. Effects of newspaper stories on the incidence of suicide in Australia. *Australian & New Zealand Journal of Psychiatry*, 1995a, 29, 480–483.

Hassan, R. *Suicide explained*. Melbourne: Melbourne University, 1995b.

Haw, C. M. A cluster of suicides at a London psychiatric unit. *Suicide & Life-Threatening Behavior*, 1994, 24, 256–266.

Ishii, K. Measuring mutual causation. *Social*

Science Research, 1991, 20, 188–195.

James, R., & Silcocks, P. Suicidal hanging in Cardiff. *Forensic Science International*, 1992, 56, 167–175.

Jobes, D. A., Berman, A. L., O'Carroll, P. W., Eastgard, S., & Knickmeyer, S. The Kurt Cobain suicide crisis. *Suicide & Life-Threatening Behavior*, 1996, 26, 260–264.

Jonas, K. Modelling and suicidal behavior. *British Journal of Social Psychology*, 1992, 31, 295–306.

King, C. A., Franzese, R., Gargan, S., Sarafa, C., Ghaziuddin, N., & Naylor, M. W. Suicidal contagion among adolescent inpatients. In D. Lester (Ed.), *Suicide '93*. Denver: AAS, 1993, 158–160.

King, C. A., Franzese, R., Gargan, S., Sarafa, C., McGovern, L., Ghaziuddin, N., & Naylor, M. W. Suicidal contagion among adolescents during acute psychiatric hospitalization. *Psychiatric Services*, 1995, 46, 915–918.

Kirch, M. R., & Lester, D. Is a spate of suicides a cluster? *Perceptual & Motor Skills*, 1990, 70, 46.

Lester, D. Do how-to-commit-suicide manuals increase the suicide rate? *Perceptual & Motor Skills*, 1994, 79, 10.

Martin, G. The influence of television suicide in a normal adolescent population. *Archives of Suicide Research*, 1996, 2, 103–117.

Martin, G., & Koo, L. Celebrity suicide. *Archives of Suicide Research*, 1997, 3, 187–198.

Marzuk, P.M., Tardiff, K., Hirsch, C. S., Leon, A. C., Stajic, M., Hartwell, N., & Portera, L. Increase in suicide by asphyxia in New York City after the publication of *Final Exit*. *New England Journal of Medicine*, 1993, 329, 1508–1510.

Marzuk, P. M., Tardiff, K., & Leon, A. C. Increase in fatal suicidal poisonings and suffocations in the year *Final Exit* was published. *American Journal of Psychiatry*, 1994, 151, 1813–1814.

Michel, K., Arestegui, G., & Spuhler, T. Suicide with psychotropic drugs in Switzerland. *Pharmacopsychiatry*, 1994a, 27, 114–118.

Michel, K., Waeber, V., Valach, L., Arestegui, G., & Spuhler, T. A comparison of the drugs taken in fatal and nonfatal self-poi-

soning. *Acta Psychiatrica Scandinavica*, 1994b, 90, 184–189.

Nowers, M., & Gunnell, D. Suicide from the Clifton Suspension Bridge in England. *Journal of Epidemiology & Community Health*, 1996, 50, 30–32.

Platt, S. The social transmission of suicide. *Crisis*, 1993, 14, 23–31.

Riaunet, A., Stiles, T. C., Rygnestad, T., & Bjerke, T. Mass-media reports of suicide and suicide attempts, and the rate of parasuicide. In T. Bjerke & T. C. Stiles (Eds.), *Suicide attempts in the Nordic countries*. Trondheim: Tapir Forlag, 1991, 157–162.

Ross, T. E., & Lester, D. Suicides at Niagara Falls. *American Journal of Public Health*, 1991, 81, 1677–1678

Simkin, S., Hawton, K., Whitehead, L., Fagg, J., & Eagle, M. Media influence on parasuicide. *British Journal of Psychiatry*, 1995, 167, 754–759.

Sonneck, G., Etzerdorfer, E., & Nagel-Kuess, S. Subway suicide in Vienna (1980–1990). In P. Crepet, G. Ferrari, S. Platt & M. Bellini (Eds.), *Suicidal behaviour in Europe*. Rome: John Libbey, 1992, 203–213.

Sorenson, S. B., & Rutter, C. M. Transgenerational patterns of suicide attempt. *Journal of Consulting & Clinical Psychology*, 1991, 59, 861–866.

Stack, S. Audience receptiveness, the media, and aged suicide, 1968–1980. *Journal of Aging Studies*, 1990a, 4, 195–209.

Stack, S. Divorce, suicide and the mass media. *Journal of Marriage & the Family*, 1990b, 52, 553–560.

Stack, S. The impact of fictional television films on teenage suicide, 1984–1985. *Social Science Quarterly*, 1990c, 71, 391–299.

Stack, S. A reanalysis of the impact of non-celebrity suicides. *Social Psychiatry & Psychiatric Epidemiology*, 1990d, 25, 269–273.

Stack, S. Social correlates of suicide by age. In A. A. Leenaars (Ed.), *Lifespan perspectives of suicide*. New York: Plenum, 1991, 187–213.

Stack, S. The effect of the media on suicide. *Suicide & Life-Threatening Behavior*, 1992, 22, 255–267.

Stack, S. The media and suicide. *Suicide & Life-Threatening Behavior*, 1993, 23, 63–66.

Stack, S. The effect of the media on suicide. *Suicide & Life-Threatening Behavior*, 1996, 26, 132–142.

Taiminen, T. J., & Helenius, H. Suicide clustering in a psychiatric hospital with a history of a suicide epidemic. *American Journal of Psychiatry*, 1994, 151, 1087–1088.

Waldron, G., Walton, J., & Helowicz, R. Copycat overdoses accidental. *British Medical Journal*, 1993, 306, 1416.

Wallace, M. D., & Kral, M. J. The effect of prior experience with suicide on attitudes toward suicide. In J. McIntosh (Ed.), *Suicide '96*. Washington, DC: AAS, 1996, 141–142.

Wasserman, I. The impact of divorce on suicide in the US, 1970–1983. *Family Perspectives*, 1990, 24(1), 61–67.

Wasserman, I. Comment on hypermedia coverage of suicide in New York City. *Social Science Quarterly*, 1993, 74, 216–218.

Wasserman, I., Stack, S., & Reeves, J. L. Suicide and the media. *Journal of Communication*, 1994, 44, 64–83.

Williams, S., Molock, S. D., & Kimbrough, R. Glamorized suicides and their contagious effects. In J. McIntosh (Ed.), *Suicide '96*. Washington, DC: AAS, 1996, 129–130.

Chapter 20

SUICIDE AND AGGRESSION

Suicidal Behavior In Murderers

Gottlieb and Gabrielson (1990) studied 52 murderers in Denmark, all guilty, nonpsychotic, and no longer in prison. Prior to the murder, 29 percent had attempted suicide. After release, 10 percent completed suicide and 8 percent attempted suicide. Suicidal behavior after release was predicted by having had prior psychiatric admissions, but not by the relationship with the victim. Suicidal behavior before the murder was not associated with pre-murder criminal violence or criminality, the relationship with the victim or age.

In a psychiatric intensive care unit, Citrome et al. (1994) found that the homicidal/assaultive patients stayed longer and had more multiple admissions than the suicidal patients.

Myers et al. (1995) found that adolescent homicidal youths had a high incidence of prior suicidal ideation (52 percent) and attempts (14 percent), but Myers did not include a comparison group. Crimmins et al. (1997) found that 41 percent of women who murdered their children had attempted suicide in the past.

Rasanen et al. (1995) found that arsonists had a higher incidence of prior suicidal ideation and attempts than murderers, as well as more alcohol abuse and Axis I

psychiatric disorders. They did not differ in Axis II disorders. Some of the arsonists had used arson to attempt suicide.

Suicides Versus Murderers

Ponzer et al. (1995) compared victims of firearms injuries in Stockholm (Sweden). The completed and attempted suicides were more often Swedish, male, and older; they more often died as compared to the murder victims and attempted murder victims, or the accident victims. They did not differ in overall convictions for crimes, but the suicides did have fewer convictions for murder and attempted murder.

Suicide After Murder

In counties in the Midwest, Palermo et al. (1997) found that the typical murder-suicide was a male assailant, white, murdering a spouse with a gun in the home.

Rosenbaum (1990) compared couples in which murder/suicide occurred with those in which only murder occurred. The perpetrators of murder/suicides were more often men, depressed, older, white, of higher social class, and married or separated; they were less often alcohol/drug abusers or drunk at the time of the act. The victims of the murder/suicides were less often alcohol/

drug abusers and less often had an antisocial personality disorder.

In Kentucky from 1985–1990, 6 percent of the homicides and one percent of the suicides were murder-suicides (Anonymous, 1991). The rate of murder-suicide was 0.3; 0.27 in whites and 0.34 in blacks. Perpetrators were primarily male, mean age 41, while victims were primarily female, mean age 35. Ninety-two percent were intraracial, and in 96 percent of the cases, the perpetrator and victim were known to each other. Seventy percent of the perpetrators were husbands, ex-husbands, or ex-boy friends; and 45 percent of them were intoxicated with alcohol or drugs or both.

In Chicago, Stack (1997) found that murder-suicide was more likely (than simple murder) if the victim was a child/spouse/ex-lover/friend, a white victim, a white offender, a female victim, an older offender, and a male offender.

Hanzlick and Koponen (1994) found that the modal murderer in Fulton County (Georgia) was male, black, using a firearm, and 34 years old; the modal victim was female, spouse or lover, same race, and 28 years old.

Wilson et al. (1995) compared murderers of spouse and children with murderers of spouses or children only. More of the familicide perpetrators were men and completed suicide after the murder than the uxoricide and filicide perpetrators.

Aderibigbe (1997) classified American murder-suicides into Marzuk's typology for murder-suicide using victim-murderer relationship. The most common types were fathers murdering children, spouses murdering each other, lovers murdering consorts, and extra-familial victims. Murders by mothers were less common than murders by fathers, and murders of children under the age of 16 were rare. Perpetrators were most often male and used firearms.

Buteau et al. (1993) found a murder-suicide rate in Quebec (Canada) in 1988–1990 of 0.18, compared with a murder rates of 2.35 and a suicide rate of 13.13. The murderer-suicides were primarily men, under the age of 40, using firearms, with recent marital separation and mental disorder. They killed spouses (32 percent), children under the age of 14 (35 percent) and strangers (23 percent).

In England from 1887–1990, Danson and Sotthill (1996) found that *The Times* reported 2274 murders, of which 6 percent were murder-suicides. Most murder-suicides were family affairs with male murderers. Men killed wives and lovers more, while women killed children more. Males also more often killed strangers.

In England, Milroy (1993) found that 5 %–10 % of murders were followed by suicide. These incidents usually were male assailants killing spouses, followed by children. Shooting was the most common method. Milroy (1995a) noted that the typical English murder-suicide involved a male assailant murdering a spouse after a breakdown in their relationship. In Australia, Milroy et al. (1997) found that typical murder-suicide had a male assailant aged 30–39 who shot a spouse/lover aged 30–49.

Easteal (1994) found that Australian murderers of intimates more often completed suicide than other murders. Among murderers of intimates, suicide was more likely if a gun was used, the murderer was born overseas, male, estranged from partner or partner was ailing, nonaboriginal, and over the age of 60. They less often used alcohol and more often killed more than one victim. They did not differ in their history of domestic violence or unemployment.

In northern Sweden, Lindqvist and Gustafsson (1995) found that 16 of 156 murders were followed by the murderer completing suicide. These murder-suicides were primarily men, with long-standing friction (usually marital) and victims known to the murderers. Thirteen of the murderers committed suicide within an hour of the murder using the same method.

Kominato et al. (1997) found that the majority of murder-suicides in one region of Japan involved family violence, primarily by men killing wives and/or children.

In British Columbia (Canada), Cooper and Eaves (1996) found that 18 percent of murderers of family members completed suicide and 5 percent made serious attempts. All of these killed partners or offspring. The completed/attempted suicides were more often males and more often killed females and biological children, and less often killed step-children. Murder-suicide was more common after separation or if the murderer was mentally ill. Violence by the victims, family conflict and financial/criminal motives were less likely to result in the suicide of the murderers. When men killed women, the suicidal murderers used firearms more often, less force, less often in the home, and more often after separation. For the filicides, none of the child-abuse cases committed suicide.

Somander and Rammer (1991) studied child victims of murder. Those whose murderers also completed suicide more often involved multiple victims, females killing children only, or males killing wives and children; the murderers less often had a criminal record or drug/alcohol abuse. In Japan, Sakuta (1995) described the modal case as a parent killing a child, at home, between 2 a.m. and 10 a.m., with the assailant in the 30s, depressed, healthy, married, suffering from illness or economic hardship, and impulsive. The victim was a healthy child. About half of the murderers were women, and about half left wills. Alder and Baker (1997) found that 25 percent of mothers who killed children completed suicide and 9 percent attempted suicide.

In Cuyahoga County in Ohio from 1970–1985, Kratcoski (1990) found that, of 179 suicides over the age of 60, 9 percent had committed suicide after murdering another. All were husbands who had murdered wives, some of whom were terminally ill.

Felthous and Hempel (1995) have reviewed research on murder-suicide.

Suicide and Aggression

Apter et al. (1991) compared samples of violent and nonviolent psychiatric patients. The risk of suicide was associated with the risk of violence in both groups. The risk of suicide (controlling for the risk of violence) was predicted by similar variables in both groups: impulsivity, anger, state and trait anxiety, fear, and sadness. Apter et al. (1993) found that psychiatric patients who had attempted suicide were more violent when on the ward. The attempters were more angry and had more trait anxiety than the nonattempters, but did not differ in state anxiety or impulsivity. Botsis et al. (1995) found that suicidal risk was associated with violence risk in psychiatric inpatients. Both kinds of risk were associated with behavioral problems in the patient and behavioral problems in first-degree relatives. Plutchik et al. (1995) compared predictors of suicidality and assaultiveness in psychiatric inpatients. The risks of these were associated positively. Depression, impulsivity, and disturbed reality testing predicted both. Sexual drive predicted assaultiveness while sexual inhibition, ego strength, and self-esteem predicted suicidality.

Hillbrand (1992) studied male psychiatric patients with histories of severe violence. In the institution, those showing both self and other-directed aggression (versus just other-directed aggression) showed more verbal and physical aggression. They more often had a diagnosis of organic disorder, but did not differ in intelligence test scores or age. Also among male forensic inpatients, Hillbrand (1995) found that those who had showed both self-destructive behavior during incarceration and prior suicidal behavior showed the most aggression toward others in the institution.

In a population of juvenile court offenders, Battle et al. (1993) found that the wish to kill oneself (found in 12 percent of the youths) was predicted by sexual abuse by an adult, alcohol abuse, cocaine use, worst unhappiness, and not having their mother/grandmother as one of their most important significant others. The wish to kill others (found in 18 percent of the youths) was predicted by sexual abuse by an adult, physical abuse, alcohol abuse, worst unhappiness, purpose-in-life scores, and juvenile court being the worst experience in life. Clearly, some of the predictors were the same, while others were different.

Greenwald et al. (1994) gave scales to predict suicide risk and violence risk to male alcoholics. Some of the predictors were similar (alcohol dependence and displacement as a defense mechanism). Other predictors were different: borderline and histrionic personality were associated with suicide risk, while antisocial and compulsive personality were associated with violence risk.

Grosz et al. (1994) compared adolescent psychiatric inpatients with a history of violence and those without. The violent adolescents had attempted suicide more, had more suicidal behavior in their families, and were rated as at higher risk for both suicide and violence.

Lehnert et al. (1994) found that adolescent suicide attempters had more anger-in, anger-out, and trait anger and had lower impulse control than high school students. In the attempters, depression was associated with impulse control and anger-in; hopelessness was associated with anger-in.

Szabo (1991) found that suicidal intent in attempted suicides was associated with more inward-directed hostility (on some measures), less criticism of others, and depression. Attempters with personality disorder (borderline, antisocial, and narcissistic) were more externally hostile than a depressed control group, but controls for age eliminated this difference. Compared to a nonclinical control group, the attempters did not differ in hostility once depression was controlled for.

Romanov et al. (1994) found that hostility (and alcohol abuse) predicted later completed/attempted suicide in a sample of Finnish twins.

Goldney et al. (1996, 1997) found that anger at self (and, less consistently, anger at society) predicted suicidal ideation four years later in students, but only for males. Initial anger did not predict subsequent attempted suicide. Suicidal ideation four years later was predicted by depression, negative mood, hopelessness, loneliness, locus of control, and employment status, but not anger. Anger also did not predict attempting suicide in the following eight years.

In a sample of violent offenders, Wong et al. (1997) found that those who were repetitively violent made attempts at suicide that were more impulsive than one-time violent offenders, and they also had less suicidal behavior in their families.

Experience in War

Fontana and Rosenheck (1995a) found that lifetime attempted suicide in Vietnam veterans was associated with combat scale scores, combat exposure, participation in atrocities, a rejecting welcome back home, conduct disorder, family instability, post-traumatic stress disorder, psychiatric disturbance, and substance abuse. In a multiple regression, only psychiatric disorder was significant.

Among the veterans with post-traumatic stress disorder, Fontana and Rosenheck (1995b) found that prior attempted suicide was associated with being white, childhood abuse, combat exposure, disciplinary actions, psychiatric symptoms, and substance abuse. These variables were poor in predicting subsequent attempts.

Sociological Studies

Lester (1991) found that the murder rate for babies was positively associated with the suicide rate (but not the homicide rate) over nations of the world. Lester (1992) found that the association between the murder rate of babies and the suicide rate was not statistically significant over the states of America.

Lester (1997a) found that the murder-suicide rate of nations was negatively associated with the murder rate. The coefficient of variation was lower for the murder-suicide rate than for the murder rate over the nations.

Over nations, Milroy (1995b) found that the higher the homicide rate, the lower the proportion of mentally ill offenders and offenders who commit suicide. Also, the rate of murder by the mentally ill and the rate of murder-suicide was stable over nations and over time. Reanalysis of his data indicates that this latter holds only over nations, not over time.

Saucer (1991) found that murder and suicide rates were in general not significantly associated over the states in each of the nine regions of the United States, although one region had a significant negative correlation

(east south central). Stolinsky and Stolinsky (1994, 1995, 1997) found no association between suicide and murder rates over 73 nations and only a weak positive association over the United States. Lester (1997b) also found no association between homicide and suicide rates over 72 nations. On the other hand, in a sample of primitive societies, Shulman (1996) found that the incidence of suicide was positively associated with the incidence of homicide and with war.

Lester (1993) found a positive association between suicide and homicide rates in the United States over the time period 1940-1989 and between yearly changes in these rates, opposite to predictions from a hypothesis by Ferri.

Over time in both Ireland and Northern Ireland, McKenna et al. (1997) found that suicide rates were positively associated with homicide rates (and with crime rates).

Guileyardo et al. (1994) found that the homicide/suicide ratio for firearm deaths in Dallas County (Texas) was highest in blacks, followed by white Hispanics, Asians, and white non-Hispanics.

Lethal Violence

Unnithan et al. (1994) hypothesized that the suicide-plus-homicide rate (the lethal-violence rate) was a function of patterned sources of frustration), while the direction of aggression (the suicide rate divided by the lethal-violence rate) was a function of structural and cultural sources of variation in causal attributions. In a study of 88 nations, they found no social correlates of the lethal-violence rate, while correlates of the direction-of-aggression rate were similar to those for the suicide rate. They also explored correlates of their two measures over the United States. Hospital bed availability was associated with the lethal-violence rate and percent rural population with the direction-of-aggression rate.

Discussion

This research continues to show that suicidal individuals are quite outwardly aggressive and that suicidal behavior is not necessarily a result of the suppression and repression of outwardly-directed anger.

REFERENCES

Aderibigbe, Y. A. Violence in America. *Journal of Forensic Sciences*, 1997, 42, 662–665.

Alder, C. M., & Baker, J. Maternal filicide. *Women & Criminal Justice*, 1997, 9(2), 15–39.

Anonymous. Homicide followed by suicide. *Morbidity & Mortality Weekly Report*, 1991, 40(38), 652–659.

Apter, A., Kotler, M., Sevy, S., Plutchik, R., Brown, S. L., Foster, H., Hillbrand, M., Korn, M. L., & van Praag, H. Correlates of risk of suicide in violent and nonviolent psychiatric patients. *American Journal of Psychiatry*, 1991, 148, 883–887.

Apter, A., Plutchik, R., & Van Praag, H. M. Anxiety, impulsivity, and depressed mood in relation to suicidal and violent behavior. *Acta Psychiatrica Scandinavica*, 1993, 87, 1–5.

Battle, A. O., Battle, M. V., & Tolley, E. A. Potential for suicide and aggression in delinquents at juvenile court in a southern city. *Suicide & Life-Threatening Behavior*, 1993, 23, 230–244.

Botsis, A. J., Plutchik, R., Kotler, M., & Van Praag, H. M. Parental loss and family violence as correlates of suicide and violence risk. *Suicide & Life-Threatening Behavior*, 1995, 25, 253–260.

Buteau, J., Lesage, A. D., & Kiely, M. C. Homicide followed by suicide. *Canadian Journal of Psychiatry*, 1993, 38, 552–556.

Citrome, L., Green, L., & Frost, R. Length of stay and recidivism on a psychiatric intensive care unit. *Hospital & Community Psychiatry*, 1994, 45, 74–76.

Cooper, M., & Eaves, D. Suicide following homicide in the family. *Violence & Victims*, 1996, 11, 99–112.

Crimmins, S., Langley, S., Brownstein, H., & Spunt, B. J. Convicted women who have killed their children. *Journal of Interpersonal Violence*, 1997, 12, 49–69.

Danson, L., & Sotthill, K. Murder followed by suicide. *Journal of Forensic Psychiatry*, 1996, 7, 310–322.

Easteal, P. Homicides-suicides between adult sexual intimates. *Suicide & Life-Threatening Behavior*, 1994, 24, 140–151.

Felthous, A. R., & Hempel, A. Combined homicide-suicides. *Journal of Forensic Sciences*, 1995, 40, 846–857.

Fontana, A., & Rosenheck, R. An etiological model of attempted suicide among Vietnam theater veterans. *Journal of Nervous & Mental Disease*, 1995a, 183, 377–383.

Fontana, A., & Rosenheck, R. Attempted suicide among Vietnam veterans. *American Journal of Psychiatry*, 1995b, 152, 102–109.

Goldney, R. D., Winefield, A. H., Saebel, J. L., Winefield, H. R., & Tiggeman, M. Anger, suicidal ideation, and attempted suicide. In J. McIntosh (Ed.), *Suicide '96*. Washington, DC: AAS, 1996, 157–159.

Goldney, R. D., Winefield, A. H., Saebel, J. L., Winefield, H. R., & Tiggeman, M. Anger, suicidal ideation, and attempted suicide. *Comprehensive Psychiatry*, 1997, 38, 264–268.

Gottlieb, P., & Gabrielson, G. The future of homicide offenders. *International Journal of Law & Psychiatry*, 1990, 13, 191–205.

Greenwald, D. J., Reznikoff, M., & Plutchik, R. Suicide risk and violence risk in alcoholics. *Journal of Nervous & Mental Disease*, 1994, 182, 3–8.

Grosz, D. E., Lipschitz, D. S., Eldar, S., Finkelstein, G., Blackwood, N., Gerbino-Rosen, G., Faedda, G. L., & Plutchik, R. Correlates of violence risk in hospitalized adolescents. *Comprehensive Psychiatry*, 1994, 35, 296–300.

Guileyardo, J. M., Carmody, T. J., Lene, W.

J. W., & Stone, I. C. Racial and ethnic patterns in firearm deaths. *American Journal of Forensic Medicine & Pathology*, 1994, 15, 328–330.

Hanzlick, R., & Koponen, M. Murder-suicide in Fulton County, Georgia, 1988–1991. *American Journal of Forensic Medicine & Pathology*, 1994, 15, 168–173.

Hillbrand, M. Self-directed and other-directed aggressive behavior in a forensic sample. *Suicide & Life-Threatening Behavior*, 1992, 22, 333–340.

Hillbrand, M. Aggression against self and others in violent psychiatric patients. *Journal of Consulting & Clinical Psychology*, 1995, 63, 668–671.

Kominato, Y., Shimada, I., Hata, N., Takizawa, H., & Fujikura, T. Homicide patterns in the Toyama prefecture, Japan. *Medicine, Science & the Law*, 1997, 37, 316–320.

Kratcoski, P. C. Circumstances surrounding homicides by older offenders. *Criminal Justice & Behavior*, 1990, 17, 420–430.

Lehnert, K. L., Overholser, J. C., & Spirito, A. Internalized and externalized anger in adolescent suicide attempters. *Journal of Adolescent Research*, 1994, 9, 105–119.

Lester, D. Murdering babies. *Social Psychiatry & Psychiatric Epidemiology*, 1991, 26, 83–85.

Lester, D. The murder of babies in American states. *Psychological Reports*, 1992, 71, 1202.

Lester, D. A test of Ferri's hypothesis about suicide and homicide rates. *Psychological Reports*, 1993, 72, 1122.

Lester, D. Homicide-suicide rates and homicide rates. *Perceptual & Motor Skills*, 1997a, 85, 178.

Lester, D. Economic development, suicide and homicide. *Perceptual & Motor Skills*, 1997b, 85, 458.

Lindqvist, P., & Gustafsson, L. Homicide followed by the offender's suicide in northern Sweden. *Nordic Journal of Psychiatry*, 1995, 49, 17–24.

McKenna, C., Kelleher, M. J., & Corcoran, P. Suicide, homicide, and crime in Ireland. *Archives of Suicide Research*, 1997, 3, 53–64.

Milroy, C. M. Homicide followed by suicide (dyadic death) in Yorkshire and Humberside. *Medicine, Science & the Law*, 1993, 33, 167–171.

Milroy, C. M. Reasons for homicide and suicide in episodes by dyadic death in Yorkshire and Humberside. *Medicine, Science & the Law*, 1995a, 35, 213–217.

Milroy, C. M. The epidemiology of murder-suicide. *Forensic Science International*, 1995b, 71, 117–122.

Milroy, C. M., Dratsas, M., & Ranson, D. L. Homicide-suicide in Victoria, Australia. *American Journal of Forensic Medicine & Pathology*, 1997, 18, 369–373.

Myers, W. C., Scott, K., Burgess, A. W., & Burgess, A. G. Psychopathology, biosocial factors, crime characteristics, and classification of 25 homicidal youths. *Journal of the American Academy of Child & Adolescent Psychiatry*, 1995, 34, 1483–1489.

Palermo, G. B., Smith, M. B., Jenzten, J., Henry, T. E., Konicek, P. J., Peterson, G. F., Singh, R. P., & Witeck, M. J. Murder-suicide of the jealous paranoia type. *American Journal of Forensic Medicine & Pathology*, 1997, 18, 374–383.

Plutchik, R., Botsis, A. J., & Van Praag, H. M. Psychopathology, self-esteem, sexual, and ego functions as correlates of suicide and violence risk. *Archives of Suicide Research*, 1995, 1, 27–38.

Ponzer, S., Bergman, B., & Brismar, B. Sociodemographic characteristics and criminality in victims of firearm injuries. *Journal of Trauma*, 1995, 38, 845–850.

Rasanen, P., Hakko, H., & Vaisanen, E. The mental state of arsonists as determined by forensic psychiatric examinations. *Bulletin of the American Academy of Psychiatry & Law*, 1995, 23, 547–553.

Romanov, K., Hatakka, M., Keskinen, E., Laaksonen, H., Kaprio, J., Rose, R. J., & Koskenvuo, M. Self-reported hostility and suicidal acts, accidents, and accidental deaths. *Psychosomatic Medicine*, 1994, 56, 328–336.

Rosenbaum, M. The role of depression in couples involved in murder-suicide and homicide. *American Journal of Psychiatry*, 1990, 147, 1036–1039.

Sakuta, T. A study of murder followed by suicide. *Medicine & Law*, 1995, 14, 141–153.

Saucer, P. R. Regional correlations between

suicide and homicide rates for 1986. *Psychological Reports*, 1991, 68, 938.

Shulman, E. The suicide-homicide relationship across societies. In J. McIntosh (Ed.), *Suicide '96*. Washington, DC: AAS, 1996, 123–124.

Somander, L. K. H., & Rammer, L. M. Intra- and extrafamilial child homicide in Sweden 1971–1980. *Child Abuse & Neglect*, 1991, 15, 45–55.

Stack, S. Homicide followed by suicide. *Criminology*, 1997, 35, 435–453.

Stolinsky, D. C., & Stolinsky, S. A. Guns in the home. *New England Journal of Medicine*, 1994, 330, 1157–1159.

Stolinsky, D. C., & Stolinsky, S. A. Strict firearm laws have been claimed to reduce rates of suicide and homicide. *Journal of Trauma*, 1995, 38, 464.

Stolinsky, D. C., & Stolinsky, S. A. Suicide and homicide rates are not correlated with each other. *Journal of Trauma*, 1997, 42, 573.

Szabo, P. F. *The role of hostility against self in suicide attempt*. Doctoral dissertation, University of Windsor, 1991.

Unnithan, N. P., Huff-Corzine, L., Corzine, J., & Whitt, H. P. *The currents of lethal violence*. Albany: SUNY Press, 1994.

Wilson, M., Daly, M., & Daniele, A. Familicide. *Aggressive Behavior*, 1995, 21, 275–291.

Wong, M., Fenwick, P., Fenton, G., Lumsden, J., Maisey, M., & Stevens, J. Repetitive and nonrepetitive violent offender behavior in male patients in a maximum security hospital. *Medicine, Science & the Law*, 1997, 37, 150–160.

Chapter 21

THE PERSONALITY, ATTITUDES, AND BEHAVIORS OF SUICIDAL PEOPLE

Acculturation

Hovey and King (1996) found that suicidal ideation was associated with depression and acculturation stress in Latino adolescents, but not with family functioning. Rasmussen et al. (1997) found that depression, self-esteem, sex, and acculturation predicted suicidal ideation in Mexican-American eighth graders – the more-acculturated students were more suicidal.

Affect Regulation

Westen et al. (1997) found that psychiatric patients with prior attempts had less positive affect, more negative affect, more externalization defenses, less avoidant defenses, and less reality-focused responses. Zlotnick et al. (1997) found that, among adolescent psychiatric inpatients, those who had attempted suicide had worse affect regulation.

Alexithymia

Lester (1991a) found that alexithymia was associated with past and present suicidality in a sample of college students, but not after controls for depression. Taiminen et al. (1996) found that suicidal intent and suicidal lethality were not associated with alex-ithymia scores in a sample of attempted suicides, nor associated with difficulties identifying or describing feelings.

Alienation

Lester and Miller (1990) found that current suicidal ideation was positively associated with alienation in teenagers, but not with shyness or grade point average. Controls for depression scores eliminated the association.

Anger

Van Elderen et al. (1996) found that attempted suicides who were repeaters had higher trait anger and internalization-of-anger scores than community controls and less control of anger.

Anhedonia

Oei et al. (1990) found that suicidal depressed patients were more depressed, more anxious (state and trait), and more anhedonic (a reduced capacity for pleasure) than nonsuicidal depressed patients. On the other hand, Loas et al. (1995) found that current suicidal ideation was not associated with anhedonia in the general population.

Anomia

Schaller and Schmidtke (1995) found that suicidal ideation and anomia were associated in a community sample of the elderly.

Anxiety

In a sample of suicide attempters, Chance et al. (1994) found that only trait anxiety and a negative world view predicted suicidal intent (not depression, state anxiety, or over-all psychopathology). Ohring et al. (1996) found that adolescent psychiatric inpatients who had attempted suicide had higher state and trait anxiety than those who had not done so. After controls for depression, the difference in trait anxiety was still found.

Attitudes Toward Physician-Assisted Suicide

Jacobson et al. (1995) found that 16 percent of deceased patients would have liked aid in dying according to their significant others, a decision associated with the deceaseds' personal characteristics.

In a community survey in Detroit, Lichtenstein et al. (1997) found that blacks were less in favor of assisted suicide than were whites. Approval of assisted suicide was predicted by religiosity, but not sex, age, or education.

Duberstein et al. (1995) found that females saw suicide as rational more than did men. Family physicians disapproved more of assisted suicide than did other groups. In Scandinavia, nursing students' attitudes toward voluntary active euthanasia were negatively associated with religiosity and conservative political views (Sorbye et al., 1995). Kearl (1996) found that approval of physician-assisted suicide was strongest in white males and weakest in black females (and matched the rank ordering of suicide

rates).

Emanuel et al. (1996) found that oncology patients and the general public were more in favor of physician-assisted suicide than were oncologists.

Attributional Style

Spirito et al. (1991) found that adolescent suicide attempters were more likely to attribute good events to global causes, but did not differ from nonsuicidal psychiatric patients in seven other scores of attributional style. The groups did not differ in depression, hopelessness, or internal attributions.

Priester and Clum (1992) found that suicidal ideation was associated in college students with attribution style – internal for positive events, and stable and global for negative events. Suicidal ideation was also associated with depression and hopelessness, but not with exam grades.

Joiner and Rudd (1995) found that suicidal ideation in college students was predicted by a negative attribution style for interpersonal events, as well as hopelessness and negative interpersonal stressors. An increase in suicidality over time was also associated with a negative attribution style for interpersonal events and the occurrence of such events.

Jack (1991; Jack and Williams, 1991) found that female self-poisoners did not differ from controls in how they viewed positive events; for negative events they made more stable and global attributions, although there were no differences in internal attributions. They had also experienced more stressors in the prior seven days and were more psychologically disturbed.

Bereavement

Szanto et al. (1997) found that suicidal ideation in recently bereaved people was associated with depression, hopelessness, anxiety, complicated grief, and less interpersonal support.

Burn-Out

Samuelsson et al. (1997) found that suicidal ideation (but not prior attempts) was associated with burn-out in psychiatric nurses, but not with the quality of work or a negative work environment.

Caffeine

Szekeley (1997) hypothesized that caffeine (a central nervous system stimulant) might protect against nonimpulsive suicide, but not against impulsive suicide.

Chocolate

Lester and Bernard (1991) found that past and current suicidality was not associated with liking chocolate or candy.

Circadian Activity Rhythm

Verkes et al. (1996a, 1996b) found that those who repeated attempted suicide did not show a circadian activity rhythm (using a wrist monitor), but did have higher levels than controls of suicidal ideation, hopelessness, personal pathology, impulsiveness, and borderline traits.

Coffee

Kawachi et al. (1996) found that nurses who drank two or more cups of coffee a day had a lower suicidal risk than nondrinkers. No association was found for tea.

Coherence

Petrie and Brook (1992) found that suicidal ideation in a sample of attempters was negatively associated with a sense of coherence (comprehensibility, manageability, and meaning), as well as hopelessness, depression, and self-esteem. The sense of coherence predicted suicidal ideation six months later, while the sense of coherence along with age, unemployment, living alone, and prior attempts predicted attempted/completed suicide

Coping

Curry et al. (1992) found that prior suicidal ideation/attempts in adolescents was associated with depression, but not social maladjustment. For coping mechanisms, suicidality was associated only with problem solving (negatively), but not with logical analysis, information seeking, affective regulation, or emotional discharge.

In adolescent psychiatric inpatients, Puskar et al. (1992) found that the suicidal patients used affective-oriented methods of coping more than problem-oriented methods, while the nonsuicidal patients used both styles equally often.

Josepho and Plutchik (1994) compared psychiatric inpatients who had attempted suicide with those who had not. The attempters had more interpersonal problems and used suppression more and replacement less as coping styles. Suicidal ideators used substitution more than controls.

Wilson et al. (1995) found that adolescent suicide attempters used fewer strategies for coping and were more likely to generate maladaptive coping strategies (and had more recent stressors) than normals. The groups did not differ in intelligence, problem-solving scores, or coping solutions generated.

Horesh et al. (1996) found that psychiatric patients who had attempted suicide used minimizing and mapping less often as a coping style than nonattempters. They did not differ in the use of suppression, help seeking, replacement, blame, substitution, or reversal.

Spirito et al. (1996) found that suicidal and nonsuicidal adolescent psychiatric patients showed more social withdrawal (but not nine other coping responses) to hypothetical situations than attempted suicides seen in an emergency room or normal controls. The psychiatric patients were also less anxious and less sad, but did not differ in suicidality.

Creativity

Lester (1993g) explored differences between creative women who completed suicide and those who did not, finding that psychiatric disturbance was the most obvious difference.

Cynicism

Nierenberg et al. (1996) found that suicidal ideators in a sample of depressed outpatients were more cynical, but did not differ in hostile affect or attacks, angry responses or attacks, life experiences, or depression.

Dating Behavior

Migeot and Lester (1996) found that students who had experienced abuse in their dating relationships were more depressed, but not more suicidal, than those who had not.

Death Attitudes and Anxiety

Orbach et al. (1991) found that suicidal adolescents had more attraction to death and repulsion by life than nonsuicidal psychiatric patients, but similar repulsion by death and attraction to life. Orbach et al. (1993) found

that suicidal adolescents had less fear of losing self-fulfillment as a result of death, less fear of self-annihilation, and less fear of the unknown than nonsuicidal psychiatric controls (but did not differ in fear of consequences to family or loss of personal identity). Suicidality and fears were negatively associated in the suicidal patients, not associated in the psychiatric controls, and positively associated in normal subjects. Orbach et al. (1995a, 1995b) found differences on all four scales between attempted suicides and nonsuicidal-but-depressed adolescents.

Cotton and Range (1990, 1993) found that suicidality in children aged 6–13 was not associated with attitudes (attraction and repulsion) toward life and death, nor with hopelessness or age. Payne and Range (1996b) found that suicidality in 8–13 year olds was predicted by depression and attitude toward life, but not by family cohesion or adaptability.

Payne and Range (1995) found that suicidality in college students was associated with attraction to death and repulsion by life, as well as negative life events (but not positive life events). In a mixed sample of students and adolescent patients, Cotton and Range (1996) found that hopelessness and repulsion to life predicted suicidality. Payne and Range (1996a) found that suicidality in college students was predicted by repulsion by death, attraction to life, and family cohesion, but not by depression, family adaptability, attraction to death, or repulsion by life.

Osman et al. (1993a) found that college students who had attempted suicide had less attraction to life and more repulsion by life and attraction to death than nonsuicidal students (but did not differ in repulsion by death). Osman et al. (1994) found that suicidal psychiatric patients had less attraction to life, more repulsion by life, and more attraction to death than nonsuicidal patients (but not more repulsion by death). Similar correlations were obtained with prior suicidal threats and ideation.

D'Attilio and Campbell (1990) found no association between death anxiety and suicidality in a sample of adolescents.

Brubeck and Beer (1992) found that current suicidal ideation in high school students was associated with death anxiety, as well as depression, self-esteem, and grade-point average (negatively). Students with current suicidal ideation from divorced versus nondivorced parents did not differ in death anxiety, sex, or suicidal ideation, but those with divorced parents did have lower grade point averages and self-esteem, and higher depression scores.

Abruzzi et al. (1994) found that adolescent suicide attempters had a less-mature understanding of death than did controls.

Lester (1996c) found that students' estimates of their probability of committing suicide if they were dying of cancer was associated with their fear of death and dying, but not with the hypothetical pain of the cancer or pain from chemotherapy.

Rohde et al. (1996) found that death-related items (in the areas of health, injury and self; and thoughts, feelings, and actions) predicted past suicidal ideation.

Defensive Style

Recklitis et al. (1992) studied adolescent psychiatric patients. Those who had attempted suicide or who were suicidal ideators did not differ in the use of turning against others, projection or principalization. The suicidal patients used turning against the self more and reversal less. After controls for diagnosis, the difference in turning against the self remained significant. Apter et al. (1997) found that suicidal adolescent psychiatric inpatients used displacement more and com-

pensation less than psychiatric controls. Suicidal patients who were not also violent used repression and introjection more.

Delinquency

Sorensen and Johnson (1996) classified delinquents into five types. Prior attempted suicide was most common in the distressed and least in the nondistressed. Current suicidality was most common in the distressed and least in the alienated, insecure-anxious, and nondistressed types.

In a sample of juvenile delinquents, Rohde et al. (1997a, 1997b) found that prior attempted suicide was more common in females, school dropouts, and those with dysthymia, major depressive disorders, and anxiety disorders. It was less common in those with cannabis use/dependence, and less common in girls with conduct disorder, and more common in boys with conduct disorder. Prior attempts were associated with current suicidal ideation and depression, worse global functioning, and past suicidal ideation, but not with offense type or number or comorbidity. Past attempts were associated in the boys with current suicidal ideation, not living with a biological parent, and ineffective coping; and associated in the girls with stressors, impulsivity, and not living with a biological parent. The correlates of prior suicidal ideation were somewhat different.

Depression/Manic Experience

In college students, Kaplan and Lester (1994) found that depressive but not manic-like-experiences were associated with prior suicidal ideation and attempts.

Developmental Stage

Borst et al. (1991) compared adolescent suicide attempters with controls and found the attempters were more often at Loevinger's conformist stage of development and less often at the preconformist stage. None were at the postconformist stage. The attempters were also more often female and more often had an affective disorder.

Dissociation

Orbach et al. (1995a, 1995b) found that adolescent suicide attempters showed more control dissociation, but not affect or cognitive dissociation, than nonsuicidal depressed adolescents. They showed more of all three kinds of dissociation than normal adolescents. Both psychiatric groups showed more negative attitudes toward their bodies than the normal adolescents.

Eating Behavior

Van Strien et al. (1995) found that female students whose eating was triggered by emotional states (such as being upset) had higher scores on a factor grouping of traits including suicidality. Eating triggered by external cues was not associated with this factor score. Pook et al. (1996) found that scores of students on an eating-disorder scale were associated with past and current suicidal ideation (but not past attempted suicide), but not after controls for depression. Williams and Lester (1996) found that scores on screening measures for eating disorders were associated with prior suicidality in a sample of college students.

Ego Identity

Bar-Joseph and Tzuriel (1990) found that adolescents who had threatened suicide had lower ego-identity scores (which measured committment/purposefulness and solidarity/continuity) than did normal controls.

Emotional Expression

Diggs and Lester (1996) found that general emotional expressiveness was negatively associated with prior suicide ideation, but measures of emotional control were not associated with current or prior suicidal ideation.

Emotional Health

Ahmadi et al. (1992) found that prior suicidal ideation and attempts were associated with poor emotional health in a sample of prep school students.

Extraversion

Lester (1991e) found that Lynn's measure of national levels of extraversion (but not neuroticism) in industrialized nations was associated with national suicide rates. In a study of nations, Lynn and Martin (1995) found that nations in which samples of the population had higher extraversion scores had lower suicide rates (but neuroticism and psychoticism scores were not associated with suicide rates).

Straub et al. (1993) found that female attempters using violent methods were less introverted, less inhibited, more achievement-oriented and more action-oriented than those using nonviolent methods.

On the other hand, Ashton et al. (1994) found that attempted suicides were more introverted, depressed, anxious, and hopeless than normal controls and had higher neuroticism and psychoticism scores. Repeaters were more hopeless and introverted than first-timers.

Duberstein et al. (1994; Duberstein, 1995) had survivors of completed suicides complete a personality test on behalf of the deceased. The suicides were judged to have had higher introversion, lower openness scores, and higher neuroticism scores than controls (but did not differ in agreeableness or conscientiousness). Younger suicides (under the age of 50) were more open and less conscientious than older suicides.

Fear of Attachment

Lester (1991f) found that past and current suicidal ideation was not associated with fears of individuation or attachment, but a history of attempted suicide was associated with less fear of attachment.

Firesetting

Repo et al. (1997) found that firesetters who had attempted suicide more often abused alcohol and had a major mood disorder, but did not differ in pyromania or personality disorder from nonattempters. The attempters more often had alcoholic fathers and more often set fires with a suicidal motive. They did not differ in age, intelligence, recidivism, or absent parents.

Future Orientation

Schmidtke and Schaller (1993b) found no differences between suicide attempters and psychiatric controls in time estimation, but attempters were more future oriented.

Gambling

Phillips et al. (1996) found that visitors to three SMSAs (in Nevada and New Jersey) with gambling facilities had higher suicide rates than visitors to other SMSAs. Furthermore, the residents in those SMSAs, both native-born and migrant, had higher suicide rates.

Giftedness

Metha and McWhirter (1997) found that gifted and normal seventh and eighth graders did not differ in suicidality and that suicidality in both groups was associated with depression and stress. Baker (1995) found no differences in suicidal ideation or depression between exceptional, gifted, and normal children.

Height

Stack and Wasserman (1996) found that short men (under 5'6") had higher suicide rates after controls for other variables. Suicide rates were also higher in the non-married, blacks, and those with high levels of alcohol consumption.

Helplessness

Reich et al. (1996) found that suicidal ideation in a sample of the elderly was associated with helplessness, health decline, self-esteem, fatalism, and confused thinking.

Hopelessness

Mendonca and Holden (1996) found that hopelessness scores were more strongly associated with suicidal ideation items concerned with frequency and acceptance of the wish to die and less with items to do with the method of self-harm. Suicidal ideation was also associated with unusual thinking on a symptom checklist.

Young et al. (1996) measured baseline hopelessness (the level when not depressed) and the sensitivity (the rate of increasing hopelessness as depression increased) in a sample of depressive disorder patients. The baseline level was associated with being female and with dissatisfaction with life, stress, and introversion. Sensitivity was associated with being Christian and with causal attributions for mood (negatively). Only the baseline measure was associated with prior and subsequent attempted suicide.

Enns et al. (1997) found that suicidal intent in adolescent psychiatric inpatients who had attempted suicide was predicted better by hopelessness scores for Canadian whites and by depression scores for native Canadians.

MacLeod et al. (1997) found that attempted suicides anticipated fewer positive future experiences, but did not differ in their anticipation of future negative experiences as compared to healthy controls. The attempters tended to expect more negative outcomes in the next week, but not in the next few years.

Negron et al. (1997) studied adolescents in the emergency room. Attempters were more hopeless than ideators before the event (but not more depressed or angry), did not differ during the event, and were less angry after the event. During the event, the attempters were more isolated and less often communicated their suicidality to others.

Overholser et al. (1997) found that hopelessness and depression (but not alcohol/drug use) were associated with suicidal intent in a sample of adolescent psychiatric inpatients who had attempted suicide.

Weber et al. (1997) found that suicidal ideation in college students was associated with hopelessness, depression, loneliness, and stress.

Brittlebank et al. (1990) followed up a sample of suicide attempters. Those who repeated their attempts were more hopeless, more intropunitive, and more extrapunitive, but did not differ in dominance. The same differences were found in a comparison of the attempters who had made previous attempts and the first timers. However, suicidal intent for the index attempt was not associated with any of the personality trait scores.

Hostility

Marazziti and Conti (1991) found that attempted suicides scored higher than depressed patients and healthy controls on the Buss and Durkee Hostility Inventory for the total score and the guilt score; they tended to score higher on the other scales too, but not significantly.

Simonds et al. (1991) found that suicide attempters had higher scores on almost all scales of the Buss and Durkee Hostility Inventory than normal controls (significant on resentment, suspicion, verbal hostility, guilt, assault, and irritation). They also had higher depression, hopelessness, and role-definition scores.

Castrogiovanni et al. (1990) found that attempted suicides scored higher on indirect hostility than depressives, but did not differ on the other seven scales.

Woods et al. (1991) found that current suicidal ideation in high school students was associated with suppressed and expressed anger and with psychosomatic symptoms. In Swedish college students, Eskin (1993) found that suicidal ideation was associated with hostility and hopelessness, but not with a negative self-evaluation.

Impostor Feelings

Lester and Moderski (1995) found that a history of suicidal ideation was associated with feelings of being an impostor, even after controls for depression.

Impulsivity

Lester (1990a) found that college students who had previously threatened to commit suicide obtained higher scores on a measure of impulsivity than those who had not, even after controls for depression scores. Having previously thought about or attempted suicide was not associated with impulsivity. Lester (1993b) found that suicidality was more strongly associated with functional impulsivity than with dysfunctional impulsivity once depression was taken into account.

Kaplan et al. (1992) found that clinically rated suicidal risk was associated with impulsivity, anger, depression, hopelessness, attraction to death, and attraction to life (negatively) in a sample seen at a military mental health clinic. In Israeli soldiers given psychiatric examinations, Koslowsky et al. (1922) found that suicidal risk was predicted by impulsivity, anger, violence, and depression.

Kashden et al. (1993) found that suicidal adolescent psychiatric inpatients had higher depression and hopelessness scores, and higher impulsiveness on one of three tests of the construct. They did not differ in problem-solving ability.

Kotler et al. (1993) found that psychiatric inpatients who had attempted suicide were more impulsive than nonattempters (as well as having more anger, suicide risk, and violence risk and less use of minimalization as a coping scale). They did not differ on seven other methods of coping, diagnosis or social support (or sex, race, and marital status).

Herpertz et al. (1995) found that depressed suicide attempters and impulsive self-mutilators were more impulsive than premeditated self-mutilators and depressed nonsuicidal patients. The self-mutilators had more anger, but the four groups did not differ in depression scores. Evans et al. (1996) found that repeaters were more impulsive on a psychological test than first-time attempters, even after controls for sex and age. Horesh et al. (1997) found that suicidal and nonsuicidal psychiatric inpatients were more angry than healthy controls, but the suicidal inpatients were more impulsive. In all groups, suicidal risk was positively associated with both anger and impulsivity. Korn et al. (1997) found that suicidal risk and impulsivity were associated in a sample of panic disorder patients.

On the other hand, Schmidtke and Schaller (1994a, 1994b) found no differences between suicide attempters and psychiatric controls in measures of impulsivity (or verbal or performance intelligence test scores). Female attempters were more impulsive than male attempters, and repeaters more impulsive than one-timers. Attempters did not differ from controls in rigidity, field dependence, or dichotomous thinking. They did not differ either in depression, hopelessness, anxiety, or locus of control.

Intelligence

Walters (1990) reported cases of suicidal ideation and attempts in severely mentally retarded patients. Villasana et al. (1992) found that, while the majority of children attempting suicide had normal intelligence (82 percent), there were more with below-average intelligence than above average (16 percent versus 3 percent).

Schmidtke (1992) and Schmidtke and Schaller (1992) found no differences in intelligence-test scores between nonsuicidal patients, one-time attempters, and repeaters. Schaller and Schmidtke (1993) studied elderly people living at home. Those with current suicidal ideation did not differ from those without in intelligence, physical condition, short-term memory, anomie, hopelessness, or loss of personal control. Schmidtke and Schaller (1993a) found no differences between attempters and psychiatric controls in intelligence or scores on a matching-figures test (which measures impulsivity).

Milling et al. (1997) found that a clinician's estimate of the intelligence of children who were psychiatric inpatients was not associated with their suicidality, but parent ratings of verbal intelligence were positively associated with the child's suicidality.

Interpersonal Trust

Lester and Gatto (1990) found that current suicidal ideation was positively associated with interpersonal trust and depression in adolescents.

Kleptomania

Sarasalo et al. (1996) found that 32 percent of a sample of kleptomaniacs had previously attempted suicide.

Knowledge About Suicide

Leenaars et al. (1991) found that younger adults had more accurate knowledge about suicide than the elderly, but knowledge did not differ by sex or occupation. Leenaars and Lester (1922) found that Canadian and American students did not differ in their accuracy of knowledge about suicide. Lester and Akande (1994) found that American students had more accurate knowledge about suicide than Nigerian (Yoruban) students.

Lester (1991b) found that accurate knowledge about suicide was associated with viewing suicide more often as rational and less often as moral. Lester and Pitts (1991) found that accuracy of knowledge about suicide in police officers was associated with a history of suicidal ideation, but not with age, sex, race, or rank. Cruikshanks and Slavich (1993–1994) found that college students' accurate knowledge about suicide was not associated with sex or race. Lester and Castromayor (1994) found that

Philippine nurses had less-accurate knowledge about suicide than American nurses. Lester et al. (1994) found that age, sex, and locus of control were not associated with accuracy of knowledge about suicide in American, Turkish, or Philippine students, but depression was associated with accuracy scores for American students.

Lester and Mielish (1990) found that belief in myths about suicide and irrational thinking were negatively associated in college students. Lester (1993d) found no association between belief in myths about suicide and extraversion or neuroticism.

Lester (1995b) found that knowledge about suicide in general was associated with knowledge about childhood suicide, while Lester (1996b) found no association of either score with age, sex, extraversion, or neuroticism.

Locus of Control

Strang and Orlefsky (1990) found that suicidal ideation in college students was associated with an external locus of control, greater hopelessness, and less-secure interpersonal attachments. Goldney et al. (1991) found that an external locus of control, depression, self-esteem, anomie, and hopelessness were associated with suicidal ideation in those leaving school four and eight years after they left. These variables were less successful in predicting attempted suicide. Simonds et al. (1991) found that attempters had a greater external locus of control than normal controls, more attempted suicide in their families, more recent breakups with lovers and more arrests. They did not differ in physical problems or social desirability scores. Lester (1991d) found the more seriously suicidal high school students were more likely to be above the median score both for depression and for external locus of control. In college students, Pearce and Martin (1993) found that suicidal ideators and attempted suicides were more external. Akande and Lester (1994) found that prior suicidal ideation was associated with an external locus of control in Nigerian students, but not in American students. Depression predicted prior suicidality in both sets of students. Lester et al. (1991a) found that an external locus of control was associated with prior attempted suicide in American and Philippine students and with prior suicidal ideation in Turkish students.

On the other hand, Lester (1993c) found that suicidality was not strongly associated with locus of control in high school students. But, after controls for age, sex, and depression, those with prior suicidal ideation had lower external scores.

However, Lester and Pitts (1990) found no association between locus of control or depression and a history of suicidal preoccupation in police officers. McCollaum and Lester (1997) found no association between past and current suicidal ideation and locus of control, or depression in a sample of Korean workers. Schmidtke and Schaller (1997) found that suicide attempters did not differ from psychiatric controls in intelligence, locus of control or field dependence. Versus normal controls, the attempters were more introverted and less field dependent, but for the adolescents only and not the adults.

Leisure

Malkin et al. (1989) found that suicidal women had less leisure satisfaction than nonsuicidal psychiatric controls, less life satisfaction, less perceived freedom of leisure, more depression, and more hopelessness. Leisure satisfaction and depression and hopelessness were correlated only for the seriously suicidal group.

Loneliness

Weber and Metha (1995) found that loneliness was the strongest correlate of suicidal ideation in college students, with cognitive development and stressors playing a smaller role. Yang and Clum (1995) found that loneliness (as well as life stress and depression), but not social support, was associated with suicidal ideation in Asian students. Joiner and Rudd (1996) found that loneliness (as well as depression and hopelessness) was associated with current suicidal ideation in students and also associated ten weeks later.

Meaning in Life

Buchanan (1994) found that suicidal ideation in elderly psychiatric patients and in normals was associated with meaning-in-life scores as well as depression.

Kinnier et al. (1994) found that suicidal ideation was associated with purpose in life and self-esteem (negatively); and self-derogation, substance abuse, and depression (positively). The associations were stronger in normal high school students than in adolescent psychiatric patients.

Memory

Williams et al. (1996) found that attempted suicides had fewer specific memories to cue words and were less specific about the future compared to non-depressed controls.

Meta-Contrast

Fribergh et al. (1992) presented patients with conflicting stimuli via a tachistoscope. The suicide attempters did not differ in performance from depressed patients. In follow-up testing, the attempters showed more stereotypy and less mature performance.

Music Preferences

Martin et al. (1993) found that suicidal ideation was less common in high school pupils preferring pop music than in those preferring rock/heavy metal. Those students preferring rock/heavy metal more often were delinquent, risk-takers, and drug users; came from broken homes; and had less close family relationships.

Lester and Whipple (1996) found that preference for alternative rock and heavy-metal music was associated with past (but not current) suicidal ideation in college students.

Stack (1996) found that approval of suicide was associated with being a heavy-metal music fan, but this did not hold up in a multiple-regression analysis (where marital status, sex, education, conservatism, and church attendance predicted approval of suicide). Stack (1997) found that liking blues music was associated with suicide acceptance, but not after controls for education, political ideology, and church attendance.

Myers-Briggs Typology

Komisin (1992) found that the INFP type (among college students) had the highest incidence of suicidal ideation and attempts, while the ESTJ type had the least. Street and Kromrey (1994) found that prior suicidality was more common in college students of type ISF, INP, and ENJ for males and IP for females.

Near-Death Experiences

Greyson (1991) found that suicide attempters who had a near-death experience in the attempt were more often Christian, were more religious, and had more prior

knowledge about near-death experiences than attempters who did not have the experience; they did not differ in psychopathology or prior suicidality. Greyson (1992–1993) found that those who had nearly died and had a near-death experience were more antisuicide than those who did not have the experience.

Neuropsychological Tests

Lester (1993h) suggested that suicide may have a neuropsychological basis similar to that occasionally proposed for outwardly directed violence.

Ellis et al. (1992) found no differences between suicide attempters and nonsuicidal psychiatric patients on a variety of neuropsychological tests (Peabody Picture-Vocabulary Test, Wisconsin Card-Sorting Test, and a finger-tapping test) except that the attempters performed worse on a trail-making test. The groups did not differ in depression or hopelessness. Zimmerman (1993) found no differences between adolescent attempted suicides and nonattempters on a neuropsychological screening battery.

However, Burns et al. (1994) found that suicidal depression and scores on the Luria Nebraska Neuropsychological Battery (such as expressive speech and memory) were positively associated in brain-damaged patients.

Pain Tolerance

Orbach et al. (1996a, 1996b) found that suicidal psychiatric inpatients tolerated electric shocks and thermal pain better than the nonsuicidal patients. In the emergency room, attempted suicides tolerated pain better than accident victims and community subjects. (They were also more depressed and anxious and less hardy psychologically.) Orbach et al. (1997) reported that adolescent psychiatric patients who had attempted suicide had higher pain tolerance; more dissociation, hope-lessness, and depression; a higher attraction to death and repulsion by life; and lower attraction to life and repulsion by death.

Perfectionism

Hewitt et al. (1992) found that current suicidal depression in psychiatric patients was associated with hopelessness and socially prescribed perfectionism for the self (but not self-perfectionism or other perfectionism). In a later study, Hewitt et al. (1994) reported that self-perfectionism or other perfectionism also contributed to the prediction, both in psychiatric patients and in normals. Hewitt et al. (1997) reported that sex, socially prescribed perfectionism and hopelessness were associated with suicidal ideation in adolescent psychiatric inpatients.

Adkins and Parker (1996) found that suicidal ideation and perfectionism scores were associated in college students, strongest with passive perfectionism (procrastination out of fear of making mistakes).

Dean and Range (1996) found that suicidality was associated with stress, depression, hopelessness, reasons for living, and state anxiety but not perfectionism. Dean et al. (1996) found that suicidal ideation was associated with stressors, depression, hopelessness, reasons for living, and perfectionism.

Physical Activity

In a 24–year follow-up study of Harvard University alumni, Paffenbarger et al. (1994) found that physical activity did not predict later suicide, whereas depression, alcohol consumption, and smoking did.

Physiognomy

Lester et al. (1993) found that naive judges could not tell suicides from non-suicides using photographs of their faces.

Problem Solving

Orbach et al. (1990) compared suicide attempters and ideators with emergency room controls for their problem-solving ability. The suicidal people were less versatile in their problem solving; used less direct confrontation; and had less relevant solutions, positive affect, future orientation, and self-reliance. The attempters and controls were more active than the ideators. The groups did not differ on authoritarianism, depression, or creativity.

Rotheram-Borus et al. (1990) compared minority female adolescents who had attempted suicide with nonsuicidal psychiatric patients. The attempters had worse problem-solving skills (that is, generated fewer alternatives), were more focused on the problems, used wishful thinking and self-blame more and sought social support less often. They did not differ in the use of minimizing the threat or being emotion-focused. The groups did not differ in depression, intelligence test scores, or recent stressors.

Evans et al. (1992) found that attempted suicides had fewer and less-effective problem-solving strategies than surgical controls, as well as having more over-general memories, and greater anger and hopelessness.

Priester and Clum (1993a, 1993b) found that suicidality in college students after exams was more weakly associated with problem-solving ability than were depression or hopelessness scores. Thus, the weak associations with suicidality were probably a result of the greater depression and hopelessness in the suicidal students. Suicidal ideation after the exams was associated with preexam suicidality, getting a D or F grade, and problem-solving ability. Clum and

Febbraro (1994) found that suicidal ideation was associated with only one of seven measures of problem solving (confidence). Life stress and loneliness were not associated with suicidal ideation.   Yang and Clum (1994) found that suicidal ideation in Asian students was predicted by some problem-solving scores, as well as by depression, hopelessness, loneliness, and stressful events. Clum et al. (1996) found no differences in scores on a social problem-solving inventory between college students who were high and low in suicidality, after controls for depression. Clum et al. (1997) found that, among depressed college students, those with suicidal ideation were more lonely and had poorer problem-solving ability (only on finding generalized relevant alternatives) and lower self-rated problem-solving ability. They did not differ in stressors.

Dixon et al. (1994) found that suicidality in psychiatric outpatients was associated with hopelessness, problem-solving confidence, and approach avoidance.

In a sample of college students, Mraz and Runco (1994) found that divergent thinking (as well as perceived stress and attitudes toward suicide) was associated with suicidal ideation. Suicidal ideation appeared to be associated with greater problem-generation fluency and worse problem-solving flexibility.

In a sample of psychiatric outpatients, Rudd et al. (1994) found that suicidal ideation was associated with problem-solving skills (as well as negative life stress, hopelessness, and intelligence). Attempters did not differ from ideators in these measures (except for more negative life stress in the attempters).

Kehrer and Linehan (1996) found that poor performance on a means-end problem-solving test predicted subsequent attempted suicide in a group of chronically suicidal women with borderline personality disorder. Emotional problem-solving stories were

better predictors of subsequent attempted suicide than were interpersonal problem-solving stories. Problem-solving style did not predict subsequent attempts.

Lester (1996d) found that current suicidal ideation was associated positively with the use of compromising as an interpersonal problem-solving style and negatively with competing.

Joiner et al. (1997) found that suicidal ideation was associated with problem-solving scores, hopelessness, and depression, but not stressors, in a sample of young inpatients and outpatients.

However, Ivanoff et al. (1992) found no differences between currently suicidal and nonsuicidal inmates in problem solving in a sample of male inmates, all of whom had attempted suicide in the past. The currently suicidal inmates were more depressed and hopeless. In a sample of nonsuicidal inmates, a history of prior attempts was not associated with any of these measures.

Psychoticism

Nordstrom et al. (1995) found that attempted suicides scored higher than surgical controls on psychoticism, neuroticism, hopelessness, somatic anxiety, and muscular tension and were less socialized; they were no different in extraversion, or hostility (indirect, verbal, irritability, suspiciousness or guilt).

Purpose in Life

Lester and Badro (1992) found that current and past suicidality were negatively associated with purpose-in-life scores in a sample of college students, even after controls for depression.

Reasons for Living Scale

Connell and Meyer (1991) found that

suicidality in college students was negatively associated with scores on the reasons for living inventory and some subscales, but social desirability scores were also associated with reasons for living scores. Steele and McLennan (1995), Ellis and Jones (1996), and Hirsch and Ellis (1996) found that suicidality was associated with some reasons for living subscales, along with recent stress (Hirsch and Ellis, 1996); Osman et al. (1996) found the same result using a briefer version of the scale for adolescents.

Dyck (1991) found that suicidal ideation in college students and in psychotherapy patients was negatively related to reasons for living scores (and positively with hopelessness scores). Kralik and Danforth (1992) found that students with prior suicidality and those with none differed on some scales of the reasons for living inventory and the non-suicidal students also used a wider variety of coping strategies. Osman et al. (1993b) found that suicidal ideation and scores for some reasons for living were negatively associated after controls for psychopathology.

Ellis and Range (1991) found that, among college students in general, blacks endorsed the reasons for living more than whites and women more than men. Ellis and Smith (1991) found that reasons for living scores were associated in normal college students with spiritual well-being and social desirability scores, while Ellis and Russell (1992) found that having divorced parents did not affect the total score on the scale, although age at time of divorce was associated with scores.

Turzo and Range (1991) found that making normal students either elated or depressed increased their reasons for living scores over those with no induced mood. Ellis and Range (1992) found that making students elated increased their scores on the reasons for living scale over those from students who were made depressed. Neyra et al. (1990) subjected students to success or failure experiences. Under success conditions, suicidal ideators did not differ from nonideators in their reasons for living score; but under failure conditions, the ideators had a lower score.

Bjerke et al. (1992) found that adrogynous students had less depression and more reasons for living than nonandrogynous students.

Rich et al. (1992) found that female high school students had more fear of death and injury than males, whereas the males had more fear of social disapproval. In multiple regressions, suicidal ideation was associated in both males and females with reasons for living scores, hopelessness, depression, and substance abuse.

In a sample of attempted suicides, Strosahl et al. (1992) found that the strongest correlate of suicidal intent was the survival and coping scale of the reasons for living inventory. Depression, hopelessness, and negative life events were also associated with suicidal intent.

Westerfeld et al. (1992) found that self-reported suicidal risk was associated with the total score on a college student version of the scale and with four of the six subscales. Range and Penton (1994) found that four of the six subscales were associated with suicidality in college students, along with depression and hope.

Lester and O'Neill (1995) found that some of the reasons for living were positively associated with scores on a measure of irrational thinking (and with self-esteem).

Osman et al. (1992) confirmed the original factor structure of the scale and found that females scored higher than males on all scales, significantly so on three.

Religiosity

Lester and Francis (1993) found that religiosity predicted suicidality in college students, but not after controls for neuroticism.

Self-Defeating Personality

Lester and Hoffman (1992) found that self-defeating personality scores were associated with current and prior suicidality in a sample of college students, even after controls for depression. Lester and Schaeffler (1993) found that the association between self-defeating personality and suicidality was stronger in college students than in high school students, and that the association differed for male and female college students.

Self-Esteem

Reynolds (1991) found that suicidal ideation was associated with lower self-esteem; higher depression, hopelessness, and anxiety; and prior attempted suicide. Cole et al. (1992) found that suicidal ideation in the past year in high school students was associated with lower self-esteem, more life stress, and more loneliness. In Zuni adolescents, Bee-Gates et al. (1996) found that suicidal ideation was associated with lower self-esteem as well as psychological symptoms and seeking help. Vella et al. (1996) found that self-esteem was associated with suicidality in college students, even after controls for depression.

Marciano and Kazdin (1994) found that psychiatric inpatient children who had attempted suicide were more depressed and hopeless than psychiatric controls. They had lower self-esteem, but not after controls for depression. Overholser et al. (1995) found that self-esteem (along with depression and hopelessness) was associated with both suicidal ideation and attempts in adolescent psychiatric inpatients and in high school students. Milling et al. (1996) found that depression was associated with prior suicidal

ideation in child psychiatric inpatients while self-esteem was associated with prior attempted suicide, although additional correlates included hopelessness, but not aggressive behavior.

Pinto and Whisman (1996; Pinto et al., 1996) found that adolescent psychiatric inpatients who had suicidal ideation were more hopeless and had a worse self-concept than nonsuicidal patients (and more often had a diagnosis of major depression or dysthymia), but they did not differ in depression and anxiety. Attempters did not differ from the controls. Among the suicidal patients, however, suicidality was associated with depression and anxiety and not with hopelessness, anger, or self-concept.

Self-Monitoring

Lester (1990b) found that self-monitoring was not associated with past or present suicidality in college students.

Self-Object Representation

Chance et al. (1996) found that suicidal intent in a group of attempters was positively associated with less differentiated self-object representation, less emotional investment in relationships, more depression, and more prior attempts.

Self-Transcendence

Buchanan et al. (1995) found that geriatric patients with high self-transcendence scores (success in meeting multiple changes in later life) less often wished to die, but did not differ in current suicidal ideation and prior attempted suicide.

Separation Anxiety

Feldman and Wilson (1997) found that

suicidal adolescents (with and without a conduct disorder) had more separation anxiety than nonsuicidal conduct disorder adolescents, but not more than normal controls.

Smoking

Beratis et al. (1997) found that attempted suicides smoked more than matched normal and psychiatric controls. Among Greek adolescents, Kokkevi et al. (1997) found that prior attempted suicide was more common in those who smoked or used alcohol (and even higher in those who used illicit drugs). Windle and Windle (1997) found that attempting suicide in high school students was associated with use of cigarettes, marihuana, alcohol, and drugs; higher levels of stress and depression; less family support; and having more substance-abusing peers.

Suicide Attitudes

Boldt (1982–1983) found that Canadian school students were more accepting of suicide than were their parents.

Lester and Icli (1990) found that Turkish and American students did not differ in their views on the morality of suicide. The American students had thought and attempted suicide more in the past and believed in fewer myths about suicide.

Lester et al. (1991b) found that judgments about the rationality and morality of suicide were associated with depression and prior suicidal preoccupation, but not with the sex and age of the respondent or the sex of the protagonist.

Monte (1991) found that the percentage of respondents in the General Social Survey who approved of suicide increased from 1977 to 1986, and approval was greater in those who were liberal in politics, were Jewish or had no religion, favored freedom of expression, and were less religious.

Lester (1990–1991) found that people thought it would be harder to express sympathy toward the spouse of hypothetical suicides whose suicide notes contained a great deal of self-blame. (They did not differ in blame assigned to spouse, the spouse's responsibility, or the suicide's disturbance.) The sex of the suicide or the respondent had no effect on attitudes toward the suicide.

Hammond and Deluty (1992) found no differences in whether professionals had a positive attitude toward suicide based on whether they had experienced thoughts of suicide themselves.

Lester and Bean (1992a) found that commitment to assisting and preventing suicide were not associated, and the desire to prevent suicide was greater than the desire to assist suicide. On the Keirsey-Bates Inventory, the desire to prevent suicide was positively associated with intuiting scores.

Lester and Bean (1992b) found that locus-of-control or irrational-thinking scores did not predict the theory of suicide held by subjects (intrapsychic, interpersonal, or societal causes) or the attitude toward suicide.

Lester et al. (1991–1992) found that students judged suicidal ideation, attempted suicide, and completed suicide to be inappropriate responses to crises. Condemnation of suicide as a response to crises was associated with lower scores on a test of irrational thinking.

In Israeli adolescents, Stein et al. (1992) found that attitudes toward suicide varied with sex, religious involvement, and suicidal ideation, but not with exposure to suicidal behavior in others.

Finch (1993) found that psychologists with religious views were less accepting of suicide, while those who had a friend or family member commit suicide were more accepting of and more knowledgeable about suicide.

Fiske (1993) found that college students viewed the suicide of an old woman whose husband was deceased as more acceptable than the suicide of a healthy young man whose girl friend had broken up with him.

Greening and Dollinger (1993) asked high school students to predict the risk of suicide for "someone like you." Public high school students rated the risk as higher than did parochial students, and females rated the risk higher than did boys.

Kalb (1993) found that psychiatric patients with a history of suicide attempts saw suicide as having more positive aspects and fewer negative consequences, and they saw the alternatives as having more disadvantages (but no differences in advantages). Thus, Kalb argued, suicide was a subjectively rational act since the advantages outweighed the disadvantages.

Domino et al. (1995) found that Americans and Chinese residents differed in suicide attitudes, with the Chinese seeing the role of mental illness as stronger and disapproving more of the right to die. Both samples, however, showed similar associations with conservatism, positive with the role of mental illness and negative with the right to die. Domino and Su (1994–1995) also found differences between Americans and Taiwanese-Americans. Suicidal ideation in both samples was positively associated with belief in the right to die and the normality of suicide, and negatively associated with religious views and viewing suicide as a moral evil. Both also showed similar associations between conservatism and attitudes toward suicide. Leenaars and Domino (1993) found differences in attitudes toward suicide in Windsor (Canada) and Los Angeles, with the Canadians being more accepting of suicide.

Lester (1993a) used REP Grids to explore how individuals perceived different methods for suicide.

Lester (1992–1993) found that the stigma felt toward suicidal individuals was greater than that toward ethnic and religious groups.

Zonda (1993) interviewed attempted suicides in Hungary and found that those from a region with a high suicide rate judged suicide to be more acceptable, would be more likely to attempt suicide again, and had more relatives and friends who had attempted or completed suicide than those from a region with a low suicide rate.

Kaplan and Ross (1994, 1995) found that opposition to suicide was positively associated with political conservatism, intrinsic religiosity, and belief that life belongs to God, but not with locus of control.

Lester and Akande (1994) found that Nigerian (Yoruban) students had more negative attitudes toward suicide than American students.

Linblad et al. (1994) found that students with more recent stress saw suicide more often as a chronic state and externally caused. Students scoring higher on a measure of Type A behavior were more accepting of suicide and saw anger as a motivating force.

King et al. (1996) found that approval of suicide was greater/stronger in those with no religious affiliation and who had attempted suicide and for cases of terminal/chronic illness and depression.

Ellis and Hirsch (1995) found that opinions about a case of suicide depended on the reason for the suicide. Suicide was seen as more appropriate when the stressors were not under personal control (such as cancer or being a robbery victim). Ellis and Lane (1995) found that male students blamed the parents of a child suicide more than females did, but the age of the child (10, 13, or 17) played no role in opinions.

Eskin (1995) found that Swedish students

had more liberal attitudes toward suicide than Turkish students, but that the Turkish students were more accepting of a suicidal peer.

Lester (1995a) found that the moral acceptability of suicide was not consistently associated with measures of locus of control, hostility, factual knowledge about suicide, depression, or past or current suicidality.

LoPresto et al. (1994–1995) found that college students saw suicide as more acceptable if the person was male and suffering from a terminal illness. Students with low religiosity and high depression also rated suicide as more acceptable.

Seidlitz et al. (1995) found that men, whites, those with higher income, and those for whom religion was not important had more favorable attitudes toward suicide and assisted suicide.

Stack and Wasserman (1995) found that married men (but not married women) showed less approval of suicide in the majority of nations surveyed. In the United States, approval of suicide was lower in the married, those attending church, and those with less education; approval was higher in feminists, both blacks and whites. The greater approval of suicide by males and by those with no children was found only for whites.

Dahlen and Canetto (1996) found that men were more supportive than women of a decision to attempt suicide, while the sex of the person in the vignette did not play a role.

Lester (1996a) found that suicide was viewed as similar to drug addiction (as an unstable and uncontrollable phenomenon), and less like AIDS, cancer, and PTSD in veterans. Lester (1996–1997) found that students increased their probability of suicide, if they had AIDS, both as the level of pain increased and the probability of survival for one year decreased, suggesting that the hypothetical decision was a rational

one. Lester and Yang (1996) found that the estimated probability of committing suicide if one had cancer varied with the anticipated pain from chemotherapy and the probability of survival.

In young German adults, Siegrist (1996) found that approval of suicide was associated with church nonattendance, not being Catholic, more education, and having an acquaintance commit suicide, but not with sex.

In a sample of elderly people in the community, Cicirelli (1997) found that the hypothetical choice of suicide was associated with race, sex, marital status, social class, religiosity, quality of life, fear of death, and loneliness; it was not associated with age, health locus of control, depression, self-esteem, or social support.

Parker et al. (1997) found no association of race or sex with positive attitudes toward suicide in elderly city-housing residents.

Peeters et al. (1997) classified subjects into optimists, pessimists, and realists regarding future problems and found that the majority (about 80 percent) were optimists regarding suicide and other future problems such as alcohol abuse and prison.

Stack (1996–1997) found that married people and those with children (for all marital statuses except being single) were less accepting of suicide. Acceptance of suicide was also associated with being Catholic, church attendance, education, and gender. In China, Stack and Cao (1997–1998) found that acceptance of suicide was less in those financially satisfied, as well as older residents. Marriage, children, and church attendance were not associated with suicide acceptance.

Sympathetic Predominance

In a sample of high school students, Lester (1991c) found no association between current suicidal ideation and scores on a questionnaire measure of sympathetic-parasympathetic predominance.

Tedium

Lester (1993e) found that suicidality was positively associated with scores on a measure of tedium.

Thinking

Bartfai et al. (1990) found that male suicide attempters scored lower than normal controls on intelligence tests, reasoning, and design fluency, but did not differ in a test on synonyms, a block test, the Stroop Test, the Wisconsin Card-Sorting Test, a perceptual maze, and a test on the use of objects. They concluded that suicidal people had a reduced ability to generate new ideas.

Malkin (1990, 1991) found that highly suicidal female psychiatric inpatients did not differ in dichotomous thinking from less suicidal patients, although they were more depressed and hopeless and viewed life as less positive and active on the Semantic Differential.

Woods et al. (1991) found that current suicidal ideation in college students and high school students was associated with irrational thinking, anxiety, depression, and hopelessness. (The high school students had more current suicidal ideation than the college students.)

Schmidtke (1992) found no differences between suicide attempters and nonsuicidal psychiatric patients in rigidity of thought or field dependence. The repeaters had higher cognitive impulsivity. Schmidtke and Schaller (1992) found no significant differences between suicide attempters and non-suicidal psychiatric controls in cognitive rigidity, dichotomous thinking, field dependence, state and trait anxiety, depression, extraversion, or neuroticism.

Hughes and Neimeyer (1993) found that subsequent suicidal ideation in psychiatric inpatients was predicted by pessimism, while subsequent suicide attempts were predicted by self-negativity, constricted thinking, differentiation, and polarized construing on the REP Grid and problem-solving ability.

Wolfersdorf and Niehus (1993) found that, among a sample of psychiatric depressed inpatients, those with prior suicidal ideation or attempts had more narrow thinking (as well as more depression, hopelessness, and suicides in their families, but did not differ in diagnosis).

Lehnert et al. (1996) found that suicidal ideation in adolescent psychiatric patients was predicted by measures of cognition (complex/abstract thinking, problem-focussed thinking and a negative world/self view) as well as low self-esteem, depression, and hopelessness.

Rogers (1992) suggested that alcohol may play a role in precipitating suicidal behavior by affecting the thought processes, since alcohol may reduce the ability to engage in inferential thought and reduce the range of perception (an alcohol-induced myopia).

Time Perspective

Lennings (1994) found that current suicidal ideation was associated with a negative temporal attitude (and depression), but not with time perspective (or impulsivity).

MacLeod and Tarbuck (1994) found that attempted suicides were more depressed, hopeless, and anxious (both trait and state) than medical controls. The attempters felt that future negative events were more likely, and they were less able to give reasons why such events might not happen.

Touching

Pearce et al. (1995) found that adolescents

who reported receiving negative touching from friends/family (such as punches) were more depressed and suicidal (ideation and attempts) in the prior six months. Positive touching (such as hugs) was negatively associated with depression and recent suicidality only for girls.

Values

Lester (1991h, 1993f) found no associations in college students between suicidality and scores on the Rokeach Survey of Values.

Standardized Personality Scales

Eysenck's Personality Test

Benjaminsen et al. (1990) found that attempted suicides did not differ from psychiatric controls in extraversion or psychoticism, but did have lower neuroticism scores. The suicide attempters did not differ in oral or obsessive test scores, but did have lower hysterical scores. They also did not differ in having a narcissistic personality and differed in only two personality traits out of 20 measured (less superego severity and suggestibility).

Lolas et al. (1991) studied a sample of female attempted suicides and found that current suicidal ideation was associated with psychoticism and neuroticism (but not with extraversion) scores, while prior attempts were associated only with psychoticism.

Freiburg Personality Inventory

Kuda (1992) found that college students with suicidal ideation were less inhibited and dominant and more depressed and nervous than nonsuicidal students. From a content analysis of verbal behavior, the suicidal students had more inward-directed hostility,

mutilation anxiety, diffuse anxiety and covert outward-directed hostility, and less shame anxiety, separation anxiety, guilt anxiety, and death anxiety. They did not differ in outward-directed hostility or ambivalent hostility.

Marke-Nyman Temperament Scale

Engstrom et al. (1996) found that attempters using violent methods had higher solidity scores on this scale than those using nonviolent methods, and male attempters had higher stability scores than female attempters. Repeaters did not differ from first-timers.

Millon Clinical Multiaxial Inventory

McCann and Gergelis (1990) found that only one of the 25 scales differentiated suicide attempters from ideators (the ideators showed less denial of problems), and so the inventory seemed to be of little use. The attempters had no peaks on the profile, while the ideators had peaks on avoidant, passive-aggressive, self-defeating, borderline, dysthymia, and debasement scales.

Hull et al. (1992) found that suicidal ideation was predicted by passive-aggressive-negativistic, dysthymic, and paranoid scores.

The MMPI

Botsis et al. (1990) found that Greek military inductees who had suicidal ideation had higher D and Pd scores than nonsuicidal inductees, were more hopeless and hostile (both introverted and extraverted hostility), and had experienced more stressful life events.

Craig and Olsen (1990) compared drug addicts who had attempted suicide with those who had not. The attempters had higher scores on F, D, Hy, Pd, Mf, Pa, Pt, and Sc; lower scores on K; and did not differ on Ma. The most common profiles for the attempters were 18/81, 29/92, 43, and 59; common profiles for the nonattempters were 2, 5, 9, 19, 62, and 89.

Hyer et al. (1990) compared Vietnam veterans with post-traumatic stress disorder who had attempted suicide with those who had not. The attempters had higher F, Pa, and Sc scores. MMPI scores were not associated with PTSD severity or community adjustment. The attempters had more survivor guilt and cried more, but did not differ in flashbacks, nightmares, suicidal ideation, or fights.

Boone (1995) found that scores of psychiatric inpatients on a suicide probability scale were associated with D scale scores on the MMPI-2, positively for the full and obvious scale, but negatively with the subtle scale.

Minarik et al. (1997) found that suicidal differed from violent adolescents on the Adolescent Multiphasic Personality Inventory in scoring higher on hypochondria, psychasthenia, paranoia, schizophrenia, and social introversion.

Rorschach

Alboretti et al. (1990) compared attempted suicides with psychiatric controls and found differences on only four Rorschach scores and no differences on 67 scores. The attempted suicides more often had color shock, self-criticism, more than three morbid responses, and pair responses.

Rydin et al. (1990) compared attempters using violent methods with those using nonviolent methods and psychiatric controls. Those using violent methods had more color shading, a greater paranoid attitude, more primitive thought, less tolerance for

dysphoric affect, reduced reality testing, and poorer handling of conflict. Those using violent methods differed from the controls in having more morbid content, a lower developmental level, more immature cognition, and more hostility. After four years, the subsequent completed suicides came only from those using violent methods.

Sibberg and Armstrong (1992) found no difference on the Exner scale between suicidal and nonsuicidal depressed adolescent psychiatric inpatients. However, six new variables did differentiate the groups, especially $CF+C < FC$, vista responses > 0 and $M- > 1$. In a review of research on the Exner system of scoring and interpretation, Wood et al. (1997) found that the prediction of suicide was not well validated.

Conti et al. (1996) found that attempted suicides gave more content relevant to devitalization, dismemberment, and aggression than psychiatric controls, but did not differ in formal scoring, refusals, or latency.

In an 8-24 year follow-up study of medical students, Thomas et al. (1997) found that the Rorschach predicted suicide less well than it predicted four other disorders. (It worked best for predicting mental illness.)

Based on Rorschach scoring, Lester (1991g) found evidence for an increase in dark shading in the poems of Anne Sexton prior to her suicide.

Other Tests

Lester et al. (1990) found that the rating of spinning responses on a multiple-choice test by students as "disliked" was negatively associated with current and prior suicidal ideation, but not with a history of attempted suicide.

Discussion

The research in this area has clearly

included a wide variety of traits and behaviors. Many have not been studied sufficiently to permit drawing reliable conclusions. For the areas that have been studied extensively (such as locus of control and reasons for living), there needs to be a good meta-analysis of the results so that the reliability (consistency) of the associations can be assessed. For other areas (such as attitudes toward suicide), scales that are widely acceptable and accepted need to be developed so that the results of the different studies can be compared with one another. At the moment, too much of the research into some of these areas (such as thinking and problem solving) is chaotic in the choice of measures used, so that reliable conclusions cannot be drawn.

REFERENCES

Abruzzi, W., Tuthill, R., Wieckowski, E., & Abruzzi, M. Immature death attitudes. In D. Lester (Ed.), *Suicide '94*. Denver: AAS, 1994, 32.

Adkins, K. K., & Parker, W. Perfectionism and suicidal preoccupation. *Journal of Personality*, 1996, 64, 529–543.

Ahmadi, K. S., Goethe, J. W., Mirabile, C. S., & Wright, J. S. Prep school students. In D. Lester (Ed.), *Suicide '92*. Denver: AAS, 1992, 85–86.

Akande, A., & Lester, D. Suicidal preoccupation, depression and locus of control in Nigerians and Americans. *Personality & Individual Differences*, 1994, 16, 975.

Alboretti, S., Vitali, A., Calchi Novati, N., Rapollar, M., & Rabizzoni, F. Predicting suicide risk using the Rorschach inkblot test. In G. Ferrari, M. Bellini & P. Crepet (Eds.), *Suicidal behavior and risk factors*. Bologna: Monduzzi-Editore, 1990, 735–741.

Apter, A., Gothelf, D., Offer, R., Ratzoni, G., Orbach, I., Tyano, S., & Pfeffer, C. R. Suicidal adolescents and ego defense mechanisms. *Journal of the American Academy of Child & Adolescent Psychiatry*, 1997, 36, 1520–1527.

Ashton, C. H., Marshall, E. F., Hassanyeh, F., Marsh, V. R., & Wright-Honari, S. Biological correlates of deliberate self-harm. *Acta Psychiatrica Scandinavica*, 1994, 90, 316–323.

Baker, J. A. Depression and suicidal ideation among academically gifted adolescents. *Gifted Child Quarterly*, 1995, 39, 218–223.

Bar-Joseph, H., & Tzuriel, D. Suicidal tendencies and ego identity in adolescence. *Adolescence*, 1990, 25, 215–223.

Bartfai, A., Winberg, I. M., Nordstrom, P., & Asberg, M. Suicidal behavior and cognitive flexibility. *Suicide & Life-Threatening Behavior*, 1990, 20, 254–266.

Bee-Gates, D., Howard-Pitney, B., LaFromboise, T., & Rowe, W. Help-seeking behavior of native American Indian high school students. *Professional Psychology*, 1996, 27, 495–499.

Benjaminsen, S., Krarup, G., & Lauritsen, R. Personality, parental rearing behavior, and parental loss in attempted suicide. *Acta Psychiatrica Scandinavica*, 1990, 82, 389–397.

Beratis, S., Lekka, N. P., & Gabriel, J. Smoking among suicide attempters. *Comprehensive Psychiatry*, 1997, 38, 74–79.

Bjerke, T., Stiles, T. C., & Svarva, K. *Sex role identity, depressive tendencies, and reasons for living among university students*. 4th European Symposium on Suicidal Behavior, Odense, Denmark, 1992.

Boldt, M. Normative evaluations of suicide and death. *Omega*, 1982–1983, 13, 145–147.

Boone, D. Differential validity of the MMPI-2 subtle and obvious scales with psychiatric inpatients. *Journal of Clinical Psychology*, 1995, 51, 526–531.

Borst, S. R., Noam, G. G., & Bartok, J. A. Adolescent suicidality. *Journal of the American Academy of Child & Adolescent Psychiatry*, 1991, 30, 796–803.

Botsis, A. J., Soldatos, C. R., Kokkevi, A., & Lyrintzis, S. Suicidal ideation in military draftees. In D. Lester (Ed.), *Suicide '90*. Denver: AAS, 1990, 294–296.

Brittlebank, A. D., Cole, A., Hassanyeh, F., Kenny, M., Simpson, D., & Scott, J. Hostility, hopelessness, and deliberate self-harm. *Acta Psychiatrica Scandinavica*, 1990, 81, 280–283.

Brubeck, D., & Beer, J. Depression, self-esteem, suicidal ideation, death anxiety, and GPA in high school students of divorced and nondivorced parents. *Psychological Reports*, 1992, 71, 755–767.

Buchanan, D. M. Meaning-in-life, depression, and suicide in older adults. In D. Lester (Ed.), *Suicide '94*. Denver: AAS, 1994, 175–176.

Buchanan, D. M., Farran, C., & Clark, D. Suicidal thought and self-transcendence in older adults. *Journal of Psychosocial Nursing*, 1995, 33(10), 31–34.

Burns, S., Kappenberg, R., McKenna, A., & Wood, C. Brain injury. *Brain Injury*, 1994, 8, 413–427.

Castrogiovanni, P., Fabiani, R., Toschi, D., Marazziti, D., & Conti, L. Aggressive behavior and suicidal attempts. In G. Ferrari, M. Bellini & P. Crepet (Eds.), *Suicidal behavior and risk factors*. Bologna: Monduzzi-Editore, 1990, 749–755.

Chance, S. E., Kaslow, N. J., & Baldwin, K. Anxiety and other predictors of suicidal intent in urban psychiatric inpatients. *Hospital & Community Psychiatry*, 1994, 45, 716–718.

Chance, S. E., Reviere, S. L., Rogers, J. L., Jannes, M. E., Jessee, S., Rojas, L., Hatcher, C. A., & Kaslow, N. J. An empirical study of the psychodynamics of depression. *Depression*, 1996, 4(2), 89–91.

Cicirelli, V. G. Relationship of psychosocial and background variables to older adults' end-of-life decisions. *Psychology & Aging*, 1997, 12, 72–83.

Clum, G. A., Canfield, D., Arsdel, M. V., Yang, B., Febbraro, G., & Wright, J. An expanded etiological model for suicide behavior in adolescents. *Journal of Psychopathology & Behavior Assessment*, 1997, 19, 207–222.

Clum, G. A., & Febbraro, G. Stress, social support, and problem-solving appraisal skills. *Journal of Psychopathology & Behavior Assessment*, 1994, 16, 69–83.

Clum, G. A., Yang, B., Febbraro, G., Canfield, D., & Van Arsdel, M. An investigation of the validity of the SPSI and

SPSI-R. *Journal of Psychopathology & Behavior Assessment*, 1996, 18, 119–132.

Cole, D. E., Protinsky, H. O., & Cross, L. H. An empirical investigation of adolescent suicidal ideation. *Adolescence*, 1992, 27, 813–818.

Connell, D. K., & Meyer, R. G. The Reasons-for-Living Inventory and a college population. *Journal of Clinical Psychology*, 1991, 47, 485–489.

Conti, L., Giannoni, A., Falco, P., Rossi, A., & Tognazzo, D. P. Death between reality and imagination. *Italian Journal of Suicidology*, 1996, 6, 83–91.

Cotton, C. R., & Range, L. M. Hopelessness and attitudes toward life and death in children. In D. Lester (Ed.), *Suicide '90*. Denver: AAS, 1990, 227–229.

Cotton, C. R., & Range, L. M. Suicidality, hopelessness, and attitudes toward life and death in children. *Death Studies*, 1993, 17, 185–191.

Cotton, C. R., & Range, L. M. Suicidality, hopelessness, and attitudes toward life and death in clinical and nonclinical adolescents. *Death Studies*, 1996, 20, 601–610.

Craig, R. J., & Olsen, R. E. MMPI characteristics of drug abusers with and without histories of suicide attempts. *Journal of Personality Assessment*, 1990, 55, 717–728.

Cruikshanks, D. R., & Slavich, S. P. Further investigation of popular misconceptions about suicide. *Omega*, 1993–1994, 28, 219–228.

Curry, J. F., Miller, Y., Waugh, S., & Anderson, W. B. Coping responses in depressed, socially maladjusted, and suicidal adolescents. *Psychological Reports*, 1992, 71, 80–82.

Dahlen, E. R., & Canetto, S. Gender, context, and meanings of suicidal behavior In J. McIntosh (Ed.), *Suicide '96*. Washington, DC: AAS, 1996, 173–174.

D'Attilio, J. P., & Campbell, B. Relationship between death anxiety and suicide potential in an adolescent population. *Psychological Reports*, 1990, 67, 975–978.

Dean, P. J., & Range, L. M. The escape theory of suicide and perfectionism in college students. *Death Studies*, 1996, 20, 415–424.

Dean, P. J., Range, L. M., & Goggin, W. C. The escape theory of suicide in college students. *Suicide & Life-Threatening Behavior*, 1996, 26, 181–186.

Diggs, K. A., & Lester, D. Emotional control, depression, and suicidality. *Psychological Reports*, 1996, 79, 774.

Dixon, W. A., Heppner, P. P., & Rudd, M. D. Problem-solving appraisal, hopelessness and suicide ideation. *Journal of Counseling Psychology*, 1994, 41, 91–98.

Domino, G., Lin, J., & Chang, O. Attitudes toward suicide and conservatism. *Omega*, 1995, 31, 237–252.

Domino, G., & Su, S. Conservatism and attitudes toward suicide. *Omega*, 1994–1995, 30, 131–143.

Duberstein, P. R. Openness to experience and completed suicide across the second half of life. *International Psychogeriatrics*, 1995, 7, 183–198.

Duberstein, P. R., Conwell, Y., & Caine, E. D. Age differences in the personality characteristics of suicide completers. *Psychiatry*, 1994, 57, 213–224.

Duberstein, P. R., Conwell, Y., Cox, C., Podgorski, C. A., Glazer, R. S., & Caine, E. D. Attitudes toward self-determined death. *Journal of the American Geriatric Society*, 1995, 43, 395–400.

Dyck, M. J. Positive and negative attitudes mediating suicidal ideation. *Suicide & Life-Threatening Behavior*, 1991, 21, 360–373.

Ellis, J. B., & Hirsch, J. K. Attitudes of traditional and nontraditional college students towards suicide. *College Student Journal*, 1995, 29, 445–448.

Ellis, J. B., & Jones, L. N. Adaptive behavior in suicide ideators and non-ideators. *Social Behavior & Personality*, 1996, 24, 309–320.

Ellis, J. B., & Lane, D. How young men and women assess parents of a child suicide victim. *Social Behavior & Personality*, 1995, 23, 29–34.

Ellis, J. B., & Range, L. M. Differences between blacks and whites, women and men in reasons for living. *Journal of Black Studies*, 1991, 21, 341–347.

Ellis, J. B., & Range, L. M. Mood influences on reasons for living in older adolescents. *Psychiatry*, 1992, 55, 216–222.

Ellis, J. B., & Russell, C. D. Implications of divorce on reasons for living in older adolescents. *Journal of Divorce & Remarriage*, 1992, 18(3–4), 197–205.

Ellis, J. B., & Smith, P. C. Spiritual well-being, social desirability, and reasons for living. *International Journal of Social Psychiatry*, 1991, 37, 57–63.

Ellis, T. E., Berg, R. A., & Franzen, M. D. Neuropsychological performance and suicidal behavior in adult psychiatric inpatients. *Perceptual & Motor Skills*, 1992, 75, 639–647.

Emanuel, E. J., Fairclough, D. L., Daniels, E. R., & Clarridge, B. R. Euthanasia and physician-assisted suicide. *Lancet*, 1996, 347, 1805–1810.

Engstrom, G., Nyman, G. E., & Traskman-Bendz, L. The Marke-Nyman Temperament (NMT) Scale in suicide attempters. *Acta Psychiatrica Scandinavica*, 1996, 94, 320–325.

Enns, M. W., Inayatulla, M., Cox, B., & Cheyne, L. Prediction of suicide intent in Aboriginal and non-Aboriginal adolescent inpatients. *Suicide & Life-Threatening Behavior*, 1997, 27, 218–224.

Eskin, M. Swedish translations of Suicide Probability Scale, Perceived Social Support from Friends and Family Scales, and the Scale for Interpersonal Behavior. *Scandinavian Journal of Psychology*, 1993, 34, 276–281.

Eskin, M. Adolescents' attitudes toward suicide, and a suicidal peer. *Scandinavian Journal of Psychology*, 1995, 36, 201–207.

Evans, J., Platts, H., & Liebenau, A. Impulsiveness and deliberate self-harm. *Acta Psychiatrica Scandinavica*, 1996, 93, 378–380.

Evans, J., Williams, J. M. G., O'Loughlin, S., & Howells, K. Autobiographical memory and problem-solving strategies of parasuicide patients. *Psychological Medicine*, 1992, 22, 399–405.

Feldman, M., & Wilson, A. Adolescent suicidality in urban minorities and its relationship to conduct disorders, depression, and separation anxiety. *Journal of the American Academy of Child & Adolescent Psychiatry*, 1997, 36, 75–84.

Finch, I. A. Religion and psychologists' attitudes toward suicide. In D. Lester (Ed.), *Suicide '93*. Denver: AAS, 1993, 168–169.

Fiske, A. Attitudes toward young-versus-old suicidal individuals. In D. Lester (Ed.), *Suicide*

'93. Denver: AAS, 1993, 180–182.

Fribergh, H., Traksman-Bendz, L., Ojehagen, A., & Regnell, G. The meta-contrast test. *Acta Psychiatrica Scandinavica*, 1992, 86, 473–477.

Goldney, R. D., Smith, S., Winefield, A. H., Tiggerman, M., & Winefield, H. R. Suicidal ideation. *Acta Psychiatrica Scandinavica*, 1991, 83, 115–120.

Greening, L., & Dollinger, S. J. Rural adolescents' perceived personal risks for suicide. *Journal of Youth & Adolescence*, 1993, 22, 211–217.

Greyson, B. Near-death experiences precipitated by suicide attempt. *Journal of Near-Death Studies*, 1991, 9, 183–188.

Greyson, B. Near-death experiences and antisuicide attitudes. *Omega*, 1992–1993, 26, 81–89.

Hammond, L. K., & Deluty, R. H. Attitudes of clinical psychologists, psychiatrists, and oncologists toward suicide. *Social Behavior & Personality*, 1992, 20, 289–293.

Herpertz, S., Steinmeyer, S. M., Marx, D., Oidtmann, A., & Sass, H. The significance of aggression and impulsivity for self-mutilative behavior. *Pharmacopsychiatry*, 1995, 28, (Suppl. 2), 64–72.

Hewitt, P. L., Flett, G. L., & Turnbull-Donovan, W. Perfectionism and suicide potential. *British Journal of Clinical Psychology*, 1992, 31, 181–190.

Hewitt, P. L., Flett, G. L., & Weber, C. Dimensions of perfectionism and suicide ideation. *Cognitive Therapy & Research*, 1994, 18, 439–460.

Hewitt, P. L., Newton, J., Flett,. G. L., & Callander, L. Perfectionism and suicide ideation in adolescent psychiatric inpatients. *Journal of Abnormal Child Psychology*, 1997, 25, 95–101.

Hirsch, J. K., & Ellis, J. B. Differences in life stress and reasons for living among college suicide ideators and nonideators. *College Student Journal*, 1996, 30, 377–386.

Horesh, N., Rolnick, T., Iancu, I., Dannon, P., Lepkifker, E., Apter, A., & Kotler, M. Coping styles and suicide risk. *Acta Psychiatrica Scandinavica*, 1996, 93, 489–493.

Horesh, N., Rolnick, T., Iancu, I., Dannon, P., Lepkifker, E., Apter, A., & Kotler, M. Anger, impulsivity, and suicide risk. *Psychotherapy & Psychosomatics*, 1997, 66, 92–96.

Hovey, J. D., & King, C. A. Acculturative stress, depression, and suicidal ideation among immigrant and second-generation Latino adolescents. *Journal of the American Academy of Child & Adolescent Psychiatry*, 1996, 35, 1183–1192.

Hughes, S. L., & Neimeyer, R. A. Cognitive predictors of suicide risk among hospitalized psychiatric patients. *Death Studies*, 1993, 17, 103–124.

Hull, J. S., Range, L. M., & Goggin, W. C. Suicide ideas. *Death Studies*, 1992, 16, 371–375.

Hyer, C. L., McCranie, E. W., Woods, M. G., & Boudewyns, P. A. Suicidal behavior among chronic Vietnam theater veterans with PTSD. *Journal of Clinical Psychology*, 1990, 46, 713–721.

Ivanoff, A., Smyth, N. J., Grochowski, S., Jang, S. J., & Klein, K. E. Problem-solving and suicidality among prison inmates. *Journal of Consulting & Clinical Psychology*, 1992, 60, 970–973.

Jack, R. L. *Women and attempted suicide.* Hove, UK: Lawrence Erlbaum, 1991.

Jack, R. L., & Williams, J. M. The role of attribution in self-poisoning. *British Journal of Clinical Psychology*, 1991, 30, 25–35.

Jacobson, J. A., Kasworm, E. M., Battin, M. P., Botkin, J. R., Francis, L. P., & Green, D. Decedent's reported preference for physician-assisted death. *Journal of Clinical Ethics*, 1995, 6, 149–157.

Joiner, T. E., & Rudd, M. D. Negative attribution style for interpersonal events and the occurrence of severe interpersonal disruptions as predictors of self-reported suicidal ideation. *Suicide & Life-Threatening Behavior*, 1995, 25, 297–304.

Joiner, T. E., & Rudd, M. D. Disentangling the interrelations between hopelessness, loneliness, and suicidal ideation. *Suicide & Life-Threatening Behavior*, 1996, 26, 19–26.

Joiner, T. E., Rudd, M. D., & Rajab, M. H. The Modified Scale for Suicidal Ideation. *Journal of Abnormal Psychology*, 1997, 106, 260–265.

Josepho, S. A., & Plutchik, R. Stress, coping, and suicide risk in psychiatric inpatients. *Suicide & Life-Threatening Behavior*, 1994, 24,

48–57.

Kalb, R. Rational aspects of suicidal attempts. In K. Bohme, R. Freytag, C. Wachtler & H. Wedler (Eds.), *Suicidal behavior.* Regensburg: S Roderer, 1993, 694–697.

Kaplan, K., & Ross, L. T. Life ownership and attitudes toward abortion, suicide, doctor-assisted suicide, and capital punishment. In D. Lester (Ed.), *Suicide '94.* Denver: AAS, 1994, 151–152.

Kaplan, K., & Ross, L. T. Life ownership and attitudes toward abortion, suicide and capital punishment. *Journal of Psychology & Judaism,* 1995, 19, 177–193.

Kaplan, S., & Lester, D. Depression, mania, and suicidal preoccupation. *Psychological Reports,* 1994, 74, 974.

Kaplan, Z., Bennebishty, R., Waysman, M., Solomon, Z. & Bleich, A. Clinician's assessments of suicide risk. *Israel Journal of Psychiatry,* 1992, 29, 159–166.

Kashden, J., Fremouw, W. J., Callahan, T. S., & Franzen, M. D. Impulsivity in suicidal and nonsuicidal adolescents. *Journal of Abnormal Child Psychology,* 1993, 21, 339–353.

Kawachi, I., Willett, W. C., Colditz, G. A., Stampfer, M. J., & Speizer, F. E. A prospective study of coffee drinking and suicide in women. *Archives of Internal Medicine,* 1996, 156, 521–525.

Kearl, M. C. Dying well. *American Behavioral Scientist,* 1996, 39, 336–360.

Kehrer, C. A., & Linehan, M. M. Interpersonal and emotional problem-solving skills and parasuicide among women with borderline personality disorder. *Journal of Personality Disorders,* 1996, 10, 153–163.

King, S. R., Hampton, W. R., Bernstein, B., & Sichor, A. College students' views on suicide. *Journal of American College Health,* 1996, 44, 283–287.

Kinnier, R. T., Metha, A. T., Keim, J. S., Okey, J. L., Adler-Tabia, R. L., Berry, M. A., & Mulvenon, S. W. Depression, meaninglessness, and substance abuse in normal and hospitalized adolescents. *Journal of Alcohol & Drug Education,* 1994, 39(2), 101–111.

Kokkevi, A., Politikou, K., & Stefanis, C. The relationship of suicide attempts to licit and illicit drug use. In A. J. Botsis, C. R. Soldatos & C. N. Stefanis (Eds.), *Suicide.* Amsterdam: Elsevier, 1997, 55–63.

Komisin, L. K. Personality type and suicidal behaviors in college students. *Journal of Psychological Type,* 1992, 24, 24–32.

Korn, M. L., Plutchik, R., & Van Praag, H. M. Panic-associated suicidal and aggressive ideation and behavior. *Journal of Psychiatric Research,* 1997, 31, 481–487.

Koslowsky, M., Bleich, A., Apter, A., Solomon, Z., Wagner, B., & Greenspoon, A. Structural equation modelling of some of the determinants of suicide risk. *British Journal of Medical Psychology,* 1992, 65, 157–165.

Kotler, M., Finkelstein, G., Molcho, A., Botsis, A. J., Plutchik, R., Brown, S. L., & Van Praag, H. M. Correlates of suicide and violence risk in an inpatient population. *Psychiatry Research,* 1993, 47, 281–290.

Kralik, K. M., & Danforth, W. J. Identification of coping ideation and strategies of preventing suicidality in a college-age sample. *Suicide & Life-Threatening Behavior,* 1992, 22, 167–186.

Kuda, M. The relevance of anxiety and aggression for the suicidality of students. In P. Crepet, G. Ferrari, S. Platt & M. Bellini (Eds.), *Suicide behaviour in Europe.* Rome: John Libbey, 1992, 119–129.

Leenaars, A. A., & Domino, G. A comparison of community attitudes towards suicide in Windsor and Los Angeles. *Canadian Journal of Behavioural Science,* 1993, 25, 253–266.

Leenaars, A. A., & Lester, D. Facts and myths of suicide in Canada and the United States. *Journal of Social Psychology,* 1992, 132, 787–789.

Leenaars, A. A., Saunders, M., Balance, W. D., & Wenckstern, S. Knowledge about facts and myths of suicide in the elderly. *Gerontology & Geriatrics Education,* 1991, 12(1), 61–68.

Lehnert, K. L., Overholser, J. C., & Adams, D. M. The cognition rating form. *Psychological Assessment,* 1996, 8, 172–181.

Lennings, C. J. Time perspective, mood disturbance, and suicide liberation. *Omega,* 1994, 29, 153–164.

Lester, D. Impulsivity and threatened suicide. *Personality & Individual Differences,*

1990a, 11, 1097–1098.

Lester, D. Self-monitoring, depression, and suicidal ideation. *Psychological Reports*, 1990b, 67, 410.

Lester, D. Attitudes toward the survivors of suicides as a function of motive for suicide. *Omega*, 1990–1991, 22, 215–218.

Lester, D. Alexithymia, depression, and suicidal preoccupation. *Perceptual & Motor Skills*, 1991a, 72, 1058.

Lester, D. Accurate knowledge about suicide and judgments about suicide. *Perceptual & Motor Skills*, 1991b, 72, 1018.

Lester, D. Depression, suicidal ideation, and autonomic reactivity. *Perceptual & Motor Skills*, 1991c, 73, 294.

Lester, D. A test of Lester's depression paradox hypothesis of suicide. *Psychological Reports*, 1991d, 68, 1254.

Lester, D. National measures of extraversion and neuroticism and suicide and homicide rates. *Psychological Reports*, 1991e, 69, 434.

Lester, D. Depression and fears of individuation and attachment. *Transactional Analysis Journal*, 1991f, 21, 218–219.

Lester, D. Dark-shading in the poems of Anne Sexton. *Perceptual & Motor Skills*, 1991g, 73, 366.

Lester, D. Depression, suicidal preoccupation, and scores on the Rokeach Value Survey. *Psychological Reports*, 1991h, 69, 998.

Lester, D. The stigma against dying and suicidal patients. *Omega*, 1992–1993, 26, 71–75.

Lester, D. How do different people perceive the different methods for suicide? *Death Studies*, 1993a, 17, 179–184.

Lester, D. Functional and dysfunctional impulsivity and depression and suicidal ideation in a subclinical population. *Journal of General Psychology*, 1993b, 120, 187–188.

Lester, D. Depression, suicidal ideation, and locus of control. *Perceptual & Motor Skills*, 1993c, 76, 1282.

Lester, D. Accurate knowledge about suicide and personality. *Psychological Reports*, 1993d, 73, 506.

Lester, D. Tedium, depression, and suicidal preoccupation. *Psychological Reports*, 1993e, 73, 622.

Lester, D. Depression, suicidal preoccupation, and scores on the Rokeach Value Survey. *Psychological Reports*, 1993f, 73, 1202.

Lester, D. *Suicide in creative women.* Commack, NY: Nova Science, 1993g.

Lester, D. The neuropsychology of violence and suicide. *Corrective & Social Psychiatry*, 1993h, 39, 11–13.

Lester, D. The moral acceptability of suicide. *Perceptual & Motor Skills*, 1995a, 81, 1106.

Lester, D. Myths about childhood suicide. *Psychological Reports*, 1995b, 77, 330.

Lester, D. An attributional analysis of suicide. *Journal of Social Psychology*, 1996a, 136, 399–400.

Lester, D. Accurate knowledge about suicide and personality. *Psychological Reports*, 1996b, 79, 218.

Lester, D. Fears of death and the probability of suicide. *Psychological Reports*, 1996c, 79, 510.

Lester, D. Interpersonal problem solving, subclinical depression and suicidal ideation. *International Journal of Psychology Research*, 1996d, 1(1), 33–35.

Lester, D. AIDS and rational suicide. *Omega*, 1996–1997, 34, 333–336.

Lester, D., & Akande, A. Attitudes about suicide among the Yoruba of Nigeria. *Journal of Social Psychology*, 1994, 134, 851–853.

Lester, D., & Badro, S. Depression, suicidal preoccupation, and purpose in life in a subclinical population. *Personality & Individual Differences*, 1992, 13, 75–76.

Lester, D., & Bean, J. Attitudes toward preventing versus assisting suicide. *Journal of Social Psychology*, 1992a, 132, 125–127.

Lester, D., & Bean, J. Attribution of causes to suicide. *Journal of Social Psychology*, 1992b, 132, 679–680.

Lester, D., & Bernard, D. Liking for chocolate, depression, and suicidal preoccupation. *Psychological Reports*, 1991, 69, 570.

Lester, D., & Castromayor, I. Myths about suicide in American and Philippine nurses. *Psychological Reports*, 1994, 75, 538.

Lester, D., Castromayor, I., & Icli, T. Locus of control, depression, and suicidal ideation among American, Philippine, and Turkish students. *Journal of Social Psychology*, 1991a, 131,

447–449.

Lester, D., Decker, J., Eisenberg, R. J., Ecker, C., Guerriero, J., & Mielish, C. Association between whirling responses on psychological tests and suicidal preoccupation. *Perceptual & Motor Skills*, 1990, 71, 1105.

Lester, D., & Francis, L. J. Is religiosity related to suicidal ideation after personality and mood are taken into account? *Personality & Individual Differences*, 1993, 15, 591–592.

Lester, D. Fraser, D., & Turoff, M. Recognizing suicides from photographs. *Perceptual & Motor Skills*, 1993, 77, 506.

Lester, D., & Gatto, J. L. Interpersonal trust, depression, and suicidal ideation in teenagers. *Psychological Reports*, 1990, 67, 786.

Lester, D., Guerriero, J. M., & Wachter, S. M. The suicide attitude vignette experience. *Death Studies*, 1991b, 15, 435–441.

Lester, D., & Hoffman, S. Self-defeating behavior, depression, and suicidal preoccupation. *Psychological Reports*, 1992, 70, 1106.

Lester, D., & Icli, T. Beliefs about suicide in American and Turkish students. *Journal of Social Psychology*, 1990, 130, 825–827.

Lester, D., Icli, T., & Castromayor, I. Who has accurate knowledge about suicide? *Psychological Reports*, 1994, 75, 1306.

Lester, D., McCabe, C., & Cameron, M. Judging the appropriateness of completed suicide, attempted suicide, and suicidal ideation. *Omega*, 1991–1992, 24, 75–79.

Lester, D., & Mielish, C. Belief in myths about suicide and irrational thinking. *Psychological Reports*, 1990, 67, 1050.

Lester, D., & Miller, C. Depression and suicidal preoccupation in teenagers. *Personality & Individual Differences*, 1990, 11, 421–422.

Lester, D., & Moderski, T. The impostor phenomenon in adolescents. *Psychological Reports*, 1995, 76, 466.

Lester, D., & O'Neill, B. G. Is it rational to have reasons for not committing suicide? *Perceptual & Motor Skills*, 1995, 81, 94.

Lester, D., & Pitts, J. Depression and locus of control in police officers. *Psychological Reports*, 1990, 67, 826.

Lester, D., & Pitts, J. Do police officers have accurate information about suicide?

Psychological Reports, 1991, 69, 830.

Lester, D. & Schaeffler, J. Self-defeating personality, depression, and suicidal ideation in adolescents. *Psychological Reports*, 1993, 73, 113–114.

Lester, D., & Whipple, M. Music preference, depression, suicidal preoccupation, and personality. *Suicide & Life-Threatening Behavior*, 1996, 26, 68–70.

Lester, D., & Yang, B. An approach for examining the rationality of suicide. *Psychological Reports*, 1996, 79, 405–406.

Lichtenstein, R. L., Alcser, K. H., Corning, A. D., Bachman, J. G., & Doukas, D. J. Black/white differences in attitudes toward physician-assisted suicide. *Journal of the National Medical Association*, 1997, 89, 125–133.

Linblad, J., Koury, D., Trapani, L., & Lester, D. Stress and attitudes toward suicide. *Psychological Reports*, 1994, 75, 1082.

Loas, G., Fremaux, D., Gayant, C., & Boyer, P. Anhedonia, depression, and suicidal ideation. *Perceptual & Motor Skills*, 1995, 80, 978.

Lolas, F., Gomez, A., & Suarez, L. EPQ-R and suicide attempt. *Personality & Individual Differences*, 1991, 12, 899–902.

LoPresto, C. T., Sherman, M. F., & Di Carlo, M. A. Factors affecting the unacceptability of suicide and the effects of evaluator depression and religiosity. *Omega*, 1994–1995, 30, 205–221.

Lynn, R., & Martin, T. National differences for 37 nations in extraversion, neuroticism, psychoticism and economic, demographic, and other correlates. *Personality & Individual Differences*, 1995, 19, 403–406.

MacLeod, A. K., Pankhania, B., Lee, M., & Mitchell, D. Parasuicide, depression, and the anticipation of positive and negative future experiences. *Psychological Medicine*, 1997, 27, 973–977.

MacLeod, A. K., & Tarbuck, A. F. Explaining why negative events will happen to oneself. *British Journal of Clinical Psychology*, 1994, 33, 317–326.

Malkin, M. J. Cognitive evaluation patterns of suicidal women. In D. Lester (Ed.), *Suicide '90*. Denver: AAS, 1990, 43–45.

Malkin, M. J. Cognitive evaluations of

suicidal women. *Therapeutic Recreation Journal,* 1991, 25(1), 34–49.

Malkin, M. J., Howe, C. Z., & Del Rey, P. Psychological disability and leisure dysfunction of female suicidal psychiatric clients. *Therapeutic Recreation Journal,* 1989, 23(1), 36–46.

Marazziti, D., & Conti, L. Aggression and suicide attempts. *European Neuropsychopharmacology,* 1991, 1, 169–172.

Marciano, P. L., & Kazdin, A. E. Self-esteem, depression, hopelessness, and suicidal intent among psychiatrically disturbed inpatient children. *Journal of Clinical Child Psychology,* 1994, 23, 151–160.

Martin, G., Clarke, M., & Pearce, C. Adolescent suicide. *Journal of the American Academy of Child & Adolescent Psychiatry,* 1993, 32, 530–535.

McCann, J. T., & Gergelis, R. E. Utility of the MCMI-II in assessing suicidal risk. *Journal of Clinical Psychology,* 1990, 46, 764–770.

McCollaum, B., & Lester, D. Locus of control, depression, and suicidality in Korean workers. *Psychological Reports,* 1997, 80, 1282.

Mendonca, J. D., & Holden, R. R. Are all suicidal ideas closely linked to hopelessness? *Acta Psychiatrica Scandinavica,* 1996, 93, 246–251.

Metha, A., & McWhirter, E. H. Suicide ideation, depression, and stressful life events among gifted adolescents. *Journal for the Education of the Gifted,* 1997, 20, 284–304.

Migeot, M., & Lester, D. Psychological abuse in dating, locus of control, depression, and suicidal preoccupation. *Psychological Reports,* 1996, 79, 682.

Milling, L., Campbell, N. B., Bush, E., & Laughlin, A. Affective and behavioral correlates of suicidality among hospitalized preadolescent children. *Journal of Clinical Child Psychology,* 1996, 25, 454–462.

Milling, L., Giddan, J. J., Campbell, N. B., Bush, E., & Laughlin, A. Preadolescent suicidal behavior. *Child Psychiatry & Human Development,* 1997, 28, 103–115.

Minarik, M. J., Myatt, R., & Mitrushina, M. Adolescent Multiphasic Personality Inventory and its utility in assessing suicidal and violent adolescents. *Suicide & Life-Threatening Behavior,* 1997, 27, 278–284.

Monte, P. Attitudes toward the voluntary taking of life. *Sociological Spectrum,* 1991, 11, 265–277.

Mraz, W., & Runco, M. A. Suicide ideation and creative problem solving. *Suicide & Life-Threatening Behavior,* 1994, 24, 38–47.

Negron, R., Piacemtini, J., Graae, F., Davies, M., & Shaffer, D. Microanalysis of adolescent suicide attempters and ideators during the acute suicidal episode. *Journal of the American Academy of Child & Adolescent Psychiatry,* 1997, 36, 1512–1519.

Neyra, C. J., & Range, L. M., & Goggin, W. C. Reasons for living following success and failure in suicidal and nonsuicidal college students. *Journal of Applied Social Psychology,* 1990, 20, 861–868.

Nierenberg, A. A., Ghaemi, S. N., Clancy-Colecchi, K., Rosenbaum, J. F., & Fava, M. Cynicism, hostility, and suicidal ideation in depressed outpatients. *Journal of Nervous & Mental Disease,* 1996, 184, 607–610.

Nordstrom, P., Schalling, D., & Asberg, M. Temperamental vulnerability in attempted suicide. *Acta Psychiatrica Scandinavica,* 1995, 92, 155–160.

Oei, T. I., Verhoeven, W. M. A., Westenberg, H. G. M., Zwart, F. M., & van Pee, J. M. Anhedonia, suicide ideation, and dexamethasone nonsuppression in depressed patients. *Journal of Psychiatric Research,* 1990, 24, 25–35.

Ohring, R., Apter, A., Ratzioni, G., Weisman, R., Tyano, S., & Plutchik, R. State and trait anxiety in adolescent suicide attempters. *Journal of the American Academy of Child & Adolescent Psychiatry,* 1996, 35, 154–157.

Orbach, I., Bar-Joseph, H., & Dror, N. Styles of problem-solving in suicidal individuals *Suicide & Life-Threatening Behavior,* 1990, 20, 56–64.

Orbach, I., Kedem, P., Gorchover, O., Apter, A., & Tyano, S. Fears of death in suicidal and nonsuicidal adolescents. *Journal of Abnormal Psychology,* 1993, 102, 553–558.

Orbach, I., Kedem, P., Herman, L., & Apter, A. Dissociative tendencies in suicidal, depressed, and normal adolescents. *Journal of Social & Clinical Psychology,* 1995a, 14, 393–408.

Orbach, I., Lotem-Peleg, M., & Kedem, P. Attitudes toward the body in suicidal, depressed, and normal adolescents. *Suicide & Life-Threatening Behavior*, 1995b, 25, 211–221.

Orbach, I., Mikulincer, M., King, R., Cohen, D., & Stein, D. Thresholds and tolerance of physical pain in suicidal and nonsuicidal adolescents. *Journal of Consulting & Clinical Psychology*, 1997, 65, 646–652.

Orbach, I., Milstein, I., Har-Even, D., Apter, A., Tyano, S., & Elizur, A. A multi-attitude suicide tendency scale for adolescents. *Psychological Assessment*, 1991, 3, 398–404.

Orbach, I., Palgi, Y., Stein, D., Har-Even, D., Lotem-Peleg, M., Asherov, J., & Elizur, A. Tolerance for physical pain in suicidal subjects. *Death Studies*, 1996a, 20, 327–334.

Orbach, I., Stein, D., Palgi, Y., Asherov, J., Har-Even, D., & Elizur, A. Perception of physical pain in accident and suicide attempt patients. *Journal of Psychiatric Research*, 1996b, 30, 307–320.

Osman, A., Barrios, F. X., Grittman, L. R., & Osman, J. R. The Multi-Attitude Suicide Tendency Scale. *Journal of Clinical Psychology*, 1993a, 49, 701–708.

Osman, A., Barrios, F. X., Panak, W. F., Osman, J. R., Hoffman, J., & Hammer, R. Validation of the Multi-Attitude Suicide Tendency Scale in adolescent samples. *Journal of Clinical Psychology*, 1994, 50, 847–855.

Osman, A., Gifford, J., Jones, T., Lickliss, L., Osman, J., & Wenzel, R. Psychometric examination of the Reasons for Living Inventory. *Psychological Assessment*, 1993b, 5, 154–158.

Osman, A., Gregg, C. L., Osman, J. R., & Jones, K. Factor structure and reliability of the Reasons for Living Inventory. *Psychological Reports*, 1992, 70, 107–112.

Osman, A., Kopper, B. A., Barrios, F. X., Osman, J. R., Besett, T., & Linehan, M. M. The Brief Reasons for Living Inventory for adolescents. *Journal of Abnormal Child Psychology*, 1996, 24, 433–443.

Overholser, J. C., Adams, D. M., Lehnert, K. L., & Brinkman, D. C. Self-esteem deficits and suicidal tendencies among adolescents. *Journal of the American Academy of Child & Adolescent Psychiatry*, 1995, 34, 919–928.

Overholser, J. C., Freiheit, S. R., & DiFilippo, J. M. Emotional distress and substance abuse as risk factors for suicide attempts. *Canadian Journal of Psychiatry*, 1997, 42, 402–408.

Paffenbarger, R. S., Lee, I. M., & Leung, R. Physical activity and personal characteristics associated with depression and suicide in American college men. *Acta Psychiatrica Scandinavica*, 1994, (Suppl. 377), 16–22.

Parker, L. D., Cantrell, C., & Demi, A. S. Older adults' attitudes toward suicide. *Death Studies*, 1997, 21, 289–298.

Payne, B. J., & Range, L. M. Attitudes toward life and death and suicidality in young adults. *Death Studies*, 1995, 19, 559–569.

Payne, B. J., & Range, L. M. Family environment, depression, attitudes toward life and death, and suicidality in young adults. *Death Studies*, 1996a, 20, 237–246.

Payne, B. J., & Range, L. M. Family environment, attitudes toward life and death, depression, and suicidality in elementary school children. *Death Studies*, 1996b, 20, 481–494.

Pearce, C. M., & Martin, G. Locus of control as an indicator of risk for suicidal behavior among adolescents. *Acta Psychiatrica Scandinavica*, 1993, 88, 409–414.

Pearce, C. M., Martin, G., & Wood, K. Significance of touch for perceptions of parenting and psychological adjustment among adolescents. *Journal of the American Academy of Child & Adolescent Psychiatry*, 1995, 34, 160–167.

Peeters, G., Cammaert, M. F., & Czapinski, J. Unrealistic optimism and positive-negative asymmetry. *International Journal of Psychology*, 1997, 32(1), 23–34.

Petrie, K., & Brook, R. Sense of coherence, self-esteem, depression, and hopelessness as correlates of reattempting suicide. *British Journal of Clinical Psychology*, 1992, 31, 293–300.

Phillips, D. P., Welty, W. R., & Smith, M. M. Elevated suicide levels associated with legalized gambling. *Suicide & Life-Threatening Behavior*, 1996, 27, 373–378.

Pinto, A., & Whisman, M. A. Negative affect and cognitive biases in suicidal and nonsuicidal hospitalized adolescents. *Journal of the American Academy of Child & Adolescent Psychiatry*, 1996, 35, 158–165.

Pinto, A., Whisman, M. A., & McCoy, K. Suicidal ideation in hospitalized adolescents. In J. McIntosh (Ed.), *Suicide '96*. Washington, DC: 1996, 160–161

Pook, R., Conti, T., & Lester, D. Eating disorders, depression and suicidal preoccupation in a nonclinical sample. *Psychological Reports*, 1996, 79, 302.

Priester, M. J., & Clum, G. A. Attribution style as a diathesis in predicting depression, hopelessness, and suicide ideation in college students. *Journal of Psychopathology & Behavior Assessment*, 1992, 14, 111–122.

Priester, M. J., & Clum, G. A. Perceived problem-solving ability as a predictor of depression, hopelessness, and suicidal ideation in a college population. *Journal of Counseling Psychology*, 1993a, 40, 79–85.

Priester, M. J., & Clum, G. A. The problem-solving diathesis in depression, hopelessness, and suicidal ideation. *Journal of Psychopathology & Behavioral Assessment*, 1993b, 15, 239–254.

Puskar, K., Hoover, C., & Miewald, C. Suicidal and nonsuicidal coping methods of adolescents. *Perspectives in Psychiatric Care*, 1992, 28(2), 15–20.

Range, L., M., & Penton, S. R. Hope, hopelessness, and suicidality in college students. *Psychological Reports*, 1994, 75, 456–458.

Rasmussen, K. M., Negy, C., Carlson, R., & Burns, J. M. Suicide ideation and acculturation among low socioeconomic status Mexican American adolescents. *Journal of Early Adolescence*, 1997, 17, 390–407.

Recklitis, C. J., Noam, G. G., & Borst, S. R. Adolescent suicide and defensive style. *Suicide & Life-Threatening Behavior*, 1992, 22, 374–387.

Reich, J. W., Newsom, J. T., & Zautra, A. J. Health downturns and predictors of suicidal ideation. *Suicide & Life-Threatening Behavior*, 1996, 26, 282–291.

Repo, E., Virkkunen, M., Rawlings, R., & Linnoila, M. Suicidal behavior among Finnish fire setters. *European Archives of Psychiatry*, 1997, 247, 303–307.

Reynolds, W. M. Psychometric characteristics of the Adult Suicidal Ideation Questionnaire in college students. *Journal of Personality Assessment*, 1991, 56, 289–307.

Rich, A. R., Kirkpatrick-Smith, J., Bonner, R. L., & Jans, F. Gender differences in the psychosocial correlates of suicidal ideation among adolescents. *Suicide & Life-Threatening Behavior*, 1992, 22, 364–373.

Rogers, J. R. Suicide and alcohol. *Journal of Counseling & Development*, 1992, 70, 540–543.

Rohde, P., Lewinsohn, P. M., Seeley, J. R., & Langhinrichsen-Rohling, J. The Life Attitudes Schedule Short Form. *Suicide & Life-Threatening Behavior*, 1996, 26, 272–281.

Rohde, P., Mace, D. E., & Seeley, J. R. The association of psychiatric disorders with suicide attempts in a juvenile detention sample. *Criminal Behavior & Mental Health*, 1997a, 7, 187–200.

Rohde, P., Seeley, J. R., & Mace, D. E. Correlates of suicidal behavior in a juvenile detention population. *Suicide & Life-Threatening Behavior*, 1997b, 27, 164–175.

Rotheram-Borus, M. J., Trautman, P. D., Dopkins, S. C., & Shrout, P. E. Cognitive style and pleasant activities among female suicide attempters. *Journal of Consulting & Clinical Psychology*, 1990, 58, 554–556.

Rudd, M. D., Rajab, M. H., & Dahm, P. F. Problem-solving appraisal in suicide ideators and attempters. *American Journal of Orthopsychiatry*, 1994, 64, 136–149.

Rydin, E., Asberg, M., Edman, G., & Schalling, D. Violent and nonviolent suicide attempts. *Acta Psychiatrica Scandinavica*, 1990, 82, 30–39.

Samuelsson, M., Gustavsson, J. P., Petterson, I. L., Arnetz, B., & Asberg, M. Suicidal feelings and work environment in psychiatric nursing personnel. *Social Psychiatry & Psychiatric Epidemiology*, 1997, 32, 391–397.

Sarasalo, E., Bergman, B., & Toth, J. Personality traits and psychiatric and somatic morbidity among kleptomaniacs. *Acta Psychiatrica Scandinavica*, 1996, 94, 358–364.

Schaller, S., & Schmidtke, A. Hopelessness, attribution style, and depressive suicidal tendencies in the elderly. In D. Lester (Ed.), *Suicide '93*. Denver: AAS, 1993, 150–151.

Schaller, S., & Schmidtke, A. Anomia, hopelessness, and well-being in the elderly. In D. Lester (Ed.), *Suicide '95*. Washington, DC: AAS, 1995, 100–101.

Schmidtke, A. The influence of mood factors

on cognitive styles during suicidal crises. In D. Lester (Ed.), *Suicide '92*. Denver: AAS, 1992, 220–221.

Schmidtke, A., & Schaller, S. Covariation of cognitive styles and mood factors during crises. In P. Crepet, G. Ferrari, S. Platt & M. Bellini (Eds.), *Suicide behaviour in Europe*. Rome: John Libbey, 1992, 225–233.

Schmidtke, A., & Schaller, S. Cognitive impulsivity and repeated suicidal behavior. In K. Bohme, R. Freytag, C. Wachtler & H. Wedler (Eds.), *Suicidal behavior*. Regensburg: S. Roderer, 1993a, 763–768.

Schmidtke, A., & Schaller, S. Time perspective and time estimation of suicidal patients. In D. Lester (Ed.), *Suicide '93*. Denver: AAS, 1993b, 161–162.

Schmidtke, A., & Schaller, S. Impulsivity and suicidal behavior. In D. Lester (Ed.), *Suicide '94*. Denver: AAS, 1994a, 142–144.

Schmidtke, A., & Schaller, S. The role of cognitive factors in suicidal behavior. In U. Bille-Brahe & H. Schiodt (Eds.), *Intervention and prevention*. Odense: Odense University Press, 1994b, 104–124.

Schmidtke, A., & Schaller, S. Megargee's concept of the "overcontrolled individual" and suicidal behavior. In J. McIntosh (Ed.), *Suicide '97*. Washington, DC: AAS, 1997, 94–95.

Seidlitz, L., Duberstein, P. R., Cox, C., & Conwell, Y. Attitudes of older people toward suicide and assisted-suicide. *Journal of the American Geriatrics Society*, 1995, 43, 993–998.

Sibberg, J. L., & Armstrong, J. G. The Rorschach test for predicting suicide among depressed adolescent inpatients. *Journal of Personality Assessment*, 1992, 59, 290–303.

Siegrist, M. Church attendance, denomination, and suicide ideology. *Journal of Social Psychology*, 1996, 136, 559–566.

Simonds, J. F., McMahon, T., & Armstrong, D. Young suicide attempters compared with a control group. *Suicide & Life-Threatening Behavior*, 1991, 21, 134–151.

Sorbye, L. W., Sorbye, S., & Sorbye, S. W. Nursing students' attitudes toward assisted suicide and euthanasia. *Scandinavian Journal of Caring Sciences*, 1995, 9, 119–122.

Sorensen, E., & Johnson, E. Subtypes of incarcerated delinquents constructed via cluster analysis. *Journal of Child Psychology & Psychiatry*, 1996, 37, 293–303.

Spirito, A., Francis, G., Overholser, J., & Frank, N. Coping, depression, and adolescent suicide attempts. *Journal of Clinical Child Psychology*, 1996, 25, 147–155.

Spirito, A., Overholser, J., & Hart, K. Cognitive characteristics of adolescent suicide attempters. *Journal of the American Academy of Child & Adolescent Psychiatry*, 1991, 30, 604–608.

Stack, S. Heavy metal, religiosity, and suicide attempts. In J. McIntosh (Ed.), *Suicide '96*. Washington, DC: AAS, 1996, 136–137.

Stack, S. Does being a parent affect suicide ideology? *Omega*, 1996–1997, 34, 71–80.

Stack, S. Blues fans and suicide acceptability. In J. McIntosh (Ed.), *Suicide '97*. Washington, DC: AAS, 1997, 154–158.

Stack, S., & Cao, L. The effect of financial satisfaction on female suicide attempts in China. *Omega*, 1997–1998, 36, 161–167.

Stack, S., & Wasserman, I. The effect of marriage, family, and religious ties on African American suicide ideology. *Journal of Marriage & the Family*, 1995, 57, 215–222.

Stack, S., & Wasserman, I. Height and risk of suicide. *Journal of Social Psychology*, 1996, 136, 255–256.

Steele, A. A., & McLennan, J. Suicidal and countersuicidal thinking. *Australian Psychologist*, 1995, 30, 149–152.

Stein, D., Witztum, D., Brom, D., DeNour, A. K., & Elizur, A. The association between adolescents' attitudes toward suicide and their psychosocial background and suicidal tendencies. *Adolescence*, 1992, 27, 949–959.

Strang, S. P., & Orlefsky, J. L. Factors underlying suicidal ideation among college students. *Journal of Adolescence*, 1990, 13, 39–52.

Straub, R., Wolfersdorf, M., & Hole, G. Motivational and volitional dysfunction, personality disposition, and suicidal behavior in depressed women. In K. Bohme, R. Freytag, C. Wachtler & H. Wedler (Eds.), *Suicidal behavior*. Regensburg: S. Roderer, 1993, 775–778.

Street, S., & Kromrey, J. D. Relationships between suicidal behavior and personality types. *Suicide & Life-Threatening Behavior*, 1994, 24, 282–292.

Strosahl, K., Chiles, J. A., & Linehan, M. Prediction of suicide intent in hospitalized parasuicides. *Comprehensive Psychiatry*, 1992, 33, 366–373.

Szanto, K., Prigerson, H., Houck, P., Ehrenpreis, L., & Reynolds, C. F. Suicidal ideation in elderly bereaved. *Suicide & Life-Threatening Behavior*, 1997, 27, 194–207.

Szekeley, T. Caffeine as a stimulant against suicide. *Archives of Internal Medicine*, 1997, 157, 243–244.

Taiminen, T. J., Saarijarvi, S., Helenius, H., Keskinen, A., & Korpilahti, T. Alexithymia in suicide attempters. *Acta Psychiatrica Scandinavica*, 1996, 93, 195–198.

Thomas, C. B., Suhori, T. R., & Graves, P. L. Psychological precursors of disorders. *Psychological Reports*, 1997, 81, 1227–1231.

Turzo, A. P., & Range, L. M. Reasons for living. *Journal of Applied Social Psychology*, 1991, 21, 1161–1168.

Van Elderen, T., Verkes, R. J., Arkesteijn, J., & Komproe, I. Psychometric characteristics of the self-expression and control scale in a sample of recurrent suicide attempters. *Personality & Individual Differences*, 1996, 21, 489–496.

Van Strien, T., Schippers, G. M., & Cox, W. M. On the relationship between emotional and external eating behavior. *Addictive Behaviors*, 1995, 20, 585–594.

Vella, M. L., Persic, S., & Lester, D. Does self-esteem predict suicidality after controls for depression? *Psychological Reports*, 1996, 79, 1178.

Verkes, R. J., Kerkhof, G. A., Beld, E., Hengeveld, M. W., & Van Kempen, G. Suicidality, circadian activity rhythms, and platelet serotonergic measures in patients with recurrent suicidal behavior. *Acta Psychiatrica Scandinavica*, 1996a, 93, 27–34.

Verkes, R. J., Pijl, H., Meinders, A. E., & Van Kempen, G. Borderline personality, impulsiveness, and platelet monoamine measures in bulimia nervosa and recurrent suicidal behavior. *Biological Psychiatry*, 1996b, 40, 173–180.

Villasana, A. E., Gonzales, J. J., & Ortiz, A. *Children parasuicide*. 4th European Symposium on Suicide, University of Odense, 1992.

Walters, R. M. Suicidal behavior in severely mentally handicapped patients. *British Journal of Psychiatry*, 1990, 157, 444–446.

Weber, B. C., & Metha, A. Loneliness and suicidal ideation in college students. In D. Lester (Ed.), *Suicide '95*. Washington, DC: AAS, 1995, 98–99.

Weber, B., Metha, A., & Nelsen, E. Relationships among multiple suicide ideation risk factors in college students. *Journal of College Student Psychotherapy*, 1997, 11(3), 49–64.

Westen, D., Muderrisoglie, S., Fowler, C., Shedler, J., & Koren, D. Affect regulation and affective experience. *Journal of Consulting & Clinical Psychology*, 1997, 65, 429–439.

Westerfeld, J. S., Cardon, D., & Deaton, W. L. Development of the college student Reasons for Living Inventory. *Suicide & Life-Threatening Behavior*, 1992, 22, 442–452.

Williams, D., & Lester, D. Eating disorder and manic-depressive tendencies. *Psychological Reports*, 1996, 78, 794.

Williams, J. M. G., Ellis, N. C., Tyers, C., Healy, H., Rose, G., & MacLeod, A. K. The specificity of autobiographical memory and imageability of the future. *Memory & Cognition*, 1996, 24, 116–125.

Wilson, K. G., Stelzer, J., Bergman, J. N., Kral, M. J., Inayatullah, M., & Elliott, C. A. Problem-solving, stress, and coping in adolescent suicide attempts. *Suicide & Life-Threatening Behavior*, 1995, 25, 241–252.

Windle, R. C., & Windle, M. An investigation of adolescent substance use behaviors. *Journal of Child Psychology & Psychiatry*, 1997, 38, 921–929.

Wolfersdorf, M., & Niehus, E. M. Depressive inpatients and suicidal behavior. *Schweizer Archiv fur Neurologie & Psychiatrie*, 1993, 144, 575–583.

Wood, J. M., Nezworski, M. T., & Stejskal, W. J. The comprehensive system for the Rorschach. *Psychological Science*, 1997, 7, 3–10.

Woods, P. J., Silverman, E. S., Gentilini, J. M., Cunningham, D. K., & Grieger, R. M. Cognitive variables related to suicidal contemplation in adolescents with implications for long-range prevention. *Journal of Rational Emotive & Cognitive Behavioral Therapy*, 1991, 9, 215–245.

Yang, B., & Clum, G. A. Life stress, social

support, and problem-solving skills predictive of depressive symptoms, hopelessness, and suicidal ideation in an Asian student population. *Suicide & Life-Threatening Behavior*, 1994, 24, 127–139.

Yang, B., & Clum, G. Measures of life stress and social support specific to an Asian student population. *Journal of Psychopathology & Behavioral Assessment*, 1995, 17, 51–67.

Young, M. A., Fogg, L. F., Scheftner, W., Fawcett, J., Akiskal, H., & Maser, J. Stable trait components of hopelessness. *Journal of Abnormal Psychology*, 1996, 105, 155–165.

Zimmerman, J. K. Adolescent suicidality and neuropsychological impairment. In D. Lester (Ed.), *Suicide '93*. Denver: AAS, 1993, 43–45.

Zlotnick, C., Donaldson, D., Spirito, A., & Pearlstein, T. Affect regulation and suicide attempts in adolescent inpatients. *Journal of the American Academy of Child & Adolescent Psychiatry*, 1997, 36, 793–798.

Zonda, T. The suicidal attempt in Hungary. In K. Bohme, R. Freytag, C. Wachtler & H. Wedler (Eds.), *Suicidal behavior*. Regensburg: S. Roderer, 1993, 656–658.

Chapter 22

SUICIDAL TYPES

Empirical Studies

Completed Suicides

Van Hoesel (1983; Reynolds and Berman, 1995) classified 404 suicides into the major typologies proposed by scholars. A cluster analysis revealed five major types: escape, depression/low self-esteem, alienation, confusion, and aggression. Differences were found between the types. For example, the alienated suicides had fewest females and the depressed suicides most. Dyadic suicides were more often aggressive, while jail suicides were more often the escape type. Differences were found by age, race, drug abuse, method, precipitating cause, and prior attempts.

Attempted Suicides

Dancer (1990) compared the profiles of normals, psychiatric inpatients, and attempted suicides on a suicide-probability scale. The attempters had 27 different profiles, the psychiatric inpatients six and the normals five. Thus, the attempters were the most diverse group.

Ellis and Rudd (1993) identified two clusters of individuals using the Millon Clinical Multiaxial Inventory given to a sample of Army psychiatric referrals for suicide attempts, a history of suicidal behavior, or suicidal ideation: (1) negativism and antisocial and (2) avoidant, schizoid, negativistic, and dependent. The second type was more seriously suicidal than the first type.

Ellis and Rudd (1994) found three clusters of suicidal military personnel using the Millon Clinical Multiaxial Inventory: (1) negativistic-avoidant-schizoid, (2) avoidant-dependent-negativistic, and (3) antisocial. Ellis et al. (1996) reported four clusters of suicidal psychiatric outpatients using the same inventory: (1) negativistic/avoidant/ schizoid, (2) avoidant/dependent/ negativistic (a group with more agoraphobics), (3) antisocial (a group with more alcohol abusers), and (4) histrionic/ narcissistic (a group with more alcohol abusers and fewer bipolar disorders and panic disorders).

Kienhorst et al. (1993) factor analyzed data from adolescent suicide attempters and identified two types: (1) psychological well-being, with depression, hopelessness, low self-esteem, repeated attempts, and poor relationships with parents; and (2) problematic behaviors, with repeated attempts, use of soft drugs, deaths of friends and family members, divorced parents, and residing at vocational training schools.

Engstrom et al. (1996) found six clusters of attempters based on scores on the Karolina Scales of Personality and the Eysenck Personality inventory: (1) and (2) normals; (3) neurotic introvert; (4) anxious, aggressive, and impulsive; (5) psychotic and impulsive; and (6) anxious and guilty. Engstrom et al. (1997) reported four types: (1) and (2) normal, (3) neurotic introverts, and (4) anxious impulsive. These four types did not differ in CSF levels of HVA, 5-HIAA or MHPG or blood levels of MAO. The first type of normals had a greater response to DST cortisol, while types (3) and (4) were the most hopeless and suicidal.

De Leo et al. (1990) carried out a cluster analysis of several hundred attempted suicides who were repeaters. They identified three clusters: (1) 24–26 years old, drug addicted, single, unemployed, with three-to-five prior attempts; (2) 28–35 years old, with a personality disorder, single, unemployed, with two-to-three prior attempts; and (3) 20–24 years old, with a personality disorder or neurotic depression, single, student or worker, with only one prior attempt.

Suicidal Ideators

Steer et al. (1993a) found that psychiatric outpatients who were suicidal ideators were more depressed, anxious and hopeless than those who were not; they more often had a mood disorder and less often an anxiety disorder. The ideators fell into four types: hopeless, anxious-depressed, below average, and severely suicidal. These four types did not differ in age or sex.

Suicidal Intent

Kingsbury (1993) factor analyzed Beck's suicidal-intent scale for a sample of adolescent suicide attempters. He found four factors and noted that the items measuring actual behaviors were only weakly associated with self-report items. Mieczkowitz et al. (1993) found two factors for the Beck scale, which they labelled lethal intent and planning.

Steer et al. (1993b) found three factors from the suicide-intent scale responses from psychiatric inpatients: desire for death, preparation for suicide, and active suicidal desire.

Spirito et al. (1996) found three factors of suicidal intent in a sample of adolescent suicide attempters. Expected outcome and planning activities were associated with depression, hopelessness, and suicidal ideation; isolation behaviors were associated with none of these traits.

Review

Arensman and Kerkhof (1996) reviewed 32 recent studies on typologies of attempted suicides and found only two consistent groupings: mild and severe.

Non-Empirical Ideas

Berman (1996) classified dyadic deaths (murder-suicides and double suicides) as erotic-aggressive, unrequited love, dependent-protective, and symbiotic.

Lester (1990) proposed a classification of nonfatal suicidal types based on a classification proposed for self-defeating behavior: failed suicide, deliberate self-harm (with no intention to die), subintentional self-harm (where the positive consequences outweigh the negative consequences), counter-productive self-harm (where there are unforeseen negative consequences), and pseudo self-harm (suicidal gestures).

Jobes (1995) proposed two types of suicide completers: (1) intrapsychic, with internal pain, an Axis I diagnosis, and suiciding privately; and (2) exteropsychic, with external pain, an Axis II diagnosis, and suiciding publicly.

Orbach (1997) proposed three types of suicidal individuals: (1) depressed-perfectionist, (2) impulsive, and (3) disintegrative.

Orbach did not make it clear whether the typology was for completed or attempted suicides.

Assisted Suicide

Muller et al. (1995) found that the majority of assisted suicides in the Netherlands occurred in nursing homes. Those choosing this mode of death were more likely than other nursing home patients to have cancer, to be in their low 70s, and to be men. They had been in the nursing home for an average of 13 months.

Bindells et al. (1996) studied male homosexuals in the Netherlands who had AIDS and died. Twenty-three percent died from euthanasia/assisted suicide and 13 percent as a result of medical decisions concerning the end of life. The euthanasia/assisted suicides were older and had known their diagnosis for longer periods. They did not differ in symptoms or severity of symptoms, and most would have died within a month.

In the Netherlands, Van der Wal and Onwuteaka-Philipsen (1996) found that patients requesting euthanasia or assisted-suicide had cancer, AIDS, multiple sclerosis, and amyotrophic lateral sclerosis more often than comparable patients; they had respiratory system and circulatory diseases less often.

Discussion

This is a neglected area of research. Most research classifies suicidal people on the basis of their psychiatric diagnosis. More meaningful typologies based on characteristics other than diagnosis need to be devised. Clearly, all suicides are not alike, and meaningful research requires a sound typology.

REFERENCES

Arensman, E., & Kerkhof, A. Classification of attempted suicide. *Suicide & Life-Threatening Behavior*, 1996, 26, 46–67.

Berman, A. L. Dyadic death. *Suicide & Life-Threatening Behavior*, 1996, 26, 342–350.

Bindells, P. J., Krol, A., van Ameijden, E., Mulder-Folkerts, D., van den Hoek, J., van Griensven, G., & Coutinho, R. Euthanasia and physician-assisted suicide in homosexual men with AIDS. *Lancet*, 1996, 347, 499–504.

Dancer, L. S. Suicide prediction and the partial order scalogram analysis of psychological adjustment. *Applied Psychology*, 1990, 39, 479–497.

De Leo, D., Degli Stefani, M., Dalcin, B., Cadamuro, M., Caneva, A., & Banon, D. The problems of suicidal repetition. In G. Ferrari, M. Bellini & P. Crepet (Eds.), *Suicidal behavior and risk factors*. Bologna: Monduzzi-Editore, 1990, 505–514.

Ellis, T. E., & Rudd, M. D. A cluster analysis of suicide psychiatric outpatients. In D. Lester (Ed.), *Suicide '93*. Denver: AAS, 1993, 145–146.

Ellis, T. E., & Rudd, M. D. Cluster analysis update. In D. Lester (Ed.), *Suicide '94*. Denver: AAS, 1994, 172–174.

Ellis, T. E., Rudd, M. D., Rajab, M. H., & Wehrly, T. E. Cluster analysis of MCMI scores of suicidal psychiatric patients. *Journal of Clinical Psychology*, 1996, 52, 411–422.

Engstrom, G., Alling, C., Gustavsson, P., Oreland, L., & Traskman-Bendz, L. Clinical characteristics and biological parameters in temperamental clusters of suicide attempters. *Journal of Affective Disorders*, 1997, 44, 45–55.

Engstrom, G., Alsen, M., Gustavsson, P., Schalling, D., & Traskman-Bendz, L. Classification of suicide attempters by cluster analysis. *Personality & Individual Differences*, 1996, 21, 687–695.

Jobes, D. A. The challenge and promise of

clinical suicidology. *Suicide & Life-Threatening Behavior*, 1995, 25, 437–449.

Kienhorst, C. W., De Wilde, E. J., Van Den Bout, J., Van Der Burg, E., Diekstra, R. F. W., & Wolters, W. H. G. Two subtypes of adolescent suicide attempters. *Acta Psychiatrica Scandinavica*, 1993, 87, 18–22.

Kingsbury, S. J. Clinical components of suicidal intent in adolescent overdose. *Journal of the American Academy of Child & Adolescent Psychiatry*, 1993, 32, 518–520.

Lester, D. A classification of acts of attempted suicide. *Perceptual & Motor Skills*, 1990, 70, 1245–1246.

Mieczkowitz, T. A., Sweeney, J. A., Haas, G. L., Junker, B. W., Brown, R. P., & Mann, J. J. Factor composition of the Suicide Intent Scale. *Suicide & Life-Threatening Behavior*, 1993, 23, 37–45.

Muller, M. T., van der Wal, G., van Eijk, J., & Ribbe, M. W. Active euthanasia and physician-assisted suicide in Dutch nursing homes. *Age & Aging*, 1995, 24, 429–433.

Orbach, I. A taxonomy of factors related to suicidal behavior. *Clinical Psychology*, 1997, 4, 208–224.

Reynolds, F. M. T., & Berman, A. L. An empirical typology of suicide. *Archives of Suicide Research*, 1995, 1, 97–109.

Spirito, A., Sterling, C. M., Donaldson, D. L., & Arrigan, M. E. Factor analysis of the Suicide Intent Scale with adolescent suicide attempters. *Journal of Personality Assessment*, 1996, 67, 90–101.

Steer, R. A., Beck, A. T., Brown, G. K., & Beck, J. S. Classification of suicidal and nonsuicidal outpatients. *Journal of Clinical Psychology*, 1993a, 49, 603–614.

Steer, R. A., Rissmiller, D. J., Ranieri, W. F., & Beck, A. T. Dimensions of suicidal behavior in psychiatric inpatients. *Behavior Research & Therapy*, 1993b, 31, 229–236.

Van der Wal, G., & Onwuteaka-Philipsen, B. D. Cases of euthanasia and assisted suicide reported to the public prosecutor in North Holland over 10 years. *British Medical Journal*, 1996, 312, 612–613.

Van Hoesel, F. M. T. *An empirical typology of suicide.* Master's thesis, Catholic University, 1983.

Chapter 23

OTHER SELF-DESTRUCTIVE BEHAVIORS

Stanley et al. (1992) argued that suicidal behavior, self-mutilation, and minor forms of self-abuse such as trichotillomania formed a continuum of impulsive aggressive self-harm and could be studied as a continuum.

Depression

Mendlovic et al. (1997) argued that depression may lead to immunological dysfunction, increasing the vulnerability of the body by reducing immune responses and promoting autoimmune responses that damage the body. Thus, depression itself may be (unconsciously) "suicidal."

Driving

Grossman et al. (1993) compared completed suicides aged 16–35 with licensed drivers. The suicides had more past psychiatric hospitalizations, more hospitalizations for any injury, more for assaults, and more for attempted suicide; they had more car crashes, both single car and any type.

Rockett et al. (1991) compared attempted suicides with injured drivers seen at a trauma center. The drivers were more often white and male, and their traumas occurred more often in the summer and from 6 p.m. to midnight. The suicide attempts occurred more often on Tuesdays. The groups did not differ in religion or social class.

Roehrig and Range (1995) found that neither dangerous driving nor cigarette use/drug use/bad company predicted suicidal ideation in college students; foolhardiness, depression, and reasons for living did.

Drug Overdoses

Kjelsberg et al. (1995) followed up adolescent psychiatric patients and compared those completing suicide with those dying of drug overdoses. The suicides were more often suicidal, with learning difficulties and psychotic symptoms, and less often drug dependent, risk-takers, and with poor impulse control. Kjelsberg concluded that the drug overdoses were most likely not suicides, but rather accidents.

Nondeliberate Self-Harm

Upadhyaya et al. (1989) found that elderly who engaged in nonfatal deliberate self-harm also often had serious suicidal intent (64 percent) and a depressive illness (56 percent), and so gestures should not be viewed as trivial.

Recklessness

Clark et al. (1990) found that adolescents

373

who scored high on a scale of recklessness reported more suicidal ideation than low scorers. Suicidal ideation was also more common in those who drove dangerously, abused drugs, smoked, and associated with "bad company."

Risk-Taking

Windle et al. (1992) found that suicidal ideation and attempts were more common in junior high school children who engaged in high-risk behaviors and who engaged in heavy alcohol use.

Seat Belt Use

In adolescents seen at a clinic, little or no seat belt use was associated with both depression and prior suicidal ideation (Schichor et al. (1990).

Self-Destructiveness

Lester and Desch (1990) found that scores on a measure of general self-destructiveness were not associated with scores on a measure of Type A behavior (but were negatively associated with age and were higher in males).

Boudewyn and Liem (1995) found that college students, self-reports of suicidal ideation and attempts were positively correlated with scores for self-destructiveness. Lewinsohn et al. (1995) found that prior attempted suicide in high school students was associated with scores on a measure of general self-destructiveness.

Self-Mutilation

Bongar et al. (1990) found that suicidal patients seen at an emergency mental health center had a borderline personality disorder and were self-mutilators more often than the

other patients. They did not differ in alcohol abuse or a diagnosis of bipolar affective disorder or schizophrenia. Lester (1993) noted that recent self-mutilation and lifetime attempted suicide were associated in this sample. In a sample of adolescent psychiatric inpatients, Zlotnick et al. (1997) found that those who had attempted suicide had self-mutilated more in the prior year, but did not differ in risk-taking behaviors. On the other hand, Simeon et al. (1992) found that self-mutilators with and without a personality disorder did not differ in their prior suicide attempts.

Sonneburn and Vanstraelen (1992) compared suicide attempters and self-mutilators, all of whom burned themselves. The attempters more often used inflammable liquids and set fire to their clothes; the self-mutilators used matches and lighters more and made direct burns. They did not differ in past psychiatric history or prior suicide attempts. The attempters more often had an affective disorder, while the self-mutilators more often had a personality disorder.

Garrison et al. (1993) studied nonsuicidal physically self-damaging acts in 12–14 year olds. Those committing such acts tended more often to have suicidal ideation, a history of attempted suicide, major depressive disorders, obsessive-compulsive disorder, and impulsivity.

Soloff et al. (1994) found that patients with borderline personality disorder who self-mutilated were also more likely to attempt suicide and have more serious suicidal ideation, although they were not more depressed. The suicidal behavior of the self-mutilators was more manipulative but not more lethal.

Among a sample of patients with body dysmorphic disorder, Phillips and Taub (1995) found that suicidal ideation and attempting suicide were not associated with skin picking. Christenson and Mitchell

(1991) found no differences in self-injury (burning, choking, and cutting) in bulimics versus controls.

Fulwiler et al. (1997) found that prison inmates who self-mutilated repeated the acts more than those who attempted suicide, more often had a mixed anxiety/dysthymia disorder, and less often a major affective disorder; more often they were hyperactive/learning disabled as children. They did not differ in age, sex, education, head injuries, neurological abnormalities, drug/alcohol abuse, or conduct disorder as children.

Discussion

The relationship between self-destructive behaviors and suicidal behavior has not been explored thoroughly, and the relationship needs to explored further, especially from a theoretical point of view.

REFERENCES

Bongar, B., Peterson, L., Golann, S., & Hardiman, J. Self-mutilation and the chronically suicidal patient. *Annals of Clinical Psychiatry*, 1990, 2, 217–222.

Boudewyn, A. C., & Liem, J. H. Psychological, interpersonal, and behavioral correlates of chronic self-destructiveness. *Psychological Reports*, 1995, 77, 1283–1297.

Christenson, G. A., & Mitchell, J. E. Trichotillomania and repetitive behavior in bulimia nervosa. *International Journal of Eating Disorders*, 1991, 10, 593–598.

Clark, D. C., Sommerfeldt, L., Schwarz, M., Hedeker, D., & Watel, L. Physical recklessness in adolescence. *Journal of Nervous & Mental Disease*, 1990, 178, 423–433.

Fulwiler, C., Forbes, C., Santaangelo, S. L., & Folstein, M. Self-mutilation and suicide attempt. *Journal of the American Academy of Psychiatry & Law*, 1997, 25, 69–77.

Garrison, C. Z., Addy, C. L., McKeown, R. E., Cuffe, S. P., Jackson, K. L., & Waller, J. L. Nonsuicidal physically self-damaging acts in adolescents. *Journal of Child & Family Studies*, 1993, 2, 339–352.

Grossman, P. C., Soderberg, R., & Rivara, F. P. Prior injury and motor vehicle crash as risk factors for youth suicide. *Epidemiology*, 1993, 4, 115–119.

Kjelsberg, E., Winther, M., & Dahl, A. A. Overdose deaths in young substance abusers. *Acta Psychiatrica Scandinavica*, 1995, 91, 236–242.

Lester, D. Borderline personality disorder and suicidal behavior. *Psychological Reports*, 1993, 73, 394.

Lester, D., & Desch, R. Self-destructiveness and Type A personality. *Psychological Reports*, 1990, 67, 746.

Lewinsohn, P. M., Langhinrichsen-Rohling, J., Langford, R., Rohde, P., Seeley, J. R., & Chapman, J. The Life Attitudes Schedule. *Suicide & Life-Threatening Behavior*, 1995, 25, 458–474.

Mendlovic, S., Doron, A., & Eilat, E. Can depressive patients exploit the immune system for suicide? *Medical Hypotheses*, 1997, 49, 445–446.

Phillips, K. A., & Taub, S. L. Skin picking as a symptom of body dysmorphic disorder. *Psychopharmacology Bulletin*, 1995, 31, 279–288.

Rockett, I. R. H., Spirito, A., Fritz, G. K., Riggs, S., & Bond, A. Adolescent risktakers. *International Journal of Social Psychiatry*, 1991, 37, 285–292.

Roehrig, H. R., & Range, L. M. Recklessness, depression, and reasons for living in predicting suicidality in college students. *Journal of Youth & Adolescence*, 1995, 24, 723–729.

Schichor, A., Beck, A., Bernstein, B., & Crabtree, B. Seat-belt use and stress in adolescents. *Adolescence*, 1990, 25, 773–779.

Simeon, D., Stanley, B., Frances, A., Mann, J. J., Winchel, R., & Stanley, M. Self-mutilation in personality disorder. *American Journal of Psychiatry*, 1992, 149, 221–226.

Soloff, P. H., Lis, J. A., Kelly, T., Cornelius,

J., & Ulrich, R. Self-mutilation and suicidal behavior in borderline personality disorder. *Journal of Personality Disorder*, 1994, 8, 257–267.

Sonneburn, C. K., & Vanstraelen, P. M. A retrospective study of self-inflicted burns. *General Hospital Psychiatry*, 1992, 14, 404–407.

Stanley, B., Winchel, R., Molcho, A., Simeon, D., & Stanley, B. Suicide and the self-harm continuum. *International Review of Psychiatry*, 1992, 4, 149–155.

Upadhyaya, A. K., Warburton, H., & Jenkins, J. C. Psychiatric correlates of nonfatal deliberate self-harm in the elderly. *Journal of Clinical & Experimental Gerontology*, 1989, 11(3/4), 131–143.

Windle, M., Miller-Tutzawer, C., & Domenico, D. Alcohol use, suicidal behavior, and risky activities among adolescents. *Journal of Research on Adolescence*, 1992, 2, 317–330.

Zlotnick, C., Donaldson, D., Spirito, A., & Pearlstein, T. Affect regulation and suicide attempts in adolescent inpatients. *Journal of the American Academy of Child & Adolescent Psychiatry*, 1997, 36, 793–798.

Chapter 24

SUICIDAL BEHAVIOR IN LOWER ANIMALS

The word "suicide" continues to be used for a variety of organisms and substances not human, including suicide substrates, substances that bind to the active sites of an enzyme, irreversibly inactivating the enzyme. The enzyme is seen as committing suicide (Burke et al., 1990). Bonness et al. (1994) described the behavior of the pokeweed antiviral protein as suicide when it thwarts "viral attack by acting as a local suicide mechanism for compound cells" (p. 180). Suicide is also used to refer to cell behavior (Duke et al., 1996), such as the phenomenon in which T-cells attach themselves to target cells in the body, programming them for death (T-cell mediated cytolysis) (Chayen, et. al, 1990; Scott et al., 1996), and to the occasional behavior of red cells (Scott and Eaton, 1995). Cellular suicide has also been described in the nematode and fruit fly (Steller, 1995).

Waser and Price (1993) described pollen that commits suicide by foregoing an attempt at fertilization, while Takeuchi et al. (1955) have described suicide in seeds.

Suicide has been described in a ciliated protozoa (Simon and Meyer, 1992), in aeromonads (Guimaraes et al., 1996; Namdari and Cabelli, 1990) and in mammalian cells (Ucker, 1991). Kataoka et al. (1992) described suicide in plant ribosomes in which an antiviral protein shuts down the protein synthesis of its own cells when it spreads into the cytoplasm because of breaks in the cells. Thus, it is a defensive agent that induces viral resistance through the suicide of its own cells.

McAllister et al. (1990) reported suicide in pea aphids (after parasitization, they actively increase their risk of dying) and Lemoneck (1996) in male praying mantises after they have copulated.

Muller and Schmid-Hempel (1992) saw as suicide the behavior of bumblebees in which workers infected with parasites remain outside of the nest, thereby dying sooner. Patel et al. (1995) viewed as suicide the behavior of female wasps, who die without reproducing after pollinating tree figs. Suicide has also been described in spiders (Andrade, 1996) and termites (Bordereau et al., 1997).

If there is right ventricular outflow tract obstruction from the heart, it is called "suicide right ventricle" (Kroshus et al., 1995).

Abdulali (1995) documented the frequent occurrence of birds in Assam (India) killing themselves en masse by flying into walls and lights. This could be suicide or the result of the birds trying to get to safety as a result of the high winds.

Discussion

The term suicide has been increasingly applied to lower organisms in the 1990s, and this trend probably will continue.

REFERENCES

Abdulali, H. The mystery of "mass suicides" by birds. *Journal of the Bombay Natural History Society*, 1995, 92, 125-126.

Andrade, M. Sexual selection for male sacrifice in the Australian red back spider. *Science*, 1996, 271, 70-72.

Bonness, M. S., Ready, M. P., Irvin, J. D., & Mabry, T. J. Pokeweed antiviral protein inactivates pokeweed ribosomes. *Plant Journal*, 1994, 5, 173-183.

Bordereau, C., Robert, A., Van Tuyen, V., & Peppuy, A. Suicidal defensive behavior by frontal gland dehiscence in Globitermes Sulphureus Haviland soldiers. *Insectes Sociaux*, 1997, 44, 289-297.

Burke, M. A., Maini, P. K., & Murray, J. D. On the kinetics of suicide substrates. *Biophysical Chemistry*, 1990, 37(1-3), 81-90.

Chayen, J., Pitsillides, A. A., Bitensky, L., Muir, I. H., Taylor, P. M., & Askonas, B. A. T-cell mediated cytolysis. *Journal of Experimental Pathology*, 1990, 71, 197-208.

Duke, R. C., Ojcius, D. M., & Young, J. Cell suicide in health and disease. *Scientific American*, 1996, 275(6), 80-87.

Guimaraes, M. S., Neves, M. S., & Nunes, M. P. Prevention of suicide phenomenon in aeromonads. *European Journal of Microbiology & Infectious Diseases*, 1996, 15, 420-422.

Kataoka, J., Habuka, N., Miyano, M., Masuta, C., & Koiwai, A. Adenine depurination and inactivation of plant ribosomes by an antiviral protein of Mirabilis jalapa (MAP). *Plant Molecular Biology*, 1992, 20, 1111-1119.

Kroshus, T. J., Kshettry, V. R., Hertz, M. I., Everett, J. E., & Bolman, R. M. Suicide right ventricle after lung transplantation for Eisenmenger syndrome. *Annals of Thoracic Surgery*, 1995, 59, 995-997.

Lemoneck, M. D. Sex as suicide. *Time*, 1996, 147(3), 60.

McAllister, M. K., Roitberg, B. D., & Weldon, K. L. Adaptive suicide in pea aphids. *Animal Behavior*, 1990, 40, 167-175.

Muller, C. B., & Schmid-Hempel, R. To die for host or parasite? *Animal Behavior*, 1992, 44, 177-179.

Namdari, H., & Cabelli, V. J. Glucose-mediated catabolic repression of the tricarboxylic acid cycle. *Journal of Bacteriology*, 1990, 172, 4721-4724.

Patel, A., Anstett, M. C., Hossaert, M., & Kjellberg, F. Pollinators entering female dioecious figs. *Journal of Evolutionary Biology*, 1995, 8, 301-313.

Scott, D. W., Grdina, T., & Shi, Y. T cells commit suicide, but B-cells are murdered. *Journal of Immunology*, 1996, 156, 2352-2356.

Scott, M. D., & Eaton, J. W. Thalassaemic erythrocytes. *British Journal of Haematology*, 1995, 91, 811-819.

Simon, E. M., & Meyer, E. D. Suicide is not the inevitable outcome of perpetual selfing in tetrahymenines collected from natural habitats. *Developmental Genetics*, 1992, 13(1), 47-52.

Steller, H. Mechanisms and genes of cellular suicide. *Science*, 1995, 267, 1445-1449.

Takeuchi, Y., Omigawa, Y., Ogasawara, M., Yonegama, K., Konnai, M., & Worsham, A. D. Effects of brassinosteroids on conditioning and germination of clover broomrape (Orobanche minor) seeds. *Plant Growth Research*, 1995, 16, 153-160.

Ucker, D. S. Death by suicide. *New Biologist*, 1991, 3(2), 103-109.

Waser, N. M., & Price, M. V. Crossing-distance effects on prezygotic performance in plants. *Oikos*, 1993, 68, 303-308.

Chapter 25

THEORIES OF SUICIDE

Physiological Theories

Lester (1990a) applied Lee Ellis's neuro-hormonal theory of criminal behavior to suicide and found that the theory suggested interesting areas worthy of future investigation. Lester and Goldney (1997) presented an analysis of suicidal behavior from an ethological perspective.

De Catanzaro (1995) tested his socio-biological theory of suicide by showing that, in the general public and in high-risk groups, suicidality was predicted by loneliness and a feeling that one was a burden to one's family. Suicide was more common in psychiatric patients, the elderly, and homosexuals, in the elderly with health and financial problems, in males aged 18–30 who were less sexually active, and in homosexual males whose heterosexual experiences had been bad.

Psychological Theories

Baumeister (1990) has tried to generate a theory of suicide based on viewing suicide as an escape. He proposed six steps: (1) the person experiences recent problems where the outcomes fall below expectations (that is, there is failure); (2) the person makes internal attributions (blames himself or herself for the failures); (3) the person has an aversive state of self-awareness, especially self-blame; (4) there is negative affect (emotions); (5) the person tries to escape from meaningful thought or cognitive construction (such as concrete, short-term thinking with the removal of meaning from awareness); and (6) the person experiences a reduction in inhibitions.

Lester (1990b) proposed a series of theories of suicide modeled after the classic theories of crime and delinquency proposed by criminologists. Lester (1991b) reviewed the major systems of psychotherapy for what each theorized about suicidal behavior.

Rogers and Carney (1994) proposed a social learning theory of attempted suicide.

Lester (1997) analyzed suicide from a communitarian perspective. Yang and Lester (1996; Lester and Yang, 1997) presented several models of suicide based on economic theories. Lester and Yang (1991b) explored the differences in microsocionomic and macrosocionomic approaches to the study of suicidal behavior. Mishara (1996) presented a model of suicide based on models of open systems in physics and chemistry proposed by Prigogine (1980).

Lester (1996a) explored the relationships (empirical and theoretical) between attempted and completed suicide. Lester (1990c) explored a feminist perspective on suicidology, which included, among other issues, a proposal for the replacement of the terms "completed" and "attempted" suicide by "fatal" and "nonfatal" suicide. Lester (1996b) explored sexism in suicidology in general.

Lester (1995) rated 30 famous suicides for each of Leenaars' eight core elements of suicide. The older suicides showed less interpersonal conflict, less aggression turned inward, and less ego strength. Associations with sex, experience of loss, year of birth, and nationality were not significant.

Rationality

Lester and Yang (1991a) compared Gary Becker's two definitions of irrationality (doing what you have done before and behaving randomly) to two types of suicidal people (chronic and acute).

Lester and Yang (1995) showed that subjects reacted rationally when presented with cancer scenarios in which the anticipated pain from the chemotherapy and the probability of survival were varied, since subjects changed their estimated likelihood of committing suicide in accord with these factors.

Comparing Theories

Lester (1991a) rated 30 suicides for the presence of elements of ten major theories of suicide. A factor analysis of the scores revealed that Adler's theory and Binswanger's theory were very different

from each other and very different from the remaining eight theories. Lester (1993) found that Jung's theory was less applicable to men; Jung's, Murray's and Sullivan's theories were less applicable to the elderly, while Binswanger's theory was more applicable; and Adler's and Zilboorg's theories applied better to those who had experienced early loss.

Lester (1994) enlarged the sample of theories to 15 and identified five clusters of theories. He also found that success of the theories depended upon the sex, year of birth, experience of loss, European versus non-European origin, and age of the suicides.

Discussion

Some scholars think that theory is crucial for advancing the understanding of a phenomenon; empirical research without a theoretical basis is not very useful. Thus, it is striking that very little has appeared in recent years on theories of suicide, and there has been almost no research to test theories that have been proposed. Suicidologists have remained content to propose a list of psychological factors that increase the risk of suicide, combining the factors in a simple additive-regression model. Our understanding of suicide will not advance until better theories are proposed and tested.

REFERENCES

Baumeister, R. F. Suicide as escape from self. *Psychological Review*, 1990, 97, 90-113.

De Catanzaro, D. Reproductive status, family interactions, and suicidal ideation. *Ethology & Sociobiology*, 1995, 16, 385-394.

Lester, D. The relevance of Ellis's neurohormonal theory of crime and delinquency to suicide. *Personality & Individual Differences*, 1990a, 11, 1201-1206.

Lester, D. *Understanding and preventing suicide*. Springfield, IL: Charles Thomas, 1990b.

Lester, D. The study of suicide from a feminist perspective. *Crisis*, 1990c, 11, 38-43.

Lester, D. The study of suicidal lives. *Suicide & Life-Threatening Behavior*, 1991a, 21, 164-173.

Lester, D. *Psychotherapy for suicidal clients*. Springfield, IL: Charles Thomas, 1991b.

Lester, D. Ten theories of suicide and their applicability to older suicides. In K. Bohme, R. Freytag, C. Wachtler & H. Wedler (Eds.), *Suicidal behavior.* Regensburg: S. Roderer, 1993, 157-160.

Lester, D. A comparison of fifteen theories of suicide. *Suicide & Life-Threatening Behavior,* 1994, 24, 80-88.

Lester, D. An examination of Leenaars's theory of suicide. *Perceptual & Motor Skills,* 1995, 80, 578.

Lester, D. On the relationship between fatal and nonfatal suicidal behavior. *Homeostasis,* 1996a, 37, 122-128.

Lester, D. Sexism in suicidology. *Homeostasis,* 1996b, 37, 83-88.

Lester, D. Communitarianism and suicide prevention. *Crisis,* 1997, 18, 118-123.

Lester, D., & Goldney, R. D. An ethological perspective on suicidal behavior. *New Ideas in Psychology,* 1997, 15, 97-103.

Lester, D., & Yang, B. Suicidal behavior and Becker's definition of irrationality. *Psychological Reports,* 1991a, 68, 655-656.

Lester, D., & Yang, B. Microsocionomics versus macrosocionomics as a model for examining suicide. *Psychological Reports,* 1991b, 69, 735-738

Lester, D., & Yang, B. An economic approach for examining the rationality of suicide. *Proceedings of the Pennsylvania Economic Association,* 1995, 299-304.

Lester, D., & Yang, B. *The economy and suicide.* Commack, NY: Nova Science, 1997.

Mishara, B. L. A dynamic developmental model of suicide. *Human Development,* 1996, 39, 181-194.

Prigogine, I. *From being to becoming.* San Francisco: Freeman, 1980.

Rogers, J. R., & Carney, J. V. Assessing the modeling effect in parasuicidal behavior. *Crisis,* 1994, 15, 83-89.

Yang, B., & Lester, D. Conceptualizing suicide in economic models. *Applied Economics Letters,* 1996, 3, 139-143.

Chapter 26

CONCLUSIONS

It is not easy to draw simple conclusions from the review of this vast body of research. In the first edition of this book, I quoted Kahne (1966) who was extremely disenchanted with the research on suicide up until that point. However, suicidologists in the 1960s and 1970s witnessed the identification of interesting issues in suicide research, some great research and some attempts to derive new theories to supplement the classic theories of suicide. The 1990s have not continued these trends. There has been poor research, an absence of theorizing, and no new issues opened up for research.

With regard to the genetics of suicidal behavior, no studies have appeared on identical twins reared apart nor on cross-fostering, let alone studies that have controlled for the inheritance of psychiatric disorder. (If identical twins reared apart are more similar in suicidal behavior than non-identical twins, this could result from the inheritance of an affective disorder.)

In physiological studies of suicide, most of the research appears to be conducted to elucidate the physiological basis of depression. Therefore, the control subjects are typically normals. Such studies fail to advance our understanding of suicide because of the confounding factor of psychiatric disorder and, in particular, depression. There have also been few meta-analyses to identify consistent trends in the research.

With regard to studies of adolescent suicide, psychiatric disorder, and personality traits, most studies take a sample already collected for other purposes (typically of psychiatric patients) or form a new sample (typically of school or college students), throw in a number of variables, and search for correlates of suicidal behavior. The same variables are used, and the same results are typically found. Suicidal individuals are more depressed, disturbed, and hopeless. They have lower self-esteem, come from dysfunctional families, and have suffered stress.

The most promising researchers in these fields are John Mann and David Brent, and we look forward to their work in the 21st century.

There have been no new theories of the sex difference in suicidal behavior and almost no research to test the existing theories. There have been very few studies that endeavor to identify perinatal, infant, and childhood predictors of later suicidal behavior.

Few adequately designed studies have appeared to test the classic sociological theories of suicide (although almost every research paper pretends to be a test of Durkeim's theory), and the same is true for psychological theories. Few typologies of suicidal behavior have appeared, save those that classify suicidal individuals based on their psychiatric diagnosis.

Several "fads" are observable. There has been a growth in research into sexual abuse and suicidal behavior; almost all of that research fails to control for the possibility that sexual abuse increases the level of psychiatric disturbance which causes increased suicidal behavior. There has also been an increase in studies of suicidal behavior in AIDS patients, replacing the interest in cancer patients in the 1980s.

Research has continued on the choice of methods for suicide and on the issue of whether restricting access to lethal methods for suicide might reduce the suicide rate.

In my previous volumes reviewing research, I identified the major contributors to the field. The criteria for a major contribution include making a substantial contribution (that is several research studies or a complex theory), greatly increasing our knowledge in the field, having relevance for future research, and identifying a new area of study. The following is my judgment concerning the major contributions to the field of suicidology:

1800s: Emile Durkheim – sociological theory

1950s: Andrew Henry and James Short – sociopsychological theory

1960s: Edwin Shneidman and Norman Farberow – psychological studies
Charles Neuringer – the thought processes of the suicidal individual
Alex Pokorny – the study of climate

1970s: Aaron Beck – hopelessness in suicidal individuals
David Phillips – imitation effects

1980s: Antoon Leenaars – the study of suicide notes
David Lester – psychiatric epidemiology, availability of methods, and theories of suicide
Stephen Platt – unemployment and suicide
Steven Stack – sociological studies of suicide and imitation effects

1990s: –

REFERENCES

Kahne, M. J. Suicide research. *International Journal of Social Psychiatry*, 1966, 12, 177–186.